edited by
JOSEPH T. FROOMKIN
Joseph Froomkin, Inc.

DEAN T. JAMISON
The World Bank

ROY RADNER
University of California,
Berkeley

Education as an Industry

A Conference of the
Universities-National
Bureau Committee for
Economic Research

Published for the
NATIONAL BUREAU OF
ECONOMIC RESEARCH, Inc.,
by BALLINGER PUBLISHING
COMPANY, Cambridge, Mass.
A Subsidiary of
J. B. Lippincott Company
1976

Library of Congress Cataloging in Publication Data
Main entry under title:
Education as an industry.

(Universities-National Bureau conference series; 28)
Papers presented at the National Bureau of Economic Research's
conference held in Chicago in June 1971.
Includes index.
1. Education—Economic aspects—United States—Congresses.
I. Jamison, Dean. II. Froomkin, Joseph. III. Radner,
Roy. IV. Universities-National Bureau Committee for Economic Re-
search. V. National Bureau of Economic Research. VI. Series.

LC66.E254   370'.973   76-29631

ISBN 0-87014-269-0

Relation of the National Bureau Directors to
Publications Reporting Conference Proceedings

Since the present volume is a record of conference proceedings, it has been exempted from the rules governing submission of manuscripts to, and critical review by, the Board of Directors of the National Bureau.

(Resolution adopted July 6, 1948,
as revised November 21, 1949,
and April 20, 1968)

Funds for the economic research conference program of the National Bureau of Economic Research are supplied by the National Science Foundation.

Contents

Introduction   xi

Part I   EDUCATIONAL PRODUCTION

1. The Ph.D. Production Process
   David W. Breneman   3
2. Scholastic Achievement: Its Determinants and
   Effects in the Education Industry
   Dennis J. Dugan   53
   Comments:
   Barbara L. Heyns   84
   Frank Levy   90
3. Graduation, Graduate School Attendance,
   and Investments in College Training
   Lewis J. Perl   95
   Comments:
   Leonard Baird   136
   Alvin K. Klevorick   141
4. Concepts of Economic Efficiency and Educational
   Production
   Henry M. Levin   149
   Comments:
   Eric A. Hanushek   191
   Harold W. Watts   197

Part II   COMPENSATORY EDUCATION

5. Cost and Performance of Computer-Assisted
   Instruction for Education of Disadvantaged
   Children

Dean T. Jamison, J. Dexter Fletcher, Patrick
Suppes, and Richard C. Atkinson 201
    Comments:
      Allen C. Kelley 240
      David E. Wiley 245
6. A Study of the Relationship of Instructional
Process and Program Organization to the Success
of Compensatory Education Projects in California
Herbert J. Kiesling 249
    Comments:
      Thomas I. Ribich 282
      Burton A. Weisbrod 286

Part III HIGHER EDUCATION

7. Demand for Higher Education in the United
States: A Second Progress Report
Leonard S. Miller 293
    Comments:
      Stephen A. Hoenack 346
8. Productivity Trends in Higher Education
June O'Neill 349
    Comments:
      George B. Weathersby 366
9. Instructional Costs of University Outputs
Robert M. Oliver and David S. P. Hopkins 371
    Comments:
      Colin E. Bell 405
      Estelle James 408
10. Faculty-Student Ratios in U.S. Higher
Education
Roy Radner 415
    Comments:
      Gus Haggstrom 445
      Kenneth D. Roose 450

Part IV POLICY ISSUES

11. Policy Issues in the Education Industry
Joseph N. Froomkin 455
    Comments:
      Jerry Miner 474
      J. Alan Thomas 478
Index 481

Introduction

This volume contains eleven papers that were presented at the National Bureau of Economic Research's conference, "Education as an Industry," which was held in Chicago in June 1971. As the name suggests, the focus of the conference was on the internal workings of the educational system—its production functions, cost functions, and productivity. Thus, the conference was a natural sequel to the 1968 NBER Conference on Education and Income,* held at the University of Wisconsin, at which the papers, with one exception, dealt with the effects of education.

Part One of this volume contains four papers dealing with educational production. The papers by Breneman, Dugan, and Perl estimate educational production functions at a number of levels in the education system, using a variety of measures of output. The fourth paper, by Levin, is a detailed critique of the methodology and relevance of educational production-function analysis.

Part Two contains two early attempts to apply the methods of economic analysis to problems of compensatory education for disadvantaged students. Kiesling examines a range of compensatory education programs in California in an attempt to identify features common to the successful ones. Jamison, Fletcher, Suppes, and Atkinson examine in more detail the cost and effectiveness of a single method of compensatory education—computer-assisted instruction.

Part Three contains studies of problems of higher education. In the first paper, Miller examines factors influencing demand for higher education by using newly developed empirical techniques for estimating choice probabilities over discrete sets of options. The next three papers

---

* The proceedings of the conference were published in *Education, Income, and Human Capital*, Studies in Income and Wealth 35 (New York: NBER, 1970).

deal in one way or another with the costs of higher education. O'Neill examines how productivity (in a sense, unit cost) has varied over the period 1930–67; Oliver and Hopkins examine costs from a much more microanalytic viewpoint, applying techniques of operations research. Finally, Radner examines the determinants of what is itself the most important determinant of per student costs, the faculty-student ratio.

In the concluding paper to this volume, Froomkin discusses policy issues that are illuminated by research that views education as an industry and suggests lines that further research should take.

Discussion at the conference was lively—often sharp—and some of the flavor of that discussion comes through in the comments included in this volume. Yet, since more than the usual amount of time has elapsed between the conference and the publication of this volume, several of the original papers have been revised and updated in ways that make some of the comments partially inapplicable. We have, in these few cases, let the original comments stand; the spirit of the conference is thus preserved in the volume, though the papers have been updated.

PART ONE | Educational Production

1

**DAVID W.
BRENEMAN**
Amherst College

The Ph.D. Production Process

INTRODUCTION

Microeconomic theory of nonprofit institutions is currently a relatively underdeveloped area of analysis. In an attempt to expand this body of theory, the present paper applies the economic model of rational behavior to the Ph.D. production process within the university. In particular, economic analysis is used to explain the marked disciplinary differences in mean time to degree and in student attrition that have been the subject of much recent discussion.[1] I think that the theory developed is broadly applicable, although the data have been drawn primarily from the University of California at Berkeley.

Section I contains data documenting departmental differences in Ph.D. production, Section II develops the theory of departmental behavior, and Section III presents evidence in support of that theory. It should be noted that the present paper has been distilled from a considerably larger study, and much of the empirical work has been deleted. The interested reader should refer to the author's dissertation[2] for more complete treatment of the topic.

I. DIFFERENCES IN DEPARTMENTAL PERFORMANCE

In a 1966 study[3] prepared for the Graduate Division of the University of California at Berkeley, sociologist Rodney Stark analyzed five cohorts of

3

graduate students beginning graduate work at three-year intervals in each of four Berkeley departments, English, History, Political Science, and Chemistry. The success rates for each group, as of 1966, are presented in Table 1. Note the sharp contrast between Chemistry and the

TABLE 1. The Outcome of Doctoral Studies by Department and Year of Admission, Berkeley

	Year of Admission				
	1951	1954	1957	1960	1963
Political Science Department					
Received Ph.D.	17%	14%	14%	4%	0%
Withdrew after M.A.	24	23	29	35	26
Withdrew—no degree	59	60	51	39	21
Still registered (1966)	0	3	6	14	53
On leave of absence	0	0	0	8	0
Number of students	29	35	49	49	42
Chemistry Department					
Received Ph.D.	86%	77%	76%	68%	0%
Withdrew after M.A.	7	6	10	8	0
Withdrew—no degree	7	17	12	16	2
Still registered (1966)	0	0	2	6	96
On leave of absence	0	0	0	2	2
Number of students	28	35	51	50	50
English Department					
Received Ph.D.	13%	16%	15%	6%	0%
Withdrew after M.A.	23	25	24	14	24
Withdrew—no degree	58	55	58	29	36
Still registered (1966)	3	0	3	37	34
On leave of absence	3	4	0	14	6
Number of students	31	38	53	49	50
History Department					
Received Ph.D.	27%	12%	29%	8%	0%
Withdrew after M.A.	15	27	13	18	14
Withdrew—no degree	52	54	52	31	46
Still registered (1966)	6	0	4	23	32
On leave of absence	0	7	2	20	8
Number of students	33	26	48	51	50

SOURCE: Unpublished study by Rodney Stark, prepared for the Dean of the Graduate Division, Berkeley, 1966.

other three departments with respect to the per cent of successful Ph. D. completions.

Table 2 contains the number of enrolled-graduate-student-years that must be charged against the degree output of the four departments in the Stark study. For the English, History, and Political Science departments, the figures represent the combined results of the 1951, 1954, and 1957 cohorts, while the 1960 cohort was also included for the Chemistry Department, since that group was virtually complete by 1966. Note the much shorter average time to degree in chemistry and the early occurrence of attrition in the program. By contrast, unsuccessful students in the other three departments were not terminated or did not drop out

TABLE 2 **Enrolled Student Time per Degree, 1951–54–57 Cohorts,[a] Four Departments, Berkeley**

	Number of Students	Enrolled Student-Years	Average Years per Outcome
Political Science Department			
Received Ph.D.	6	44	7.3
Received M.A.	26	85	3.3
Received no degree	50	183	3.6
Total	82	312	
Chemistry Department			
Received Ph.D.	94	358	3.8
Received M.A.	14	27	1.9
Received no degree	17	23	1.4
Total	125	408	
English Department			
Received Ph.D.	9	61	6.8
Received M.A.	27	80	3.0
Received no degree	45	114	2.5
Total	81	255	
History Department			
Received Ph.D.	16	108	6.8
Received M.A.	16	51	3.2
Received no degree	42	108	2.5
Total	74	267	

SOURCE: Stark study, Berkeley, 1966.
[a] Limited to students who enrolled with B.A. or B.S. only. Chemistry includes the 1960 cohort.

until an average of two to three years had been completed in the program.

Data limitations prohibited preparation of similar cohort studies for a larger number of Berkeley departments. However, degree-enrollment ratios for the seven-year period 1961–67, presented in Table 3, indicate the range of departmental variation.

Evidence that the differential pattern of attrition and time to degree observed in Berkeley departments is not unique to that campus is found in Joseph Mooney's recent study of attrition among Woodrow Wilson Fellows.[4] Mooney examined success rates as of 1966 for the 1958–60 entering cohorts of Woodrow Wilson Fellows, and found the same pattern that Berkeley displays—high success rates in the physical and biological sciences, followed by the social sciences, with the humanities a poor third.

Explanation of these differences found in the literature typically focus upon such factors as variation in financial support, intrinsic differences in fields, different traditions, and so forth. In particular, departments are implicitly viewed as passive organizations lacking objectives regarding the number of Ph.D.'s to award. No attempt has been made in previous work to analyze departmental objectives and the constraints under which departments operate, and to relate these factors to Ph.D. production. The following theory attempts to fill that gap.

II. A THEORY OF DEPARTMENTAL BEHAVIOR

The system that we wish to analyze is far from simple. The production of Ph.D.'s involves the joint and interacting behavior of two groups, faculty and students, whose objectives may be more in conflict than in agreement. Furthermore, individual faculty members have personal objectives, from which we must construct a description of departmental objectives. Thus, our theory must consider student and faculty motivation, and combine these into a theory of departmental behavior.

In Section A, a theory of graduate student behavior will be presented, followed in Section B by a theory of faculty motivation. The second section will also examine the relation of faculty objectives to departmental objectives. Section C will discuss the factors that enter into the department's objective function, and in Section D the elements of analysis will be synthesized into a theory that explains departmental differences in pattern and timing of graduate student attrition.

TABLE 3 Seven-Year Enrollment and Degree Totals, University of California, Berkeley, 1961-67

Department	Column A Ph.D. Degrees Awarded	Column B Ph.D. Student-Years[a]	Degrees per Student-Year (Col. A/Col. B)	Student-Years per Degree (Col. B/Col. A)
Entomology	79	397	.198	5.02
Chemistry	335	1,802	.185	5.38
Chemical Engineering	75	404	.185	5.39
Electrical Engineering	175	1,032	.169	5.90
Civil Engineering	129	763	.169	5.91
Physics	380	2,438	.155	6.42
Zoology	94	634	.148	6.74
Botany	52	352	.147	6.77
Geology	37	270	.137	7.30
Biochemistry	63	469	.134	7.44
Geography	21	158	.132	7.52
Mechanical Engineering	94	716	.131	7.62
Psychology	162	1,238	.130	7.64
Astronomy	32	246	.130	7.69
Spanish	18	150	.120	8.33
History	177	1,517	.116	8.57
Math	194	1,680	.115	8.66
Classics	13	118	.110	9.08
German	24	219	.109	9.12
Bacteriology	17	157	.108	9.24
Economics	137	1,316	.104	9.61
Anthropology	69	720	.095	10.43

TABLE 3 (concluded)

Department	Column A Ph.D. Degrees Awarded	Column B Ph.D. Student-Years[a]	Degrees per Student-Year (Col. A/Col. B)	Student-Years Per Degree (Col. B/Col. A)
Political Science	96	1,026	.093	10.69
Physiology	24	267	.089	11.12
English	105	1,374	.076	13.09
Sociology	57	753	.075	13.21
French	28	374	.074	13.36
Philosophy	27	507	.053	18.78

SOURCE: Office of Institutional Research, University of California, Berkeley.

[a] Enrollment figures are understated for those departments that require doctoral students first to earn the M.A. degree; those student-years are not recorded. Enrollments include both degree winners and nondegree students.

A. The Graduate Student

I assume that the vast majority of graduate students view the decision to enter graduate school as an investment, much as the human capital literature suggests. However, in the case of the Ph.D., for those people intent upon an academic career the relevant variable is not necessarily the rate of return calculated in money terms, but the investment in a life-style. Inasmuch as the Ph.D. is the required "union card" of the college professor, one might view the investment decision from the student's point of view as a step function (see Figure 1). The student may study for several years, but if he fails to earn the degree, his payoff is effectively zero, thereby making his investment extremely costly to him.[5]

In considering this model of the student's view of the value of incomplete degree work, it is important to remember the reason for the discontinuity in the function; apart from income considerations, the step signifies that the degree winner is properly certified and acceptable for types of employment not open to individuals without the degree. We shall assume this factor to be of primary importance to students and shall continue to represent the investment as having a sharp discontinuity.

Given the investment model of student behavior, economic theory would suggest that students as potential investors will gather information regarding the costs of investment, the anticipated benefits (pecuniary and nonpecuniary), and the risks surrounding successful completion of the program, and will embark upon graduate study only if the present value of the benefits, adjusted for risk, exceeds the present value of the costs. Certain costs can be determined with some precision; these include the opportunity cost of forgone earnings, tuition, and out-of-pocket costs. Other elements in the cost-benefit analysis however, are subject to considerable uncertainty. In evaluating factors such as the length of time required to earn a degree, sources of financial support, and the probability of successful completion, the student must rely upon information he can gain from the department and other sources such as friends already in the program. One of the most important items of information needed for an informed decision is the probability of successful completion. This is unknown for any individual student, but a reasonable proxy would be the historical experience of students in the department; if y students have enrolled over the past several years and x students have earned the doctorate, then a reasonable probability estimate of successful completion would be x/y. Unfortunately, this rudimentary piece of information is not generally available, leaving the student unable to make an informed estimate of the risk involved.

Knowledge of the demand for one's services upon successful completion of the doctorate would be an additional piece of information needed

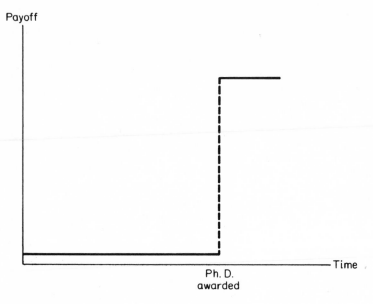

Payoff

Ph. D.
awarded

Time

FIGURE 1

for an informed investment decision. Hard information on this item is essentially unavailable to the student for at least two reasons. First, studies of the academic markets[6] have all commented on the limited information available to participants in these markets. Most universities do not publicly advertise their openings, and no central clearinghouse exists to provide complete job coverage. Second, the length of the production cycle (approximately five years) means that a student would need a forecast of demand five years hence, a difficult prospect at best. Demand in governmental and industrial markets may be better advertised, but the need to forecast years ahead again clouds the picture.

The lack of specific information regarding market demand for Ph.D.'s has probably not been a deterrent to students during the 1950s and 1960s, because of a general belief that the country was desperately short of Ph.D.'s. The baby boom, the tremendous expansion of college enrollments, and the increasing proportion of the 18 to 21 age group going on to college during this period resulted in a series of crisis forecasts, sparked by the National Education Association biennial surveys,[7] which appear to have been widely circulated and believed. Hence, it is reasonable to assume that during the period under study, students believed that many employers would demand their services, regardless of their field.

The following implications for rational student behavior can be deduced from the investment model of student motivation coupled with the discontinuity in the payoff function. (We assume that students can control within limits the speed with which they progress through the program and are free to withdraw at any point.) From the standpoint of the cost of earning the doctorate, of which much is borne by the student, we might conclude that all students will proceed through the program as rapidly as possible, i.e. students will take full course loads, prepare for examinations as rapidly as possible, and not waste time getting started and finishing the dissertation. However, given the nature of the payoff function, rational behavior may result in a decision to proceed more slowly in order to maintain higher grades, improve class standing, earn or keep fellowships, and so forth. To the extent that these factors operate in all fields, we should not expect any departmental differences in the time to degree to arise from this source. However, because opportunity costs do differ between fields, we might expect, ceteris paribus, that students in disciplines with high starting Ph.D. salaries would be less willing to slow their own progress than would students in less well-paying fields. For example, a chemistry student planning to enter industry sees the cost of an additional year in the program as $15,000, while the philosophy student may see a cost of $9,000 for an additional year's work. Furthermore, the philosophy student is presumably aiming at an academic position, and he may rationally calculate that an additional year's work on his thesis may result in an offer from a more prestigious university, thereby increasing the psychic return on the investment.

The preceding analysis suggests that students acting rationally may stretch out their degree programs, and argues that this decision may be related to the type of employment sought by the Ph.D. candidate and to the opportunity costs related to that employment. However, regardless of field, this analysis does not explain the differences in attrition between departments as a function of student decisions. Thus, we must look elsewhere for our theoretical explanation of the large differences in attrition among the disciplines.

The proposed model of student behavior is summarized as follows:

1. The student, regardless of field or sex, is viewed as an investor rather than a consumer of graduate education.

2. The investment requires the earning of the Ph.D. degree for its successful completion, i.e. the student attaches little if any value to incomplete degree work.

3. The investment is not properly evaluated in money terms alone, but is viewed by the student as an investment necessary for entry into certain occupations requiring the doctorate.

4. The potential graduate student has very limited information regarding his probability of successfully completing the degree and regarding the demand for his services upon completion of the program. He undertakes the investment in the face of this uncertainty, because he assumes that the department will treat him justly and that satisfactory employment will be available, i.e. he assumes that the demand for Ph.D.'s in his field will be strong when he graduates.

5. The rational student may have sound reasons for lengthening his time to degree, and departmental differences in average time to degree may be partly explained by the differences in opportunity costs seen by students in different fields. However, analysis of student behavior does not provide an explanation for departmental differences in attrition.

B. The Individual Faculty Member and the Department

My ultimate aim is to propose a theory of departmental behavior, but I must first explain my use of the term "the department." For present purposes, the members of the department are defined to include all faculty members, tenured and nontenured, who are employed full time by the university. I exclude from this definition students, teaching assistants, associate lecturers, and other nonregular faculty ranks. Thus, in seeking a theory of departmental behavior, I must propose a theory of faculty behavior and determine whether goals of individual professors blend consistently into a unified set of goals for the department.

The fundamental assumption of the analysis is that behavior of the faculty members may be explained by the theory of utility maximization. Let us assume that the representative faculty member at a university such as Berkeley, regardless of field and rank, seeks to maximize his own prestige. Using Merton's distinction, faculty members at a large university such as Berkeley are "cosmopolitans" rather than "locals," i.e. primary loyalty is to the discipline rather than to the employing institution. Prestige, therefore, is understood to mean a professor's professional reputation within the discipline as judged by peers in the same field in other universities. Reputation is enhanced by the quality of a person's research publications and by the quality of the graduate students who serve as apprentices to the professor.

It seems reasonable to assume that nearly all faculty members at Berkeley accept this value system or behave as if they do. Initially, a considerable self-selection process operates to minimize the number of faculty members on the staff not interested in research. Furthermore, the university discards those members who fail to produce by refusing tenure offers. Thus, survival on the faculty requires adherence to the values of research, or an uncanny ability to disguise one's true interests and still produce the minimum acceptable amount of research work.

In addition to these negative considerations, however, faculty members have many positive reasons for prestige maximizing. As a professor's prestige increases, his value to the institution also increases. Thus his bargaining power increases and he can command a higher income, faster promotion, a reduced teaching load, and other perquisites. In addition, increased prestige renders him potentially more valuable to a number of competing universities, who will bid for his services, thereby increasing his independence and mobility. In those fields where external funding of research projects is common, increased prestige will result in easier access to these funds. Increased prestige also enhances self-esteem, which is of no small value to people in intellectual occupations. In short, most of the objects that philosophers have recognized as desired by people—power, income, independence, self-esteem—accrue to the academic who successfully maximizes prestige.

If we assume that the prestige of an academic department is simply the sum of the prestige levels of its faculty members, then prestige-maximizing behavior on the part of each professor is consistent with the maximization of departmental prestige. The following passage from Caplow and McGee's *The Academic Marketplace* describes the symbiotic relationship between professor and department:

> The relationship between departmental prestige and the personal prestige of department members is reciprocal. Over a period of time, each man's personal prestige in his discipline is a partial function of his department's prestige, and vice versa. It becomes vitally important, then, to maintain the prestige of the department by hiring only individuals who seem likely to enhance it, since a decline in departmental prestige will be experienced by each individual member as a decline in his own prestige.[8]

Thus, in the remaining analysis, we shall speak of the department's goal of prestige maximization, grounded in the rational, self-regarding behavior of individual professors.

Departmental prestige is not, of course, an absolute measure but is determined on a relative scale by comparison with departments in the same discipline in other universities. Surveys, such as the 1966 Cartter Report,[9] are published periodically, ranking departments by the quality of faculty, thereby establishing relative prestige ratings. To the extent that ratings are reported by simple numerical orderings, departments are forced into a competitive zero sum game, i.e. in order for one department to rise in the ratings, another department must fall. Thus, in order to maximize departmental prestige, a department must compete successfully for prestigious faculty, and this requires resources. From the department's perspective, the Dean is the primary supplier of resources, and the competitors are the other academic departments under the Dean's jurisdiction. Therefore, it seems certain that each department will discover the basis for resource acquisition within the university, and will behave in accordance with the incentive system in order to maximize command over resources.

Specification of resources is reasonably straightforward, and includes the number of full time equivalent (FTE) faculty, teaching and research assistantship (T.A. and R.A.) positions, salary money, funds for research, space, computer time, funds for library acquisitions, and so forth. In particular, it is assumed that departments are highly motivated to maintain or increase their number of faculty FTE positions, for in this way new people can be brought into the department periodically, thereby insuring against stagnation. A desire for increased faculty can be understood as allowing increased specialization, broader coverage of the discipline, reduced teaching loads, and increased prestige.

The connection between graduate students and prestige must now be introduced. Unlike undergraduates and M.A. candidates, doctoral students are part of the prestige system, since many new Ph.D.'s remain in academia. The apprentice system, whereby a Ph.D. candidate completes his research under the guidance of a faculty adviser, tends to link the two individuals so that the work produced will reflect credit or discredit upon them jointly, if not equally. Thus, the prestige-maximizing professor has a definite incentive to seek out the best graduate students and to avoid the worst, hoping that some other professor will be foolish enough to adopt that burden. If a professor is successful in this strategy for several years, his reputation as an effective and desirable adviser will result in the better students seeking him out. Similarly, a professor who has consistently been willing to work with the poorer students, may find himself unable to attract any of the better students. Thus, the quality of student research with which the latter man is associated will decline, and his prestige in the field will suffer correspondingly.[10]

Note that the major visible test of the quality of the student and his work is the job placement which he achieves. The student's thesis is actually read by very few people, and thus judgment must be made in a derivative manner by assuming that the "best" students will be hired by the "best" universities. Thus, within the profession, the quality of job placement reflects credit or discredit on the student, his adviser, and the department. Given this analysis, we can conclude that a number of less able graduate students who manage to reach the dissertation stage each year may experience difficulty in securing a thesis adviser.[11] Nor will it be in the interest of the department to insure that such students complete the degree, for the department rationally seeks to attract the best students, award the Ph.D. degree to those students who can be placed well in other universities, and discourage those students who could only be placed in low-prestige positions. A department that successfully pursues this policy will enhance its own prestige and will be able to attract better students than those departments foolish enough to produce Ph.D.'s for low-prestige institutions.

Consideration of the quality of placement of new Ph.D.'s directs our attention to the job market faced by graduates in each field. In certain disciplines, such as the humanities, virtually the only acceptable employment available is college or university teaching, whereas graduates in the sciences may enter industrial or governmental employment as well. Ph.D.'s who accept employment in government or industry are outside the academic prestige system entirely, meaning that the majority of these placements will have a neutral impact on the department's prestige. The implication for our model of departmental behavior is to make the optimal output of the prestige-maximizing department a function of the demand conditions in the job market for each discipline. The department can regulate the supply of new Ph.D.'s produced by controlling variables such as admission and performance standards, the number and type of requirements included in the curriculum, the use of teaching and research assistantships, and the allocation of fellowships. Because control over the process is lodged within the department, we must look at departmental objectives and the institutional constraints in order to develop a plausible theory of the determinants of Ph.D. production.

Before summarizing this section, a more specific discussion of the control variables available to the department may be in order. These variables can be organized under four headings: admissions, curriculum, information, and use of resources.

Admissions

Until very recently, each academic department at Berkeley set its own graduate admissions standards and determined the number of Ph.D. candidates to admit. Thus, the number of Ph.D. students was a variable largely under departmental control.

Curriculum

The department exercises virtually complete control over the curriculum, including the number of required courses, their sequence, grades and grade requirements, standards exacted on screening and qualifying examinations, and the nature of the dissertation required. The curriculum will affect attrition in two ways. First, the timing of examinations and the standards set will directly affect attrition patterns in the obvious way. The decision on standards determines rather precisely the number allowed to continue, and the timing obviously affects the number of years a student spends before being rejected. Second, in a clumsier and less controllable manner, the longer, the less precise and less articulated the curriculum, the higher the likelihood of attrition. A student who feels that he is making no clear progress toward the degree may experience frustration and discouragement, and will reduce his estimate of the probability of success, possibly reaching a point where the expected present value of the benefits does not exceed the present value of the costs.

Information

The department can exert a strong influence on the individual student's estimate of the probability of success by controlling information needed by the student in making that estimate. Periodic evaluations of the student's progress, interpretation of test results, even chance comments, are the data points which the student uses in constantly revising his estimate of the risk factor. A department that wants to keep a student in the program must provide feedback designed to maintain the student's estimate of the probability of success at a high level.

Resources

Given the resources available for student support in each field, we assume that departments may organize their fellowships, teaching assistantships, and research assistantships in a variety of ways, and some ways may be better than others, judged by the criterion of Ph.D. production. One would expect the more productive departments to have a policy of financial support designed to provide funds in the most useful way to a student at each phase of the program.

Our analysis of the faculty member and the department can be summarized:

1. The faculty member is assumed to be rationally attempting to maximize his own prestige, and this behavior on the part of all

members of a department is consistent with maximization of departmental prestige.

2. Departmental prestige is a function of resources and the quality of placement of its Ph.D. students within the prestige system. Individuals who accept industrial or governmental jobs are outside the academic prestige system and this type of placement is viewed as neutral, or in some cases, positively prestigious.

3. Considerations of the quality of placement forces the analysis to include the nature of demand for new Ph.D.'s in each field as a determinant of the prestige-maximizing level of doctoral output.

4. The department was shown to have control over the factors assumed to affect the rate and timing of attrition. These include admissions policy, curriculum design, information, and organization of resources for financial support.

C. Analysis of the Department's Objective Function

In the previous section it was argued that departmental prestige is a function of two variables: (1) resources; (2) quality of Ph.D. placement. We must now examine these two variables in order to understand how they are determined.

In California, the following formula has been developed with the State Department of Finance to determine the numbers of FTE faculty positions that the state will fund:[12]

$$\text{FTE Faculty} = \frac{1.0\,LD + 1.5\,UD + 2.5\,OG + 3.5\,AD}{28}$$

where

LD = number of FTE lower-division students enrolled;
UD = number of FTE upper-division students enrolled;
OG = number of FTE Master's candidates and first-year doctoral students enrolled; and
AD = number of FTE advanced doctoral students enrolled.

In other words, the state is committed in principle to a weighted 28 to 1 student-faculty ratio. Note that each advanced doctoral student enrolled brings the campus ⅛ FTE faculty position.

Internally, there is considerable evidence indicating that allocation of FTE positions to departments closely follows the same weighted enrollment formula. Interviews with Budget Office personnel revealed that departmental requests for new positions are often bolstered by enrollment figures, and cross-section regression analysis indicated that weighted enrollments "explain" approximately 82 per cent of the variation in departmental staffing. Therefore, although the formula expressed in equation 1 is not followed mechanically at the departmental level, it seems reasonably clear that departments are awarded faculty positions on the basis of weighted student enrollments. Once the number of faculty positions for each department has been determined, other resources such as office space and nonacademic personnel can be functionally related to the faculty numbers. Thus, the resource allocation process can be viewed as a two-stage process (see Figure 2).

The second element of the department's prestige function is the quality of placement achieved by the department's doctoral students. Quality of placement for each year's group of students will be a function of the number produced and the demand for Ph.D.'s in a field. The following simple model may clarify the process of placement.

We begin with the following assumptions:

1. Assume that at any point in time a department can rank its graduate students from best to worst.
2. Assume also that a department and its graduate students would generally agree on a ranking of university, college, and junior-college departments according to prestige. (We might think of a clustering of colleges and universities into five broad groups, rated along the scale from high, positive prestige to low, negative prestige.)
3. Assume that regardless of the rate of attrition, the department will view those students who complete the Ph.D. as its best students. In other words, assume that the awarding of Ph.D.'s follows the student rank ordering, so that if 3 students out of 10 receive the doctorate, the department will view the successful candidates as the 3 best students.
4. Considering just the academic market, assume a strong positive correlation between the prestige ordering of job offers and the department's rank ordering of its successful Ph.D. candidates.
5. Assume that a student with multiple offers will accept the most prestigious position.

Given these assumptions, our model of the market's functioning as viewed by the department is depicted as in Figure 3.

Since it has been argued that the department controls the number of Ph.D.'s it produces, the decision problem facing the department is to determine where in the rank ordering of students it should draw the line. The actual number cannot be precisely controlled because of random factors, but one can assume that a department knows approximately how much attrition a particular curriculum, set of standards, and level of financial support will produce. In other words, the department is pre-

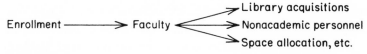

FIGURE 2

sumed to have considerable knowledge of its production function. The fundamental hypothesis is that the decision on where to draw the line is a function of the department's perceived demand curve for its graduates. In Figure 3, a department wishing to maximize prestige by avoiding placement in schools with negative prestige would only award Ph.D. degrees to the six "best" students, resulting in an attrition rate of 50 per cent.

The introduction of another large employing sector, such as industry, provides the department with an escape hatch from the prestige system. In the previous example, all the department's products were forced into the academic market; thus, to avoid poor placement, a department must create a certain amount of attrition. However, a department such as Chemistry enjoys a large, nonacademic demand for its Ph.D.'s, and is therefore not under pressure to create attrition as is a department lacking that outlet.

The elements of a theory explaining differences in attrition rates by department are now complete.

D. The Theory of Departmental Attrition

The theory of departmental attrition follows in a direct and simple way from the previous discussion. In this section, a simple analytic model will be developed to explain the differences in departmental success rates. In the following section, comments on the differences in timing of attrition will be made.

The Theory of Different Success Rates

It should be stressed that this theory describes the long-run adjustment of a department. Academic departments are relatively slow in their ability to react to changing circumstances; the loose form of organization and the collegial system insures this. Furthermore, we know that much uncertainty and many random factors affect the system under discussion, while the theory describes a department operating with full information and considerable foresight. Nonetheless, the following simple model captures the essence of the optimization problem facing the department.

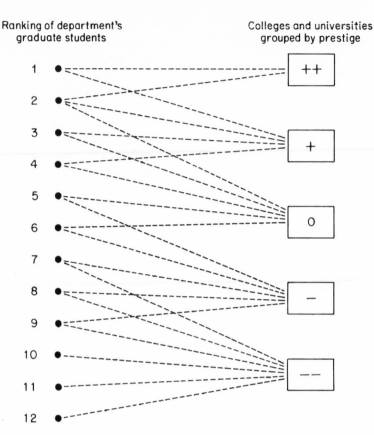

Ranking of department's
graduate students

Colleges and universities
grouped by prestige

1
2
3
4
5
6
7
8
9
10
11
12

++
+
0
−
−−

NOTE: Dotted lines indicate job offers.

FIGURE 3

We have assumed the department's objective to be prestige maximization. Prestige was discussed in terms of the department's ability to attract and hold good people, and its ability to place its doctoral students well. Following the logic of the last section, this reduced operationally to command over resources and the number of Ph.D.'s produced. The functional relationships implied can be expressed as follows:

(1)   Prestige $= f$ (resources, number of Ph.D.'s produced)

(2)   Resources $= g$ (enrollments)

(3)   Number of Ph.D.'s produced $= h$ (enrollments).

Our interest focuses on relation 3 which defines the attrition rate. I have argued that this function is not technologically determined, but is subject to departmental control. The model provides one plausible hypothesis to explain why departments differ with regard to relationship 3.

Graphically, the functions might be expressed as they are in Figures 4 through 7.

Figure 4 depicts a linear relationship between enrollments and resources over a range from X_0 to X_1, with a kink at X_1 and a leveling of the function. The kink at X_1 recognizes the fact that departments are not free to expand enrollments indefinitely, that limits are imposed by scarce resources and administrative control.

Figure 5 sketches one possible relation between doctoral enrollment and Ph.D.'s produced. Of particular interest is the angle θ, which can range over values from $0°$ to $45°$, with $0°$ representing 100 per cent attrition and $45°$ representing no attrition.

Figure 6 depicts the relation between resources and prestige. The function may or may not be linear; the only restriction is that it be monotopically increasing.

Figure 7 represents one possible relationship between the number of Ph.D.'s produced and departmental prestige. This particular graph might represent a field serving only the academic market, with the shape of the function following directly from the analysis of the previous section. This particular function is also properly interpreted as the department's perceived demand curve for its Ph.D. products. The shape of the function will vary according to the nature of the market served.

These functions are now linked together as a system to show how the department's prestige-maximizing behavior determines the optimal attrition rate. The French and Chemistry departments, representing the extremes of departmental behavior, will be examined.

The French Department is a typical humanities department whose Ph.D.'s only enter academia. For the past twenty-one years, the department at Berkeley has awarded between one and five Ph.D.'s a year despite a rising enrollment. Our theory suggests that this behavior would be consistent with a perceived demand curve of the type sketched in quadrant III of Figure 8. Given a stable market without large fluctuations in demand, the department's prestige-maximizing long-run equilibrium output would be three Ph.D.'s per year, with small expected variance caused by random factors. This output rate will insure P_2 units of prestige from placement.

The combination of quadrants I and II indicate that the department will enroll the maximum allowable, E_1, in order to receive R_1 resources, producing P_1 units of prestige.

The angle θ_1 in quadrant IV, the department's optimal attrition rate,

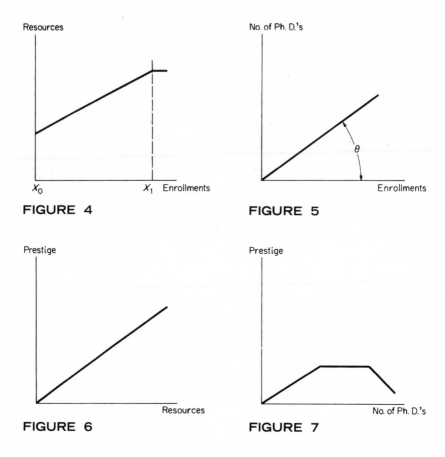

Resources

X_0 X_1 Enrollments

FIGURE 4

No. of Ph. D.'s

θ

Enrollments

FIGURE 5

Prestige

Resources

FIGURE 6

Prestige

No. of Ph. D.'s

FIGURE 7

is now completely determined by the intersection of the prestige-maximizing enrollment and output decisions from quadrants I and III. Maximum prestige possible, $P_1 + P_2$, is attained with the department not having to trade off one determinant of prestige against the other.

Regardless of department, quadrants I and II remain essentially unchanged, i.e., departments have incentive to maintain enrollments at a maximum. Thus, the market will determine the angle θ for each department.

Relative to a field such as French, the market during the 1950s and 1960s for Ph. D. chemists was very strong and diversified. Fewer than 50 per cent of the chemists produced by graduate departments accepted academic positions,[13] as industrial firms sought to hire these individuals. In this circumstance, one might assume that the Chemistry Department would view the demand for their Ph.D.'s as unlimited, with each stu-

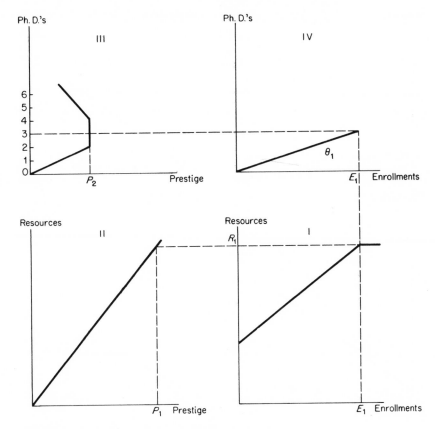

FIGURE 8   Case 1, French Department

dent receiving multiple offers, all of them satisfactory placements. A discipline in this fortunate position would have no need to organize the program to insure a certain level of attrition; in fact, every effort would be made to produce as many Ph. D.'s as possible, resulting in an angle θ_2 very near to 45°. This field would be graphed as follows in Figure 9.

The two polar cases demonstrate how market forces operate upon prestige maximizing departments to produce different rates of attrition. We must now turn our attention to the differences in timing of attrition observed among departments.

The Theory of Differences in Attrition Patterns

As mentioned earlier, Stark's study[14] revealed two disturbing aspects of attrition at Berkeley, the differences in departmental success rates and

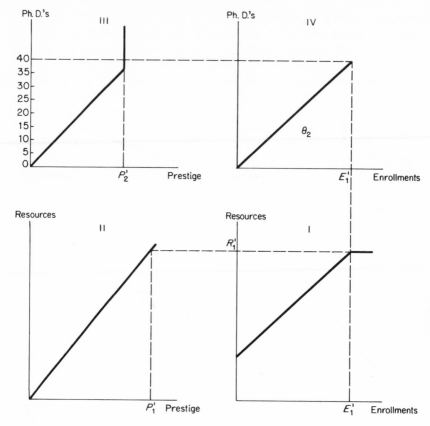

FIGURE 9 Case 2, Chemistry Department

the differences in timing of attrition. Thus, not only did the Chemistry Department have a high success rate, but the attrition occurred almost entirely within the first year. By contrast, the other three fields had numerous students enrolled for two, three, or even four years before leaving without a degree. The theory presented in the first part of this section explained differences in success rates; the purpose of this section will be to present a theory to explain the differences in timing of attrition.

As in the first part, the theory will concentrate upon the department's role, with emphasis placed upon the production functions in each field and the internal economy of departments. The nature of faculty input and the role of physical capital in the production process will be relevant factors, as well as the graduate student's role in the department's economy.

Consider first the economy of the French Department. Previously it was suggested that the demand for Ph.D.'s in French is not great and has been reasonably stable during the last several years, relative to many other disciplines. It was argued that this fact explains the low success rate in French. Weakness in the market also explains the lack of financial support available to graduate students in French. The department, however, has a demand for graduate students based on its need to produce student credit hours to maintain its claim over university resources. Furthermore, the presence of numerous graduate students generates demand for advanced courses in highly specialized areas of French literature, the type of courses that faculty members like to teach. The department's demand for graduate students coupled with the minimal demand for French Ph.D.'s would pose a serious problem were it not for the presence of Letters and Science undergraduates who are required to complete four quarters of a foreign language.[15] This requirement generates a large demand for teaching assistants and solves the department's problem of providing financial support for graduate students. Thus, the economy of this department rests, somewhat perilously, on the demand for undergraduate instruction artificially created by breadth requirements.

The technology of Ph.D. production in this field is reasonably simple, and from the department's point of view, inexpensive. Faculty input is limited to course offerings, testing, and thesis advising; capital requirements are classroom space and library facilities, provided by university funds. The department has no incentive to economize on the use of resources required to produce Ph.D.'s; in fact, there is every incentive to maximize use and control over such resources.

From the perspective of the French faculty, then, the graduate student must be viewed as a very valuable member of the department's economy. Not only does the graduate student teach the dull introductory courses, but he is a source of student credit hours and demand for advanced instruction. Departmental technology is such that having graduate students in residence for several years is costless to the faculty, and not without certain advantages. First, the experienced teaching assistant requires minimal supervision; if graduate turnover were high, faculty would be forced to spend more time working with the fledgling teachers. In addition, second- and third-year graduates can be expected to enroll in more advanced courses, thereby allowing increased faculty specialization. Consequently, in this type of department, faculty members have no incentives to make rapid decisions to terminate Ph.D. aspirants. Graduate students are particularly valuable assets to such departments and will be kept in residence as long as possible. Eventually, fatigue, financial pressures, or the dissertation will produce the necessary attrition.

25 | David W. Breneman

Linking the analysis of the first part with the above, we have a picture of a humanities department desiring a high attrition rate, but not wanting this to occur within the early years of the student's graduate career. If this is an accurate description of the department's objectives, we would expect to find the following features of the graduate program:

1. Critical hurdles designed to eliminate candidates in the late rather than in the early stages of the program.
2. A curriculum sufficiently ambiguous and fuzzy to keep students mildly confused about their rate of progress toward the degree.
3. Conscious minimization of the student's feeling that he is a member of a particular graduate class or cohort. A student should have a minimum of checkpoints by which to measure his progress.
4. Feedback from the department designed to keep the student's estimate of success high.
5. Extremely demanding requirements for the dissertation, this being the final hurdle for the degree.
6. Use of the same individuals as teaching assistants for several years.
7. Absence of discussion or information related to the job market for Ph.D.'s.
8. A general lack of information about the historical success rates of graduate students, attrition patterns, and so forth. The best policy for the department would be to minimize information flows to the students.
9. A tendency for the department not to keep detailed records on the experiences of past graduate students.
10. Little evidence of major curriculum revisions.

By way of contrast, let us now consider a natural science department such as Chemistry. Stark's study demonstrated that virtually all of the attrition in this field occurs in the first year. Why might this be?

First, our earlier analysis suggested that this department, having faced an excellent market during the 1950s and through most of the 1960s, would have had little reason to want any particular level of attrition; in fact, market factors alone may have dictated a zero attrition rate as optimal. Under these circumstances, the department would have no incentive to delay a decision on a student until the second or third year. Students who appear short on intelligence or motivation should be spotted quickly and removed to make room for others who will be successful.

Departmental technology also plays an important role in this type of field. Unlike the humanities, a doctoral student in chemistry may easily require thousands of dollars worth of expensive equipment for dissertation research. This equipment is often purchased from the funds of a professor's research grant. The professor, having hired the student as a research assistant, cannot afford to have someone incompetent working with equipment purchased from his grant, since the funding agency expects satisfactory research results. Should a student in this situation fail to produce, the professor would bear a large part of the cost. Therefore, the department must do its screening early to protect against this type of embarrassment. Even if the Chemistry Department faced a poor job market, the above considerations suggest that attrition would occur early in the program. The inclusion of expensive capital equipment in the production function plus a heavier involvement of faculty time makes attrition in the third or fourth year too expensive for the department to bear.

Note the fundamental difference between the cost functions in French and Chemistry departments. An advanced doctoral student in French may need expensive library resources, funded through the university budget. This cost is not borne by any professor in the French Department, i.e., the cost is not included in the professor's or the department's cost function. If the student fails to complete the dissertation, the department will still benefit from the enlarged French collection in the library. By contrast, chemistry professors are directly accountable to the external funding agencies which support their research; thus, the performance of graduate students is incorporated into the individual professor's cost function, providing the professor with incentive to see that the work is done.

Although both departments have a demand for graduate students as an input in the production of student credit hours, the Chemistry Department primarily needs graduate students for research assistance, while the French Department's primary need is for teaching assistance. Given the research orientation of the Ph.D. degree, it is obvious that the needs of the Chemistry Department coincide with the degree requirements much more closely than do those of the French Department.

Our analysis of the Chemistry Department's technology suggests that the department will screen its students closely during the first year, eliminating from the program students who might be poor research risks. That done, one would expect a rationally organized curriculum designed to get students through quickly and into the market.

III. EVIDENCE SUPPORTING THE THEORY

A. The Demand for Ph.D.'s

Writing in 1966, Allan Cartter made the following observation:

> Considering the importance of the problem to higher education, and the
> many hundreds of millions of dollars appropriated by the federal government
> for the expansion of graduate education over the last few years, it is rather
> astonishing that we know so little about the present and probable supply and
> demand of college teachers.[16]

Cartter was referring to our ignorance regarding aggregate supply and
demand for Ph.D.'s; he later comments that we know even less about
supply and demand by field.[17] In particular, we lack reliable time series
data on demand for Ph.D.'s by discipline.

In his 1965 study, *Academic Labor Markets*,[18] prepared for the U.S.
Department of Labor, David Brown proposes several measures for comparing excess demand across fields:[19]

1. starting salaries of newly graduated Ph.D.'s;
2. extent of salary increase;
3. salaries paid to full professors in 1962–63;
4. academic rank of newly graduated Ph.D.'s;
5. unfilled positions as a percentage of all positions;
6. percentage of newly graduated Ph.D.'s entering college teaching;
   and
7. expansion demand as a percentage of all hiring.

Brown argues that none of the above measures taken separately
adequately captures the relative supply-demand balance across fields;
however, survey data Brown collected allowed him to rank 23 disciplines
on each of the seven measures. These separate rankings were then
combined into a single shortage index for 1964, reproduced as Table 4.
In commenting on these rankings, Brown stresses that, "The individual
discipline markets are tighter in the expanding fields and in those fields
where the opportunities outside the academic community are
greatest."[20]

In considering Brown's data, we merely note that those fields in high
demand in 1964, the hard sciences and engineering, are the fields with
minimal attrition and shorter time-to-degree at Berkeley, while the
fields with lesser demand, the humanities, are the high attrition, lengthy
time-to-degree programs at Berkeley. Thus, these data are consistent
with the demand-oriented theory of Ph.D. production. Further reference to these data will be made as we turn to the supply side of the
market.

TABLE 4 Brown's Ranking of 23 Disciplines by Excess Demand,[a] 1964

Discipline	Shortage Index
Electrical Engineering	1
Educational Services and Administration	2
Mechanical Engineering	3
Mathematics	4
Physics	5
Economics	6
Civil Engineering	7
Chemistry	8
Counseling and Guidance	9
Clinical Psychology	10
Sociology	11
Art	12
Secondary Education	13
Political Science	14
Earth Sciences and Geology	15
General Biology	16
Biochemistry	17
Physical Education and Health	18
Music	19
General Zoology	20
English and Literature	21
History	22
French	23

SOURCE: David Brown, *Academic Labor Markets*.
[a] Rank of 1 means excess demand greatest in that discipline.

B. The Supply of Ph.D.'s

Although we have no precise method for determining the demand schedule for Ph.D.'s by field over time, annual figures are available on the supply of new doctorates. In assessing departmental performance, a comparison of Berkeley's doctoral output with national production of Ph.D.'s adds to the plausibility of our market-oriented theory.

Data were collected on doctorates awarded annually by field for the 21-year period, 1947–48 to 1967–68. In addition to total production, degrees awarded by the top 20 quality ranked schools[21] in each discipline were recorded. Table 5 presents the 21-year totals for each field. Examination of the column headed "Berkeley % of Top 20" demonstrates that Berkeley is a significant producer in all subject areas. For example, Berkeley's forty-one Ph.D.'s in Spanish (an average of two per

TABLE 5 Total Ph.D. Degrees Produced by U.S. Universities, 28 Fields, 1947–48 to 1967–68 (21-year totals)

Field	No. of Ph.D.'s Awarded in U.S.	No. of Ph.D.'s Awarded by 20 Top Quality Schools[a]	No. of Ph.D.'s Awarded by Berkeley	% of Total Produced by 20 Top Quality Schools	Berkeley % of Total	Berkeley % of Top 20
Classics	775	638	25	82.3	3.2	3.9
English	9,161	5,349	209	58.4	2.3	3.9
French	1,399	1,074	53	76.8	3.8	4.9
German	1,021	696	53	68.2	5.2	7.6
Spanish	1,036	649	41	62.6	4.0	6.3
Philosophy	2,190	1,381	66	63.1	3.0	4.8
Anthropology	1,316	1,197	119	91.0	9.0	9.9
Economics	6,077	3,538	300	58.2	4.9	8.5
Geography	1,115	936	51	83.9	4.6	5.4
History	7,910	4,695	364	59.4	4.6	7.8
Political Science	4,472	2,839	194	63.5	4.3	6.8
Sociology	3,728	2,118	95	56.8	2.5	4.5
Bacteriology	3,247[b]	1,286[b]	85	39.6	2.6	6.6
Biochemistry	3,857[b]	1,655[b]	198	42.9	5.1	12.0
Botany	2,947	1,485	130	50.4	4.4	8.8
Entomology	1,710	1,408	188	82.3	11.0	13.4
Physiology	1,727[b]	721[b]	95	41.7	5.5	13.2
Psychology	14,157	5,448	351	38.5	2.5	6.4
Zoology	3,915[b]	1,989[b]	236	50.8	6.0	11.9

Astronomy	533	487	65	91.4	12.2	13.3
Chemistry	23,418	10,412	778	44.5	3.3	7.5
Geology	3,542	2,414	92	68.2	2.6	3.8
Mathematics	7,097	3,635	313	51.2	4.4	8.6
Physics	12,699	6,616	811	52.1	6.4	12.2
Chemical Engineering	4,142	2,236	103	54.0	2.5	4.6
Civil Engineering	2,405	1,684	142	70.0	5.9	8.4
Electrical Engineering	5,617	3,755	244	66.8	4.3	6.5
Mechanical Engineering	2,846	1,760	146	61.8	5.1	8.3
Total, 28 fields	134,059	72,101	5,547	53.8	4.1	7.7

SOURCE: U.S. Department of Health, Education and Welfare, Office of Education, *Earned Degrees Conferred*, 1947–48 to 1967–68.

[a] Ranked in *Assessment of Quality* (Cartter Report 1966).

[b] Totals are understated because certain universities did not list their degrees under this category.

year) still represents 6.3 per cent of the production by the top 20 schools. In terms of sheer numbers, a recent publication of the National Research Council, *Report on Doctoral Programs,* shows that Berkeley ranked fifth out of 184 institutions in total doctorate production for the period 1958–62, and first out of 213 for the period 1963–67.[22] Of the fields considered in this study, Berkeley's lowest departmental ranking in terms of Ph.D. output for the period 1963–67 was thirteenth out of 102 in the English and American Language and Literature category.[23] In virtually every other field, Berkeley ranked within the top four producers. Forgetting departmental enrollments and looking just at output, there would seem to be little cause for concern.

Shifting to individual fields, consider the supply of French Ph.D.'s, reported in Table 6. Note that Berkeley's output of two to three Ph.D.'s per year generally accounted for 4 to 6 per cent of top 20 production. One realizes how thin the market for French Ph.D.'s is by recalling that Brown's shortage index ranked this field last in terms of excess demand during the middle 1960s; in fact, Brown referred to French as one of the surplus disciplines. And yet, during that period, total production averaged only seventy Ph.D.'s, per year with the top 20 schools averaging approximately fifty Ph.D.'s. If, during 1963–64, Berkeley's department, with a graduate enrollment of over ninety students, had produced a reasonable number of Ph.D.'s for that enrollment (say fourteen instead of four), Berkeley's per cent of the top 20 production would have risen from 6.0 per cent to 18.2 per cent. I submit that an increase of such magnitude would not have gone unnoticed in a very thin market. One can imagine the department facing a very difficult marketing operation; not only might the jobs not be there, but within the fraternity of French departments, such an increase might have been interpreted as a reduction in quality. The department might have found it very difficult to regain its reputation as a quality program.

Two additional representative tables are presented, covering the supply of Ph.D.'s in German (Table 7) and Political Science (Table 8). Since both fields are typified by high attrition rates at Berkeley, the reader is encouraged to consider the effect that tripling the department's output would have had upon the market in each field. I believe that these figures reveal a major determinant of each department's decision regarding the desirable number of Ph.D.'s to produce.

C. Placement of Berkeley Ph.D.'s

Earlier it was hypothesized that departments at Berkeley are not interested in producing Ph.D.'s for all segments of the academic market, but operate instead to produce a number that can be placed reasonably

TABLE 6 Annual U.S. Production of Ph.D. Degrees in French, 1947–48 to 1967–68

Year	No. of Ph.D.'s Awarded in U.S.	No. of Ph.D.'s Awarded by 20 Top Quality Schools[a]	No. of Ph.D.'s Awarded by Berkeley	% of Total Produced by Top 20 Schools	Berkeley % of Total	Berkeley % of Top 20
1967–68	159	119	5	74.8	3.1	4.2
1966–67	118	83	5	70.2	4.2	6.0
1965–66	94	69	6	73.4	6.4	8.7
1964–65	80	57	2	71.2	2.5	3.5
1963–64	88	67	4	76.1	4.5	6.0
1962–63	63	50	3	79.4	4.8	6.0
1961–62	63	48	3	76.2	4.8	6.2
1960–61	51	35	2	68.6	3.9	5.7
1959–60	63	51	3	81.0	4.8	5.9
1958–59	70	55	3	78.6	4.3	5.4
1957–58	41	35	2	85.4	4.9	5.7
1956–57	50	43	3	86.0	6.0	7.0
1955–56	59	48	2	81.4	3.4	4.2
1954–55	53	40	2	75.5	3.8	5.0
1953–54	58	35	1	60.4	1.7	2.9
1952–53	57	43	2	75.4	3.5	4.6
1951–52	52	46	2	88.5	3.8	4.3
1950–51	44	35	1	79.5	2.3	2.8
1949–50	58	51	1	87.9	1.7	2.0

TABLE 6 (concluded)

Year	No. of Ph.D.'s Awarded in U.S.	No. of Ph.D.'s Awarded by 20 Top Quality Schools[a]	No. of Ph.D.'s Awarded by Berkeley	% of Total Produced by Top 20 Schools	Berkeley % of Total	Berkeley % of Top 20
1948–49	48	39	0	81.2	0.0	0.0
1947–48	30	25	1	83.3	3.3	4.0
Total, 21 years	1,399	1,074	53	76.8	3.8	4.9

NOTE: Other statistics based upon 21-year totals:

	Total U.S. Universities	Berkeley
French degrees as % of total degrees awarded in all 28 fields	1.04	0.95
% of degrees in French awarded to men	64.8	81.1

SOURCE: H.E.W., *Earned Degrees Conferred*; Berkeley degrees gathered from dissertation records.
[a] Ranked by the Cartter Report.

TABLE 7 Annual U.S. Production of Ph.D. Degrees in German, 1947–48 to 1967–68

Year	No. of Ph.D.'s Awarded in U.S.	No. of Ph.D.'s Awarded by 20 Top Quality Schools[a]	No. of Ph.D.'s Awarded by Berkeley	% of Total Produced by Top 20 Schools	Berkeley % of Total	Berkeley % of Top 20
1967–68	122	69	4	56.6	3.3	5.8
1966–67	100	67	4	67.0	4.0	6.0
1965–66	95	49	4	51.6	4.2	8.2
1964–65	68	46	4	67.6	5.9	8.7
1963–64	78	51	2	65.4	2.6	3.9
1962–63	37	28	1	75.7	2.7	3.6
1961–62	46	34	5	73.9	10.9	14.7
1960–61	38	26	1	68.4	2.6	3.8
1959–60	24	17	0	70.8	0.0	0.0
1958–59	29	26	2	89.6	6.9	7.7
1957–58	35	27	5	77.1	14.3	18.5
1956–57	32	25	5	78.1	15.6	20.0
1955–56	33	17	3	51.5	9.1	17.6
1954–55	26	19	2	73.1	7.7	10.5
1953–54	46	35	4	76.1	8.7	11.4
1952–53	37	33	1	89.2	2.7	3.0
1951–52	56	43	0	76.8	0.0	0.0
1950–51	31	22	1	70.1	3.2	4.5
1949–50	40	30	3	75.0	7.5	10.0

TABLE 7 (concluded)

Year	No. of Ph.D.'s Awarded in U.S.	No. of Ph.D.'s Awarded by 20 Top Quality Schools[a]	No. of Ph.D.'s Awarded by Berkeley	% of Total Produced by Top 20 Schools	Berkeley % of Total	Berkeley % of Top 20
1948–49	27	14	0	51.8	0.0	0.0
1947–48	21	18	2	85.7	9.5	11.1
Total, 21 years	1,021	696	53	68.2	5.2	7.6

NOTE: Other statistics based upon 21-year totals:

	Total U.S. Universities	Berkeley
German degrees as % of total degrees awarded in all 28 fields	0.76	0.95
% of degrees in German awarded to men	78.6	86.8

SOURCE: H.E.W., *Earned Degrees Conferred.*
[a] Ranked by the Cartter Report.

TABLE 8 Annual U.S. Production of Ph.D. Degrees in Political Science, 1947-48 to 1967-68

Year	No. of Ph.D.'s Awarded in U.S.	No. of Ph.D.'s Awarded by 20 Top Quality Schools[a]	No. of Ph.D.'s Awarded by Berkeley	% of Total Produced by Top 20 Schools	Berkeley % of Total	Berkeley % of Top 20
1967-68	457	267	17	58.4	3.7	6.4
1966-67	390	213	20	54.6	5.1	9.4
1965-66	336	192	15	57.1	4.5	7.8
1964-65	304	181	16	59.5	5.3	8.8
1963-64	263	171	12	65.0	4.6	7.0
1962-63	228	134	9	59.2	3.9	6.7
1961-62	214	142	7	66.4	3.3	4.9
1960-61	217	153	10	70.5	4.6	6.5
1959-60	201	137	7	68.2	3.5	5.1
1958-59	191	118	6	61.8	3.1	5.1
1957-58	170	104	8	61.2	4.7	7.7
1956-57	156	106	8	67.9	5.1	7.5
1955-56	203	126	9	62.1	4.4	7.1
1954-55	181	114	6	63.0	3.3	5.3
1953-54	153	109	9	71.2	5.9	8.2
1952-53	164	114	7	69.5	4.3	6.1
1951-52	147	121	11	82.3	7.5	9.1
1950-51	152	104	6	68.4	3.9	5.8
1949-50	127	85	3	66.9	2.4	3.5

TABLE 8 (concluded)

Year	No. of Ph.D.'s Awarded in U.S.	No. of Ph.D.'s Awarded by 20 Top Quality Schools[a]	No. of Ph.D.'s Awarded by Berkeley	% of Total Produced by Top 20 Schools	Berkeley % of Total	Berkeley % of Top 20
1948–49	119	75	4	63.0	3.4	5.3
1947–48	99	72	4	72.7	4.0	5.6
Total, 21 years	4,472	2,839	194	63.5	4.3	6.8

NOTE: Other statistics based upon 21-year totals:

	Total U.S. Universities	Berkeley
Political science degrees as % of total degrees awarded in all 28 fields	3.33	3.49
% of degrees in political science awarded to men	92.2	92.8

SOURCE: H.E.W., *Earned Degrees Conferred.*
[a] Ranked by the Cartter Report.

well within the prestige system. Underlying this view was the assumption that quality of doctoral student placement reflects positively or negatively upon the prestige of the producing institution; it was argued that if a department "overproduced" to the extent that significant numbers of its placements were in inferior quality schools, the department's reputation would suffer. These assertions are open to empirical test, the purpose of this section.

In the theoretical section, it was suggested that conceptually one could categorize the colleges and universities in this country into five prestige classes, ranking them symbolically ++, +, 0, −, and −−. The argument was made that Berkeley departments control their output so that the vast majority of placements will be made within the first three groups; placements in the − and −− categories would be avoided by not overproducing. To give meaning to these classifications, we turn again to David Brown's publication *Academic Labor Markets*.[24]

For his own purposes, Brown produced a Prestige Index, by which he ranked 1,121 U.S. colleges and universities. With numerous caveats, he proposed the following eight factors as measuring elements of academic prestige:[25]

1. percentage of faculty with Ph.D.'s;
2. average compensation (salary and fringe benefits) per faculty member;
3. percentage of students continuing to graduate school;
4. percentage of students studying at the graduate level;
5. number of volumes in library per full-time student;
6. total number of full-time faculty members;
7. faculty-student ratio; and
8. total current income per student.

Every school was ranked from 1 to 1,121 on each factor, and an average rank, or composite rating, was computed for each institution. The schools were then broken into six groups, labeled A through F, with group A being the most prestigious, group F the least prestigious.

Brown's classification was accepted for the present study, with one major change. The ++ category in our conceptualization was reserved for universities ranked 1 through 10 in each field by the Cartter Report, for it was felt that the very highest prestige accrues to placement in such schools. Brown's "A" ranking included colleges such as Amherst and Swarthmore, which, while prestigious in their own way, do not have the status of graduate-oriented research institutions. Consequently, Table 9 sets forth the definitions of our proposed prestige rating system.

It is not feasible to reproduce the list of all 1,121 schools; the interested reader is referred to Brown's book.[26] To give an idea of the type of school included in each category, a few examples are provided:

TABLE 9   Definition of College and University Prestige
             Groupings

Group	Definition	No. of Institutions
+ +	Top 10 Cartter Report schools in each field	10
+	Brown's groups A and B plus schools ranked 11–20 in Cartter Report	65 (approximate)
0	Brown's groups C and D	335
−	Brown's group E	283
− −	Brown's group F	428
	Total	1,121

SOURCE: Cartter Report, and Brown, *Academic Labor Markets.*

+ +   Refer to Cartter Report for each field—generally the well-known universities, such as Harvard, Yale, Princeton, Michigan, etc.

+   Amherst, Swarthmore, Williams, Wellesley, Rochester, University of California at San Diego, Tulane.

0   Antioch, Colorado College, George Washington University, University of Colorado, Kansas, Rutgers, Ohio State, Temple.

−   University of Alabama, Arizona, Butler, Central Michigan, Clemson, East Texas State, Elmira College, San Diego State, University of San Francisco, Southern Oregon.

− −   Abilene Christian, California State Polytechnic, Brigham Young, University of Dayton, DePaul, Florida A&M, Golden Gate College, Slippery Rock, Memphis State, Seton Hall, Washburn University.

Data on first academic position taken by Berkeley doctorates were gathered from the National Academy of Sciences, "Survey of Earned Doctorates."[27] Beginning with fiscal year 1967, the computerized data list the name of the first academic employer or postdoctoral institution; thus, data on two years' placement (1967, 1968) were available for the twenty-eight departments. A total of 466 academic appointments were listed; of these, seventy-four new Ph.D.'s remained at Berkeley, presumably for postdoctoral work. These seventy-four were excluded from the ratings. The remaining 392 were ranked according to prestige groupings described in Table 9. Results for the total placements are presented in Table 10. Comparing the number of placements in each category to the number of schools in each prestige group (Table 9), we note that nearly half (47.5%) of Berkeley's graduates accepted first positions in

TABLE 10   Number of Berkeley Academic Placements in
Each Prestige Grouping, 1967, 1968

Group	No. of Placements	% of Total
++	85	21.7
+	101	25.8
0	157	40.0
−	37	9.4
− −	12	3.1
Total	392	100.0

SOURCE: National Academy of Sciences, "Survey of Earned Doctorates," computer tape for University of California, Berkeley.

schools ranked either ++ or +, although these two categories encompass only 75 colleges and universities. Furthermore, of the 428 institutions listed as − − schools, only 12 secured the services of a Berkeley Ph.D. The 410 schools representing ++, +, and 0 categories employed 87.5 per cent of the Berkeley graduates entering academia; the fact that only 49 Berkeley doctorates (12.5%) accepted positions in one of the 711 institutions carrying a − or − − rating suggests that the departments have not been interested in serving this sector of the market.

Our understanding of academic placement is enhanced by examining the positions accepted from 1962–63 to 1969–70 by the graduates of Berkeley's English Department, a large department (492 graduate students enrolled in 1965–66) with attrition from the doctoral program in excess of 80 per cent. Information was gathered from the annual departmental reports of the Committee on Placements.[28] Table 11 lists the schools where jobs were taken, by prestige grouping. Note that of the 136 placements ranked on the prestige index, 118 (87%) were in schools in the top three categories. Clearly, during the 1960s, Berkeley's English Department was not producing Ph.D.'s for the vast, less prestigious portion of the academic market.

D.   Interviews with Faculty and Students

The purpose of interviewing faculty and students in several departments was simply to gain more understanding of the factors perceived by the participants as affecting time to degree and attrition. The theory of Section II was not directly presented to the interviewees because we did not wish to bias the response; instead, the differences in departmental performance were described and interviewees were asked how they

TABLE 11 Placement of Berkeley English Ph.D.'s, 1962–63 to 1969–70, by Prestige Grouping

Year	++	+	0	–	– –	Unranked
1962–63	Harvard (2) Stanford Princeton Indiana	Virginia Amherst U.S.C. UCLA (2)	Rutgers	Hunter		
1963–64	Yale (2) Columbia (2) Indiana (2) Cornell	Reed (2) Williams Smith Dartmouth Stony Brook	Texas Bucknell Rutgers			
1964–65	Columbia Indiana	UCLA Tufts Pomona UC-Santa Cruz UC-Irvine St. John's UC-S. Barbara Wellesley	Carleton Mich. State Texas Massachusetts Colorado			McGill
1965–66	Harvard Princeton Chicago Columbia Yale Wisconsin	Virginia UC-Riverside	Kansas Buffalo Kentucky New Mexico University of Illinois, at Chicago Circle	Boston U.		McGill Victoria (2) University of British Columbia

1966–67	Chicago Cornell Wisconsin Indiana	Washington (2) Minnesota M.I.T. (2) Pennsylvania (2) Tufts Michigan	U. of Pacific Kansas Buffalo (2) Massachusetts	Hunter (2) Boston U. San Jose State	University of British Columbia
1967–68	Stanford Wisconsin	UCLA (2) Williams Washington Pennsylvania Pittsburgh Dartmouth UC-Santa Cruz	Nebraska (2) Texas Colorado (2) Rutgers Penn. State Mich. State Temple Buffalo	Boston U. (2) Harpur-SUNY Richmond-CUNY San Diego State San Jose State	
1968–69	Columbia Yale Chicago	Illinois UC-Riverside	Temple Penn. State (2) S.M.U. Colorado Hawaii Buffalo Fresno State Rutgers	Conn. (2) Indiana Northern Villanova	CSC at Dominguez Hills
1969–70 [a]	UC-Berkeley (Rhetoric) Harvard Indiana	Minnesota UCLA Illinois (2)	Texas (2) Rutgers Buffalo	California State University at San Francisco	

SOURCE: Berkeley English Department reports of the Committee on Placements.
[a] Interim Report, Jan. 20, 1970. Ten other students had received at least one offer and were still negotiating.

would explain the relative performance of their department. Two senior professors in each of five fields were interviewed separately for an hour or more. The men were chosen for their knowledge of the program; in all but one instance, the professors had been members of the Berkeley faculty for 15 years or more. Students were interviewed in groups of three to five, representing different amounts of time in the program. Highlights of the interviews in three fields follow.

Chemistry

From faculty interviews, a clear picture of the economy of a Chemistry Department emerged. A faculty member must publish in order to gain a reputation so that he may acquire research grants with which to support graduate students who help him produce more research so that larger grants can be acquired allowing more students to be supported, etc.—a true vicious circle. The department simply could not afford to have a nonproductive faculty member, since each professor is expected to generate enough funds to support several students in a research group.

> In this field, publish or perish is an understatement. I spend half my time supervising graduate students, making sure that the work gets done, and the other half in Washington begging for more money. My knuckles are raw from bowing and scraping in front of those agencies. I think it's a great tribute to our faculty that we manage to do as good a teaching job as we do under these circumstances.[29]

The economic pressure to publish felt by faculty members in this field has led to an efficient organizational adaptation in which faculty members suggest topics and provide guidance and the graduate students do the actual research. The final product is published jointly under both names, with benefits flowing to both parties. The faculty member expands his publication list, thereby increasing his reputation and ability to earn more grants, while the student gains his Ph.D. and a first publication. The student is thus a critical input into the faculty member's research production function, freeing the professor from the tedious work in the laboratory and allowing him to operate more productively as a source of research proposals and as a fund raiser.

> Back in the early 1940s when I was a young assistant professor at Berkeley working 90 hours a week to get tenure, I actually did a research project by myself one summer and published it under just my name. So many people quizzed me about that at the professional meetings, questioning my sanity and so forth, that I learned never to make that mistake again, and haven't published solo since then.

One can understand why course work is kept to a minimum—the student is simply much more valuable in the laboratory than in the classroom.

The departmental decision regarding the number of graduate students to admit has been dictated primarily by the availability of extramural faculty grants which support graduate students and their research; hence, external resources appear to be more important to the department than internal resources. However, the department is keenly aware of the work-load measures used by the university's budget personnel:

> Even though our students take very few formal courses, they're all enrolled for the maximum course load in 298's and 299's.[30] Believe me, we produce more than our share of student credit hours.

The market's influence on departmental decisions governing the output rate of Ph.D.'s was brought out in several comments:

> When we're considering a marginal student in an oral exam, we know that if we pass him he'll be able to get a job in an industrial lab somewhere and will probably be a damn good chemist, so we generally let such students through. Of course, if we had to place all our students in academic jobs, we'd have to change our requirements and eliminate marginal students. We couldn't let as many through.

> As far as prestige is concerned, we view a placement in Bell Labs, or at Dupont or General Electric, as very acceptable, almost as good as a top academic position. In general, however, we hope that our best students take academic jobs.

Queried about the department's response to the currently worsened job market, one professor expressed uncertainty as to whether this was a temporary decline or represented a more permanent change. Should the decline be long-lived, he thought the department would reduce enrollments somewhat (although noting that this would be resisted by many professors), and that the curriculum would be revised to include more course work in order to train less specialized, more flexible chemists. The clear implication was that the product would be adapted to enhance its marketability.

Two other factors importantly related to student success rates emerged from the discussions. First, both professors stressed the value of the student's belonging to a specific research group, a place where the student could "hang his hat." This affiliation means that a professor is concerned with the student's progress from the beginning and provides a supportive group to bolster the student's confidence when the work becomes discouraging. Secondly, it was very apparent that the faculty expect and want the students to succeed; we were told that if there were any doubt concerning the ability of an applicant to earn the degree, he would not be admitted. Thus, the faculty does not expect a high attrition rate, an expectation that becomes self-fulfilling.

The chemistry students' description of the program was virtually identical with the faculty description. The students agreed that there was only one critical test—the ability to perform research adequately.

> We don't sweat course work or exams or the German requirement. The only thing that matters to the faculty is what we produce in the lab. The students who are asked to leave are the ones who spend a year trying to do research and make no progress.

When asked about student response to the worsening job market, it was observed that students are beginning to stay in Berkeley for a fifth year. By working as a T.A., the student can avoid the 25 per cent pay reduction accorded R.A.'s;[31] furthermore, it was noted that several faculty members have not reduced student pay if the research being done is useful. We asked the first-year student whether the worsening market had affected his decision to enroll:

> I don't give a damn about the poor market—who knows what it will be like four years from now? I just don't think about it because I'm doing what I want to do now. I want to teach when I finish, and I figure something will be available then.

Asked for their attitude toward the joint authorship of research, the students responded favorably, indicating that it was, "a help in establishing a scientific career." Departmental organization into research groups was strongly supported for giving the student a sense of belonging. Morale in the department appeared to be very high.

English

We began both faculty interviews by inquiring into department policies regarding graduate enrollments; we wanted to know how faculty explained the growth of the department to 492 graduate students during the 1965–66 academic year. The first professor was not aware of any conscious policy regarding departmental size. He had noticed, however, a tendency for enrollment growth to correspond rather closely to increased faculty size. He did not express an opinion regarding the direction of causality.

The second professor offered numerous explanations. He stated that the department had established objective criteria for admission and felt obligated to accept all qualified applicants, noting the absence of physical constraints such as laboratory space and facilities that would restrict enrollments. Next, he observed that English professors display near "missionary zeal" regarding the teaching of their subject, seeing their duty as rescuing the country from "cultural barbarism and illiteracy." Presumably, this made it harder for the department to reject applicants. Finally, he commented:

> In reality, I suspect our growth had a lot to do with the way the University keeps its books—you know, that weighted enrollment formula. While this was never overtly discussed when considering applicants, I know we all had in the back of our minds the knowledge that more graduate students meant more faculty. I'm sure most department members would never admit this, but I think you should adopt a behavioral approach—don't go by what we say, but by what we did.

This professor felt that the department had gotten far too large in terms of both students and faculty.

> What sense of community can you have when the chairman's annual cocktail party for faculty, teaching assistants, and wives is attended by over 250 people? Why, we have to rent space off campus just to house the affair. . . . There are assistant professors who have been in the department for two or three years whose names I don't even know. It's a bit embarrassing when I pass them in the hall.

He felt that the department would be much better off if graduate enrollments were reduced to a number small enough so that all students could be supported. The loss of faculty positions that such a policy would entail was viewed as an acceptable cost, perhaps even a move in the right direction. "Perhaps we could regain a feeling of community."

The other professor did not express a desire for such substantial change. Shocked by the worsening job market, he indicated that the department was aiming for a steady-state enrollment of 340 Ph.D. students, with 75 to 100 new doctoral students admitted each year. When asked how many Ph.D.'s the department would want to award annually when in that steady state, he indicated that "with the new program we hope to reduce attrition to an acceptable level and award 30 to 40 Ph.D.'s each year."

Note that these figures imply an attrition rate in excess of 50 per cent, and yet the professor clearly indicated that such performance would be viewed by the English faculty as optimal. The pronounced difference between faculty expectations in the English and Chemistry departments certainly helps to explain why attrition rates differ so markedly. Of course, my fundamental argument is that these divergent faculty attitudes are a reflection of the different markets being served.

The English graduate students described the program as "a series of hurdles accompanied by continual anxiety and humiliation." A third-year student stressed the "feeling that you are not fully accepted by the department until you've neared the end of the program." A second-year student stated that, "the feeling in this department is, they're out to fail you." She noted that during the first year in the program she met few of her fellow students, largely because the intense competition was not conducive to friendships. And yet the students were stunned when shown the data from Stark's study; they had no idea that so few students actually earned the Ph.D.

The students described the Comprehensive and Oral examinations as the major obstacles in the program. The open-ended nature of the Comprehensive exam, coupled with the awareness that the department would fail some of the students, made that exam a particularly frightening experience. Although the brochure states that students must take the Comprehensive between the fourth and sixth quarter, the students knew several people who had managed to postpone the exam until the seventh or eighth quarter for fear of failure. (In keeping with the theory of Section II, such behavior may be perfectly rational given the all-or-nothing nature of the investment; an extra quarter's study is well spent if it makes the difference between passing and failing. Faculty attitudes are critical, for if the students know a certain number will be flunked, the incentive is to expand study time and minimize that risk.)

The language requirements were not viewed as a direct cause of attrition although it was felt that the Latin requirement does contribute to the "disgust" which finally causes some people to leave the program. The forced study of Latin is apparently viewed by many students as highly irrelevant; one student commented that:

> The faculty has preserved the Latin requirement because they view it as a hurdle which demonstrates the high quality of the Berkeley graduate program in English.

An advanced student argued that the department was constantly comparing its program to that of Yale and Harvard (the English departments ranked number one and two ahead of Berkeley in the Cartter Report), trying to outdo those two schools in the rigor of the doctoral program.

The Oral Examination was viewed as somewhat less an ordeal now that the student's area of interest occupies a larger portion of the exam. The students still characterized the exam as sadistic, marked by petti-

budgeting approach based on degrees granted rather than on enrollment levels.

At Berkeley, the Graduate Division now has the power to set graduate enrollment ceilings for each department, and a simple debit-credit system has been created to monitor departmental performance (departments are debited for each enrolled student-year and credited for each Master's degree and Ph.D. awarded). The Graduate Division determines enrollment levels and the allocation of student financial support, to a degree, on the basis of this monitoring system.

Changes in the environment and in the incentive system would be expected to modify departmental performance, and an update of this study would be most interesting. Investigation into the economic behavior of nonprofit institutions remains a challenging and intriguing area of research.

NOTES AND REFERENCES

1. Bernard Berelson, *Graduate Education in the United States* (New York: McGraw-Hill, 1960); Joseph D. Mooney, "Attrition Among Ph.D. Candidates: An Analysis of a Cohort of Recent Woodrow Wilson Fellows," *Journal of Human Resources* 3 (Winter 1968): 47–62; Kenneth Wilson, *Of Time and the Doctorate—Report of an Inquiry into the Duration of Doctoral Study* (Atlanta: Southern Regional Education Board, 1965).
2. David W. Breneman, "The Ph.D. Production Process: A Study of Departmental Behavior" (Ph.D. diss., University of California at Berkeley, 1970).
3. Rodney Stark, *Graduate Study at Berkeley: An Assessment of Attrition and Duration* (Berkeley: Survey Research Center, University of California, Berkeley, 1966).
4. Joseph Mooney, "Attrition Among Ph.D. Candidates," pp. 47–62.
5. A less extreme assumption allowing positive payoff to incomplete degree work would not alter the analysis as long as a significant discontinuity between no degree and degree is present.
6. David Brown, *Academic Labor Markets* (a report to the U.S. Department of Labor, Washington, D.C., September 1965); and T. Caplow and R. McGee, *The Academic Marketplace* (New York: Basic Books, 1958).
7. National Education Association, "Teacher Supply and Demand in Universities, Colleges, and Junior Colleges" (published biennially from 1955 to 1965, Washington, D.C.).
8. Caplow and McGee, *The Academic Marketplace*, p. 92.
9. Allan Cartter, *An Assessment of Quality in Graduate Education* (American Council on Education, Washington, D.C., 1966). (Known also as the Cartter Report.)
10. In a different form and context, this description of a university's functioning was suggested to me by C. B. McGuire.
11. This fact was noted in a recent study of Berkeley doctoral students. See Ann M. Heiss, "Berkeley Doctoral Students Appraise Their Academic Programs," *Educational Record* 48 (Winter 1967): 40.
12. This formula has not been met in very recent years because of the state's decision to reduce the level of funding for the University of California.

13. National Academy of Sciences, *Doctorate Recipients from United States Universities 1958–1966* (Publication 1489, Washington, D.C., 1967), p. 82.
14. Stark, *Graduate Study at Berkeley.*
15. In May 1970, this requirement was eliminated. The analysis of this section helps explain why the change was bitterly contested by the language departments.
16. Allan Cartter, "The Supply of and Demand for College Teachers," *Journal of Human Resources* 1 (Summer 1966): 22.
17. Ibid., p. 38.
18. Brown, *Academic Labor Markets.*
19. Ibid., p. 87.
20. Ibid., p. 92.
21. Reported in the Cartter Report.
22. National Research Council, *Report on Doctoral Programs* (Washington, D.C., 1968): pp. 16–17.
23. Ibid., p. 17.
24. Brown, *Academic Labor Markets.*
25. Ibid., p. 337.
26. Ibid., pp. 341–352.
27. National Academy of Sciences, "Survey of Earned Doctorates" (Washington, D.C.; computer tape for Berkeley graduates, 1958–67, supplied by Graduate Division, University of California, Berkeley).
28. Department of English, University of California, Berkeley, "Report of the Committee on Placements" (provided by the English Department, 1962–1970).
29. Extracts are reproduced from notes.
30. Research seminars and individual research for graduate students for which course credit is given.
31. To provide an incentive for students to finish in four years, the department reduces an R.A.'s stipend by 25 per cent in the fifth year.

2

DENNIS J.
DUGAN
University of Notre Dame
and U.S. General
Accounting office

Scholastic Achievement: Its Determinants and Effects in the Education Industry

I. INTRODUCTION

Economists traditionally look upon scholastic achievement, for a given level of educational attainment, as a quality factor that differentiates a person's productive capacity in the labor market. The competitive economic system rewards such quality differentials by high wage rates or salaries. This effect of scholastic achievement upon economic activity has been verified in the literature, most recently in an article by Hansen, Weisbrod, and Scanlon.[1] Research that established the positive relationship between the level of educational attainment and level of earnings have generally acknowledged the importance of scholastic achievement as a determininant of the level of earnings, although most efforts have

NOTE: This paper is an outgrowth of a joint research effort carried out with Ernest Bartell, congregation of Holy Cross; Arthur Corazzini; Henry Grabowski; John Keith; and Alvin Klevorick for the State of Massachusetts' Board of Higher Education. The author wishes to thank all the gentlemen, especially Arthur Corazzini and Henry Grabowski, for numerous suggestions and helpful comments. Naturally, the remaining errors belong to the author. The author also wishes to thank the State of Massachusetts for granting the funds which made this research possible.

not been able to isolate its quantitative impact with any great degree of precision.[2]

This study focuses upon a different role that scholastic achievement plays—the role it plays within the education industry. In our educational system, scholastic achievement may be a vital factor that clears the path to higher levels of educational attainment. This may be especially important when a student reaches the high school plateau in his educational career and decides to pursue a college education. In fact, a number of institutions of higher learning have admission requirements directly related to the level of scholastic achievement of potential students. This paper presents a model that describes the role that scholastic achievement plays in securing a space in an institution of higher learning, and the model is empirically tested using sample data on 1969 high-school seniors in the Boston Metropolitan Area. The analysis considers not only the actual enrollment rates for these high-school seniors but also relationships between aspirations and plans and scholastic achievement of the students. Once these relationships are established, the determinants of scholastic achievement are discussed, and this permits us to discuss the policy issue of how scholastic achievement may be influenced to ensure "the quality of educational opportunity."

Although some research[3] has considered the relationship between scholastic achievement and college enrollment rates, it has generally been within the context of a demand model for higher education. In such analysis scholastic achievement is treated as a "taste" factor which represents the notion that intellectually capable individuals seek academic fulfillment and correspondingly desire to pursue higher levels of educational attainment. However, scholastic achievement may represent a form of nonmarket rationing that is used by some suppliers of educational services as a mechanism that brings demand and supply factors into equilibrium. Indeed, it is well known that some institutions of higher learning maintain stringent admission standards based on estimates of student potential (generally measured by scores on the Scholastic Aptitude Test [SAT]) and academic background. The analysis that follows takes into account the supply side characteristics of this market and attempts to isolate the magnitude of the nonmarket rationing that takes place in the market-clearing process.

A public policy issue then presents itself. If education is a vehicle of social mobility and a tool that enables the general populace to pull itself up by the bootstraps, and if nonmarket rationing exists, to ensure "the equality of educational opportunity" all segments of society ought to have equal access to scholastic achievement insofar as it is not an inherited trait. Thus, a model of scholastic achievement is presented and empirically tested to isolate those factors which have the greatest impact upon scholastic achievement and are most susceptible to public policy.

In the next section the determinants of aspirations, plans and actual enrollment in colleges are theoretically and empirically analyzed. Section III discusses the nonmarket rationing that takes place through the use of admission standards. A model of scholastic achievement is presented in Section IV, and the final section considers the implications of the analyses and policy issues. A 1969 survey of 4,000 high school seniors in the Boston Standard Metropolitan Statistical Area (SMSA) and a follow-up study in the next year provide sufficient data to test the hypotheses presented.[4]

II. DECISIONS GOVERNING ENROLLMENT IN HIGHER EDUCATION

When a high school graduate enters college, it may appear that he is simply taking another step in a long series of steps up the educational ladder. However, several barriers have to be overcome by a student before he actually enrolls in college. Indeed, tuition charges, opportunity costs, and admission requirements, to mention a few factors, divert some students with a high school diploma who desire to pursue a higher education. In fact, the original study of the Boston SMSA high school seniors in 1969 indicated that high school seniors do not pursue a college education in a random fashion and that their decision to attend or not attend an institution of higher learning is complex. Certain behavioral patterns emerged from the study that indicated that family income, tuition charges, scores on scholastic aptitude tests, and labor-market conditions acted as deterrents to more education. Furthermore, academic requirements used by some institutions of higher learning in allocating their available spaces among potential students act as a rationing device.

Although some deterrents and rationing devices exert their influence at a particular moment in time (e.g., when a high school student receives notice of acceptance or rejection at a college during the spring of his senior year), others reflect influences that encompass a number of years if not the entire lifetime of the student. The very nature of rationing is such that it should be considered a long-run phenomenon. It is not unreasonable to assume that nearly all parents have some desire for their newborns to attend college, but many potential collegiates are gradually excluded along the way.

Some of the determinants of enrollment may exert their influence at a particular moment in time, or may have a cumulative effect over time, or may be a combination of the two. For example, family income is a determinant of the decision to attend college and one which reflects a whole set of environmental factors that are not limited to one particular year or segment of the student's career. Such income has a cumulative effect during the preschool and formal-school years of a student. Conceptually, this cumulative effect is much different than the financial effect of family income representing the amount of family resources available to the high school graduate for his higher educational pursuits. The former effect may influence the student's desire to attend college and may prepare him for academic accomplishment in his educational career. The financial aspect of the family income variable plays a definite role when the student is gathering together resources to meet the cost of attending college.

Thus, the process by which a student decides to attend college is undoubtedly sequential or a step process. Educational decisions are made at various time during the elementary and secondary school years of the student. An early decision concerning higher education may deny the student the opportunity to make other decisions later in his educational career. For example, a decision on the part of a high school student to drop out of school before graduation generally precludes a later decision to attend college. A sequence of these decisions may be made throughout the student's high school career, e.g. when he chooses his educational track or decides not to drop out of school or studies diligently to get good grades. Accordingly, we conceptualize the decisions to attend college to be a sequential decision process. The sequence of decisions may begin in the preschool environment where parents may or may not provide the atmosphere which is conducive to academic achievement and, in the final analysis, to enrollment at an institution of higher learning. The choice of grade school and high school may also be instrumental in the final decision to attend college. Surely, parental encouragement and the home environment during grade school and high school have a positive influence upon the likely success of a student pursuing a higher education.

Data which would make possible empirical investigation of each of these decision junctures are not available for the Boston Metropolitan Area. Therefore, in the analysis that follows, two stages in the decision process are isolated and the determinants of those decisions are analyzed and evaluated. The final "either-or" decision that is made after high school graduation and immediately before enrollment is also discussed and its determinants are statistically evaluated. Of particular interest in this study are the relative impacts of the home, school, and community determinants upon the aspirations, plans, and actual enrollment. In the second stage, actual enrollment is analyzed as dependent upon these same home, school, and community factors. As the final "either-or" decision draws near for the potential college student, certain environmental factors may play a more dominant role and the nature of the rationing taking place is clarified. In this section of the paper, the levels of aspirations, plans, and actual enrollment are explained by a number of community, home, and school influences. In the next section, the amount of rationing taking place, the difference between the number pursuing college at one stage of the decision process and the number of students at another stage, is isolated and empirically identified.

Methodology

The focus here is upon those factors which have an impact upon the levels of students' aspirations toward college, their plans for attending, and their actual enrollment rates. If the student employs rational investment criteria, these higher education decisions are based upon a comparison of the present value of the benefits of pursuing a higher education (discounted at an appropriate rate) and the discounted present values of the direct and opportunity costs of doing so. For the Boston Metropolitan Area, the factors that influence these decisions must capture the distinctive characteristics of the communities within the Boston Standard Metropolitan Statistical Area (SMSA). One such factor is the home environment and its empirical counterpart in this study is family income,[5] which represents the economic well-being of the student's family. This factor has several diverse impacts upon the decision variables, and although it is not possible to separate out all of these impacts empirically, it is worth our while to mention these aspects here. First of all, as has been previously stated, family income represents a source of financial aid to the potential college student, for it is from this source of funds that tuition, board, and room fees may be paid. If family income is high, a priori one would expect this student to be in a better position to obtain financial support than a student whose family income is lower. Secondly, family income may also be an indication of the general lifestyle of the student and thus it provides resources for goods and services that may incline the student to higher education. Furthermore, a family with a high income may provide stimulus-response-reinforcement activities in the home, even in the preschool years, that help the student achieve scholastically at a high rate in school and to be inclined toward scholastic endeavors. To be specific, certain activities such as reading in the home may reinforce the student's school experience, the natural outgrowth of this being the pursuit of more education rather than less.

Another home factor that has a real impact upon these decisions is family size. This variable has a financial aspect along with environmental implications. Financially, family size represents the number of persons among whom education funds may be spread. A student from a smaller family is more likely to command education resources of the family than a student from a large family, since a large family must allocate its scarce educational resources over a large number of individuals. Outside the realm of direct financial considerations associated with higher education, small family size may provide an incentive and motivation to attend college to the student because he has closer contact with his parents and easier access to them. Again, this variable may have a differential impact upon the decisions, depending upon whether the decision is actual attendance or aspiration. For the empirical analysis that follows, the family size and income variables are kept separate since they conceptually have different impacts upon the decision. Although it is possible to combine these two variables into one, namely, income per family member, they are separated for the analysis to isolate their differential impacts.

A community variable, per cent nonwhite, represents those characteristics which are not caught by the other influences upon the decision variables and additional factors that pertain to minority groups. These particular factors may be economic or racial discrimination or traits particular to a racial group. The school influences are captured in the aggregate by current expenditures per pupil in average daily attendance and pupil-teacher ratios. Quality aspects of a particular school are represented by teacher experience (the mean number of years the teachers currently teaching in the system have spent in that system and the mean number of years the teachers currently teaching in a system have spent in public school teaching) and the educational attainment of the teachers (the mean highest level of education attained by teachers in a particular school system).

Another variable that has a vitally important impact upon the higher education decision is the Scholastic Aptitude Test (SAT) score of the student. Not only is that score an indication of the student's aptitude toward academic achievement and aptitude for furthering his education, but it is also a criterion for entry into a number of institutions of higher learning. It is common knowledge that SAT scores have high predictive power concerning success in college, and furthermore they are used as a rationing device by colleges to allocate their number of available spaces.

To relate the decision variables to their explanatory variables, regression analysis is employed. There are several different relations which are plausible, both from the standpoint of the variables to be included and the nature of the functional form to be used. A linear functional form with a limited number of independent variables will be considered here. The relationship between the decision variable and its determinants may be derived from an underlying relation pertaining to the individual student.

Consider the following relation between a student's higher education decision and his other characteristics

(1) $$D_{ij} = a_1 + a_2 N_{ij} + |a_3 F_{ij} + a_4 Y_{ij} + a_5 E_j + U_{ij}$$

where D_{ij} is the particular decision variable of the ith student in the jth school. The output variable is not a continuous variable but a 0-1 binary variable which takes on the value 1 when a certain condition is met, such as planning to attend an institution of higher learning, and 0 otherwise.

N_{ij} = a binary variable assigned the value 1 if the ith student in the jth school is nonwhite and 0 otherwise;
F_{ij} = the family size of the ith student in the jth school;
Y_{ij} = the family income of the ith student in the jth school;
E_j = the current expenditures per pupil in the jth school; and
U_{ij} = a randomly distributed error term.

Equation 1 relates each student decision to his own personal and environmental situation. Since the data are at the school level, a similar relation is derived for each school. Accordingly, for the jth school, equation 1 is summed over its n senior students, and dividing by n the following relation results

(2) $$\frac{1}{n} \sum_{i=1}^{n} D_{ij} = a_1 + a_2 \frac{1}{n} \sum_{i=1}^{n} N_{ij} + a_3 \frac{1}{n} \sum_{i=1}^{n} F_{ij} + a_4 \frac{1}{n} \sum_{i=1}^{n} Y_{ij}$$
$$+ a_5 \frac{1}{n} \sum_{i=1}^{n} E_j + \frac{1}{n} \sum_{i=1}^{n} |U_{ij}$$

For the binary decision variables and the nonwhite variable, the sum of all positive entries divided by the total number of students becomes the percentage of students in the school population satisfying this particular condition. Thus, equation 2 may be rewritten as a relation between mean values and percentage variables in the following manner

(3) $$\overline{D}_j = a_1 + a_2 \overline{N}_j + a_3 \overline{F}_j + a_4 \overline{Y}_j + a_5 \overline{E}_j + \overline{U}_j$$

where a bar over a variable denotes a mean or percentage over the jth school. Equation 3 is in such a form that multiple regression analysis may be applied and the forty-seven schools in the Boston SMSA provide the empirical base.[6]

Since the means are calculated over schools whose senior classes vary significantly in size, a weighting procedure based on the size of each school's population is employed to obtain efficient estimators. This procedure involves weighting by the square root of each school's senior population and is described in standard statistical sources.[7]

Several decision variables are available, and chosen were those to represent distinct stages in the decision process. The first variable concerns the aspirations of the students toward higher education, the second concerns their plans as of April 1969, and the third their actual choice in September 1969. Variants of the three are used and the total number of decision variables comes to seven (7). Aspirations are considered at two levels: those aspiring to four-or-more years of college and those aspiring to two-or-more years of college. Plans are broken down as to whether they were definite or probable. Finally, the actual decision to attend is considered for those attending four-year institutions and for those attending two-or-four-year institutions. Also falling into this latter category is a decision variable which represents those deciding not to attend college and entering the labor force. On a priori grounds, the independent variables should have the reverse effect on "working only" as it has upon actual enrollment.[8] Thus, we have chosen seven decision variables which include the following: (1) per cent aspiring to four-or-more years of college; (2) per cent aspiring to two-or-more years of college; (3) per cent definitely planning to attend college; (4) per cent definitely or probably planning to attend college; (5) per cent attending college; (6) per cent attending universities and four-year colleges; and (7) per cent working.

Since there is no "one" particular specification of the decision that has overwhelming a priori appeal, several different specifications are made to isolate different types of determinants of the higher education decision. The first approach was theoretically stated above, the second considers the same home and community variables plus disaggregated school variables, and the third approach introduces a measure of scholastic ability or achievement together with the home and community variables.

In Table 1, regression results are presented for the seven decision variables when per cent nonwhite, family size, family income, and an aggregate measure of the school resources available to the student are included, representing home, school, and community influences. As expected, mean family income has a positive effect upon these decisions with one exception—the "working only" variable where the opposite

TABLE 1 Family, Environmental, and School Influences upon Higher Education Decisions

Dependent Variable (D_j)	a_1 Constant	a_2 Per Cent Nonwhite	a_3 Family Size	a_4 Mean Family Income	a_5 Expenditures per Pupil	$\bar{R}^2$
D_1 (% aspiring to 4+ years)	-6.11	.502[b] (.21)	-4.309 (4.19)	.0114[b] (.002)	.0057 (.007)	.686
D_2 (% aspiring to 2+ years)	22.0	.397[a] (.19)	-5.222[c] (3.80)	.009[b] (.002)	.0056 (.006)	.721
D_3 (% definitely planning)	-7.584	.23 (.21)	-4.66 (4.29)	.0123[b] (.002)	.0022 (.007)	.675
D_4 (% definitely or probably planning)	36.14	.42[a] (.18)	-4.087 (3.60)	.007[b] (.002)	.004 (.006)	.765
D_5 (% actually attending college)	13.0	.101 (.20)	-7.805[a] (4.01)	.0096[b] (.002)	.0131[a] (.006)	.709
D_6 (% attending universities and 4-year colleges)	-8.46	.229 (.26)	-1.33 (5.25)	.0063[a] (.003)	.0222[a] (.0099)	.431
D_7 (% working)	60.5	-.272[c] (.20)	5.286[c] (4.0)	-.0071[b] (.002)	-.0087[c] (.006)	.411

NOTE: Numbers in parentheses indicate standard error of regression coefficient. $\bar{R}^2$ is the coefficient of determination, adjusted for degrees of freedom.
[a] Statistical significance at 5% level using t statistic.
[b] Statistical significance at 1% level using t statistic.
[c] Statistical significance at 10% level using t statistic.

reaction to family income would be anticipated. Family income was highly significant statistically in all the decision equations. The size of the family income coefficients are very similar for those aspiring to four-or-more years of college, the students definitely planning to attend, and the per cent actually attending, college. The impact of family income is less on those aspiring to two-or-more years and those definitely or probably planning, and this would indicate that the obstacles, financial and other, perceived by the aspirant and planner are less when several different levels of college are available and choices are not limited to four-year institutions. The family size variable works in the direction expected a priori and indicates that size of family acts as a deterrent to higher education either as a financial consideration or as a home environment factor. Although this variable is not statistically significant in all cases, it exhibits substantial stability with regard to sign and magnitude. Of special interest here is the large impact of this variable upon the attendance decision. This may be one indication that in the final stages of the decision-making process, this variable becomes more and more influential and exerts a larger impact. Family size, because of its obvious affect upon family resources, may be a relatively latent factor until the funds for higher education are actually needed.

The nonwhite variable is significant in three of the seven decision equations, and it generally has a positive impact upon the decisions. It is statistically significant in the aspirations and planning equations, and this may be an indication that the nonwhite group perceives higher education as "a vehicle to social mobility" and is in pursuit of it. It is interesting to speculate why the nonwhite variable becomes statistically insignificant as the final higher education decision is approached. Perhaps, that group attempts to keep all of its options open, and it is only at the final juncture of the decision process that financial and other constraints interfere with their desire to attend college.

The impact of the school environment upon the decision variables is demonstrated by the size of the coefficient of current expenditures per pupil. This aggregate measure of the school resources available to the student is not statistically significant for either aspirations or planning, but it does have a positive and a statistically significant impact upon the per cent attending colleges and the per cent attending universities and four-year colleges. This result seems to indicate that indeed the school does play an integral part in influencing its students' college attendance, and this influence has its greatest impact in the final selection process. Furthermore, this school influence has its largest impact upon the per cent attending universities and four-year colleges.

The disaggregated school variables, the pupil-teacher ratio, and mean years in system and education of teachers, yielded mediocre results which are presented in Table 2. The home and community variables performed in a fashion similar to the results presented in Table 1, while "mean years in system" was statistically significant and had a positive impact upon the actual decision to attend college. This result coincides with our a priori notion that teacher experience exerts a positive influence upon the decision variables. The education-of-teacher variable was deleted from the results because it was never statistically significant, which is not surprising due to the minimal amount of variation exhibited by that particular variable.

Since one of the admissions requirements to four-year colleges and universities is performance of a certain level on SAT exams, and since those scores represent in some cases the interest of the student in an academic career, a combination of verbal and math scores was introduced into the decision equations along with the family and community environment variables. This specification of the decision equation yielded the best results of the empirical analyses and the per cent of the variation explained by this specification was substantial—in the neighborhood of 80 per cent in most cases. These results are presented in Table 3. In that table, taken in its entirety, all the variables are significant at least at the 5 per cent level except for two variables which are statistically significant at the 10 per cent level. Per cent nonwhite has a positive influence upon the decision variables (except working) and the size of its coefficient remains close to .5 in all cases except the actual attendance equation. The family size variable exhibits its usual negative impact upon the decision variables, and family income shows a strong and positive influence. The coefficient of the SAT variable is positive and statistically significant at the 1 per cent level in each equation. It is worth noting that this variable has its greatest impact upon the decision variables that represent the final stages of the whole process. Furthermore, its greatest impact is upon the per cent who attend universities and four-year colleges, confirming the well-known fact that admission requirements to these institutions of higher learning are most stringent.

In conclusion, the family, the school, and scholastic achievement play significant roles not only in the actual enrollment rates but also in the aspirations and plans of high school students for their pursuit of higher education. In fact, these variables also have an influence, in the opposite direction, upon the decision to enter the labor market (per cent working) instead of pursuing more education. The latter result reinforces the results obtained for the decision variables pertaining to higher education itself.

TABLE 2 Family, Environmental, and Disaggregated School Influences upon Higher Education Decisions

Dependent Variable (D_j)	Constant	Per Cent Nonwhite	Family Size	Mean Family Income	Pupil-Teacher Ratio	Mean Years in System	$\bar{R}^2$
D_1 (% aspiring to 4+ years)	-24.6	.343[c] (.21)	-3.557 (4.24)	.014[b] (.003)	-.257 (.76)	1.135[c] (.81)	.689
D_2 (% aspiring to 2+ years)	20.06	.267[c] (.20)	-4.933 (3.89)	.0105[b] (.003)	-.430 (.70)	.719 (.75)	.718
D_3 (% definitely planning)	-7.93	.171 (.22)	-4.50 (4.41)	.0129[b] (.003)	-.224 (.79)	.346 (.84)	.668
D_4 (% definitely or probably planning)	27.86	.302[a] (.18)	-3.616 (3.66)	.0086[b] (.002)	-.304 (.66)	.788 (.70)	.765
D_5 (% actually attending college)	-.761	-.164 (.21)	-7.214[a] (4.11)	.0133[b] (.003)	-.595 (.74)	1.457[a] (.79)	.704
D_6 (% attending universities and 4-year colleges)	-13.42	.255 (.28)	-2.295 (5.60)	.0108 (.004)	-.493 (1.01)	1.023 (1.08)	.365
D_7 (% working)	51.63	-.119 (.21)	5.346[c] (4.14)	-.0084[b] (.003)	.632 (.74)	-.585 (.80)	.391

NOTE: Numbers in parentheses indicate standard error of regression coefficient. $\bar{R}^2$ is the coefficient of determination, adjusted for degrees of freedom.
[a] Statistical significance at 5% level using t statistic.
[b] Statistical significance at 1% level using t statistic.
[c] Statistical significance at 10% level using t statistic.

TABLE 3 Family, Environmental, and Aptitude Influences upon Higher Education Decisions

Dependent Variable (D_j)	a_1 Constant	a_2 Per Cent Nonwhite	a_3 Family Size	a_4 Mean Family Income	a_5 Mean Verbal-Math SAT	$\bar{R}^2$
D_1 (% aspiring to 4+ years)	−74.238	.687[b] (.17)	−7.435[a] (3.45)	.0086[b] (.002)	.213[b] (.05)	.792
D_2 (% aspiring to 2+ years)	−27.911	.521[b] (.17)	−7.589[a] (3.42)	.0071[b] (.002)	.157[b] (.05)	.780
D_3 (% definitely planning)	−56.545	.379[a] (.19)	−6.809[a] (3.95)	.0099[b] (.002)	.153[b] (.05)	.730
D_4 (% definitely or probably planning)	−9.621	.542[b] (.16)	−6.204[a] (3.25)	.0051[b] (.002)	.143[b] (.04)	.813
D_5 (% actually attending college)	−54.122	.223[c] (.17)	−11.277[b] (3.44)	.0078[b] (.002)	.212[b] (.045)	.791
D_6 (% attending universities and 4-year colleges)	−97.66	.679[b] (.22)	−6.956[c] (4.45)	.0046[a] (.002)	.286[b] (.06)	.595
D_7 (% working)	120.655	−.405[a] (.17)	8.240[a] (3.48)	−.005[b] (.002)	−.189[b] (.046)	.565

NOTE: Numbers in parentheses indicate standard error of regression coefficient. $\bar{R}^2$ is the coefficient of determination, adjusted for degrees of freedom.

[a] Statistical significance at 5% level using t statistic.
[b] Statistical significance at 1% level using t statistic.
[c] Statistical significance at 10% level using t statistic.

III. MARKET AND NONMARKET RATIONING IN THE HIGHER EDUCATION DECISION

The empirical investigation in the previous section was directed toward the question of why potential college students cease the pursuit of higher education at certain junctures in their educational careers. The decision analysis indicated that the school, the family environment, and scholastic achievement not only influence the final decision to enter college but also a high school student's desire, in the first instance, to investigate and entertain the idea of pursuing a higher education. Thus, within the total framework of finding a place at colleges or universities, the high school students who finally pursue the opportunity are in no sense a random sample of the entire student population. The students who move along the path toward higher education encounter several crossroads at which decisions to attend institutions of higher learning are encountered. Some of these individual decisions in the sequential decision-making process are: (1) initial aspirations to acquire a higher education; (2) search efforts, such as taking the Scholastic Aptitude Test, to meet academic requirements; (3) actual plans concerning enrollment; (4) choice of type of institution of higher learning; and (5) the final step of actually enrolling and becoming a college student. Although previous analysis explained the level of aspirations and plans and enrollment, a far more crucial question remains unanswered. Why do some high school students who aspire or plan to pursue higher education end up not attending? Rephrasing the question in terms of the current study: What has happened in the relatively short period of time between aspirations and enrollment or between plans and enrollment that would prohibit some high school students from attending a college or university? Undoubtedly, a number of factors could become apparent to the potential higher education student that would interfere with his aspirations or plans. These factors can be conveniently broken into three categories: (1) financial ability to attend an institution; (2) scholastic ability to attend; and (3) other nonmarket characteristics that would act as a barrier to enrollment.

The interval between aspirations or plans and the actual enrollment in an institution of higher learning allows for a limited number of factors to interfere or divert the potential student away from the college campus. On the financial side, the economic situation of the family is important and may emerge as a major constraint as the final decision approaches. The family unit has a limited amount of resources to spend on education compared to other economic commodities, and the size of the family budget and the size of the family itself are primary determinants of the financial ability of the family to support the education of one of its members. Capital market imperfections and lack of work opportunities may also interfere and present some difficulty in acquiring the financial resources necessary for higher education.

Scholastic achievement is another factor that will play a role in the decision that is made in the time interval between the senior year in high school and enrollment at college the following autumn. This factor may discourage the potential student from certain institutions because he is not "academically qualified." The student may be bumped from a space at four-year institution because he lacks academic credentials, and thus he may have to settle at a level below his original aspirations. Since junior and community colleges do not have academic requirements besides the high school degree, scholastic achievement need not bump a potential student out of his pursuit for higher education, although even in this situation, poor scholastic achievement may discourage the student because the likelihood of success may seem quite low to him. Nevertheless, scholastic achievement, which is sometimes looked upon as a student's taste for education, surely enters into his decision process between aspirations and enrollment. It is likely to interfere with the realization of aspirations, and it is doubtful that a high schooler's taste for higher education changes over such a short period of time. Rationing of spaces by institutions of higher learning, on the basis of scholastic achievement, is a likely candidate for the influence of scholastic achievement during the interval between aspirations and enrollment.

Finally, nonmarket characteristics besides scholastic achievement may play a role in the decision. Community attitudes and racial characteristics may be important in this regard.

Methodology

A more stringent test of the decision processes concerning higher education is now undertaken. This is accomplished by considering two levels in the decision process, say "those aspiring to 4+ years of college" and "the number actually attending college." Our interest converges upon the difference between the levels, i.e.

(4) $$R^1_{ij} \equiv D^1_{ij} - D^5_{ij}$$

where D_{ij} is the particular decision variable of the ith student in the jth school, and R_{ij} is the ith student in the jth school who does not realize his aspirations or plans. Each of these variables are 0-1 binary, variables which take on the value 1 when a certain condition is met and 0 otherwise. In this case, D^5_{ij} takes on a 1 if his aspirations are realized and he enters college, and a 0 if he does not. Since the data are at the school level, a similar relation is derived for each school. Accordingly, for the jth school, equation 4 is summed over its n senior students who aspired to 4+ years of college, and dividing by n the following relation results

$$(5) \qquad \frac{1}{n} \sum_{i=1}^{n} R^1_{ij} \equiv \left| \frac{1}{n} \sum_{i=1}^{n} D^1_{ij} - \left| \frac{1}{n} \sum_{i=1}^{n} D^5_{ij} \right.\right.$$

For the binary decision variables, the sum of all positive entries divided by the total number of students who aspired to attend college becomes the percentage of students in the appropriate school population satisfying this particular condition. Thus equation 5 may be rewritten in the following manner

$$(6) \qquad \overline{R}^1_j = 1 - \overline{D}^5_j$$

where the bar over a variable denotes a percentage over the jth school. Equation 6 is thus interpreted simply as the per cent of high school seniors rationed in the decision process and is one minus the per cent of students actually attending college. The R variable is the concern of the analysis and will be determined by the variables elaborated in the previous section. Using an analysis similar to that developed in the previous section, it is possible to relate the R variable (the rationing that takes place) to average family income, average family size, per cent nonwhite and average SAT scores in the following manner

$$(7) \qquad \overline{R}^1_j = b_1 + b_2 \overline{N}_j + b_3 \overline{F}_j + b_4 \overline{Y}_j + b_5 \overline{SAT}_j + \overline{U}_j$$

where $\overline{N}_j$, $\overline{F}_j$, $\overline{Y}_j$, $\overline{SAT}_j$, and $\overline{U}_j$ are per cent nonwhite, average family size, average family income, average SAT score, and an average statistical error term respectively. Again, since the means are calculated over schools whose senior classes vary significantly in size, a weighting procedure based on the applicable number in each school's population is employed to obtain efficient estimators.

Several rationing variables qualify for this type of empirical analysis, and three different rationing variables were developed, two for the rationing of aspirations and a third for the rationing of plans. The first concerns the rationing that takes place between the aspirations to attain four-or-more years of college that were prevalent in April 1969 and the enrollment in September 1969. The second applies to the aspirations to attain two-or-more years, and the third applies to plans for college made in the spring of 1969. Thus, the three rationing variables are the following: (1) per cent of 4+ year aspirants who were rationed (i.e., the rationed aspirants to 4+ years divided by aspirants to 4+ years); (2) per cent of 2+ year aspirants who did not enroll; and (3) per cent of plans (probable plus definite) to attend college that were diverted. These rationing variables are determined by several sets of independent variables in the following section.

The Statistical Results

There is no "one" particular specification of the rationing process that has overwhelming a priori appeal, and three different specifications are made to isolate different types of determinants of the rationing variables. The first approach is exploratory and includes only home and community determinants. The second approach adds the school environment to the first, and the third approach introduces a measure of scholastic achievement along with the home and community variables.

In Table 4, the preliminary results are presented, and the per cent nonwhite variable is the only one that is consistently significant. The variable had a positive impact on rationing, indicating that the nonwhite group has certain characteristics besides family size and income which make it susceptible to being diverted from the fulfillment of its aspirations and plans for higher education. This result may be due to the particular specification of the equation, since the impact of school is excluded. It is common knowledge that the nonwhite students generally receive fewer educational resources in terms of expenditures per pupil than their white counterparts. Furthermore, nonwhite students do not perform as well as white students on scholastic achievement tests. The third approach introduces scholastic achievement directly into the analysis, and the discussion of the nonwhite variable is appropriately postponed until the results of that approach are evaluated.

The results of Table 4 also indicate that a larger family size is associated with more rationing and fewer high school students pursuing higher education. The result was expected on a priori grounds. Although this variable had the expected sign, it was not statistically significant. The family income variable is statistically significant for the rationed plans group, and the result indicates that the lack of finances enters the picture and acts as a deterrent to higher education. The family income variable was not statistically significant for the other two approaches.

The school influences are added to the previous specification of the rationing equations, and the empirical results of this are presented in Table 5. The nonwhite variable is again highly significant with a positive impact upon rationing for all three approaches. The family size variable has the right sign, but it is not statistically significant. Family income has a statistically significant negative impact upon the rationed plans group, and it was not significant for the other groups. Expenditures per pupil

TABLE 4 Preliminary Regression Results of Higher Education Rationing

Dependent Variable (R_j)	b_1 Constant	b_2 Per Cent Nonwhite	b_3 Family Size	b_4 Family Income	$\bar{R}^2$
R_1 (Rationed aspirants to 4+ years/aspirants)	−29.85 (32.36)	.685[b] (.26)	6.646 (5.44)	.0008 (.003)	.103 [2.325]
R_2 (Rationed aspirants to 2+ years/aspirants)	19.98 (29.27)	.431[a] (.244)	5.03 (4.98)	−.0038[c] (.0026)	.141 [2.89]
R_3 (Rationed plans/plans)	38.41[c] (27.58)	.418[a] (.227)	6.15[c] (4.69)	−.0065[b] (.0024)	.312 [6.22]

NOTE: Numbers in parentheses indicate standard error of regression coefficient. Numbers in brackets are F statistics. $\bar{R}^2$ is the coefficient of determination adjusted for degrees of freedom.

[a] Statistical significance at 5% level using t statistic.
[b] Statistical significance at 1% level using t statistic.
[c] Statistical significance at 10% level using t statistic.

TABLE 5 Family, Environmental, and School Influences upon Higher Education Rationing

Dependent Variable (R_j)	b_1 Constant	b_2 Per Cent Nonwhite	b_3 Family Size	b_4 Family Income	b_5 Expenditures per Pupil	$\bar{R}^2$
R_1	−28.62 (32.43)	.741 [b] (.27)	5.834 (5.515)	.0022 (.0032)	−.009 (.01)	.101 [2.03]
R_2	21.09 (29.17)	.496 [a] (.25)	4.12 (5.03)	−.0022 (.0029)	−.01 (.009)	.148 [2.60]
R_3	40.21 [c] (27.0)	.506 [b] (.228)	4.91 (4.64)	−.0043 [a] (.0027)	−.015 [a] (.0087)	.342 [5.78]

NOTE: Numbers in parentheses indicate standard error of regression coefficient. Numbers in brackets are F statistics. $\bar{R}^2$ is the coefficient of determination adjusted for degrees of freedom.
[a] Statistical significance at 5% level using t statistic.
[b] Statistical significance at 1% level using t statistic.
[c] Statistical significance at 10% level using t statistic.

added to the realization of plans and exhibits a significant coefficient. The rationed plans group yielded three significant variables and a coefficient of variation of 34.2 per cent.

In Table 6, the empirical results are presented for the impact of home, community, and scholastic achievement variables upon the ra-

TABLE 6 Family, Environmental, and Aptitude Influences upon Higher Education Rationing

Dependent Variable (R_j)	b_1 Constant	b_2 Per Cent Nonwhite	b_3 Family Size	b_4 Family Income	b_5 Mean SAT	$\bar{R}^2$
R_1	−22.804 (40.15)	.664 [a] (.276)	7.031 (5.64)	.0012 (.003)	−.022 (.073)	.084 [1.84]
R_2	55.64 [c] (35.7)	.319 [c] (.248)	6.69 [c] (4.98)	−.002 (.003)	−.111 [a] (.007)	.177 [2.97]
R_3	80.06 [b] (33.02)	.281 (.227)	8.08 [a] (4.6)	−.0044 [a] (.0025)	−.130 [b] (.061)	.365 [6.28]

NOTE: Numbers in parentheses indicate standard error of regression coefficient. Numbers in brackets are F statistics. R^2 is the coefficient of determination, adjusted for degrees of freedom.
[a] Statistical significance at 5% level using t statistic.
[b] Statistical significance at 1% level using t statistic.
[c] Statistical significance at 10% level using t statistic.

tioning variables. Since this specification of the rationing model has the most appeal, with its inclusion of mean SAT scores, more explicit attention will be given to the results. The determinants of 4+ year rationing explain a small 8.4 per cent of the variation, and only one variable is statistically significant, the per cent nonwhite. This result indicates that, after adjustment for family characteristics and scholastic achievement, the nonwhite community gets rationed disproportionately in their pursuit of higher education. The results of the 2–4 year rationing equation indicate that scholastic achievement is a significant factor and that rationing occurs on the basis of academic requirements at institutions of higher learning. Exactly how this rationing due to academic standards takes place is not readily apparent, although a "bumping down" phenomenon might be expected. That is, the very best schools with their high standards turn away or bump down a large number of students who then pursue their higher education at a lower-quality institution; a continuation of the bumping down through all levels of higher education finally leads to some individuals being "bumped out." The other variables had the expected signs on the coefficients, and per cent nonwhite and family size were statistically significant at the 10 per cent level.

The final rationing equation for the plans to attend college yielded the best overall results. The determinants explained 36.5 per cent of the variation in the rationing variable and most of the independent variables were statistically significant. The per cent nonwhite variable had the expected sign although it was not significant. The family size acted as a deterrent to the realization of plans for college, whereas family income and scholastic achievement acted as impetuses to the actualization of plans. The latter three variables were all statistically significant.

Thus, even under the stringent specification of the rationing process, several factors play key roles and can be identified as having significant impacts upon the rationing that takes place in the higher education decision process.

IV. DETERMINANTS OF SCHOLASTIC ACHIEVEMENT

An obvious implication of the previous analysis is that scholastic achievement, as measured by SAT scores, is instrumental in determining the success of a student in his pursuit of a higher education. Low SAT scores can act to frustrate student expectations with respect to college attendance. Not only is scholastic achievement an influential factor in the decision process at the aspirations, plans, and enrollment junctures but it is also a significant determinant of the rationing that takes place between the decision junctures. From the point of view of public policy that seeks to guarantee "the equality of educational opportunity," the fact that scholastic achievement is a primary determinant of students' decision to attend college presents the following policy problem: Is it possible to mould scholastic achievement and make it equally accessible to all segments of society? This section sets forth to identify and empirically estimate the extent to which home, community, and school factors influence performance on the Scholastic Aptitude Test. School variables are most susceptible to public policy, while the home and community environment sometimes cannot be affected in such a straightforward fashion. Thus, an attempt will be made to measure the separate influence of each of these factors.

Methodology

Identifying factors that contribute to the scholastic success of students is within the realm of educational production-function studies.[9] The production function, since it is a mathematical function relating system inputs and outputs, forces the researcher to be very specific with regard to the goal of the educational process, the nature of the inputs and the quantity and quality of the resulting outputs. The empirical results of two previous sections direct our search for an appropriate output variable to SAT, since this measure of scholastic achievement is a primary determinant of the decision to enroll in college. Relating system inputs to mean SAT yields empirical estimates of the significance and impact of such inputs, thus indicating the productivity of the educational process in the area of scholastic achievement.

Several input variables that attempt to capture the separate environmental influences on the student emanating from his home, community, and school are now present. The home environment variable has for its empirical proxy both the income of the student's family and family size. An environmental factor reflecting the community environment is per cent nonwhite. The most obvious candidates for the school inputs are current expenditures per student, empirical variables related to the teacher—experience and educational attainment—and the pupil-teacher ratio. Teacher experience and educational attainment have as empirical counterparts the mean number of years the teachers currently teaching in a system have spent in the system and the mean highest level of education attained by teachers in a particular school system.

The unit of analysis for this empirical test is the school, and multiple regression analysis is employed to isolate those inputs that are statistically significant determinants of mean SAT and to identify the magnitude of the influences. In a manner similar to that used in the previous sections, the relationship between mean SAT and mean input variables is derived from an underlying relation pertaining to the individual student. Summing over the basic relationship for all seniors in a high school and dividing by this number yields the following

(8) $$\overline{SAT}_j = c_1 + c_2 \overline{N}_j + c_3 \overline{F}_j + c_4 \overline{Y}_j + c_5 \overline{E}_j + \overline{U}_j$$

where $\overline{SAT}_j$ is the mean SAT score for the jth school. Since these means are calculated over schools which vary significantly in size, a weighting procedure based upon the size of each senior class is again employed to obtain efficient estimators.

This linear equation has the disadvantage of specifying a constant change in output to a given change in inputs over the entire range of inputs. However, diminishing returns may be an important factor and would eventually set in, especially with regard to family income and current expenditures. Thus the above analysis was expanded for nonlinear regression. Accordingly, it is assumed that each student is operating under the following quadratic form

(9) $$SAT_{ij} = c_1 + c_2 N_{ij} + c_3 F_{ij} + c_4 Y_{ij} + c_5 Y^2_{ij} + c_6 E_{ij} + c_7 E^2_{ij} + U_{ij}$$

Diminishing returns imply that c_5 and c_7 have negative signs. Summing over all the students in a particular school and dividing by those students, the following equation results

(10) $$\overline{SAT}_j = c_1 + c_2 \overline{N}_j + c_3 \overline{F}_j + c_4 \overline{Y}_j + c_5 \frac{1}{n} \Sigma Y^2_{ij} + c_6 \overline{E}_j$$
$$+ c_7 \frac{1}{n} \Sigma E^2_{ij} + \overline{U}_j$$

Using the statistical identity to obtain a measure of average square of family income

(11) $$\frac{1}{n} \Sigma Y^2_{ij} = G^2_Y + \overline{Y}^2$$

substituting the estimate of G^2_Y for each high school sample and adding it to $\overline{Y}^2$ for an estimate of the average square of family income in equation 10.

The Empirical Results

Three formulations of the scholastic achievement model were empirically tested and the results are presented in Table 7. The first specification of the model included the home and community variables and

TABLE 7 Empirical Determinants of Mean SAT Scores

	c_1 Constant	c_2 Per Cent Nonwhite	c_3 Family Size	c_4 Family Income	c_5 Expenditures per Pupil	c_6 Pupil/ Teacher	c_7 Teacher Experience	c_8 Teacher Education	c_9 (Family Income)^2	c_{10} (Expenditures per Pupil)^2	$\bar{R}^2$
1.	315.13^b (63.13)	−1.402^b (.54)	17.412^c (11.02)	.0098^c (.006)	.05^b (.02)						.933 [129.98]
2.	315.13^a (182.84)	−1.312^a (.56)	15.605^c (11.93)	.0113 (.009)		−3.037^c (2.18)	1.18 (2.63)	9.676 (20.72)			.927 [84.04]
3.	808.57^a (400.34)	−1.638^b (.56)	15.861^c (11.04)	−.134 (.11)	.109 (.09)				9.93×10^{-6} (7.5×10^{-6})	-26.61×10^{-6} (37.31×10^{-6})	.934 [93.86]

NOTE: Numbers in parentheses indicate standard error of regression coefficient. Numbers in brackets are F statistics. $\bar{R}^2$ is the coefficient of determination, adjusted for degrees of freedom.

[a] Statistical significance at 5% level using t statistic.
[b] Statistical significance at 1% level using t statistic.
[c] Statistical significance at 10% level using t statistic.

current expenditures per student, which represents the aggregate educational resources available to the student. The second formulation introduced disaggregated school variables in place of current expenditures per pupil. The final specification is the nonlinear equation with squared family income and squared current expenditures per pupil. All three formulations yielded significant coefficients of variation, adjusted for degrees of freedom, in the neighborhood of .93.

The per cent nonwhite variable was statistically significant in each specification of the model and had a coefficient circa −1.4 in each case. This indicates that a 1 per cent increase in the per cent of a high school being nonwhite yields a decrease of one and four-tenths points on the SAT. This result is not unusual for educational production-function studies and reinforces the notion that the public education system does not provide the same educational services for different racial groups, even if it spends an identical amount of dollars on that group.

Expenditures per pupil is statistically significant in the linear formulation of the model and the elasticity of SAT with respect to expenditures, computed at the means, is .088. This elasticity demonstrates the positive impact of expenditures on SAT but it indicates a relatively inelastic response of the output measure to school inputs. This inelastic response, however, is not atypical or surprising when educational output variables are involved. These outputs are a cumulative function of a long history of past inputs in the student's home and school environment, and tend to be only marginally responsive to current inputs influencing student performance—such as family income flows and current school expenditures. The disaggregated school inputs yielded coefficients with the right direction of impact, although only the pupil-teacher ratio was close to being significant at the 5 per cent level. The negative coefficient of the pupil-teacher ratio demonstrates that manipulation of school inputs, in particular, greater amounts of teacher-pupil contact, does increase the output of the system. Teachers' experience and their educational attainment also produce better scores on SAT.

Family size has a positive impact upon scholastic achievement in all three formulations of the model, although it is not significant at the 5 per cent level in any case. This positive impact runs contrary to the results of most educational production-function studies. The standard result is generally interpreted as follows: when family size is large, the economic resources of the family that can be devoted to educational activities is limited because of the other needs of the family. Thus, small family size allows more time, effort, and resources to be devoted to the educational pursuits of the children. The results obtained here, running contrary to other studies, may possibly be interpreted in terms of externalities that accrue to large families due to the interactions among the members which may contribute to educational achievement. For example, one youngster, upon mastering the phonics system, may easily teach a younger brother or sister and free the parents for other educational interactions with their children.

The family income variable is close to statistical significance at the 5 per cent level in the linear formulation of the model and has a positive impact on SAT, as expected a priori. However, that variable is not significant in the other specifications of the model, in fact it has a negative sign in the nonlinear equation. On the whole, the nonlinear model yielded only mediocre empirical results.

The empirical results of the SAT model indicate that scholastic achievement can be influenced by school, home, and community variables. However, increasing scholastic achievement is not at present an easy or inexpensive policy solution because the output of the system is so inelastically related to school expenditures and family income.

V. IMPLICATIONS OF THE ANALYSES AND POLICY CONSIDERATIONS

The nonwhite segment of the Boston SMSA high school seniors in 1969 sought to hold open the possibility of attaining a college education until the last possible moment. With home and school influences held constant, this nonwhite segment portrayed special aspirations and plans to attain a college education. Yet, when the final enrollment tally was complete, the unique desire of this group was not realized. One interpretation of this result is that the nonwhite group places considerable stock in the belief that higher education is a vehicle of social mobility and a way of "pulling themselves up by the bootstraps," and accordingly they desired to keep the higher education option open to themselves as long as possible. However, in the final stage of the decision process, these aspirations were frustrated.

This example of a barrier that confronts high school students who aspire to a college education does not exhaust the list of barriers that they must overcome before enrollment in college takes place. Family income and size, school and community environment, and scholastic achievement influence the individual's education decision. Some of these factors, such as family income and current expenditures per student, are the standard economic forces that play a role in the marketplace. However, scholastic achievement may be considered a nonmarket force if it is used by the suppliers of educational services as a market-clearing mechanism. A rationing model developed in the text demonstrated that academic requirements were being used by the suppliers of educational services in that manner.

The analysis of rationing also confirms the notion that minority groups are frustrated in their plans to enroll in college. In the rationing model, the per cent nonwhite variable was statistically significant, and the direction of its impact indicated that the greater the per cent of the nonwhite student population, the more likely that rationing would occur between springtime of the senior year in high school and fall enrollment in college. Although it has been argued that such a variable may be capturing the inadequate academic backgrounds of nonwhite students, as measured by SAT scores, the inclusion of scholastic achievement in the analysis together with the per cent nonwhite variable yielded identically significant results. Those results indicated that the nonwhite group was rationed disproportionately, explicit consideration of its academic credentials notwithstanding. One implication for policy is that any financial program for higher education should take into explicit account the racial characteristics of the student population that it covers, for one racial segment of the population may have unique characteristics that make it more difficult for that group to attain a college education.

College requirements, specifically certain levels of scholastic achievement, act as a deterrent to enrollment in college. Such requirements act to frustrate aspirations and plans to pursue the Great American Dream. As long as admissions policies are used by institutions of higher learning, rationing vis-à-vis the decision process will continue and a certain proportion of aspirations to attend college will be frustrated.

APPENDIX A

The Boston Metropolitan Area Sample

In the original April 1969 sample, there were fifty-six schools in the Boston Metropolitan Area with adequate educational expenditure data and a sufficient number of returned questionnaires to be used as the basis for empirical analysis. The same fifty-six schools were examined carefully for possible inclusion in the follow-up study. In the original Boston Metropolitan Area (BMA) study, these fifty-six schools accounted for 2,209 questionnaires. The follow-up study yielded a total of 1,450 returns from the original total, 1,082 of which were mail returns and the rest compiled from information gathered in phone interviews. Thus, 65.6 per cent of the original sample were recontacted in the follow-up survey, and 49.2 per cent of that original population from the fifty-six schools returned their questionnaires in usable form.

Since the entire population did not respond to the follow-up questionnaire, it seemed likely that some biases existed in the response rates of the various schools. In fact, a simple regression of per cent returns on mean family incomes for the fifty-six schools yielded an R^2 of .227, the regression equation read: % Total Return = 11.9 + .0077 Income, and the income coefficient was significant at the .01 level. Thus, the respondents on the average were from families with higher incomes. This result may be one indication that college students responded in greater proportion than the others in the population. To counteract this possible bias in the response rate, a criterion was established to insure a minimum response rate per school. The following test was established to insure a sufficiently large number of observations within each school. At least twenty returns from each school were necessary for a school to be included in the empirical analysis. If that "absolute-number-criterion" was not met, an alternative criterion could qualify a school for inclusion: a return of over 60 per cent for the school. Although the criterion is substantial, only nine of the fifty-six schools were eliminated because of it. A simple regression of per cent returns on family income for the forty-seven schools yielded the following regression equation: % Total Returns = 30.1 + .00567 Income, with the income coefficient statistically significant at the .01 level. These forty-seven schools yielded an income coefficient .0021 smaller than the income coefficient for the fifty-six schools. This result indicates that the criterion employed above eliminated some of the bias that existed in the returns. Approximately 30 per cent of the bias was deleted through the exclusion of the nine schools.

Of the remaining forty-seven schools in the sample, six were from Boston and forty-one from the surrounding communities. These forty-seven schools provide a substantial degree of variation for empirical analysis, both with regard to the percentage of students aspiring to attend, and actually attending, college, and also with respect to the school, home, and community environments that surround them.

APPENDIX B

Statistical Characteristics of the Boston Metropolitan Area Data

Forty-seven schools in the Boston Metropolitan Area provide the basis for the empirical analysis in this paper. Although there are more high schools in the BMA, some did not provide the expenditure and other educational information necessary for inclusion in the analysis. In Table B-1 the descriptive statistics for the forty-seven schools included in the sample are presented for the decision, input, and mean SAT variables. For the decision variables, the table shows that 52.4 per cent of the 1969 high school seniors in the Boston Metropolitan Area were attending universities or four-year colleges in the 1969–70 academic year, 10.8 per cent were attending two-year colleges, and 21.9 per cent were working full time. Over 73 per cent of the total number of students aspired to two or more years of college. Table B-1 also presents data concerning the dispersion for the decision, input, and mean Scholastic Aptitude

TABLE B-1   Dispersion of Variables

Variable	Mean	Coefficient of Variation
A. Decision variables		
1. % aspiring to 4 or more years of college	65.66	.213
2. % aspiring to 2 or more years of college	73.17	.166
3. % definitely planning to attend college	65.0	.224
4. % definitely or probably planning to attend college	75.87	.14
5. % attending college	63.24	.229
6. % attending universities and 4-year colleges	52.43	.311
7. % working	21.9	.549
B. Input variables		
1. Family income (dollars)	7,123.70	.114
2. Family size	3.811	.112
3. % nonwhite	3.76	2.039
4. Mean verbal SAT	472.96	.071
5. Mean math SAT	508.11	.078
6. Expenditures/pupil	861.63	.260
7. Pupil/teacher	22.49	.116
8. Mean age of teachers	37.547	.096
9. Mean years in system	7.21	.422
10. Mean years in public school	9.07	.299
11. Teacher education	9.989	.030
C. SAT variable		
Mean SAT: (Verbal + Math)/2	490.53	.071

Test (SAT) variables. The coefficient of variation, an index of dispersion, is the ratio of the standard deviation to the mean value of a variable. The dispersion of all the variables provides sufficient variation to include them in the analysis. The small dispersion for the mean verbal SAT, mean math SAT, and mean SAT is to be expected, since these scores are drawn from a normal population which has a tendency to cluster close to the population mean.

As in most studies of education, it is necessary to investigate the possibility that the independent variables are "clumped" together and so highly correlated that they exhibit little independent variation. If such a situation exists, it becomes very difficult to discriminate among their effects. Table B-2 presents the matrix of simple correlation coefficients. While the correlations between the school input variables and the environment variables are often statistically significant, they do not seem large enough to present a severe multi-collinearity problem. The most severe multi-collinearity occurs among some of the alternative measures of teacher age and experience. These high correlation coefficients between mean age of teachers, mean number of years in the system, and mean number of years in public education indicate that these variables are substitute measures of teacher experience, and little can be gained by employing more than one of these measures in any statistical analysis. Mean math and mean verbal SAT scores are also highly correlated, and this indicates that either one adequately describes the scholastic aptitude of students. Except for these variables, the independent variables exhibit enough independent variation to be jointly employed in a statistical analysis.

Table B-2 also provides some insights into the structure of these variables for the Boston SMSA. They indicate that school allocations (e.g. high expenditures per pupil and low pupil-teacher ratios) tend to be positively related to those environmental and background influences which contribute to a successful educational experience on the part of students (high family income and small family size). Thus, in the Boston SMSA school allocations tend on balance to reinforce any inequalities arising from the nonschool environment. Another structural feature of the simple correlations is the positive relationship between teacher age and experience and expenditures per pupil. At the same time, these teacher experience variables are negatively related to family income, indicating that the prosperous communities tend to employ younger teachers.

Finally, Table B-2 yields positive correlations between SAT scores and expenditures per pupil and between SAT scores and family income. These relationships are expected a priori and from previous research into the determination of scholastic achievement. However, a word of

TABLE B-2 Simple Correlations of Input Variables

	Family Income	Family Size	Mean Verbal	Mean Math
Family size	−.194			
Mean verbal SAT	.353	.055		
Mean math SAT	.275	.030	.885	
Expenditures/pupil	.314	−.198	.378	.376
Pupil/teacher	−.453	.025	−.275	−.169
Mean age of teachers	−.419	−.175	−.093	−.024
Mean years in system	−.647	−.013	−.291	−.162
Mean years in public education	−.374	−.192	−.118	−.047
Teacher education	.346	−.262	.263	.165
% nonwhite	−.346	.089	−.353	−.282

caution is in order. If SAT scores and family income are used to determine simultaneously the decision variables, it may be difficult to isolate the independent influence of these variables because their inclusion may "muffle" their separate impacts. Indeed, family income is a determinant of SAT, but SAT and family income have, conceptually, separate impacts that may be difficult to isolate in the empirical analysis. The severity of this simultaneous-equation bias may be minimal in this case, but it should be noted.

NOTES AND REFERENCES

1. W. Lee Hansen, Burton A. Weisbrod, and William J. Scanlon, "Schooling and Earnings of Low Achievers," *American Economic Review* 60 (June 1970): 409–418.
2. For example, Gary Becker in his work on rates of return to education assumed that approximately one-third of the earnings differential between high school and college degree holders was attributable to scholastic achievement. See Gary Becker, *Human Capital* (New York: NBER, 1964), pp. 79–90.
3. For an indication of some of the research that is currently taking place in this area, see R. Radner and L. S. Miller, "Demand and Supply in U.S. Higher Education: A Progress Report," *American Economic Review, Papers and Proceedings* (May 1970): 326–334.
4. Arthur J. Corazzini et al., *Higher Education in the Boston Metropolitan Area: A Study of the Potential and Realized Demand for Higher Education in the Boston SMSA* (Boston: Board of Higher Education, 1969), pp. 27–43.

Expenditures per Pupil	Pupil/ Teacher	Mean Age of Teacher	Mean Years in System	Mean Years in Public Education	Teacher Education
−.323					
.171	.148				
.005	.271	.882			
.205	.141	.938	.886		
.431	−.067	.326	.080	.400	
.099	.048	.397	.498	.341	−.074

5. The 1969 survey of the high school seniors of the Boston SMSA provided information concerning the father's age, occupation, and level of educational attainment. These data were then used to construct a family-income figure by relating those characteristics to income of males 14 years and older, nonwhite and white, for the Northeast Region of the U.S. as shown in U.S. Census of Population, *Occupation by Earnings and Education* (Washington, D.C., 1965), PC (2)-7B, Table 2, pp. 196–219. These data provided two age categories, eight occupational categories, and six education categories to arrive at a proxy for the family-income figure used in the local analysis.

6. See Appendix A for the criteria upon which the selection of the forty-seven schools was made.

7. For example, E. Malinvaud, *Statistical Methods of Econometrics* (Chicago: Rand McNally, 1966), pp. 254–258.

8. The following argument could be put forth: "By definition 'those attending' and 'those not attending' add to the total high school graduates, and this identity dictates that the 'working only' group be influenced in the exact opposite direction as those forces which influence enrollment." However, these two groups do not encompass the entire population, and housewives, persons in the armed forces, those attending noncollege institutions and others are not included in the above division of students between "working only" and those actually attending college.

9. There have been a number of such studies in recent years, one of which is S. Bowles and H. M. Levin, "The Determinants of Scholastic Achievement—An Appraisal of Some Recent Evidence," *Journal of Human Resources* 3 (Spring 1968): 1–24.

2 | COMMENTS

Barbara L. Heyns
University of California

It is reassuring to observe the increased interest in educational research and policy shown by economists; it is, however, disheartening to see the degree to which professionals within disciplines maintain departmental specializations and forgo efforts at interdisciplinary research and communication. While economists are surely not alone in this tendency, there is a large body of sociological literature relevant to the concerns of this Conference, and to the issues raised by Dugan.

The present research conceptualizes scholastic achievement as a factor in both the demand and supply of higher education. The demand for higher education, measured by aspirations, plans and college enrollment, is conceived as a "taste" factor, reflecting a propensity to consume schooling. The supply of education, or the admissions policies of colleges and universities, is subject to "nonmarket" rationing, due in part to differential achievement and, perhaps, to discrimination. The approach adopted appeals to me. It is more sophisticated conceptually than traditional economic models.

The institutional constraints are, at least, acknowledged by the inclusion of a concept of rationing. In contrast, achievement is traditionally assumed to reflect either qualitative differences in educational attainment or an output measure in production-functions for schools.

The framework of Dugan's analysis is straightforward. The model presented is generally well reasoned and explicit. In general, my comments are directed toward clarification in light of a rather different body of literature, so perhaps my remarks should be weighed by a different scale. My criticism is divided into three parts, not equally important in my mind; questions of methodology, of substantive interpretation, and of concepts and policies.

The methodological problems should, perhaps, be dealt with first, since they are generally less interesting. The relationships presented by Dugan are calculated from school data, and represent aggregate relationships, not individual differences. Consistently, however, the interpretations offered refer to differences between individuals, and not between schools. A considerable literature exists on the pitfalls of ecological analysis,[1] and the fallacies involved in making inferences to individuals based on correlations among aggregates. The equations provided by Dugan offer, perhaps, an empirical example. The partial regression coefficient for per cent nonwhite in all of the equations examined is positive, except those depicting rationing. The effects are largely insignificant, except for the models which include mean SAT scores. Interpreting these effects as representing differences between racial groups, would force one to conclude that nonwhite students were more likely to aspire to, to plan for, and to attend a college or university than whites. There is some support for higher aspirations among nonwhites, however no research I am familiar with has yet demonstrated higher attendence rates, regardless of controls used. The conclusion which is correct, however, is that those schools which had a higher proportion nonwhite sent more pupils to college. Inferring that nonwhites as a group were more likely to enroll is incorrect, and testable only with data disaggregated by race. The conclusion about schools may be somewhat misleading, since many other characteristics of such schools are not known. Aggregated data tend to be more highly correlated than do relationships between individuals; ecological correlations, even when weighted, can be biased estimators of the actual relationships, even to the extent of having the opposite sign. Introducing them into a regression equation tends to increase both the degree of multicollinearity, and the proportion of variance explained.

Equally important, significance levels for coefficients computed from aggregated data depend not on the sample size, but on the degrees of freedom present. Restricting observations to group means substantially reduces both the variance to be explained, and the degrees of freedom. Weighting school means by the size of the within-group sample does not justify imputing a substantially lower standard error based on individual observations. For the Boston Metropolitan Area data, the sample actually consists of 47 schools, not 1,450 individuals.[2]

Such complaints may reflect the quibbling of sociologists, who rarely explain as much as half the variance between individuals. A model such as that presented by Hauser[3] would have been substantially more informative, even at the sacrifice of explanatory power. While the models presented are intriguing, conclusions as well as policy recommendations await a more refined analysis.

Several substantive criticisms also seem in order. It is not surprising that the relationships between school variables such as per pupil expenditures, pupil-teacher ratios, and the age and experience of teachers are not powerful predictive variables; a large number of studies have shown such results.[4] The justification generally offered for their inclusion, despite trivial and erratic coefficients, is that school variables can be more easily manipulated through social policy, than can background factors. Policy recommendations, such as equalizing resources, or altering college admissions are indicative of both the state of the art, and the value judgments of the researcher. If achievement is viewed as the product of schools, and certain characteristics of schools are associated with higher achievement, it is often difficult to consider alternative explanations. Relationships between teacher experience, per pupil expenditure, and academic outcomes are a case in point.[5] Dugan interprets these relationships as demonstrating that schools do "play an integral part in influencing students attending college."

An alternative interpretation could be made. A typical career pattern for many teachers is to accept first positions at relatively disadvantaged schools, with low-achieving pupils, and to transfer to more affluent and desirable districts after acquiring some experience.[6] The association between teacher experience and achievement could be entirely due to the teaching profession's preference for highly motivated, academically oriented students, rather than teacher experience having an independent effect on achievement. Since years of experience is a prime ingredient in determining salaries, and since 85 per cent of the average school budget is allocated to personnel, inequalities between schools in expenditures may reflect the same pattern. Equalizing school resources would seem to mean either restricting the mobility of teachers, or increasing the staff at disadvantaged schools. While there may be some merit in such policies, the expected impact on achievement, aspirations, or college attendance would be negligible. Such examples serve only to make the point that the educational process is quite complex and subtle, and that there is every reason to believe that models currently available are inadequate for different schools, districts, or groups of pupils.[7]

The pattern of coefficients in different equations is interpreted as representing sequential decisions of students, or stages of educational aspirations. The actual survey included only one follow-up, however, and we are never told how consistent the respondents are in either responses or behavior. The general similarity of models strikes me as being as noteworthy as the slight changes in coefficients in separate equations. I suspect that the dependent variables are quite highly intercorrelated, and that they are measuring similar propensities between schools. One could imagine a perfect correlation between the proportion aspiring to higher education and the proportion attending college between schools, while large numbers of students in every school decide not to continue. The series of equations refers to neither a sequential process, since the same students are involved, nor to individual decision making, insofar as this is inadequately reflected in changing proportions relative to other schools. The degree to which individuals are sorted on the basis of income and race cannot be determined with such data. The changes represent either changes in individual plans, individual misreporting, or differential reliabilities between schools. Research on the aspirations of high school seniors indicates we have much to learn about the formation and change of aspirations.[8] The model of educational rationing presented could also be criticized from this perspective. If the correlation between decision variables is high, one would expect differences in proportions between schools to contain substantial error variance. The precipitous decline in the proportion of variance explained in Tables 4, 5, and 6 could be explained if one assumed much of the difference was error, rather than real changes in either the demand or supply of higher education.

Operationalizing a concept such as rationed admissions on any criteria is extremely difficult. Historically, the expansion of opportunities for higher education has grown as quickly as has the increasing proportions of students completing high school. Continuation rates do not indicate a substantial bottleneck at college admission, nor do trends point to an increased difficulty in enrolling.[9] It is possible that aspirations among high school graduates have increased relative to the supply of higher education but one would need a time series of such relationships to reach this conclusion. What is clear from a variety of sources is that aspirations exceed attainment at almost every level of education. In high schools, fewer students are assigned to a college preparatory course than report aspiring to, or planning for, college.[10] It is also true that lower class and nonwhite students are differentially "cooled out"; that is, the gap between aspirations and attainment is inversely related to social class.

Schools are the principal institution for social selection and differentiation, and this necessarily implies rationing at many levels. The paradox would seem to be demanding equality of opportunity from institutions designed to channel students into a highly stratified society. Changing admissions policies alone would not necessarily alter the life changes of many pupils, nor insure a larger degree of upward mobility. The returns to education are by no means equally distributed by class or race. The total amount of schooling is presently more equally distributed than is income, and the trend seems to be toward greater equality. What I find disturbing is the implicit assumption that more accessible educational institutions would provide more equal opportunity.

Sociological models of occupational mobility point to the importance of education as a mediating factor between the status of sons and that of fathers.[11] Duncan has argued that American society allows for a considerable amount of social mobility and that no evidence exists which suggests this is declining. It is also true that a considerable degree of inequality can and does exist simultaneously, and also shows little tendency to change. The latter point is important precisely because policy makers often assume that increasing social mobility will reduce inequality. Education does facilitate individual mobility, at least relative to the importance of parental status. However, the large component of unexplained variance suggests that many factors other than schooling are important.

The substantive conclusions reached by Dugan can be questioned both methodologically and conceptually. The findings discussed seem in general to be consonant with much social science research. Policy considerations, however, depend on the extent to which manipulating factors will produce different outcomes.

The process through which education is rationed can be criticized from many perspectives. If the desired outcome was to promote opportunity, it is quite doubtful that a perfectly competitive market for higher education would do so. The situation in which the only determinant of college admission is the ability to purchase it seems highly unlikely to allow many children from lower-class families entrance.

Equality of opportunity minimally implies that the allocation of scarce resources depends on some individual characteristics rather than, or in addition to, parental wealth. Any such social constraint would involve nonmarket rationing, at least until such time as education is neither a scarce commodity nor a determinant of wealth or status. The critical policy question is how, and to what degree, such rationing will occur. Some consideration of alternatives seems called for.

The question of how selection should operate is fundamental, and re-solves itself into the question of what are relevant criteria. As Dugan argues, scholastic achievement has become a principal mechanism for differentiating pupils. In part, this is because it is presumed to measure past achievements, and because it is highly predictive of future academic success. Equally, it seems to differentiate between children of different social class and racial groups. What can well be overlooked, however, is that it does not predict occupational success or income later in life very well, except through the strong relationship to years of schooling.[12]

· Although Dugan points to the role of achievement as restricting the options open to certain children, a critique of those criteria would also be relevant. The arguments regarding cultural bias in tests are well made elsewhere. Let us assume that a principal ability measured by such tests is an ability to take tests. This form of interpersonal competition is considerably more prevalent and better rewarded in schools than in the labor market. The diversity of talents and aptitudes required to perform many jobs competently is neither well measured nor part of the curriculum. Potentially, this is a possible explanation for the negligible independent effect of ability. The criticism is not so much that schools are irrelevant to students' futures; but that the bases of selection and recruitment are strictly academic and do not reflect the broad spectrum of human potential. A case could be made for the usefulness of tests to predict *academic* success. It is obviously more efficient to admit students who show more "promise" than students who need special attention. Perhaps higher education should remain academic, rather than relevant, but then surely other channels of upward mobility could be established—with nonscholastic determinants.

The question of the degree of rationing seems to me to depend on the amount of educational subsidies available. If the only criteria for admission were aspirations, it would be equivalent to open enrollment. Such a policy has much to recommend it, except perhaps the costs involved. It is not clear to me whether Dugan would advocate open enrollment or prefers a rationing model based on equal admission rates for different groups of students. What I find lacking in the analysis is an explicit description of policy alternatives, and some feeling for the sociological impact such policies might have.

One final point deserves mention. At a conference entitled "Education as an Industry," one would like to hear discussion of the potential impact economic analyses have on school administrators and educational systems. In *Education and the Cult of Efficiency*,[13] Callahan brilliantly documents the disastrous effects of considering education as an industry during the early twentieth century. "Scientific" management, efficiency, and cost accounting seem more applicable to production systems in which there is certain knowledge of the process; unfortunately, we lack such knowledge entirely when it comes to learning. As a social scientist, one's minimal responsibility would be to admit the state of the art and to try to avoid the most blatant errors of the past.

NOTES AND REFERENCES

1. See W. S. Robinson, "Ecological Correlations and the Behavior of Individuals," *American Sociological Review* 15 (June 1950): 251–357; Leo A. Goodman, "Ecological Regressions and Behavior of Individuals," *American Sociological Review* 18 (December 1953): 663–664; Leo A. Goodman, "Some Alternatives to Ecological Correlation," *American Journal of Sociology* 64 (May 1959); Otis D. Duncan, Ray P. Cozzort, and Beverly Duncan, *Statistical Geography* (Glencoe, Ill.: Free Press, 1961); Hayward R. Alker, Jr., "A Typology of Ecological Fallacies," Mattei Dogan and Stein Rokkan, eds., *Quantitative Ecological Analysis in the Social Sciences* (Cambridge, Mass.: M.I.T. Press, 1969).
2. It should be noted that a correlation based on 47 cases must be larger than .288 to be significant at the 5% level and greater than .372 at the 1% level; among the zero-order correlations presented in the appendix less than half are larger than .288.
3. Robert M. Hauser, "Family, School, and Neighborhood Factors in Educational Performances in a Metropolitan School System" (Ph.D. diss., University of Michigan, 1968); and Hauser, "Schools and the Stratification Process," *American Journal of Sociology* 74 (May 1969): 587–611.
4. Christopher Jencks, "The Coleman Report and the Conventional Wisdom," in Frederick Mosteller and Daniel P. Moynihan, eds., *On Equality of Educational Opportunity* (New York: Random House, 1971); Edward L. McDill, Edmund D. Meyers, Jr., and Leo C. Rigsby, "Institution Effects on the Academic Behavior of High School Students," *Sociology of Education* 40 (Winter 1967): 181–199; Stephan Michelson, "The Association of Teacher Resources with Children's Characteristics," in U.S. Department of Health, Education, and Welfare, Office of Education, *Do Teachers Make A Difference?* OE-58042 (Washington, D.C., 1970), Chapter 6; James S. Coleman, Ernest Q. Campbell, Carol J. Hobson, James McPartland, Alexander N. Mood, Frederick D. Weinfeld, and Robert L. York, *Equality of Educational Opportunity* (Washington, D.C.: Government Printing Office, 1966).
5. Christopher Jencks, Marshall Smith, Henry Acland, David Cohen, Herbert Gintis, Barbara Heyns, and Stephan Michelson, *Inequality* (New York: Basic Books, 1972).
6. Howard Becker, "The Career of the Chicago Public School Teacher," *American Journal of Sociology* 57 (1952): 470–477.
7. See for example, Henry Levin's paper, "Concepts of Economic Efficiency and Educational Production," this volume.
8. William H. Sewell and Vimal P. Shah, "Socioeconomic Status, Intelligence, and the Attainment of Higher Education," *Sociology of Education* 40 (Winter 1967): 1–23; Sewell and Shah, "Social Class, Parental Encouragement, and Educational Aspirations," *American Journal of Sociology* 73 (March 1968): 559–572; Sewell and Shah, "Parents' Education and Children's Educational Aspirations and Achievements," *American Sociological Review* 33 (April 1968): 191–209.
9. Beverly Duncan, "Trends in Output and Distribution of Schooling," in Eleanor B. Sheldon and Wilbert E. Moore, eds., *Indicators of Social Change* (New York: Russell Sage Foundation, 1968), Chapter 12.
10. Barbara Heyns, "Social Selection and Stratification Within Schools," *American Journal of Sociology* 79 (May 1974): 1434–1451.
11. Peter M. Blau and Otis D. Duncan, *The American Occupational Structure* (New York: John Wiley, 1967).
12. Otis D. Duncan, "Ability and Achievement," *Eugenics Quarterly* 15 (March 1968): 1–11.
13. Raymond Callahan, *Education and the Cult of Efficiency* (Chicago: University of Chicago Press, 1962).

Frank Levy

University of California
at Berkeley

Dugan has provided a good framework in which to analyze college-going decisions. His separate analysis of college aspirations, planning for college, and actual college attendance is conceptually far more satisfying than an analysis of a simple go–no-go decision.

To discuss Dugan's application of this framework to the data at hand, it will be useful to divide his findings into two general groups: those that do not have direct relevance to current educational policy debates and those that do. In the first group, I include Dugan's findings that when SAT scores are controlled, the student's propensity to plan for and go to college depends positively on family income and negatively on family size. These findings certainly seem plausible. While we might not like their implications, it seems that no alternative method of college financing, including the Brewster-Zacharias Plan, will change the findings very much.

In the second group, I include two other of Dugan's findings. First, he argues that even when SAT scores are controlled, nonwhite students are disproportionately rationed in their desire to go to college (Table 6 and pp. 77–78). Second, Dugan argues that the SAT scores themselves, an important element in the rationing process, can be raised through additional expenditure in the schools (Table 7, regression 1). Both of these findings may be correct but I believe each will require further exploration before the issues are closed.

I shall begin with the rationing finding. There are something like four variables in which one might be interested when measuring the propensity toward college of a class of seniors:

1. the number of students in the class;
2. the number of students who aspire to go to college;
3. the number of students who are seriously planning to go to college (by which, I mean, they have read catalogues, filled out applications, and so on); and
4. the number of students who actually do go to college the following fall.

If I were to investigate the presence of current discrimination by either the colleges or the college and noncollege sources of financial aid, I would look at the ratio of (4) to (1). I would want to see whether there was a difference in that ratio between white and nonwhite classes when other factors were controlled. Dugan performs such an analysis in regressions D_5 and D_6 of Table 3. He finds no current discrimination of the type I have suggested. When the class is controlled for family size, family income, and SAT scores, Dugan finds that the proportion of nonwhite students has a *positive* impact on the proportion attending all colleges and the proportion attending four-year institutions (though the all-college coefficient is significant only at the 10 per cent level).

Dugan's conclusion on rationing comes not from the ratio of (4) to (1) but from the ratio of (4) to (3) and especially (4) to (2),—that is, the number of seniors who actually go to college as a proportion of those who were planning to go to college or who aspired to go to college in their senior year of high school (Table 6—all regressions).

Dugan finds that when family background and SAT scores are controlled, a relatively large proportion of nonwhites who want to go to college do not make it. Given the positive relationship between proportion nonwhite and proportion admitted to college noted above, this rationing relationship can be true only if the proportion nonwhite has an even larger positive impact on the proportion who want to go to college. This is in fact what Dugan shows in Table 3, regressions D_1-D_4.

It is here, I think, that caution must enter. Many other studies have shown a similar relationship: that when background factors are controlled, nonwhite children have higher aspiration levels than do white children.[1] For precisely this reason, it is important to find out whether aspiration means the same thing for both groups. Consider asking a high school senior the following two questions:

1. Do you want to go to college?
2. Have you ever seen a college catalogue or written for an admissions application?

If the senior answered yes to the first question but no to the second, I would be suspicious as to how serious his aspirations were. To be sure, intervening problems could exist. Inadequate counselling advice would be an example. But I would have to know more before I considered the failure of such a student to get into college to be a national problem.

In Dugan's data, there is a hint, no more, that something like this may be going on. Consider the regressions in Table 3. The proportion of nonwhite students in a class has a smaller impact on the proportion of students definitely planning to go to college (regression D_3) than it does on the proportion of students aspiring to go to college (regressions D_1 and D_2). These results appear again in Table 6. The impact of rationing on nonwhite students who were planning to go to college (R_3) appears to be substantially weaker than the impact of rationing on nonwhite students who aspired to go to college (R_1). There certainly are interpretations of this aspirations-planning gap which do not rely upon the "unserious aspiration" model I have suggested, but I believe the question needs to be more fully investigated before we know the answer.

Even if Dugan's rationing conclusion is based on unserious aspirations, there are other rationing questions in his data which are worthy of exploration. Dugan shows that when SAT scores are controlled, the proportion of students in a class who attend college is positively related to their mean family income and negatively related to their family size (Table 3, regressions D_5 and D_6). I noted above that when these factors were also held constant, nonwhites were favored, but we can ask whether they were favored enough. For example, we might want a scholarship policy which took explicit recognition of the fact that blacks come, on average, from larger families with lower incomes than whites. Dugan might then ask whether there is a gap in black-white college attendance when SAT's are controlled but when family size and family income are assumed equal. If there is, then the mechanism producing this gap should be further explored.

In discussing the determinants of college attendance, Dugan shows that SAT scores play an important part in the college attendance process (Table 3, D_5, D_6). This finding leads him to explore the determinants of SAT scores themselves (Section IV). One of his findings is the positive relationship between expenditure per child in the school and the average level of SAT scores of the students. Thus it appears that another way of helping a group of students into college (though as Dugan notes, an extremely costly way) might be to spend more money on schools to boost the students' SAT scores (Table 7, regression 1).

We know from other educational production-function literature that such findings must be interpreted with great caution. Investigators such as Bowles (1970) and Hansheck (1968) have found that when input characteristics are carefully disaggregated—for example, classifying teachers by their verbal ability—some relationship between school inputs and student achievement can be found. However, the majority of studies including many of the pessimistic conclusions about the Elementary and Secondary Education Act (ESEA) Title I compensatory programs offer little hope that simply spending more money in a school will boost the achievement scores of the students.

Again, an alternative model may be operating. Suppose that in Table 7, regression 1, family income is not an adequate control for family background. Suppose rather that even when income is controlled, the parents of certain communities put an exceptionally high premium on their children's education. Suppose they show this concern first by giving their children exceptional attention within the home, and second by voting high school budgets in the (incorrect) belief that the size of expenditures per child has a positive effect on achievement. In such a situation, it may be the home attention that is really causing the high SAT scores but statistically it will appear that expenditure is important.

Here, too, some further exploration seems both warranted and possible. In note 5, Dugan notes that his income figure is constructed data: that originally he had information on father's occupation and father's years of education and that these were transformed into income figures through figures in *Occupation by Earnings and Income*. If my alternative argument is correct, then the original occupation and education data may offer a slightly better control for background than do the derived income figures. Regressions using the original background data may be in order.

As I said at the outset, I believe Dugan has developed a good approach with which to analyze who goes to college and when those who do not go become diverted. I believe, however, that he will have to do more work with the data he has, and perhaps with other data, before the approach can yield policy conclusions in which we have confidence.

NOTE

1. See, for example, Coleman et al. (1966) Table 2.43.1 (p. 193) for white and nonwhite responses similar to those in Dugan's data. Despite achievement test and other differences between whites and nonwhites, percentage responses to definitely planning and probably planning to go to college questions are essentially equal.

REFERENCES

Bowles, Samuel, "Towards an Educational Production Function," in W. Lee Hansen, ed., *Education, Income and Human Capital* (New York: NBER, 1970).

Coleman, James S. et al., *Equality of Educational Opportunity* (Washington, D.C.: U.S. Department of Health, Education, and Welfare, 1966).

Hansheck, Eric Alan, "The Education of Negroes and Whites" (Ph.D. diss., Massachusetts Institute of Technology, August, 1968).

3

**LEWIS J.
PERL**

National Economic
Research Associates

Graduation, Graduate School Attendance, and Investments in College Training

I. INTRODUCTION

It has often been suggested by economists and other social scientists that the educational system may conveniently be viewed as a production process.[1] The primary output of this process is an increase in the student's stock of knowledge and skill, an output which acquires value by augmenting the individual's ability to produce other goods and services. The inputs to this process include the student's time (the productivity of which depends upon a previously acquired stock of human capital), the time of instructors, and a variety of forms of capital equipment which augment the instructional process. When students acquire their education in groups, it may be well to recognize that the input to this process by one student may affect not only his own output but the output of other students as well.[2]

In order to examine the usefulness of this view, I have attempted in this study to estimate the relationship between specific measures of the output of the educational process at the college level and proxies for each of the dimensions of input specified above. These estimates are derived by postulating rather simple functional relationships between these input and output measures—referred to as educational production functions—and using multiple regression analysis to estimate the parameters of these functions. These parameters are estimated from data describing the input and outputs of the college experience for a large sample of students entering college in 1960.

There are three primary objectives of this effort that attempts to estimate the parameters of these production functions. As suggested above, this analysis provides a means for evaluating the viability of viewing the educational system as a production process. The failure to observe consistent relationships between the supposed inputs and outputs of this process would cast doubt on the usefulness of this view.

If this approach does produce consistent input-output relationships, the production function provides a useful device for evaluating the efficiency of alternative patterns of investment. In particular, this production function may provide a guide for students, educational administrators, and the public generally in attempting to improve the efficiency of educational investment.

Finally, since the output of the educational system, once produced, cannot be freely bought and sold, the process by which educational services are produced has important implications for the distribution of educational services. For a variety of reasons, students from high-income family backgrounds possess a larger stock of human capital upon entry to college than students from low-income family backgrounds. In addition, these students are capable of making larger financial investments in college than those from low-income backgrounds. The production function provides a mechanism for evaluating the importance of each of these advantages and enables us to assess the usefulness of alternative means for achieving a more egalitarian distribution of educational output.

The remainder of this study is divided into four parts. First, the results of a number of other studies of the relationships between specific inputs and outputs of the college process are examined. In Section III, the model and estimating procedure used in this study are discussed in some detail; and, in Section IV, the estimated parameters of that model are evaluated. Section V summarizes the primary policy implications of this study.

II. OTHER STUDIES

While a number of other studies have examined the relationship between educational inputs and outputs, it is difficult to generalize from the results of these studies. Thus, a study by Hunt [16] examines, for a sample of college graduates, the relationship among earnings in 1947, ability level, and expenditure per pupil at the college they attended. This study suggests that after controlling for the student's ability level, expenditure per pupil has little effect on earnings. In examining the relationship between earnings and school expenditures, Hunt controls for several factors which may themselves be responsive to college quality. These include the student's likelihood of graduation from college, the student's decision to attend graduate school, as well as certain aspects of the student's career choice. Moreover, expenditure per pupil at these colleges as of a point in time is used to measure college quality over the period of nearly half a century. Both of these factors may have reduced the magnitude and statistical significance of the relationship between college quality and earnings. On the other hand, another aspect of the model operates in the opposite direction. Hunt uses both the average ability of the student body and expenditure per pupil to measure college quality, but these measures are not examined simultaneously. Consequently, the estimated effect on earnings of increasing expenditure per pupil at a college may include the effect of increasing the quality of the student body at the college.

Weisbrod and Karpoff [26] examine the relationship among the earnings of college graduates, their ability, and the quality of the college they attended. In their study, both of these inputs appear related to earnings, but the authors do not test the statistical significance of this relationship. Moreover, since the measure of college quality is a subjective one, it would be difficult to use these results to evaluate the efficiency of alternative patterns of educational investment.

The most recent examination of this relationship is that of Daniere and Mechling [11]. In this study they construct an earnings composite for each of a number of colleges. This composite, which is based on the graduation rate at each college and the career pattern of graduates observed five years after graduation, is then related to the average ability of the student body and the level of expenditure per pupil at these colleges. The results indicate positive returns on increased expenditure per student and a particularly high return in low-expenditure, high-ability institutions. Unfortunately, Daniere and Mechling fail to test the statistical significance of these relationships. Moreover, the use of expenditures as the single measure of college quality may, as we suggested above, overestimate the returns to educational investment.

A number of studies examine the relationship between the quality of the inputs to a student's undergraduate experience and the likelihood of attaining a Ph. D. degree. Knapp and Goodrich [19] suggest that there is a substantial difference between high- and low-quality colleges in this regard. However, as other authors point out, this study fails to control for differences in the student's input to this process. Holland [15], Thistlethwaite [25], and Astin [1] all try to remedy this deficiency, and their studies suggest a more modest role for college quality. Astin's study does suggest that increasing the ratio of faculty to students increases the fraction of entrants who receive Ph. D. degrees.

One of the most complex models of the educational process is that examined by Astin in a recent article in *Science* [2]. In this study, the output measures are the student's scores on the Graduate Record Examination's achievement tests in the natural sciences, humanities, and the social sciences. The scores on these tests by each of 669 students in 38 colleges and universities are related to nearly 170 measures of educational input. These include over 100 measures of student input such as the student's scores on aptitude tests administered prior to college entry, measures of the student's socioeconomic background, characteristics of the high school attended, and measures reflecting the student's career choice. In measuring the characteristics of the student's college, the study included the average ability level of students in that college, measures of expenditure per student in the college, enrollment level, academic competitiveness, and the region and size of the community in which the college is located. In addition, a number of measures were included reflecting interaction among these variables.

On the basis of regressions relating these inputs to each of the three output measures, the study concludes that college characteristics have little effect on student achievement. This conclusion is based on the fact that after controlling for measures of student input, only two measures of college input—library expenditures and a composite reflecting total affluence of the college—have a significant effect on college output.

This conclusion may be misleading. Given the number of variables used in this analysis, it is not surprising that many of the school input measures have no significant effect on student performance. Due to the high degree of multicollinearity among these input measures, there is little independent variance in any of the school inputs. Therefore, the effects of these inputs can only be estimated with substantial error. Consequently, although Astin is not able to reject the hypothesis that the effect of these variables is zero, he would also be unable to reject the hypothesis that they have a substantial effect. This should not be taken as evidence that these variables have no effect, but as evidence that Astin's model is far too complex to be evaluated with the data available. [3]

In summary, the literature on relating college inputs and outputs is rather inconclusive with respect to the impact of increasing college quality. Those studies which have failed to show a significant relationship between the level of investment per student and measures of output all appear to have examined measures of input which may have been too highly disaggregated, given the quality of the available data. On the other hand, studies which show a substantial return on these investments have generally failed to test for statistical significance or have used input measures which are so highly aggregative as to be of questionable usefulness.

III. THE MODEL

Data Sources

In analyzing the production of educational services, data on students from the Project Talent data bank were used.[4] The students included in the sample are males who were high school seniors in 1960, who responded to both follow-up questionnaires, and who had entered four-year colleges as full-time students in September of that year. Various forms of nonresponse and the requirement that each student in the final sample attend a college attended by at least ten other students from the sample reduced the final sample to about 3,000 students attending 200 different colleges. The data on these students from the Project Talent Survey is supplemented by data on the colleges they attended from the Higher Education General Information Survey.[5]

Measures of Output

In assessing the college output of these students, two dichotomous measures are used. The first of these is a variable which takes on the value one if the student graduates within five years and is zero otherwise. The second measure, which is assessed only for students who graduate within five years, takes on the value one if the student goes on to graduate school and is zero otherwise. The estimated relationship between these measures and various inputs reflects the effects on the *probability* of college graduation or graduate school attendance of varying each of these inputs, while holding all other inputs constant.

There are two primary drawbacks to these variables as measures of college output. First, they clearly do not represent a complete specification of the output of the college process. There are many other dimensions of success in college which are not reflected either by graduation or graduate school attendance. This, of course, limits the ability to generalize from the results of this study. If no significant relationship between these measures and the inputs to the educational process is found, it may not follow that the production model is inappropriate to the educational process but only that these are inappropriate measures of output. On the other hand, if significant relationships are uncovered in this analysis, this should serve to encourage application of this model to other indexes of output as well.

A second difficulty stems from the subjective nature of these output measures. The standards for graduation may vary from institution to institution and from student to student, and moreover, these standards may themselves be an increasing function of the inputs to the educational process. Similarly, while the model explored in this study suggests that a student's likelihood of attending graduate school depends upon the quality of his undergraduate experience, it is also likely to depend upon the student's assessment of the attractiveness of the other opportunities available to him at the time of graduate school attendance. The quality of these opportunities may also depend upon the quality of the student's undergraduate experience. Consequently, the estimated relationships between these output measures and the inputs to the educational process are likely to underestimate the effect of these inputs on the quality of the undergraduate experience.

Despite these limitations, there are good reasons for using these variables as measures of output. After adjustment for the costs of these investments, students with graduate training earn more than graduates who do not go into graduate school, and both of these groups earn more, on average, than college entrants who do not graduate. The relationship between these events and earnings suggests that college graduates have acquired more productive capacity from college than dropouts and that students attending graduate school have acquired more than those who terminate their formal education upon graduation. If, as has often been alleged, the objective of investment in education is to increase productive capacity, then it should be useful to explore the relationship between the level of this investment and the likelihood of these events. Moreover, given the relationship between these events and lifetime earnings, they should be of interest to students even if they are unrelated to productivity.

Even in the absence of a relation to earnings, these events represent viable measures of college output. In the current context, a student who fails to graduate is generally dissatisfied with the college he attends or has been found a less-than-satisfactory student by the faculty of that college. By the same token, graduate school attendance is a reflection of a high level of satisfaction with the educational process. The prospective graduate student is sufficiently satisfied with his undergraduate experience to extend this process. The graduate or professional school, in admitting this student, is expressing satisfaction with the caliber of his undergraduate program and his performance in that program. In both cases, it is useful to see whether increasing the level of input to the educational process can reduce the probability of unsatisfactory outcomes while increasing the likelihood of more satisfactory outcomes.

Functional Form and Estimation Procedure

The output measures used in this analysis are assumed to be linear, additive functions of the inputs to the educational process. That is

(1) $Y_i = \beta_0 + \beta_1 X_{1i} + \beta_2 X_{2i} + \ldots + \beta_n X_{ni} + \epsilon_i$

where

Y_i = a dummy variable which takes on the value one if the ith entrant (graduate) graduates (attends graduate school) and is zero otherwise;

X_{ji} = a measure of the jth input to the educational process for the ith student;

β_j = the parameters of the model; and

ϵ_i = a stochastic term.

Multiple regression analysis is used to estimate the parameters of this model. Assuming the expected value of ϵ_i is 0, ordinary least squares or regression would produce unbiased estimates of these parameters. However, given the limited nature of the dependent variable, these estimates would clearly not be minimum variance. The variance of ϵ_i is

(2) $VAR(\epsilon_i) = (X'_i \beta) - X'_i \beta)$

where

X_i = the vector of input values for the ith student; and

β = the vector of parameters;

which clearly depends upon the value of X_i. Homoscedasticity can be restored by redefining the model as

(3) $\gamma_i Y_i = \gamma_i X'_i \beta + \gamma_i \epsilon_i$

where

(4) $\gamma_i = \dfrac{1}{X'_i \beta (1 - X'_i \beta)}.$

Estimates of β made by applying least squares regression to this model will be minimum variance, and if the assumptions of the model hold, weighting by γ_i will not change the expected value of the regression coefficients. To estimate the parameters of this modified model, an estimate of the parameters of these equations using ordinary least squares was first obtained. These are then used to estimate γ_i, and each student's input and output measures are multiplied by the appropriate value of γ_i. Minimum variance estimates of β are obtained by applying least squares regression to these modified data.[6]

In addition to these statistical difficulties, the linear additive model precludes the possibility that the productivity of inputs to the educational process depends upon their own level or the level of other inputs. In part, this problem is dealt with by measuring these inputs in a manner which takes account of certain forms of nonlinearity. For example, by including a variable and the square of that variable as input measures, the possibility that the productivity of that variable depends upon its level is considered. To explore the possibility of other forms of nonlinearity, the students are divided into subsamples in which the range of specific inputs is restricted. By estimating the parameters of the production function separately for each of these subsamples and comparing these parameters, the extent and magnitude of interaction among the inputs to the educational process is examined.

Measures of Input

In this model, it is assumed that these output measures are functions of three dimensions of input: the time and effort each student brings to the educational process, the quality of the faculty and facilities available to each student at the college attended, and the quality of the other students in the college attended. Each of these dimensions of input is measured by a number of separate variables. The means and standard deviations of these measures for all students and for students in public and private colleges are described in Tables 1 and 2.

The quality of the effort the student brings to the educational process depends upon the quality of the academic skills he has acquired prior to college entry. These skills have been measured for the students in our sample by a battery of ability tests administered about six months prior to college entry. Principal components analysis has been used to measure the separate dimensions of ability reflected in these tests, and the students' scores on these principal components are used as input measures.[7] Preliminary analysis suggested that a number of these components were not related to success in college, and these were dropped from subsequent analyses.[8]

At the time the student decides whether or not to attend graduate school, these skills have been altered by the nature of the undergraduate

TABLE 1 Means and Standard Deviations of the Input and Output Measures for the Sample of Students Entering College in 1960

	All Students		Students in Public Colleges		Students in Private Colleges	
	Mean	Standard Deviation	Mean	Standard Deviation	Mean	Standard Deviation
Ability measure 1 (percentiles)	72.06	21.11	70.77	21.48	75.73	19.60
Ability measure 2 (percentiles)	63.65	24.29	62.01	24.66	68.33	22.60
Ability measure 3 (percentiles)	49.32	26.95	49.15	26.96	49.79	26.93
Ability measure 4 (percentiles)	47.22	27.11	47.44	27.05	46.58	27.30
Ability measure 5 (percentiles)	58.76	28.02	57.39	28.11	62.66	27.39
Ability measure 12 (percentiles)	43.47	25.73	43.64	25.39	42.97	26.66
Average ability (percentiles)	72.21	10.70	70.70	9.91	76.47	11.65
Living expenses (hundreds of dollars)	6.23	4.24	6.02	3.87	6.81	5.09
Working for pay[a]	.506	.500	.504	.500	.513	.500
Hours worked per week for pay	11.68	14.57	11.55	14.46	12.04	14.86
Living at home[a]	.416	.493	.384	.486	.531	.499
Student-faculty ratio	21.12	7.40	20.40	6.46	23.10	9.32
Expenditure per student on instruction-related activities (hundreds of dollars)	13.25	5.29	12.52	4.49	15.33	6.65
Expenditure per student on organized research and extension (hundreds of dollars)	8.25	9.75	8.04	9.10	8.83	11.39
Enrollment (thousands)	15.3	10.5	17.5	10.8	9.1	6.4
Enrollment² (thousands)	344.3	438.1	421.9	477.1	124.3	158.9
Proportion graduating[a]	.644	.479	.616	.486	.725	.446
Sample size	3,155		2,317		806	

[a] In the analysis, these were dummy variables which took on the value one if the event in question occurred and zero if it did not occur. Their means and standard deviations reflect the proportion of students for whom the variable took on the value one.

TABLE 2 Means and Standard Deviations of Input and Output Measures for the Sample of Students Entering College in September 1960 and Graduating by November 1965

	All Students		Students in Public Colleges		Students in Private Colleges	
	Mean	Standard Deviation	Mean	Standard Deviation	Mean	Standard Deviation
Ability measure 1 (percentiles)	76.19	18.51	74.85	18.65	79.32	17.86
Ability measure 2 (percentiles)	67.41	22.57	65.53	23.16	71.93	20.46
Ability measure 3 (percentiles)	50.38	26.62	50.19	26.67	51.05	26.44
Ability measure 4 (percentiles)	46.31	26.74	47.05	26.66	44.57	26.83
Ability measure 10 (percentiles)	30.63	20.76	30.96	20.28	29.82	21.47
Average ability (percentiles)	73.95	10.64	72.09	9.65	78.31	11.61
Grades	7.88	1.71	7.85	1.69	7.93	1.75
Living at home [a]	.377	.485	.341	.474	.450	.497
Working for pay [a]	.469	.499	.470	.499	.463	.499
Hours worked for pay (per week)	9.11	12.05	9.05	11.83	9.28	12.66
Student-faculty ratio	20.6	7.06	20.4	7.03	21.1	8.41
Expenditure per student on instruction-related activities (hundreds of dollars)	13.93	5.62	12.89	4.55	16.36	6.97
Expenditure per student on organized research and extension (hundreds of dollars)	9.30	10.48	8.82	9.44	10.42	12.52

	15.6	10.6	18.4	10.8	8.8	6.2
Enrollment (thousands)						
Enrollment^2 (thousands)	354.6	438.4	455.6	480.1	118.9	151.2
College major						
Math & physical sciences [a]	.254	.436	.261	.439	.239	.427
Social sciences & humanities [a]	.315	.465	.306	.461	.337	.473
Prelaw, premedicine, predentistry [a]	.013	.111	.012	.110	.014	.116
Engineering [a]	.020	.146	.024	.152	.010	.097
Proportion attending graduate or professional schools [a]	.537	.499	.521	.500	.568	.495
Sample size	2,453		1,717		736	

[a] See Table 1, note *a*.

experience. Given the substantial differences in the rate of student development in college, ability at the time of college entrance may be a poor predictor of the student's ability at the time of college graduation. Consequently, in estimating the likelihood of graduate school attendance, the student's grades in college are included as an additional measure of student input to the educational process. These may be viewed as an intermediate output of the educational process which then exerts an effect on the student's desire and ability to gain entrance to graduate school.[9]

In addition to these skills, the quality and quantity of the effort the student brings to the educational process depends upon the nature of the student's living environment while in college. About half the students in our sample worked for pay while in college, and those students worked an average of 22 hours per week during the school year. It seems reasonable to suppose that, at least in excess of some reasonable number of hours, working for pay reduces the time the student spends on the educational process. Hence, the model includes as a negative input a variable measuring the number of hours the student worked for pay while in college. In order to take account of the possibility that the adverse effects of working for pay do not begin until the student works in excess of a certain number of hours, a dummy variable which takes on the value one if the student works and is zero otherwise is also included.

In addition, the students in the sample varied in the nature of their living environments while in college. About 40 per cent of the students in the sample described in Table 1 lived at home while attending college. While living at home may reduce the financial costs of college attendance, it may also reduce the input to the student's college program by limiting his contact with the informal education process which takes place among those students who live at school. To reflect this possibility, the model includes a variable which takes on the value one if the student lives at home while in college and is zero otherwise.

Students also differ in the amount that they spend on their living accommodations while in college. While the average student in the sample reported spending about $600 per year on room, board, and other college expenses, 13.2 per cent spent $1,000 or more per year, and 33 per cent spent less than $300. These differences reflect the fact that a student may reduce his living expenditures by substituting time for money in structuring his living environment, or by reducing the quality of that environment. However, these adjustments are likely to reduce either the quantity or the quality of the effort the student brings to the educational process. Thus, by living in overcrowded or dilapidated housing, the costs of college attendance are reduced, but this may deprive the student of an adequate place to study or to relax from studying. The extent of this relationship is explored by examining the relationship between annual living expenditures and the rate of college graduation. This variable was initially included as an input in estimating the probability of graduate school attendance. However, its effect was small and not statistically significant and was dropped from that model.

The second dimension of input examined in this study reflects the quantity and quality of the instructional facilities available at the college attended by each of the students in the sample. These resources are measured by the level of current expenditure per pupil at these colleges, and these expenditures are separated into three components. First, expenditures which have been specifically earmarked for organized research and other noninstructional activities have been separated from all other expenditures. Thus, while there may be important complementarities between research and teaching, it seems reasonable to suppose that research expenditures will have less effect on the quality of the instructional process than other components of expenditure. Moreover, to the extent that research and teaching are competitors for faculty time and facilities, increasing research expenditure may actually diminish the output of the instructional process.

The remaining expenditures, which include expenditures for faculty and other personnel, library expenditures, and expenditures for the maintenance of buildings and equipment, were separated into two components. First, these expenditures were adjusted to reflect the level which would have prevailed at a student-faculty ratio of 20:1.[10] The actual student-faculty ratio is included as a separate input measure. The student-faculty ratio has been separated from other instructional facilities for two reasons. Its effect, if any, is reasonably easy to interpret. If reducing this ratio increases either the rate of graduation or graduate school attendance, this would suggest that reducing class size or otherwise increasing student-faculty contact increases the output of the educational process. The data available on the other components of instructional expenditure are already too highly aggregated to clearly interpret the policy implications of its effect on output. On the other hand, other studies of the educational process suggest that reducing class size has little or no effect on the output of the educational process. If this is the case, the effects of other components of expenditures would be obscured by combining them in a single expenditure measure which would be heavily influenced by the student-faculty ratio.

While the above resources were measured on a per-student basis, it does not seem reasonable to suppose that the quality of these resources increases linearly with the level of expenditure per pupil. For example, it probably costs less per student to maintain an adequate library in a large than in a small school. On the other hand, beyond a certain size, further increases in the size of the student population may produce an impersonality deleterious to the educational process. In order to measure these economies and diseconomies of scale, both enrollment and the square of enrollment are included as inputs to the educational process.

The quality of a college may depend not only on the quality of its facilities but on the quality of the student body. Students clearly learn from each other as well as from their instructors, and moreover, the quality of the student body influences the level of instruction which is possible. Consequently, as a third dimension of input, a measure of the average ability level of the students at each of the colleges in this sample has been included. This measure is the mean score on the first principal component of ability of the students in the Talent sample attending each of these colleges. Since the Project Talent sample from which these students are drawn is roughly representative of the high school population, the students in this sample at each college are roughly representative of the student body at those colleges.[11]

In estimating the relationship between these inputs and the rate of graduate school attendance, an effort has been made to hold constant the student's choice of undergraduate major. Other studies have shown that students in some fields are much more likely to go on to graduate school than others. Since these fields of study may also vary in the ability level of the students they attract, it is necessary to control for this choice in order to avoid biasing the effect of other variables. Undergraduate majors have been grouped into four categories: mathematics and the physical sciences, the social sciences and humanities, engineering, and professional fields requiring postgraduate training (law, medicine, dentistry, and so forth). Dummy variables are used to reflect the student's presence in each of these categories. Students not included in any of these majors were recorded as zero on all four of these variables.

IV. EMPIRICAL RESULTS

The Linear Model

Tables 3 and 4 describe the estimated parameters relating each input measure to the rates of graduation and graduate school attendance respectively. In each case, the regression coefficients described in these tables have been scaled to reflect the effect of a unit change in each of

TABLE 3 Regression Coefficients Relating Measures of Educational Input[a] to the Relative Frequency with which Entrants Graduate from College

	All Schools			Public Schools			Private Schools		
	Regression Coefficient	Standard Error	Significance Level[b]	Regression Coefficient	Standard Error	Significance Level[b]	Regression Coefficient	Standard Error	Significance Level[b]
Constant	−11.08	7.49	.141	−15.44	9.04	.087	7.62	18.49	.681
Ability measure 1 (percentiles)	.449	.045	.000+	.442	.052	.000+	.448	.097	.000+
Ability measure 2 (percentiles)	.307	.036	.000+	.294	.042	.000+	.336	.070	.000+
Ability measure 3 (percentiles)	.105	.030	.000+	.127	.036	.000+	.065	.051	.204
Ability measure 4 (percentiles)	.079	.032	.013	.115	.039	.003	.004	.057	.944
Ability measure 5 (percentiles)	.103	.034	.002	.130	.041	.002	.015	.063	.810
Ability measure 12 (percentiles)	.121	.033	.000+	.092	.041	.025	.147	.058	.012
Average ability (percentiles)	.128	.097	.187	.229	.124	.066	.021	.197	.912
Living expenses	.220	.190	.250	.340	.250	.183	−.090	.300	.757
Work/not work	19.07	2.16	.000+	18.41	2.67	.000+	17.48	3.87	.000+
Hours worked per week	−1.16	.074	.000+	−1.10	.086	.000+	−1.18	.154	.000+
Live at home/at school	−4.08	1.76	.021	−5.72	2.15	.008	.489	3.27	.880
Student/faculty ratio	−.045	.115	.697	−.027	.165	.873	−.396	.217	.068
Expenditure per student on instruction-related activities	−.200	.210	.332	−.630	.290	.031	−.610	.480	.200

TABLE 3 (concluded)

	All Schools			Public Schools			Private Schools		
	Regression Coefficient	Standard Error	Significance Level[b]	Regression Coefficient	Standard Error	Significance Level[b]	Regression Coefficient	Standard Error	Significance Level[b]
Expenditure per student on organized research and extension	.220	.100	.030	.230	.120	.066	.320	.230	.167
Enrollment	.028	.244	.912	−.150	.361	.674	3.57	.916	.000+
Enrollment^2	−.003	.006	.667	.003	.008	.704	−.140	.038	.000+
R^2	.468			.325			.667		
F	159.50			64.73			91.48		
Number	3,089			2,297			792		
Efficiency ratio[c]	.967			.971			.966		

[a] The means and standard deviations of these input measures are described in Table 1. The regression coefficients reflect the change in the per cent of entrants graduating for a unit change in each input. Ability is measured in percentiles and all expenditures are in hundreds of dollars. Enrollment is measured in thousands.

[b] Probability of observing a coefficient this far from zero, if that were the true value of this parameter.

[c] The ratio of the standard error of estimate after correcting for heteroscedasticity to the standard error of estimate before this correction was made.

TABLE 4 Regression Coefficients Relating Measures of Educational Input[a] to the Relative Frequency with which College Graduates Attend Graduate and Professional Schools

	All Schools			Public Schools			Private Schools		
	Regression Coefficient	Standard Error	Significance Level[b]	Regression Coefficient	Standard Error	Significance Level[b]	Regression Coefficient	Standard Error	Significance Level[b]
Constant	−70.12	10.09	.000+	−87.49	11.26	.000+	−13.58	28.29	.631
Ability measure 1 (percentiles)	.116	.078	.139	.076	.087	.384	.209	.166	.207
Ability measure 2 (percentiles)	.165	.045	.000+	.185	.052	.000+	.178	.092	.052
Ability measure 3 (percentiles)	.046	.035	.187	−.048	.040	.234	.263	.066	.000+
Ability measure 4 (percentiles)	−.017	.037	.660	.057	.044	.186	−.127	.071	.073
Ability measure 10 (percentiles)	.083	.059	.152	.181	.068	.008	−.091	.113	.424
Average ability (percentiles)	.151	.127	.234	−.034	.154	.825	−.089	.285	.757
Grades in college	5.64	.514	.000+	8.29	.670	.000+	2.11	.817	.010
Work/not work	10.63	2.88	.002	10.39	3.36	.002	7.89	5.49	.152
Hours worked	−.723	.112	.000+	−.618	.130	.000+	−.826	.218	.000+
Live at home/at school	6.16	1.98	.000+	6.63	2.32	.004	3.58	3.92	.362
Student/faculty ratio	.772	.165	.000+	.928	.211	.000+	.417	.340	.222
Expenditure per student on instruction-related activities	1.150	.270	.000+	1.740	.360	.000+	.040	.670	.960
Expenditure per student on organized research & extension	−.010	.140	.920	.040	.160	.794	.340	.310	.267

TABLE 4 (concluded)

	All Schools			Public Schools			Private Schools		
	Regression Coefficient	Standard Error	Significance Level[b]	Regression Coefficient	Standard Error	Significance Level[b]	Regression Coefficient	Standard Error	Significance Level[b]
Enrollment	.949	.319	.003	.827	.476	.084	3.16	1.14	.006
Enrollment²	-.022	.008	.005	-.022	.010	.032	-.128	.047	.007
College major									
Math & physical sciences	12.61	2.36	.000+	9.77	2.74	.000+	14.31	4.45	.001
Social sciences & humanities	5.45	2.22	.014	5.26	2.59	.042	.116	4.19	.984
Prelaw, premedicine, predentistry	13.96	7.76	.073	24.58	9.20	.008	-7.72	14.16	.589
Engineering	6.84	7.02	.332	7.33	7.48	.327	8.50	17.49	.624
R^2	.320			.359			.306		
F	56.79			47.19			15.67		
Number	2,433			1,705			728		
Efficiency ratio[c]	.982			.962			1.000		

[a] The means and standard deviations of these input measures are described in Table 2. The regression coefficients reflect the change in the per cent of entrants graduating for a unit change in each input. Ability is measured in percentiles and all expenditures are in hundreds of dollars. Enrollment is measured in thousands.
[b] See Table 3, note b.
[c] See Table 3, note c.

the inputs on the number of graduates (graduate school attenders) per 100 entrants (graduates). Consequently, unit changes in these output measures are referred to as changes of 1 percentage point in the *rate* of graduation or graduate school attendance.

The results of these tables indicate that the quality and quantity of the effort the student brings to the educational process have pronounced effects on the student's likelihood of graduation and graduate school attendance. Considering the rate of graduation first, note that each of the six components of ability examined has a statistically significant effect on this output measure. A 10 percentile increase in the first of these components would appear to result in a 4.5 percentage point increase in the graduation rate, while a 10 percentile increase in the second component would increase the graduation rate by 3.1 percentage points. The significance of these magnitudes becomes apparent if they are used to examine the probable graduation rate of students currently not attending college. Students not attending college in 1960 have ability scores 42 percentiles lower on the first ability measure and 23 percentiles lower on the second than those attending college. As a result of this difference, if those not attending were to attend college, they would have a graduation rate 25 percentage points lower than the average student currently enrolled.

Examining the effect of these ability measures on the rate of graduate school attendance involves estimating both the direct effect of these inputs and any indirect effects which ability exerts on graduate school attendance through its effect on grades in college. In order to determine these indirect effects, the relationship between these test scores and grades in college are estimated in Table 5. Including both direct and indirect effects, a 10 percentile increase in these ability measures would increase the rate of graduate school attendance by 2.5 percentage points in the case of ability measure one and 1.9 percentage points in the case of ability measure two. The effects of the other ability measures examined, both direct and indirect, are quite modest.

The amount of time the student spends working for pay while in college also appears to affect adversely his chances of graduation and graduate school attendance. In the case of graduation, this adverse effect does not begin unless the student works in excess of 16 hours per week. However, each hour worked in excess of 16 reduces the rate of graduate school attendance by nearly 1.2 percentage points. In the case of graduate school attendance, the adverse effects of working for pay begin after 14 hours per week and reduce the rate of graduation by .8 percentage points per hour worked.

The impact of other components of the student's living environment while in college is less straightforward. Living expenditure, which is not

TABLE 5 Regression Coefficients Relating Grades in College[a] to Measures of Input to the Educational Process

	Variable Mean	Regression Coefficient	Standard Error	Significance Level[b]
Constant	1.0	5.47	.574	.000+
Ability measure 1 (percentiles)	76.3	.025	.002	.000+
Ability measure 2 (percentiles)	67.4	.005	.002	.009
Ability measure 3 (percentiles)	50.6	.007	.001	.000+
Ability measure 4 (percentiles)	53.7	.000+	.002	.865
Ability measure 5 (percentiles)	62.0	−.003	.002	.037
Average ability 1 (percentiles)	73.2	−.006	.006	.337
Average ability 2 (percentiles)	63.5	−.009	.004	.042
Average ability 3 (percentiles)	51.8	−.002	.005	.631
Average ability 4 (percentiles)	51.1	−.011	.005	.028
Work/not work	.472	.077	.117	.515
Hours worked	9.21	−.011	.004	.030
R^2	.118			
F	13.59			
Number	2,245			

[a] Grades are measured on a twelve-point scale from D− to A+.
[b] See Table 3, note b.

included in the equation estimating the rate of graduate school attendance, has a quite modest positive effect on the rate of graduation, and the high standard error of estimate makes it difficult to generalize about the effect of this variable. Living at home has a pronounced effect on both graduation and graduate school attendance but in opposite directions. The student who lives at home has a graduation rate 4.1 percentage points lower, and (if he does graduate) a rate of graduate school attendance 6.2 percentage points higher, than a similar student who does not live at home. There are several plausible explanations for the apparent inconsistency in the effect of this variable. Other analyses of this data which we have conducted suggest that the adverse effects of living at home occur primarily for low-ability students. Consequently, the average ability of college graduates who live at home may be greater than that of graduates who live at school. This would explain the positive relationship between living at home and graduate school attendance. Moreover, since living at home reduces the costs of college attendance, students who live at home may be able to finance the costs of graduate school attendance more easily than students from similar backgrounds who live at school.

In examining the effect of college characteristics, we find sharp differences between the effect of these measures on the rates of graduation and graduate school attendance. Of these measures, only research expenditures has a statistically significant effect on the graduation rate, and its effect is so modest—each $100 increase in research expenditures results in a .2 percentage point increase in the graduation rate—that it may be ignored. Increasing the average ability level of other students and reducing the student-faculty ratio both have positive effects on the graduation rate, but these effects are not statistically significant. While the effect of increasing instructional expenditures is also not statistically significant, it has an unexpected sign. Altering the enrollment level had little or no effect on the graduation rate.

The rate at which graduates attend graduate and professional schools appears sensitive to changes in the level of instructional expenditures per student. Each $100 increase in this component of input raises the rate of graduate school attendance by 1.2 percentage points. Since the colleges in our sample range from those spending as little as $350 to those spending nearly $4,000 on these inputs, the importance of this measure of college quality in explaining variations in the rate of graduate school attendance is substantial. Neither research expenditure nor average student ability has either large or statistically significant effects on the rate of graduate school attendance. On the other hand, the effect of varying the student-faculty ratio is substantial, significant, and has an unexpected sign. The model suggests that reducing the student-faculty ratio from 30:1 to 20:1 *reduces* the rate of graduate school attendance by nearly 7.7 percentage points.

It should also be noted that altering the enrollment level, while it has no effect on the rate of graduation, does affect the rate of graduate school attendance. This effect is nonlinear. Increasing enrollment from 5,000 to 10,000 students increases the rate of graduate attendance by 2.3 percentage points; an increase from 10,000 to 15,000 students results in an increase of 1.4 percentage points; and an increase from 13,000 to 20,000 students increases this rate by only .3 percentage points. Increasing enrollment beyond 20,000 students appears to reduce the rate of graduate school attendance.

While these estimates provide some useful insights into the workings of the educational process, several of these results call into question the plausibility of this framework for evaluating the educational process. First, the estimated parameters of these equations suggest that none of the college characteristics examined has any significant effect on the rate of graduation. Secondly, the model suggests that decreasing the student-faculty ratio would reduce the rate of graduate school attendance. If these conclusions are allowed to stand, either the graduation rate and the rate of graduate school attendance are inappropriate measures of output, or the production model used in this study is an unreasonable description of the educational process. Several alternative explanations of these results are explored below.

Public and Private Colleges Compared

As is suggested at the outset, degree standards vary from institution to institution. If colleges with high levels of expenditure per student also impose high degree standards, this may obscure any positive relationship which would exist between the components of expenditure per student and the graduation rate, holding degree standards constant. The relationship between degree standards and expenditure per student is less likely to obscure the relationship between these expenditures and the graduation rate in private than in public colleges. This is true because private colleges can raise degree standards without altering the graduation rate by raising admission requirements. In contrast, public colleges are often precluded by law from altering admission standards, and consequently, raising degree standards in public colleges would tend to reduce the graduation rate. To explore this possibility, the parameters of the college production function for public and private colleges have been estimated separately.

Examining the parameters of the production function estimated for students attending private colleges, we find that reducing the student-faculty ratio from 30:1 to 20:1 appears to increase the graduation rate by nearly 4.0 percentage points, and this effect is significant at the .07 level. While increasing instructional expenditures continues to have an unexpected sign, the effect of this variable is not statistically significant. On the other hand, in public colleges, reducing the student-faculty ratio has no effect on the graduation rate, and increasing instructional expenditures reduces the graduation rate by .6 percentage points per $100 of expenditure. This effect is significant at the .03 level. Two important conclusions emerge from these comparisons. First, at least under certain circumstances, one component of expenditure per student—the student-faculty ratio—has a significant and appreciable effect on the graduation rate in the expected direction. Secondly, the relationship between degree standards and expenditures provides a plausible explanation of the failure to observe a significant relationship between expenditures and the graduation rate for the sample as a whole.

Several other differences which emerge between public and private colleges are also worthy of note. The enrollment level, which has no significant effect on the rate of graduation in public colleges, is significant in private colleges. Increasing enrollment appears to increase the graduation rate until enrollment reaches 12.7 thousand students, but further increases in enrollment diminish this output. As an illustration of the magnitude of this effect, an increase in enrollment from 5,000 to 10,000 students would increase the graduation rate by nearly 7.0 percentage points. Secondly, while in public colleges increasing the average ability of other students appears to increase each student's chances of graduation, this is not the case in private colleges. Finally, the adverse effects of living at home while in college appear to occur only in the case of students attending public colleges.

There appears to be a fairly wide difference between otherwise comparable public and private colleges in their rates of graduation. The model suggests that a private college whose input level was the average for the sample of all colleges would have a graduation rate nearly 11 percentage points higher than a similar public college. Given the differences in the effect of specific variables between public and private colleges, the magnitude of this differential depends upon the input level at which the comparison is made. The difference is wider for students who live at home than for those who live at school and narrower in colleges where enrollment is less than 5,000 students or greater than 20,000 than for colleges of average size (15,000). Since increasing the student-faculty ratio has an effect in private but not in public colleges, this differential is also narrower in colleges where the ratio is high. Since public and private colleges differ widely with respect to the student-faculty ratio, enrollment, and the per cent of students living at home, it is difficult to determine whether differences in the graduation rate between public and private colleges reflect nonlinearities in the effect of these variables or structural differences between public and private colleges.

The greater homogeneity of the student body within private colleges suggests one possible explanation for this difference. At every ability level, there appears to be less variation in ability within private colleges than within public colleges. Consequently, if the same degree standards were applied at public and private colleges where the average ability of students was the same, more students would fail to meet those standards at the public than at the private colleges. This suggests that developing a more differentiated public college system, in which students of different ability levels attended different colleges, would reduce the rate of attrition in public colleges.

We also have estimated separately for students in public and private colleges the parameters of the model relating educational inputs to the rate of graduate school attendance (see Table 4). Once again, there are sharp differences in these parameters between public and private colleges, particularly with respect to the components of expenditure per pupil. Increasing instructional expenditures per pupil has a pronounced effect on the rate of graduate school attendance in public schools—each $100 increase in these expenditures increases the rate of graduate school attendance by 1.7 percentage points—but little or no effect in private colleges. This is true for a number of other variables as well, and in general, the model is less successful in relating the rate of graduate school attendance to these inputs in private than in public colleges. In part, this may reflect the fact that our sample consisted of relatively few students in private colleges, and the inputs for private colleges are substantially more collinear than those for public colleges. Alternatively, graduate school attendance may simply be a less valid measure of output for students attending private colleges than for those attending public colleges.

Nonlinearities

It also seems possible that some of the anomalies in the estimated effects of the inputs to the educational process reflect nonlinearities in the relationship between these inputs and outputs. To explore this possibility, the parameters of this model have been estimated separately for subsamples in which the range of specific inputs is restricted. In estimating the parameters of the model for these subsamples, however, no effort was made to adjust for heteroscedasticity. Moreover, when the range of specific inputs to this model is restricted, this also alters the average level of other input measures. Consequently, it is not possible to use this approach to establish with precision the impact of altering the level of specific inputs. Nevertheless, these comparisons are suggestive of certain patterns of interaction. The most revealing of these comparisons are described in Tables 6, 7, and 8.

In Table 6, the relationship between these inputs and the rate of graduation is examined for students attending colleges where the student-faculty ratio was less than or equal to 20:1 and those attending colleges where this ratio was greater than 20:1. It should be noted that the colleges where the student-faculty ratio was low may also be described as high input in other respects as well. The students in these colleges scored higher on ability tests and were less likely to work for pay while in college than those attending colleges where the student-faculty ratio was high. These colleges also spent more on both instruction and research-related activities than those with high student-faculty ratios. The most striking result to emerge from Table 6 is the difference in the apparent effect of the student-faculty ratio between these two subsamples. In schools where the student-faculty ratio was in excess of 20:1, each unit reduction in this ratio appears to *increase* the graduation rate by .4 percentage points. In schools where the student-faculty ratio was below 20:1, each unit reduction appears to *reduce* the graduation rate by 1.0 percentage points. Both of these effects are significant at the .05 level. This apparently "U-shaped" effect of reducing the student-faculty ratio provides an alternative explanation for the failure to discern a significant relationship in the sample of all students.

It is also interesting to note that a number of other input measures appear to be complements of the student-faculty ratio.[12] The adverse effects of working for pay while in college begin after fewer hours of work and more severely affect the rate of graduation in colleges with low than in colleges with high student-faculty ratios. Moreover, increasing the average ability level of the student population has a greater effect on the graduation rate in colleges where the student-faculty ratio is low than in those where it is high. On the other hand, living expenditures and the other inputs to the educational process appear to be substitutes. In low-input colleges, each $100 increase in these expenditures increases the graduation rate by .8 percentage points. This effect is more modest and not statistically significant in the high-input subsample.[13]

In Tables 7 and 8, the parameters of the model relating these inputs

TABLE 6 Regression Coefficients Relating Measures of Educational Input to the Relative Frequency with which Entrants Receive College Degrees in Colleges with Varying Student-Faculty Ratios[a]

| | Colleges Where the Student-Faculty Ratio Is: | | | | | | | |
| | Less Than or Equal to 20:1 | | | | Greater Than 20:1 | | | |
	Mean	Regression Coefficient	Standard Error	Significance Level[b]	Mean	Regression Coefficient	Standard Error	Significance Level[b]
Constant	1.0	−48.7	14.8	.000+	1.0	−16.0	10.6	.131
Ability measure 1 (percentiles)	75.4	.482	.073	.000+	69.5	.397	.061	.000+
Ability measure 2 (percentiles)	63.8	.249	.056	.000+	63.6	.312	.048	.000+
Ability measure 3 (percentiles)	50.5	.161	.045	.000+	48.4	.111	.043	.010
Ability measure 4 (percentiles)	47.1	.133	.049	.007	47.3	.114	.046	.014
Ability measure 5 (percentiles)	60.0	.118	.053	.025	57.8	.129	.049	.009
Ability measure 12 (percentiles)	42.1	.076	.052	.144	44.5	.125	.047	.009
Average ability (percentiles)	75.9	.463	.155	.003	69.5	.254	.152	.095
Living expenses	6.97	.340	.260	.193	5.67	.800	.280	.004
Work/not work	.451	16.75	3.53	.000+	.548	19.6	3.61	.000+
Hours worked	9.2	−1.21	.135	.000+	13.5	−1.11	.119	.000+
Student-faculty ratio	14.5	1.02	.394	.010	26.0	−.412	.204	.044
Expenditure per student on instruction-related activities	15.25	−.300	.270	.257	11.76	.070	.530	.897
Expenditure per student on research and extension	13.79	.160	.130	.226	4.09	.060	.370	.873
Enrollment	13.6	−.823	.535	.126	16.6	−.284	.398	.478
Enrollment²	258.3	.028	.015	.057	408.8	.002	.008	.841
R^2	.216				.163			
F	24.54				23.30			
Number	1,351				1,804			

[a] An F statistic testing the hypothesis that the slope coefficients of these two regressions are the same is 1.88 with 15 and 3,125 degrees of freedom. This is significant at the 5 per cent level.

[b] See Table 3, note b.

TABLE 7 Regression Coefficients Relating Measures of Educational Input to the Relative Frequency with which College Graduates Attend Graduate and Professional Schools from Colleges with Varying Levels of Instructional Expenditure per Pupil[a]

| | Students Attending Colleges Where Instructional Expenditure per Student Is: | | | | | | | |
| | Greater Than $1,200 | | | | Less Than or Equal to $1,200 | | | |
	Variable Mean	Regression Coefficient	Standard Error	Significance Level[b]	Variable Mean	Regression Coefficient	Standard Error	Significance Level[b]
Constant	1.0	−88.3	18.6	.000+	1.0	−86.5	15.8	.000+
Ability measure 1 (percentiles)	80.7	.021	.115	.857	71.1	.099	.106	.352
Ability measure 2 (percentiles)	70.5	.193	.067	.004	64.0	.176	.064	.006
Ability measure 3 (percentiles)	50.4	.046	.050	.362	50.4	−.019	.052	.711
Ability measure 4 (percentiles)	45.8	.082	.054	.129	46.8	−.016	.055	.771
Ability measure 10 (percentiles)	28.0	.055	.085	.515	33.6	.093	.083	.256
Average ability (percentiles)	79.4	.414	.214	.054	67.7	.185	.183	.312
Grades in college	8.02	6.25	.766	.000+	7.71	8.74	.885	.000+
Living at home/at school	.345	6.17	2.87	.032	.414	1.26	2.98	.674
Work/not work	.449	5.56	4.49	.219	.491	8.83	4.49	.050
Hours worked per week	8.20	−.676	.203	.000+	10.14	−.536	.175	.002
Student-faculty ratio	18.6	.583	.253	.021	22.9	.247	.254	.332
Expenditure per student on instruction-related activities	17.81	1.021	.400	.010	9.55	2.16	1.080	.044
Expenditure per student on research and extension	14.42	.100	.160	.509	3.54	−1.42	.410	.000+
Enrollment	18.9	.858	.453	.060	11.8	1.27	.565	.025
Enrollment²	488.0	−.018	.010	.082	203.9	−.032	.015	.033
College major								
Math & physical sciences	.274	10.2	3.29	.002	.232	13.9	3.59	.000+
Social sciences & humanities	.304	5.48	3.14	.082	.328	1.89	3.25	.562
Prelaw, premedicine, predentistry	.017	24.8	10.14	.015	.008	−15.5	15.54	.322
Engineering	.024	−1.00	8.54	.914	.016	28.3	11.22	.012
R²	.137				.170			
F	10.83				12.27			
Number	1,306				1,158			

[a] An F statistic testing the hypothesis that the slope coefficient of these two regressions are the same is 2.10 with 20 and 2,424 degrees of freedom. This is significant at the 1 per cent level.
[b] See Table 3, note b.

TABLE 8 Regression Coefficients Relating Measures of Educational Input to the Relative Frequency with which College Graduates Attend Graduate and Professional Schools from Colleges with Varying Levels of Research Expenditure per Pupil[a]

| | Students Attending Colleges Where Expenditure per Student on Research and Extension Is: | | | | | | | |
| | Greater Than $1,000 | | | | Less Than or Equal to $1,000 | | | |
	Variable Mean	Regression Coefficient	Standard Error	Significance Level[b]	Variable Mean	Regression Coefficient	Standard Error	Significance Level[b]
Constant	1.0	-83.4	21.1	.000+	1.0	-74.0	13.5	.000+
Ability measure 1 (percentiles)	80.5	-.038	.131	.772	73.3	.104	.097	.280
Ability measure 2 (percentiles)	69.0	.178	.076	.019	66.3	.194	.059	.000+
Ability measure 3 (percentiles)	52.8	.066	.058	.256	48.8	-.017	.047	.711
Ability measure 4 (percentiles)	46.1	.054	.063	.395	46.4	.011	.049	.818
Ability measure 10 (percentiles)	26.3	.019	.099	.841	33.5	.091	.075	.222
Average ability (percentiles)	79.2	.435	.242	.072	70.5	.193	.164	.242
Grades in college	8.04	6.69	.863	.000+	7.77	7.66	.781	.000+
Living at home/at school	.255	5.93	3.37	.078	.459	1.39	2.66	.603
Work/not work	.417	4.56	5.09	.368	.503	8.78	4.10	.032
Hours worked per week	7.0	-.677	.249	.007	10.5	-.587	.159	.000+
Student-faculty ratio	16.3	.147	.358	.682	23.5	.266	.236	.256
Expenditure per student on instruction-related activities	18.05	1.110	.410	.006	11.18	1.372	.490	.005
Expenditure per student on research and extension	19.00	.300	.180	.093	2.83	-1.50	.630	.016
Enrollment	18.3	.242	.537	.653	13.7	1.15	.475	.015
Enrollment[2]	459.4	-.001	.012	.912	284.6	-.023	.012	.061
College major:								
Math & physical sciences	.294	8.51	3.61	.019	.228	14.69	3.26	.000+
Social sciences & humanities	.274	9.52	3.71	.010	.343	.374	2.86	.897
Prelaw, premedicine, predentistry	.015	16.23	11.99	.177	.011	12.51	11.89	.294
Engineering	.030	3.52	8.63	.682	.013	22.73	10.96	.038
R^2	.188				.150			
F	11.83				13.60			
Number	986				1,478			

to the rate of graduate school attendance are examined. In Table 7 the sample has been divided into students attending schools spending in excess of $1,200 per year and those attending schools spending less than this amount. Four results of importance emerge from examining the relation between inputs and outputs for these two subsamples. First, as the level of expenditure per student increases, the effect of this variable appears to diminish: a $100 increase in instructional expenditures in schools spending less than $1,200 per student increases the rate of graduate school attendance by 2.2 percentage points; in colleges spending in excess of $1,200, a $100 increase in expenditures increases the rate of graduate school attendance by only 1.0 percentage points.

Second, the effect of reducing the student-faculty ratio, while it continues to have an unexpected sign, is substantially smaller in both of these subsamples than in the sample as a whole. This suggests a possible explanation for the effect of this variable. The student-faculty ratio is inversely related to instructional expenditures, and the effect of instructional expenditures diminishes as the level of instructional expenditures increases. The apparently adverse effect of decreasing the student-faculty ratio may, in part, reflect these nonlinearities in the effect of instructional expenditures.

Third, as is the case when the graduation rate is the output measure, the effects of increasing average ability and diminishing the number of hours worked for pay are greater in high- than in low-input colleges. For students in schools spending over $1,200, increasing the average ability of other students by 10 percentiles increases the rate of graduate school attendance by 4.1 percentage points, and this effect is significant at the .05 level. In colleges spending less than $1,200, this increase would affect a 1.9 percentage point increase in the rate of graduate school attendance, and this effect is significant only at the .31 level. The adverse effects of working for pay while in college begin after 8.2 hours per week in colleges spending over $1,200, but in schools spending less than $1,200, this effect does not begin until the student works in excess of 16 hours. Moreover, in the high-input colleges, each hour worked reduces the rate of graduate school attendance by .68 percentage points. This reduction is .54 percentage points per hour worked in low-input colleges.

There is, finally, a rather striking difference evidenced in this table between low- and high-input schools in the impact of research expenditures. In schools spending less than $1,200 per student on instruction-related activities, each $100 increase in research expenditures appears to reduce the rate of graduate school attendance by 1.4 percentage points, and this effect is statistically significant at the .001 level. In schools spending over $1,200, the level of research expenditures has little or no effect on the rate of graduate school attendance. Of course, it is unclear whether the difference between these two subsamples in the effect of research expenditures results from the variation in the level of instructional expenditures, the level of research expenditures, or some other difference between these two subsamples. Thus, a similar difference is found in the effect of this variable between the two subsamples examined in Table 8. In this table, the students have been divided into those attending schools spending less than $1,000 on research and extension activities and those spending in excess of this amount. However, it seems reasonable to infer from these results that in schools where inputs are generally in short supply—either because instructional expenditures are low, or because student quality is low, or because research expenditures are low—research competes with instruction for available resources with the result that increasing research expenditures diminishes the output of the instructional process. On the other hand, in resource-rich schools, the expansion of research activities has no deleterious effects on the instructional process, and there may even be positive spillover from research to instruction.

The negative impact of research expenditures suggests another factor contributing to the apparently adverse effect on the rate of graduate school attendance of reducing the student-faculty ratio. In measuring the student-faculty ratio, no effort was made to distinguish between faculty involved in the program of resident instruction and those involved primarily in research or extension activities. If the level of research expenditure per student is inversely related to the rate of graduate school attendance, and if schools with low student-faculty ratios are those in which a substantial component of faculty time is devoted to research, this may account for the adverse effect on the rate of graduate school attendance of reducing the student-faculty ratio. This explanation receives some support from the results of Table 8. Controlling for the level of research expenditures further reduces the effect of alterations in the student-faculty ratio. The effect of reducing the student-faculty ratio is more adverse in the subsample in which research expenditures have a negative effect on the rate of graduate school attendance than in the subsample in which research expenditures have no effect.

V. CONCLUSIONS

The estimated parameters of this model have implications for both public and private educational decisions. First, for the student deciding whether or not to attend college, the model suggests that the success of this investment depends heavily on the student's ability level and the financial capital available to him for this investment. Students whose ability level is low or who, because of inadequate financing, must work for pay while they are in college are substantially less likely to graduate or to attend graduate school than those with adequate financing and precollege training. Living at home to reduce the costs of college attendance also reduces the student's likelihood of college graduation. A student attending the average college in our sample who scored in the ninetieth percentile in each of the first two ability measures, who lived at school, and did not work for pay while in college, would have a probability of graduation of .860, and if he does graduate, a probability of graduate school attendance of .501. A student attending the same college who scored in the thirtieth percentile on each of these ability measures, who lived at home, and who worked 25 hours per week for pay while in college, would have a .251 probability of graduation—and if he did graduate, a .178 probability of attending graduate school. If the probabilities of graduation and graduate school attendance are important determinants of the attractiveness to students of college attendance, these relationships help to explain the positive association of the rate of college attendance with both ability and family income.

The model also provides some guidelines for the student choosing among alternative colleges. Among private colleges and colleges where the student-faculty ratio is in excess of 20:1, attending colleges where the student-faculty ratio is low increases the student's likelihood of college graduation. For students interested in graduate study, these data suggest that there are advantages in choosing a college which has a high level of instructional expenditure per pupil and in which the enrollment level is relatively high. The impact of increasing enrollment diminishes as enrollment increases and reaches an optimum at 20,000 for public colleges and 12,500 for private colleges. For students of high ability, or among colleges where expenditure per student is high, the likelihood of both graduation and graduate school attendance can be increased by choosing colleges where *average* ability is high.

These prescriptions may also be interpreted as guides for college administrators concerned with reducing the rate of student attrition or increasing the rate of graduate school attendance. Thus, colleges in which the student-faculty ratio is currently in excess of 20:1 could diminish student attrition by reducing this ratio. The model suggests that by increasing instructional expenditures, these colleges could increase the rate at which their graduates attend graduate and professional schools.

The implications of the model with respect to average ability of the student body are of particular interest. In colleges where the level of expenditure per student is high, increasing the average ability level of the student body increases each student's chances of graduation and graduate school attendance. Thus, offering scholarships as inducements to high-ability students may represent a reasonable investment in the quality of the undergraduate program.

Finally, the model may be viewed as a guide to public educational policy. One apparent objective of public investment in education is to assure a more egalitarian distribution of educational output. The model suggests that improving the quality of the capital market for students investing in education might improve the educational opportunities of low-income students. To the extent that low-income students attend college, they keep the cost of this investment low by living at home, by working for pay, by living in low-quality housing, or by attending low-input colleges with low tuition levels. However, these reductions in input also reduce these students' chances of graduation and graduate school attendance. Greater availability of loans might encourage these students to increase the size of their investment and thereby improve the quality of their output.

In addition to financial constraints, low-income students are also handicapped in college by low-ability levels. Reducing the correlation between ability and income by redistributing investment in primary and secondary schools would also produce a more egalitarian distribution of college outputs. Alternatively, the inputs to the college process could be redistributed in favor of low-income (low-ability) students. The difference in the rates of graduation and graduate school attendance between high- and low-income students could be narrowed by increasing the level of instructional expenditure per student and reducing the student-faculty ratio in schools attended by low-income students. Sending low-income students to colleges where average ability (and family income) is high might also increase their chances of graduation and graduate school attendance. However, these two forms of redistribution differ in their implications for the average level of college output. Since the schools currently attended by low-income students tend to have low levels of expenditure per student, and since the components of expenditure appear to exhibit diminishing returns, increasing expenditures in these schools would have a greater return than a similar increase in schools which currently have high levels of expenditure per pupil. On the other hand, there was some evidence that the effect of increasing average ability was greatest in high-input schools. Thus, it may be that increasing average ability has greater effects on high- than on low-ability students. If this were the case, increasing the variance in the distribution of ability at each college would reduce the variance in educational output, but it would also lower the average level of educational output.

APPENDIX A

Principal Components Analysis

In measuring the ability level of the students in this sample, scores on the principal components of a battery of 22 ability tests were used. In selecting the components to use in this analysis, the relationship between the output measures and each of the 22 ability components was estimated. Only those components which had a substantial effect were used in the final analysis. The results of those preliminary analyses are described in Tables A-1 and A-2. It should be noted in the case of Table A-1 that since the components are measured by raw scores, the signs and magnitude of the regression coefficients are difficult to interpret. Standardized regression coefficients provide a better guide to the magnitude of these effects.

In Table A-3, the factor loadings of each of the initial test scores on each of the first four principal components are described. These loadings may provide some insight into the appropriate interpretation of these components.

APPENDIX B

Logit Analysis

An alternative approach which avoids some of the statistical and conceptual difficulties posed by the linear model is logit analysis. This model assumes a linear relationship between the inputs to the educational process and the log odds of graduation and graduate school attendance. In order to compare the results of this form of analysis with those derived from the linear model, the log odds of graduation and graduate school attendance have been estimated for each of the colleges in this sample. Multiple regression analysis was used to estimate the relation between these measures and each of the inputs to the educational process. Since the data are now grouped by college, a limited set of input measures is examined. In particular, it was no longer possible to distinguish between individual and average ability levels, and the coefficient on the ability measures for the students in each college reflects the combination of these influences. Measures of student environment—living at home, working for pay, and living expenditures have also been omitted—since aggregating across the students in each

TABLE A-1 Estimated Relationship between the Rate with which Entrants Graduate College and the Student's Score on Each of Twenty-two Principal Components of Ability, Controlling for Various Other Inputs to the Educational Process

	Variable Mean	Regression Coefficient	t-Statistic	Beta Coefficient[b]
Principal component 1[a]	−107.931	−.4575	−3.37	.1047
Principal component 2[a]	−16.567	−1.2118	−7.62	.1049
Principal component 3[a]	−2.129	.7486	4.07	.0611
Principal component 4[a]	25.406	−.5448	−3.06	.0417
Principal component 5[a]	−15.488	−.5205	−2.47	.0426
Principal component 6	−13.805	.1980	.61	.0111
Principal component 7	−16.031	−.4251	−2.22	.0281
Principal component 8	−.083	−.2375	.72	.0114
Principal component 9	−26.275	−.2673	−.96	.0135
Principal component 10	28.268	.1064	.33	.0060
Principal component 11	13.284	−.1684	−.65	.0084
Principal component 12[a]	21.505	−1.0422	−3.66	.0531
Principal component 13	10.206	−.0438	−.15	.0018
Principal component 14	1.862	.4828	1.61	.0202
Principal component 15	−47.023	.0477	.20	.0004
Principal component 16	10.283	.3310	1.08	.0160
Principal component 17	5.317	−.7617	2.32	.0270
Principal component 18	4.431	.0328	.12	.0016
Principal component 19	1.505	.5245	−1.55	.0235
Principal component 20	−12.471	.1748	.52	.0079
Principal component 21	−64.580	.1137	−.61	.0191
Principal component 22	−4.268	1.0570	−3.18	.0327
Other input measures[c]				
Live at home/at school	.354	−6.99	−4.67	−
Work/not work	.504	17.65	8.28	−
Hours worked per week	11.490	−1.14	−15.23	−
Living expenses	656.48	.003	1.58	−
Research expenditure as a per cent of total expenditure	12.80	.070	1.15	−
Expenditure per pupil	22.47	.010	.66	−
Per cent male	62.015	−.070	−1.69	−
Enrollment (thousands)	13.548	−.100	−1.97	−
Rate of graduation	66.7	−	−	−

[a] These principal components were used as measures of ability in subsequent analysis of the relationship between educational inputs and the rate of college graduation. The criterion for selecting these measures was primarily the size of the beta coefficient. At this preliminary stage of the analysis, the principal components were measured by raw scores rather than percentiles.

[b] This is the regression coefficient multiplied by the ratio of the standard deviation of the independent variable to the standard deviation of the dependent variable. This measure is useful in comparing the effect of various principal components, since it converts their effect into comparable units.

[c] At the stage of the analysis in which all the principal components were included in the model, these variables constituted the other inputs examined. In subsequent analysis, some of these measures were dropped and others were modified.

TABLE A-2 Estimated Relationship between the Rate with which College Graduates Attend Graduate and Professional Schools and the Student's Score on Each of Twenty-two Principal Components of Ability, Controlling for Other Inputs to the Educational Process

	Variable Mean	Regression Coefficient	t-Statistic
Principal component 1[a]	23.628	−.4596	−3.09
Principal component 2[a]	32.565	−.2236	−3.58
Principal component 3[a]	30.571	.1318	2.45
Principal component 4[a]	53.733	−.0712	−1.37
Principal component 5	37.971	−.0329	−.52
Principal component 6	47.818	−.0640	−.99
Principal component 7	38.948	−.0184	−.38
Principal component 8	54.745	−.0513	−.90
Principal component 9	37.384	−.0179	−.30
Principal component 10[a]	69.850	−.2609	−3.14
Principal component 11	57.115	−.0354	−.69
Principal component 12	58.406	−.0535	−.96
Principal component 13	47.291	−.0185	−.39
Principal component 14	59.852	.0076	.16
Principal component 15	34.419	.0743	−.95
Principal component 16	64.028	.0034	.05
Principal component 17	61.188	.0200	.40
Principal component 18	61.080	.0055	.09
Principal component 19	43.534	.0276	.48
Principal component 20	43.980	.1537	−2.58
Principal component 21	28.517	.0273	.20
Principal component 22	43.561	.0752	1.37
Other input measures			
Living expenditure	655.88	.002	.59
Work/not work	.472	6.60	1.89
Hours worked	9.210	−.578	−4.00
Expenditure on faculty	590.93	.003	1.17
Average ability	68.32	.092	.784
Enrollment	16.58	.761	3.03
Enrollment²	438.97	−.011	−2.42

[a] These variables were included as measures of ability in subsequent analyses of the relationship between educational inputs and the rate with which graduates attend graduate and professional schools. The criterion used for selection was the magnitude of the regressive coefficients. At this stage of the analysis the principal component scores were measured in percentile terms.

TABLE A-3 Coefficients (Factor Loadings) Relating the First Four Principal Components of Ability to Each of Twenty-two Ability Tests

Test Title	After Rotation to Maximize Variation in these Weights			
	(1)	(2)	(3)	(4)
1. General information	.823	.243	.299	.111
2. Knowledge of literature	.804	.079	.319	.090
3. Knowledge of music	.763	.094	.221	.046
4. Knowledge of vocabulary	.756	.235	.368	.081
5. Knowledge of social studies	.748	.115	.362	.042
6. Reading comprehension	.717	.317	.317	.179
7. Disguised words	.611	.274	.108	.224
8. Knowledge of physical science	.590	.277	.532	.034
9. Scientific attitude	.557	.214	.271	.063
10. Creativity	.545	.508	.145	.182
11. Knowledge of English usage	.502	.162	.490	.337
12. Visualization in three dimensions	.150	.780	.246	.021
13. Mechanical reasoning	.276	.764	.230	.062
14. Visualization in two dimensions	.091	.747	.073	.078
15. Abstract reasoning	.284	.601	.365	.106
16. Mathematics test I	.338	.240	.822	.133
17. Mathematics test II	.259	.193	.817	.081
18. Knowledge of mathematics	.455	.223	.763	.072
19. Arithmetic reasoning	.380	.310	.624	.176
20. Word functions in sentences	.389	.249	.560	.225
21. Memory for sentences	.022	.100	.042	.853
22. Memory for words	.286	.066	.289	.633

college would alter the meaning of these variables. Since these alterations affect the parameters of the model, the parameters of the linear additive model are also estimated using this limited subset of inputs. The estimated parameters of the logit model are described in Table B-1 and those for the linear model in Table B-2. In both cases, the data were weighted to adjust for the heteroscedasticity which results from grouping.

In order to compare the results of these two models, the effect of a unit change in each of the input measures on the rates of graduation and graduate school attendance has been estimated from the logit model. These estimates were made holding each of the other input measures constant at their mean levels. These estimates are generally less than one standard deviation away from the estimate derived from the linear

TABLE B-1 Regression Coefficients Relating Measures of Educational Input to the Log Odds of Entrants Graduating and Graduates Attending Graduate and Professional Schools—Estimates Based on Data Grouped by College Attended

	Log Odds of Graduation					Log Odds of Graduate School Attendance				
	Mean	Regression Coefficient	Standard Error	Significance Level[a]	Δ% Graduation[b] ΔX_i	Mean	Regression Coefficient	Standard Error	Significance Level[a]	Δ%Attendance[b] ΔX_i
Constant	1.0	-4.14	.662	.000+	-	1.0	-2.60	.875	.003	-
Ability measure 1 (percentiles)	70.4	.029	.008	.000+	.725	70.4	.010	.011	.352	.250
Ability measure 2 (percentiles)	62.0	.025	.007	.000+	.625	62.0	.014	.009	.100	.350
Ability measure 3 (percentiles)	51.1	.013	.006	.031	.325	51.1	-.019	.008	.019	-.475
Ability measure 4 (percentiles)	49.2	.006	.007	.368	.150	49.2	.002	.009	.817	.050
Ability measure 5 (percentiles)	56.1	.011	.008	.138	.275	56.1	.013	.010	.180	.325
Student-faculty ratio	21.3	-.029	.008	.000+	-.725	21.3	.029	.010	.007	.725
Expenditure per student on instruction-related activity	12.81	.0001	.016	.999+	.003	12.81	.039	.022	.080	.975
Expenditure per student on organized research and extension	7.03	.005	.008	.502	.125	7.03	.004	.011	.726	.100
Enrollment	11.9	-.029	.017	.091	-.725	11.9	-.002	.022	.936	-.050
Enrollment²	234.1	.0004	.0004	.238	.010	234.1	-.0001	.0005	.872	-.002
Log odds of graduation	.296					.046				
Log odds of graduate school attendance						.283				
R²	.569					.283				
Number	169					169				

[a] See Table 3, note b.
[b] Estimated at the mean for each of the input measures.

Since: $\ln P(x)/1 - P(x) = a + bx$

$dP(x)/dx = b [P(x) - P(x)^2]$

where: $P(x)$ = the probability of graduation (graduate school attendance) for entrants (graduates), with input characteristics described by the vector x. Resultant derivatives have been scaled by 100 to reflect change in *per cent* graduating or attending graduate school.

TABLE B-2 Regression Coefficients Relating Measures of Educational Input to the Rate with which Entrants Graduate and Graduates Attend Graduate and Professional Schools—Estimates Based on Data Grouped by College Attended

	Rate of Graduation				Rate of Graduate School Attendance			
	Mean	Regression Coefficient	Standard Error	Significance Level[a]	Mean	Regression Coefficient	Standard Error	Significance Level[a]
Constant	1.0	−34.7	12.6	.006	1.0	−9.96	15.6	.528
Ability measure 1 (percentiles)	70.4	.673	.164	.000+	70.4	.116	.203	.569
Ability measure 2 (percentiles)	62.0	.499	.126	.000+	62.0	.311	.157	.048
Ability measure 3 (percentiles)	51.1	.245	.118	.038	51.1	−.367	.147	.012
Ability measure 4 (percentiles)	49.2	.163	.129	.207	49.2	.080	.160	.617
Ability measure 5 (percentiles)	56.1	.158	.144	.271	56.1	.413	.179	.020
Student-faculty ratio	21.3	−.566	.157	.000+	21.3	.525	.194	.007
Expenditure per student on instruction-related activity	12.81	−.294	.323	.362	12.81	.908	.401	.023
Expenditure per student on organized research and extension	7.03	.169	.166	.307	7.03	.000+	.002	.865
Enrollment	11.9	−.382	.330	.246	11.9	.140	.409	.733
Enrollment²	234.1	.006	.008	.435	234.1	−.005	.009	.631
Per cent of entrants graduating	55.4							
Per cent of graduates attending graduate and professional schools					49.6			
R²		.779				.634		
Number		169				169		

Note: The regression coefficients reflect the change in the rate of graduation for a unit change in each of these input measures. The ability variables are measured in percentiles; living expenditures, research expenditures. Instructional expenditures are measured in hundreds of dollars and enrollment is measured in thousands of students.

[a] See Table 1, note b.

model. Moreover, since at the mean value of each of these inputs the estimated probabilities of graduation and graduate school attendance are about .5, the effects of each input estimated from the logit model reflects the maximum effect of that variable. Since these estimates are generally above those derived from the linear model, choosing other input values would produce estimates closer to those derived from the linear model. While the estimates of R^2 for each of these models suggest that the linear model fits the data better than the logit model, no rigorous comparison of fit has been made.

NOTES

1. This view underlies the work in this area of Becker, Schulz, Thurow, Weisbrod, and others. For the most explicit discussion, see Yoram Ben Porath, "The Production of Human Capital and the Life Cycle of Earnings," *Journal of Political Economy* 75 (August 1967): 352–365.
2. This possibility has often been ignored by economists but not by sociologists. See, for example, James S. Coleman et al., *Equality of Educational Opportunity* (Washington, D.C.: Government Printing Office, 1966); and Alexander W. Astin, "Undergraduate Achievement and Institutional Excellence," *Science* 161 (August 16, 1968): 611–617.
3. For a useful discussion of the difficulties inherent in the approach used by Astin to assess the importance of inputs to the educational process, see Samuel Bowles and Henry M. Levin, "The Determinants of Scholastic Achievement—An Appraisal of Some Recent Evidence," *Journal of Human Resources* 3 (Winter 1968): 3–24; Glen C. Cain and Harold W. Watts, "Problems in Making Policy Inferences from the Coleman Report," *American Sociology Review* 35 (April 1970): 228–241; Samuel Bowles and Henry M. Levin, "More on Multicollinearity and the Effectiveness of the Schools," *Journal of Human Resources* 3 (Summer 1968): 393–400.
4. The Project Talent data bank is a cooperative effort of the U.S. Office of Education, the University of Pittsburgh, and the American Institute for Research. This data bank is based on a survey of about 400,000 students who were enrolled in nearly 1,000 high schools in 1960. An extensive battery of aptitude and personality tests and a questionnaire assessing family background, plans, and interests were administered to these students in May of 1960. These data have been augmented by follow-up surveys administered to these students one and five years after their scheduled date of high school graduation. In acknowledging the contribution of Project Talent, I would like to point out that the design and interpretation of the research reported herein are solely my own responsibility.
5. The Higher Education General Information Survey is an ongoing project of the National Center for Educational Statistics of the U.S. Office of Education. It is an annual survey of all institutions of higher education in the United States and contains data on the enrollment levels, the employees, the finances, degrees granted, and the growth plans of these institutions. In this study, I used data on finances, enrollment, and employees from the 1966 HEGIS.
6. For a discussion of this method, see J. Johnston, *Econometric Methods* (New York:

McGraw-Hill, 1962), pp. 227–228. An alternative approach to the problem of heteroscedasticity, logit analysis, is explained in Appendix B.

7. The high collinearity among the original tests resulted in high standard errors in their estimated effects. Since these principal component scores are orthogonal measures of ability, their separate effects can be measured with precision. For a discussion of principal components analysis, see Donald F. Morrison, *Multivariate Statistical Analysis* (New York: McGraw-Hill, 1967), pp. 221–258.

8. The results of these preliminary analyses are described in Appendix A.

9. A separate function was used to estimate the relationship between grades and other inputs to the educational process. The parameters of this function are described in Table 5.

10. This estimate was computed as follows

$$IE^*_i = IE_i + FE_i \ \frac{IE_i}{TE_i} \left(\frac{SIF_i}{20} - 1 \right)$$

where

IE^*_i = instruction-related expenditures which would prevail at the ith college if that college had a student-faculty ratio of 20:1;

IE_i = actual instruction-related expenditures at the ith college;

FE_i = total expenditures on faculty at the ith college;

S/F_i = the ratio of faculty to students at the ith college; and

TE = total expenditures at the ith college.

11. As noted previously, colleges attended by less than ten students from the Project Talent sample were excluded from this analysis. Assuming a normal distribution of ability scores at each college and viewing the samples of students at each college as if they were drawn randomly from the population of students at each college, the probability of our estimate being more than four percentiles from the true college mean would be less than .05. Of course, since the Talent data were gathered from a stratified, random sample of schools and a cluster sample of students, the actual variance of sample means might be a little larger or smaller than that estimated from these data. However, since 80 per cent of the variance in ability test scores occurs within rather than between high schools, the effect of cluster sampling on the distribution of ability scores is quite modest. The precise effect of stratification is unclear.

12. The increase in the productivity of these inputs may also be attributed to complementarity with other components of input. Thus, similar interaction was observed when the sample was divided with respect to the ability level of the students. If the marginal product of these variables increased as their level increased, this would also account for the difference in the regression coefficients between these subsamples. Other comparisons suggest that this last possibility was unlikely.

13. The reduction in the effect of living expenses between these two subsamples may also reflect diminishing returns to successive increases in the level of this variable.

REFERENCES

1. Astin, Alexander W. "Productivity of Undergraduate Institutions." *Science* 126 (April 13, 1962): 129–135.

2. ———. "Undergraduate Achievement and Institutional Excellence." *Science* 161 (August 16, 1968): 611–617.

3. Becker, Gary S. *Human Capital: A Theoretical and Empirical Analysis with Special Reference to Education.* New York: NBER, 1974.

4. Ben Porath, Yoram. "The Production of Human Capital and the Life Cycle of Earnings." *Journal of Political Economy* 75 (August 1967): 352–365.

5. Blau, Peter M., and Duncan, Otis D. *The American Occupational Structure.* New York: John Wiley and Sons, 1963.

6. Bowles, Samuel. "Towards an Educational Production Function." In W. Lee Hansen, ed., *Education, Income, and Human Capital.* New York: NBER, 1970.

7. Bowles, Samuel, and Levin, Henry M. "The Determinants of Scholastic Achievement—A Review of Some Recent Evidence." *Journal of Human Resources* 3 (Winter 1968): 1–24.

8. ———. "More on Multicollinearity and the Effectiveness of the Schools." *Journal of Human Resources* 3 (Summer 1968): 393–400.

9. Cain, Glen C., and Watts, Harold W. "Problems in Making Inferences from the Coleman Report." *American Sociological Review* 35 (April 1970): 228–241.

10. Cartter, Allan M. "The Economics of Higher Education." In Neil W. Chamberlain, ed., *Contemporary Economic Issues.* Homewood, Illinois: Richard D. Irwin, 1969.

11. Daniere, Andre, and Mechling, Jerry. "Direct Marginal Productivity of College Education in Relation to College Aptitude of Students and Production Costs of Institutions." *Journal of Human Resources* 5 (Winter 1970): 51–70.

12. Flanagan, J. C., et al. *The American High School Student* (U.S. Office of Education, Cooperative Research Project No. 635). Pittsburgh: University of Pittsburgh, 1964.

13. ———. *Project Talent One-Year Follow-Up Studies* (U.S. Office of Education, Cooperative Research Project No. 2333). Pittsburg: University of Pittsburgh, 1966.

14. Havemann, Ernest, and West, Patricia S. *They Went to College.* New York: Harcourt Brace, 1952.

15. Holland, J. L., "Undergraduate Origins of American Scientists." *Science* 126 (September 6, 1957): 433–437.

16. Hunt, Shane. "Income Determinants for College Graduates and the Return to Educational Investments." *Yale Economic Essays* 3 (Fall 1963): 305–358.

17. Iffert, Robert E. *Retention and Withdrawal of College Students* (U.S. Department of Health, Education and Welfare). Washington, D.C.: Government Printing Office, 1958. Bulletin 1958, no. 1.

18. Johnston, J. *Econometric Methods.* New York: McGraw-Hill, 1962.

19. Knapp, R. H., and Goodrich, H. B. *Origins of American Scientists.* Chicago: University of Chicago Press, 1952.

20. Lansing, John B.; Lorimer, Thomas; and Moriguchi, Chikashi. *How People Pay for College.* Ann Arbor: University of Michigan Survey Research Center, 1960.

21. Marshak, Jacob, and Andrews, William, Jr. "Random Simultaneous Equations and the Theory of Production." *Econometrica* 12 (July, October 1964): 143–205.

22. Morrison, Donald F. *Multivariate Statistical Methods.* New York: McGraw-Hill, 1967.

23. Perl, Lewis J., and Katzman, Martin. *Student Flows in California's System of Higher Education.* Berkeley: University of California, Office of the President, 1968.

24. Summerskill, John. "Dropouts from College." In N. Sanford, ed., *The American College.* New York: John Wiley and Sons, 1962.

25. Thistlethwaite, D. L. "College Environments and the Development of Talent." *Science* 136 (July 10, 1959): 71–75.

26. Weisbrod, Burton A., and Karpoff, Peter. "Monetary Returns to College Education, Student Ability, and College Quality." *Review of Economics and Statistics* 50 (November 1968): 491–510.

3 | COMMENTS

Leonard Baird
Educational Testing Service

There are many good reasons besides the current financial crisis for acquiring a comprehensive knowledge of the effects of higher education. Without such knowledge, we cannot organize new colleges or reorganize old ones to exert more effective influence. The present practice of making decisions by rule of thumb or through political pressure tends to support the status quo or to encourage the following of fads. Moreover, this knowledge is needed to make the training of our limited supplies of talented people, as well as the use of supporting resources, more productive.

However, such knowledge requires a long-term effort and a recognition of the many complexities involved in assessing the effects of college. I should now like to outline some of the basic elements needed to carry out such assessments, endeavoring to relate these elements to Perl's study. There are six such elements. First, we need to know what colleges are trying to accomplish, that is, their goals. Second, we need to know what students are like when they enter college, because their final status is usually highly dependent on their initial status. Third, and related to the first two elements, we need to know the criteria that represent an adequate approximation of a college's aims for its students. Fourth, we need to know how to describe the characteristics of the college environment both empirically and in terms of theory. Fifth, we need to know the technical or statistical models that are most appropriate for assessing effects. And sixth, we need to know who is going to use this information and for what purposes.

Clearly, these elements cannot be presented adequately in fifteen minutes. Books and monographs (e.g., Feldman and Newcomb, 1969; Astin, 1970) have been written about these issues. But I should like to analyze the elements as they apply to the paper under discussion.

First, the goals of higher education have been the subject of a great deal of rhetoric and a very small amount of research (Peterson, 1970). However, it is clear that most institutions would consider their goals to include a good deal more than the processing of students to maximize their standing according to some objective economic measure. Of course, no single study can study every goal, but it should be remembered that institutions often emphasize a variety of goals, such as contributing to knowledge, providing leadership for various organizations, meeting local needs, general public service, vocational preparation, social activism, students' intellectual development, and students' personal development. Some of these goals have economic implications, some do not. Any study should be seen in the general context of the variety of institutional goals and functions, and, before its results are taken as guides for action, it should be examined in terms of the variety of goals that it does not consider, as well as those that it does.

The second element, adequately assessing student input in order to assess students' progress, also requires a recognition of variety. Various studies have shown that entering classes differ widely with respect to such variables as academic potentials, educational and vocational aspirations, life goals, potentials for original accomplishment, personality traits, values, parental attitudes, and socioeconomic status. (Again, see Feldman and Newcomb, 1969.) In particular, a variety of these characteristics have been related to college graduation and to postgraduate education (e.g., Astin and Panos, 1969; Snyder, 1969). Even more particularly, Project Talent data have been used to relate cognitive *and* noncognitive variables to college graduation (Bayer, 1968; Schoenfeldt, Bayer, and Brown, 1970). I wonder why this study did not use the Project Talent measures of interests, personality, and socioeconomic status, since they were presumably available. The last variable mentioned especially merits inclusion. Other basic characteristics, such as sex and ethnic group, could also have been used for breakdowns of the analyses. The study would have been much stronger if these features had been included. As it now stands, there are a number of unanswered questions.

A variety of inputs is also important to an assessment of the factors involved in meeting the requirements of the third element, defining criteria of student outcomes. Again, the chief purpose of mentioning this element is to help place the study in context. While it is difficult to place some criteria in operational terms, a number of them can be operationalized: actual subject-matter knowledge (Rock, Baird, and Linn, 1971); values (see Feldman and Newcomb); career plans and aspirations (Davis, 1965); and such variables as participation in organizations (Pace, 1969) or changes on personality scales (Chickering, 1969). This diversity of criteria of student outcomes is especially critical in drawing policy conclusions from college impact research. Caution is especially advisable because the college characteristics that seem to be positively related to one of these criteria may be negatively related to others. For example, a recent study (Rock, Baird, and Linn), found that even within the relatively well defined area of academic knowledge, different environmental characteristics were related to achievement in the humanities versus the social sciences. Furthermore, not one college was in both the group of colleges most effective in fostering knowledge of humanities and the group most effective in fostering knowledge of social science. To revert to the criteria used in the study we are discussing, it would have been a better study if it had differentiated between students who dropped out voluntarily, and those who flunked out, and between those who entered relatively high-quality graduate programs and those entering lower-quality programs. For the purposes of manpower distribution, these distinctions may make little difference, but for students choosing various educational careers, they may be critical.

The fourth element, describing the characteristics of the institutional environment is a most vexing one, as evidenced by the great variety of approaches used (Astin, 1965, 1968; Pace, 1968; Feldman, 1971). In general, however, it is useful to distinguish between: (1) measures based on the aggregate characteristics of the people *in* the environment (e.g., Holland and Astin, 1961; Richards et al., 1970), and those based on the characteristics of the environment as distinct from the people in it (Baird, 1971); (2) measures of *between* college environmental variables (e.g., Pace, 1968) and *within* college variables (Pace and Baird, 1966); and (3) variables useful for *understanding* the environment and those useful for decision making (Baird, 1971; Cain and Watts, 1970). The present study seems to focus on variables potentially useful for decision making, but it does not treat *within* college experience variables (working, and so on) differently from *between* college variables (enrollment, and so on). (This is related to the problem of the unit of analysis, to be discussed in a moment.) I think the study would have been made much stronger if some of the variety of other *between* college measures had been used, such as those in Astin's 1965 book, or those available through the American Council on Education's data bank. The variety of information is too great to be discussed here, but many of the variables would have policy implications.

Let me observe that it is quite striking that virtually every approach that has been used to study college environment has been basically empirical, lacking anything but the vaguest of implicit theoretical ideas. It would be useful to both researchers and decision makers to know not only *what* is happening in colleges but *why* it is happening, so that they will have a better basis for recommending or making decisions. This is not to fault the present paper in any way, but merely a wistful hope for better days ahead.

The problems of the fifth element, finding the most appropriate technical or statistical model for assessing efforts, is a topic of heated debate in research and statistical circles (e.g., Astin, 1970; Feldman, 1970). The literature and issues are too complex to go into in a brief time, but one issue seems more important than others—that is, the unit of analysis used in the data. As Astin (1970) has pointed out, there has been considerable controversy about the most appropriate use of multivariate analysis in analyzing student input, environmental, and student output information. Perl (along with such authors as Werts and Watley, 1969) pools all input and environmental variables in a single analysis rather than using a two-stage input-environment analysis—that is, developing some predictions based on student data, then, in a second stage, studying how institutions affect or add to those predictions, using either the college as a unit, or the student, depending on the question asked. The resulting regression coefficients in the single regression analysis are taken to reflect the "independent contribution" of various input and environmental variables in accounting for variation in the output variable. One interpretive difficulty with this method is that the various input and environmental variables may not be independent. As Astin (1970) writes: "The problem here is essentially one of what happens to the confounded variance. Since this variance must be reflected in the regression coefficients, there is no way to determine merely from these coefficients just how much of the confounded versus unique variance has been allotted to any independent variable or class of variables." (Of course, the study under discussion does try to develop different results for different groups of colleges, but this is a relatively costly and inefficient strategy.) Another problem is that the regression coefficients do not show whether a particular variable is acting directly on the output variable or whether it is operating primarily as a suppressor variable by accounting for extraneous variance in other independent variables.

These are difficult problems for which I have no perfect solutions, but I think the paper might take cognizance of them. However, several other methods may be useful, and should be mentioned. One method (Rock, Baird, and Linn, 1971) that seems to eliminate some of the problems of regression analysis is to: (1) develop regression lines for each institution, using the best predictors for the whole sample as variables; (2) use a grouping or clustering technique, such as Ward's (1963); (3) employ multiple-group discriminant functions using the regression lines as data, to see if colleges are in fact different; and, (4) employ discriminant functions using college descriptive measures. This seems to be one useful way to study the relative effects of colleges for the purposes of studying between-college effects. Another approach might be the use of path analysis (Blalock, 1964; Duncan, 1966).

This brings us to the sixth element, determining who is going to use the results of studies for what purposes. There are at least three groups of users of research results: the first is the private or public agency that would like aids for deciding which institutions or programs to support, and at what level. For these users, the institution or program might be the most useful unit of analysis, with between-college variables that have fairly direct monetary or policy implications emphasized. A second group of users of research results consists of the local administrator or decision maker who wants to alter his institution's environment so that it may be more effective in reaching the criteria he values. For these users, the unit of analysis may be programs within *and* between institutions, with variables that assess relatively specific aspects of the institution. The third user is the student who is choosing a college or a course of action within a college. In choosing a college he is not overly concerned about the policy implications of a measure but rather with whether it affects characteristics of the environment he is interested in or that are related to outcomes he values. Thus, using the college as a unit, the between-college measures can refer to rather subjective characteristics such as friendliness, as long as they are reliable and available for the colleges he is interested in. He may also wish to know the influences of working, for example, so he can guide his actions. For these, the unit of analysis may again be the within-college experience, perhaps analyzed across colleges with studies of the interaction of experience and between-college differences. Perl's paper seems to try to say something for each of these groups of users. It might be useful to focus the analyses for one of the purposes, rather than touching on all of them.

In this critique, I have tried to describe some of the complexities of studying institutional impact. I should repeat that no single paper can do all the things that I have mentioned. Overall, Perl's paper seems to be a useful contribution to the long-term enterprise of understanding how our higher education system works.

REFERENCES

Astin, A. W. *Who Goes Where to College*. Chicago: Science Research Associates, 1965.

———. *The College Environment*. Washington, D.C.: American Council on Education, 1968.

———. "The Methodology of Research on College Impact, Part One." *Sociology of Education* 43 (1970): 223–254.

———. "The Methodology of Research on College Impact, Part Two." *Sociology of Education* 43 (1970): 437–450.

Astin, A. W., and Holland, J. L. "The Environmental Assessment Technique: A Way to Measure College Environments." *Journal of Educational Psychology* 52 (1961): 306–316.

Astin, A. W., and Panos, R. J. *The Educational and Vocational Development of College Students*. Washington, D.C.: American Council of Education, 1969.

Baird, L. L. "The Functions of College Environmental Measures." *Journal of Educational Measurement* 8 (1971): 83–86.

Bayer, A. E. "The College Drop-Out: Factors Affecting Senior College Completion." *Sociology of Education* 41 (1968): 305–316.

Blalock, H. M., Jr. *Causal Inferences in Non-experimental Research*. Chapel Hill, N.C.: University of North Carolina, 1964.

Cain, G. C., and Watts, Harold W. "Problems in Making Inferences from the Coleman Report." *American Sociological Review* 35 (1970): 228–241.

Chickering, A. W. *Education and Identity*. San Francisco: Jossey-Bass, 1969.

Darlington, R. B. "Multiple Regression in Psychological Research and Practice." *Psychological Bulletin* 69 (1968): 161–182.

Duncan, O. D. "Path Analysis: Sociological Examples." *American Journal of Sociology* 72 (1966): 1–16.

Feldman, K. A. "Studying the Impacts of Colleges on Students." *Sociology of Education* 42 (1969): 207–237.

———. "Measuring College Environments: Some Uses of Path Analysis." *American Educational Research Journal* 8 (1971): 51–70.

Feldman, K. A., and Newcomb, T. M. *The Impact of Colleges on Students*. San Francisco: Jossey-Bass, 1969.

Pace, C. R. "College Environments." Pp. 169–173 in R. L. Ebel, ed., *Encyclopedia of Educational Research*. 4th ed. London: Macmillan, 1969a.

———. *College and University Environment Scales: Technical Manual*. 2nd ed. Princeton, N.J.: Educational Testing Service, 1969b.

Pace, C. R., and Baird, L. L. "Attainment Patterns in the Environmental Press of College Subcultures." Pp. 215–242 in T. M. Newcomb and E. K. Wilson, eds., *College Peer Groups*. Chicago: Aldine, 1966.

Peterson, R. E. *The Crisis of Purpose: Definition and Uses of Institutional Goals*. Washington, D.C.: ERIC Clearinghouse of Higher Education, 1970.

Richards, J. M., Jr.; Seligman, R.; and Jones, P. K. "Faculty and Curriculum as Measures of College Environment." *Journal of Educational Psychology* 61 (1970): 324–332.

Rock, D. A.; Baird, L. L.; and Linn, R. L. "Interaction between College Effects and Students' Aptitudes." *American Educational Research Journal* 9 (Winter 1972): 149–161.

Schoenfeldt, L. F.; Bayer, A. E.; and Brown, M. D. "Delayed and Normal Progress College Students: A Comparison of Psycho-Social Characteristics and Career Plans." *American Educational Research Journal* 7 (1970): 235–249.

Snyder, E. E. "A Longitudinal Analysis of the Relationship between High School Student Values,

Social Participation, and Educational-Occupational Achievement." *Sociology of Education* 42 (1969): 261–270.

Ward, J. H., Jr. "Hierarchical Grouping to Optimize an Objective Function." *Journal of the American Statistical Association* 58 (1963): 236–244.

Werts, C. E., and Watley, D. J. "A Student's Dilemma: Big Fish–Little Pond or Little Fish–Big Pond." *Journal of Counseling Psychology* 16 (1969): 14–19.

Alvin K. Klevorick
Yale University

Lewis Perl's paper "Graduation, Graduate School Attendance, and Investments in College Training" presents a new model of the production process in the college sector of the education industry. The model's novelty derives from the new measures of the output of the college production process and the new collection of measures of the inputs to the process that are used. Employing this model and a broad data base, derived from the Project Talent Survey and the Higher Education General Information Survey, Perl examines the relationship between the inputs to the college production activity and the educational outputs of that activity.

His empirical results are interesting. In particular, one welcomes the plausible but sometimes hard-to-find result that both individual-student and school-quality factors are important in the production process. Furthermore, as the author indicates, the results of this study have implications for educational policy decisions at several levels: the individual student, college administrators, and public educational policy makers. Because Perl intends his production-function results as a guide to these several sets of decision makers in their joint attempts to improve the efficiency of educational investment, it is most important that we examine carefully the model and the particular estimates upon which these recommendations are based.

1. THE MEASURES OF EDUCATIONAL OUTPUT

To begin, consider the measures of educational output used in the model: graduation and graduate-school attendance. One wonders whether these are adequate measures of the output of the college sector. Different degrees—differentiated by field, by school, and so on—are explicitly, or at least implicitly, given different weights when they are taken as measures of productive capacity. Even if one were to take the view, as some people have, that most productive training takes place on the job, it is still the case that the

NOTE: I am grateful to my colleague Kim Peck for his helpful discussions.

background characteristics with which an individual comes to a job will be evaluated by potential employers on the basis of what degree he has as well as whether or not he has a degree. The probability that the individual will get a particular job and his future earnings in that job will depend on the type of degree he has earned. But Perl's measure does not distinguish among different types of degrees.[1]

Stated in extreme terms, if we accept Perl's measures of educational output, and if, as a policy goal, we desire to increase that output, there is a very simple policy to follow. Specifically, all colleges should lower their degree standards and all graduate schools should lower their admission standards. At an individual level, ceteris paribus, it would be optimal for a student to attend a school whose admissions standards and degree standards were far below his own ability. One must wonder about an output measure with such implications.

Perl's output measure treats education of undergraduates as the production of a homogeneous commodity—graduates. In contrast, the agents in the education industry—both consumers and producers—view the industry as producing a collection of heterogeneous outputs—graduates of different quality.[2] The variation in school input levels observed in Perl's sample may be directly related to the multidimensionality of college education output that has been lost in his reduction of output to one dimension. And, the difference in the structure of his estimated relationship that emerges when the sample is divided according to the level of a particular input may be a reflection of the differentiated-product nature of this educational output. For example, if a degree from a small college is regarded as a product different from a degree from a large school, and if size of school is highly correlated with student-faculty ratio, then it could be the differentiated-product character of the output that led to differences between the structures of the regression for schools with high student-faculty ratios and for schools with low student-faculty ratios.

It is true that as economists we often simplify, especially in our empirical work, and regard products that differ in some attributes as the same product. But this reduction of all attributes to one seems highly inappropriate in the case of measurement of educational output. It is difficult to believe that any *one* index of output, and particularly attainment of a degree, will suffice to measure the output of the college sector of the education industry.

2. THE DETERMINANTS OF GRADUATION AND GRADUATE SCHOOL ATTENDANCE

Let us suppose, nevertheless, that one did want to measure the output of colleges by the number of degrees that were granted. What factors affect the probability of graduation for an individual student? Following Perl, the relevant elements can be divided into two categories: student factors and school factors. Among the student factors would be included (1) ability and (2) effort, with effort itself being a function of (a) motivation, (b) the time available for study, and (c) the student's living environment. While the author is very careful about his inclusion and his measurement of student ability, he pays no attention to student motivation. The student, however, undoubtedly arrives at college with some motivation, just as he arrives with some ability. The college can affect his motivation just as it can affect his ex post (after-college) ability (for which Perl uses grades as a proxy). It may be difficult to disentangle ability from motivation with the available data, but surely motivation requires some mention. In future studies of this type where students are given a battery of ability tests, perhaps it would be worthwhile to subject them as well to the tests psychologists have developed to measure motivation.[3]

The time a student has available for study and the nature of his living environment are probably strongly affected by the financial resources he has available. The author uses four variables to measure these dimensions of student input: (1) whether or not the student works, (2) how many hours a week the student works if he does, (3) whether or not he lives at home, and (4) the student's annual living expenses. Curiously, neither family income nor any measures of the scholarship aid the student is receiving or the amount he is borrowing ever enter the model constructed by Perl. Yet one would think that the entire financing picture—in particular, the way in which the student is raising the funds needed for his education and the extent of family financial resources—would affect the student's available time and his living environment and, hence, his probability of graduating. Indeed, Perl talks in several places (for example, page 00) about the student's financial capital and the importance of such capital in determining the success of his college-education investment. The information he uses concerning students' financial situations does not seem adequate to the conclusions he wants to draw.

Turning to those aspects of the individual school that affect the student's probability of graduation, one would include: (1) standards of admission, (2) standards of graduation, (3) resource inputs including both (a) instruction-related activities and (b) research and other noninstructional activities, (4) enrollment, (5) ability of other students, and (6) financial aid provided—both the total amount and the composition according to type of aid. Some comments are in order concerning the way in which the author treats several of these factors.

Perl notes that his output measure is quite subjective because standards of graduation may vary across institutions and may be an increasing function of the school inputs. He pays particular heed to this problem in discussing the differences between private and public colleges. Different schools do have different admissions and degree standards, and it seems clear that differences in these policies will have an important effect on the probability that a given student graduates. Hence, a study of the college education process that focuses on the role of student inputs and school resources should control for such differences in admissions and graduation standards. As a first approximation, this suggests the inclusion of two other independent variables

1. $\dfrac{\text{number of graduates from student's entering class}}{\text{number of admissions in student's entering class}}$

and

2. $\dfrac{\text{average ability (at time of admission) of student's entering class}}{\text{average ability (at time of admission) of graduates from student's entering class}}$

The author's treatment of the resources the college devotes to producing a graduate also raised some questions in my mind. First, I wondered why instructional expenditures per student and research expenditures per student were included as separate variables, each measured in dollar terms. Presumably, when measured in dollar values, these variables are highly correlated. If they are highly correlated, this might explain some of the difficulty encountered in obtaining significant plausible values for the expenditure parameters in the graduation regression. At the same time, Perl seems quite right in supposing that research expenditures and instructional expenditures have different effects on the graduation rate. But, then, why not measure the school's financial input by its total expenditure per student and have another variable measure the proportional division between instructional and research expenditures?[4]

It is also not clear why normalization of the instructional expenditures to reflect the level that would have obtained at a 20:1 student-faculty ratio is appropriate. The selection of (1) a level of instructional expenditures per student, (2) a level of research expenditures per student, and (3) a student-faculty ratio represents the choice of an education technique from the available education technology. The selection of a particular input triad should be considered an optimizing choice. Normalizing to a standard student-faculty ratio only obscures the different input combinations chosen by different schools. The particular normalization employed by the author would be appropriate only in the presence of certain types of education technology and no argument is presented that the actual technology takes such a form.

Two further points should be raised concerning the measurement of the college's resource inputs. First, since the paper is concerned with the output of undergraduate education, the appropriate data on expenditures and student-faculty ratios are data on the resources devoted to undergraduates and the undergraduate student-faculty ratio. It is not clear from the paper that the data available to the author were sufficiently disaggregated between undergraduate and graduate education to enable him to obtain the most appropriate figures. Second, one is almost always dubious about measures of student-faculty ratios. As Perl points out, he has made no effort to distinguish between faculty involved in resident instruction and faculty involved primarily in research or extension activities. An added difficulty results because different colleges report the status of teaching assistants and the like in different ways when computing faculty size. It is difficult, therefore, to know exactly how much teaching input to associate with a given student-faculty ratio.

3. THE PRODUCTION FUNCTION

Perl assumes that the output measures he employs are linear, additive functions of the inputs to the college education process he considers. He recognizes that such a model precludes the possibility that the productivity of an input depends upon the level at which it is employed or on the level of other inputs. To provide for some degree of nonlinearity, the author includes both a linear and a quadratic term in enrollment, and he estimates the parameters of his model separately for subsamples in which the range of particular inputs is restricted. These separate estimates seem quite suggestive of important complementarity relationships among inputs to the college education process. I would have preferred to see more explicit account taken of these interactions.

My own prior belief is that it is far more likely that marginal rates of substitution between education factors vary with changes in input levels than it is that these rates of technical transformation are constant. Some multi-input Cobb-Douglas production function would seem to me to be a more appropriate model. Alternatively, one might have chosen an intermediate position. First, an aggregate student input would be formed as a linear combination of the student factors and an aggregate school input would be formed as a linear combination of the school factors. Then, the two aggregate inputs would enter a two-factor Cobb-Douglas function. In any event, nonlinearities in the educational production process—both in terms of diminishing returns to a single input and in terms of substitute-complement relations between inputs—seem important, and they deserve more explicit attention than the author's model has given them.

4. THE ESTIMATION TECHNIQUE

In estimating his linear additive model, Perl uses a two-step procedure to correct for the heteroscedasticity resulting from the dichotomous nature of his dependent variables. While this two-step regression procedure provides efficient estimates of the parameters of his linear probability function, there remains an important problem with the use of the linear probability function model.[5] Specifically, this model allows EY_i (the conditional probability of graduation or of graduate school attendance, given the input vector X_i) to lie outside the range $[0,1]$. This is, of course, inconsistent with the definition of Y and with the interpretation of EY_i as a probability. There will be vectors of inputs, X_i, for which the conditional probability of graduation $EY_i = X_i' \hat{\beta}$ is greater than one and others for which it is less than zero. There may even be vectors of inputs in the sample itself for which the estimated conditional probability $\hat{Y}_i$ will not lie in the [0, 1] interval. It would seem that the appropriate statistical model to employ in the case of Perl's production function with a dichotomous output measure is multivariate probit analysis.[6] This is a maximum likelihood estimation method that takes explicit account of the dichotomous nature of the dependent variable and that ensures that EY_i is restricted to the [0,1] interval.[7]

5. MULTICOLLINEARITY AND THE INTERPRETATION OF THE EMPIRICAL RESULTS

Let us, finally, consider some of the difficulties that may confront us in interpreting Perl's results and in attempting to convert these results into policy recommendations. The major difficulty arises because one suspects that there exists a high degree of collinearity among the measures of school inputs. The author confirms this suspicion for private colleges when he cites the collinearity problem as a probable cause of the less satisfactory performance of his private-college equation. In addition, he shows us that when the sample is stratified by the level of some specific school input—for example, student-faculty ratio or instructional expenditures per student—it turns out that colleges that are high (low) input on this criterion are also high (low) input in terms of the other school factors. While this evidence does not confirm any suspicions of collinearity, it surely strengthens those misgivings. If, indeed, there is a high degree of collinearity among the inputs to the education process, it is of course difficult to disentangle the effect of particular inputs and any policy recommendations are placed on a somewhat less-than-solid foundation.

The collinearity problem is perhaps exacerbated by the way in which the author selected the principal components of ability to include in his final analysis of the production of graduates and graduate school attendance. First Perl regressed each output measure on all twenty-two ability components and all the other exogenous variables (the nonability student inputs and the school inputs). He then retained for use in the final analysis only those ability components that had a "substantial effect" in the preliminary regressions. By definition, the omitted principal components are orthogonal to those retained, and hence there is no chance that the explanatory power of the components excluded from the final analysis is shifted to the retained components. But if the nonability exogenous variables are correlated with the omitted principal components of ability and if these omitted components were contributing any explanatory power in the preliminary regression, then the final regressions will impute too much importance to the nonability exogenous variables.

One last caution may be in order for the policy maker who would base his recommendations on the results of the present paper. To ensure that his sampling from any one college was reasonable in size, Perl required that each student in his final sample attend a college attended by at least ten other students who (1) were in the original Project Talent sample and (2) responded to both follow-up questionnaires. This exclusion of all colleges having fewer than eleven students in the modified Project Talent sample in its student body probably yields a bias against small colleges. To the extent that this bias exists and to the extent that college characteristics other than enrollment differ systematically between small and large colleges, the regression results may be misleading in their implications for the efficacy of certain policy measures.

6. A CONCLUDING COMMENT

In summary, Perl has provided us with an interesting new model of the college sector of the education industry. As with anything novel, however, there are some serious questions about the innovations that must be answered before we are willing to buy and to use the product.

NOTES

1. For example, his measure draws no distinction between "degree mills" and other institutions. While such distinctions are difficult to make, they have been found necessary and they have been made, for example, in the Bundy plan for New York State aid to private colleges.
2. This statement of producers' concerns already ignores the fact that universities may view themselves as having more than the education of undergraduates as their goal. They are also concerned, for example, about the contributions they make to scholarship, their production of Ph.D.'s, and so on.
3. For example, one might use the tests developed by David McClelland and his associates to measure need for achievement.
4. This procedure was actually used by Perl in his preliminary regression (Table A-1), which included all twenty-two ability components. One wonders why it was not used in the final regression as well.
5. For a more complete discussion of the linear probability function, see Arthur S. Goldberger, *Econometric Theory* (New York: John Wiley and Sons, 1964), pp. 248–251.
6. For a description and discussion of this procedure, see James Tobin, "The Application of Multivariate Probit Analysis to Economic Survey Data," Cowles Foundation Discussion Paper No. 1, 1955.
7. It should be noted that in an appendix to his paper, Perl uses logit analysis to reestimate the relationship between the output of the college education production process and the inputs to that process. Specifically, he groups his data by college and estimates the parameters of a linear relationship between the student and school inputs to college education and the log odds of graduation (or graduate school attendance). The logit-analysis approach does avoid some of the statistical and conceptual problems created by the linear probability function. Had Perl been willing to use nonlinear estimation techniques, however, he would not have had to group his data by college. That is, using nonlinear estimation procedures and a particular specification of the error term would have enabled the author to retain the individual student as his unit of observation. This would have provided him with parameter estimates that were more directly comparable with his original estimates for the linear probability function.

4

**HENRY M.
LEVIN**
Stanford University

Concepts of Economic Efficiency and Educational Production

I. INTRODUCTION

The education industry has two characteristics which make it a prime candidate for a study of efficiency: size and rising costs. Education represents one of the largest industries in the nation with estimated total direct expenditures of about $108 billion in 1974–75, representing about eight per cent of the gross national product (Bell 1974). During the same period, estimated employment was over 3 million for student enrollments of about 59 million. Beyond its sheer magnitude, the education industry has experienced very steep increases in costs. For example, between 1961–62 and 1971–72 the current expenditure per pupil in *real* terms (1971–72 dollars) rose from $569 to $934 at the elementary-secondary level and from $1,676 to $2,367 at the college level (U.S. Department of Health, Education and Welfare 1972: 3). These represent increases in real costs over the decade of about 64 per cent and 41 per cent respectively.

Of course, one possible explanation for rising costs might be qualitative increases in educational output. Yet, there seems to be no evidence of such a trend. Rather there appears to be increasing concern with the quality of schools as reflected in public opinion surveys (Gallup 1970), educational critiques (Silberman 1970; Greer 1972; Carnoy 1972), and voter support. For example, in 1962 voters approved about 80 per cent of school bond issues, while in 1969 the proportion of approvals had declined to only 44 per cent (Gallup 1970: p. 100).

The substantial increase in resource costs, coupled with growing dissatisfaction with the schools, has surely raised important questions about the performance of the educational sector. In response, economists have increasingly devoted their attentions to studying the internal efficiency of the educational sector, and their early efforts suggest a natural bifurcation into camps of optimism and pessimism.

The pessimists have suggested that the very nature of such activities as education must inevitably lead to higher real costs per unit of output. William Baumol has systematized this analysis by viewing education as a "technologically unprogressive" activity, where the latter term is applied to those activities which cannot benefit from innovation, capital accumulation and economies of large scale (Baumol 1967). According to Baumol, the labor intensive nature of education is an end in itself, so that the possibilities for capital-labor substitution are limited severely. Assuming that money wages rise according to increases in labor productivity within the technologically progressive industries, these increases are passed along to the nonprogressive sectors such as education in the form of higher real costs per unit of output. Baumol concludes that the real costs of even a constant level of output for nonprogressive industries such as education will increase indefinitely and without limit. Note that the Baumol model does not see costs rising because of inefficiency; rather they are rising because of inevitability. Accordingly, his palliative seems to be: "Don't send advice, send money."

Nevertheless, since economists have a greater predilection for providing advice than for fund raising, most economists who have concerned themselves with the educational sector have tactitly assumed that productivity in education can be improved. They are the optimists, since they see their own approaches as ones which will lead to greater efficiency in educational spending. While both Adam Smith and Milton Friedman belong in this school, it is primarily the economists who have attempted to estimate educational production functions that are included in the present analysis.[1] Their studies have generally been addressed to estimating the production set for education with the hope that the marginal products obtained can be compared with prices to obtain a least-cost solution to educational production (Bowles 1970; Katzman 1971; Perl 1973; Winkler 1972; Thomas 1971; Burkhead et al. 1967; Brown and Saks 1975; Kiesling 1967; Hanushek 1968, 1972; Levin 1970a, 1970b; Michelson 1970; Murnane 1974). The tacit assumption underlying such investigations is that schools are allocatively inefficient, and that these studies can lead to the information necessary for better resource allocation in the educational sector. Some of the formidable obstacles to estimating these relationships have also been explored in some detail (Bowles 1970; Bowles and Levin 1968a and 1968b; Michelson 1970; Levin 1970a and 1974). Moreover the findings of these studies have been discussed in a public policy context (Guthrie, Kleindorfer, Levin, and Stout 1971; Kiesling 1971; Hanushek 1972; Bowles 1970; Levin 1970b; Hanushek and Kain 1972; Cain and Watts 1970; and Jencks et al. 1972).

Yet, in my opinion, scant attention has been devoted to the relevance of these approaches to questions of efficiency in educational production. The purpose of this paper is to explore several concepts of efficiency with regard to their role in enabling us to evaluate the production of education. That is, if the purpose of the educational production-function literature is to derive prescriptive decision rules for improving the effectiveness of resource use in the educational sector, it is crucial that we examine the nature of the problem and the relevance of our tools for solving it *before* applying them to the evaluative task.

Educational Production Functions

The general production function that appears common to most educational studies is reflected in (1).

(1) $A_{it} = g\,(F_{i\,(t)}, S_{i\,(t)}, P_{i\,(t)}, O_{i\,(t)}, I_{it})$

The i subscript refers to the ith student; the t subscript in parentheses (t) refers to an input that is cumulative to time period t.

A_{it} = a vector of educational outcomes for the ith student at time t;

$F_{i\,(t)}$ = a vector of individual and family background characteristics cumulative to time t;

$S_{i\,(t)}$ = a vector of school inputs relevant to the ith student cumulative to time t;

$P_{i\,(t)}$ = a vector of peer or fellow-student characteristics cumulative to time t;

$O_{i\,(t)}$ = a vector of other external influences (community, etc.) relevant to the ith student cumulative to time t; and

I_{it} = a vector of initial or innate endowments of the ith student at the time t.

We might view (1) as a capital-embodiment approach to education, since output in time period t is mainly a function of inputs cumulative to t from some earlier time.[2] That is, clearly the educational outcomes at a point in time for an individual, a school, or a larger social collectivity are influenced not only by present observed circumstances but by past ones as well. It is reasonable to believe that from the time a child is conceived various environmental characteristics combine with his innate characteristics to mold his behavior. In the context of (1) the educational outcome for the individual is determined by the cumulative amounts of "capital" embodied in him by his family, his school, his community, and his peers as well as by his innate traits. The greater the amount and the quality of investment from each of these sources, the higher will be the output. More specifically, the family provides a material, intellectual, nutritional, and emotional set of inputs which are embodied in the child; and the schools, peer groups, media, and so on also provide flows of inputs over time which increase capital embodiment.[3]

The operational formulation of (1) is subject to large errors in the equations and in the variables (Bowles 1970; Michelson 1970; Levin 1970a). Most studies have used only a single measure of output, scores on standardized achievement tests, despite the fact that schools are expected to produce a variety of attitudes and skills. Specification of the input structure has been based in part upon what data are available, in part upon the researcher's hunch, and only to a very small degree on theories of development and learning.[4]

Family and background inputs generally include such measures of social class as parental education, father's occupation, family possessions, family structure, race and sex of students. School characteristics have included such facilities as libraries, laboratories, age and nature of buildings; personnel inputs (with special emphasis on class size) and such teacher traits as experience, education, attitudes, and verbal aptitudes. Peer influences include the social class and racial characteristics of fellow students, and other influences include community variables and certain residual variables. The difficulty of obtaining valid measures of innate characteristics has meant that such variables have been omitted from the econometric models. These omissions have probably resulted in an upward bias in the estimated coefficients of family and background variables.[5]

In all of these studies, student background measures appear to be highly related to educational achievement.[6] Among school characteristics, some facilities measures appear to show significant statistical relationships, but the most consistent relations are found between teacher variables and academic achievement. Specifically, virtually all of the studies that have measured teacher verbal aptitudes have found that variable to be significantly related to student achievement (Coleman 1966; Hanushek 1972; Bowles and Levin 1968; Michelson 1970; Levin 1970a). Indeed, the consistency of this finding is buttressed by the fact that separate studies have been carried out at several grade levels and for samples of black, white, and Mexican-American students (Hanushek 1972). Of course, it is important to point out that in the light of specification biases, the teacher's verbal score may be a proxy for a large number of possible cognitive and personal traits of the teacher; so that the observed relationship between the teacher's verbal pattern and student achievement may derive from these associated traits rather than the teacher's verbal proficiencies per se (Griliches, 1957).

While teacher experience has also been found to be related to student achievement on a fairly regular basis, the teacher's degree level has rarely shown such an effect. Moreover, variables reflecting the teacher's certification status on the basis of existing state requirements seem to show no apparent association with student achievement. Finally, most studies have found no statistical effect of differences in class-size on pupil performance.

II. SOME CONCEPTS OF EFFICIENCY

Technical and Allocative Efficiency in Educational Production

It is useful at the outset to define two types of efficiency, technical and allocative. *Technical efficiency* refers to organizing available resources in such a way that the maximum feasible output is produced. That is, no alternative organization would yield a larger output. *Allocative efficiency*, or price efficiency, refers to use of the budget in such a way that, given relative prices, the most productive combination of resources is obtained. That is, no alternative combination of resources, given the budgetary constraint, would enable the organization to produce a higher output (Farrell 1957; Leibenstein 1966).

One of the major assumptions that tacitly underlies the estimation of educational production functions is that schools are technically efficient, that is, that they are maximizing output given the input mix that they have selected.[7] In Figure 1 the production frontier is depicted by the production isoquant $AoAo'$, where the individual observations can be thought of as schools using various combinations of S_1 and S_2 to produce constant educational output Ao. Schools a, b, and c are on the production frontier and are thus technically efficient. All of the other schools are to the northeast of the production frontier suggesting that they are not technically efficient. That is, all schools other than a, b, and c require higher levels of factor inputs to obtain the output Ao. The reasons for such inefficiencies will be suggested below, but if technically inefficient schools are prevalent, then statistical estimates of the educa-

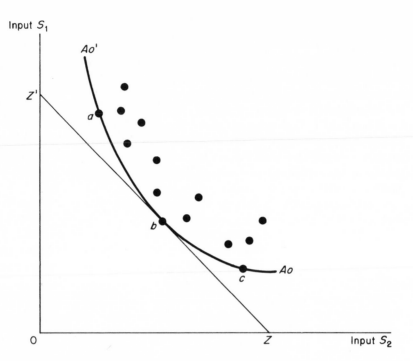

FIGURE 1   Production Frontier for Schools

tional production will not be frontier ones even in the absence of errors in the equations or variables.

If we assume that $Z'Z$ is the relative price or iso-cost line facing all schools for the two factors, only school b is both technically efficient and price or allocatively efficient. Firms a and c are technically efficient, but they are clearly allocatively inefficient since they require a higher budget to achieve output Ao' than would be required if they were at point b. Indeed, the underlying goal of the educational production function studies is that of determining where point b lies on the production function.

Social Welfare Efficiency in Educational Production

Figure 1 assumes a single-valued output for the educational firm that is signified by A. Yet, schools are multi-product firms, so $A = (a_1, a_2, a_3, \ldots, a_n)$. By assuming a value for A, the analysis overlooks another important efficiency aspect which we might call overall social efficiency. That is, somehow the A obtained for any given budget must maximize social welfare. Since the various outputs comprising A probably have different corresponding values for different individuals, it may be impossible to derive a structure of outputs for any given input that maximizes individual welfare and total social welfare (Arrow 1951; Little 1950; Dahl and Lindblom 1953). Perhaps even more important, without having some way of communicating true "social" preferences among outcomes to the schools, it is possible that emphasis on productive efficiency may lead simply to the efficient production of nonoptimal bundles of outputs (Williams 1970).

Figure 2 illustrates this situation for the two output case. AA' represents a product transformation schedule between educational outputs a_1 and a_2. I_0 and I_1 represent social indifference curves for the two outputs such that I_1 represents a higher level of satisfaction than I_0. It is obvious that given the production possibilities and community preferences, the highest level of welfare is represented by E_1.

Now suppose that the actual combination of outputs produced is represented by E_0. E_0 represents an efficiently produced bundle of outputs since it lies on the production frontier. It is evident that E_0 gives the community less satisfaction than E_1, but more importantly any choice of outputs within the shaded portion of the diagram (e.g., E_2) will yield a higher level of welfare than E_0. That is, a large number of subfrontier choices make the community happier than any point on the frontier except E_1. Stated another way, it may be better to produce inefficiently that which is highly desirable to the community than to produce with perfect efficiency that which is of low value.[8]

Efficiency and Scale

Thus, we have identified three types of efficiency which might be applied to an analysis of the educational sector: technical efficiency, allocative efficiency, and social welfare efficiency. A fourth type is one that we shall not explore here in detail, that of size efficiency. Even given technical and allocative efficiency as well as the "correct" choice of outputs for all firms in the education industry, inefficiencies might be introduced if the firms are too large or too small. Given the enormous size variation of individual schools and school districts, it is possible that both economies and diseconomies of scale exist.[9] Empirical work in this area has been carried out, but findings must be heavily qualified, given the enormous errors that are imposed by lack of a sound theoretical structure and measurement problems (Kiesling 1967; Kiesling 1968; Riew 1966; Cohn 1968).

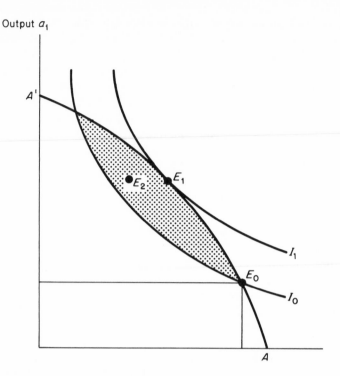

Output a_1

A'

E_2

E_1

I_1

E_0

I_0

A

FIGURE 2 Social Welfare and Choice of Output Combinations

III. BEHAVIORAL ASSUMPTIONS FOR EDUCATIONAL FIRMS

The major reason for believing that private firms are efficient derives from market theory. The incentive of profit maximization in combination with the pressure of competition can be reasonably expected to move firms (and the industry) towards both technical and allocative efficiency, provided that certain other conditions exist. Moreover, the existence of market prices for outputs enables the multi-product firms (and the industry) to evaluate all outputs in terms of their contribution to revenue.[10]

Let us list explicitly a few of the conditions which underlie our expectations of efficiency in the private sector.[11] While these categories are not mutually exclusive, each emphasizes an aspect of competitive supply that can be scrutinized for its applicability to educational suppliers in the public sector. The first two categories refer to technical efficiency considerations; the next two refer to assumptions on market structure and market information; and the final two refer to the existence and visibility of managerial incentives that relate to the outcomes of the firm. Technical efficiency for an industry presumes that there exist:

1. managerial knowledge of the technical production process;
2. substantial managerial discretion over input mix;
3. a basic competitive environment with all of its attendant assumptions (freedom of entry, many firms, perfect information);
4. managerial knowledge of prices for both inputs and outputs;
5. an objective function that is consistent with maximizing output such as profit maximization; and
6. clear signals of success or failure (profits, losses, sales, costs, rate of return, share of market).

Of course, to the degree that these do not hold, private firms can be expected to be inefficient, both technically and allocatively and with regard to scale. Indeed, in recent years economists have recognized increasingly the possibilities of technical inefficiency for firms, a possibility that was once assumed away by the textbook version of pure competition (Farrell 1957; Leibenstein 1966; Nerlove 1965, Chapter 7; Aigner and Chu 1968; Timmer 1969 and 1971; Comanor and Leibenstein 1969; Lau and Yotopoulas 1971 and 1973).

The question that we wish to pose is: Do parallel conditions exist for such public firms as schools or school districts that would ensure efficient behavior in producing education? The answer seems to be a resounding No. For virtually every condition stipulated above, the schools appear to be at the opposite end of the spectrum from that of the supplier in the competitive marketplace.

1. *The educational managers at all levels lack knowledge of the production set for obtaining particular outcomes.* The educational process is so complex and outputs are so diverse that relations between inputs and outputs are difficult to derive whether by casual observation or research. Salter defines three levels of technological knowledge that relate to production: (a) the basic principles of physical (or behavioral) phenomena; (b) the application of these principles to production, the engineering level; and (c) the level that relates to day-to-day operations (Salter 1960, p. 13). The sparsity of data at all three levels confronts the educational manager, just as it confronts the educational researcher. Moreover, schools do not possess management information systems that are sophisticated enough to obtain even approximate relationships between changes in practices and educational outcomes (Hanushek and Levin 1969). The result is that neither science nor trial and error yields much insight to the educational manager on the nature of the production set.

2. *Substantial management discretion does not exist over which inputs are obtained and how they are organized in educational production.*

School administrators make very few decisions regarding the purchase and organization of school inputs. In part, this dereliction is due to direct limitations on managerial discretion; in part it derives from the lack of knowledge of the production set; and in part it derives from an inbred reverence for existing practices. Each of these phenomena reinforces the other, for when production relations are ambiguous and organizations are governed by mandates, managers learn to avoid decisions and obey the rules. Any violation of the rules or the status quo is a risk for which educational payoffs can rarely be demonstrated convincingly to all observers.

The "rules" for operating the schools derive from many sources, federal, state, local, and the vast legacy of traditional and, thus, sacrosanct practices. At the federal level there exist particular guidelines for the expenditure of federal educational funds for each category for which funds are available. More inhibiting is the fact that in many states the laws regulating the schools fill so many volumes that they require a substantial bookshelf for nesting. These codes affect virtually every portion of school operations from the important to the minuscule. In addition, the state departments of education possess their own labyrinths of operational minutiae which are imposed upon local school systems. While matters of personnel licensing and personnel ratios are two of the better known areas of control, most states can even dictate the specific books that will be used in a particular class.[12]

Other factors that circumscribe the ability of managers to make substantial changes include local regulations and regional accreditation requirements. Moreover, negotiated contracts with educational personnel have increasingly been used to stipulate in great detail the most uniform system of employment for a productive activity that lacks inherent uniformity. Finally, as we shall note below, the reward structure for managers discourages risk taking, since salaries and promotion are based primarily on seniority and docility rather than on any educationally meaningful sense of leadership. All of these factors inhibit substantial managerial discretion in operating educational institutions.

3. *Little or no competition exists among schools.* With the exception of nominal competition among school districts for families who can afford to migrate, there is no competition for students.[13] Usually the school that a child attends is determined simply by the attendance area in which he lives. Rarely does he have a choice of schools to attend, even among those within the school district. Thus, most schools possess monopoly powers that would be the envy of any monopolistic industry. The combination of assignment practices and compulsory attendance

laws promises a clientele for the school no matter how poorly the school performs. Indeed, as we shall see below, these factors assure that good performance goes unrewarded and poor performance is uncensured, since a captive audience is always guaranteed.[14]

Of course, the schools are not market institutions, but political ones. Thus, one must ask what system of political sanctions exists for an individual family or group of citizens to ensure that schools will be responsive. The answer to this must surely be that the public has very little ability to affect what is happening in the schools. First, the public lacks information on both local schools and education itself as evidenced by extensive public opinion sampling (Gallup 1969, pp. 4–7). Moreover, many states have laws preventing citizens from "interfering" in school operations in any way including visiting of schools without permission, and the schools seem to be exceedingly deficient in providing desirable data on the educational process (Gallup 1969, pp. 8–9; Hanushek and Levin 1969; Coleman and Karweit 1969; Wynne 1972). Second, the school boards themselves seem to lack the ability to respond to demands, since they tend to identify more with the educational professionals than with their citizens on matters of educational policy, and they themselves lack the sanctions to change most outcomes (Lyke 1970; Gittell 1967; Iannacone 1967).

Perhaps worst of all, the school bureaucracies have generally shown themselves to be incapable of carrying out major changes in policy, whether these be school desegregation, curriculum reform, or compensatory education (Rogers 1968; Schrag 1967; Gittell and Hollander 1968). Indeed, they can best be described as suffering from "organizational sclerosis," a malady that makes a movement from the status quo both painful and unnatural (Jencks 1966; Rogers 1968). This frustration is characterized by demands for accountability, and even the pressures for community control of schools are principally a reaction to the red tape thrown in the paths of citizens who seek information about, or changes in, the traditional school regimen (Levin 1970c).

4. *Prices of both inputs and outputs are not readily available to educational managers.* In part, this is due to the inadequacy of school information systems, but in larger measure it is due to the complexity of the markets for educational inputs and outputs. On the input side, most of the characteristics that have been associated with higher educational productivity have been such teacher traits as attitudes, verbal score, and so on. Clearly, it is difficult to disembody these particular characteristics for purposes of pricing, and it may also be difficult to obtain more of any one of these characteristics per se without obtaining others that are embodied in the same person (Levin 1968, Chapters 6–8). Available data on costs are not related to homogeneous inputs. Rather, they are

linked to line-item accounts or to objects that are not standardized with regard to quality, such as principals' salaries, materials, and so on (U.S. Department of Health, Education and Welfare 1957). Even the planning, programming, and budgeting systems that have been designed for the schools do not begin to make inroads into the quests for obtaining specific prices or unit costs (Hartley 1968; Mushkin and Pollak 1970).

Prices for outputs are nonexistent in a market sense. Yet, the schools are expected to produce a large number of outcomes including job preparation, literacy, transmission of knowledge, and democratic values.[15] In theory, referendums and representative governance of schools might be used to reasonably reflect priorities among outputs in the absence of prices. Unfortunately, the political realities suggest that the values of significant proportions of the population are not reflected in the decision process because of imperfect information, inadequate political institutions, and communication gaps between those whose values should be considered and those who actually implement the decisions (Lyke 1970; Jencks 1966; Gittell 1970; Rogers 1968).

5. *The incentive or reward structures characteristic of schools seem to have little relation to the declared educational goals of those institutions.* Financial rewards and promotions for school personnel are handed out primarily on the basis of seniority and accumulation of college credits rather than on demonstrated effectiveness. Individual schools, teachers, or administrators who are successful in achieving important educational goals are treated similarly to those who are unsuccessful, mediocre, or incompetent. In lockstep fashion, the schools reward equally all personnel with the same nominal characteristics, regardless of differences in performance (Kershaw and McKean 1962; Levin 1968). That is, success is not compensated or formally recognized, and the reward structure is divorced systematically from educational outcomes.[16]

In contrast, commercial enterprises tend to compensate their personnel on the basis of the contributions of employees to the effectiveness of the organization. Commissions for sales personnel, bonuses, promotions, profits, and salary increases all represent rewards for individual or organizational proficiencies that do not seem to have their counterparts, in an output-oriented sense, in the schools.

6. *Finally, there are no clear signals of success or failure for the schools that are comparable to sales, profits, losses, rates of return, or shares of market.* Such standard measures as test scores and proportion of students graduating or gaining college entry are so heavily determined by factors beyond the school's control, such as students' social class and cultural antecedents, that it is difficult to disentangle school influences from nonschool influences.[17] Moreover, since education is essentially a dynamic process, the effects of present policy changes may

only be discernible in the distant future. Furthermore, observation of dynamic effects is obscured by mobility and dynamic changes in social structure that prevent observations on how well school policies have succeeded or failed. Moreover, the multiplicity of outcomes and the lack of concise measures for most of them substantially limit the ability just to observe the school's effects, even if the influence of other factors could be removed. Thus, informational feedback on operational performance of the schools is neither visible nor easily obtainable from existing data.

Standardized Achievement as Educational Output

But if schools cannot be appropriately viewed as acting like competitive suppliers, it is erroneous to assume that they are maximizing the socially optimal mix of educational outputs for any given set of resources. This fact becomes especially important when one considers that most studies of educational production functions have simply assumed that schools are maximizing a single output, the achievement scores of their students. Even those analyses that do acknowledge the multi-product nature of schools generally limit their inquiry exclusively to test scores (Hanushek 1972, pp. 20–26). The usual presumption is that we know very little about the nature of measurement of other outputs in comparison with our understanding of, and ability to measure, cognitive skills. Yet the omission of other outputs in the estimation of educational production functions will lead to a biased set of estimated production coefficients *even for the achievement output* if the other outputs are not strict complements of achievement in the production process.

The evidence suggests that schools are not attempting to maximize achievement scores even when their official rhetoric indicates this as a goal. This is best illustrated by the experience under Title I of the Elementary and Secondary Education Act of 1965. Since 1965–66 over one billion dollars a year has been allocated by the federal government to schools educating children from low-income families. In applying for the money local school districts were required to state the purposes and design of their Title I programs, and they were required to evaluate the results of their efforts. Thus, we can take for granted that the school's specific goals under the program were the ones that they stated, and we can focus on those outcomes. Moreover, the funds allocated to such programs represented approximately half again as much as what was presently being spent on each eligible child, so one might have expected their marginal impact to be substantial.

Since most of the programs concentrated on reading skills, it is useful to evaluate the effect of Title I funds on that outcome. In evaluating the

1966–67 and 1967–68 Title I funded reading programs, the U.S. Office of Education found that on the basis of reading test scores, "a child who participated in a Title I project had only a 19% chance of a significant achievement gain, a 13% chance of a significant achievement loss, and a 68% chance of no change at all [relative to the national norms]" (Picariello 1969, p. 1). Further, the projects included in the investigation were "most likely to be representative of projects in which there was a higher than average investment in resources. Therefore more significant achievement gains should be found here than in a more representative sample of Title I projects."

This inability to create even a nominal direct impact on specific objectives appears to be endemic. Among many thousands of Title I project evaluations, the U.S. Office of Education selected the 1,000 most promising for purposes of further scrutiny by an independent research contractor. Of these, only 21 seemed to have shown sufficient evidence of significant pupil achievement gains in language or numerical skills (Hawkridge, Chalupsky, and Roberts 1968). A more recent analysis has shown a similar pattern of failure to improve test scores (Wargo et al. 1972).

Moreover, studies of school processes and organization suggest that there are other agenda that dominate the educational production function (Jackson 1968; Dreeben 1968). Gintis (1971) has found that grades and other social rewards of schooling are more consistently correlated with the personality attributes of students than with their cognitive achievement scores. It is not even apparent that the cognitive component of schooling as reflected by student test scores has as large an economic impact as other outputs of the educational process. For example, studies of earnings functions suggest that the inclusion of a variable measuring the cognitive performance of individuals (as reflected in test scores) reduces by only a modest amount the observed earnings coefficient for schooling (Taubman and Wales 1973; Griliches and Mason 1972; and Gintis 1971). Presumably, the explanation for this phenomenon is that the other outputs of education that are quite independent of test scores tend to be the ones that have the principal impact on earnings (Bowles and Nelson 1974; Bowles and Gintis 1973).

A more insightful analysis of the relationship between educational production and labor market success seems to be reflected in the recent work of Bowles (1972) and Gintis (1971) and Bowles and Gintis (1975). These studies suggest that the principal purpose of schools is to reproduce the social relations of production, and that achievement scores are only one component of the productive hierarchy. "The school is a bureaucratic order with hierarchical authority, rule-orientation, stratification of 'ability' (tracking) as well as by age, role differentiation by sex (physical education, home economics, shop) and a system of external incentives (marks, promise of promotion, and threat of failure) much like pay and status in the sphere of work" (S. Bowles, 1973, p. 353). This analysis suggests that educational achievement is only one of the many outputs of schooling, and it is not necessarily the most important one.

Yet, in order to estimate a production function for educational achievement, we must assume that all schools are operating on the production frontier for *this* output, so that the observed relations represent the maximum output that can be produced with the inputs that are being utilized. The fact that schools are producing other outputs besides cognitive achievement raises serious questions about this assumption, since it is reasonable to believe that the production of other outputs reduces the amount of cognitive learning that will be produced. In this case, it is obvious that statistical estimates among existing schools that consider only the achievement score outcomes of students will not give us estimates of the production frontier, since more achievement could be obtained by reducing the levels of all noncomplementary outputs to zero.

The obvious answer to estimating production functions in the multiproduct case is to specify a system of equations that takes into account all of the outputs of schooling. Unfortunately, our overall ignorance of the conceptual outputs of schools, their measurement, and their structural relationships to one another and to inputs, limits our ability to include nonachievement outputs in the analysis. The result of these limitations is that almost every study that has attempted to estimate educational production functions has considered only educational achievement as an output.[18] In most cases, the obvious problems involved are either ignored or the assumption is made that all other outputs are produced as perfect joint products in exact fixed proportion to achievement scores. As we noted, there is no empirical substantiation for this assumption.

IV. TECHNICAL INEFFICIENCY IN PRODUCING STUDENT ACHIEVEMENT AND ITS IMPLICATIONS FOR EVALUATION

In the previous section we noted that there are many reasons for believing that schools are not technically efficient in producing achievement and that the inefficiencies may be substantial.[19] There is no counterpart for the competitive environment of firms that would stimulate the production of achievement. Even if the school attempted to maximize achievement, the effort would be limited by the imperfect knowledge and limited discretion of school managers. Moreover, other outputs compete with achievement for school resources. Yet, attempts to estimate educational production functions that use achievement as the output are based upon the tacit assumption that schools are producing as much achievement as can be obtained with their resources. That is, they are producing on the "achievement" frontier. But given the high probability of technical inefficiency, estimates of the production functions on this output are likely to yield biased coefficients and misleading implications.

This situation is shown in Figure 3, which represents a hypothetical input-input space where S_1 and S_2 represent two different school inputs into the production of student achievement. Each observation represents the combination of S_1 and S_2 that a particular school is using to produce a given amount of achievement output, Ao. That is, each school in the sample is using a different input mix, even though the apparent output is the same.

Isoquant Ao_1 represents the production frontier defined as the locus of all observations that minimize the combinations of S_1 and S_2 required to produce constant product Ao. Presumably, these schools are producing only the socially minimal required levels of other school outputs.[20] Since Ao_1 is a mapping of the most efficient points for producing achievement Ao, it is the production frontier. All observations to the northeast of Ao_1 are of "inefficient" schools that are using higher input levels to produce the same achievement.[21] Now assume that we fit the observations statistically via normal regression procedures. We obtain the statistical equivalent of Ao_2 for all schools (both efficient and inefficient ones). Of course, all points on Ao_2 are farther from the origin than those on Ao_1, showing that the average production relationship is a less efficient one than the frontier relationship.

Since virtually all estimates of educational production have been based on the performance of both average and efficient schools rather than efficient ones only, the existing statistical studies of educational production are not production function studies in the frontier sense. Moreover, their results may suggest erroneous conclusions about which combination of inputs (programs) maximizes achievement for a given budget constraint. For example, assume the two-input production function

(2) $\quad A = h(S_1, S_2)$

In equilibrium, we would wish to satisfy the conditions set out in (3), where P_1 and P_2 represent the prices of S_1 and S_2 respectively.

(3) $\quad \dfrac{\partial A / \partial S_1}{P_1} = \dfrac{\partial A / \partial S_2}{P_2}$

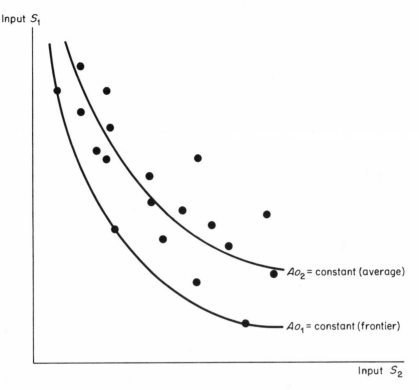

FIGURE 3   Frontier and Average Production Isoquants for Student Achievement

or

$$\frac{h'_1}{P_1} = \frac{h'_2}{P_2}$$

Now consider two different values for h'_1 and h'_2. At the frontier, $h'_1 = \hat{h}'_1$, and for the average of all schools, $h'_1 = \overline{h}'_1$. The symbols for h'_2 can be defined in the same way.

(4)
$$\frac{\hat{h}'_1}{\hat{h}'_2} = \frac{\overline{h}'_1}{\overline{h}'_2} = \frac{P_1}{P_2}$$

(4) reiterates the necessary conditions for a maximum, both for frontier estimates and for average estimates of the production function. In both

cases, we wish to select the combination of inputs that equates the ratios of marginal products (first derivatives) to the ratios of prices.

Efficiency Implications of the Estimates

If we estimate only the average production function or only the frontier production function, can the optimal ratio of inputs derived from one estimate also apply to the other? The answer to this question clearly depends on whether there are differences in the structural parameters associated with each input.

For example, it is possible that the inefficiencies of nonfrontier schools are neutral among inputs so that at every level of input and for every combination of inputs the ratios of the marginal products are identical for both frontier and average functions. That is, (5) holds.

(5)
$$\hat{h}_i' = \gamma \bar{h}_i' \quad (i = 1,2)$$
$$\gamma \geqslant 1$$

This can be represented by Figure 4, where Ao_1 signifies the production isoquant for Ao for all efficient schools and Ao_2 represents the same level of output for the entire set of schools, efficient and inefficient. B_1B_2 and C_1C_2 represent budget or iso-cost lines reflecting the various combinations of S_1 and S_2 obtainable for two given cost constraints, B_1B_2 and C_1C_2, where $C_1C_2 > B_1B_2$. The slope of the iso-cost lines is determined by the ratio of the prices, P_2/P_1. Thus, E and F represent equilibrium points which reflect (4). That is, the combination of S_1 and S_2 that obtains Ao for budget constraint B_1B_2 is determined by the tangency of Ao_1 to B_1B_2 at point E for efficient or frontier schools and of Ao_2 to C_1C_2 at point F for schools on the average.

It can be shown that the relative intensities of the two inputs will be identical for both groups of schools if a ray drawn from the origin intersects both points of tangency. $0\,M$ satisfies that condition, so the same ratio of S_1/S_2 is optimal for both groups of schools. Whether we use the estimates of frontier schools or of all schools, the findings on the optimal combinations of S_1 and S_2 will be binding for both. In such a case it does not matter which group we use to estimate the production function, although the absolute product will be higher for the set of schools at the frontier for any input level.

The situation depicted in Figure 4 and defined by (5) is a kind of happy state of affairs which would be desirable indeed for purposes of evaluation. Yet, there is no evident reason that such a fortuitous case should hold (Bowles 1970, pp. 16–17). Given technical inefficiencies in the production of education, it is likely that such inefficiencies are not

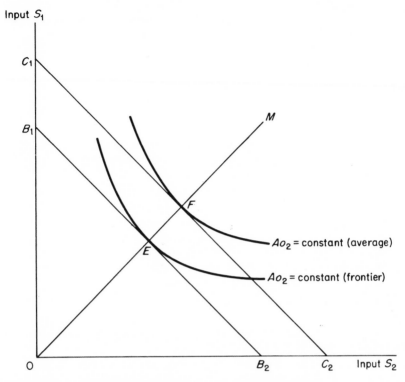

FIGURE 4 Technical Inefficiency that is Neutral between Inputs

neutral among inputs. That is, the inefficient school may be organized in such a way that the relative inefficiency in the use of one input may be greater than for another.[22] This can be shown in Figure 5, and it is also evident in Figure 3. Here the relative inefficiency in the use of S_1 appears to be greater than that for S_2. For example, if S_1 represents physical school facilities and S_2 represents teachers, Figure 5 suggests that the organizational arrangements in inefficient schools are relatively more harmful to the productivity of the facilities in increasing student achievement than to that of the teachers. In this case, a ray drawn through the origin representing a constant ratio of inputs will not intersect both points of tangency. That is, the optimal ratio of S_1/S_2 for frontier schools represented by $0\,M$ intersecting point E will not intersect point F; rather it intersects the production isoquant for the average schools at point G, which is a more costly combination of inputs than that represented at F. In short, the optimal ratio of S_1/S_2 for frontier schools will be different from that for nonfrontier ones, and if we impose

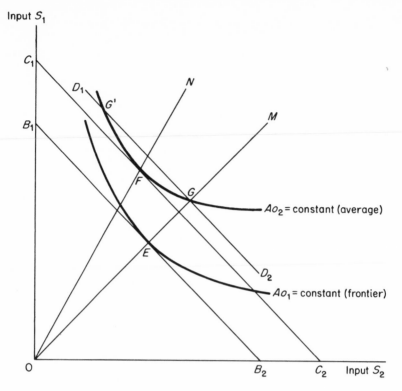

FIGURE 5   Technical Inefficiency that Is Biased between Inputs

that input ratio (represented by 0 M) on the nonfrontier production set, we shall recommend an *allocatively inefficient* set of inputs for the nonfrontier firms.

Of course, the obverse is also true. If we were to base our estimates of the production set on the entire group of schools, and we derived an optimal input ratio based upon 0 N which intersects tangency point F, we would impose an allocatively inefficient decision on frontier firms. That is, in either case, the results that we obtain for one group of schools cannot be applied to the other group. Rather each set of schools will have its own optimal combination of S_1/S_2 depending on the relative efficiencies with which these inputs are used. The point to be emphasized is that even with estimates based upon perfectly specified systems of equations for educational achievement, the input combinations that might be considered optimal for the industry will actually lead to a reduction in allocative efficiency for some educational firms. More specifically, those schools on Ao_2 using any combination of inputs within

$G G'$ would operate with greater price or allocative efficiency by ignoring the advice of economic studies of "frontier" firms.

Now it becomes obvious that under reasonable conditions, the advice of economists using econometric approaches to estimating production functions can actually lead to recommendations that *would decrease the allocative efficiency* of the educational sector. Even with the same set of prices, if every firm has a different set of marginal products such that the marginal rates of substitution of factors differ from firm to firm, then any prescriptive decision rule on optimal input combinations for the educational sector would have a high probability of producing a decrease in allocative efficiency.

This prospect becomes clearer if we depict an industry composed of three firms, Z_1, Z_2, and Z_3. If we assume that each firm is operating on its own "production function," we can depict the individual unit product isoquants for each firm as in Figure 6. Each firm is producing the same level of achievement output, but the mappings of feasible factor combinations differ. The assertion of this kind of idiosyncratic behavior derives primarily from our contention that educational managers lack the competition, incentives, information, and discretion to move toward the production frontier for achievement in any consistent way.

Further, assume that we wish to obtain a unit production isoquant for the industry. Fitting a convex hull to points a, b, and c, we obtain an approximation to the industry production frontier, ac.[23] Though in this case every firm's production surface is on the industry frontier, this condition should not be assumed ordinarily. Rather the unit production isoquants of some firms will be tangent to the frontier, while for others this will not be true. Such a situation is perfectly consistent with that described in Figure 1.

Figure 7 shows the conditions for maximizing allocative efficiency in this three-firm case. If we assume that $B_1 B_2$ is the relative price or iso-cost line facing the industry, then tangency with ac is at point b. That is, at point b it would appear that we would be obtaining the optimal combination of S_1/S_2 for maximizing allocative efficiency. Now assume that each educational firm accepts the recommendation of this industry evaluation with regard to the optimal ratio of S_1/S_2 for maximizing its allocative efficiency. Line $0 M$ is drawn from the origin through point b to indicate the constant ratio of S_1/S_2 that was derived for the industry. In following this recommendation, firm Z_1 would select combination R; firm Z_2 would select combination b; and firm Z_3 would select combination Q. What is the effect on allocative efficiency for each firm?

By coincidence, the iso-cost line $B_1 B_2$, the production isoquant for firm Z_2, and the estimated frontier for the industry ac are all tangent at the same point. Therefore the choice of b is allocatively efficient for firm Z_2. Following the evaluation recommendations, firm Z_1 selected point R

Input S_1

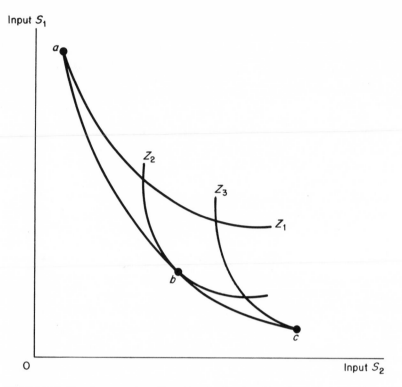

FIGURE 6 Approximating the Industry Production Surface for Three Firms

on iso-cost line aR. Yet it is obvious that Z_1 would be more efficient by producing at R_1 which is tangent to iso-cost line $C_1 C_2$. Indeed, even if firm Z_1 were not at point R_1, the choice of combination R could decrease its efficiency; for any selection of input combinations between point a and point R would be superior to R.

A similar situation exists for firm Z_3. The manager of Z_3 believes fully in using the findings of "scientific" research and evaluation activity in making his choices. Accordingly, he selects input combination Q with the expectation that his firm will be allocatively efficient. Yet, factor combination Q_1 is tangent to a lower iso-cost line $D_1 D_2$, and any input combination between c and W would be superior to Q.

Introducing Further Inefficiencies in Educational Production

In summary, by believing and implementing the results of the industry evaluation, the industry became less efficient rather than more efficient.

Input S_1

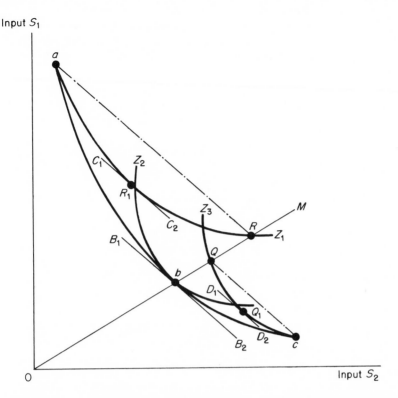

FIGURE 7 Maximizing Allocative Efficiency for the Three-Firm Industry

Yet, the techniques of evaluation were based upon the enormously useful tools of microeconomic analysis. Further, as Figure 7 suggests, no single estimate of the industry's production function for achievement will solve this problem. That is, optimal factor proportions will vary from firm to firm, and a uniform adoption for the industry will reduce overall allocative efficiency. Moreover, even this analysis has assumed that there will be no errors in the estimation of the relationships and that the same relative prices are applicable to each firm. The fact that neither of these assumptions are valid buttresses further the argument that efficiency recommendations based upon statistical production functions of student achievement for the education industry (or a segment of it) can be more harmful than beneficial to sectoral efficiency.

Bear in mind that at the present time we cannot identify or measure most educational outputs, and we are woefully ignorant of the proper specification and measurement of the input structures. Further, since the lion's share of the school budget is spent on personnel, one must raise the question whether teacher "prices" are the same for every school or school district. Among labor markets this is not likely to be so, but even within a school district a set of teachers with given characteristics are not indifferent about the schools in which they teach. For the same salary level, teachers prefer to work in schools attended by middle-class youngsters, and in suburban areas, rather than those attended by lower-class and minority youngsters in rural or highly urbanized areas (H. Becker 1952; Herriott and St. John 1966, Chapter 5). As one might expect, the relative preferences of teachers for specific school sites is reflected in the salaries required to obtain teachers for particular schools.[24]

For the very reasons stated above, it is not possible to test adequately the hypothesis that the production set differs among educational firms. Such a test would require a better specified model than the present state of the art will support. Nevertheless, for those who like the feel of numbers (even unreliable ones), I have used the appendix to compare estimates of educational production functions at the "frontier" with those for a large sample of sixth graders, in toto. Such an empirical operation is relegated to the appendix because it is meant to be provocative rather than definitive. Indeed, no numerical result derived from this exercise should be taken seriously.[25]

Of course, it is possible that parallel and serious problems arise in an analysis of private sector industries, leaving those studies open to erroneous conclusions. Yet, there is a quantum difference in the possible impact of erroneous findings in those cases in comparison with such findings in an evaluation of the education industry. The main difference is that private firms will tend to decide their input combinations on the basis of the peculiar circumstances facing them rather than on average "results" for the industry.[26] Further, the higher the level of aggregation of firms, the more inapplicable the results would appear to any reasonably proficient manager. Since most studies of the industry production function use state averages as units of observation, it would be unlikely that any particular firm would identify with such results.[27]

For example, Griliches carried out a set of studies on agricultural production functions (Griliches 1963, 1964). Using 39 states as "firms" and an unrestricted Cobb-Douglas equation, he found a ratio of marginal revenue product to marginal cost of about 3 to 5 for fertilizer (Griliches 1964). At the time, he notes that fertilizer use was growing at a tremendous rate in reaction to the disequilibrium (p. 968). What is noteworthy here is that Griliches saw natural market forces moving agriculture toward allocative efficiency in a dynamic setting. He did not intend his study to be used by individual farmers to make decisions. Rather he tacitly viewed their managerial behavior as being a function of stimuli much closer to their productive operations and more influential than the pages of economic journals. Indeed, it would be exceedingly foolish for any farmer to base his factor hiring decisions on the results of such studies.

The situation is entirely different for the schools and other public enterprises. The U.S. Office of Education, state departments of education, educational researchers, and school managers search out the uniform decision or recommendation with the hope of applying it generally. This penchant for standardizing input proportions is reflected in the laws of many of the states that require very specific ratios of administrators to teachers, and of teachers and other professional staff to students. It is reflected in the policy prescriptions of most educational reports.[28] Moreover, the fact that results derived from modern analytic tools often go unquestioned because many decision makers lack training in these areas just intensifies the problem. There is an increasing desire to try on the "emperor's new clothes" by educational managers who find this attire preferable to the dull and monotonous garb which makes them indistinguishable from other bureaucratic chieftains.

V. SUMMARY

Rising costs of education in conjunction with persistent concerns about quality have raised questions about the efficiency of the educational sector. One approach to improving the effectiveness of resource use in education is to estimate the technical production set for educational output; to relate the technical coefficients to prices of the inputs; and to make policy recommendations on the basis of these analyses that will raise the allocative efficiency of the educational enterprise. Within recent years a large number of studies have estimated an educational production function for student achievement, and an attempt has been made to compare marginal products with prices.

But, in order for observed statistical relations between inputs and outputs to reflect the maximum amount of input that can be obtained with the resources being utilized, all firms in the sample must be on the production frontier. In conventional analyses of industry production functions, it is assumed that the nature of a competitive environment in conjunction with the goal of profit maximization would tend to ensure that firms operating in competitive industries would be both technically and allocatively efficient. But, schools neither operate in a competitive environment nor do they have most of the other characteristics that we ascribe to competitive firms. Accordingly, it is not reasonable to believe that schools are operating on the production frontiers for the particular outputs that we believe that they *should be* producing.

Virtually all attempts to estimate educational production have specified educational achievement as reflected in test scores as the appropriate output of the educational process. We have shown that there is abundant evidence in conflict with the view that schools are attempting to maximize achievement scores. Accordingly, it does not seem reasonable that educational firms are operating on the production frontier for student achievement, and estimates of production functions among schools will not be likely to yield the appropriate technical coefficients that show the maximum amount of educational achievement that can be obtained with a given set of resource inputs. Moreover, it is likely that using the results of such studies for policy could decrease the economic efficiency of the educational industry with respect to the production of achievement rather than improving it.

It would seem that a more productive approach to future research in this area would be to attempt to ascertain a behavioral theory of schools that describes what schools are producing and how they are doing it.[29] Such studies would investigate the internal processes of educational enterprises as well as the various types of outcomes that they produce. They would also study the interface between schools and their external environment in order to determine the types of political sanctions and other characteristics that create the existing operations of the schools (Bowles and Gintis, 1975; Carnoy and Levin, 1976). This type of study might also begin to explain what aspects of schooling in addition to cognitive achievement affect adult income and other social outcomes. At the present time, our understanding of these relations is so inadequate that we are applying concepts derived from the competitive theory of the firm to bureaucratic, nonmarket institutions, and such an application seems unjustified.

An important start in this direction is reflected in the work of Gintis (1971) and Bowles (1972 and 1973). According to their analyses, schools serve to reproduce the social relations of production required by capitalist enterprise. They trace the evolution of the American schools through two periods of great change in the capitalist order (1830–90 and 1890–1930), and they assert that the changes in characteristics of schooling tended to mirror the changes in the demands of capitalist enterprises (Bowles and Gintis 1975). They have also related the internal activities of schooling, including school organization and grading practices, to worker characteristics that have been linked to productivity and earnings in hierarchical work settings. At the very least, their findings suggest that the function of schools is considerably more complex than the maximization of student achievement. It would seem that research endeavors in this direction would yield much more information about efficiency in the production of schooling than the present naive approach to "estimating" production sets. The most that can be said about the present production function studies is that they are interesting and harmless; unfortunately, they may also be misleading.

APPENDIX

A Temerarious Empirical Application

The major difficulty in demonstrating some of the empirical implications of the foregoing analysis is that the necessary relationships are much easier to obtain mathematically and geometrically than they are statistically. The particular problems in deriving educational production functions have been described elsewhere, so they will not be detailed here (Bowles 1970; Michelson 1970; Cain and Watts 1970; Levin 1970a). Yet it is useful to note that the statistical work in this area is subject to errors in the equations as well as errors in the variables. In the former case, the proper specification of the model is still in the exploratory stage. The structure of the model, the specific variables to be included, and their relationship to one another have not been well established, and there are many gaps in our knowledge. Moreover, most of the operational variables used in the models are subject to varying degrees of measurement error.

Thus, no strict application of our findings to public policy is warranted. Rather, the empirical aspects are meant to be provocative in generating new directions and thought on the process of evaluation. The results that we derive must surely be subject to replication and further analysis before they can be considered acceptable for policy evaluation.

The Sample

The data set used in this analysis represent a subsample drawn from the Survey on Equal Educational Opportunity of the U.S. Office of Education for the school year 1965–66. Specifically, it is composed of some 597 white sixth graders who had attended only the school in which they were enrolled at the time of the survey.[30] These data were reanalyzed and recoded extensively for purposes of estimating the present relationships, so they differ in important ways from other studies that have utilized information from the same survey. There are some 29 schools represented in the sample, and teacher characteristics represent the averages for each school for all teachers who were assigned to grades 3 through 5. These averages were intended to reflect the teacher characteristics that had influenced student behavior up to the time of the survey. Moreover, it was assumed that the observed measures of family background and other educational influences were related systematically to the cumulative impacts of each of these variables.

The equation that we will use to explore differences between frontier and average estimates will be a linear equation based on (1). Linearity not only violates our assumptions about the second derivative, but it also runs counter to our intuition about the real world. Yet, the difficulties of estimating particular nonlinear functions and the risk of greater specification biases in the coefficients by imposing another arbitrary functional form suggest that the linear equation might yield reasonable first approximations to the estimates that we seek. Of course, this limits our comparison of the frontier and average estimates to that of the linear marginal products and price ratios.

The variables in the equation are shown in Table A-1. These variables are taken from the reduced-form equation for verbal achievement derived from a four-equation system encompassing three simultaneous equations and one that represents a recursive relationship. Once that system is estimated one can solve for the reduced-form equation for any of the three endogenous variables. Since the estimation of that system is discussed elsewhere, we shall concern ourselves only with the reduced form of the verbal equation.[31] This equation was fitted to the entire sample of observations. Consequently, it represents the average production relation for the sample of schools. Results are shown for this estimate in the right column of Table A-2.

Obtaining Frontier Estimates

Using the same set of data and variables, we wish to obtain estimates of the equation for only the most efficient observations, those on the frontier. While there are several ways of doing this, we have chosen the programming approach in input-output space suggested by Aigner and Chu (1968). Since our individual observations are students rather than schools, we wish to seek those students who show a particular outcome with the lowest application of resources. Using the general notation from (1), the problem is to minimize (1-a).

$$(1\text{-}a) \quad \sum_{i=0}^{n} \hat{\alpha}_i \overline{X}_i$$

where $\hat{\alpha}_i$ is the parameter for the ith input, $\overline{X}_i$ is the mean of X_i, and $\overline{X}_o$

TABLE A-1 List of Variables

Name of Variable	Measure of:	Coding
Verbal score	Student performance	Raw score
Sex	Male-female differences	Male = 0, female = 1
Age	Overage for grade	Age 12 or over = 1, less than 12 = 0
Possessions in student's home	Family background (socioeconomic status)	Index of possessions: television telephone dictionary encyclopedia automobile daily newspaper record player refrigerator vacuum cleaner (Yes = 1, No = 0, for each; index is sum)
Family size	Family background	Number of people in home
Identity of person serving as mother	Family background	Real mother at home = 0, real mother not living at home = 1, surrogate mother = 2
Identity of person serving as father	Family background	Real father at home = 0, real father not living at home = 1, surrogate father = 2
Father's education	Family background	Number of years of school attained
Mother's employment status	Family background	Has job = 1, no job = 0
Attended kindergarten	Family background	Yes = 1, no = 0

TABLE A-1 (concluded)

Name of Variable	Measure of:	Coding
Teacher's verbal score	Teacher quality	Raw score on vocabulary test
Teacher's parents' income	Teacher socioeconomic status	Father's occupation scaled according to income (000's of dollars)
Teacher experience	Teacher quality	Number of years of full-time experience
Teacher's undergraduate institution	Teacher quality	University or college = 3, teacher institution = 1
Satisfaction with present school	Teacher's attitude	Satisfied = 3, maybe prefers another school = 2, prefers another school = 1
Per cent of white students	Student body	Percentage estimated by teachers
Teacher turnover	School	Proportion of teachers who left in previous years for reasons other than death or illness
Library volumes per student	School facilities	Number of volumes divided by school enrollment

TABLE A-2 Frontier and Average Production Relations for White Sixth Graders, Eastmet City

Variable	Frontier Function				Average Function
	Run 1	Run 2(− 9)	Run 3(− 23)	Run 4(− 38)	
Sex	0.0	1.649	0.982	0.01956	0.817
					(1.41)
Age	−7.714	−4.642	−4.769	−5.553	−6.010
					(4.49)
Family size	−0.502	−0.500	−0.089	−0.770	−0.552
					(3.50)
Father's identity	0.0	0.0	−0.283	−0.420	−0.327
					(0.64)
Mother's identity	−0.878	−1.342	−1.190	−1.202	−0.433
					(1.90)
Father's education	0.509	0.179	0.0	0.103	0.273
					(3.22)
Mother's employment	−1.726	−2.293	−1.089	−0.951	−0.509
					(1.31)
Possessions	1.865	1.464	1.070	1.020	1.229
					(5.08)
Kindergarten	0.0	2.866	1.920	2.106	2.372
					(2.47)
Teacher's verbal ability	0.810	0.218	0.695	0.791	0.250
					(1.70)
Teacher's parents' income	0.0	0.0	0.0	−0.00006	−0.118
					(0.65)
Teacher's undergraduate institution	3.736	5.269	1.991	8.307	6.525
					(2.09)

TABLE A-2 (concluded)

Variable	Frontier Function				Average Function
	Run 1	Run 2(− 9)	Run 3(− 23)	Run 4(− 38)	
Teacher experience	0.0	−0.500	−0.264	−0.616	0.787 (4.93)
Teacher satisfaction	3.630	7.078	4.666	3.608	1.960 (1.50)
Per cent white students	0.0	−0.500	−0.264	−0.178	−0.047 (0.25)
Library volumes per student	0.0	0.571	0.509	0.156	0.565 (1.53)
Teacher turnover	0.0	0.0	0.0	−0.035	−0.101 (1.27)
Constant	0.0	0.0	−0.944	−4.051	−7.902 (0.84)
					$n = 597$ $R^2 = .48$

NOTE: t statistics are in parentheses.

= 1 in order to obtain a constant term. More specifically, we wish to minimize (1-a) which can be rewritten as (2-a) subject to the constraints (3-a).

(2-a)   Min. $\hat{\alpha}_o + \hat{\alpha}_1 \overline{X}_1 + \ldots + \hat{\alpha}_n \overline{X}_n$

subject to:

(3-a)
$$\hat{\alpha}_o + \hat{\alpha}_1 X_{11} + \ldots + \hat{\alpha}_n X_{n1} \geq Y_1$$

$$\vdots$$

$$\hat{\alpha}_o + \hat{\alpha}_1 X_{im} + \ldots + \hat{\alpha}_n X_{nm} \geq Y_m$$
$$\hat{\alpha}_i \geq 0$$

Since this is essentially a linear programming problem, there will be as many "efficient" observations as there are inputs into the production function (assuming that no two observations are identical). Yet, clearly some of these firms will appear to be efficient when in fact the figures represent measurement errors.[32] Accordingly, a problem arises in that it is impossible for us to know a priori whether a particular observation is efficient or spurious. Following Timmer we have discarded extreme observations in order to eliminate what might be spurious points (Timmer 1969). This is particularly important for the frontier estimates, since very few observations determine the structural coefficients.

Table A-2 contrasts the frontier estimates with those for the average function. Each of the coefficients represents the first derivative or marginal product of the function.[33] Four linear programming runs were used to obtain frontier estimates. Run 1 eliminated no observations; Run 2 discarded the nine most "efficient" points; Run 3 eliminated 23 observations; and Run 4 discarded the 38 most extreme points (or about 6 per cent of the sample). We shall focus on the comparisons between the frontier function from Run 4 and the average function. In doing this we shall examine two properties of the estimates: (1) the relative magnitudes of the coefficients; and (2) implications for allocative or price efficiency.

Recall that in order for evaluation findings of optimal input intensities to yield the same relative applications of inputs for both average and frontier schools, the marginal products for both functions must bear a constant relation to each other as reflected in (5). Table A-3 shows the ratios of marginal products for the two sets of estimates for all of the school variables. According to this table, there is no obvious systematic relationship between the two sets, and some of the coefficients, such as teacher's verbal score, are different at statistically significant levels. At the frontier, such inputs as the teacher's verbal facility and the propor-

Ratio of Marginal Products at "Frontier" to
Marginal Products for Entire Sample

School Variables	MP (frontier) / MP (average)
Kindergarten	.888
Teacher's verbal ability	3.164
Teacher's parents' income	.001
Teacher's undergraduate institution	1.273
Teacher experience	.783
Teacher satisfaction	1.841
% white students	3.787
Library volumes per student	.276
Teacher turnover	.347
Constant	.513

tion of white students show marginal products that are more than three times their counterparts derived for the sample as a whole. On the other hand, such variables as teacher turnover, teacher experience, and library volumes per student show much smaller coefficients for the frontier function.

If these estimates are truly unbiased, the implications are that so-called frontier schools are more efficient in the use of some inputs and less efficient in the use of others. Thus any optimal combination of inputs for any set of schools or any individual school is likely to be nonoptimal for any other set of schools or individual ones. In other words, for any given array of prices $(P_1, P_2, \ldots, P_n)$ the optimal set of factor or input proportions may vary significantly from school to school.

For purposes of generalization, this is the worst of all possible worlds. That is, while we might be able to derive the optimal input structure for frontier schools or for schools on the average as represented by equilibrium conditions stated in (4), it is likely that the desirable combination of input intensities will differ between the two sets of schools (and in all probability will differ significantly from school to school).

An illustration of this is found in Table A-4, which shows the estimated ratios of prices of two inputs as well as the two sets of marginal products for those inputs. The prices reflect the increments to annual teacher salaries for each of the characteristics as derived from an equation relating teacher attributes to earnings in the Eastmet teacher market.[34] The marginal products associated with a unit change in teacher verbal score and teacher experience are taken from Table A-2. In equilibrium the ratios of the marginal products of the inputs should be

TABLE A-4 Relative Prices and Marginal Products for Teacher Experience and Teacher Verbal Score

	Teacher Verbal Score (1)	Teacher Experience (2)	Ratio (1) ÷ (2) (3)
Price	$24.00	$79.00	0.303
Marginal product at frontier	0.791	0.616	1.284
Marginal product on average	0.250	0.787	0.317

equal to the ratios of their respective prices. For the average production estimates these ratios are almost identical, so that allocative or price efficiency is implied even though the average estimates are assumed to be based upon technically inefficient (nonfrontier) schools.

On the other hand, the frontier estimates show a ratio of marginal products four times as great as the price ratio for the two inputs. This suggests that the utilization of more verbally able teachers yields four times as much output per dollar as the utilization of additional teacher experience. If this is correct, the schools on the frontier could increase total output by reallocating their budgets in favor of teacher verbal score while reducing teacher experience.[35]

The significant aspect of this analysis is that the output maximizing combination of inputs differs between the two estimates. If these differences persist among schools of different efficiencies, the hope of obtaining general rules for decision making which can be applied across schools seems to be frustrated. That is, the lack of similarities among the production techniques used by different schools may mean that neither average nor frontier findings can be applied to any particular school. Indeed, in the extreme case each individual school is on its own production function, and evaluation results for any group of schools will not be applicable to individual schools in the sample.

NOTES

1. Both Smith and Friedman are concerned about inefficiencies that result when state-run schools have little or no incentive to fulfill their stated objectives. (Smith 1937, p. 737; Friedman 1955 and 1962).
2. The rudiments of this specification were first suggested by Hanushek 1968.
3. For a more literal interpretation see Dugan (1969). Dugan has calculated the monetary value of parents' educational investment in their offspring by calculating the opportunity cost or market value of such services. The values of father's educational

investment, mother's educational investment, and school investment (all measured in dollars) seem to have high combined predictive value in explaining achievement levels. Also see Leibowitz, 1974.

4. These "theories" are essentially "black-box" hypotheses, based upon correlational findings or upon man-machine analogies. They do not specify general input-output structures or the physical, psychological, biological, and physiological processes underlying them. Indeed, there is no engineering knowledge of the educational process that is remotely analogous to those in agriculture and manufacturing. See for example, Bloom (1964).

5. The reasons for this assertion are found in Levin (1970a, pp. 65–66).

6. For general reviews of findings see Bowles (1970); Guthrie et al. (1971, Chapter 3); Kiesling (1971); and Averch et al. (1974).

7. This assumption has been questioned by Michelson (1970, pp. 134–149); Bowles (1970, pp. 16–17); and Levin (1970a, pp. 57–59).

8. Certainly this can be related to the criticisms of the schools made by many commentators who see the schools focusing on the wrong outputs. For a more sophisticated, but related, social welfare argument see Gintis (1969 and 1971) and Levin (1974a).

9. School districts in the United States vary in enrollments from a handful of students to the over 1 million enrollees in New York City. Individual schools show enrollments varying from a few children into the 10,000 student range. There were some 19,000 operating school systems and 44.5 million public-school students in 1969. Of these systems, only 1 per cent of them had 25,000 or more pupils. Yet, almost one-third of the students were in the 25,000 and over category while less than 2 per cent were in school systems with less than 300 pupils (Sietsema and Mongello, 1970, p. 6).

10. For an analysis of the production decisions faced by the multi-product firm generally and the joint product firm specifically, see Sune Carlson (1956, Chapter V); and Pfouts (1961).

11. The conventional "theory of the firm" has come increasingly under attack by those who charge that it is a theory of an environment rather than a theory of behavior. See Cyert and Hedrick (1972) for a review of this controversy.

12. In California, the state department of education even prints many of the books required at the elementary level. The cumbersomeness of this arrangement has resulted in a perennial ritual by which several hundred thousand youngsters have lacked their reading and arithmetic books for periods of up to two or three months following the opening of school. For greater detail on the degree of external control see Levin (1974a).

13. While Tiebout has suggested that such a public market exists, its efficiency must be questioned. Costs of migration are high, preventing frequent movement in response to disequilibria. Moreover, zoning and other impediments limit the usefulness of the housing market as a vehicle for educational choice. (See Tiebout 1956.) Of course, private alternatives exist for those willing and able to make substantial financial sacrifices.

14. For some approaches to implementing competition among the public schools see Downs (1970). Data on the voucher-inspired federal experiment in San Jose, California, are found in Weiler et al. (1974).

15. For an extensive taxonomy of educational objectives see Bloom (1956); and Krathwohl, Bloom, and Masia (1964).

16. For a more general analysis of the relation between institutional performance and incentive structures see Schultze (1968) and Rivlin (1971). Educational applications are found in Pincus (1974).

17. Multicollinearity among such inputs is a major basis of criticism for some of the

earlier work done in the area of estimating educational production. See Bowles and Levin (1968a and 1968b).

18. Exceptions to this are the multi-product estimations of Levin (1970a) and Michelson (1970), as well as the work of Boardman et al. (1973).

19. Of course, many private firms are likely to be technically inefficient to the degree that the competitive assumptions do not hold for them. See Leibenstein (1966) for a variety of examples illustrating substantial differences in technical efficiency or "x-efficiency" of firms. Nevertheless, while the inefficiency club is not an exclusive one, it would appear a priori that public schools have even fewer of the characteristics that would promote efficient production than do private firms. See Aigner and Chu (1968); Timmer (1971); and Farrell (1957).

20. In theory, schools on the frontier for student achievement are producing no other outputs. That is, the production of other outputs is assumed to detract from the production of student achievement. But, in fact, it is likely that there is a socially minimal level of other outputs (such as citizenship, work attitudes, and so on) that all schools produce. In this case, the schools that appear to be on the achievement frontier are on a "modified frontier," which assumes a socially minimal level of other outputs. That is, short of an experiment, we are unable to obtain production data on schools that are producing only student achievement.

21. Inefficiency is used here in a very narrow way. Specifically, it refers to the case in which more of a particular output could be obtained by reallocating existing resources from other outcomes to the one under scrutiny. The case of "technical inefficiency" or "x-inefficiency" is just a misnomer for this condition. Under conditions of technical inefficiency, it appears that more output could be obtained with the same level of inputs. But, as we have shown elsewhere (Levin and Muller, 1973), the physical laws of production must surely behave according to the principles of conservation of mass and energy, so that nothing is "lost" in the production process. One is always on the production frontier in that there is a mapping of outputs on inputs for any production process. When a steel mill is producing less steel for a given set of inputs than another mill, it is producing more heat energy or worker leisure or other outputs. It just happens that the most-valued or preferred output from the perspective of the analyst is steel rather than heat energy or worker leisure. Thus, so-called technical inefficiency can always be shown to reduce to allocative or price inefficiency, since it is a function of values rather than energy losses in a physical sense. For reference to the concept of technical efficiency or x-efficiency, see Farrell (1957) and Leibenstein (1966). In our view, the conception is erroneous for reasons mentioned above and outlined more systematically in Levin and Muller (1973). Also see Knight (1923).

22. There is an obvious similarity between this issue and the question of neutrality of technological progress. See Salter (1960); Brown (1966).

23. For discussion of techniques for deriving such a convex hull, see Aigner and Chu (1968).

24. For evidence of price differences attributable to teacher preferences for particular types of schools and teaching environments, see Toder (1972) and Levin (1968).

25. These results are also reported in Levin (1974).

26. See Hall and Winsten (1959) for a discussion of complications arising from interfirm differences in environmental conditions.

27. See the comments by Walters (1963, pp. 5–11).

28. See for example James S. Coleman et al. (1966, Chapter 1); and U.S. Commission on Civil Rights (1967). For criticism of such policy uses see Bowles and Levin (1968a), and Cain and Watts (1970).

29. There is an obvious parallel with the behavioral theory of the firm. See Cyert and March (1963) and Cyert and Hedrick (1972).
30. See Levin (1970a) for details.
31. Ibid.
32. Unfortunately each observation is a student rather than a firm. The proper approach is to seek efficient firms (schools) rather than students. The reason that students are used rather than firms is due to the limited sample size of schools, 29. Since it would require 18 of these firms to fit the frontier—given 18 parameters—one could hardly maintain that the frontier coefficients were based *only* on efficient firms.
33. Since $\alpha_i \geq 0$, those variables that showed negative coefficients for the average function represented problems for the programming estimates. The array for each such variable was multiplied by (-1) for the programming estimates, and the signs were reversed in turn when reporting the results in Table A-2. The author is indebted to Richard C. Carlson for computing the programming estimates. See his paper "Educational Efficiency and Effectiveness," May 1970, prepared for the Seminar in Economics of Education, Stanford.
34. These are taken from Levin (1968). For a similar application of these prices see Levin (1970c).
35. For a similar finding, see Levin (1970c).

REFERENCES

Aigner, D. J., and Chu, S. F. "On Estimating the Industry Production Function." *American Economic Review* 58 (Sept. 1968): 826–839.

Arrow, Kenneth. *Social Choice and Individual Values.* New York: John Wiley and Sons, 1951.

Averch, Harvey R. *How Effective is Schooling? A Critical Review of Research.* Englewood Cliffs: Educational Technology Publications, 1974.

Baumol, William. "Macroeconomics of Unbalanced Growth: The Anatomy of Urban Crisis." *American Economic Review* 57 (June 1967): 415–426.

Becker, G. S. *Human Capital.* Princeton: Princeton University Press, 1964.

Becker, Howard S. "The Career of the Chicago Public School Teacher." *American Journal of Sociology* 57 (Mar. 1952): 470–477.

Bell, Terrel. "Statement to Press on the Opening of Schools, 1974–75." Reported in *Education-Training Market Report* 10 (Sept. 16, 1974): 1.

Bloom, Benjamin S. *Stability and Change in Human Characteristics.* New York: John Wiley and Sons, 1964.

Bloom, Benjamin, ed. *Taxonomy of Educational Objectives, Handbook I: The Cognitive Domain.* New York: David McKay and Co., 1956.

Boardman, Anthony E.; Davis, Otto A.; and Sanday, Peggy. "A Simultaneous Equations Model of the Educational Process: The Coleman Data Revisited with an Emphasis upon Achievement." Paper presented at the Annual Meeting of the American Statistical Association, New York, Dec. 28, 1973.

Bowles, Samuel S. "Towards an Educational Production Function." In W. Lee Hanson, ed. *Education, Income, and Human Capital.* New York: NBER, 1970, pp. 11–60.

———. "Understanding Unequal Economic Opportunity." *American Economic Review Papers and Proceedings* 63 (May 1973): 346–356.

———. "Unequal Education and the Reproduction of the Social Division of Labor." In Martin Carnoy, ed. *Schooling in a Corporate Society.* New York: David McKay and Co., 1972a, pp. 36–66.

Bowles, Samuel, and Gintis, Herbert. "IQ in the U.S. Class Structure." *Social Policy* 3 (Nov./Dec. 1972, Jan./Feb. 1973).

Bowles, Samuel, and Gintis, Herbert. *Schooling in Capitalist America*. New York: Basic Books, Inc., 1975.

Bowles, Samuel, and Levin, Henry M. "The Determinants of Scholastic Achievement—A Critical Appraisal of Some Recent Evidence." *Journal of Human Resources* 3 (Winter 1968): 3–24.

———. "More on Multi-collinearity and the Effectiveness of Schools." *Journal of Human Resources* 3 (Summer 1968b): 393–400.

Bowles, Samuel, and Nelson, Valerie. "The 'Inheritance of IQ' and the Intergenerational Reproduction of Economic Inequality." *Review of Economics and Statistics* 56 (Feb. 1974): 39–51.

Brown, Byron, and Saks, Daniel. "The Production and Distribution of Cognitive Skills Within Schools." *Journal of Political Economy* Vol. 83, No. 3 (1975): 571–594.

Brown, Murray. *On the Theory and Measurement of Technological Change*. New York: Cambridge University Press, 1966.

Burkhead et al. *Input and Output in Large City High Schools*. Syracuse: Syracuse University Press, 1967.

Cain, Glen G., and Watts, Harold. "Problems in Making Policy Inferences from the Coleman Report." *American Sociological Review* 35 (Apr. 1970): 228–242.

Carlson, Richard C. "Educational Efficiency and Effectiveness." Paper prepared for the Seminar in Economics of Education, Stanford University (May 1970).

Carlson, Sune. *A Study on the Pure Theory of Production*. New York: Kelley and Millman, 1956.

Carnoy, Martin, ed. *Schooling in a Corporate Society*. New York: David McKay and Co., 1972.

Carnoy, Martin, and Levin, Henry M. *The Limits of Educational Reform*. New York: David McKay and Co., 1976.

Cohn, Elchanan. "Economics of Scale in Iowa High School Operations." *Journal of Human Resources* 3 (Fall 1968): 422–434.

Coleman, James S., and Karweit, Nancy. "Multi-Level Information Systems in Education." Rand Document 19287-RC. Santa Monica, Calif.: Rand Corporation, 1969.

Coleman, James S., et al. *Equality of Educational Opportunity*. U.S. Office of Education, OE 38001. Washington, D.C.: GPO, 1966.

Comanor, W., and Leibenstein, H. "Allocative Efficiency, X-Efficiency, and the Measurement of Welfare Losses." *Economica* 36 (Aug. 1969): 304–309.

Cyert, R. M., and March, J. G. *A Behavioral Theory of the Firm*. Englewood Cliffs, N.J.: Prentice-Hall, 1963.

Cyert, Richard M., and Hedrick, Charles L. "Theory of the Firm: Past, Present, and Future." *Journal of Economic Literature* 10 (June 1972): 398–412.

Dahl, R. A., and Lindblom, C. E. *Politics, Economics, and Welfare*. New York: Harper and Brothers, 1953.

Downs, Anthony. "Competition and Community Schools." In Henry M. Levin, ed., *Community Control of Schools*. Washington, D.C.: Brookings Institution, 1970.

Dreeben, Robert. *On What is Learned in School*. Reading, Mass.: Addison Wesley and Co., 1968.

Dugan, Dennis. "The Impact of Parental and Educational Investment Upon Student Achievement." Paper presented at the Annual (129th) Meeting of the American Statistical Association, New York City, August 21, 1969, processed.

Farrell, Michael. "The Measurement of Productive Efficiency." *Journal of the Royal Statistical Society*, Series A (General), Vol. 120, Part 3 (1957): 253–281.

Friedman, Milton. "The Role of Government in Education." In *Capitalism and Freedom*. Chicago: University of Chicago Press, 1962, Chapter VI.

———. "The Role of Government in Education." In Robert A. Solo, ed., *Economics and the Public Interest*. New Brunswick, N.J.: Rutgers University Press, 1955.

Gallup, George. *How the Nation Views the Public Schools*. Princeton, N.J.: Gallup International, 1969.

———. "Second Annual Survey of the Public's Attitude Toward the Public Schools." *Phi Delta Kappan* 52 (Oct. 1970): 99–112.

———. Sixth Annual Gallup Poll of Public Attitudes Toward Education." *Phi Delta Kappan* 56 (Sept. 1974): 20–32.

Gintis, Herbert. "Education, Technology and the Characteristics of Worker Productivity." *American Economic Review* 61 (May 1971): 266–279.

———. "Production Functions in the Economics of Education and the Characteristics of Worker Productivity." Ph.D. diss., Howard University, 1969.

Gittell, Marilyn. *Participants and Participation*. New York: Praeger, 1967.

Gittell, Marilyn, and Hollander, T. Edward. *Six Urban School Districts: A Comparative Study of Institutional Response*. New York: Praeger, 1968.

Greer, Colin. *The Great School Legend*. New York: Basic Books, 1972.

Griliches, Zvi. "Estimates of the Aggregate Agricultural Production Function from Cross-Sectional Data." *Journal of Farm Economics* 45 (May 1963): 419–428.

———. "Research Expenditures, Education, and the Aggregate Agricultural Production Function." *American Economic Review* 54 (Dec. 1964): 961–974.

———. "Specification Bias in Estimates of Production Functions." *Journal of Farm Economics* 39 (Feb. 1957): 8–20.

Griliches, Zvi, and Mason, W. "Education, Income, and Ability." *Journal of Political Economy* 80, Supplement (May/June 1972): S. 74–S. 103.

Guthrie, James W.; Kleindorfer, George B.; Levin, Henry M.; and Stout, Robert T. *Schools and Inequality*. Cambridge: Massachusetts Institute of Technology Press, 1971.

Hall, Lady, and Winsten, C. B. "The Ambiguous Notion of Efficiency." *Economic Journal* 69 (Mar. 1959): 71–86.

Hanushek, Eric. *Education and Race*. Lexington, Mass.: D. C. Heath, 1972.

———. "The Education of Negroes and Whites." Ph.D. diss., Department of Economics, Massachusetts Institute of Technology, 1968.

Hanushek, Eric, and Kain, John F. "On the Value of Equality of Educational Opportunity as a Guide to Public Policy." In F. Mosteller and D. D. Moynihan, eds., *On Equality of Educational Opportunity*. New York: Random House, 1972, pp. 116–145.

Hanushek, Eric, and Levin, Henry M. "Educational Information Systems for Management and Evaluation—A Proposed Program." D-2073. Santa Monica, Calif.: Rand Corporation, 1969.

Hartley, Harry J. *Educational Planning, Programming, Budgeting: A Systems Approach*. Englewood Cliffs, N.J.: Prentice-Hall, 1968.

Hawkridge, David G.; Chalupsky, Albert B.; and Roberts, A. Oscar H. "A Study of Selected Exemplary Programs for the Education of Disadvantaged Children." Parts I and II, Final Report, Project No. 08-9013 for the U.S. Office of Education. Palo Alto, Calif.: American Institutes for Research, 1968, processed.

Herriott, Robert E., and St. John, Nancy H. *Social Class and the Urban School*. New York: John Wiley and Sons, 1966.

Iannacone, Laurence. *State Politics and Education*. New York: CARE, Inc., 1967.

Jackson, Philip W. *Life in Classrooms*. New York: Holt, Rinehart, and Winston, 1968.

Jencks, Christopher, et al. *Inequality: A Reassessment of the Effect of Family and School-ing in America.* New York: Harper-Row, 1973.

——."Is the Public School Obsolete?" *Public Interest,* 2 (Winter 1966): 18–27.

Katzman, Martin. *The Political Economy of Urban Schools.* Cambridge: Harvard University Press, 1971.

Kershaw, J. A., and McKean, R. N. *Teacher Shortages and Salary Schedules.* New York: McGraw Hill, 1962.

Kiesling, Herbert J. *High School Size and Cost Factors.* Final Report for the U.S. Office of Education, Bureau of Research, Project No. 6-1590, Mar. 1968, processed.

——. "Measuring a Local Government Service: A Study of School Districts in New York State." *Review of Economics and Statistics* 59 (Aug. 1967): 356–367.

——. "Multivariate Analysis of Schools and Educational Policy." P4595. Santa Monica, Calif.: Rand Corporation, 1971.

Knight, Frank. "The Ethics of Competition." *Quarterly Journal of Economics* 37 (Aug. 1923): 579–624.

Krathwohl, D. R.; Bloom, B. S.; and Masia, B. B. *Taxonomy of Educational Objectives, Handbook II: The Cognitive Domain,* New York: David McKay and Co., 1964.

Lau, Lawrence J., and Yotopoulos, Pan A. "A Test for Relative Economic Efficiency: Some Further Results." *American Economic Review* 63 (Mar. 1973): 214–223.

——. "A Test for Relative Efficiency and Application to Indian Agriculture." *American Economic Review* 61 (Mar. 1971): 94–110.

Leibenstein, Harvey. "Allocative Efficiency vs. 'X-Efficiency.' " *American Economic Review* 56 (June 1966): 392–415.

Leibowitz, Arleen. "Home Investments in Children." *Journal of Political Economy* 82 (Mar./Apr. 1974): S111–S131.

Levin, Henry M. "A Conceptual Framework for Accountability in Education." *School Review* 82 (May 1974): 363–391.

——. "A Cost-Effectiveness Analysis of Teacher Selection." *Journal of Human Resources* 5 (Winter, 1970): 24–33.

——. "Educational Reform and Social Change." *Journal of Applied Behavioral Science* 10 (Aug. 1974a): 304–320.

——. "Measuring Efficiency in Educational Production." *Public Finance Quarterly* 2 (Jan. 1974): 3–24.

——. "A New Model of School Effectiveness." In *Do Teachers Make a Difference?* U.S. Department of Health, Education and Welfare, Office of Education, OE-58042. Washington, D.C.: GPO, 1970b, Chapter 3.

——. *Recruiting Teachers for Large-City Schools.* Washington, D.C.: Brookings Institution 1968, processed.

Levin, Henry M., ed. *Community Control of Schools.* Washington, D.C.: Brookings Institution, 1970c.

Levin, Henry M., and Muller, Jurgen. "The Meaning of Technical Efficiency." Oct. 1973, processed.

Little, I. M. D. *A Critique of Welfare Economics.* Oxford: Oxford University Press, 1950.

Lyke, Robert F. "Representation and Urban School Boards." In H. M. Levin, ed., *Community Control of Schools.* Washington, D.C.: Brookings Institution, 1970, pp. 138–168.

Michelson, Stephan. "The Association of Teacher Resourceness With Children's Characteristics." In *Do Teachers Make a Difference?* U.S. Department of Health, Education and Welfare, Office of Education, OE-58042. Washington, D.C.: GPO, 1970, Chapter 6.

Murnane, Richard. "The Impact of School Resources on the Learning of Inner City Children." Ph.D. diss., Department of Economics, Yale University, 1974.

Mushkin, Selma, and Pollak, William. "Analysis in a PPB Setting." In R. L. Johns et al., eds., *Economic Factors Affecting the Financing of Education*, Vol. 2. Gainesville, Fla.: National Educational Finance Project, 1970, pp. 329–372.

Nerlove, Marc. *Estimation and Identification of Cobb-Douglas Production Functions.* Chicago: Rand McNally, 1965.

Pfouts, Ralph W. "The Theory of Cost and Production in the Multi-Product Firm." *Econometrica* 29 (Oct. 1961): 650–658.

Picariello, Harry. "Evaluation of Title I." U.S. Office of Education, Office of Program, Planning, and Evaluation, 1969, processed.

Pincus, John. "Incentives for Innovation in the Public Schools." *Review of Educational Research* 44 (Winter 1974): 113–144.

Riew, John. "Economies of Scale in High School Operation." *Review of Economics and Statistics* 48 (Aug. 1966): 280–287.

Rivlin, Alice M. "Forensic Social Science." In *Perspectives on Inequality.* Reprint Series No. 8. Cambridge: *Harvard Educational Review*, 1973, pp. 25–39.

———. *Systematic Thinking for Social Action.* Washington, D.C.: Brookings Institution, 1971.

Rogers, David. *110 Livingston Street.* New York: Random House, 1968.

Salter, W. E. G. *Productivity and Technical Change.* Cambridge: Cambridge University Press, 1960.

Schrag, Peter. *Village School Downtown.* Boston: Beacon Press, 1967.

Schultze, Charles L. *The Economics and Politics of Public Spending.* Washington, D.C.: Brookings Institution, 1968.

Sietsema, John P., and Mongello, Beatrice O. *Education Directory 1969–70 Public School Systems.* U.S. Department of Health, Education and Welfare, National Center for Education Statistics, OE-20005-70. Washington, D.C.: GPO, 1970.

Silberman, Charles. *Crisis in the Classroom.* New York: Random House, 1970.

Smith, Adam. *The Wealth of Nations.* Modern Library Edition. New York: Random House, 1937.

Taubman, Paul J., and Wales, Terence J. "Higher Education, Mental Ability and Screening." *Journal of Political Economy* 81 (Jan./Feb. 1973): 28–55.

Thomas, J. Alan. *The Productive School.* New York: John Wiley and Sons, 1971.

Tiebout, Charles M. "A Pure Theory of Local Expenditures." *Journal of Political Economy* 64 (Oct. 1956): 416–424.

Timmer, C. P. "On Measuring Technical Efficiency." Ph.D. diss., Department of Economics, Harvard University, 1969.

———. "Using a Probabilistic Frontier Production Function to Measure Technical Efficiency." *Journal of Political Economy* 79 (July/Aug. 1971): 776–794.

Toder, Eric. "The Supply of Public School Teachers to an Urban Area: A Possible Source of Discrimination in Education." *Review of Economics and Statistics* 54 (Nov. 1972): 439–443.

U.S. Department of Health, Education and Welfare, Office of Education. *Financial Accounting for State and Local School Systems.* State Educational Records and Reports Series: Handbook II, OE 22017. Washington, D.C.: GPO, 1957.

U.S. Department of Health, Education and Welfare. *Projections of Educational Statistics to 1981–82.* National Center for Educational Statistics, Office of Education. Washington, D.C.: GPO, 1972.

Walters, A. A. "Production and Cost Functions: An Econometric Survey." *Econometrica* 31 (Jan./Apr., 1963): 1–66.

Wargo, Michael J.; Tallmadge, G. Kasten; Michaels, Debbra D.; Lipe, Dewey; and Morris, Sarah J. "ESEA Title I: A Reanalysis and Synthesis of Evaluation Data

From Fiscal Year 1965 Through 1970." Palo Alto, Calif.: American Institutes for Research, March 1972.

Weiler, Daniel, et al. *A Public School Voucher Demonstration: The First Year at Alum Rock.* Santa Monica, Calif.: Rand Corporation, June 1974.

Williams, Andrew T. "Education and the Joint Product Production Function." Paper prepared for the Seminar in Economics of Education, Stanford University, 1970, processed.

Winkler, Donald R. *The Production of Human Capital: A Study of Minority Achievement.* Ph.D. diss., Department of Economics, University of California at Berkeley, 1972.

Wynne, Edward. *The Politics of School Accountability.* Berkeley, Calif.: McCutchan Publishing Co., 1972.

4 ‖ COMMENTS

Eric A. Hanushek
Yale University

It always helps to take stock periodically of what we are doing and where we are going. Educational research is certainly no exception. It is simply too easy to continue doing what we know best. However, after being forced by Levin into a reappraisal of the directions of educational research, I remain unpersuaded that drastic modification is called for. I have some serious reservations about the conclusions and implications both for research and public policy drawn from Levin's analysis, particularly as it pertains to technical inefficiency in the schools.

In many ways, Levin's viewpoint does not diverge significantly from my own. We start from the same data; there is no disagreement about the constraints on the system or about the amount of knowledge and information available to the participants in the educational process. We also agree on many of the results that develop from constraints on information and possible actions. Our major points of disagreement arise from nomenclature of observed output differences and the subsequent implications for future research and public policy.

In his taxonomy of types of inefficiency, Levin argues that there are reasons to believe that schools are not operating on the production frontier (technical inefficiency), are not operating with the best input mix (allocative inefficiency), and are not providing the desired output mix (social welfare inefficiency). The heart of his analysis is directed toward the evidence concerning technical inefficiency and its implications for research and public policy. That is also the central issue in my discussion.

Before entering that debate, however, I wish to make two points relating to allocative and social welfare efficiency. These are not points of disagreement with Levin; they are simply added to emphasize certain aspects of the discussion. First, allocate inefficiency has not only been the central concern of economists but is also almost a necessary condition for analysis. In the absence of large differences in the relative prices of inputs, allocative inefficiency is needed to analyze educational production functions. Otherwise we would observe one point on the production function, and our statistical techniques are noticeably weak at drawing multidimensional planes through one point. Second, the whole issue of social welfare efficiency, or producing the best mixture of outputs, has the same elusive character as choosing the right quantity and mixture of general public goods. The optimum marginal conditions on the social welfare function are easy enough to derive, but the operational questions have generally been beyond the economist's ability to answer. Nevertheless, in my subjective evaluation, this is probably the most important area of concern in education today. The question of whether or not schools are producing the outputs desired and needed in society remains important but unresolved. We are not sure what the outputs of schools are, how to measure the outputs, how to produce each, or what tradeoffs exist among outputs. Not only space limitations on this discussion but also the difficulty of the issue preclude my going into more detail on this.

The main message delivered by Levin is that there are compelling reasons to believe that what have paraded under the banner of educational production functions are not really production functions in the economist's usage of the term, because they do not describe the frontier of possible production. Instead they are a weighted average of the practices of efficient, or "frontier," schools and inefficient, or "nonfrontier," schools. With these average relationships, blind application of well-known optimization rules could even degrade the production by a school system which is almost universally cited as inefficient.

A crucial facet of the debate is how one should define technical inefficiency. Past discussions, for example, Leibenstein's development of X-efficiency [2] and Levin's presentation, rest heavily upon a microeconomic textbook treatment of production, where output is a function of a quantity of homogeneous capital and homogeneous labor. Then, noting that these inputs are really not homogeneous, firms with poorer "homogeneous" inputs are observed to produce less output than firms with identical quantities but better quality "homogeneous" inputs. The availability of better or worse "homogeneous" inputs can be related to incomplete labor contracts, lack of knowledge of the production function, motivational differences, or simply general managerial ability. Differences in output for "equal" inputs are used as a measure of technical inefficiency.

A real problem remains in specifically defining technical inefficiency. In reality, technical inefficiency or X-inefficiency is a measure of the strength of variables omitted from a model of the production process. These omitted variables may take the form of education, motivation, laziness, or what have you. They are just the explanations given for efficiency differences. In these terms, defining technical inefficiency becomes very difficult. Before any analysis of technical inefficiency can be developed, one must define what the base model of the production process should look like. Amounts of inefficiency then become difficult to measure, since they are a function of the chosen degree of misspecification in the base model. A common way to set the frame of reference appears to be using the model which can be developed from available data. This, of course, creates problems, because the amount of inefficiency can change over time simply due to better data becoming available.

A different way of looking at this "inefficiency," however, is to use a well-specified model as the standard and to view observed production differences in terms of model misspecification. The traditional production function that pictures output as a function of the quantity of man-hours or man-hours within given human capital classifications provides an incomplete view of the labor input to production. There are more attributes to labor than are represented in these functions. These omitted attributes often tend to be correlated with management ability or firm size or nationality in Leibenstein's international examples. Estimated production functions can then give a distorted view of the production potential. There is, however, no reason why the analyst cannot specify or attempt to specify all of the attributes that go into production. He need not be bound to specifying just those inputs as seen in a microeconomic text or those explicitly purchased by the firm.

In point of fact, this extension of the list of inputs has been the order of the day in educational research. Educational production functions of the past decade have not looked at schools as providing a given number of homogeneous teachers; nor have they looked at schools as providing only the set of purchased inputs (class size, experience, and graduate education). Instead they have looked at schools as providing a set of attributes, such as teacher verbal ability. The attributes explicitly measured may well be proxies for other attributes which have direct causal relationships with achievement. However, to the extent that a set of stable proxies which represent a fair proportion of the real teacher inputs to education have been analyzed, the importance of the technical inefficiency argument is considerably diminished.

If we map achievement outputs against only those inputs explicitly purchased by schools (class size, teacher experience, and teacher graduate education), we will certainly find the picture indicated by Levin's Figure 1. This will happen because, according to past analyses, the purchased factors have a small or nonexistent effect on output, but other nonpurchased characteristics of teachers do have an important effect. Since these other factors are not randomly distributed by schools—as shown in Levin [3], schools with apparently the same input levels will show different outputs. Yet, within the context of educational production functions, the real question is: Do schools have different outputs after the relevant teacher inputs are held constant?

It is reasonable that past discussions in fields other than education have centered upon technical inefficiency in production. This arises largely from having poorer data sources for, say, aggregate manufacturing firms than for educational firms. Research in education has been aided by having detailed measures of relevant inputs. Further, the emphasis within educational research has been on refining the measures of inputs. This is not to say that we now have perfectly specified models of educational production. We have a long way to go in that regard. It does imply that attention has been placed where I think it properly should be—on model specification and, to a certain extent, on experimental design.

The case by Levin for technical inefficiency derives chiefly from the observations that school managers do not know what the production function for education looks like and that these managers are severely constrained in their operating and hiring practices. Other factors relating to technical inefficiencies are the general lack of competition in education and lack of both incentives and clear-cut signals of success or failure.

From a specification point of view, the implications to be drawn from Levin's observations of current school operations change considerably. First, I am uncertain how the school principal, whether he knows the production function or not, affects technical efficiency. If, as past research would suggest, the main school inputs to education under the current technology are attributes of the teacher, it is hard to see how the principal affects the relationship between these attributes and achievement by very much. In terms of managing teachers, the principal may assign his best reading teacher to teach physical education; this is an allocatively poor decision that would reduce total achievement in a school for his expenditures, but not necessarily one that falls off the production frontier for education. It indicates that the analyst must be careful to separate the characteristics of the physical education teacher and the reading teacher. But, given this, there seems to be no reason to require the principal to know that he is making a mistake.

The fact that there are constraints on the manager's actions does not seem to destroy the usefulness of estimated production functions either. Constraints imply that he can only operate on a limited portion of possible input mixes. For example, a principal probably does not have the option to install a Computer-Assisted Instruction (CAI) program on his own. Nevertheless, he can attempt to suboptimize within the portion of the production frontier available to him. There is no reason to suspect that any such suboptimization attempts lead to technical inefficiency.

The other conceptual reasons for concluding that technical inefficiency is probably large produce a similar discussion. Such reasons seem to imply that schools could be allocatively very inefficient but not technically inefficient.

There is an empirical question about the importance of variables relating to facilities, curriculum, and management which may be systematically related to achievement and not generally included in production models. I have made a modest attempt to answer this question with a sample of 515 students from blue-collar families within one school system. The data sample and estimated educational models are reported elsewhere [1]. After standardizing for different teacher inputs, I attempted to find out whether there were characteristics of schools and principals which systematically affected output. For this analysis, each of twenty-three schools in the sample was allowed to have its own intercept value, and statistical tests were performed to ascertain whether these intercepts differed by school. The intercept dummy variables provide estimates of the systematic school effects, regardless of whether the components of these effects can be adequately specified or measured. These effects would be equivalent to a measure of technical efficiency.

Within this sample, only one school out of twenty-three (comprising two per cent of the students) produced significantly higher outputs after standardizing for teacher inputs.[1] This appears to be very weak evidence for the existence of important technical inefficiencies. Matched against this is the finding that the total wage bill could be reduced by approximately 22 per cent with no decrease in achievement by not hiring individuals possessing superior experience or graduate education, or by not paying for such experience and graduate education, which were shown to have no impact on achievement. (In other words, by improving allocative efficiency, a savings of 22 per cent could be realized.)

Finally, we know that there is a large random component associated with individual achievement. There is no reason to suspect that we get more or better information about educational production by looking at a smaller sample, whether by linear programming or least squares. Also, even in the context of viewing "efficient" production with linear programming, there is no reason to believe that specification problems are any less severe. If we wish to make decisions about educational production from considering "efficient" schools, we are still left with trying to decide why such schools are efficient. In other words, we are left with the same specification problems.

CONCLUSIONS

It is not evident to me that technical inefficiency is a particularly large problem, unless we use obviously misspecified models as the standard. Within the context of well-specified models, similar to those developed within the past few years, emphasis upon allocative efficiency appears warranted. I do not wish to indicate that we know all there is to know about educational production. Yet, both conceptually and empirically, allocative inefficiency seems more important than technical inefficiency.

The difference in my approach and Levin's is more than a question of semantics. First, use of the term inefficiency tends to imply that there is a free lunch, that some organizational changes within the school will bring about significant changes in outputs at little or no cost. On the other hand, when viewed in terms of omitted variables, it is immediately obvious that bringing "inefficient" schools up to the level of "efficient" schools may not be free. Second, the term technical inefficiency seems to imply that the observed differences in outputs are related almost exclusively to management differences. However, my work has led me to suspect that the real efforts should be directed toward better specifying teachers and their inputs to education. Third, the concept of technical efficiency appears vacuous from a public policy viewpoint. Even if some consensus could be arrived at as to how this inefficiency should be measured, we are at best led to trying to explain these differences in order to reduce the differentials involved.

If the problem is looked upon as one of specification problems, it leads to intensifying data collection efforts and broadening the scope of our measurement of teacher attributes. It also calls for experimentation in order to observe other parts of the production frontier. If instead, one concludes that school management in terms of approaching the production frontier is the key issue, a different course of action is called for. In this case, much more effort should be directed toward analyzing organizational behavior and the relationship between management, teachers, and facilities. In my judgment, the former course of action will have much higher payoffs.

On the other hand, Levin's observations about the definition and measurement of educational outputs cannot be disregarded. Even though cognitive ability, as measured by test scores, is undoubtedly an important aspect of elementary and secondary schools, this is not the sole output of schools. While the joint product problem is not completely developed by Levin, it represents a very important issue for future research. Unfortunately, the methodology for handling joint production when there are no prices (or weights) to combine the different dimensions of output is an underdeveloped area of economics.

NOTE

1. Another significant aspect of this estimation was the finding that the dummy variable for this school had a very low correlation with each of the included school variables. (The simple correlation was always less than .1.) This implies that even if we were to believe that the dummy variable represented some omitted management aspects for this school, its effect on the included coefficient estimates is small; that is, the amount of specification bias would be small.

REFERENCES

1. Hanushek, Eric A. *Education and Race,* Lexington, Mass.: D.C. Heath, 1972.
2. Leibenstein, Harvey. "Allocative Efficiency vs. 'X-Efficiency'," *American Economic Review* 56 (June 1966): 392–415.
3. Levin, Henry M. "Recruiting Teachers for Large-City Schools." Washington, D.C.: Brookings Institution, 1968, processed.

Harold W. Watts
University of Wisconsin

The primary conclusion Levin arrives at in this paper is that valid prescriptions for improving efficiency of the educational process (or that part of it which takes place in public schools) cannot be derived from existing estimated production functions. He argues that the world is much more complicated than the available econometric models of educational production and that naive attempts to draw normative conclusions from such models could be counter-productive. These conclusions seem appropriate enough as warnings or expressions of humility, but they also seem quite anticlimactic at the end of so many pages of analytic threshing about.

Levin opens by attempting to motivate our interest in efficiency by observing the rising costs of education combined with dissatisfaction over the quality of schools and loss of voter support for bond issues. It is quite clear that improvements in efficiency, if any are available, would offset for a while some of the increase in costs and might produce a more popular product. But the existence of inefficiency, in any of its varieties, does not imply either rising costs or consumer dissatisfaction. If inefficiency were getting worse at some steady rate, we might expect the consequences of rising costs and/or falling quality, but Levin does not provide evidence of progressive inefficiency. In no sense does the hypothesis of inefficiency provide an alternative to the "pessimistic" view of Baumol that "unprogressive" sectors will suffer cost increases as other sectors enjoy productivity gains and consequent wage increases.

But there is probably plenty of interest in efficiency as a property of the educational system and further motivation is unnecessary. Levin proceeds to use production isoquants and output transformation loci to illustrate various kinds of inefficiency and also to introduce various ways that model misspecification can foul up econometric estimates of production functions. Here one principal point is that productive units that are not using efficient techniques will not lie on the production frontier and will result in the estimation of a subfrontier production function. A second one is that output measurements may be incorrectly specified (either in one or many dimensions) and that spurious inefficiencies or "second bests" may be perceived as a consequence of that misspecification.

The next section of Levin's paper presents a long a priori argument in support of the proposition that schools must be inefficient! The main premise seems to be that they are unlike private competitive firms in a number of critical respects, and without those characteristics educational "firms" have no basis for achieving efficiency. I find myself quite convinced that the education "industry" is poles apart from the straw-man industry which has all the perfect properties of the competitive model. However, it seems that most of the real world of productive enterprises share enough of those imperfections to invalidate for them the simpleminded empirical analysis that Levin criticizes for education. Again, I can easily accept the argument that our public schools leave something to be desired in terms of efficiency, but I cannot agree that the contrast with other private or public production is particularly unfavorable.

The other part of the section spells out the limitations of standardized achievement tests as measures of school output. I fully share all Levin's reservations here and would welcome any progress toward satisfactory measures of neglected aspects, but again, this is a problem of measuring the outputs of a human-service industry and that is an unsolved problem everywhere.

The next section explores the GIGO[1] production function as applied to econometric research and derived policy prescriptions in education. Levin is quite persuasive about the various kinds of mischief that can result from a zealous application of intermediate theory to the estimated production functions for education which have appeared in respectable journals. He is motivated in this analysis by a belief that there is a real danger of these half-baked conclusions being promulgated by ukase, and even worse, that they will affect school practice.

My own appreciation of how hard it is to get any real change in the way schools and teachers behave, combined with Levin's own sense about how varied schools are, both on and off the efficiency frontier, make the threat of lockstep imitation of the latest econometric optimality formula pretty remote. Consequently, I can accept his analysis of what-if-everyone-acted-silly without agreeing on the likelihood of the premise.

In the end, Levin pleads for better models—always a popular plea—and suggests that a "behavioral theory of schools" may be under construction by Bowles and Gintis. Clearly one can begin to be relevant once a reasonably comprehensive concept of the objectives or outputs of schools has been specified; and maximum standardized achievement test scores do not fill the bill. Better models also include more attention to how observations are generated and to the implications for econometric estimation. The use of programming techniques to form "envelope" estimates is one possible improvement and Levin's numerical example shows that it may be of some importance. Clearly our economic and econometric analyses of the education industry in general and its production function in particular are very crude and are not strong enough to support policy recommendations. I am more optimistic than Levin that the work to date has been harmless and may even have been helpful in moving toward more useful models. I am quite pessimistic about the chance of an estimated second derivative ever becoming the basis of a universally followed command which will halt or reverse the upward trend of educational costs.

NOTE

1. Garbage In Garbage Out.

PART TWO

Compensatory Education

5

DEAN T.
JAMISON
The World Bank

J. DEXTER
FLETCHER
Navy Personnel Research
and Development Center

PATRICK
SUPPES
Stanford University

RICHARD C.
ATKINSON
National Science
Foundation

Cost and Performance
of Computer-Assisted
Instruction for
Education of
Disadvantaged
Children

I. INTRODUCTION

This paper discusses the potential role of computer-assisted instruction
(CAI) in providing compensatory education for disadvantaged children.
All CAI involves, to one extent or another, the interaction of students

NOTE: This research was supported in part by National Science Foundation Grant NSF-GJ-443X3 to
the Institute for Mathematical Studies in the Social Sciences, Stanford University. A. Kelley, S.
Michelson, and D. Wiley provided helpful comments on an earlier draft of this paper.

with computers. Curriculum material is stored by a computer which is provided with decision procedures for presenting the material to individual students. Typically students work at terminals, usually teletypewriters, which are located at school sites and are connected by telephone lines to a central computer. Using time-sharing techniques, a single computer may simultaneously serve more than 1,000 students at diverse and remote locations. Advances in time-sharing techniques, coupled with reductions in hardware costs and increasing availability of tested curriculum material, are beginning to make CAI economically attractive as a source of compensatory education. Pedagogically, the value of CAI is established by its capacity for immediate evaluation of student responses and detailed individualization of treatment based on accurate and rapid retrieval of performance histories.

A number of institutions in the United States have computer-assisted programs under way in varying scales of complexity. Zinn (1970) and Lekan (1971) have provided overviews of these efforts. Stanford University's Institute for Mathematical Studies in the Social Sciences (IMSSS) has been engaged in such development efforts for over ten years and now operates one of the largest CAI centers in the country. This paper discusses the Institute's efforts to use CAI to provide compensatory education for disadvantaged students. Before turning to these efforts, however, it is worthwhile to place our work in the context of the large national effort in compensatory education that has been financed, primarily, by Title I of the Elementary and Secondary Education Act of 1965.

For a number of years the federal government has spent about one billion dollars annually to provide compensatory education for disadvantaged children in the United States. Unfortunately, much of the available evidence suggests that these federally funded Title I programs have met with little success. During the period 1966–68 Piccariello (1969) conducted a large-scale evaluation of Title I reading programs and, in more than two instances out of three, found no significant achievement differences between children in control groups and children in one of the Title I programs. Further, only slightly more than half of the significant differences obtained were in a positive direction. In his widely discussed paper on IQ and scholastic achievement, Jensen (1969) surveyed a large number of studies indicating a general failure of compensatory education.

Rather than studying the typical compensatory education program, Kiesling (1971) undertook a study of those compensatory education programs that had been most successful in the State of California. Kiesling concluded that there were a number of common elements in all these successful programs, and that one could learn from their success and replicate them. Thus, while compensatory education may have been, on the average, unsuccessful in the past, Kiesling concluded that there is no reason to repeat these failures. Success could be achieved by tailoring future compensatory programs around those that have previously proven themselves. Kiesling presented a number of paradigmatic compensatory programs for both arithmetic and reading and estimated their annual cost per student to be on the order of $200 to $300 per year in addition to the normal school allotment for that student.

A different interpretation from Kiesling's of the failure of compensatory education is that what goes on in schools has little effect on the achievement of students. This view received considerable support from Coleman, Campbell, Hobson, McPartland, Mood, Weinfeld, and York (1966), and is consistent with the views of Jensen (1969). Coleman et al. concluded that factors within the schools seem to affect achievement much less than do factors outside the schools; these somewhat disheartening conclusions have been the source of vigorous debate since their initial publication. A number of recent view interpreting the data of the Coleman Report may be found in Mood (1970). The general drift of the papers in this book is that schooling is rather more important than one would conclude from the initial Coleman Report; nevertheless, there is an increasing consensus, since publication of the report, that input factors in the schooling process seem to have a good deal less effect on the outputs than had been thought previously (see Jamison, Suppes, and Wells, 1973).

Our own work, however, has led to more hopeful conclusions concerning the potential capability of the schools to affect scholastic performance. We have found strong and consistent achievement gains by disadvantaged students when they are given CAI over a reasonable fraction of a school year. Thus we are more inclined to accept Kiesling's general conclusions that compensatory education can work than the less hopeful interpretations of the Coleman Report. As Bowles and Levin (1968) pointed out: "The findings of the Report are particularly inappropriate for assessing the likely effects of radical changes in the level and compositions of resources devoted to schooling, because the range of variation in most school inputs in this sample is much more limited than the range of policy measures currently under discussion." Our evaluations of CAI provide detailed information about the output effects of a much broader variety of school inputs than the Coleman Report was able to consider.

This paper reports on the performance of three CAI programs that have performed well with underachieving children. Section II of the paper describes those programs—one in elementary arithmetic, one in initial reading, and one in computer programming for high school students. Section III reports on an evaluation of the performance of these programs. We considered two aspects of performance: achievement gain and the degree to which the program enabled disadvantaged students to close the gap between themselves and more advanced students. In order to examine this latter distributional effect, we relied in part on Gini coefficients derived from Lorenz curve representations of achievement data. We also examined the results in the light of several alternative mathematical formulations of "inequality-aversion." Section IV of the paper provides a discussion of costs. In particular, we examined the problem of making computer-assisted instruction available in rural as well as urban areas and attempted a realistic assessment of those costs. Our cost projections were for systems having about 1,000 student terminals; this number of terminals would allow 20,000 to 30,000 students to use the system per day. We computed not only dollar costs but also opportunity costs for using CAI in order to estimate the increase in student-to-teacher ratios that would be required if CAI were introduced under the constraint that expenditures per student should remain constant.

II. DESCRIPTION OF THREE PROGRAMS

A. Arithmetic

Development of elementary-school mathematics (grades 1 through 6) CAI was begun by the Institute in 1965. The intent of the program is to provide practice in arithmetic skills, especially computation, as an essential supplement to regular classroom instruction. Concepts presented by the CAI program are assumed to have been previously introduced to the students by their classroom teacher.

In the version of the mathematics curriculum discussed in this report, curriculum material for each of the six elementary-school grades was arranged sequentially in 20–27 concept blocks that corresponded in order and content to the mathematical concepts presented in several textbook series surveyed during the development of the curriculum. Each concept block consisted of a pretest, five drills divided into five levels of difficulty, and a posttest. The pre- and posttests were comprised of equal numbers of items drawn from each of the five difficulty levels in the drills. Each block contained approximately seven days of activity, one day each for the pre- and posttests and five days for the five drills. As part of each day's drill, a student also received review items drawn from previously completed concept blocks. Review material comprised about a third of a day's drill.

The level of difficulty for the first drill within a block was determined by a student's pretest performance for the block. The level of difficulty for each successive day's drill was determined by the student's performance during the preceding day. If a student's performance on a drill was 80 per cent or more correct, his next drill was one level of difficulty higher; if his performance on a drill was 60 per cent or less correct, his next drill was one level of difficulty lower.

The drill content, then, was the same for all students in a class, with only the difficulty levels varying from student to student. The content of the review material, however, was uniquely determined for each student on the basis of his total past-performance history. His response history was scanned to determine the previously completed concept block for which his posttest score was lowest, and review exercises were drawn from this block. Material from the review block was included in the first four drills for the current block, and a posttest for the review block was given during the fifth drill. The score on this review posttest replaced the previous posttest score for the review block and determined subsequent review material for the student.

Student terminals for the arithmetic curriculum were Model-33 teletypewriters without the random audio capability required for the reading program. These teletypewriters were located at school sites and were connected by telephone lines to the Institute's central computer facility at Stanford University. Students completed a concept block about every one and one-half weeks. This version of the arithmetic curriculum is described extensively in a number of publications including Suppes and Morningstar (1969) and Suppes, Jerman, and Brian (1968).

A more highly individualized mathematics strand program in arithmetic has been developed over the past several years and has replaced the program just described. Performance data in this paper are for the earlier program; a description of the more recent program was given by Suppes and Morningstar (1970).

B. Reading

CAI in initial reading (grades K–3) has been under development by IMSSS since 1965. The original intent of the reading program was to implement a complete CAI curriculum using cathode-ray tubes (CRT), light pen and typewriter input, slides, and random access audio. These efforts, described in Atkinson (1968), were successful but prohibitively expensive. Economically and pedagogically, some aspects of initial reading seemed better left to the classroom teacher. Subsequent efforts of the reading project were directed toward the development of a CAI reading curriculum that would supplement, but not replace, classroom reading instruction.

The current reading curriculum requires only the least expensive of teletypewriters and some form of randomly accessible audio. No graphic or photographic capabilities are needed and only uppercase letters are used. Despite these limitations, an early evaluation of the curriculum indicated that it is of significant value (Fletcher and Atkinson, 1972).

The version of the reading curriculum used in this report, more fully described by Atkinson and Fletcher (1972), emphasized phonics instruction. There were two primary reasons for this emphasis. First, it enabled the curriculum to be based on a relatively well-defined aspect of reading theory, making it more amenable to computer presentation. Second, the phonics emphasis on the regular grapheme-phoneme correspondences (or spelling patterns) which occur across all English orthography insured that the program appropriately supplemented classroom instruction using any initial reading vocabulary.

Instruction was divided into seven content areas or strands: O—machine readiness; I—letter identification; II—sight-word vocabulary; III—spelling patterns; IV—phonics; V—comprehension categories; and VI—comprehension sentences.

The term strand in the reading program defined a basic component skill of initial reading. Students in the reading program moved through each strand in a roughly linear fashion. Branching or progress within strands was criterion dependent; a student proceeded to a new exercise within a strand only after he had attained some (individually specifiable) performance criterion in his current exercise. Branching between the strands was time dependent; a student moved from one strand to take up where he left off in another after a certain (again, individually specifiable) amount of time, regardless of what criterion levels he had reached in the strands. Within each strand there were two to three progressively more difficult exercises that were designed to bring students to fairly high levels of performance. This criterion procedure was explained in more detail by Atkinson and Fletcher (1972).

Entry into each strand was dependent upon a student's performance in earlier strands. For example, the letter-identification strand started with a subset of letters used in the earliest sight words. When a student in the letter-identification strand exhibited mastery over the set of letters used in the first words of the sight-word strand, he entered that strand. Initial entry into both the phonics and spelling pattern strands was controlled by the student's placement in the sight-word strand. Once he entered a strand, however, his advancement within it was independent of his progress in other strands. On any given day, a student's lesson might draw exercises from one to five different strands.

Most students spent two minutes in each strand and the length of their daily sessions was ten minutes. A student could be stopped at any point in an exercise, either by the maximum-time rule for the strand or by the session time limit; however, sufficient information was saved in his history record to assure continuation from precisely the same point in the exercise when he next encountered that strand.

C. Computer Programming

Development of computer-assisted instruction in computer programming was begun by the Institute in 1968 and was initially made available to students at an inner-city high school in February, 1969. Requisite knowledge of computer languages and systems varies greatly among applications, and for this reason, general concepts of computer operations rather than knowledge of the specific languages or systems used were emphasized in the curriculum. To achieve this generality, the curriculum ranged from problems in assembly-language coding to symbol manipulation and test-processing. The three major components of the curriculum were SIMPER (Simple Instruction Machine for the Purpose of Educational Research), SLOGO (Stanford LOGO), and BASIC. Associated with each component were interpreters, utility routines, and curriculum material.

Basically, computers understand only binary numbers. These numbers may be either data or executable instructions. A fundamental form of programming is to write code as a series of mnemonics, which bear a one-to-one relationship to the binary number-instructions executable by a computer; this type of coding is called assembly-language programming. The instructions of higher order languages, such as BASIC and SLOGO, do not bear a one-to-one relationship to the instructions executed by a computer and, therefore, obscure the fundamental operations performed during program execution. The intent of SIMPER was to make available to students using teletypewriters a small computer that could be programmed in a simple assembly language. The SIMPER computer was, of course, mythical, since giving beginning students such sensitive access to an actual time-sharing computer would be both prohibitively expensive and potentially disastrous.

As simulated, SIMPER was a two-register, fixed-point, single-address machine with a variable size memory. There were sixteen operations in its instruction set. To program SIMPER, a student typed the pseudo operation "LOC" to tell SIMPER where in its memory to begin program execution, and then entered the assembly-language code that comprised his solution to an assigned problem. During execution of the student's program, SIMPER typed the effect of each instruction on its memory and registers. In this way, students received special insight into how each instruction operated and how a series of computer instructions is converted into meaningful work.

SLOGO, the Institute's implementation of LOGO, was the second major component of the curriculum. LOGO is a symbol manipulation and string-processing language developed by a major computer utilities company expressly for teaching the principles of computer programming. It is suitable for manipulating data in the form of character strings, as well as for performing arithmetic functions, and its most powerful feature is its capacity for recursive functions. It was thought that the computer applications most characteristic of the employment available to these students would be the inventory control problems that arise in filing and stock-room management, and it was these problems that were stressed in the SLOGO component of the curriculum. Students were taught not only the SLOGO languages, but the data structures needed for applications such as tree searches and string editing.

SIMPER and SLOGO were more fully documented by Lorton and Slimick (1969). They were written for the Institute's PDP-10 computer and made available to students in the spring and fall of 1969. Mixed with the usual, well-documented enthusiasm of all students for CAI was some disappointment among the computer programming students that they were not learning a computer language generally found in industry. For this reason, the ubiquitous BASIC programming language was prepared for the Institute's PDP-10 computer and made available to the students in the spring of 1970.

The BASIC course, as the SIMPER and SLOGO courses before it, was designed to permit maximum student control. Most of this control concerned the use of such optional material as detailed review, overview lessons, and self-tests. Students were aware that they would be graded only on homework and tests, and it was emphasized that their course grades would not include wrong answers made in the BASIC teaching program.

The course consisted of 50 lessons, each comprising 20 to 100 problems and each requiring one to two hours to complete. The lessons were organized into blocks of five. Each lesson was followed by a review printout and each block of five lessons was followed by a self-test and overview lesson. Students received review printouts, self-tests and overview lessons at their option. Each block was terminated by a short graded test that was evaluated partly by computer and partly by the supervising teacher.

Students were given as much time as needed to answer each problem. Since the curriculum emphasized tutorial instruction rather than drill material, students could spend several minutes thinking or calculating before entering a response; hence, there was no time limit. Because the subject matter of the course was a formal language which was necessarily unambiguous to a computer, extensive analysis of students' responses was possible and highly individualized remediation could be provided for wrong, partially wrong, or inefficient solutions to assigned problems. Significantly, individual errors and misconceptions could be corrected by additional instruction and explanation without incorporating unnecessary exposition in the mainstream of the lesson.

III. PERFORMANCE

We conceive compensatory education to have two broad purposes with respect to student achievement. The first is, of course, to increase the student's achievement level over what it would have been without compensatory education. We discuss achievement gains in III.A. The second purpose of compensatory education is to decrease the spread among students or to make the distribution of educational output more nearly equitable. The notion of equality in education has received considerable attention in recent years, and we made no attempt to review that literature here; Coleman (1968) provided a useful overview of some of the issues. Michelson (1970) discussed inequality in real inputs in producing achievement, and in a later paper (Michelson, 1971) discussed inequality in financial inputs. Our treatment differs in focusing on output inequality and, methodologically, in utilizing tools recently developed by economists for analyzing distribution of income. Section III.B discusses our results in this area.

A. Achievement Gain

Gains in Arithmetic

During the 1967–68 school year, approximately 1,000 students in California, 1,100 students in Kentucky, and 600 students in Mississippi participated in the arithmetic drill-and-practice program. Sufficient data were collected to permit CAI and non-CAI group comparisons for both the California and Mississippi students. The California students were drawn from upper-middle-class schools in suburban areas quite uncharacteristic of those for which compensatory education is usually intended. The Mississippi students, on the other hand, were drawn from an economically and culturally deprived rural area and provided an excellent example of the value of CAI as compensatory education.

The Mississippi students (grades 2 through 6) were given appropriate forms of the Stanford Achievement Test (SAT) in October, 1967. The SAT was administered to the Mississippi first-grade students in February, 1968. All the Mississippi students (grades 1 through 6) were posttested with the SAT in May, 1968. Twelve different schools were used; eight of these included both CAI and non-CAI students, three included only CAI students, and one included only non-CAI students. Within the CAI group, 1 to 10 classes were tested at each grade level, and within the non-CAI group, 2 to 6 classes were tested at each grade level. Achievement gains over the school year were measured by the differences between pre- and posttest grade placements, estimated by the SAT computation subscale. Average pretest and posttest grade placements, calculated differences of these averages, t values for these differences, and degrees of freedom for each grade's CAI and non-CAI students are presented in Table III-1. Significant t values ($p < .01$) are starred. The performance of the CAI students improved significantly more over the school year than that of the non-CAI students in all but one of the six grades. The largest differences between CAI and non-CAI students occurred in grade 1 where, in only three months, the average increase in grade placement for CAI students was 1.14, compared with .26 for the non-CAI students.

On other subscales of the SAT, the performance of CAI students, measured by improvement in grade placement, was significantly better than that of the non-CAI students on the SAT concepts subscale for grade 3 [$t(76) = 3.01$, $p < .01$], and for grade 6 [$t(433) = 3.74$, $p < .01$], and on the SAT application subscale for grade 6 ($t(433) = 4.09$, $p < .01$). In grade 4, the non-CAI students improved more than the experimental group on the concepts subscale [$t(131) = 2.25$, $p < .05$].

Appropriate forms of the SAT were administered to all the California students (grades 1 through 6) in October, 1967, and again in May, 1968. Seven different schools were used. Two of the schools included both CAI and non-CAI students, two included only CAI students, and three included only non-CAI students. Within the CAI group, 5 to 9 classes were tested at each grade level, and within the non-CAI group, 6 to 14 classes were tested at each grade level. Average pretest and posttest grade placements on the SAT computation subscale, calculated differences of these averages, t values for these differences, and degrees of freedom for each grade's CAI and non-CAI students are presented in Table III-2. As in Table III-1, significant t values ($p < .01$) are starred. The performance of the CAI students improved significantly more over the school year than that of the non-CAI students in grades 2, 3, and 5.

TABLE III-1 Average Grade-Placement Scores on the Stanford Achievement Test: Mississippi 1967–68[a]

Grade	Pretest		Posttest		Posttest–Pretest			Degrees of Freedom
	Experimental	Control	Experimental	Control	Experimental	Control	t	
1	1.41 (52)*	1.19 (63)	2.55	1.45	1.13	0.26	9.63**	113
2	1.99 (25)	1.96 (54)	3.37	2.80	1.38	0.84	4.85**	77
3	2.82 (22)	2.76 (56)	4.85	4.04	2.03	1.26	4.87**	76
4	2.34 (56)	2.45 (77)	3.36	3.14	1.02	0.69	2.28	131
5	3.09 (83)	3.71 (134)	4.46	4.60	1.37	0.89	3.65**	215
6	4.82 (275)	4.35 (160)	6.54	5.49	1.72	1.13	4.89**	433

* Values in parentheses are numbers of students.

** $p < .01$.

[a] The assumptions underlying this test of significance are, first, that the two distributions compared are distributed normally and, second, that their variances are equal. Robustness of the t test is discussed by Boneau (1960) and Elashoff (1968) among others.

TABLE III-2 Average Grade-Placement Scores on the Stanford Achievement Test: California 1967–68[a]

Grade	Pretest Experimental	Pretest Control	Posttest Experimental	Posttest Control	Posttest–Pretest Experimental	Posttest–Pretest Control	t	Degrees of Freedom
1	1.39 (58)*	1.31 (259)	2.62	2.51	1.23	1.21	0.20	315
2	2.06 (65)	2.16 (238)	3.20	2.89	1.14	0.73	4.96**	301
3	3.00 (136)	2.85 (210)	4.60	3.86	1.60	1.02	6.70**	344
4	3.40 (103)	3.49 (185)	4.87	5.00	1.46	1.51	−0.41	286
5	4.98 (149)	4.44 (90)	6.41	5.31	1.43	0.88	4.06**	237
6	5.42 (154)	5.70 (247)	7.43	7.59	2.01	1.90	0.84	399

* Values in parentheses are numbers of students.
** p < .01.
[a] The assumptions underlying this test of significance are, first, that the two distributions compared are distributed normally and, second, that their variances are equal Robustness of the t test is discussed by Boneau (1960) and Elashoff (1968) among others.

On other subscales of the SAT, the CAI students improved significantly more over the school year than did the non-CAI students on the concepts subscale for grade 3 [$t(344) = 4.13, p < .01$] and on the application subscale for grade 6 [$t(399) = 2.14, p < .05$].

A comparison of the California students with the Mississippi students suggests at least two observations worth noting. First, when significant effects were examined for all six grades, the CAI program was more effective for the Mississippi students than for the California students. Second, changes in performance level for the CAI groups were quite similar in both states, but the non-CAI group changes were very small in Mississippi relative to the non-CAI group changes in California. These observations suggest that CAI may be more effective when students perform well below grade level and are in need of compensatory education, as in the rural Mississippi schools, than when the students receive an adequate education, as in the suburban California schools.

These data do not fully reflect the breadth of educational experience permitted by CAI. Some of the Mississippi students took the Institute's beginning course in mathematical logic and algebra, which had been prepared for bright fourth- to eighth-grade students whose teachers were not prepared to teach this advanced material. At the end of the 1967–68 school year, two Mississippi Negro boys placed at the top of the first-year mathematical logic students, almost all of whom came from upper-middle-class suburban schools.

Gains in Reading

The reading data used in this report were also discussed by Fletcher and Atkinson (1972). In November of the school year, 25 pairs of first-grade boys and 25 pairs of first-grade girls were matched on the basis of the Metropolitan Readiness Test (MET). Matching was achieved so that the MET scores for a matched pair of subjects were no more than two points apart. Moreover, an effort was made to insure that both members of a matched pair had classroom teachers of roughly equivalent ability.

The experimental member of each matched pair of students received eight to ten minutes of CAI instruction per school day roughly from the first week in January until the second week in June. The control member of each pair received no CAI instruction. Except for the eight- to ten-minute CAI period, there is no reason to believe that the activities during the school day were any different for the experimental and control subjects.

Four schools within the same school district were used. Two schools provided the CAI students and two different schools provided the non-CAI subjects. The schools were in an economically depressed area eligible for federal compensatory education funds.

Three posttests were administered to all subjects in late May and early June. Four subtests of the Stanford Achievement Test (SAT), Primary I, Form X, were used: word reading (S/WR), paragraph meaning (S/PM), vocabulary (S/VOC), and word study (S/WS). Second, the California Cooperative Primary Reading Test (COOP), Form 12A (grade 1, spring) was administered. Third, a test (DF) developed at Stanford and tailored to the goals of the CAI reading curriculum was administered individually to all subjects.

During the course of the school year, an equal number of pairs was lost from the female and male groups; complete data were obtained for 22 pairs of boys and 22 pairs of girls.

Means and t values for differences in SAT, COOP, and DF total scores are presented in Table III-3. In this table t values are displayed in brackets. The t values calculated are for nonindependent samples, and those that are significant ($p < .01$, one-tailed) are starred.

The results of these analyses were encouraging. All three indicated a significant difference in favor of the CAI reading subjects. These differences were also important from the standpoint of improvement in estimated grade placement. Table III-4 displays the mean grade placement of the two groups on the SAT and COOP.

Means and t values for the differences on the four SAT subtests are presented in Table III-5. As in Table III-3, t values are displayed in brackets; t values that are significant ($p < .01$, one-tailed) are starred.

These SAT subtests revealed some interesting results. Of the four SAT subtests, the S/WS was expected to reflect most clearly the goals of the CAI curriculum; yet greater differences between CAI and non-CAI groups were obtained for both the S/WR and S/PM subtests. Also notable was the lack of any real differences for the S/VOC. One explanation for this result is that the vocabulary subtest measures a pupil's

TABLE III-3   Means and t Values[a] for the Stanford Achievement Test (SAT), the California Cooperative Primary Test (COOP), and the CAI Reading Project Test (DF)[b]

	SAT	COOP	Degrees of Freedom
CAI	112.7	33.4	64.5
	[4.22*]	[4.04*]	[6.46*]
Non-CAI	93.3	26.2	54.8

* $p < .01$, df = 43.
[a] t values are shown in brackets.
[b] The assumptions underlying this test of significance are, first, that the two distributions compared are distributed normally and, second, that their variances are equal. Robustness of the t test is discussed by Boneau (1960) and Elashoff (1968) among others.

TABLE III-4 Average Grade Placement on the Stanford Achievement Test (SAT) and the California Cooperative Primary Test (COOP)

	SAT	COOP
CAI	2.3	2.6
Non-CAI	1.9	2.1

vocabulary independent of his reading skill (Kelley et al., 1964); since the CAI reading curriculum was primarily concerned with reading skill and only incidentally with vocabulary growth, there may have been no reason to expect a discernible effect of the CAI curriculum on the S/VOC. Most notable, however, were the S/PM results. The CAI students performed significantly better on paragraph items than did the non-CAI students, despite the absence of paragraph items in the CAI program and the relative dearth of sentence items. These results for phonics-oriented programs are not unprecedented, as Chall's (1967, pp. 106–107) survey shows. Nonetheless, for a program with so little emphasis on connected discourse, they were surprising.

The effect of CAI on the progress of boys compared with the progress of girls is interesting. The Atkinson (1968) finding that boys benefit more from CAI instruction than do girls was corroborated by these data. On the SAT the relative improvement for boys exposed to CAI versus those not exposed to CAI was 22 per cent; the corresponding figure for girls was 20 per cent. On the COOP the percentage improvement due to CAI was 42 for boys and 17 for girls. Finally, on the DF the improvement was 32 per cent for boys and 13 per cent for girls. Overall, these data suggested that both boys and girls benefit from CAI instruction in

TABLE III-5 Means and t Values[a] for the Word Reading (S/WR), Paragraph Meaning (S/PM), Vocabulary (S/VOC), and Word Study (S/WS) Subtests of the Stanford Achievement Test[b]

	S/WR	S/PM	S/VOC	S/WS
CAI	26.5	23.0	21.6	41.6
	[5.18*]	[4.17*]	[.35]	[3.78*]
Non-CAI	20.1	16.3	21.2	35.7

*p < .01, df = 43.
[a] t values are shown in brackets.
[b] The assumptions underlying this test of significance are, first, that the two distributions compared are distributed normally and, second, that their variances are equal. Robustness of the t test is discussed by Boneau (1960) and Elashoff (1968) among others.

reading, but that CAI is relatively more effective for boys. Explanations of this difference were discussed by Atkinson (1968).

Achievement Gains in the Computer Programming Course

Eight weeks prior to the end of the 1969–70 school year, students who received CAI instruction in BASIC were given the SAT's mathematical computation and application sections. A control group of students from the same school was given the same test. At semester's end, the test was repeated and the following additional data were gathered: (i) verbal achievement scores from the ninth-grade-level test of the Equality of Educational Opportunity Survey, and (ii) responses to the socioeconomic status questionnaire of the EEO survey.

Sufficient pre- and posttest scores were obtained for 39 CAI students and 19 non-CAI students. Average pre- and posttest scores for the SAT computation and application subscales, average gains, and t values for differences in the average gains achieved by CAI and non-CAI students are presented in Table III-6.

The SAT tests were used here in the absence of a standardized achievement test in computer programming; gains in arithmetic achievement were, then, only a proxy for gains in the skills taught in the course. Presumably, students gained in arithmetic skill because they spent more than the usual time working on quantitative problems.

There was also a good deal of textual output at the teletype that the students needed to read and comprehend, and it was the unanimous impression of the teachers who worked with the students that they were better able to read as a result. However, scores on verbal achievement tests administered at the end of the school year showed virtually no differences between the CAI and control groups in reading ability.

In order to identify some of the sources of achievement gain, we ran a

TABLE III-6   Arithmetic Achievement for Computer Programming Course[a]

| | CAI | | | Control | | | | Degrees of |
	Pre	Post	Gain	Pre	Post	Gain	t	Freedom
SAT computation	7.97	9.11	1.14	7.97	8.41	.44	1.68	55
SAT application	7.74	8.61	.86	8.33	8.38	.05	1.73	55

[a] The assumptions underlying this test of significance are, first, that the two distributions compared are distributed normally and, second, that their variances are equal. Robustness of the t test is discussed by Boneau (1960) and Elashoff (1968) among others.

stepwise linear regression of gain scores (posttest minus pretest) against pretest scores, verbal scores, and various items from the socioeconomic status (SES) questionnaire. The dependent variable was the sum of the gain scores on the computation and applications sections of the test. Table III-7 below lists the independent variables and the coefficients estimated for them.

The results in the table are self-explanatory, but we make two comments in conclusion. First, even though the regression coefficient on CAI was not significant at standard levels, in magnitude it was substantial; failure to have had CAI during this eight-week interval would remove about .5 years (one-half of .99) of arithmetic achievement. Naturally, it would be desirable to replace the 0–1 CAI variable with actual amount of time on the system; the regression coefficient would then have a good deal more practical value. Second, the mathematics pretest had a negative coefficient; when CAI and control regressions

TABLE III-7 Determinants of Achievement Gain[a,b]

Independent Variable	Mean	Standard Deviation	Regression Coefficient	Standard Error
Constant term			4.40	
CAI {0 CAI group / 1 control group}	.35	.48	−.99	.96
Sum of pretest scores on computation and application	15.3	4.22	−.26	.14
Raw score on verbal test	27.6	9.9	.17	.06
Age in years	15.9	2.5	−.23	.20
Race {0 Caucasian / 1 Other}	.23	.42	−1.44	1.18
Number of people living in child's home	5.63	1.86	.13	.29
Total years of schooling of both parents	15.5	10.52	−.02	.05
Educational aspiration of student, in years of schooling	15.4	4.45	.07	.11
Previous math grade placement achievement of student	2.40	1.30	−.11	.39

[a] Dependent variable is the sum of students' gain scores on arithmetic and computation sections of SAT.
[b] $R^2 = .26$.

were run separately, this coefficient was negative for CAI and positive for control. This result implies that CAI in sufficient quantity would have an equalizing effect, a point to be further discussed in the next subsection. We plan, in a later paper, to analyze in more detail the interaction of CAI and student background characteristics as determinants of scholastic achievement (Wells, Whelchel, and Jamison, 1973).

B. Reduction in Inequality

Our second criterion of performance concerned the extent to which CAI is inequality reducing. Clearly, any compensatory program that has positive achievement gain, if applied only to those sectors of the population who perform least well, will have a tendency to reduce inequality. Often, however, entire schools receive the compensatory education and it is less likely that the program is inequality reducing. Our purpose in this subsection was to use techniques developed for analyzing inequality in the distribution of income to provide concrete measures of the extent to which CAI is inequality reducing. These measures are as applicable when an entire student population receives the compensatory treatment as when only some subset of the population does.

We first used a traditional measure of inequality—the Gini coefficient based on the Lorenz curve—to examine before and after inequality in CAI and control groups and to examine inequality in achievement gains. Use of the Gini coefficient as a measure of inequality has, however, a number of shortcomings that were reviewed by A. Atkinson (1970). Prominent among these is that it is not purely an empirical measure but contains an underlying value judgment concerning what constitutes more inequality. Newbery (1970) showed that it is impossible to make this value judgment explicit by means of any additive utility function. Therefore, we also used the inequality measure proposed by A. Atkinson that makes explicit the underlying value judgments.

Use of either the Atkinson measure or Gini coefficients implies that achievement test scores should be measured on a ratio scale (i.e. the achievement measure must be unique up to multiplication by a positive constant). If, for example, achievement measures were only unique up to a positive linear transformation, the Gini coefficient could be made arbitrarily small by adding an arbitrarily large amount to each individual's achievement test score. The reader is cautioned that our assumption that achievement is measured on a ratio scale is quite strong; on the other hand, a ratio scale is implicit in the assumption that one test score is better than another if—and only if—the number of problems correct on the one test is greater than the number correct on the other.

Inequality Measured by the Gini Coefficient

Consider a group of students who have taken an achievement test; each student will have achieved some score on the test, and there will be a total score obtained by summing all the individual scores. We may ask, for example, what fraction of the total score was obtained by the 10 per cent of students doing most poorly on the test, what fraction was obtained by the 20 per cent of students doing most poorly, and so on. The Lorenz curve plots fraction of total score earned by the bottom x per cent of students as a function of x.

These concepts may be expressed more formally in the notation of Levine and Singer (1970) as follows. Let $N(u)$ be the achievement-score density function. The $N(u)du$ represents the number of individuals scoring between u and $u + du$. The total number of students, N, and their average score, A, are given by

$$N = \int_0^\infty N(u)du$$

and

$$A = \frac{1}{N} \int_0^\infty uN(u)du$$

The fraction of students scoring a or less is given by

$$f(a) = \frac{1}{N} \int_0^a N(u)du$$

and the fraction of the total score obtained by students scoring a or less is

$$g(a) = \frac{\int_0^a uN(u)du}{NA}$$

The Lorenz curve plots $g(a)$ as a function of $f(a)$, and a typical Lorenz curve for our results is shown in Figure III-1 below. The $f(a)$, $g(a)$ pairs are obtained by computing these functions for all values of a. If there were a perfectly equitable distribution of achievement (everyone having identical achievement) the Lorenz curve would be the 45° line depicted in Figure III-1. The more $g(a)$ differs from the 45° line the more inequitable is the distribution of achievement. The Gini coefficient is an aggregate measure of inequality that is defined as the ratio of the area between $g(a)$ and the 45° line to the area between the 45° line and the abscissa. If the Gini coefficient is zero, the distribution of achievement is completely uniform; the larger the Gini coefficient, the more unequal the distribution.

In order to examine the extent to which the different CAI programs described in Section II of this paper were in fact inequality reducing, we

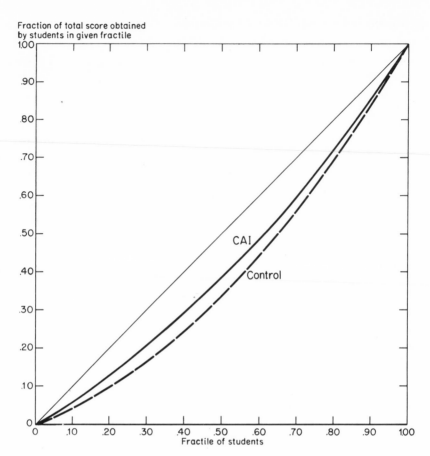

Fraction of total score obtained
by students in given fractile

CAI

Control

Fractile of students

FIGURE III-1 Typical Lorenz Curves: Distribution of Reading
Posttest Achievement (COOP)

computed Gini coefficients for the distribution of achievement before
and after the CAI was made available for both the CAI and the control
groups. In Table III-8 these Gini coefficients are presented for both the
high school level computer programming course and the elementary
arithmetic course in Mississippi and California grades 1 through 6. For
each group at each grade level, we give the Gini coefficients for the
pretest for the group as a whole, the Gini coefficients for the posttest for
the group as a whole, and the difference between those two Gini
coefficients. Similar information is given for the control group. In the
final column of the table the difference between columns 3 and 6 of the
table is shown; if this difference is positive, it indicates that there is
more of a reduction in inequality in the CAI group than in the control

TABLE III-8 Gini Coefficients for CAI and Control Groups

Group	CAI Pre (1)	Post (2)	Pre-Post (3)	Control Pre (4)	Post (5)	Pre-Post (6)	Col. (3) Minus Col. (6)
Computer Programming							
SAT COMP R.S. [a]	.113	.087	.026	.108	.096	.012	.014
SAT APPL R.S. [b]	.119	.111	.008	.084	.097	−.013	.021
SAT COMP G.P. [c]	.079	.066	.013	.075	.070	.005	.008
SAT APPL G.P. [d]	.080	.079	.001	.059	.069	−.010	.011
Math Drill [e] and Practice							
Mississippi 1967–68							
Grade 1	.057	.067	−.010	.037	.062	−.025	.015
Grade 2	.064	.039	.025	.055	.050	.005	.020
Grade 3	.016	.032	−.016	.035	.038	−.003	−.013
Grade 4	.080	.053	.027	.084	.065	.019	.008
Grade 5	.095	.070	.025	.078	.079	−.001	.026
Grade 6	.068	.077	−.009	.078	.084	−.006	−.003
California 1967–68							
Grade 1	.058	.077	−.019	.054	.075	−.021	.002
Grade 2	.075	.056	.019	.073	.062	.011	.008
Grade 3	.042	.063	−.021	.050	.060	−.010	−.011
Grade 4	.067	.053	.014	.065	.058	.007	.007
Grade 5	.056	.048	.008	.055	.068	−.013	.021
Grade 6	.077	.073	.004	.065	.070	−.005	.009

[a] Gini coefficients from Stanford Achievement Test, computations subscale, raw scores.
[b] Gini coefficients from Stanford Achievement Test, application subscale, raw scores.
[c] Gini coefficients from Stanford Achievement Test, computation subscale, grade placements.
[d] Gini coefficients from Stanford Achievement Test, application subscale, grade placements.
[e] Gini coefficients for all math drill and practice from Stanford Achievement Test, computation subscale, grade placements.

group. For the high school CAI group we computed the Gini coefficients for both raw scores and grade placement scores and the differences between those two computations can be seen in the table. We applied a sign test to the 12 arithmetic cases and the two computer programming cases that used grade placement scores to test the significance of the hypothesis that inequality was reduced more in the CAI groups than in the control groups. From column 7 of Table III-8 it can be seen that in only 3 of the 14 cases was the CAI less inequality-reducing than no CAI. The sign test then implied an acceptance of the hypothesis that CAI is inequality reducing at the .05 level.

In Table III-9 we show the Gini coefficients for CAI and control

TABLE III-9 Gini Coefficients for Reading Achievement Posttests[a]

	CAI	Control	Control − CAI
SAT	.134	.174	.040
COOP	.183	.266	.083
DF	.068	.152	.084
S/WR [1]	.140	.209	.069
S/PM [2]	.226	.396	.170
S/WS [3]	.119	.149	.030
S/VOC [4]	.170	.183	.013

[a] Due to careful matching of CAI and control groups by pretest achievement (on the Metropolitan Readiness Test—see Section III.A), pretest Gini coefficients are not shown.

groups for the various sections of the reading achievement posttests. We did not include the pretest scores since different tests were used and the results were not directly comparable. In all 7 cases in Table III-9 the Gini coefficient was less for the CAI group than for the control group; the hypothesis that CAI is inequality reducing was substantiated in this case at the .01 level. The widely held subjective impression that no students in the reading CAI groups are "lost" seems, then, to be strongly supported by these data. It is reasonable to expect that the effect of CAI on posttests would correlate positively with the Gini coefficient differences obtained from the CAI and non-CAI subjects. The difference in Gini coefficients should be greatest where the CAI treatment is greatest and this seems to be the case. The effect of CAI was statistically significant on the S/WR, S/PM and S/WS, and for these subtests the Gini coefficient differences were fairly large. There was only a slight positive effect of CAI in the S/VOC, and the Gini coefficient differences for this subtest were correspondingly small.

Value Explicit Measures of Inequality

In this section we consider a measure of inequality proposed by A. Atkinson (1970) that makes explicit the value judgment entering into the comparison of the inequality of two distributions. Atkinson drew, in his discussion of greater and lesser inequality, on a close parallel between the concept of greater risk (or greater spread) in a probability distribution and the concept of greater inequality in a distribution of income. He was thus able to apply certain results concerning the ordering by riskiness of probability distributions to ordering by degree of inequality of income distributions. He showed that a variety of conventional measures of inequality—including variance, coefficient of variation, relative mean deviation, Gini coefficient, and standard deviation of logarithms—are necessarily consistent with the ordering implied by concave utility functions. That is, one can, in general, find a concave utility function that is consistent with the ordering induced by any of the above measures.

Atkinson then proposed that the overall utility, W, of a distribution of achievement scores, $N(u)$, be represented by the following formula

$$W = \int_0^{\overline{u}} U(u)\, N(u)\, du$$

when $\overline{u}$ is the maximum score achieved on the test. It is assumed in the above that $U(u)$ is increasing and concave, i.e., that $U'(u)$ is greater than 0 and that $U''(u)$ is less than 0.[1] The concavity implies, for that particular population, that there is an aversion to inequality. Given this aversion to inequality there exists a level of achievement, u_e, that is *lower* than the average level of achievement in the population under consideration such that if everyone in the population had exactly a u_e level of achievement, the overall level of social welfare would remain constant at W. Following Atkinson, we call u_e the "equally distributed equivalent" level of achievement. Clearly, u_e, in general, depends on the form of U; however, by direct analogy with the theory of choice under uncertainty, u_e is invariant with respect to positive linear transformations of U.

If μ is the average level of achievement in the society, then a reasonable measure of inequality, I, is given by the following formula

$$I = 1 - \frac{u_e}{\mu}$$

The lower I is, the more equal is the distribution of achievement; to put this another way, as u_e gets closer to μ, the cost of having inequality gets lower. The I ranges between 0 for complete equality and 1 for complete inequality and tells us, in effect, by what percentage total achievement could be reduced to obtain the same level of W if the achievement level were equally distributed.

In order to apply the measure I we need an explicit formulation of U. In this paper we consider two classes of functions U. The first of these was suggested by Atkinson and has the property of "constant relative inequality aversion." Constant relative inequality aversion means that multiplying all achievement levels in the distributions by a positive constant does not alter the measure I of inequality. If there is constant relative inequality aversion, it is known from the theory of risk aversion that $U(u)$ must have the following form

$$U(u) = a + B\, \frac{u^{1-\epsilon}}{1-\epsilon} \text{ if } \epsilon \neq 1$$

and

$$U(u) = ln(u) \text{ if } \epsilon = 1$$

Another possibility that Atkinson considered was that of constant *absolute* inequality aversion, which means that adding a constant to each achievement level in the distribution does not affect the measure of inequality. A theorem of Pfanzagl (1959) shows that if there is constant absolute inequality aversion, then $U(u)$ must have one of the following two forms

$$U(u) = au + b$$

or

$$U(u) = a\lambda^u + b$$

Strict concavity implies the latter of these two and that $0 < \lambda < 1$.

We thus have two families of utility functions, one indexed by ϵ and the other by λ, which include a large number of qualitatively important alternatives for U. In Figure III-2, $U(u)$ is shown for several values of ϵ and in Figure III-3 $U(u)$ is shown for several values of λ. Since transforming the functions depicted in Figures III-2 and III-3 by a positive linear transformation does not affect the measure I, the height and location of the functions in those two figures is arbitrary.

It is clear from the preceding, that the measure I of inequality for any fixed distribution of achievement varies with ϵ or λ. In Figure III-3 we have constrained $U(u)$ to pass through 0 and 1 for all values of λ, implying that $U(u) = (1 - \lambda^u)/(1 - \lambda)$. For λ very close to 1, inequality is close to 0; as λ gets smaller, inequality gets larger for any fixed distribution. The way in which I varies with ϵ is just the opposite; low values of ϵ give a low measure of inequality, whereas large values of ϵ give large values for I.

Figures III-4 and III-5 illustrate I plotted as a function of ϵ and as a function of λ for one particular CAI group and its control. The distributions $N(u)$ are of posttest scores and they are for a case where there was little difference in inequality on the pretest, as measured by the Gini coefficients of the CAI and control groups.

One benefit in having a measure of inequality indexed by some parameter describing degree of inequality aversion (such as λ or ϵ) is that the control group may be judged to be more equal for some values of λ and ϵ but less equal for others. Table III-10 shows such reversals as a function of ϵ under the assumption of constant relative inequality aversion. Table III-11 shows the same information as a function of λ.

We have attempted to provide explicit measures of the extent to which the three CAI programs we reviewed are inequality-reducing. We used recent work on measurement of inequality that has appeared in the economics literature to show that, ultimately, measurement of inequality rests on either an implicit or explicit value judgment. We showed measures of inequality for CAI and control groups for several explicit

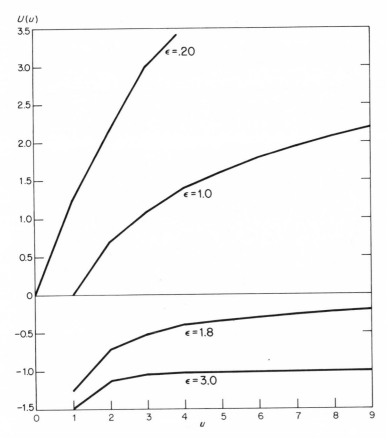

FIGURE III-2 $U(u)$ for Several Values of ϵ

classes of value judgments concerning distribution of achievement. It is perhaps worth stressing that as we were actually designing and implementing our CAI programs, we did not have inequality-reduction in mind as an explicit goal; our results, literally, just turned out this way.

The next step to take at this point, we feel, is to design patterns of CAI presentation that are optimal by some utility function U maximized to a variety of constraints. One constraint could be the distribution of prior achievement in the population to which we are providing CAI; another constraint could be the total number of terminal hours per month available to that population; still another constraint could be possible impositions from the school administration that no students get less than a certain amount of CAI or more than a certain amount of CAI per day on an average; and a final fundamental constraint could be the production function that relates time on the system and other factors to gains in

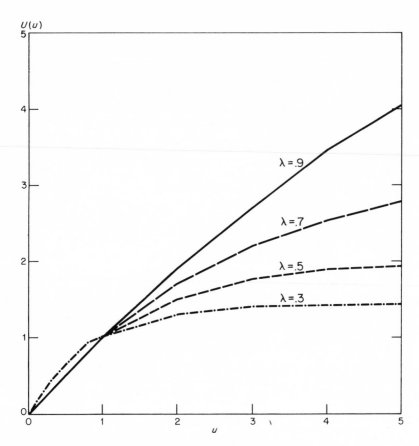

FIGURE III-3 *U(u)* for Several Values of λ

student achievement. What we plan to examine in the future is how the solution to this optimization problem varies with *U* when the constraints vary. We can then design patterns of instruction that are explicitly tailored to several separate *U*'s and empirically examine the extent to which we obtain the stated objectives. We hope that in this fashion any tradeoffs that might exist between total achievement gain and inequality-reduction can be made explicit both in terms of the underlying technology and the underlying value structure.

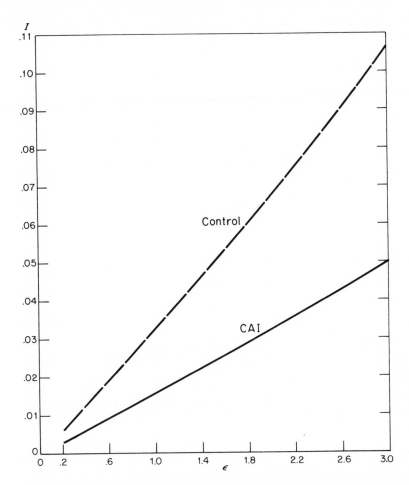

FIGURE III-4 *I* as a Function of ϵ for Fifth-Grade Arithmetic,
California, 1967–68

IV. COST OF COMPUTER-ASSISTED
INSTRUCTION

A. General Considerations

It is useful to place CAI costs into three broad categories. The first category comprises the terminal equipment used by the students. Terminals vary in complexity from a simple touch-tone pad used for telephones to a CRT with keyboard, light pen, audio, and random-access slide screen, and costs vary accordingly. The second cost category com-

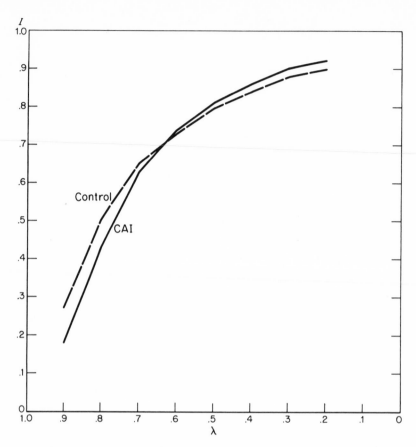

FIGURE III-5 *I* as a Function of λ for Fifth-Grade Arithmetic, California, 1967–68

prises the computer system that decides on and stores instructional presentations and evaluates student responses. This category includes the central processing unit, disc and core storage, high-speed line units, and peripheral equipment. The final cost component is the multiplexing and communication system that links the student terminals to the main computer system. This communication system can be reasonably simple when the terminals are located within a few hundred feet of the compu-ter. If the terminals are dispersed, the communication system may include a communication satellite as well as one or more small comput-ers that assemble and disassemble signals.

Up to this point we have mentioned only the cost components neces-sary to *provide* CAI and have assumed that the curriculum to be used has already been programmed. Only the cost of provision is considered

TABLE III-10 CAI Inequality Reduction: Constant Relative Inequality Aversion[a]

Student Group (Math Drill and Practice)	ϵ							
	.20	.60	1.0	1.4	1.8	2.2	2.6	3.0
Mississippi 1967–68								
Grade 1	.001	.002	.004	.005	.006	.007	.007	.007
Grade 2	.004	.012	.020	.030	.041	.054	.068	.084
Grade 3	−.002	−.005	−.008	−.012	−.015	−.019	−.024	−.029
Grade 4	.002	.005	.009	.014	.020	.028	.038	.050
Grade 5	.005	.012	.019	.023	.026	.027	.025	.022
Grade 6	.000	−.002	−.003	−.004	−.006	−.007	−.009	−.010
California 1967–68								
Grade 1	.000	.000	.000	.000	.000	.001	.002	.002
Grade 2	.002	.004	.007	.009	.011	.014	.016	.019
Grade 3	−.002	−.006	−.010	−.015	−.021	−.027	−.035	−.045
Grade 4	.004	.001	.001	.000	−.003	−.007	−.013	−.022
Grade 5	.003	.010	.017	.025	.034	.042	.052	.062
Grade 6	.002	.006	.010	.015	.022	.030	.039	.051

[a] The numbers shown in the table are $I_A - I_B$ as a function of ϵ. I_A is the difference in inequality between CAI and control after treatment (i.e., on the posttest) and I_B is the difference before treatment. If the difference is greater after treatment than before, CAI is inequality-reducing.

TABLE III-11 CAI Inequality Reduction: Constant Absolute Inequality Aversion[a]

Student Group (Math Drill and Practice)	λ							
	.90	.80	.70	.60	.50	.40	.30	.20
Mississippi 1967–68								
Grade 1	−.001	−.005	−.009	−.011	−.013	−.005	.011	.030
Grade 2	.010	.041	.090	.127	.146	.148	.139	.120
Grade 3	−.131	−.180	−.237	−.297	−.331	−.331	−.300	−.246
Grade 4	−.013	.016	.050	.054	.044	.033	.024	.017
Grade 5	.048	.006	−.010	−.007	.000	.004	.009	.016
Grade 6	−.083	−.108	−.098	−.078	−.060	−.046	−.037	−.030
California 1967–68								
Grade 1	.032	.069	.086	.086	.081	.078	.077	.076
Grade 2	−.018	−.038	−.041	−.031	−.020	−.012	−.006	.001
Grade 3	−.078	−.116	−.158	−.173	−.160	−.246	−.118	−.096
Grade 4	.050	.044	.012	−.010	−.024	−.031	−.033	−.036
Grade 5	.092	.071	.021	.002	−.004	−.004	−.005	−.006
Grade 6	−.020	.045	.045	.038	.034	.031	.029	.027

[a] The numbers shown in the table are $I_A - I_B$ as a function of λ. I_A is the difference in inequality between CAI and control after treatment (i.e., on the posttest) and I_B is the difference before treatment. If the difference is greater after treatment than before, CAI is inequality-reducing.

here. Of course, unless ways are found to share a single curriculum among many users, the per student cost of curriculum preparation can be prohibitively high. Levien (1972) discussed how to provide incentives and how to recoup costs for CAI curriculum preparation. Since a reasonably large body of tested curriculums already exists, we consider those costs sunk and do not include them here.

There appear to be two trends in design philosophy for the computer component of a CAI system. One trend is toward large, highly flexible systems capable of simultaneously providing curriculums in many subjects to a large number of simultaneous users. The other trend is toward small, special-purpose computer systems capable of providing only one or two curriculums to a few students. A large, general-purpose computer system might have 1,000 or more student terminals simultaneously in use. The proposed PLATO IV system of the University of Illinois is now aiming for about 500–3,000 fewer than originally planned (Stifle, 1972); the small special-purpose system is likely to have 8 to 32 terminals. Naturally, the number of terminals per computer has important implications for the communication system. In order to make a large system worthwhile, an extensive communication system is almost inevitable. On the other hand, even a moderate-sized elementary school could use a 16-terminal system, and only simple communications would be required. The potential scale economies of a large computer system, its broader range of offerings, and its easy updating must be balanced, then, against the lower communication costs of special-purpose systems.

Jamison, Suppes, and Butler (1970) examined the cost of providing CAI in urban areas by way of a small special-purpose computer system, the first of which is now in operation. Rather than review those costs here, we refer the reader to that paper. Costs per student per year are approximately $50 above the normal cost of educating the child, assuming that the school system in no way attempts to reduce other costs (for example, by increasing the student-teacher ratio) as a result of introducing CAI.

B. Cost of Providing CAI in Rural Areas

The most distinctive aspect of providing CAI in rural areas is that the students to be reached are highly dispersed and thus tend to be reasonably distant from a central computer. One could use small computers for rural areas at costs somewhat higher than Jamison et al. estimated for urban areas. To obtain the advantages of a large central system, however, the communication system must be sophisticated. In this section, we examine the cost of providing large-scale CAI in rural areas. To obtain per student annual-cost figures we examine each of the three cost areas mentioned above and then combine them to give the final figures. Our costs were based on the CAI system at IMSSS, using the curriculum already available; other systems could have different costs.

Terminal Costs

The cost of a Model-33 teletypewriter, including modifications, is about $850. To provide the teletypewriter terminal with a computer-controlled audio cassette would increase the cost about $150, but since this is not operational now, the additional $150 was not included in our estimates. An alternative would be to lease the teletypewriters. That cost is about $37 per teletypewriter per month and includes maintenance.

Computer Facility Costs

Cost estimates are provided for a system capable of running about 1,000 students at a time. The system would be run at "4/5 diversity," i.e., 1,250 terminals would be attached to the system under the assumption that no more than 4/5 of the 1,250 would run at any one time. The assumption of 4/5 diversity is conservative, given our past experience.

The system would comprise two PDP-10 computers, each with a 300 million 8-bit byte disc, 512K 36-bit words of core memory, a swapping drum, and appropriate I/O and interfacing devices. The system would essentially be a doubled 500-terminal system; if, however, appreciably more terminals were desired, other designs would be appropriate.

Table IV-1 shows the initial costs of the system and Table IV-2 shows annual costs. Overhead is *not* included.

In order to express all costs as annual costs, we multiplied the $3,260,000 by .15, assuming about a ten-year equipment lifetime and 10 per cent social discount rate. Thus, the annual cost of the initial equip-

TABLE IV-1 Initial Costs, Computer Components of CAI System[a]

Component	Cost
Computer system	$2,560
Spare parts and test equipment	200
Planning and installation	350
Building	150
Total	$3,260

[a] Costs in thousands of dollars.

TABLE IV-2 Annual Costs, Computer Components of CAI System[a]

Component	Annual Cost
System operation	$150
System maintenance	175
Building maintenance	20
Supplies	35
Total	$380

[a] Costs in thousands of dollars.

ment purchase is $490,000. When added to the direct annual costs, the total is $870,000 per year. With 1,250 terminals, the central facility cost is $690 per terminal per year.

Communication Costs

In an unpublished paper, Jamison, Ball, and Potter (1971) examined in some detail the cost of communication between a central computer facility and rural terminals.[2] They considered two types of systems—one using commercial phone services and one using a single transponder on a communication satellite. Costs of communicating by satellite are independent of distance whereas phone costs are distance-dependent. Thus, for longer distances, satellites are increasingly attractive. Figures IV-1 and IV-2, taken from Jamison, Ball, and Potter, show the annual cost of communication and multiplexing for satellite and terrestrial systems. Both assume that the terminals are clustered in groups of eight. The graphs assume "best estimate" satellite and phone-service costs in 1975 and eight-year equipment lifetime with 10 per cent cost of capital. They also include maintenance and system installation but do not include overhead.

The present engineering cost estimates for G, the satellite ground-station cost, is $10,000, but this is the estimate for a feasible, not optimal system—we expect much engineering improvement. Thus, Figure IV-1 shows that the annual communication cost for a satellite distribution system would be about $800,000. From Figure IV-2 we see that if D, the average distance between the central computer facility and the terminals, exceeds about 550 miles, then communication via satellite is cheaper than via telephone.[3] Since the average distance to the terminals is quite likely to exceed 550 miles, $800,000 is our estimate of communication and multiplexing cost. This comes to $640 per terminal per year.

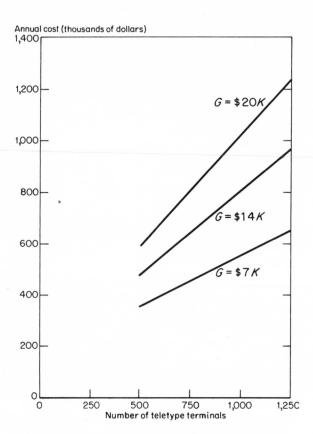

Annual cost (thousands of dollars)

FIGURE IV-1   Annual Communication and
Multiplexing Cost, Satellite
System

Per Student Costs

To obtain the annual cost of the terminal we multiplied its purchase price ($850) by .15 to obtain $130 and added 10 per cent of its purchase price to cover maintenance. The total is $215 per year. Teacher training must also be included and is typically a one-week course given at the school at a cost of about $500, plus transportation, per person. Continuing our assumption of eight terminals per school, and assuming that the course will be repeated for at least four years and that transportation costs average $300 per session, the per terminal annual charge of teacher training is $25. A final cost to be considered is that of the terminal room proctor. Much of this cost can be covered by volunteers and inexpensive help and would cost not more than $2,000 per school year or $250 per

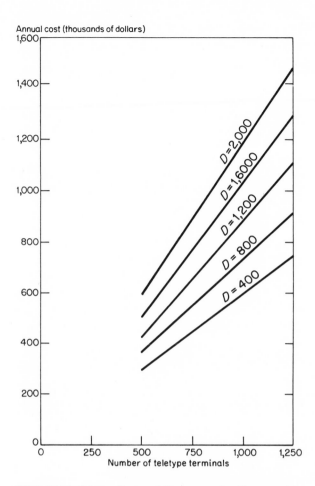

Annual cost (thousands of dollars)

Number of teletype terminals

FIGURE IV-2 Annual Communication and Multiplexing Cost, Commercial Telephone System

terminal per year. We assume space available in the schools due to a declining rural population.

Table IV-3 shows the annual costs per terminal. A utilization rate of twenty-five students per terminal per day is typical with this sort of system, so that the cost per student per year would be on the order of $75. Overhead costs might increase this to as much as $125. If the number of terminals per school were increased from eight to ten, there would be no increase in communication and multiplexing, teacher train-

235 | Dean T. Jamison

TABLE IV-3 Annual Cost in 1975 of Rural CAI per Terminal

Item	Cost
Teletype terminal	$ 215
Computer facility cost	690
Communication and multiplexing	640
Teacher training	25
Proctoring	250
Supplies and miscellaneous	25
Total	$1,845

ing, or proctoring costs, so our estimates are conservative in that respect.

Kiesling's (1971) estimates for conventional compensatory education at about the quality provided by CAI were $200 to $300 per student per year in urban and suburban areas. It would presumably be more expensive to provide this quality of compensatory education to rural areas, and salary inflation would also increase his estimates. We thus feel that CAI is a low-cost alternative for providing compensatory education to rural areas.

A possible pattern of development for rural compensatory education is to begin with satellite or long-line communications to a large central system, and then, after a cadre of experienced personnel has been trained, to convert to less expensive special-purpose systems located in the area.

C. Opportunity Cost of CAI

In the preceding discussion of cost we estimated ceteris paribus costs of adding CAI to the school curriculum. We indicated that the add-on costs of CAI are sufficiently less than those of alternative compensatory education programs so that, if additional funds were available for compensatory education, CAI appears an attractive alternative. If add-on funds are unavailable—and this is common in the present financial environment—then CAI can be introduced only at the cost of providing less of some other school resource to the students. The amount of the other resources foregone represents, then, the opportunity cost of providing CAI to the school. As teacher costs constitute by far the largest component—on the order of 70 per cent—of school costs, our purpose in this section is to examine what must be given up in terms of teacher resources in order to provide CAI for students.

The amount of teacher time required per child per year depends on average class size, average number of days per school year, and average number of class hours per school day. We assumed that length of school day and length of school year are less flexible than average class size, and examined only the effect on class size of introducing CAI. The other two variables could, however, be introduced into the analysis in a straightforward way.

Let the "instructional" cost per year for a class be the cost of its teacher's salary plus the cost of whatever CAI the class receives. Let S be the class size before CAI is introduced, T be the teacher's annual salary, and C be the cost per student per year of CAI, including all costs previously indicated in Table IV-3. We wish to compute A, the number of additional students in the class that are required to finance the CAI. With no CAI, the annual instructional cost for the class is T; with CAI, the cost is $T + C(S + A)$. We require that the per student cost with CAI be no greater than the cost without it, that is

$$\frac{T}{S} = \frac{T + C(S + A)}{S + A}.$$

Solving this equation for A we obtain

$$A = CS^2/T - CS)$$

The partial derivatives of A with respect to T, C, and S are also of interest, and those are given below

$$\frac{\partial A}{\partial C} = TS^2/(T - CS)^2$$

$$\frac{\partial A}{\partial S} = CS(2T - CS)/(T - CS)^2$$

and

$$\frac{\partial A}{\partial T} = -CS^2/(T - CS)^2$$

Table IV-4 below shows A, $\partial A/\partial S$, $\partial A/\partial C$, and $\partial A/\partial T$ for $C = \$50$ (urban) and \$75 (rural) under the assumptions that $T = \$11,000$ and $S = 26$.

A number of interesting points emerge from the table. First, even if $C = \$75$, the student-to-teacher ratio only goes from 26 to 31.6 in order to provide CAI. If the Coleman Report is correct in concluding that student performance is insensitive to student-to-teacher ratio, this would seem to be an attractive reallocation to the extent that it can be made politically feasible.[4] Second, from the values for $\partial A/\partial C$ we see that a \$10 increase in C would require about a .8 increase in A if C is \$75. Third, from the value of $\partial A/\partial S$ we see that an increase of 1 in S causes

TABLE IV-4   Increment in Class Size Required to Finance CAI

Variable	Expression[a]	Cost of CAI per Student per Year	
		$50	$75
A	$CS^2/(T - CS)$	3.5	5.6
$\partial A/\partial C$	$TS^2/(T - CS)^2$	.079	.091
$\partial A/\partial S$	$CS(2T - CS)/(T - CS)^2$	.286	.477
$\partial A/\partial T$	$-CS^2/(T - CS)^2$	-.00036	-.00062

[a] S is initial class size and it is assumed to be 26; T is annual teacher salary and it is assumed to be $11,000; C is cost per student per year of CAI, and A is the increment in class size required to finance CAI if there are to be no increases in per student annual costs.

an increase of .286 in A if C = $50 but an increase of .477 if C = $75. Finally, the last row in the table shows that a $1,000 annual increase in teacher salary would decrease A by about .36 if C is $50; it decreases A by almost twice that amount if C is $75. In general, the partial derivatives in the table seem quite sensitive to C.

We conclude this section by observing that the cost of CAI seems to have decreased sufficiently to make CAI quite attractive compared to alternative compensatory techniques with roughly similar performance. This holds whether one considers CAI as an add-on cost or as a substitute for teacher time.

NOTES

1. Sen (1972) criticized the restrictiveness of the additive functional form that Atkinson assumed for determining W. Sen provided a definition of inequality similar to Atkinson's based on a more general functional form. However, the practical usability of the additive form remains a strong argument in its favor.
2. Ball and Jamison (1973) presented updated and more detailed cost estimates for all aspects of a CAI system designed to serve rural populations; their cost estimates differ only a little from the more preliminary ones used here.
3. A further, and very important, advantage of using satellites is that it eliminates the necessity of working with poorly equipped rural telephone services. IMSSS has experienced many delays and unexpected costs as a result of working with such services in Kentucky and elsewhere.
4. Jamison, Suppes, and Wells (1974) reviewed additional evidence that indicates student performance to be insensitive to the student-to-teacher ratio; their review summarized the literature on the effectiveness of various educational technologies as well as various forms of conventional instruction.

REFERENCES

Atkinson, A. B. "On the Measurement of Inequality." *Journal of Economic Theory* 2 (1970): 221–224.

Atkinson, R. C. "Computerized Instruction and the Learning Process." *American Psychologist* 23 (1968): 225–239.

Atkinson, R. C., and Fletcher, J. D. "Teaching Children to Read with a Computer." *Reading Teacher* 25 (1972): 319–327.

Ball, J., and Jamison, D. "Computer-Assisted Instruction for Dispersed Populations: System Cost Models." *Instructional Science* 1 (1973): 469–501.

Boneau, C. A. "The Effects of Violations of Assumptions Underlying the *t*-Test." *Psychological Bulletin* 57 (1960): 49–64.

Bowles, S., and Levin, H. "The Determinants of Scholastic Achievement: An Appraisal of Some Recent Evidence." *Journal of Human Resources* 3 (1968): 3–24.

Chall, J. *Learning to Read: The Great Debate.* New York: McGraw-Hill, 1967.

Coleman, J. *The Evaluation of Equality of Educational Opportunity.* P-3911. Santa Monica, Calif.: Rand Corporation, 1968.

Coleman, J. S.; Campbell, E. Q.; Hobson, C. J.; McPartland, J.; Mood, A. M.; Weinfeld, F. D.; and York, R. L. *Equality of Educational Opportunity.* Washington, D.C.: U.S. Office of Education, 1966.

Elashoff, R. M. "Effects of Errors in Statistical Assumptions." *International Encyclopedia of the Social Sciences.* New York: Macmillan, 1968, Vol. 5, pp. 132–142.

Fletcher, J. D., and Atkinson, R. C. "An Evaluation of the Stanford CAI Program in Initial Reading (Grades K through 3)." *Journal of Educational Psychology* 63 (1972): 597–602.

Jamison, D.; Ball, J.; and Potter, J. "Communication Economics of Computer-Assisted Instruction for Rural Areas: Satellite vs. Commercial Phone Systems." Presented at the 22nd International Astronautical Congress of the International Astronautical Federation, Brussels, September, 1971.

Jamison, D.; Suppes, P.; and Butler, C. "Estimated Costs of Computer-Assisted Instruction for Compensatory Education in Urban Areas." *Educational Technology* 10 (1970): 49–57.

Jamison, D.; Suppes, P.; and Wells, S. "The Effectiveness of Alternative Instructional Media: A Survey." *Review of Educational Research* 44 (1974): 1–67.

Jensen, A. "How Much Can We Boost I.Q. and Scholastic Achievement?" *Harvard Educational Review* 39 (1969):1–123.

Kelley, T. L.; Madden, R.; Gardner, E. G.; and Rudman, H. C. *Stanford Achievement Test: Directions for Administering.* New York: Harcourt Brace Jovanovich, 1964.

Kiesling, H. *Input and Output in California Compensatory Education Projects.* R-781-CC/RL. Santa Monica, Calif.: Rand Corporation, 1971.

Lekan, H. A., ed. *Index to Computer-Assisted Instruction.* 3rd ed. New York: Harcourt Brace Jovanovich, 1971.

Levien, R. *The Emerging Technology: Instructional Uses of the Computer in Higher Education.* New York: McGraw-Hill, 1972.

Levine, D. B., and Singer, N. M. "The Mathematical Relation between the Income Density Function and the Measurement of Income Inequality." *Econometrica* 38 (1970): 324–330.

Lorton, P., and Slimick, J. "Computer-Based Instruction in Computer Programming—a Symbol Manipulation–List Processing Approach." *Proceedings of the American Federation of Information Processing Societies 1969 Fall Joint Computer Conference* 33 (1969): 535–543.

Michelson, S. "The Data: Equal Protection and School Resources." *Inequality in Education* 2 (1970): 4–16.

——. "The Political Economy of Public School Inequalities." In M. Carnoy, ed., *The Political Economy of Education: New Approaches to Old Problems*, forthcoming.

Mood, A., ed. *Do teachers make a difference?* Washington, D.C.: GPO, 1970.

Newbery, D. "A Theorem on the Measurement of Inequality." *Journal of Economic Theory* 2 (1970): 264–266.

Pfanzagl, J. "A General Theory of Measurement—Applications to Utility." *Naval Research Logistics Quarterly* 6 (1959): 283–294. Reprinted in R. Luce, R. Bush, and E. Galanter, eds., *Readings in Mathematical Psychology*, Vol. II. New York: John Wiley, 1965.

Piccariello, H. "Evaluation of Title I." Unpublished paper, 1969.

Sen, A. "On Economic Inequality." The Radcliffe Lectures at Warwick University, draft, 1972.

Stifle, J. *The PLATO IV Architecture.* Technical Report No. X-20, May, 1972. University of Illinois-Urbana, Computer-Based Education Research Laboratory.

Suppes, P., and Morningstar, M. "Computer-Assisted Instruction." *Science* 166 (1969): 343–350.

——. "Technological Innovations: Computer-Assisted Instruction and Compensatory Education." In F. Korten, S. Cook, and J. Lacey, eds., *Psychology and the Problem of Society.* Washington, D.C.: American Psychological Association, 1970.

Suppes, P.; Jerman, M.; and Brian, D. *Computer-Assisted Instruction: The 1965–66 Stanford Arithmetic Program.* New York: Academic Press, 1968.

Wells, S.; Whelchel, B.; and Jamison, D. "The Impact of Varying Levels of Computer-Assisted Instruction on the Academic Performance of Disadvantaged Students." Technical Report, Stanford University, Institute for Mathematical Studies in the Social Sciences, 1973.

Zinn, K. L. *An Evaluative Review of Uses of Computers in Instruction.* Final Report, U.S.O.E. Contract No.: OEC-5-9-32-509-0032, December, 1970, University of Michigan, Center for Research on Learning and Teaching.

5 | COMMENTS

Allen C. Kelley

Duke University

For more than a decade Patrick Suppes and his associates at Stanford have been pioneering the application of computer technology to elementary and high school education. Their imaginative and ambitious projects have included basic research in learning theory, the formulation and evaluation of programmed-instruction techniques, and the development of computer and communications systems for disseminating programmed materials. Thousands of students across the United States have been "plugged into" the Stanford CAI facility; moreover, recent advances in satellite communications technology have greatly expanded the geographic dispersion of their instructional programs. Based on the extensive data resulting from these applications, it has been demonstrated that CAI and programmed instruction are effective, under selected circumstances, in increasing student achievement; furthermore, CAI is technologically feasible in a wide range of educational settings. However, resources are scarce. Technological feasibility is only one of the conditions necessary for the utilization of CAI; this technique must also be shown to be economically efficient. The present paper by Jamison, Fletcher, Suppes, and Atkinson represents one of several recent studies which examines the economic viability of CAI.

The paper before us presents a benefit-cost analysis of CAI in three subject-matter areas—arithmetic, reading, and computer programming—with particular attention to the role of CAI in compensatory education. Several notable conclusions are reached:

1. The CAI programs have both a statistically significant and quantitatively large impact on increases in student achievement.
2. The program's benefits appear greatest at relatively low achievement levels.
3. CAI tends to narrow the inequality in the distribution of educational outputs.
4. CAI is economically efficient in selected settings, e.g., compensatory education in rural schools.

Given the high failure rate of the compensatory-education programs in the United States, the CAI system reported in the present paper might be considered as a striking success story. Not only are extremely impressive gains in student achievement shown to result from the CAI format—about a 50 per cent increase in output, but these impressive benefits are obtained at only 30 per cent of the cost of even the most successful of the currently operational programs. It sounds too good to be true; unfortunately, it probably is.

For several reasons, we must be somewhat cautious in accepting without qualification the conclusions of this study. Consider first the results showing a positive impact of CAI on student achievement. The critical question in interpreting this result relates to identifying what the experiment measures; that is, what the control group represents. In the arithmetic and reading programs, students in the control and experimental groups obtained basic instruction in concepts, application, and drill from their regular classroom teachers. In addition, those in the experimental group participated in a CAI curriculum, which, in arithmetic, emphasized drill; and which, in reading, focused on phonics. The CAI curricula were a supplement to the regular classroom arithmetic and reading programs. The impact of the CAI programs, then, must be considered *relative* to the activities of the control group during the period when the experimental students were engaged in CAI. The net value of the output of CAI is thus the difference between the *value* of the

CAI output and the output obtained by students in the control group when the experiment was taking place. To the extent that the value of the control group's time was positive, then the statistical results are an overstatement of the impact of CAI on the economic value of the student's total instruction. Indeed, it is possible that if the quantity or price of the forgone output was high enough, the statistically significant positive CAI impact could be translated into a decrease in the economic value of educational output. I realize that designing and implementing an experiment which takes into account the opportunity cost of the experimental group's time is difficult. On the other hand, the benefits of this modification in experimental design could be great. For example, if an experiment were implemented where matched pairs of students were assigned to similar activities at similar times—one with CAI mathematics drill, another with nondirected mathematics drill from, say, a programmed text—we would then be in a position to interpret the economic, as distinct from only the statistical, significance of the results.

Another qualification to the results relates to the assignment of control and experimental groups. The authors report neither the assignment procedures nor do they report a test of the homogeneity of student attributes. While a random selection of control and experimental groups is not necessary, knowledge of the assignment procedures is required to interpret the results. Similarly, since their evaluation procedures do not generally take into account the impact of CAI for various types of students, it would be appropriate to examine in detail the composition of the classes involved.

From an economics point of view, the most interesting aspect of this paper relates to the distribution of the benefits of CAI. Clearly, an assessment of the economic efficiency of any public good must examine not only the output level but also its distribution. This is because the value of output will typically vary according to who receives the output. Thus, in obtaining the total value of output deriving from an educational technique, it is necessary to examine its distribution and assign or identify values for that output for alternative students. Both of these issues, seldom confronted in the education literature, are recognized by the authors. They are to be commended for stressing its importance. However, their analytical and statistical treatment of the distribution issues requires some qualification.

The main statistical model employed in this study to assess the aggregate impact of CAI is a test on the differences in the mean performance of the "typical" student in the experimental and control groups. This model, unfortunately, conceals any of the distributional effects of CAI. For example, while a positive net increase resulting from CAI was revealed, this may have been the result of positive increases for some students and negative results for others. Paradoxically, the benefits of CAI are on a priori grounds attributed to individualization of instruction, yet the statistical models employed for analyzing its impact deal with "average" or "typical" students and abstract from any differences in individual behavior. Regression or other statistical techniques where distributional effects are explicitly considered would appear to be more appropriate to the basic research question under consideration.

Unfortunately, in the single instance where a regression was run—a stepwise regression for the computing course, the theoretical model underlying the statistical exercise was misspecified. The regression assumes that the distribution of educational achievement is invariant to the use of CAI—that is, all interaction terms between CAI and student attributes are omitted. This model is not only inconsistent with learning theory and a substantial empirical literature in education, but also with the results of the authors in previous studies. While I suspect that the authors do not believe that CAI is an equally beneficial educational technique for all students, the hypotheses they test and the statistical models they employ abstract from the key distributional questions of who gets how much and why.

The primary method employed by the authors to examine the impact of CAI on output distribution is familiar to economists: Lorenz curves and Gini coefficients. However, the results are somewhat difficult to interpret. First, without a specific norm, one cannot determine what constitutes an important change in the Gini coefficients. Second, while the authors conclude that CAI is generally egalitarian in output distribution, I am uneasy about the finding that in the Mississippi arithmetic experiment, CAI *increased* the inequality of output distribution in three out of six cases. Moreover, CAI's distributional impact was negative in the very instance where it had its most dramatic positive effect on aggregate student achievement—the Mississippi first graders. Third, even though a comparison of the CAI and control groups shows that the direction of change toward egalitarianism was statistically significant, it should be underscored that this result is specific to the output measures of the study—arithmetic drill skills and phonics. But if we assume that the opportunity cost to the students engaged in CAI was nonzero, then clearly a complete assessment of the distributional impact of CAI would appropriately employ more comprehensive output measures, including those specific study areas relevant to the control group during the period of CAI instruction. Finally, and most important, Gini coefficients and the other measures of output distribution employed in this study are not particularly interesting from either an educational or a policy point of view. They obscure the nature of the relevant redistribution taking place. For example, a zero Gini coefficient difference, given the results presented in this paper, is fully consistent with a simultaneous reallocation of educational benefits from girls to boys and from high achievers to low achievers.

While I have qualms regarding the statistical and theoretical analysis underlying the authors' examination of the distributional impact of CAI, I do support their concern with this issue. Their interest in output distribution, as well as that of government officials and the general public, is based primarily on normative grounds. As an economist interested in issues of economic efficiency, however, I am uneasy about promoting CAI or any educational technique as a *means* for redistributing output. Put differently, CAI may or may not represent an efficient technique for redistributing output, even given preferences for such a redistribution. For example, to the extent that different students respond differently to alternative production techniques—a widespread empirical finding in the education literature—then the most efficient redistribution procedure may be one which uses several different production techniques and allocates resources among them so as to maximize output subject to a distributional goal. CAI used mainly for compensatory education, given the evidence provided, may in some settings be relatively efficient both in terms of total output and its distribution. On the other hand, we must stress again that distributional goals are also multidimensional. We may wish to redistribute over some student attributes but not others. Thus, the use of CAI for all students requiring compensatory education may be inefficient, even if CAI produces greater output and allocates this toward bright youngsters who have been low achievers, if at the same time CAI reallocates output from girls to boys (probably an unpopular outcome). Again, at the empirical level, this argues for a research design and statistical models which highlight differences in individual learning styles.

Finally, a temporal dimension might also be employed in assessing the efficiency of output redistribution. While an educational technique may distribute more output to low-achieving students, it is also relevant to identify whether this output so redistributed is retained. If, for example, retention rates are lower for low-achieving students, especially in areas such as recall and recognition where the CAI drill programs appear most effective, and if *retained* value-added is a primary objective in the education industry, then we must include in our distribution analysis not only normative judgments but also long-run technological possibilities.

The shortest section of this study, and of my comments, applies to the cost analysis of CAI. The authors have examined the cost per student of *providing* the CAI curriculum to the classroom, i.e., computer and communications installation, maintenance, and operation costs. Even though they focus on the rural school setting, I would suggest that their assumptions must be considered as generally providing a lower bound on CAI costs. While I shall not examine these costs in detail, I would urge the authors to examine and present a sensitivity analysis of the cost figures to alternative key assumptions. They assume, for example, that the terminals and central processing units are highly utilized, that floor space and rooms in schools devoted to CAI have no opportunity cost, that CAI curriculum-development costs should be excluded, that costs for CAI proctoring are low or zero through the use of volunteers, and that the opportunity cost of the student's time engaged in CAI is low or zero. With these assumptions they arrive at a per student cost of $75 which compares favorably with Kiesling's study showing per student costs of comparable compensatory-education programs ranging between $200 and $300. For at least two reasons, this comparison must be qualified. First, Kiesling's cost figures are more comprehensive than those applied to CAI. Second, Kiesling's cost function varies according to the amount of output produced. If, for the several reasons discussed above, we conclude that the CAI output estimates represent an upper bound on likely long-run production possibilities of this technique, then the appropriate Kiesling cost figures must be adjusted downward.

The paper concludes with an interesting discussion of the financial feasibility of CAI in compensatory education. Recognizing that schools are unlikely to increase significantly their budgets for compensatory education, the authors compute the increase in the student-teacher ratio required to implement a CAI program without any increase in the total per pupil cost of education. Using their cost figure of $75, they find that class sizes averaging 26 increase "only" 20 per cent. If overhead is included in their CAI calculations, the class-size increase would be 40 per cent. They conclude that an increase in class size would seem to be a "quite attractive reallocation" under the assumption that student performance is insensitive to the student-to-teacher ratio. The latter assumption is critical. On the one hand, the authors attribute to individualized instruction the impressive increase in arithmetic and reading skills provided by a short ten-to-twenty minute daily contact with CAI. On the other hand, they are willing to assume, on the basis of little evidence, that a reduction in individualized instruction through a 20 per cent to 40 per cent increase in class size for the remaining five and one-half hours of instruction per day will have a negligible impact on the size and distribution of educational output. If they are right that individualized instruction provided by small class sizes in the compensatory-education setting is unimportant—and this is a testable hypothesis—then we have a long way to go to explain why the brief exposure to the computer programs is able to bestow such significant achievements through individualized instruction. Short of such an explanation, and given the nagging possibility of Hawthorne effects, we must defer our conclusion that CAI is presently, or will be in the future, an economically viable production technique.

David E. Wiley

University of Chicago

The paper by Jamison, Fletcher, Suppes, and Atkinson has three major parts: one devoted to a description of the technology, the second to an evaluation of the performance of this technology, and the last, to an assessment of its costs of application. The second section is divided into two parts; one concerning differences in level of performance for computer-assisted and conventional instruction; and the other, differences in the distribution of performances.

SOME COMMENTS ON THE ASSESSMENT OF DIFFERENTIAL PERFORMANCE

1. Mathematics

The experiment was performed in two states (California and Mississippi) in all six elementary grades. In Mississippi, twelve schools were used (8, 3, 1);

while in California, 7 were used (2, 2, 3). The gain in grade equivalents for each treatment was compared for all six grades in both California and Mississippi. Because the assignment of treatments to schools was not random, and because the process of student selection for participation in CAI in a school is not clear, some care must be taken in the interpretation of the results. The assignment and selection process has seemingly produced some differences in the previous performances of the CAI and conventional groups. The use of gain scores (in grade equivalent units) was an attempt to eliminate some of these initial differences and to increase the sensitivity of the hypothesis test. The appropriate question relates to differences between the conditional distributions of final performance for various levels of initial performance. The gain score analysis assumes that the mean of the conditional distribution is a linear function of initial status and that the slope of the regression line is one. Both assumptions seem unreasonable for these data. The authors note that the gains in Mississippi were greater than those in California. They suggest that gains may be greater for CAI when pupils are below grade level. This would imply a nonlinear relation. Also, the way in which the CAI treatments allocate resources to pupils (more resources are allocated to slow learners in an attempt to achieve more equal outcomes) would presumably make the relation between initial and final performance smaller than for conventional instruction. The metric problem is also rather bothersome. It is not clear that equal amounts of instructional effort will produce equal amounts of gain in grade-equivalent units. This problem is distinct from the one mentioned above, since the treatments are not scaled in resource or effort units. Also the grade equivalents are based on typical performances of individuals in various grades and do not represent equal amounts of learning. Finally, the utility of various final performances would presumably vary, depending on the objectives of instruction. The problem of measurement error is also crucial for an appropriate treatment of this problem.

2. Reading

The reading study used matched pairs of individuals, one of whom had received CAI; and the other, conventional instruction. Since the CAI pupils came from two schools and the conventional pupils came from two different schools, if the school averages are different, the measurement errors in the initial performance levels have different biases for each member of the pair. Since the measurement errors are large for these achievement tests, large differences in school means could produce very different results when the errors in these variables are taken into account.

3. Computer Programming

The interesting thing about the results for computer programming is the discrepancy between the results based on the gain scores and those based on the regression analysis. The regression coefficient for the sum of the pretest scores in the gain analysis is $-.26$ with a standard error of $.14$, and not zero, as is assumed in the original analysis. Also the verbal score has a significant coefficient indicating that the groups differed in verbal ability initially. None of the other coefficients is significantly different from zero. This indicates that when initial differences are taken into account there is no detectable effect of CAI (coefficient is $-.99$ with a standard error of $.96$).

COMMENTS ON THE ANALYSIS OF DIFFERENCES IN THE DISTRIBUTION OF ACHIEVEMENT

There are conceptual problems in using test scores as quantities. The total number of items on a test is fixed in any application and the score is probably better viewed as equivalent to the proportion of items correct rather than a count variable. This is especially true in using standardized achievement tests, because the items are selected so that about half the respondents will select the correct alternative for each item. These characteristics make the relations among test scores nonlinear. Recent work in test theory has produced rather strong models for test scores, which indicate that transformations of raw scores are necessary to produce variables that have appropriate ratio scale properties. It would be useful to explore the invariance of the Gini coefficients and the Atkinson models with respect to these transformations. The raw test-score metric has some characteristics which might cause some problems with these procedures. If one of the groups is relatively close in average value to the ceiling of the test, the dispersion of that group must be less than that of the other group. This linkage between mean level and dispersion may often be removed by an appropriate transformation. These problems are related to, but are conceptually distinct from, problems of invariance with respect to classes of utility functions.

Some problems exist with respect to the sign tests performed in comparing the Gini coefficients for CAI and conventional instruction. In Table III-8 the two grade-placement differences for the computer programming experiment are correlated. This violates the assumptions of the sign test. Note that all differences are correlated in Table III-9.

6

**HERBERT J.
KIESLING**
Indiana University

A Study of the Relationship of Instructional Process and Program Organization to the Success of Compensatory Education Projects in California

NOTE: The research reported in this study was jointly sponsored by the Carnegie Corporation of New York and the Rand Corporation. The manuscript as it now stands benefited from the careful readings and comments of Kent Anderson, Stephen Barro, Margaret (Polly) Carpenter, Stephen Carroll, Thomas Ribich, and Burton Weisbrod. The author also wishes to express appreciation to Harvey Averch, Ted Donaldson, and Marjorie Rapp of Rand for helpful advice, and profound gratitude to the Title I managers and other California school personnel who virtually without exception granted him their full cooperation. While the school district personnel must remain anonymous, persons who assisted from the California State Division of Compensatory Education are Tom Shellhammer, Alex Law, William McCormack, and Gerald Ryder, and from the Los Angeles County Department of Compensatory Education, William Turner and Norma Wilbur.

I. INTRODUCTION

Purpose of the Study

The study described in this report has two purposes. It is intended to advance our knowledge of compensatory education, especially with respect to issues of program design as it relates to the allocation of educational resources. In addition, I would hope that the study will prove valuable as a methodological experiment. Both objectives are important. The massive effort to overcome educational handicaps due to cultural deprivations authorized by Title I of the Elementary and Secondary Education Act of 1965 is one of the more important national social innovations of recent years. The program is costly, financed at an average of more than one billion dollars annually, and it is broad, aimed at all children coming from families officially classified as "poor."[1] Sponsors and proponents of the legislation have high hopes that it will be one significant way of drawing alienated poor and minority children into the mainstream of American life.

Despite its obvious importance, the program has been extremely difficult to evaluate. In large part, this has been because of the failure to develop a research methodology whose results would be useful to the policy maker requiring broad program evaluations. Thus, it would seem almost inevitable that any study making a contribution to our knowledge of the substantive questions involved will attempt new things in the methodology of educational research as well. Such an effort is made in this study; an evaluation of its success is left to the final section of the report, and beyond that, to the reader.

Organization of the Report

Because of the methodological interests outlined above, the first section of the report includes a discussion of the place of this study in research relating to education policy. The following section deals with the steps taken to derive a model of compensatory education. It includes a description of past findings that suggest hypotheses to test, a description of the compensatory education process (which is used to generate testable hypotheses), and a discussion of the variables collected by questionnaire. A section is reserved for the findings, and the last section is devoted to a discussion of implications for further research contained in this report.

II. METHODOLOGICAL CONSIDERATIONS

General Background

In the past, there have been two fundamental approaches to policy-relevant evaluative research in education. To use descriptive terms developed by Averch et al. (2), they are the "process" and "input-output" approaches. The process approach, which characterizes most educational research of days gone by, is usually done in carefully designed experiments, often using experimental versus control-group methodology. These studies tend to have no standard method for reporting such student characteristics as socioeconomic background, attitudinal variables, and the like (beyond merely ascertaining that such characteristics are the same for both experimental and control groups). The criterion measure, or measure of performance, is whatever the researcher chooses, and there is very little consistency from study to study in terms of criterion measures, or if there is, they are usually measures which are of little direct interest to policy makers.[2]

In the input-output approach, quantifiable output measures, such as standardized objective test scores, are related to quantities of resource inputs, with some care being taken to account, at least roughly, for student differences in learning rate due to socioeconomic characteristics. This methodology overcomes the basic weaknesses of the process approach by using large samples with the same measure of output; but at the same time, it lacks the basic strength of process studies, which is the student-specific (or at least classroom-specific) nature of the analysis. The variables used have been aggregated by school buildings or school district (often for just one grade), and, further, they have not measured the personal traits of teachers or other school personnel but, instead, what Stephen Michelson has aptly termed their "objectified characteristics," years of experience, number of degrees, and the like.[3]

An important difference between the process and input-output methodological approaches is the statistical techniques they normally employ. Well-conducted process studies have traditionally compared the means of treatment and nontreatment groups for statistically significant differences. The emphasis has been upon finding that one treatment yields results that are "better than" another, without focusing greatly upon how much better the treatment group performed. Input-output studies have, on the other hand, used multiple regression techniques which, if assumptions underlying the statistical analysis are reasonably satisfied, have the important advantage of being able to trace functional relationships between one variable and another, net of the effects of other variables entered into the regression equation. This advantage makes the approach potentially a more powerful statistical tool than the analyses of variance designs used in process research, although the latter are, perhaps, somewhat superior for studying interaction effects.

III. BUILDING A MODEL OF THE COMPENSATORY EDUCATION PROCESS

The model used in this report is based upon a descriptive analysis of the compensatory education process and upon the findings of earlier studies of compensatory education programs.

Description of the Compensatory Education Process

To begin constructing a model of compensatory education, it is useful to identify meaningful input variables through detailed analysis of the process sequence. In constructing the model for the empirical analysis, therefore, the starting point was a careful consideration of the problem of educating each child, including the organization, preparation, and actions which must be undertaken by the school from beginning to end in dealing with this problem.

In general, the "problem" of education usually begins with the realization that the pupil does not possess skills and attitudes which society wishes him to have. The education process is, of course, concerned with (effectively) dealing with the "problem" of lack of knowledge. A strategy for doing this must be picked, one which includes the training of instructional personnel, the planning of instruction, and the testing of results. In most traditional American education, preparation of instructional personnel occurs at the university, while planning and testing is the function of the individual teacher, who is not supervised to any great extent.

The education problem for children who are seriously underachieving should be viewed somewhat differently from that for normal children. Instead of "normal" lack of knowledge there is an "abnormal" lack of knowledge. The fact that the lack is "abnormal" implies that there exists some special reason for it, and the discovery of such reasons (diagnosis) becomes the important first step of compensatory education. Whether done explicitly or tacitly, formally or informally, the education of underachievers must begin with successful program diagnosis. Many states, including California, realize this and require diagnosis as a part of Title I programs.

Successful diagnosis directly implies the need for proper prescription of instructional techniques which will effectively deal with the problems found in the diagnosis. The second step in the process is, therefore, prescription.

The third step in the process is to communicate the prescription for successfully overcoming the problem to instructional personnel, who, along with program managers and other decision makers, must execute the next step, which is to design and implement instructional techniques to accomplish the desired results. The final in-process step is to evaluate the success of the program. The evaluation step, especially if there is experimentation with different techniques, provides important feedback to all the other steps in the process.[4]

Although it is conceivable that a compensatory education program could get by without coordination of project members and effective leadership by the project director (e.g. in a project completely run by a reading specialist), in almost all instances observed by the author, teamwork of project personnel has been important. For example, even when the program is completely in the hands of a specialist, it appears desirable that he or she communicate periodically with the children's regular classroom teachers.

Prior Findings

The research findings of two prior studies provide useful information about which aspects of the process just described should be contained in an input-output model. One is an earlier telephone interview study, conducted by me, of projects which were described by California State Compensatory Education personnel as highly successful.[5] Project directors were asked to describe their projects and to point out features which they considered central to program success. The second study (or, more properly, set of studies) was the painstaking review of project evaluations which was undertaken by Hawkridge and a number of associates at the American Institutes for Research (16, 17, 18). These authors first described the characteristics of studies which they could pinpoint as being successful. Then they found a number of projects which were quite similar to the successful ones in terms of objectives, basic program type, and pupil age, and attempted to ascertain which program components were associated with success and which with failure.

The findings for both of the studies just mentioned are briefly summarized in Table 1. They point to well-planned individualized instruc-

TABLE 1   Factors Associated with Successful Compensatory Education Projects According to Studies by Hawkridge and Kiesling

Hawkridge
Preschool programs
1. Careful planning, including statement of objectives
2. Teacher training in the methods of the program
3. Instruction and materials closely relevant to the objectives
Elementary programs
1. Academic objectives clearly stated
2. Active parental involvement, particularly as motivators
3. Individual attention for pupils' learning problems
4. High intensity of treatment
Secondary programs
1. Academic objectives clearly stated
2. Individualization of instruction

Kiesling
1. Individualization of instruction
2. Thorough planning and program coordination
3. Thorough in-service training of teaching personnel

SOURCES: David G. Hawkridge, G. Kasten Tallmadge, and Judith K. Lansen, *Foundations for Success in Educating Disadvantaged Children*; Final Report, U.S. National Advisory Council on the Education of Disadvantaged Children (Palo Alto, Calif.: American Institutes for Research in the Behavioral Sciences, 1968), pp. 19–20.
H. J. Kiesling, "California Compensatory Education Projects"; A Draft Report on the First Part of an Economic Analysis of Compensatory Education Projects in California. Working Note. (Santa Monica, Calif.: The Rand Corporation, 1970), p. 8.

tion as the key attribute of successful programs. Good in-service training is given prominent mention as well. Hawkridge and his associates concluded that motivation by pupils' parents was also important, at least at the elementary school level. These factors become, then, the program aspects which should be traced with special care in the analysis. In the next few pages the operation of compensatory education programs is considered in somewhat more detail as an aid to deriving workable variables.

Individualized Instruction

General Characteristics[6]

For purposes of this study, instructional techniques can be divided into two types: group and individualized. In group instruction, all members of the class encounter the same set of experiences: they hear the same teacher lectures and comments by their peers, participate in the same exercises, and so forth. Students are required to learn at some minimum rate which is the same for everyone, although upward departures from the minimum are encouraged and rewarded.

When instruction is individualized, there is a relationship or interaction of the instructor directly with the individual pupils. Assignments are based on the individual needs of the student according to his ability, motivation, learning habits, previous attainments, and so forth. Sometimes pupils are given a degree of choice concerning curriculum in light of their own goals. Individualized instruction always involves individual diagnosis and testing to ascertain the pupil's problems and strengths. Sophisticated diagnosis may suggest the kind of instructional techniques which might best be used for each child or this may be ascertained in the course of instruction with experimentation. Pupil progress is evaluated continually.[7]

While individualized instruction is a complex process, this report will focus upon three key features that are central to its working. The first is the intensity of instruction, by which is meant the amount of instruction given to the pupil, the second includes the types of personnel and methods used to deliver the instruction to the pupil, and the third is the type of instructional materials used.

Instructional Intensity

It is reasonable to expect that the amount of instruction given to pupils, other things being equal, would make a difference to program success. It is necessary to account for four sources of variations in treatment in measuring intensity: (1) the number of minutes per day per child, (2) the number of instructional sessions per week the child has, (3) the number of teaching personnel working with him, and (4) the number of pupils receiving instruction.

Instructional Design

In American public schools, there is considerably more variation in the design of instruction for compensatory education than there is in that for normal education. Since design variations can be related to program quality, this makes the analysis for compensatory education considerably more interesting. Three kinds of personnel may be used: the regular classroom teacher who is released from part of her duties so she can give additional instruction to the compensatory education child; the trained specialist; and the paraprofessional, who is enlisted in support of either classroom teachers or specialists. (Paraprofessionals are instructional personnel who are given on-the-job training and who do not have the required levels of formal education normally required for certification as a classroom teacher or as a specialist.) Also, the instruction itself is given either in the regular classroom or in some separate facility, usually a resource facility that has materials and supplies which will be discussed in the next section.

Since specialists receive training in individualized instruction techniques, it would be reasonable to expect that use of such personnel would yield better results. This view is supported by Guszak (12), who concludes that the disadvantaged child is best taught language skills by a diagnostic reading teacher who understands the variety of reading skills that exist and who can tailor instruction in skills to the individual while providing him with the emotional support that makes him wish to work and to achieve. Guszak also suggests that "the rank and file of teachers do not possess systematic knowledge of their reading skills program" (12, p. 363).

In light of the many criticisms of the role of certification in teaching effectiveness that have appeared in recent years,[8] it is also of great interest to analyze the role of the paraprofessional in the instructional process.

Instructional Materials

Finally, it is likely that the type of instructional materials used will make a difference in the instructional effectiveness of individualized instruction. There is a long list of materials and equipment that are used in much greater depth for individualized instruction than in regular classroom instruction. Equipment commonly used includes recording sets with earphones, overhead projectors, films, film strips, controlled readers, and tachistoscopes. Nonmechanical teaching aids are used in even more profusion. These include word games of various kinds, flash cards, reading series, and encoding-decoding materials. In addition, most programs use considerable material made in class by the teacher or the students.

Program Management and Coordination (or "Teamwork")

It is extremely difficult in a study with a small budget to get a good idea of the quality of program management. In this study, an attempt was made to examine program management indirectly by measuring program coordination or teamwork.

There are several benefits of teamwork. It makes possible the mutual reinforcement of goals through the dovetailing of instruction. It allows greater specialization. It encourages program personnel to share information about the problems and traits of individual children. Finally, it raises program morale. If the classroom teacher has no idea of what the specialist is doing, and no effort is being made to tell her, she may become somewhat suspicious and hostile, or, at least, indifferent. This attitude is quickly observed by the program children, and instructional effectiveness is harmed. If, on the other hand, it is obvious to the pupil that his teachers are working together, each with respect for the contribution of the other, he can respond to both without confusion.[9]

It is possible to use teamwork effectively in both group and individualized instruction, but the form that the teamwork takes in the two instances is somewhat different. In group instruction, specialization is limited mostly to areas of subject matter. Two instructors can engage in dialogue before the class, for example, or one instructor can cover material within his specialty one week, another the next, and so on. In individualized instruction, specialization and teamwork can be introduced into stages of the instruction process also. One person can diagnose the child's capabilities, another can give instruction, a third can supervise and counsel the primary instructor, and still another can evaluate the child's performance.[10]

The only program design in which it is possible to bypass most requirements for teamwork (and therefore management) is that which utilizes a highly trained and experienced specialist outside the regular classroom. He or she provides expert diagnosis, prescription, and instruction. If he or she has paraprofessional aid, it is possible for him or her to supervise them without help. And finally, he or she provides all of the ongoing evaluation and would only need a good clerk to tabulate the end of the year evaluation as well. Nonetheless, considerable teamwork is still useful in this kind of program. The specialist will often need additional diagnostic help from a psychologist or counselor. Outside evaluation is always helpful. It is almost always useful to inform both the principal and the child's regular teacher about the child's progress, needs, any special situations that require attention, and so forth. Thus, while it is possible to bypass a well-coordinated effort with this type of program, there might be a very real cost in terms of effectiveness in doing so.

Other program types require more teamwork. A program where the initial instruction is done by paraprofessionals in the regular classroom, for example, will require a specialist and/or a psychologist for diagnosis-prescription, a specialist to supervise aides, and much in-service training for aides and regular classroom teachers. A separate evaluator may be required, as well as a full-time person as manager and coordinator—an individual whose talents are, of course, crucial to program success. If carefully designed, this type of program may be much less expensive than the "pure specialist" treatment described above.

There are organizational aspects to teamwork as well. Examination of formal and informal lines of authority in these programs would seem to be a most fruitful area for further research.[11] Questions to be explored would include whether the program manager has effective control over everyone in the program and whether he makes certain that the efforts of the various instructors with whom the program children come in contact are well coordinated.

Finally, there is room for teamwork in the evaluation phase of the program. With good individualized instruction day-to-day evaluation of the child's program is almost automatic. This may be done by the specialist working alone. But from the standpoint of broad policy objectives, good overall program evaluation may then be lacking.[12]

In-Service Training

In my earlier telephone interview study, I was struck by the almost unanimous way in which respondents, upon being asked which aspect of their program did they deem most essential, answered "good in-service teacher training." In-service teacher training was mentioned in the conclusions of Hawkridge and his associates somewhat less often, although a careful rereading of a set of their key projects revealed that, indeed, the concept was present in virtually all of the successful programs and either specifically mentioned as absent, or not mentioned at all, in most of the unsuccessful programs.[13] These findings suggest that in-service training is quite important.

In-service training probably has a differential effect upon instructional personnel according to their background. For example, paraprofessionals may receive a considerable amount of in-service training but may nevertheless fail to provide instruction of the caliber of that provided by trained reading specialists (who presumably need much less in-service teacher training).

IV. DATA COLLECTION

The Sample

In the 1969–70 school year there were approximately 125,000 children in over 700 California Title I projects.[14] This study is based upon a sample which represents about 6 per cent of these projects and 10 per cent of the pupils.

To insure comparability, only projects which employed the Stanford Reading Test were used. With this restriction, the sample was chosen on a stratified random basis, according to percentage of school pupils on AFDC (Aid to Families with Dependent Children), percentage black, and percentage with Spanish surnames. The sample is reasonably representative of the state in terms of pupil distribution although blacks are somewhat overrepresented and Anglos underrepresented in terms of projects.[15] The final sample includes 42 schools in 37 school districts all over California. There was a slight overrepresentation of schools in Los Angeles and Orange counties and underrepresentation of schools in extreme northern and eastern California for reasons of travel convenience. All but two of the interviews were given in person (otherwise on the telephone) and each interview took from 45 to 60 minutes.

There are two possible sources of bias in the sample. The first is due to the limitation of the Stanford Reading Test. While the Stanford was mandated by the State of California to be used in grades 2, 3, and 6 in 1969–70, only about 35 per cent of the Title I projects used it. It is widely thought to be a "difficult" test and perhaps districts which employ it have more than average self-confidence, which may be, in turn, based on actual high quality. On the other hand, the test was in fact mandated by the state, and districts which used it may be those which are efficient enough to use the same test for two chores or, perhaps, not ambitious enough to adopt what might be considered a more responsive test for the compensatory education program.

Another potential source of bias springs from the fact that only those projects that had readable reports were picked. (Every year about 15 per cent of all projects turn in reports which are not written well enough to allow meaningful interpretation.) If poor reports are the product of poor programs, there is obvious bias.

The Questionnaire

The questionnaire was based directly upon the framework for studying the compensatory education process described above. Respondents were asked to report information on percentage minority and AFDC (these items could also be cross-checked from state sources), on instruction type, what aids were used, which personnel took part in instruction, size and length of classes, and class location. These data were double-checked since respondents were also asked to give schedules for the entire day of instruction personnel. Questions were designed to show who conducted diagnosis-prescription, to whom prescriptions were communicated, which kinds of tests were used, and length of testing time. Similar questions were asked with respect to planning and in-service training. Finally, a series of questions were asked concerning lines of authority, including who decided, and who closely helped decide, on issues concerning hiring of program personnel, choosing program children, and a number of other program characteristics.

The questionnaire was pretested twice with analysis of problems and revision occurring after each pretest. It was designed to be given in person and to require only the responses of the operating manager of the school district Title I program if that person was well informed. In large school districts, however, it was necessary to interview both the building program manager and the district program manager. In numerous other instances, as well, information was obtained from others besides the primary respondent.[16]

The questionnaire is reproduced in its entirety in (26), pp. 37–47.

V. VARIABLE CONSTRUCTION

The Performance Measure

California compensatory education projects are required to submit performance data once yearly to the Division of Compensatory Education, including information concerning program objectives, instruments used, number of project participants by grade, project length, and frequency distributions of scores at the beginning and end of the treatment period. They are also asked to provide median pre- and posttest scores and the gain in grade equivalent by grade.

As mentioned above, some 35 per cent of all the projects which submitted reports to the state used the Stanford Reading Test. This made it possible to use the gains in standard grade scores on the Stanford test for the performance measure. Since the reports also include information concerning the specific objectives of these programs, it was possible to choose the sample only from schools which put as their major objective the raising of reading scores on standardized reading tests. This made it possible to overcome to some extent one of the comparability problems which has been noted in the literature, that of studying programs with different objectives (see McDill et al., [26]).

Two performance measures were used, ending score and gain in score per month of program duration (both in grade equivalents). The latter measure was used as an effort to consider separately from program length the possibility that learning does not occur evenly over the length of the program, while the former measure was used because the use of gain scores has been criticized in the educational psychology literature. The measures were used for pupils pooled over grades 2, 3, 4, and 5, and for grade 3 alone, as that grade was the only one in which there were enough observations for meaningful analysis.

To keep this section from becoming overly long, the justification for these procedures, as well as the discussion of some other relatively minor problems concerning the performance measure, is reserved for an appendix.

Beginning Level of Performance

It is conceivable that performance gain on standardized tests is not only a function of program treatment but also of where the children started. Often this relationship is positive: the pupils who start higher gain more.[17] If there is a test ceiling or "topping out" effect at work, however, the relationship might well be negative. In either case, proper specification of the model demands that the variable be included. As used in the estimating equations, the variable was coded as the number of months the children were below the national norm at the beginning of the program plus 20.0.

Socioeconomic Variables

It is desirable to account for systematic differences in socioeconomic characteristics of pupil environments in order to assess the impact of the school program properly. Attempts were made to control for socioeconomic differences among pupils in two ways. First, respondents were asked to characterize the educational and occupational levels of the parents of their program children. This was, for several reasons, unsuccessful.[18] Second, a considerable amount of factual socioeconomic information was collected. Such data included the percentage of children in the school attendance area who were receiving aid for families with dependent children (AFDC) and the percentage' of program children belonging to minorities.

Pupil Mobility

Another characteristic that must be admitted to the analysis is the degree of mobility of program children. This may be a proxy for socioeconomic characteristics, since there are studies which show mobility to be positively related to low socioeconomic status (5). Mobility itself can be injurious to program quality, of course.[19] Thus, even though a particular child stayed in the program all year, the quality of his instruction could be affected by the fact that his teachers are constantly bothered by the comings and goings of other children in the program.

Instructional Intensity by Type of Instructor

As has been discussed above, the amount of instruction on an individual-equivalent basis was central to the analysis in this study. During the interviews, a record was made of how the pupils spent their project time, and this information was used to fashion the variables of individual-equivalent minutes spent with each child on a weekly basis by instructional personnel.

The variable as constructed allows for one measure to be constructed out of size of class, number of instructors, and length of session. As the variable was constructed, some allowance was also made for supervision time when the specialist, or classroom teacher, used one or more paraprofessional persons as assistants in actual instruction.

Here is an example of how the variable is constructed. If a single specialist sees groups of 10 pupils 30 minutes per day 5 days per week, the number of individual-equivalent minutes would be 15. (Thirty divided by 10 times 5.) If the specialist has one paraprofessional assistant for these 10 pupils, the number of individual-equivalent minutes for each pupil, ignoring supervision time, doubles. Since it is assumed that the specialist and the paraprofessional both lose 10 per cent of their time in the specialist's supervision of the paraprofessional, the number of individual-equivalent minutes for each pupil is not 30, but 27.[20]

There are of course three types of personnel used in instruction in the program, the trained reading specialist, the regular classroom teacher, and the paraprofessional. However, four types of instructor were used for constructing variables, with paraprofessionals divided into those assisting regular classroom teachers and those assisting reading specialists.

Percentage of Instruction in the Regular Classroom

Considerable importance attaches to the relative effectiveness of supplementary instruction in the regular classroom as opposed to that given in a separate facility. If effective instruction could be given in the regular classroom, the cost would be much less and the regular classroom teacher could assume a more active part. She could also receive valuable in-service training in the course of her regular duties. On the other hand, a specialist can give more undivided attention to children in a separate facility. We would expect to find a positive relationship between use of separate facilities and pupil performance, although this difference would probably be lessened in projects that have considerable teamwork and in-service training of regular teachers. The actual percentage of instruction given in the regular classroom was the variable used.

Use of Educational Materials and Equipment

The possible importance of different types of educational materials and equipment was mentioned above. In the study, however, it was impossible in practice to determine the amounts of materials and equipment used. Thus, it was found that the essential characteristics of the lists of materials and equipment obtained for each program were virtually identical (at least to the untrained eye). To be sure, there were some differences in the amounts used, but these merely reflected the fact that there were more such materials in separate facilities and that reading specialists tended to use them more than regular classroom teachers. Because of this virtually complete overlap between percentage of instruction in the regular classroom and percentage of instruction given by the trained specialists, it was decided not to include a variable in the model for type of educational equipment used. It should be remembered, however, that any positive findings for percentage of instruction in the separate facility and instruction given by trained reading specialists must necessarily include in part a finding that there is possibly some return to the heavier use of such materials and equipment.

Coordination and Leadership Variables

Several variables were used to represent program coordination. The simplest of these was hours spent in program planning per week. In the interviews, the respondents were informed what was meant by planning and by in-service training, and then asked how much of each took place. Since planning and in-service training are often difficult to separate, and also because there are problems with respondents' collective memories and with quantifying the length of informal discussions, both variables are probably subject to considerable measurement error.[21]

A variable to account for presumed weaknesses in lines of authority within the projects was also used. Teamwork should depend in part upon the degree to which all the principal actors in the project are subject to control by the same person. (Also, of course, it should depend on whether he or she uses the control wisely.) The questionnaire was designed to discover not only the formal, but more importantly the informal, "chain of command." On the basis of the information collected, a dummy variable was constructed. It was set equal to unity when conflicts in direction and purpose were reasonably possible, and zero otherwise.[22]

One additional coordination variable was defined. Respondents were asked to identify the personnel who attended planning meetings and it was hypothesized that a well-coordinated program would routinely have more key personnel present at such meetings. The percentage of attendees who were considered key people became the variable.

Use of Psychologists for Diagnosis

There was considerable variation in the amount of psychologist time used in the diagnosis and prescription phases of the programs. To test the hypothesis that intensive use of psychologist's diagnosis may be associated with better performance, a dummy variable was constructed on the basis of number of pupils per full-time-equivalent psychologist.[23]

VI. FINDINGS

The model of school performance with the best explanatory power is presented in equation 1. All other variables discussed failed to add explanatory power to the model.

$$SCORE\ 25 = 3.45 + 4.85\ PGMLENGTH* + 0.86\ BEGIN\ 25$$
$$(1.1)\quad (3.3)\quad (7.4)$$

$$- 0.013\ PCTMIN + 1.30\ SPECIEMS*$$
$$(1.0)\quad (3.1)$$

(1)

$$- 0.023\ PCTREGCR + 0.106\ TCHRPPIEMS$$
$$(1.7)\quad (2.3)$$

$$+ 2.07\ PLANHRS$$
$$(2.5)$$

$$SEE = 1.84;\ F(7,34) = 21.32;\ \text{Corrected } R^2 = .78$$

All of these models are weighted to correct for heteroscedastic error terms due to unequal numbers of pupils in each project.[24] The values given in parentheses are t statistics and variables marked with an asterisk are transformed into their logarithms.[25] Variable descriptions are given in Table 2.

TABLE 2 Means, Standard Deviations, and Description of Variables

Variable Name	Mean	Standard Deviation	Description
SCORE 25	17.46	3.36	Score at the end of program for students in grades 2, 3, 4, 5, in number of months relative to the grade level norm, coded such that the end score norm was 28.4 and the begin score norm was 20.0.
SCORE 3	17.79	3.22	Score at the end of program for students in grade 3, in number of months relative to the grade level norm, coded such that the end score norm was 27.8 and the begin score norm was 20.0.
GAINSCORE 25	0.87	0.40	Months gain on Stanford Reading Test per month of instruction, weighted average, students in grades 2, 3, 4, and 5.
GAINSCORE 3	0.84	0.56	Months gain on Stanford Reading Test per month of instruction, students in grade 3.
PGMLENGTH	8.43	1.65	Length of program in months, from pretest to posttest.
BEGIN 25	10.88	3.25	Months behind national norm of students at beginning of program, grades 2, 3, 4, and 5, plus 20.0.
BEGIN 3	10.37	2.59	Months behind national norm of students at beginning of program, grade 3, plus 20.0.
PCTMIN	59.1	27.7	Per cent of program children American Indian, black, and Spanish surname.
SPECIEMS*	18.0	13.7	Number of individual equivalent minutes (IEMs)[a] per week taught by trained reading specialists.
TCHRIEMS	16.3	10.1	Number of IEMs[a] per week taught by regular classroom teachers.
TCHRPPIEMS	8.8	8.4	Number of IEMs[a] per week taught

TABLE 2 (concluded)

Variable Name	Mean	Standard Deviation	Description
			by paid paraprofessionals assisting regular classroom teachers.
PCTREGCR	54.6	34.7	Percentage of Title I instruction given in the regular classroom.
PL ᠂NHRS	0.57	0.38	Hours per week project personnel spent in planning meetings.

[a] See page 262 for a description of individual-equivalent minutes.

Instruction both by specialists and by paraprofessionals assisting classroom teachers is related to pupil performance. For the paraprofessionals ten individual-equivalent minutes (IEMs) of instruction weekly are related to an additional month of reading performance. Specialist instruction shows a declining relationship with ten IEMs related to about 1.5 months of reading gain for the first ten or twenty minutes of instruction and then declining to less than one month of gain per ten IEMs beyond approximately 40 IEMs. The specialist variable was somewhat more statistically significant as well.

There is a small gain in performance when programs are conducted outside the regular classroom, although this variable is only barely significant at the 10 per cent level.

The only coordination-management variable which was related to performance was number of planning hours, with one hour per week of planning (which is more than most projects had) being associated with an additional 2.1 months gain. Causation cannot necessarily be inferred from the relationship, but it does suggest that some formal planning does indeed pay dividends. It is interesting to note that the in-service training variable, about which there were high hopes built on analysis of prior findings, always had the wrong sign and was never significant.

According to the variables both included and omitted from equation 1, no socioeconomic status (SES) variable is important. Of the variables not included, percentage of children with Spanish surnames had no explanatory power, while percentage black was weakly and insignificantly related to performance negatively. The percentage of children who moved, which can be considered as a proxy for one SES characteristic, was negative and usually yielded coefficients larger than their standard errors. The variable for percentage of children in the school attendance area on AFDC, which had been considered one of the more meaningful SES variables, consistently displayed the wrong sign although it, also, was not statistically significant.

The percentage minority variable was somewhat collinear with amount of instruction conducted in the regular classroom $(R = .50)$ and was somewhat more significant when that variable was not included in the model. To show this difference, equation 2 is a slightly different specification, with percentage of instruction inside the regular classroom being replaced by instruction by the regular classroom teacher.

(2)

$$SCORE\ 25 = -4.89 + 4.47\ PGMLENGTH* + 0.85\ BEGIN\ 25$$
$$(1.5) \quad (3.0) \qquad\qquad (7.0)$$

$$-\ 0.023\ PCTMIN + 1.59\ SPECIEMS*$$
$$(1.9) \qquad\qquad (3.9)$$

$$-\ 0.033\ TCHRIEMS + 0.090\ TCHRPPIEMS$$
$$(0.6) \qquad\qquad (1.4)$$

$$+\ 1.58\ PLANHRS$$
$$(1.9)$$

$$SEE = 1.91;\ F(7,34) = 19.53;\ \text{Corrected } R^2 = .76$$

In this model the per cent minority variable is significant at almost the 5 per cent level. Specialist instruction becomes even more significant than before, but instruction by paraprofessionals helping classroom teachers loses some of its significance. Since more effective individualized instruction (including use of more specialized materials and equipment) is carried on in the separate facility, the first model, represented by equation 1, is undoubtedly much preferable to that in equation 2 on a priori grounds.

As the reader will recall, it was speculated that programs which depend almost exclusively upon reading specialists for their instruction might be expected to require less management and teamwork. To test this, the model was fitted to 25 projects which did not depend heavily upon specialist instruction.[26] The results are shown in equation 3.

(3)

$$SCORE\ 25 = -7.65 + 5.33\ PGMLENGTH* + 0.81\ BEGIN\ 25$$
$$(1.3) \quad (2.0) \qquad\qquad (6.1)$$

$$-\ 0.011\ PCTMIN + 1.66\ SPECIEMS*$$
$$(0.7) \qquad\qquad (2.7)$$

$$-\ 0.0063\ PCTREGCR + 0.109\ TCHRPPIEMS$$
$$(0.3) \qquad\qquad (2.1)$$

$$+\ 1.86\ PLANHRS$$
$$(1.4)$$

$$SEE = 1.89;\ F(7,17) = 13.89;\ \text{Corrected } R^2 = .79$$

The importance of the planning hours variable is somewhat lessened instead of vice versa, and indeed this was true for all the other coordination and leadership variables as well. The hypothesis of better coordination in nonspecialist-dominated programs fails to be confirmed by the data.

Finally, because of the problems with respect to aggregating data from different grade levels mentioned above, the model was fitted to the 38 projects for which data were available for grade 3. The resultant equation, presented as equation 4, only manages to replicate the finding for the importance of specialist instruction, with the earlier significance of instruction of paraprofessionals helping classroom teachers and planning hours reduced to insignificance. This finding, therefore, introduced a note of caution into the interpretation of the meaningfulness of the latter two variables.

$$SCORE\ 3 = 5.28 + 0.53\ PGMLENGTH* + 0.78\ BEGIN\ 3$$
$$(1.0)\quad (0.2)(3.9)$$

$$- 0.0060\ PCTMIN + 1.60\ SPECIEMS*$$
$$(0.3)(2.6)$$

(4)

$$- 0.081\ PCTREGCR + 0.048\ TCHRPPIEMS$$
$$(0.9)(0.7)$$

$$+ 0.76\ PLANHRS$$
$$(0.6)$$

$$SEE = 2.59;\ F(7,30) = 4.08;\ \text{Corrected}\ R^2 = .37$$

Description of the Six Best Projects

The top-performing six projects in the study had pupil gains of at least 1.25 months per month of instruction. They averaged 1.5 months gain per month of instruction. It should be useful to outline briefly the characteristics of these six projects.

While four of the six projects had large amounts of instructional time for each pupil per week, the intensity of instruction in the other two was below average. It would appear, therefore, that large amounts of instruction are not absolutely necessary for good performance but are quite helpful.[27]

In five programs, a large proportion of the instruction was given by trained reading specialists. In the sixth, a paraprofessional who had three-years training by a specialist gave individualized instruction in a separate facility.

In the four projects in which the specialists employed paraprofessional aides, the amount of instruction given by the aide varied between one-fourth and one-third the amount given by the specialist. In all projects the specialists gave instruction in small groups no larger than 10 students. Only two projects used classroom teachers and paraprofessionals in assistance of classroom teachers, and these two projects had large doses of specialist instruction besides. Four of the six programs had all instruction in a separate facility; the other two had half of their instruction in a separate facility.

There was no discernible trend among the six projects with respect to minorities represented. Three of the projects had a very high proportion of students belonging to minority groups; while in the other three, the percentage was quite small. Two projects had high percentages of black students and four had no blacks. Two projects had a high percentage of Spanish surname children. There was also considerable variation in pupil mobility in the six projects.

Concerning some other school variables, the number of pupils per full-time program manager in all six projects was quite low. On the other hand, the number of pupils per psychologist in the projects varied widely. The number of planning hours per week and the number of hours in-service training per week also varied quite widely. In all six projects almost all key people were present at all the planning meetings.[28] In several projects, the chain of authority appeared to be somewhat muddled, and therefore this variable does not seem to be very representative of high-quality programs.

In terms of geographical setting, the projects were all medium or small in size and were all either in rural or suburban settings. There were no large urban schools represented in the six top schools in the study.

To summarize the characteristics found in all of these highly successful projects, all six had small group instruction by specialists, high ratios of managers per pupil, and a consistently large percentage of key people present at planning meetings.

Discussion of Findings

There has been wide commentary in the educational literature that compensatory education has failed; that there is no evidence to show that anything done in compensatory education programs is related to the performance of children from disadvantaged backgrounds.[29] The findings here with respect to the relationship of instruction by trained specialists to pupil performance, which maintain their significance no matter which of the meaningful subpopulations of these programs is chosen for fitting the model, clearly contradict this widely repeated set of findings. Instead, it supports the "reasonable hunch" of Guszak, based on work by

Turner and others, that the instructional procedures used by the diagnostic reading specialist are important. The evidence also suggests that instruction given by paraprofessionals helping regular classroom teachers may be effective.

Researchers who deal with disadvantaged populations often use 0.7 months per month of instruction as the "normal" rate of advance for these children, using traditional instructional methods.[30] The average gain in these projects was 0.87 months per month of gain. If the 0.7 figure is correct, the overall impact of the Title I money would be .17 months gain per month of instruction. For the projects which make heavy use of specialists giving individualized instruction, however, the gain is more. Increasing specialist instruction per child by twenty minutes per week should raise the average by at least .2 months, to a rate at which pupils would be slowly catching up. It would be dangerous to extrapolate the findings too closely in this way, but there is room for optimism based on the findings here.

Findings for the remaining aspects of the study are not nearly so positive, however. While it is true that the planning variable is significantly related to pupil performance in the main explanatory model used, the finding fails to hold up when the model is fitted to other meaningful subpopulations. Moreover, none of the other variables constructed to measure aspects of coordination and management were related to pupil performance at any time. With the possible exception of the finding for planning time, then, the general conclusion will have to stand that the strong hypotheses carried into the study with respect to the importance of coordination, teamwork, and management to program success, failed to be supported by the regression analysis. The descriptive results were somewhat more positive with respect to the importance of the amount of management input and to the percentage of key people who participated in planning sessions.

Whether the coordination variables failed because they represent reality, or because the variables are themselves too poor, remains to be seen in further studies. The latter possibility is considered highly likely although the very negative relationships found for some of the variables lead one to suspect strongly that the negative findings to some extent represent reality as well.[31] This suspicion is increased by the fact that nonspecialist-dominated programs had values for these variables which were even more negative in all cases than when the model was fitted to all projects. The same was also true for the in-service training variable, and the consistent null finding for that variable was something of a surprise and disappointment, considering all the rhetoric which I have heard in the past two years from program managers, directly and indirectly, concerning the importance of good in-service training. Perhaps the problem was that we were not able to discriminate between good in-service training and poor in-service training, or perhaps the results are in part due to the fact that specialists (who are most effective in securing good results) do not require as much in-service training as other instructional personnel.

Proper discussion of the findings for program length and beginning score fall outside of my professional competence. Program length is related to performance, and the evidence suggests that more learning is done early in the program than later, since the variable fits the data much better when transposed into its logarithm. (This is also suggested by the negative coefficient for *PGMLENGTH* in equation 1-a in Appendix A.)

It is unfortunate that the model, when fitted to the grade 3 scores, did not replicate the findings for the teacher, paraprofessional, and planning variables which obtained in equation 1. In interpreting this difference, the question of how likely it is that the aggregation of data over different grade levels will lead to error immediately arises, and this question is discussed in more detail in Appendix A. I feel that the performance levels shown by the pooled grade data represent reality more faithfully than those which are for grade 3, but some readers may disagree after reading Appendix A.

If the pooled data findings are most representative of reality, the findings in the study are not all in one direction. Instruction by the classroom teacher with his or her paraprofessional (with instruction given by the paraprofessional counting most in this case) does in fact seem to be related to performance, to a degree about two-thirds as great as that for the trained specialist. If the significance level for the paraprofessional variable were the same, we could immediately draw some rather profound economic conclusions from this, of course, but since the confidence with which we can accept the paraprofessional finding is lower, it would be a dangerous extrapolation to make.

Finally, the difference in the relationship of socioeconomic status variables to performance in this study, as compared to other input-output type studies, should be noted. While most other studies have socioeconomic status (SES) as the quality most highly related to performance, no SES variable was significant here. Part of this can probably be explained by the fact that the other studies had pupil populations with wider variation in SES. This is even true with studies, such as those of Bowles (4) and Hanushek (14, 15) in which populations were restricted by race, since there were of course middle and high SES black or Spanish surnamed children present in their samples. This is the only input-output study which used low-status children exclusively. On the other hand, the variables used may have been inadequate. Even the percentage of children in the school area on AFDC, upon which substantial hopes had been riding, completey failed to be related to performance. Much more sophisticated SES measures may be necessary for discriminating such things as verbalization in the home [see, for example, (5)], motivation, and the like. Yet, as indicated above, a procedure which depends on asking the child a straightforward question about these things is completely unacceptable for pedagogical reasons. It is perhaps surprising that the model explained as much of the variation in performance as it did, given the inadequacy of the SES variables.

VII. CONCLUDING COMMENTS

This study is the first to attempt to assess compensatory education projects with input-output methodology. A single performance measure is used across all projects and an attempt is made to account for socioeconomic differences using multiregression techniques. As with other input-output studies,[32] the largest failure of this one is that the analysis is not student-specific, or even classroom-specific. However, an attempt was made to do some things which have not been done before in input-output studies, in that program organizational characteristics and instructional organizational strategies are related to pupil performance.

Since I lacked the necessary expertise to study the internal workings of the instruction, and also the necessary budget for employing highly refined techniques with organizational relationships, it is to be emphasized that the study is only a first step and that no more is claimed for it. It was hoped that this procedure might allow us a first, rather fuzzy look at the enigmatic inner workings of schools from the standpoint of input-output methodology, but only with respect to broad organizational patterns and not in a truly student-specific way. If this kind of methodology is to be pursued further, student-specific research will have to be added next.

It is certainly important for the cost effectiveness of the nation's educational research that wise heads carefully consider the payoffs to future research of the type undertaken here. It is by no means unanimously felt that such research will, in the future, yield results worth their cost. Thus, Alcaly, in commenting on the Hanushek study mentioned above, claimed that further studies of the same genre would probably not repay the cost (1). In commenting on an earlier version of the present paper, Ribich came to much the same conclusion (29). On the other hand, Weisbrod, in commenting on the same paper, said that there were probably increasing returns for many more studies of this kind (32).

If the approach does seem viable, the findings in the present study suggest several avenues for future work. The most pressing are expansion of the analysis of differences in instructional techniques and the inclusion of student-specific analysis. Individual students must be matched to individual teachers and treatments in large enough samples and with enough control for socioeconomic differences so that findings are statistically reliable. Secondly, much more careful thought will have to be given to program organization, coordination, and management. Some progress has been made in the past using role-analysis techniques in education, but further exploration must take place. Specialists familiar with organizational characteristics of large organizations, whether public or private, should be brought in to work on these questions. Finally, much more sophisticated work will have to be done to find meaningful socioeconomic variables.

APPENDIX A

This appendix includes discussions of some statistical questions which were considered to be of insufficient general interest to be incorporated in the main text.

Use of Gain Scores

As was indicated in the text, two performance measures were used in the empirical work done in this study. One of these was gain in grade equivalents per month of elapsed program time, and since there has been considerable criticism in the educational psychology literature on the use of gain scores because of the regression to the mean phenomenon (see Cronbach and Furby, [8]), only end-score was used in the findings presented in the text. Use of gain per unit of time elapsed does allow a direct look at the rate of learning over the length of programs, however, and moreover, a presentation of the model fitted to the gain variant should give some insight into the possible damage of using gain scores. The fitted equation which is similar to equation 1 in the text is therefore presented here as equation 1-a.

$$GAINSCORE\ 25 = 0.85 - 0.031\ PGMLENGTH$$
$$(3.5)(1.3)$$

$$-\ 0.015\ BEGIN\ 25 - 0.0016\ PCTMIN$$
$$(1.0)(1.1)$$

(1-a)

$$+\ 0.16\ SPECIEMS^* - 0.0032\ PCTREGCR$$
$$(3.3)(2.0)$$

$$+ 0.017 \ TCHRPPIEMS + 0.25 \ PLANHRS$$
$$(3.2) \qquad\qquad\qquad (2.6)$$

$$SEE = .216; \ F(7,34) = 8.45; \ \text{Corrected } R^2 = .56$$

Faster rates of learning appear to take place in the beginning of the program, although the program length variable is not statistically significant. It is also noteworthy that the overall findings one would infer from equation 1-a are very similar to those one would infer from equation 1.

Pooling of Grade Data

Stanford reading scores were available for grades 2, 3, 4, 5, and 6 in various combinations from project to project. The number of valid observations for single grade levels varied from 38 in grade 3 to 15 for grade 5. Grade 3 was the only grade for which more than 50 per cent of the projects were represented. (A major reason for the large number of missing observations was that many projects changed test levels during the school year. This made their scores incomparable to the scores of projects which did not change levels.) Since achievement test scores are not necessarily comparable between grades (even when all scores are referenced to the norms by grade placement, as was done in this study) there is a possible objection to any procedure which pools data for different grades. On the other hand, if data were only used for the single usable grade, more than half of the performance data gathered in the study would have to be discarded. Discarding so much otherwise useful information is a step which should be avoided if at all possible.

The solution to this problem which was adopted was to use pooled data if no apparent differences could be found between grade results after analyzing grade differences statistically. The test used involved two steps. First, end-score was regressed against beginning-score for each grade to see if there were any discernible differences in this relationship by grade. There were not. Then, each grade was compared to grade 3, using a dummy variable for grade effect and covarying for beginning-score. (It was not necessary to covary for program length, since it was always virtually the same in the same school.) As an example of the procedure used, if there were twenty schools which had scores for both grades 3 and 4, the equation would have 40 cases and would be

$$SCORE = a_1 + a_2 \ (BEGIN \ SCORE) + a_3$$

where a_3 is the coefficient of a dummy variable set equal to 1.0 if the observation were for grade 4 and zero otherwise.

The coefficients corresponding to a_3 for the four grade effects, with the t statistics for their standard errors, are

	Coefficient	t
Grade 2	− 0.08	0.42
Grade 4	− 0.09	0.33
Grade 5	0.06	0.20
Grade 6	0.42	1.52

Since the coefficient for the grade 6 effect was large and almost significant statistically, grade 6 scores for 440 pupils for 19 projects were excluded. All the other grades were retained and a weighted pooled average of both end-score and beginning-score was constructed.

What are the possibilities of this procedure leading to serious error? Differences in grade level effects could obtain because of different levels of resource inputs used at different grade levels, or because of differences resulting from test construction. Since we have statistical evidence that there is no difference between the four grades used, the kind of errors that could remain in the presence of this null finding would be offsetting errors, that is, increased resources might be used at a grade in which this factor is offset by the effect of test construction which biases gains downward. However, considerable care was taken in the interviews to check for differences in inputs by grade level, and there were not many instances in which they obviously differed (this is especially true with respect to grade 2, somewhat less true, perhaps, with respect to the findings for grades 4 and 5).

I doubt that this pooling procedure has led to serious error. Readers who disagree will have to use the findings presented in equation 4 and disregard the rest.

Other Minor Problems in Constructing the Performance Measure

There were a number of relatively minor problems to overcome in using the Stanford Test Scores in this data set. First, it was found necessary to use the median performance scores as the measure of central tendency, since some projects failed to include frequency distributions in their reports. (Such frequency distributions would have been required to compute means.) This procedure allows for some bias, but careful investigation showed that the difference between mean and median grade equivalents (many districts reported both) were nonexistent or negligible.

A second problem arose because it was not possible to obtain summary scores for individual schools from some of the school districts. Twenty-two of the 42 school projects fell into this category. Half of the 22 had district reports in which the school project being studied accounted for less than half of the pupils covered in the report. The method used to attempt to overcome this potentially serious data problem was to request the respondent to choose a school that was "closest to the district average" in performance. Some such choice was usually possible, and since district-evaluation personnel often have a good feel for the performance levels of their project schools, the error introduced by the mismatch was probably lessened considerably by this procedure.

It may be of interest to some readers to see the model fitted to only those 31 projects where the mismatch problem was—in terms of percentages, anyway—relatively minor. This is done in equation 2-a.

$$SCORE\ 25 = -3.32 + 4.35\ PGMLENGTH^*$$
$$(0.7)\quad (1.9)$$

$$-\ 0.206\ BEGIN\ 25 - 0.0040\ PCTMIN$$
$$(1.7)\qquad\qquad (0.2)$$

(2-a)
$$+\ 1.48\ SPECIEMS^* - 0.022\ PCTREGCR$$
$$(3.1)\qquad\qquad (1.3)$$

$$+\ 0.089\ TCHRPPIEMS + 0.80\ PLANHRS$$
$$(1.8)\qquad\qquad (0.8)$$

$$SEE = 1.77;\ F(7,23) = 4.22;\ \text{Corrected}\ R^2 = .43$$

Except for the less significant *PLANHRS* variable the equation is not greatly different from equation 1.

Finally, there was a problem with respect to the question of competing program outputs. The California Division of Compensatory Education requires that Title I projects teach both mathematics and reading. It was not possible to obtain comparable achievement data on mathematics for 18 of the 42 projects,[33] however, and with this many missing observations it was simply not feasible to study mathematics programs directly. Instead a careful attempt was made to limit the study to resources going into reading.

Weighting

A problem well known to econometricians concerns the fact that regression equations fit to sample populations, where the expected error terms from properly specified models are not the same size along some important dimension of the analysis, are not efficient. That is to say, other estimators can be found for which there is less error variance. There is one dimension in educational analysis like this study where such expected error variance must surely differ, and that is program size. This is because mean scores of groups of pupils are used and the expected error variance of means of small groups is greater than those for large groups, as everyone who has studied sampling theory knows.

In studying educational projects of this kind, there is one additional quirk to the analysis which has not been pointed out before in the educational input-output literature.[34] There are two potential sources of randomness, a program effect applying to each student in the program, and a random effect which differs for each student and which arises from the vagaries of achievement testing. In symbols $u_{ij} = v_i + e_{ij}$ where u_{ij} is the stochastic term for the jth student in the ith program, v_i is the effect of the ith program, and e_{ij} is a random term. The variance of the average test score across all students in the ith program depends on the number of students (size of program), because the sum of e_{ij} depends upon the number of students. The variance v_i due to program effects may or may not depend on size of program. (In point of fact, I would suspect that it does, since the law of large numbers works with teacher's effects and the like, as well as with pupil performance on tests.) If v_i is independent of size of program, the question then becomes: "How much of the total error term u_{ij} varies by program size and how much does not?" If a large percentage did not vary, it might be more correct not to weight, or to use only a partial weight.

It should be possible to gain some insights concerning the propriety of weighting fully merely by performing the well-known test for heteroscedasticity. The projects were divided into four groups of 10, 11, 11, and 10, respectively, ranged by sample size, and the variance of the error term multiplied by a constant was computed for equation 1-a. The result was as follows, where N equals the number of pupils in the project whose scores were averaged.

$1/N \times 1000$	Variance $\times$ 100
5.8	36.4
13.1	38.4
23.3	49.4
54.2	129.6

Variance obviously increases consistently with decreased sample size. If a regression line of variance is hand fitted to $1/N$, the resulting line has a steep slope and an intercept fairly close to zero. This seems to indicate strongly that full weighting on the basis of sample size is proper.

NOTES

1. The Report on Title I for the 1968 fiscal year gives the number of children in poor families as 7,700,000 (29, p. 66). Of these, 89 per cent are in schools which receive Title I aid, and about 52 per cent are participating in some form of Title I program (29, p. 14 and p. 87).

2. For example, many of the criterion measures of teacher performance are ratings by their superiors as to the quality of their performance. There is seldom any effort to obtain correlations of ratings by superiors and actual classroom performance.

3. Two exceptions to these remarks must be noted. One Rand-sponsored study, by Hanushek (15), has matched pupils in grades 2 and 3 with their teachers. Also a number of studies, including those based on the Coleman Report and the Hanushek study just mentioned, have had variables for teacher performance on a simple verbal abilities test.

4. See Rapp (28).

5. The success criterion used was gains in cognitive reading tests which approached two times what was considered "average" for low socioeconomic status (SES) children. See Kiesling (23).

6. The following discussion has benefited greatly from the series of monographs on the subject of individualized instruction which have been written at the Far Western Regional Laboratory (9).

7. Despite what may seem logical in the matter, class size for individualized instruction is *not* necessarily smaller than that for group instruction. It is the teaching technique, not the class size that is important. Group instruction, with virtually no individualized instruction at all, could be carried on (and often is, for example, in graduate courses) with classes of four or five. Individual instruction techniques often include giving the child a short assignment and sending him off to do it. A good specialist instructor can probably give individualized instruction to 20 children at once. In actual practice, it is probably seldom that either type of instruction is given in pure form. For example, if a specialist instructor worked directly with an instructional aide, it was assumed that 10 per cent of the time of both was spent in discussion between themselves for reasons of supervision, and not in actual instruction of children.

8. See Kiesling (25, p. 34).

9. The individualized instruction that a pupil receives as part of the program is likely to be a pleasant experience, because he feels that someone cares enough to get to know him personally and to be his friend. If he feels that his regular classroom teacher is highly sympathetic to his compensatory instruction, he may relate his pleasant experience to his regular school program, resulting in a much improved attitude to all of his schoolwork.

10. Some of the instruction can be performed separately in group instruction, too. Separate people can supervise and evaluate, for example. In practice, however, this is seldom done.

11. Some work along these lines has been done. See, for example, Halpin (13), or Katz and Kahn (22).

12. For a good discussion of how this can be done, see Rapp (28).

13. Hawkridge, *et al.*, (18).

14. It should be noted that two schools in the same school district are considered to be two projects.

15. This is because a disproportionate number of blacks were in a few large schools.

16. Often as I conducted my interview and came to a section of questions which the respondent did not feel competent to answer, he or she would get me a quick

appointment with someone who knew the answers (or at least give me his name and telephone number for a telephone query later) or pick up the telephone and call someone to find out while I waited. An advantage of giving the questionnaire in person is that it is quickly ascertained to the mutual agreement of both interviewer and interviewee when the latter is weak with respect to knowledge of some program aspects. As noted in my acknowledgment, I received a degree of cooperation from almost all school personnel which I think rather amazed my colleagues at the Rand Corporation.

17. In an earlier study of mine, gains in performance from grade 4 to grade 6 were highly correlated with score in grade 4. See (24).

18. Data concerning family characteristics which might bear upon pupil motivation are simply not collected. The reason for this is understandable. Many children in Title I programs come from homes which, unfortunately, have characteristics about which they feel embarrassed. Many program instructors feel that merely asking children questions concerning their home environment causes an adverse effect upon pupil morale and pupil achievements.

It seems to me that it should be possible, however, to overcome this problem by administering instruments or questions to the children which might, directly or indirectly, assess such characteristics as amount of verbalization in the home, and so forth, without directly embarrassing the child if there is some problem. The use of one such test is described in (6).

19. It should be noted that mobility does not directly affect the performance outcomes, since test scores were reported by the projects only for pupils present both at the beginning and the end of the program.

The question that was asked to obtain mobility rate was: "What percentage of those children who were initially placed in the program at the beginning of the program year were still in the program at the end of the program year?"

20. The convention used was to deduct 10 per cent of the instructional time of supervising teacher and paraprofessional for each of the first two paraprofessional aides, and 5 per cent for each aide after that.

21. As was explained to the respondents, planning was defined to include the kinds of topics and skills program personnel should be covering during the coming week or weeks for individual children (by name). By in-service training was meant explanations concerning why project personnel should take various educational steps, how and when a certain skill requires that another kind of skill be taught immediately prior, and so forth. Demonstrations concerning classroom techniques suited to teaching skills which the program leaders desire to be taught are also included.

22. An example of the "no conflict" situation would be where the program is directed by an Assistant Superintendent with line authority who is not too busy to devote a reasonable amount of time to the program. Thus, no coordination problem need ever arise: all personnel concerned, including specialists, building principal, and so forth, are directly responsible to the Assistant Superintendent.

A majority of the actual programs were included in the "conflict possible" category, however. Often, for example, the program director has a rank equal to the building principal and has no "line" authority. The Director might supervise the specialist within a given school, while the building principal supervises the classroom teacher and paraprofessionals. The success of such a program depends crucially upon how closely the Director and the building principal cooperate. Even if these two individuals are good friends, chances are that the effects of the specialist and regular classroom teacher may not be well coordinated. At least, this is our supposition. A variation of this pattern exists when a person has the control but has too many other duties to effectively use it to coordinate the program.

23. There were very few projects which had a ratio of pupils to full-time-equivalent psychologists near 1000:1. Since most projects fell either clearly above or below this figure, if the ratio was below 1000:1 the dummy variable was set equal to unity and if above, to zero.

24. Weighting is further discussed in Appendix A.

25. For 34 degrees of freedom, significance levels are: 5 per cent 2.0; 1 per cent 2.7; .1 per cent 3.5.

26. The criteria used in making the distinction were that more than half of total instruction was accomplished by specialists together with paraprofessionals assisting specialists; and at the same time, more than half of all instruction took place in a separate facility.

27. The average number of IEMs for all 42 projects was 44 and the two projects mentioned as below average had 37 and 25 IEMs respectively. The difference in instructional intensity between the best and worst projects is striking, however. The average number of IEMs for the six best projects, including the two just mentioned, was 70. The average for the 10 worst projects, which had an average gain of about .4 months per month of instruction, was only 32. The difference in the amount of instuction given by trained specialists is even more striking: 30 IEMs in the best projects as opposed to 12 in the worst.

28. This was not true in the ten worst projects, where the per cent of key people average was 75. It is notable that, in these ten projects, for those in which the percentage of key people present was large, the actual planning time was small.

29. To cite only two: "Compensatory education has been tried and it apparently has failed"—Jensen (20, p. 2). "Negative residual gain-scores for most 'participating' groups in all grades seem to indicate that even when a lower 'starting point' is considered, participants did not progress at the same rate as nonparticipants"—Glass et al. (10, Chapter 6, p. 148).

30. The figure found in the Coleman Report was that disadvantaged children who reach grade 12 are about 3 grade levels behind. This would imply a figure of .75 months per month of instruction for those *who do not drop out*.

31. A cynical explanation, which I would be inclined to reject, is that all projects had uniformly bad management so there was nothing good to measure. I would also be inclined to reject the opposite explanation that all projects had management that was uniformly good.

32. Except Hanushek's (15), which was classroom specific.

33. Some districts did not include mathematics in their annual reports and others did not use the Stanford mathematics tests.

34. I owe this point to Joseph Newhouse.

REFERENCES

1. Alcaly, Roger. "Discussion." *American Economic Review: Papers and Proceedings* 61 (1971): 301–302.

2. Averch, Harvey, et al. *What Do We Know About Educational Effectiveness?*, R-956-PCSF/RC. Santa Monica, Calif.: The Rand Corporation, 1972.

3. *Annual Report*. Officers of Local Assistance, Department of General Services, State of California, Sacramento, 1970.

4. Bowles, Samuel. "Educational Production Function." In W. L. Hansen, ed., *Education, Income, and Human Capital*. New York: NBER, 1970, pp. 11–61.

5. Bogue, Donald J. *Principles of Demography.* New York: John Wiley and Sons, 1969, pp. 770–771.
6. Carver, Ronald P. "Use of a Recently Developed Listening Comprehension Test to Investigate the Effect of Disadvanterent on Verbal Proficiency." *American Educational Research Journal* (Mar. 1969): 263–270.
7. Coleman, James S., and Karweit, Nancy L. *Measures of School Performance,* R-488-RC. Santa Monica, Calif., The Rand Corporation, 1970.
8. Cronbach, Lee J., and Furby, Lita. "How We Should Measure 'Change'—Or Should We?" *Psychological Bulletin* 74 (1970): 68–80.
9. Far West Laboratory for Educational Research and Development. *Individualized Instruction Information Unit.* Berkeley, Calif., 1971.
10. Glass, Gene V., et al. *Education of the Disadvantaged: An Evaluative Report on Title I, Elementary and Secondary Education Act of 1965, Fiscal Year 1969.* Boulder: University of Colorado, 1970.
11. Gordon, E. W., and Wilkerson, D. *Compensatory Education for the Disadvantaged.* New York: CEBCO Standard Publishing, 1966.
12. Guszak, Frank J. "The Diagnostic Reading Teacher for the Disadvantaged Child." In J. L. Frost and G. R. Hawkes, eds., *The Disadvantaged Child.* Boston: Houghton Mifflin, 1970, pp. 361–378.
13. Halpin, Andrew W., and Croft, Dan B. "The Organizational Climate of Schools." St. Louis, Mo.: Washington University, 1962, processed.
14. Hanushek, Eric A. *The Education of Negroes and Whites.* Ph.D. diss., M.I.T., 1968.
15. ———. *The Value of Teachers in Teaching.* RM-6362-CC/RC. Santa Monica, Calif.: The Rand Corporation, 1970.
16. Hawkridge, David; Chalupsky, Albert B.; and Roberts, A. Oscar H. *A Study of Selected Exemplary Programs for the Education of Disadvantaged Children.* Final Report, U.S. Department of Health, Education, and Welfare. Palo Alto, Calif.: American Institutes for Research in the Behavioral Sciences, 1968.
17. Hawkridge, David; Campeau, Peggie L.; DeWitt, Kathryn M.; and Trickett, Penelope K. *A Study of Further Selected Exemplary Programs for the Education of Disadvantaged Children.* U.S. Department of Health, Education, and Welfare. Palo Alto, Calif.: American Institutes for Research in the Behavioral Sciences, 1969.
18. Hawkridge, David; Tallmadge, G. Kasten; and Larsen, Judith K. *Foundations for Success in Educating Disadvantaged Children.* Final Report, U.S. National Advisory Council on The Education of Disadvantaged Children. Palo Alto, Calif.: American Institutes for Research in the Behavioral Sciences, 1968.
19. Jaeger, R. M. "The 1968 Survey on Compensatory Education." Paper presented at the American Educational Research Association Meeting, 1969, Los Angeles, Calif.
20. Jensen, Arthur R. "How Much Can We Boost I.Q. and Scholastic Achievement?" *Harvard Education Review* 39 (1969): 1–123.
21. Johnston, J. *Econometric Methods.* New York: McGraw-Hill, 1960.
22. Katz, Daniel, and Kahn, Robert L. *The Social Psychology of Organizations.* New York: John Wiley and Sons, 1966, Chapter 7.
23. Kiesling, Herbert J. "California Compensatory Education Projects: A Draft Report on the First Part of an Economic Analysis of Compensatory Education Projects in California." Working Paper. Santa Monica, Calif.: The Rand Corporation, 1970.
24. ———. *The Relationship of School Inputs to Public School Performance in New York State.* P-4211. Santa Monica, Calif.: The Rand Corporation, 1969.

25. ———. "Multivariate Analysis of Schools and Educational Policy." P-4595. Santa Monica, Calif.: The Rand Corporation, 1971.

26. ———. *Input and Output in California Compensatory Education Projects*, R-781–cc/rc, Santa Monica, Calif.: The Rand Corporation, 1971.

27. McDill, Edward; McDill, Mary; and Sprehe, Timothy. *Strategies for Success in Compensatory Education: An Appraisal of Evaluation Research*. Baltimore: Johns Hopkins University Press, 1969.

28. Posner, J. "Evaluation of 'Successful' Projects in Compensatory Education." U.S. Office of Education, Office of Planning and Evaluation, Occasional Paper No. 8, 1968.

29. Rapp, Marjorie. *Evaluation as Feedback in the Program Development Cycle*. P-4066. Santa Monica, Calif.: The Rand Corporation, 1969.

30. Ribich, Thomas I. "Comment on a Paper by H. J. Kiesling." Conference on Education as an Industry, National Bureau of Economic Research, Chicago, June 4–5, 1971. [This volume.]

31. *Statistical Report for Fiscal Year 1968: A Report on the Third Year of Title I*. U.S. Office of Education, Department of Health, Education, and Welfare, Washington, D.C.: GPO, 1969.

32. U.S. Office of Education, Department of Health, Education, and Welfare. *Evaluative Report on Title I, Elementary and Secondary Education Act of 1965, Fiscal Year 1968*. Washington, D.C.: GPO, 1970.

33. Weisbrod, Burton A. "Comment on a Paper by H. J. Kiesling." Conference on Education as an Industry, National Bureau of Educational Research, Chicago, June 4–5, 1971. [This volume.]

6 | COMMENTS

Thomas I. Ribich

University of North Carolina, Chapel Hill

Before getting into the specifics of the paper presented by Kiesling, I should like to state my general position on the matter of educational production-function studies. Briefly, I'm a grouch. Part of the reason for my present predisposition can be found in the sort of technical problems and social-strategy arguments posed by Henry Levin in the opening paper of this conference, and part is present in the line of criticism developed by John Brandle more than two years ago at another conference on the economics of education sponsored by the NBER. But there are other things as well. Some

---

EDITORS' NOTE: A number of the objections raised to Kiesling's original paper in Ribich's discussion have been taken into account in the version of Kiesling's paper which appears in this volume.

of them are very general, some seemingly incidental and just barely germane. I would like to mention them briefly, if, for no other reason, than to make it clear that the specific criticisms I have of the paper under consideration may be due mainly to a bias against the genre rather than hostility toward this particular study.

To start with what may be the most incidental of all, I am a teacher as well as someone who does research about the economics of education. As a teacher, associating regularly with other teachers of the same general subject matter, I am convinced there are just about as many valid ways to teach a course as there are teachers. There also seem to be about as many ways to run an economics department as there are department chairmen. Production function studies have not, and probably never will, change my mind about that. Now, perhaps it is a different story when it comes to education and the administration of education at lower levels, but I tend to doubt it. There are different teaching styles and different administrative styles, based largely on personality and the like, and they tend to employ various "resource inputs" with greatly different degrees of efficiency. I believe that this view is widely shared, though rarely (if ever) articulated in "professional" discussions of educational production function. Nevertheless, such studies (especially those like Kiesling's, which go into considerable detail on instructional technique) will, I think, continue to be unpersuasive to a good many of those on the frontlines because of this basic problem.

Second, I cannot help feeling that a lot of the educational production-function studies are forced flowers, stimulated in a hurry as a result of the startling findings of the Coleman Report, and of several other studies appearing about the same time, indicating that educational inputs as a whole were dwarfed by socioeconomic variables when it came to explaining educational outcomes. The consequent search for educational inputs that do have a statistically significant effect on educational outcomes has turned up some apparently interesting results, but the manipulations and strainings of statistical tools required to make sense out of very imperfect data has led to complexity so bewildering as to leave the uninvolved onlooker (like myself) deeply uncertain about whether there is any meaning at all in the tables repeatedly confronted. On top of that, much of the analysis and controversy has been conducted in a vaguely tense atmosphere having to do with preserving or impugning the honor of the educational establishment. That, plus the sheer tedium of wading through mounds of theoretically ungirded statistical analysis has given the whole subject (to me at least) the emotional content of prolonged trench warfare.

There are a few other things I could mention—my feeling that the theory economists are presently getting into, in order to shore up the statistics, is of an "engineering" sort, for which economists have no special insight and expertise, and my hunch is that important truths and the means of their discovery should be simpler and prettier than the kinds of things we are turning up and the ways we are employing to do it. But I think what I've said already should be more than enough to certify me as an authentic grouch, and the specific criticisms I turn to now should be considered accordingly.

To anticipate by paraphrasing the title of Jim Bouton's new volume, "I'm glad the author is not going to take it personally."

The following has only a rough logical sequence, and the points are clearly separable, so I'll rely on the crutch of enumeration. The criticisms are not mortal blows but rather a pointing out of ambiguities and ironies, not unlike the kind that can be enumerated for most studies of this sort. There are at least a few special twists, however.

1. The statistical proceedings in Kiesling's paper make me no less uneasy than do most other papers on educational production functions. He states that he has gone to a small survey format in order to duck some of the problems he views as inherent in a "massive survey" approach or present in the context of a small "controlled" experiment. Yet in the course of explaining his methodology and his results, we are confronted with one instance after another of arbitrary assumptions, apologies for the crudeness of the data, and difficult-to-unravel statistical conundrums. One almost gets the feeling that the small survey approach manages to combine the problems that exist in the small experiments and large surveys more than it succeeds in slipping between the horns of the dilemma.

2. It is hardly comforting that the input which by calculation appears to be twice as cost effective as anything else—i.e., "better teamwork"—is not even statistically significant. Kiesling states at one point that his "intuitive judgement" is that "the magnitude of returns to expenditures on management (and thereby teamwork) is not overstated." But in summarizing his earlier regressions, upon which the cost-effectiveness estimates depend, he notes that "the effect of better teamwork between program personnel seems to be positive, although it is not possible to ascertain the magnitude of the effect." Moreover, Kiesling avoids using the teamwork variables in the construction of his isoquants later on. The issue is never resolved, and the basis for resolution is never spelled out, though it seems apparent that it is buried in the multiple ambiguities of the imperfect measures of teamwork, the question of how much teamwork can be deliberately encouraged, and the arbitrariness of the cost estimate.

3. Taking a brief look at the isoquant analysis, the diagram summarizing the results suggests strongly to me that most schools are using too many specialists. Surely the most technically efficient firms are by and large in that position if the efficiency frontier is to be taken seriously. Yet the regression analysis, converted into cost-effective terms, suggests that *not enough* specialists are being used, in that they could be substituted for individual instruction time provided by regular teachers with the result that test-score gains will rise without an increase in costs. Kiesling seems to give precedence to the isoquant results noting that "while average relationships are the proper ones to explore for making descriptive generalizations about Title I projects in California, it is only the most efficient projects which are of interest for finding the true relationship of output to differing factor combination." Since, however, few schools seem very close to the efficiency frontier (in fact, they could not be anything else, in light of the apparent contradiction between the isoquants and the regressions) it seems to me apparent

that most schools can ignore the isoquant advice, unless they plan on becoming models of efficiency at the same time they are making factor substitutions.

4. Though Kiesling never does give any specific policy advice, a school administrator might still be inclined to start adding specialists to his staff—not understanding entirely that even after several years of collective effort on the part of economists, production-function studies might be best classed as simply in "the exploratory stage." But if the administrator thought for a moment, he would realize there are several very good reasons to reject the implicit policy recommendation, even if he was not bothered by the technical problems of the analysis. First, going back to my remarks at the beginning of this comment, he could argue that he simply is not the sort of administrator that works well with specialists. Second, he could say that it was the in-the-know administrators who hired a lot of specialists, realizing that was the hottest approach, the newest conventional wisdom. Such administrators are sufficiently more clever and energetic than others so that their programs would have done better in any event. Third, those programs that hire more reading specialists simply emphasized the overall goal of reading more than he tends to do, even though all those in the sample answered the survey's multiple choice question about goals the same way: that is, they all ranked improving reading scores as the first priority. The ordinal answer fails to distinguish between those administrators who saw that goal as just barely more important than some other things, and the administrators who were bent on pursuing that goal almost exclusively. The substantially different emphasis on specialists among programs suggests different degrees of emphasis; and those that hired more specialists probably tended to turn all their efforts more strongly in the direction of improving reading test scores, to the possible detriment of other educational values.

5. Though Kiesling seems to regard the programs he deals with as especially effective, and apologizes for the possible bias that this might introduce, and though he feels that the detailed survey he undertook results in more sophisticated answers, the calculated general level of success attained by these programs seems about the same as that measured earlier with a much cruder methodology. Note that the .87 of the month's gain per month of instruction highlighted in the "summary of the findings" is not the figure we are looking for. That is not a number that describes the net impact of the programs, but one which only verifies that individuals in these programs are still advancing their reading skills less rapidly than the national norm. The figures that are more relevant are the cost-effectiveness ones, and according to the information in Table 6, they suggest that the programs, on the average, give rise to a test-score gain of about 2 per cent of a year for every additional $100 spent per student. That turns out to be very close to the outcome of the most archetypical and closely controlled of compensatory education programs in operation before Title I of the 1965 Elementary and Secondary Education Act even went into effect—the New York Higher Horizons program. Whether Higher Horizons, or the California project were "successful" programs or not can be debated, but it might be noted that the

lifetime-income-earning effect of a learning gain of that size comes out to be (by the best calculations I am aware of—my own) only about half the size of the costs involved.

All the above does not lead to some grand "main point." There are a few related things that are mildly suggested for future work in this area, however. The first is that we probably should try to rely more heavily on corroborative evidence than we presently do. Every set of observations and every known technique for uncovering "what works" in education is flawed in a number of ways; and the improvements in basic data and the means for manipulating information are not undergoing such startling improvement that earlier observations deserve to be ignored. Besides going back to see if current work jibes with past observations, it would seem especially advisable to seek corroboration of findings derived from statistical inference by seeing if the same results emerge with deliberate experimentation. The problems of deliberate experiments are imposing, but they do appear more amenable to resolution—by the exercise of scrupulous care—than are the more fundamental problems involved in statistical inference. Finally, we should, perhaps, not worry excessively if production-function work never does yield clear answers that can be adopted mechanistically by school administrators. Perhaps it is enough that we simply provide concrete illustrations of how logical thinking on the question of input mix should be introduced, letting the unique circumstances and temperaments of local administrators dictate the manner in which such rules of thought are adapted.

Burton A. Weisbrod

University of Wisconsin, Madison

Herbert Kiesling has told us a number of things about "Education as an industry":

1. While the industry produces many "products" for many markets, the process of producing *one* product, reading achievement, for one market, the educationally disadvantaged, can be examined fruitfully.
2. Firms that produce this product for this market use varying production techniques—that is, different combinations and organizations of inputs.
3. Not all of these production techniques are (a) equally *effective* in producing outputs, nor are they (b) equally *efficient*, in the economic sense that higher-cost input combinations are sometimes used when equally productive but lower-cost inputs are available.

Kiesling sets for himself the goals of *understanding* the production function (i.e., the set of technically feasible production techniques) for producing improved reading achievement for the disadvantaged, and then of distinguishing the efficient from the inefficient techniques.

Consider first the "output" side of the production function. No one, including Kiesling, claims that reading achievement is, or should be, the only output objective of schooling or even of the Title I program. Indeed, Kiesling also refers to (although he does not deal quantitatively with) two other outputs: one for which a frequently used ordinal measure exists, mathematics achievement; and one for which an ordinal (let alone a cardinal) scale is not generally accepted, self-esteem.[1] My point in mentioning the multiplicity of goals is to remind us to consider the likelihood and consequences of *conflicts among goals*; actions that contribute to achievement of one goal may interfere with achievement of some other goal. Thus, while Kiesling's effort to discover whether one goal—improved reading achievement—is attainable for the disadvantaged is an essential first step, it must be followed by a questioning of the assumption implicit in his analysis that the various goals (outputs) of schooling are separable. If production of reading achievement contributes external diseconomies (or economies) for the production of another school output, the investigator who fails to recognize the externality will, by such piecemeal analysis, urge an inefficiently high (low) level of inputs to reading achievement.

This possibility of goal conflict is quite likely in the type of educational production process studied by Kiesling, since that process involves not only using additional instructional and physical capital resources, but also involves using additional student time. The average of "40 minutes of individualized instruction" per student per week may well mean that the student has less class time available for work that might contribute to achievement of a goal other than reading achievement.

The presence of multiple goals or multiple outputs poses a problem for the interpretation of data on the variety of production (teaching) techniques used among schools. If schooling has multiple objectives or multiple outputs, if various groups of consumers attach different relative values to the various outputs, and if the same inputs enter the production function for more than one of the outputs, then examination of the production function for any *single* output—e.g. reading achievement—would yield biased input-output coefficients. Under such conditions we would find—and indeed we *do* find—apparently widely divergent levels of efficiency in resource use among schools. The problem, of course, is the usual identification problem: do observed differences in input combinations reflect disparate economic efficiency in pursuing a given goal—the interpretation given by Kiesling—or differences in the ends being pursued?

Turning back to the objective that Kiesling considers, the production function for reading achievement, the first problem is to define "reading achievement" operationally. The fact that the State of California has "solved" that problem by requiring the use of the Stanford Reading Test may be all that a school administration needs to know, and thus it may be all that Kiesling's body of data permits him to analyze, but it by no means resolves such questions as: (1) Insofar as students' performances on the various widely used reading tests are not perfectly correlated, then how sensitive are our production-function estimates to the choice of a particular measure of reading output? (2) To what extent are instructors "teaching to the test"—that is, in effect, giving children the answers to the test so as to achieve high "performance" levels (at least in a single year)? In order to cope with this latter problem, Office of Economic Opportunity, in its experimentation with "performance contracting" for compensatory education of the disadvantaged, selected randomly from a set of five examinations to be administered to each school group. There is a dilemma, however, which even this procedure cannot escape. On the one hand, insofar as the various tests provide results that are strongly and positively correlated and the teachers know it, using multiple output measures is of small value—teaching to one test is teaching to all of them. On the other hand, insofar as the results are *not* highly correlated, the measured "success" of any teaching effort (producing technique) will depend on the particular measure of output (reading achievement) that is used!

Kiesling does appear to be uneasy about the particular output measure used in his study, for he refers repeatedly to the "difficulty" of the Stanford Reading Test. Unfortunately he does not tell us what he means by "difficult" although I might guess that he means that an improved performance level on *this* test is associated with a greater relative improvement in performance on some *other* reading tests. By this interpretation, the different improvement factors (*output* or achievement-added) on the various reading tests do indeed pose a problem for anyone trying to estimate the production function for the product, "reading achievement." With the product being the improvement in test score, the choice of a particular test becomes important. It would be desirable, indeed, to know how sensitive Kiesling's productivity estimates are to the choice among output (test) measures.

Turn now from output to the inputs. I stated above that we could think of "disadvantaged" students as the *market* for the Title I compensatory education programs. But at the same time, the student is also an *input* to the production process, as is frequently the case with personal services. He is an input in the sense that he must be present (physically) at the point of production and must "cooperate" (mentally) with other inputs.

Which *specific* characteristics of an individual student are important for determining the degree to which he will benefit from exposure to a particular set of instructional inputs? Kiesling hypothesizes that the important characteristics are, or at least have as their proxies, the following three: (1) being black (or a member of some other "minority"), (2) being on AFDC, (3) having moved recently or being in a group with many other students who have moved recently. Kiesling is convinced that the lack of importance that he finds for these "socioeconomic variables is attributable to the fact that undoubtedly . . . they are too crude." Perhaps he is right. But perhaps socioeconomic class is simply unimportant for explaining variance in reading achievement—once a "more fundamental" variable is taken into account. The more fundamental variable to which I am referring is the achievement level from which the student *began* his participation in the remedial program. Indeed, the variable, "beginning-score," was one of the most statistically significant variables considered by Kiesling. (While the significance level was high, the actual quantitative importance was more modest; for each ten months in which the student was below the reading norm for his grade, participation in the group contributed approximately an additional one-third month to the increase in reading performance during the remedial program.)

The significance of the beginning-score variable—as an indicator of student achievement at the onset of the program—deserves more attention than Kiesling gave to it. Whereas he considers it only as a variable entering additively with other variables, there is a distinct possibility that such variables interact with, and hence, condition, the effect of other input variables, such as the type of instructional approach used. Indeed, my colleagues, W. Lee Hansen and Allen Kelley, and I, in a 1970 article,[2] pointed to evidence of such an interaction effect, although involving higher education. We noted that a given instructional technique might vary considerably in effectiveness among students of differential initial achievement levels, and, referring to some current experimental work by Kelley, we noted that one new instructional technique was consistently most effective (in terms of enhanced performance on a standardized achievement test) for students at the highest initial levels of achievement.

But the inputs which Kiesling appears to have most interest in, and most faith in, are the planning, coordination, leadership, and teamwork variables. His faith does not appear to be shaken by the statistically insignificant coefficients he finds for variables reflecting time spent in planning and in-service training, percentage of key people who are involved in planning, and the degree of teamwork. I suggest that Kiesling's faith in these variables is misplaced, not because they are necessarily unimportant—he is probably right in blaming "poor data"—but because they are not now *instrumental variables*. Coordination, leadership, and teamwork are not variables that can easily be added to or subtracted from a production process; we know so little about how to produce these important inputs. I believe that Kiesling is implicitly recognizing this when he admits that "teamwork is an extremely difficult thing to quantify," and that "it is also difficult to correctly represent the degree of informal meeting and discussing that occurs" among regular teachers, specialists, and leaders in some remedial programs.

To say that these variables are difficult to quantify is to say, in effect, that we do not know how to vary them. Thus, even if Kiesling is right in his faith in something called "leadership, coordination, and teamwork," we cannot depend on those variables for successful remedial programs for the educationally disadvantaged until we discover how to produce them.

A final word concerning the *dating* of variables in the production function. Kiesling implicitly set out to estimate a production function for remedial reading in a manner analogous to the production function for corn or wheat: inputs are applied during a period and a single output (crop) comes at the end of the period. As a first approximation this is an attractive approach, but it is probably a considerable simplification of reality. Learning is probably more of an *investment* process in which "outputs" from one year of schooling continue to flow for perhaps many years, thereby affecting ability to learn in subsequent school years. That is, just as inputs used in growing bananas (unlike corn and wheat) will contribute not only to the output of bananas in that year but will contribute to banana production in subsequent years, so remedial schooling inputs in one year may have effects beyond that year. Indeed, we hope that is the case!

Unfortunately, we cannot be certain that such future "output" effects will be positive. They can be negative. Analyses of OEO Head Start Programs, for example, has disclosed that output (reading level achievement) did increase during the period of the program, but one or two years later most or all of the added achievement had apparently vanished; there was no longer a difference between the achievement level of students who had been part of the Head Start Program and the achievement of a control group of students who had not. There are, of course, various interpretations of these findings; the point is only that "outputs" can be quite different, depending on the date at which they are examined.

We—economists or educators—know so little about the production function for any type of educational output for any market segment that empirical studies such as Kiesling's can be usefully multiplied manyfold even before diminishing returns set in—and, of course, we should not stop there. As this work proceeds, though, we need to place greater emphasis, I believe, on building models in which (1) schooling is treated as an investment process yielding multi-period returns in terms of learning; in which (2) interactions among inputs are considered; in which (3) inputs that can be subject to control are emphasized; and eventually (4) on building models which account for conflicts and complementarities among multiple goals.

NOTES

1. The much-praised "Sesame Street" television program has come under attack for its alleged failure to develop students' self-esteem. See, for example, *Newsweek,* May 24, 1971, p. 52.
2. W. Lee Hansen, Allen C. Kelley, and Burton A. Weisbrod, "Economic Efficiency and the Distribution of Benefits from College Instruction," *American Economic Review* 60 (May 1970): 364–369.

PART THREE

Higher Education

7

LEONARD S.
MILLER
University of California,
Berkeley

Demand for Higher Education in the United States: A Second Progress Report

This paper is the second report on demand estimates for higher education in the United States from our Project on Econometric Models of Higher Education, supported by the Carnegie Commission on the Future of Higher Education.[1] In this report I address the problem of estimating the joint probability distribution of freshman attendance at alternative types of higher education institutions.

A student's post-secondary-school alternatives are, by and large, a set of mutually exclusive possibilities. The choice of a "best" post-secondary-school alternative is dependent upon the characteristics of all the possibilities available to the chooser. Previous studies of the demand for higher education have found relationships describing the percentage of total enrollment and the percentage of enrollment at a particular type of institution. To account for the mutual interdependency between alternative institutional types, the costs of alternative choice types, these previous studies have incorporated as individual explainants in single equation regressions. In our study a more explicit account of the joint dependency of the post-secondary alternatives is made. The exploration of how the distribution of attending alternative post-secondary-school choices is related to individual and institutional characteristics is reported here.

Stochastic choice theory underlies our demand estimates. A strict model establishes a relationship between utilities and probabilities. A specific form of the utility function, the exponential of a linear sum of variables describing the chooser and his or her choices, is assumed. This function, coupled with the constraints of the choices and the strict model, allows for maximum likelihood estimates of the parameters of the resulting probability distribution function. These estimates are called conditional logit estimates.

The estimated probability functions contain two variables. The first variable represents alternative estimates of the ratio of the cost of a particular post-secondary-school choice, to the student's family income. The second variable is an estimate of the student's SAT (Scholastic Aptitude Test) score multiplied by an estimate of the average freshman SAT score of the particular post-secondary-school choice, divided by 1,000. We call the first the "cost-to-income" variable, and the second the "student-institution achievement interaction" variable.

The original data source was a subsample of SCOPE (School to College: Opportunities for Post Secondary Education). Only a portion of the SCOPE observations had a reliable family-income estimate. The subsample was divided into two groups; one with a reliable income estimate, referred to as Sample II, and one without a reliable estimate, referred to as Sample I (II has more information than I). Sample II was biased; its students had higher achievement scores and higher student-reported family income. As an attempt to understand the biases that would eventually enter our final results we computed demand estimates for both samples.

An aggregation of the observations by state yielded poor results. The "cost-to-income" coefficient was negative and often significant, as anticipated. But the coefficient on the "student-institution achievement interaction variable" fluctuated considerably. Sample I seemed to yield better results than Sample II. Because of our sampling design, it was likely that Sample I was more homogeneous than Sample II. This result suggested that more homogeneous groups might yield better demand estimates.

State observations were pooled and four achievement groups were constructed in each sample. Two significant patterns emerged. The first was that the "cost-to-income" coefficients were significantly negative; and as achievement rose the value of the coefficient became less negative. The low-achievement group had a relatively elastic demand for higher education with respect to cost and income, and the high-achievement group to a significantly positive coefficient for the high-tion with respect to cost and income.

The second pattern to emerge was that the coefficients on the "student-institution achievement interaction variable" also had a trend. This trend went from a significantly negative coefficient for the low-achievement group to a significantly positive coefficient for the high-achievement group. The middle groups were in between. Students who had low achievement measures were marginally repelled from better schools, while students who had high achievement measures were marginally attracted to better schools.

Variations in the conditional logit estimates were introduced with additional information about the high school seniors. As one would expect, direct information such as high school curriculum and the student's college plans cause the greatest alterations in the demand model's predicted probabilities. The educational objectives of parents for their children, and other measures related to the perceptions students have about the relationship between education and the future labor market cause some marginal shifts in the demand probability predictions.

Section I presents a review and critique of the previous studies. Section II presents the model and a description of the estimated demand specifications. We include a short description of the data and sampling in Section III. A more complete discussion appears in an appendix which is available from the author. A presentation of the results is accompanied by a discussion of the research process in Section IV. Section V extends the model and considers how additional information about the chooser (student) alters the probability distribution associated with his or her choices.

SECTION I: REVIEW AND CRITIQUE OF THE LITERATURE

In 1967, the process of finding empirical estimates for the demand for higher education in the United States began. Campbell and Siegel were the first to generate enough information to make the first empirical demand description.[2] Their published result consists of a regression of R_t (defined as the proportion of people between age 18 and 24 enrolled as resident degree undergraduates in 4-year institutions), on Y_{Ht}, and P_t (defined, respectively, as an estimate of real disposable income per household and an index of tuition costs deflated by the consumer price index). Their linear log specification yielded an elasticity of 1.2036 for the proportion enrollment with respect to household disposable income, and an elasticity of $-.4404$ for the proportion of enrollment with respect to tuition costs. Both elasticities were significantly different from zero at the .025 level, and 93 per cent of the variance was explained by the regression. Nine observations between 1927 and 1963 served as the estimation data in the Campbell-Siegel work.

One problem with this first study is that an identification problem probably exists in their analysis. Consequently, their demand estimates are probably biased. If equilibrium is assumed in the enrollment market, annual enrollment equals the annual supply of places. R_t, then, is also the probability that an enrollment place in higher education will be supplied to someone between 18 and 24 years old. Like demand, supply R_t could be related to Y_{Ht} and P_t. Due to the likelihood that any increase in the public sector's supply of places would be related to taxable per capita income, Y_{Ht} would be positively related to R_t. P_t could be positively related to R_t for the usual reason that more places will be offered as price rises.

On the other hand, an identification problem might not exist. Many of the most sought after 4-year institutions (those institutions where applicants exceed capacity) are not in a simple price equilibrium. Rather than expand institutional capacity, suppliers apply greater selectivity to applicants. To the extent that the supply schedule reflects this group of institutions, the price parameter may be absent. Here, the demand schedule is identified.

It is my feeling that the results themselves suggest some bias. Consider the income distribution associated with a unit increase of disposable per capita income in relation to the dependent variable in the Campbell-Siegel formulation. One portion of the income increase accrues to families whose children do not presently attend 4-year colleges, and the other portion accrues to families whose children are presently enrolled in 4-year colleges. None of the portion of the income increase accruing to the enrollees can logically increase enrollment. Some of the income may go to increased expenses, but that is not the dependent variable. Any 4-year college enrollment increase attributed to an income increase can only come from students enrolled in less than 4-year colleges, and from nonstudents. We expect, then, that the percentage of 4-year college enrollment with respect to disposable income elasticity will be less than one. The enrollment elasticity computed by Campbell and Siegel, however, was 1.20.

I am acquainted with two other econometric demand studies which attempt to determine income and price responses to enrollment. Both studies were the result of state-level attempts to impose rational planning on a state higher-education system. One study, by Stephen A. Hoenack, was done for the Office of Analytical Studies, at the University of California.[3] The other study was produced by a team of consultants for the Metropolitan Area Planning Council for the Commonwealth of Massachusetts, Board of Higher Education.[4]

Since each study had different objectives, their equation specifications were different. Hoenack's task was to determine the California high school seniors' demand for freshman places in the University of California (UC). Hoenack estimated two sets of demand specifications with data on 1965 California high school seniors. One set of specifications used information on Los Angeles area eligibles and their attendance at the University of California at Los Angeles (UCLA). This set was used to represent the demand function of all freshmen commuters for any UC campus. A second set of demand functions represented the enrollment demand of UC eligibles for UC campuses outside their high school residence communities. Separate equations were estimated for the UC campuses at Davis, Berkeley, and Santa Barbara, and an aggregate function was estimated for attendance at UCLA, Riverside (UCR), and Irvine (UCI). The aggregate demand for each campus was set equal to the weighted sum of the commuter plus noncommuter demand.[5] Hoenack determined a UC aggregate demand function by summing the separate campus functions. The actual demand function achieved was not presented, however.

In his study the dependent variable was the percentage of freshmen enrolled at specific UC campuses out of the total UC eligibles from each high school, E. The independent variables were: (1) various combinations of the cost of attending alternative UC campuses, P (campus); (2) the cost to the high school senior of attending the nearest state and junior college, P_{SC} and P_{JC} respectively; (3) estimates of the median income of families in each high school's census area, Y; (4) the number of graduating seniors from a high school, G; and (5) unemployment and wage rate data on the high school's region, U and W. The commuter equations included an estimate of the daily commuting cost. Students' time was valued at $2.40 per hour.

Alternative demand specifications were tried; they were usually linear logarithmic, although sometimes some of the independent variables were not logged. Ordinary least squares were performed on combined income brackets and on various combinations of income quartile disaggregations.

To give a flavor of Hoenack's results I include one of his estimated equations as an example.

$$\log \left(\frac{A_{UCR+UCI+UCLA}}{E}\right) = 19.11 + .002G + 1.992 \log P_{UCB} - 5.740 \log P_{UCLA}$$
$$(9.21) \quad (1.86) \quad (3.48) \quad (-3.44)$$
$$+ 1.9866 \log P_{UCSB} + 1.5473 \log P_{SC}$$
$$(3.20) \quad (2.32)$$

$$+ \ .98 \log P_{JC} + \ .69 \log Y$$
$$\quad (1.70) \qquad\qquad (1.81)$$
$$+ \ .05 \log U - 2.45 \log W$$
$$\quad (.20) \qquad\quad (-3.07)$$
$$- \ .000126 \ (P_{UCB} + P_{UCSB}) \log Y$$
$$(-3.28)$$
$$+ \ .000346 \ P_{UCLA} \log Y$$
$$\quad (3.43)$$
$$- \ .00067 \ P_{SC} \log Y - \ .00007 \ P_{JC} \log Y$$
$$\quad (-2.27) \qquad\qquad\quad (-1.77)$$

$R^2 = .99$; $DW = 2.10$; all income brackets; 90 observations; t values in parentheses.[6]

Hoenack finds a demand elasticity of $-.85$ for the percentage of enrollment with respect to price for UC campuses. This value varies from -1.12 for the lowest income bracket to $-.71$ for the highest. Hoenack reports that state colleges appear to be a close substitute for UC campuses. If state college prices rise simultaneously with UC price rises, but with increases only two-thirds of the UC price increase, the students' price elasticity for UC diminishes substantially. Average UC price elasticity values fall from $-.85$ to $-.51$; the lowest income group's values decrease from -1.12 to $-.68$, and the highest income group's values decrease from $-.71$ to $-.48$.

The decision to commute or to live away from home was apparently significantly affected by the wage rates prevailing in the hometown area. They were not affected by the unemployment rate.[7]

Income elasticities are not reported. However, the elasticity implied by the sample equation above is approximately .7.

Hoenack made a limited attempt at extending his demand formulation to the state and junior colleges in California. No estimates are actually presented, but Hoenack claims to have been unsuccessful at explaining attendance at the state college geographically nearest to each high school, and successful at explaining the proportion of high school seniors attending their nearest junior college. The junior college tuition-enrollment result given is that a $100 increase in junior college tuition would diminish enrollment by approximately 7 per cent.

The Massachusetts–Metropolitan Area Planning Council study on higher education took as its task the development of a coordinated and comprehensive public policy for higher education in the state. They saw the question of attending versus not attending any higher education institution as their principal problem. The dependent variable in this study was the percentage of 1960 tenth-grade high school students who attended college in 1963.

The following independent variables were used: (1) junior college tuition, P_j; (2) public 4-year university tuition, P_u; (3) tuition at teachers' college, P_c; (4) private 4-year university tuition, P_p; (5) father's education, which was supposed to proxy for family income, E; (6) average income of production workers, a proxy for opportunity cost, Y; (7) ability as measured by performance on achievement tests, A; and (8) unemployment, U.

The Massachusetts study presented regressions for percentage enrollees; percentage enrollees by sex; and because of possible nonlinearities, percentage of enrollees by quartiles of father's education. From lowest to highest these quartiles are denoted by *LSES, 2SES, 3SES, HSES*. Their results are reported in the table on page 300.[8]

In the equation explaining the aggregate enrollment percentage level only the coefficient on teachers' college tuition is not significantly different from zero. The computed percentage enrollment elasticities with respect to price are: $-.09$ for junior colleges, $-.18$ for 4-year state public universities, and $-.19$ for 4-year private universities in the state. Percentage of enrollment appears to be twice as price inelastic for junior colleges as it is for public universities or for 4-year private institutions.

The unemployment coefficient was significant in this equation and the wage rate was not. This result is just the opposite of that found by Hoenack.

The authors of the Massachusetts study caution against a direct use of the father's education to compute an income elasticity. However, the reader is provided with almost all the figures to do so, and the temptation was simply too great. Assuming the mean family income of the college-age population as ten thousand dollars, the implied income elasticity is .28.

When the sample was stratified by sex, we find males showing almost twice the marginal price responsiveness towards public universities as females. Similarly, the marginal responsiveness to ability is almost twice as high for men as for women. Disaggregating by sex highlights the results of institutional sexism (discrimination according to sex). Both results, price responsiveness and ability responsiveness, are consistent with the finding that males have higher rates of return on education than do females. The price result suggests that men attend college for more economic reasons than women, while the ability result suggests that women do not behave as if their abilities will be valued as much as men's abilities will be valued.

Computed Elasticity of Total Percentage Enrollment with Respect to Price

	Junior College	Public University	Private 4-Year College
Males	$-.096$	$-.27$	$-.23$
Females	$-.081$	$-.11$	not significant

Regression Results

Per Cent Enrolled	Constant	P_j	P_u	P_c	P_v	E	Y	A	U	R^2
E_T	14.431	−.0111 (−3.14)	−.0265 (−2.32)	.0081 (1.26)	−.0087 (−2.06)	2.839 (4.21)	−3.622 (−1.03)	.176 (5.72)	.834 (2.04)	.769
E_{TM}	13.993	−.0132 (−3.42)	−.0438 (−2.39)	.0009 (1.04)	−.0116 (2.17)	3.265 (4.87)	−2.066 (−1.81)	.208 (5.22)	1.553 (2.16)	.806
E_{TF}	5.094	−.0093 (−2.96)	−.0153 (−3.60)	−.0231 (−1.37)	.0106 (.87)	2.576 (2.87)	−1.041 (−1.19)	.131 (3.67)	.427 (1.41)	.721
E_{LSES}	1.573	−.0072 (−2.06)	−.0125 (−1.71)	−.0059 (1.04)	.0018 (.57)	1.762 (2.52)	−1.347 (2.29)	.041 (1.56)	.776 (1.34)	.537
E_{2SES}	4.156	−.0093 (−1.49)	−.0137 (−1.81)	−.0122 (.96)	−.0014 (−1.09)	.853 (2.17)	−1.590 (1.08)	.053 (2.02)	.316 (1.22)	.412
E_{3SES}	5.912	−.0051 (−1.19)	−.0097 (−1.91)	−.0017 (−1.36)	−.0045 (−1.74)	.907 (2.08)	−1.003 (.96)	.069 (2.12)	−.315 (−.58)	.450
E_{HSES}	5.590	.0006 (.57)	−.0126 (1.68)	.0055 (.86)	−.0041 (2.09)	.267 (1.21)	.668 (.54)	.045 (2.23)	−.065 (−1.89)	.491

NOTE: t statistics are in parentheses.

When the Massachusetts sample was stratified by father's education, a proxy for socioeconomic status (SES), most of the variables stop being significant. For example, only the junior college price is significant for the lowest SES group, and only the private college price is significant for the highest SES group. The two middle groups have no significant price coefficients. Father's education (SES) is significant for the lower three quartiles, the wage rate is negatively significant for the lowest SES group, unemployment is never significant, and ability rather uniformly affects the upper three groups.

Uncertainty about the Campbell-Siegel estimates arises out of the fact that the model used to describe their problem is incomplete. One aspect of this incompleteness is the question of whether the supply function required specification. In addition, if the reader will recall, there was some difficulty interpreting the per capita income coefficient, given the 4-year-enrollment dependent variable. This latter difficulty arose because the specification of the problem was incomplete in yet another way.

Many different types of higher education institutions exist. One would like to have known how additions to per capita income, or how the changes in the cost of attending a specific type of institution affected enrollment in all higher educational types. To some extent the models offered by Hoenack and the Massachusetts study improved on the Campbell-Siegel effort. Neither of the former two studies had identification problems, for both used cross-sectional data and assumed short-run fixed supply. And, both attempted to get at the existence of alternative higher education institution types by incorporating the costs of alternative institutions as independent explainants. However, none of the studies reported address themselves to the problem of explaining the joint dependency of the demand for these different institutional types. The reported 35 per cent drop in UC's own price elasticity when state college prices change dramatically illustrates the interdependency of demand decisions concerning higher education.

Individual choices are made within a framework of jointly dependent post-secondary-school alternatives. These include the alternative institutional possibilities and the choice of not going on to college. These possibilities can be described by attributes; items like cost and quality are perhaps among some of the more important of these attributes. This jointly dependent decision-making framework will be developed in the sections to follow.

Before proceeding, however, one further note is necessary. In addition to market forces, nonmarket forces affect higher education institutional choice, and some comment on this matter is called for. Galper and Dunn studied the short-run nonmarket effect of the rate of growth of the armed services on the Campbell-Siegel undergraduate enrollment series.[9] Their contribution to the demand estimation problem is an estimate of the effect the armed forces play on 4-year college enrollment. They estimated the elasticity of enrollment with respect to the annual rate of growth of the armed services at $-.26$, and their enrollment elasticity with respect to discharges was .13. One should add that their income elasticity estimate was .69, a value consistent with our previous argument, and similar to that found in Hoenack's example.

After estimating the probability distribution of attending alternative types of schools, principally as a function of economic and achievement variables, our attention is addressed to more noneconomic aspects of the higher education choice decision. Specifically, we compute how our estimates of the probability distribution are altered by additional information about the chooser. This analysis appears in the final section.

SECTION II: THE MODEL

Each graduating high school senior faces a supply of higher education institutions to which he or she is eligible. We shall call this institutional collection, along with the alternative of not going on to higher education, the individual's feasible choice set. Individuals have a multiple-choice problem. They choose one and only one of these separate alternatives from their feasible choice set. We are dealing, therefore, with a demand more like that for houses or automobiles than for butter or beer, in the sense that the choice is among a small number of discrete alternatives rather than among different quantities of a divisible good. Estimating the freshman demand for higher education becomes a problem of specifying and estimating this choice process.

Choosers and their choice sets will be described with personal and institutional variables, respectively. We will assume that the objective function will be the same for the entire population; only the variables describing the people or their alternatives will alter any individual's selection of "best." However, our descriptions are rather simplistic. And, it will often be the case that similarly described people choosing from similarly described feasible choice sets differ in their assessment of the best alternative.

The usual theory of choice would infer in this situation that the chooser or choosers are indifferent among the choices; they perceive the same subjective benefit from them. This is so even when nine out of every ten students choose one alternative and the tenth chooses another. An appeal to data insufficiencies might be made, but such recourse does not solve the underlying logical problem: similarly described students may not choose the same best choice, and we should not infer that students are indifferent between all the chosen alternatives.

The demand functions reported on here are based on a model of *stochastic choice theory*. The logical framework of this theory explicitly accounts for this indifference problem. The selection of the best post-secondary-school alternatives will be viewed as a stochastic utility-maximization problem. In this section the underlying theory for the freshman demand functions is presented. In addition, the section includes a brief account of the specifications, the estimation technique, and some discussion of the expected signs of the parameters.

Stochastic Choice Theory

Let A be a finite set of discrete post-secondary alternatives, and let J_i be the feasible choice set for individual i, $J_i \subset A$. Imagine that we are either dealing with one chooser who makes repeated choices, or that we are dealing with many choosers assumed to behave alike. It is likely that the utility derived from choice j is greater than the utility derived from choice k, when both j and k are in the feasible choice set, and j is chosen nine out of ten times over k. Stochastic choice theory asserts this likelihood, while absolute choice theory establishes indifference between the two choices.[10] There are many models of stochastic choice theory; they differ according to the specificity of the ordering relation and the probabilistic assumptions between the choices. All models begin by assuming that the basic axioms of probability theory apply to the elements J of the feasible choice set for individual i, J_i, where $J_i \subset A$.

(1) $\text{Prob}(j \,|\, j \epsilon J_i) \geqq 0$

(2) $\sum_{j \epsilon J_i} \text{Prob}(j \,|\, J_i) = 1$

The simplest stochastic theory, a weak stochastic model, asserts that when the utility of j is greater than the utility of k, there is a tendency to choose j over k. Formally, there exists a constant real-valued vector U over A such that: $U(j) \geqq U(k)$ IFF $\text{Prob}(j \,|\{\, j,k \}) \geqq \frac{1}{2}$. U is called a weak utility function.[11]

The stochastic model actually used to achieve our demand equations imposed more structure on the choice set and the ordering relation than is imposed by the weak model. A *strict utility model* was used, which is defined as follows: There exists a constant positive real-valued vector U over the feasible set J, $J \subset A$, such that for any j, $k \epsilon J$

(3) $U(j)/U(k) = \text{Prob}(j|J)/\text{Prob}(k|J)$

Block and Marschak have shown that a strict model implies, but is not implied by, a weak model.[12]

From equation 2 the probability of individual i choosing institutional type j is expressed as

(4) $\text{Prob}(j|J_i) = \text{Prob}(j|j \in J_i)/\sum_{k \in J_i} \text{Prob}(k$

The strict utility model states that utilities are proportionate to probabilities. The probability that individual i chooses choice type j, ϕ_{ij}, can be rewritten as:

(5) $\phi_{ij} = \text{Prob}(j|J_i) = U_i(j)/\sum_k U_i(k)$

A specific form for the utility function $U_i(j)$ allows one to relate the descriptions of the student choosers and their alternative choices to utility and relative frequency. Estimation of the parameters of the model are based on a maximum likelihood process.

Let Z_{ij}^h and β^h represent the hth variable and hth constant, respectively, in a linear sum

(6) $f_{ij} = \sum_h \beta^h Z_{ij}^h$

It is assumed that the utility or subjective benefit to individual i from institutional type j is given by the explicit equation

(7) $U_i(j) = F_{ij} = \exp(f_{ij})$

The probability of i choosing j, equation 5, can be expressed as

(8) $\phi_{ij} = \dfrac{F_{ij}}{\sum\limits_{k \subset J_i} F_{ik}} = \dfrac{\exp(\sum\limits_h \beta^h Z_{ij}^n)}{\sum\limits_k \exp(\sum\limits_h \beta^h Z_{ik}^h)}$

For n individuals, $i = 1, 2, \ldots, n$, let

$X_{ij} = \begin{Bmatrix} 1 \\ 0 \end{Bmatrix}$ according as $i \begin{Bmatrix} \text{has} \\ \text{has not} \end{Bmatrix}$ chosen j

The likelihood function, $L(\beta^h)$ is given by

(9) $L(\beta^h) = \pi_i \pi_{j \in l_i} \phi_{ij}^{X_{ij}}$

The maximum likelihood estimates, b^h of β^h, are those values of b^h that maximize $L(\beta^h)$. McFadden has produced a computer program to estimate these parameters and has explored the properties of these estimates.[13]

The availability of data, and the results of experiments with different formulations, led us to concentrate on the following variables whose precise definitions can be found in the appendix available from the author:

A_i = an achievement score for student i (an estimate of i's SAT score);

Y_i = a measure of family income for student i;

S_j = a measure of the "academic selectivity" or "quality" of alternative j; and

C_{ij} = the out-of-pocket dollar cost to i of going to j (set equal to zero for the alternative "no school").

We define Z^1_{ij} and Z^2_{ij}, in equation 6 above, in terms of these variables.

$$Z^1_{ij} = C_{ij}/Y_i, \text{ and } Z^2_{ij} = A_i S_j/1000$$

and, for the convenience of discussion, we have given these variables the names "cost-to-income" and "student-institutional achievement interaction" respectively.

The greater the "cost-to-income," the less the individual wants the alternative. Thus, the sign of the estimate b^1 for β^1 is unambiguously anticipated as negative.

For any given individual, the better the quality of the institution the higher is the value of the "student-institution achievement interaction" variable. The perceived benefits of a better quality school can occur in the form of greater intellectual and social amenities, or in the form of a higher rate of monetary return upon completion. The perceived costs of a better school can occur in the form of either increased competition, or an increased probability of failure. If an individual interprets his or her net subjective benefits from an alternative as positive, we expect the sign of the coefficient on "student-institution achievement interaction" to be positive. Alternatively, if the individual interprets the costs as exceeding the benefits, we expect the sign of the coefficient on the interaction variable to be negative.

Discussion of the conditional logit estimates focuses on marginal and elasticity terms. What follows is a derivation of these terms from the joint probability distribution function of the demand model. Given an individual's feasible choice set J_i, the probability of individual i choosing alternative j, is given by equation 8.

$$\phi_{ij} = \exp(\beta^1 Z^1_{ij} + \beta^2_2 Z^2_{ij})/ \sum_{k \in J_i} \exp(\beta^1 Z^1_{ik} + \beta^2 Z^2_{ik})$$

Differentiation of equation 8 with respect to an individual's achievement, A_i, an institution's quality, S_j, an institution's cost, C_{ij}, or the student's family income, Y_i, yields the marginal responses with respect to these variables.

$$\frac{\partial \phi_{ij}}{\partial A_i} = \beta^2 \frac{\phi_{ij}}{1,000} \left[S_j - \sum_{k \in J_i} S_k \phi_{ik} \right]$$

$$\frac{\partial \phi_{ij}}{\partial S_j} = \beta^2 \frac{A_i}{1,000} \phi_{ij}(1 - \phi_{ij})$$

$$\frac{\partial \phi_{ij}}{\partial C_{ij}} = \beta^1 \frac{1}{Y_i} \phi_{ij}(1 - \phi_{ij})$$

$$\frac{\partial \phi_{ij}}{\partial Y_i} = \frac{-\beta^1}{Y_i^2} \phi_{ij}\left[C_{ij} - \sum_{k \in J_i} C_{ik} \phi_{ik}\right]$$

Denoting $\eta_{\phi_{ij}, w}$ as the elasticity of the probability of individual i choosing choice j with respect to the variable W, the elasticities for the four marginals derived above are

$$\eta_{\phi_{ij}, A_i} = \frac{\beta^2 A_i}{1,000} \left[S_j - \sum_{k \in J_i} S_k \phi_{ik}\right]$$

$$\eta_{\phi_{ij}, Y_i} = \frac{-\beta^1}{Y_i} \left[C_{ij} - \sum_{k \in J_i} C_{ik} \phi_{ik}\right]$$

$$\eta_{\phi_{ij}, C_{ij}} = \beta^1 \frac{C_{ij}}{Y_i} (1 - \phi_{ij})$$

$$\eta_{\phi_{ij}, S_i} = \beta^2 \frac{A_i S_j}{1,000} (1 - \phi_{ij})$$

$$\eta_{\phi_{ik}, C_{ij}} = -\beta^1 \frac{C_{ij}}{Y_i} \phi_{ik}$$

$$\eta_{\phi_{ik}, S_j} = -\beta^2 \frac{A_i S_j}{1,000} \phi_{ij}$$

Two cross elasticities are of particular interest. One indicates the percentage change in ϕ_{ij} caused by a 1 per cent change in the cost of choice k, $k \in J_i$. The other indicates the percentage change in ϕ_{ij} caused by a 1 per cent change in the quality of choice k, $k \in J_i$. The appropriate marginals are obtained by differentiating equation 8

$$\frac{\partial \phi_i}{\partial S_k} = -\beta^2 \frac{A_i}{1,000} \phi_{ij}, \phi_{ik}$$

$$\frac{\partial \phi_{ij}}{\partial C_{ik}} = -\beta^1 \frac{1}{Y_i} \phi_{ij}, \phi_{ik}$$

Their elasticities are given by

$$\eta_{\phi_{ij}, S_k} = -\beta^2 \frac{A_i S_k}{1,000} \phi_{ik}$$

and

$$\eta_{\phi_{ik}, C_{ij}} = \frac{\partial \phi_{ik}}{\partial C_{ij}} \frac{C_{ij}}{\phi_{ik}} = -\beta^1 \frac{C_{ij}}{Y_i} \phi_{ij}$$

Hoenack found that the elasticity of the percentage of University of California enrollees with respect to University of California cost was lower for low-income groups than for high-income groups. Since the formula for the enrollment elasticity with respect to cost contains income in the denominator, the conditional logit results will always reproduce Hoenack's finding.

SECTION III: DATA AND SAMPLING

Estimating the proposed model required data unlike any used in previous demand studies. To my knowledge, no information about the feasible choice sets of a population existed. Two data sources contained the actual post-secondary choice selected by high school seniors, and seemed to have sufficient information to estimate the model if the feasible choice sets for observations were constructed. These sources were Project TALENT, and SCOPE (School to College: Opportunities for Post Secondary Education).

Analysis of Project TALENT data had shown that ability and family income were highly correlated, and also correlated with college attendance. Although Project TALENT probably had a better analysis of the nonreporting biases in their follow-up studies, they would not release the residency location of their subjects. Knowing the locally available higher education options was one of the determinants of an individual's feasible choice set. Since SCOPE was willing to release these data, I decided to proceed with the SCOPE information.

SCOPE is an ongoing longitudinal study, conducted at the Center for Research and Development in Higher Education, University of California, Berkeley. I was provided with a subsample, 4,434 observations of 1966 high school seniors in California, Illinois, Massachusetts, and North Carolina.

In addition to high school residency and the post-secondary-school alternative chosen, the relevant information on each SCOPE observation was an achievement measure and the observation's estimate of family income. Further income information had been obtained with a follow-up mail questionnaire to parents in 1967. Unfortunately, mailed questionnaires never produce unbiased samples.

Of the families queried, 31.6 per cent responded (1,402 out of the 4,434 in the sample). A comparison of the students' achievement test scores with their high school answers to the family-income question showed that the sample of youngsters with parent responders had higher achievement. They were also from higher-income families (determined by the students' twelfth-grade self-reporting of family income).

These were significant biases. We could not adequately take the income-reporting bias into account with a corrective sampling procedure. The relationship between parent-reported income and student-reported income was not strong enough. In addition, other differences between the parent reporters and nonreporters undoubtedly existed. In an attempt to understand the biases which would appear in our final results, we decided to make demand estimates for both the reporter and the nonreporter populations. An income predictor for the nonreporters was required for the demand specification.[14] In addition, we decided to sample from both populations in a way that would reasonably assure coverage of the full range of student achievement and students' family income.[15]

Demand samples were drawn in the following manner:

1. The reporter population in each state was allocated into cells determined by quartiles of achievement and six income ranges. The entire achievement-income range was covered by sampling four observations from each cell wherever possible. This sample will be referred to as Sample II.

2. The nonreporter population in each state was allocated into cells determined by quartiles of achievement and six predicted income ranges. Income was then predicted for the Sample II observations and the rather uniformly distributed achievement-income sample was allocated into achievement–predicted-income cells. Sample II's new cell frequency count determined the number of non-reporters that were drawn from the nonreporter achievement–predicted-income distributed population. This sample is referred to as Sample I (I has less information than II).

SECTION IV: RESULTS

Introduction

Results are presented within a twofold context. First, I want to convey what I have learned about higher education demand functions to date. Second, I should like to convey to the reader some of the process Roy Radner and I have gone through to obtain these results. The inclusion of a discussion of the research process may aid readers in interpreting the results, and may also be of value to future investigators.

Our first demand estimates were derived from individuals aggregated on the basis of the state in which they attended high school. We began with this aggregation because: (1) we processed the individual observations on a state basis (and we were anxious to see if this estimation process would work), and, (2) we believed that the demand functions in the different states might actually be different. The basis for this belief was a kind of reverse of Say's law. Here, the argument concludes, "Demand creates its own supply." Since there have been historical differences between the extent of the public higher-education effort in the four states, this very well might be evidence for the existence of different higher-education demand functions in the separate states.

In general, these state aggregation specifications were not satisfactory. The coefficient on the cost-to-income ratio was almost always negative and often significant; the coefficient on the "student-institution achievement interaction variable" was sometimes negative, sometimes positive, and was significant about as often as it was not. No definite pattern emerged. The more homogeneous income sample, Sample I, was probably yielding the best results. We decided to pool state observations and disaggregate on the basis of achievement. This produced more homogeneous groups and allowed us to experiment with the idea that the achievement interaction might vary according to the achievement distribution in the student population. The small number of our observations did not allow us to maintain the state level disaggregation, so we were never able to test successfully whether demand functions varied between states. Four averaged SAT groupings were constructed. The ranges for each group were based on an impression acquired of approximate homogeneous decision-making groups.

Under the achievement aggregation, two significant patterns emerged. The cost-to-income coefficients were significantly negative and contained a trend over the achievement groups. The enrollment elasticities with respect to cost and income ranged from elastic values for low-achievement students to inelastic values for the high-achievement students. The student-institution achievement interaction coefficients also had a trend over the achievement groups. The marginal effects for the low-achievement students were negative, the marginal effects for the high-achievement students were positive, and the marginal effects for the middle-achievement groups were in between. It appears that the higher-achieving students are attracted to better schools and the lower-achieving students are repelled from these schools. Apparently their history of relative academic failure is such as to marginally shift them away from a continuation of experiences like those they have already had.

Alternative Specifications

As I have previously stated, the demand specifications contained two variables. One variable, which for convenience we named the "cost-to-income" variable, measured the ratio of institutional cost estimates to student family-income estimates. The other variable, named the student-institution achievement interaction variable, measured the product of the student's achievement, A_i, and our estimate of the average SAT score of the freshman class at the choice under consideration, S_j, divided by 1,000 (to convert the units back into the SAT range).

For Sample II, we had four income estimates: (1) reported income, Y; (2) predicted income, YH; (3) an estimate of disposable reported income, DY; and (4) an estimate of disposable predicted income, DYH. For Sample I, the reported income estimates, (1) and (3), were not available. A rather complete discussion of these variables, and others introduced below, appears in the appendix available from the author.

Two cost estimates were available for each group; the out-of-pocket costs, C, and the C value with an opportunity cost estimated at $3,000 added to each choice, except the choice of not going to a higher-education institution. This cost was represented by the symbol CO. Combining the two cost estimates with the four possible income estimates produced eight possible cost-to-income ratios for Sample II. Combining the two possible cost estimates with the two possible income estimates produced four possible cost-to-income ratios for Sample I.

Detailed State Aggregation Results

Table 1 contains the results of estimating the demand function parameters with one variable in the conditional logit estimation function. Each variable previously discussed was estimated separately. A brief glance at Table 1 shows:

1. The C/Y coefficients always yield negative significant results. California and Illinois estimates are about the same, North Carolina's estimates are half as large as California's and Illinois's, and Massachusetts's is two-thirds of North Carolina's.
2. The C/YH coefficients again yield negative significant results (except in the case of the Massachusetts Sample II), but (a) the estimates are about 75 per cent larger than the C/Y estimates for the Sample II groups, and (b) the comparisons of Sample I and Sample II range from fairly similar estimates for California to quite different estimates for North Carolina.
3. The disposable income and predicted income specifications, C/DY and C/DYH, do not seem to contribute much understanding. These estimates are not significant in half of the states.
4. Adding the opportunity cost to the out-of-pocket cost seems to reproduce the results found in the four specifications already commented on. There are, of course, differences in the values of the coefficient estimates.

TABLE 1 Estimates of Coefficients on Individual Variables

Sample (Observations)	CAL I 96	CAL II 96	ILL I 91	ILL II 90	MASS I 91	MASS II 94	NC I 91	NC II 95
C/Y		-4.000 (.934)		-4.584 (.906)		-1.405 (.613)		-2.231 (.657)
C/YH	-5.312 (1.126)	-7.501 (1.354)	-11.273 (1.544)	-8.185 (1.267)	-7.600 (1.374)	$-.874$ (.775)	-15.418 (2.048)	-3.644 (1.043)
C/DY		$-.231 \cdot 10^{-1}$ ($.904 \cdot 10^{-2}$)		$-.870 \cdot 10^{-2}$ ($.515 \cdot 10^{-2}$)		$-.164 \cdot 10^{-1}$ ($.800 \cdot 10^{-2}$)		$-.143 \cdot 10^{-1}$ ($.567 \cdot 10^{-2}$)
C/DYH	$-.606 \cdot 10^{-2}$ ($.557 \cdot 10^{-2}$)	$-.201$ ($.805 \cdot 10^{-1}$)	-1.166 (1.167)	$-.688$ (.119)	$-.855$ (.149)	$+.420 \cdot 10^{-2}$ ($.899 \cdot 10^{-2}$)	-1.559 (.220)	$-.215 \cdot 10^{-1}$ ($.165 \cdot 10^{-1}$)
CO/Y		$-.402$ (.162)		-1.245 (.303)		$-.605$ (.274)		$-.578$ (.199)
CO/YH	$-.310$ (.169)	$-.905$ (.419)	-4.997 (.536)	-2.669 (.455)	-4.306 (.520)	$-.990$ (.443)	-5.488 (.563)	$-.893$ (.464)
CO/DY		$-.422 \cdot 10^{-2}$ ($.200 \cdot 10^{-2}$)		$-.371 \cdot 10^{-2}$ ($.207 \cdot 10^{-2}$)		$-.631 \cdot 10^{-2}$ ($.267 \cdot 10^{-2}$)		$-.420 \cdot 10^{-2}$ ($.175 \cdot 10^{-2}$)
CO/DYH	$-0.116 \cdot 10^{-2}$ ($.181 \cdot 10^{-2}$)	$-.385 \cdot 10^{-2}$ ($.463 \cdot 10^{-2}$)	$-.488$ ($.571 \cdot 10^{-1}$)	$-.181$ ($.384 \cdot 10^{-1}$)	$-.432$ ($.558 \cdot 10^{-1}$)	$+.342 \cdot 10^{-3}$ ($.456 \cdot 10^{-2}$)	$-.518$ ($.616 \cdot 10^{-1}$)	$-.506 \cdot 10^{-2}$ ($.359 \cdot 10^{-2}$)
Achievement interaction	$-.299 \cdot 10^{-1}$ ($.445 \cdot 10^{-2}$)	$-.129 \cdot 10^{-1}$ ($.389 \cdot 10^{-2}$)	$-.175 \cdot 10^{-1}$ ($.402 \cdot 10^{-2}$)	$-.133 \cdot 10^{-1}$ ($.370 \cdot 10^{-2}$)	$-.252 \cdot 10^{-2}$ ($.418 \cdot 10^{-2}$)	$+.397 \cdot 10^{-2}$ ($.396 \cdot 10^{-2}$)	$-.309 \cdot 10^{-1}$ ($.527 \cdot 10^{-2}$)	$-.100 \cdot 10^{-1}$ ($.393 \cdot 10^{-2}$)

NOTE: Figures in parentheses are standard errors of the coefficient estimates.

5. The student-institution achievement interaction coefficient estimate appears to be negative and significant in all cases except Massachusetts Sample II again. Frankly, we had not anticipated this result.

These five points tentatively suggested that most of our understanding will be derived from the out-of-pocket cost, the reported income, and the predicted income variables. The additional work that went into creating the other variables produced virtually no payoff. Furthermore, we are rather skeptical of single variable specifications.

Results of estimating the specifications with both variables included for Sample II and Sample I, by state, are presented in Table 2. The Sample II results are quite diverse. If one variable is significant in one specification, the other variable, more often than not, is not significant. The variable which is significant in any specification also varies between states. Sample II's estimates had only three specifications in which both variables were significant, the C/DY specification in California, the C/YH specification in Illinois, and the C/Y specification in Massachusetts. In these three cases, the cost-to-income coefficient was always negative, but the achievement interaction coefficient was negative in California and positive in the other two states. To repeat, not much consistency.

The Sample I estimates are less diverse than the Sample II estimates. In California, all the student-institution coefficients were negative and significant, and no cost-to-income coefficient was significant. For North Carolina we have an apparently opposite result: no student-institution coefficient was significant, while all the cost-to-income coefficients were negative and significant. The Illinois and Massachusetts results were a researcher's dream. Both coefficients were significant in every specification. Moreover, their estimates appeared to be reasonably consistent with one another. Both had positive, similar magnitudes on the student-institution variable, and both had negative, similar magnitudes on the cost-to-income variable.

All things considered, it was a very unsatisfactory state of affairs. A comparison of the results of Sample I and Sample II, however, did suggest how to proceed.

Our sampling control for Sample II had assured an achievement and income dispersion. While we could not really know the true income dispersion of Sample I, it was extremely likely that the Sample I groups were more homogeneous in economic status, within each ability group, than were the Sample II groups. Since the demand specifications worked less well in the more diversely designed sample (Sample II), we concluded that it may have been just too simplistic on our part to have expected rather different people to function as if they had similar decision-making functions. In Sample I, where we had less diverse

TABLE 2-A Demand Estimates by State and by Sample (California Sample II)

Achievement Interaction	C/Y	C/YH	C/DY	C/DYH	CO/Y	CO/YH	CO/DY	CO/DYH
$.255 \cdot 10^{-2}$	-4.346^*							
$(.513 \cdot 10^{-2})$	(1.18)							
$.103 \cdot 10^{-1}$		-9.638^*						
$(.527 \cdot 10^{-2})$		(1.82)						
$-.847 \cdot 10^{-2*}$			$-.175 \cdot 10^{-1*}$					
$(.419 \cdot 10^{-2})$			$(.842 \cdot 10^{-2})$					
$-.792 \cdot 10^{-2}$				$-.122$				
$(.454 \cdot 10^{-2})$				$(.766 \cdot 10^{-1})$				
$-.942 \cdot 10^{-2*}$					$-.234$			
$(.440 \cdot 10^{-2})$					$(.166)$			
$-.100 \cdot 10^{-1*}$						$-.309$		
$(.447 \cdot 10^{-2})$						$(.310)$		
$-.107 \cdot 10^{-1*}$							$-.235 \cdot 10^{-2}$	
$(.416 \cdot 10^{-2})$							$(.203 \cdot 10^{-2})$	
$-.122 \cdot 10^{-1*}$								$-.149 \cdot 10^{-2}$
$(.396 \cdot 10^{-2})$								$(.446 \cdot 10^{-2})$

NOTE: Figures in parentheses are standard errors of the estimates. An asterisk indicates at least .05 level of significance.

TABLE 2-B Demand Estimates by State and by Sample (Illinois Sample II)

Achievement Interaction	C/Y	C/YH	C/DY	C/DYH	CO/Y	CO/YH	CO/DY	CO/DYH
$.249 \cdot 10^{-2}$ ($.492 \cdot 10^{-2}$)	-4.953^* (1.178)							
$.117 \cdot 10^{-1*}$ ($.539 \cdot 10^{-2}$)		-10.739^* (1.788)						
$-.117 \cdot 10^{-1*}$ ($.384 \cdot 10^{-2}$)			$-.729 \cdot 10^{-2}$ ($.552 \cdot 10^{-2}$)					
$.568 \cdot 10^{-2}$ ($.529 \cdot 10^{-2}$)				$-.780^*$ (.163)				
$-.523 \cdot 10^{-2}$ ($.468 \cdot 10^{-2}$)					$-.952^*$ (.364)			
$.106 \cdot 10^{-1}$ ($.646 \cdot 10^{-2}$)						-3.840^* (.813)		
$-.125 \cdot 10^{-1*}$ ($.384 \cdot 10^{-2}$)							$-.158 \cdot 10^{-2}$ ($.218 \cdot 10^{-2}$)	
$-.342 \cdot 10^{-2}$ ($.517 \cdot 10^{-2}$)								$-.158^*$ ($.510 \cdot 10^{-1}$)

NOTE: See note to Table 2-A.

TABLE 2-C Demand Estimates by State and by Sample (Massachusetts Sample II)

Achievement Interaction	C/Y	C/YH	C/DY	C/DYH	CO/Y	CO/YH	CO/DY	CO/DYH
$.108 \cdot 10^{-1}$* $(.469 \cdot 10^{-2})$	-2.369* $(.821)$							
$.694 \cdot 10^{-2}$ $(.474 \cdot 10^{-2})$		-1.674 (1.066)						
$.591 \cdot 10^{-2}$ $(.416 \cdot 10^{-2})$			$-.200 \cdot 10^{-1}$* $(.901 \cdot 10^{-2})$					
$.242 \cdot 10^{-2}$ $(.398 \cdot 10^{-2})$				$.377 \cdot 10^{-2}$ $(.901 \cdot 10^{-2})$				
$.104 \cdot 10^{-1}$* $(.470 \cdot 10^{-2})$					-1.072* $(.393)$			
$.123 \cdot 10^{-1}$* $(.493 \cdot 10^{-2})$						-1.988* $(.653)$		
$.560 \cdot 10^{-2}$ $(.410 \cdot 10^{-2})$							$-.745 \cdot 10^{-2}$* $(.296 \cdot 10^{-2})$	
$.246 \cdot 10^{-2}$ $(.398 \cdot 10^{-2})$								$.684 \cdot 10^{-3}$ $(.486 \cdot 10^{-2})$

NOTE: See note to Table 2-A.

TABLE 2-D Demand Estimates by State and by Sample (North Carolina Sample II)

Achievement Interaction	C/Y	C/YH	C/DY	C/DYH	CO/Y	CO/YH	CO/DY	CO/DYH
$-.719 \cdot 10^{-3}$	-2.170^*							
$(.484 \cdot 10^{-2})$	$(.787)$							
$-.395 \cdot 10^{-4}$		-3.634^*						
$(.521 \cdot 10^{-2})$		(1.380)						
$-.681 \cdot 10^{-2}$			$-.112 \cdot 10^{-1*}$					
$(.417 \cdot 10^{-2})$			$(.565 \cdot 10^{-2})$					
$-.899 \cdot 10^{-2*}$				$-.143 \cdot 10^{-1}$				
$(.401 \cdot 10^{-2})$				$(.138 \cdot 10^{-1})$				
$-.500 \cdot 10^{-2}$					$-.475^*$			
$(.433 \cdot 10^{-2})$					$(.198)$			
$-.715 \cdot 10^{-2}$						$-.492$		
$(.431 \cdot 10^{-2})$						$(.351)$		
$-.758 \cdot 10^{-2}$							$-.364 \cdot 10^{-2*}$	
$(.413 \cdot 10^{-2})$							$(.187 \cdot 10^{-2})$	
$-.940 \cdot 10^{-2*}$								$-.405 \cdot 10^{-2}$
$(.396 \cdot 10^{-2})$								$(.346 \cdot 10^{-2})$

NOTE: See note to Table 2-A.

TABLE 2-E Demand Estimates by State and by Sample (California Sample I)

Achievement Interaction	C/YH	C/DYH	CO/YH	CO/DYH
$-.253 \cdot 10^{-1}$*	-1.271			
$(.594 \cdot 10^{-2})$	(1.24)			
$-.296 \cdot 10^{-1}$*		$-.233 \cdot 10^{-2}$		
$(.451 \cdot 10^{-2})$		$(.486 \cdot 10^{-2})$		
$-.301 \cdot 10^{-1}$*			$.145 \cdot 10^{-1}$	
$(.474 \cdot 10^{-2})$			$(.126)$	
$-.303 \cdot 10^{-1}$*				$.891 \cdot 10^{-3}$
$(.454 \cdot 10^{-2})$				$(.182 \cdot 10^{-2})$

NOTE: See note to Table 2-A.

groups, the specifications either worked, as in the cases of Illinois and Massachusetts, or for some unknown reason, one variable dominated the explanation, as in the cases of California and North Carolina.

There seemed to be very little discrepancy about the sign of the cost-to-income variable no matter what group or state was considered. But the estimate of the achievement interaction variable differed both within states, by sample, and between states. We thought that we needed more homogeneous achievement groups. We did not have the resources to extend our sample, so we aggregated the state observations and disaggregated the student observations into four achievement groups. The ranges selected for each achievement group were not totally arbitrary; they were based on impressions about homogeneous student decision-making. The lowest-achievement group contained the students

TABLE 2-F Demand Estimates by State and by Sample (Illinois Sample I)

Achievement Interaction	C/YH	C/DYH	CO/YH	CO/DYH
$.198 \cdot 10^{-1}$*	-16.689*			
$(.584 \cdot 10^{-2})$	(2.412)			
$.187 \cdot 10^{-1}$*		-1.720*		
$(.584 \cdot 10^{-2})$		$(.263)$		
$.488 \cdot 10^{-1}$*			-10.905*	
$(.829 \cdot 10^{-2})$			(1.247)	
$.389 \cdot 10^{-1}$*				$-.960$*
$(.788 \cdot 10^{-2})$				$(.121)$

NOTE: See note to Table 2-A.

TABLE 2-G Demand Estimates by State and by Sample (Massachusetts Sample I)

Achievement Interaction	C/YH	C/DYH	CO/YH	CO/DYH
$.232 \cdot 10^{-1}$*	-12.527*			
$(.530 \cdot 10^{-2})$	(1.908)			
$.233 \cdot 10^{-1}$*		-1.373*		
$(.527 \cdot 10^{-2})$		$(.210)$		
$.468 \cdot 10^{-1}$*			-9.476*	
$(.687 \cdot 10^{-2})$*			(1.026)	
$.409 \cdot 10^{-1}$*				$-.887$*
$(.657 \cdot 10^{-2})$*				$(.105)$

NOTE: See note to Table 2-A.

with average SAT scores of less than 400. The middle-lower group had SAT's average greater than or equal to 400, but less than 475. The upper-middle group covered the range up to 550, and the upper group's average SAT scores were 550 or above.

Achievement Aggregation Results

Table 3, like Table 1 before, contains the results of estimating the demand functions separately for each variable in the utility function. Since we have argued that we are not very interested in these single variable specifications, we shall not dwell on their detailed results. They

TABLE 2-H Demand Estimates by State and by Sample (North Carolina Sample I)

Achievement Interaction	C/YH	C/DYH	CO/YH	CO/DYH
$.441 \cdot 10^{-2}$	-16.493*			
$(.611 \cdot 10^{-2})$	(2.585)			
$.181 \cdot 10^{-2}$		-1.604*		
$(.611 \cdot 10^{-2})$		$(.270)$		
$.676 \cdot 10^{-2}$			-6.011*	
$(.651 \cdot 10^{-2})$			$(.820)$	
$-.620 \cdot 10^{-3}$				$-.512$*
$(.604 \cdot 10^{-2})$				$(.792 \cdot 10^{-1})$

NOTE: See note to Table 2-A.

TABLE 3 Single Variable Specifications on Achievement Group Samples

	I	II	I	II	I	II	I	II
	SAT < 400	SAT < 400	$400 \leq$ SAT < 475	$400 \leq$ SAT < 495	$475 <$ SAT < 550	$475 \leq$ SAT < 550	SAT ≥ 550	SAT ≥ 550
Observations	164	162	92	84	67	72	46	57
C/Y		-7.138^* (.962)		-2.700^* (.735)		-2.803^* (.865)		$-.116$ (.373)
C/YH	-17.247^* (1.844)	-4.975^* (.837)	-7.610^* (1.284)	-6.832^* (1.255)	-5.805^* (1.506)	-5.780^* (1.350)	-2.795^* (1.646)	1.354 (1.386)
C/DY		$-.387 \cdot 10^{-1*}$ ($.115 \cdot 10^{-1}$)		$-.132 \cdot 10^{-1*}$ ($.520 \cdot 10^{-2}$)		$-.168 \cdot 10^{-1*}$ ($.835 \cdot 10^{-2}$)		$-.368 \cdot 10^{-2*}$ ($.542 \cdot 10^{-2}$)
C/DYH	$-.611^*$ ($.939 \cdot 10^{-1}$)	$-.725 \cdot 10^{-2}$ ($.599 \cdot 10^{-2}$)	$-.539 \cdot 10^{-2}$ ($.863 \cdot 10^{-2}$)	$-.406^*$ (.101)	$-.636^*$ (.165)	$-.165$ (.102)	$-.338^*$ (.160)	$.133$ (.134)
CO/Y		-2.121^* (.279)		$-.321^*$ (.149)		$-.502^*$ (.209)		$-.907 \cdot 10^{-2}$ (.225)
CO/YH	-4.003^* (.381)	-1.414^* (.324)	-2.879^* (.471)	-1.872^* (.476)	-2.905^* (.624)	-1.559^* (.540)	-1.823^* (.809)	$.914$ (.946)
CO/DY		$-.910 \cdot 10^{-2*}$ ($.246 \cdot 10^{-2}$)		$-.282 \cdot 10^{-2}$ ($.169 \cdot 10^{-2}$)		$-.573 \cdot 10^{-2*}$ ($.247 \cdot 10^{-2}$)		$-.972 \cdot 10^{-3}$ ($.295 \cdot 10^{-2}$)
CO/DYH	$-.730 \cdot 10^{-2*}$ ($.315 \cdot 10^{-2}$)	$-.251 \cdot 10^{-2}$ ($.216 \cdot 10^{-2}$)	$-.196 \cdot 10^{-2}$ ($.313 \cdot 10^{-2}$)	$-.452 \cdot 10^{-1*}$ ($.190 \cdot 10^{-1}$)	$-.299^*$ ($.652 \cdot 10^{-1}$)	$-.686 \cdot 10^{-2}$ ($.893 \cdot 10^{-1}$)	$-.182^*$ ($.663 \cdot 10^{-1}$)	$.880^*$ ($.941 \cdot 10^{-1}$)
Ach. int.	$-.878 \cdot 10^{-2}$ ($.789 \cdot 10^{-2}$)	$-.279 \cdot 10^{-1*}$ ($.491 \cdot 10^{-2}$)	$-.457 \cdot 10^{-1*}$ ($.526 \cdot 10^{-2}$)	$-.138 \cdot 10^{-1*}$ ($.424 \cdot 10^{-2}$)	$-.296 \cdot 10^{-2}$ ($.402 \cdot 10^{-2}$)	$-.113 \cdot 10^{-1*}$ ($.377 \cdot 10^{-2}$)	$.115 \cdot 10^{-1*}$ ($.417 \cdot 10^{-2}$)	$.182 \cdot 10^{-1*}$ ($.395 \cdot 10^{-2}$)

NOTE: Asterisks indicate significance at .05 level. Figures in parentheses are standard errors of estimates.

are presented because they clearly illustrate two of the most interesting aspects of higher-education demand functions that we have found to date, namely, that there are trends in the coefficient estimates as one moves from the low-achievement group to the high-achievement group. These trends exist in almost every cost-to-income specification, and in the student-institution achievement interaction specification, and in both samples.

First, for the cost-to-income coefficients, the trends run from relatively high negative coefficient estimates for low-achievement groups to relatively low negative coefficient estimates for the high-achievement group. The high-achievement group's values are almost always not significantly different from zero. Second, the student-institution achievement interaction coefficients trend from statistically significant negative values for the low-achievement group to statistically significant positive values for the high-achievement group.

The sign reversal in the student-institution achievement interaction coefficients, going from negative for low-achievement students to positive for high-achievement students indicates a complete reversal in the marginal effect of quality. Given the students' eligibility, low-achievement students are repelled from better schools and high-achievement students are attracted to them.

Table 4 presents the achievement-group aggregation estimations with both variables. The general results found for the single variable specifications appear again. For Sample II, the C/Y specification has both coefficients significant in the lowest and the highest SAT groups. The cost-to-income coefficients are more negative for the low-achievement group than for the high-achievement group. The achievement variable offers a negative influence on the lower group and a positive influence on the higher group. The two middle achievement groups have their cost-to-income variable coefficients negative and significant, and their magnitude places them in the trend from elastic demand for lower-achieving students to inelastic demand for higher-achieving students with respect to cost and income. The trend in the student-institution achievement coefficient places the middle achievement group coefficients close to zero in magnitude. Their estimates did indeed turn out not significantly different from zero.

In Sample II, none of the derived cost-to-income variables offers as consistent results as the specification that used the reported income directly. The results of Sample II's predicted income specifications present the same pattern as was found in the reported income results. Their estimates are not as consistent, however. As with the reported specification, two of the four C/YH specifications are significant on both variables. As achievement rises, there is a downward trend in the C/YH coefficient,

TABLE 4 Demand Estimates by Achievement Groups and by Sample

	Achievement Interaction	C/Y	C/DY	Sample II Achievement Groups CO/Y	CO/DY
SAT < 400	$-.328 \cdot 10^{-1}$**	-3.592*			
162 Observations	$(.774 \cdot 10^{-2})$	(1.116)			
	$-.494 \cdot 10^{-1}$*		$-0.103 \cdot 10^{-1}$		
	$(.603 \cdot 10^{-2})$		$(.704 \cdot 10^{-2})$		
	$-.406 \cdot 10^{-1}$*			$-.709$*	
	$(.746 \cdot 10^{-2})$			$(.316)$	
	$-.504 \cdot 10^{-1}$*				$-.248 \cdot 10^{-2}$
	$(.602 \cdot 10^{-2})$				$(.200 \cdot 10^{-2})$
SAT ≥ 400	$-.244 \cdot 10^{-2}$	-2.450*			
SAT < 475	$(.557 \cdot 10^{-2})$	$(.907)$			
84 Observations	$-.106 \cdot 10^{-1}$*		$-.921 \cdot 10^{-2}$		
	$(.451 \cdot 10^{-2})$		$(.509 \cdot 10^{-2})$		
	$-.118 \cdot 10^{-1}$*			$-.146$	
	$(.468 \cdot 10^{-2})$			$(.156)$	
	$-.131 \cdot 10^{-1}$*				$-.734 \cdot 10^{-3}$
	$(.452 \cdot 10^{-2})$				$(.186 \cdot 10^{-2})$
SAT ≥ 475	$-.325 \cdot 10^{-2}$	-2.364*			
SAT < 550	$(.406 \cdot 10^{-2})$	(1.037)			
72 Observations	$-.928 \cdot 10^{-2}$*		$-.100 \cdot 10^{-1}$		
	$(.396 \cdot 10^{-2})$		$(.736 \cdot 10^{-2})$		
	$-.875 \cdot 10^{-2}$*			$-.214$	
	$(.412 \cdot 10^{-2})$			$(.174)$	
	$-.946 \cdot 10^{-2}$*				$-.374 \cdot 10^{-2}$
	$(.398 \cdot 10^{-2})$				$(.256 \cdot 10^{-2})$

TABLE 4 (continued)

	Achievement Interaction	C/YH	C/DYH	Sample II Achievement Groups CO/YH	CO/DYH
SAT ≥ 550 57 Observations	$.211 \cdot 10^{-1**}$ $(.423 \cdot 10^{-2})$ $.205 \cdot 10^{-1**}$ $(.415 \cdot 10^{-2})$ $.203 \cdot 10^{-1*}$ $(.415 \cdot 10^{-2})$ $.196 \cdot 10^{-1*}$ $(.413 \cdot 10^{-2})$	-1.031^* $(.589)$	$-.132 \cdot 10^{-1*}$ $(.684 \cdot 10^{-2})$	$-.393$ $(.201)$	$-.476 \cdot 10^{-2}$ $(.310 \cdot 10^{-2})$
SAT < 400 162 Observations	$-.503 \cdot 10^{-1*}$ $(.660 \cdot 10^{-2})$ $-.537 \cdot 10^{-1*}$ $(.593 \cdot 10^{-2})$ $-.518 \cdot 10^{-1*}$ $(.626 \cdot 10^{-2})$ $-.538 \cdot 10^{-1*}$ $(.593 \cdot 10^{-2})$	$-.392$ $(.537)$	$.423 \cdot 10^{-2}$ $(.500 \cdot 10^{-2})$	$-.571 \cdot 10^{-1}$ $(.139)$	$.214 \cdot 10^{-2}$ $(.255 \cdot 10^{-2})$
SAT ≥ 400 SAT < 475 84 Observations	$.130 \cdot 10^{-1**}$ $(.673 \cdot 10^{-2})$ $-.938 \cdot 10^{-2*}$ $(.452 \cdot 10^{-2})$ $-.369 \cdot 10^{-2}$ $(.819 \cdot 10^{-2})$ $-.142 \cdot 10^{-1*}$ $(.449 \cdot 10^{-2})$	-9.431^* (1.874)	$-.691 \cdot 10^{-1}$ $(.383 \cdot 10^{-1})$	-1.532^* $(.890)$	$-.125 \cdot 10^{-1}$ $(.858 \cdot 10^{-2})$

SAT ≥ 475 **SAT < 550** **72 Observations**	$.289 \cdot 10^{-2}$ $(.515 \cdot 10^{-2})$ $-.970 \cdot 10^{-2}*$ $(.422 \cdot 10^{-2})$ $-.688 \cdot 10^{-2}$ $(.552 \cdot 10^{-2})$ $-.108 \cdot 10^{-1}*$ $(.388 \cdot 10^{-2})$	$-6.514*$ (1.894)	$-.473 \cdot 10^{-1}$ $(.702 \cdot 10^{-1})$	$-.817$ $(.764)$	$-.814 \cdot 10^{-2}$ $(.965 \cdot 10^{-2})$
SAT ≥ 550 **57 Observations**	$.232 \cdot 10^{-1}**$ $(.451 \cdot 10^{-2})$ $.223 \cdot 10^{-1}**$ $(.446 \cdot 10^{-2})$ $.262 \cdot 10^{-1}**$ $(.491 \cdot 10^{-2})$ $.244 \cdot 10^{-1}**$ $(.471 \cdot 10^{-2})$	$-3.873*$ (1.735)	$-.323*$ $(.166)$	$-3.721*$ (1.255)	$-.287*$ $(.109)$
SAT < 400 **164 Observations**	$-.438 \cdot 10^{-1}**$ $(.119 \cdot 10^{-1})$ $-.847 \cdot 10^{-1}*$ $(.807 \cdot 10^{-2})$ $-.814 \cdot 10^{-1}*$ $(.863 \cdot 10^{-2})$ $-.867 \cdot 10^{-1}*$ $(.798 \cdot 10^{-2})$	$-9.593*$ (2.460)	$-.265 \cdot 10^{-1}$ $(.233 \cdot 10^{-1})$	$-.261$ $(.211)$	$-.158 \cdot 10^{-2}$ $(.213 \cdot 10^{-2})$
SAT ≥ 400 **SAT < 475** **92 Observations**	$-.460 \cdot 10^{-1}*$ $(.575 \cdot 10^{-2})$ $-.460 \cdot 10^{-1}*$	$.551 \cdot 10^{-1}$ $(.536)$	$.141 \cdot 10^{-2}$		

TABLE 4 (concluded)

	Achievement Interaction	C/YH	C/DYH	Sample II Achievement Groups CO/YH	Sample II Achievement Groups CO/DYH
	$(.534 \cdot 10^{-2})$		$(.703 \cdot 10^{-2})$	$.873 \cdot 10^{-1}$	$.337 \cdot 10^{-2}$
	$-.467 \cdot 10^{-1}$*			$(.225)$	$(.366 \cdot 10^{-2})$
	$(.591 \cdot 10^{-2})$				
	$-.467 \cdot 10^{-1}$*				
	$(.539 \cdot 10^{-2})$				
SAT ≥ 475 SAT < 550 67 Observations	$.148 \cdot 10^{-1}$**	-9.704*	-1.017*	-7.331*	$-.629$*
	$(.514 \cdot 10^{-2})$	(2.125)	$(.231)$	(1.225)	$(.120)$
	$.138 \cdot 10^{-1}$**				
	$(.511 \cdot 10^{-2})$				
	$.297 \cdot 10^{-1}$**				
	$(.657 \cdot 10^{-2})$				
	$.228 \cdot 10^{-1}$**				
	$(.614 \cdot 10^{-2})$				
SAT ≥ 550 46 Observations	$.224 \cdot 10^{-1}$**	-8.787*	$-.933$*	-7.809*	$-.527$*
	$(.486 \cdot 10^{-2})$	(2.319)	$(.258)$	(1.511)	$(.126)$
	$.233 \cdot 10^{-1}$**				
	$(.486 \cdot 10^{-2})$				
	$.330 \cdot 10^{-1}$**				
	$(.618 \cdot 10^{-2})$				
	$.257 \cdot 10^{-1}$**				
	$(.540 \cdot 10^{-2})$				

NOTE: Figures in parentheses are standard errors of estimates. Single asterisks indicate .05 level of significance. Double asterisks indicate .01 level of significance.

and an upward trend on the $A_iS_j/1,000$ coefficient. But, the lower group did not have its C/YH coefficient significant, and the lower-middle group has its achievement interaction coefficient positively significant. Apparently the achievement variable becomes positive faster than it does in the reported income specification, so it is never statistically different from zero.

Comparing the reported and predicted income coefficients for the upper achievement group shows similar magnitudes on the student-institution achievement estimates, and a response to predicted income two and one-quarter times the response to reported income.

The pattern of the Sample I achievement groups estimates was somewhat the same as the pattern of the Sample II achievement groups estimates. There were some minor variations, however, as the lowest achievement group had both coefficients significant in the Sample II C/Y specification. The lower-middle group had its achievement coefficient significant instead of its C/YH coefficient. The trend in the student-institution achievement variable was somewhat augmented by the fact that the lower-middle group's estimate was too low. This is undoubtedly due to the fact that the C/YH coefficient was not significant. An important variation is that the trend in the cost-to-income coefficient over the achievement groups was absent.

The reason the coefficient values for Sample I's cost-to-income specifications are all approximately equal to the C/YH coefficient in Sample II's lower-middle achievement group is a mystery. Is it possibly related to the sampling design of Sample I? Or is it related to some attribute about the reporting versus the nonreporting families?

Elasticities

It is our opinion that the C/Y and the C/YH specifications of the cost-to-income variable, in conjunction with the student-institution achievement interaction variable, are the best demand specifications we found. Our guess is that, of the two, the reported income is probably better than the predicted specification, but we shall have to do more work to determine which specifications are actually better in each achievement group.

Table 5 contains means and standard deviations of the income and achievement measures by achievement group, and by sample. Also included are the samples' achievement-income correlation coefficients.

There is, in general, a decline in the mean income estimates as the achievement level declines. But the hypothesis that the mean samples significantly differ in mean income is flatly rejected.

TABLE 5 Means, Standard Deviations, and Correlation Coefficients

Achievement Group	Achievement: Mean and Standard Deviation		Income: Mean and Standard Deviation			Correlation Coefficient between Achievement and Income in Achievement Group		
	Sample II	Sample I	Sample II Reported	Sample II Predicted	Sample I Predicted	Sample II Reported	Sample II Predicted	Sample I Predicted
High	611.6 (37.7)	602.2 (42.4)	16,912.8 (17,711.9)	16,921.0 (14,825.1)	17,040.8 (15,391.8)	0.116	0.228	0.502
Medium high	509.8 (22.1)	513.5 (20.7)	13,379.3 (14,170.4)	11,919.3 (5,826.9)	13,685.7 (7,698.6)	−0.059	−0.081	0.070
Medium low	440.9 (22.0)	440.8 (20.8)	12,656.0 (11,606.8)	11,021.0 (3,838.3)	11,103.4 (3,901.7)	0.066	0.078	−0.023
Low	317.4 (55.8)	307.5 (63.2)	14,030.0 (16,675.9)	10,318.6 (3,158.9)	10,537.0 (4,131.5)	0.060	0.183	0.131

NOTE: Standard deviations are in parentheses.

The correlation coefficients indicate the efficacy of the sampling design (see Section III). In all groups except Sample I's high ability group, a rather high degree of independence between the income and achievement measures was obtained. The income heterogeneity in each achievement group coupled with the four achievement samples implies that the estimates do cover the student income-achievement plane.

The following list establishes a correspondence between the post-secondary-school type number and its description. The list will aid the reader in interpreting Tables 6, 7, and 8 which follow.

Description	Type Number
No higher education	1
Low cost–low achievement	2
Low cost–medium achievement	3
Low cost–high achievement	4
Medium cost–low achievement	5
Medium cost–medium achievement	6
Medium cost–high achievement	7
High cost–low achievement	8
High cost–medium achievement	9
High cost–high achievement	10

Table 6 presents the relative frequencies of the chosen institution types with the demand model's predicted relative frequencies for the reported and predicted income specifications in each sample and achievement group.

The choosers' relative frequencies correspond rather well to the model's predicted frequencies, but the level of disaggregation by institution type is probably taxing the limits of the model's ability. Table 10 in Section V compares eight institutional types, and aggregates the ability groups. The deviations between observed and predicted relative frequencies in that table are, of course, much less. Approximate average cost and average institutional quality values for the samples' feasible choice sets appear in Table 7. The information contained in Tables 4, 5, 6, and 7, the conditional logit estimates, the sample means, the predicted relative frequencies, and the average cost and quality, respectively, enable computation of the probability of enrolling elasticities with respect to achievement, quality, cost and income. Tables 8 and 9 display the income and cost elasticities, respectively, for twelve possible student types: three by family income, $6,000, $12,000, and $18,000, and four by student achievement score, 375, 475, 575, and 650. Those elasticities are based on the Sample II estimates.

TABLE 6 Observed and Predicted Relative Frequencies

Type	Sample II			Sample I	
	Observed Relative Frequency	Predicted Relative Frequency with Reported Income	Predicted Relative Frequency with Predicted Income	Observed Relative Frequency	Predicted Relative Frequency with Predicted Income
			High Achievement		
1	0.0877	0.0294	0.0292	0.1739	0.0673
2	0.0877	0.0559	0.0622	0.1304	0.0999
3	0.0877	0.0715	0.0779	0.0435	0.1453
4	0.0	0.0435	0.0572	0.0217	0.0842
5	0.0351	0.0584	0.0571	0.0217	0.0710
6	0.1579	0.1336	0.1404	0.1739	0.1090
7	0.1404	0.2035	0.2268	0.1304	0.2095
8	0.0175	0.0006	0.0004	0.0	0.0
9	0.0526	0.1751	0.1458	0.0217	0.1014
10	0.3333	0.2285	0.2031	0.2826	0.1124
			Medium-High Achievement		
1	0.1806	0.2398	0.2432	0.2836	0.1760
2	0.2500	0.1692	0.1905	0.1194	0.1772
3	0.0556	0.0700	0.0945	0.0296	0.1535
4	0.0556	0.0201	0.0311	0.0149	0.0294
5	0.1806	0.1676	0.1492	0.1045	0.0995
6	0.1667	0.1288	0.1216	0.1343	0.1527
7	0.0417	0.0519	0.0643	0.1791	0.1020
8	0.0278	0.0021	0.0013	0.0	0.0

9	0.0139	0.1314	0.0901	0.0597	0.0884
10	0.0278	0.0191	0.0142	0.0746	0.0208

Medium-Low Achievement

1	0.2024	0.2641	0.2705	0.5544	0.5175
2	0.3452	0.1831	0.2241	0.1957	0.1729
3	0.0595	0.0872	0.1542	0.0217	0.0178
4	0.0119	0.0028	0.0056	0.0109	0.0001
5	0.1786	0.1501	0.1109	0.0978	0.1862
6	0.1310	0.1455	0.1379	0.0544	0.0504
7	0.0119	0.0084	0.0121	0.0	0.0001
8	0.0119	0.0027	0.0011	0.0326	0.0034
9	0.0238	0.1499	0.0799	0.0326	0.0510
10	0.0238	0.0063	0.0037	0.0	0.0007

Low Achievement

1	0.5617	0.5134	0.4940	0.7744	0.6828
2	0.1728	0.2304	0.2050	0.1281	0.2046
3	0.0370	0.0160	0.0103	0.0122	0.0120
4	0.0	0.0002	0.0001	0.0	0.0
5	0.1420	0.1549	0.1925	0.0366	0.0729
6	0.0309	0.0384	0.0374	0.0366	0.0192
7	0.0	0.0001	0.0001	0.0	0.0
8	0.0247	0.0028	0.0066	0.0061	0.0003
9	0.0247	0.0433	0.0537	0.0061	0.0083
10	0.0062	0.0005	0.0003	0.0	0.0000

TABLE 7 Average Costs and Quality

Type	Cost ($)	Quality (SAT)
1	0	374.4
2	402.5	426.5
3	487.4	499.8
4	542.3	561.9
5	1,607.6	445.0
6	1,700.4	496.5
7	1,462.6	562.0
8	2,574.6	426.2
9	2,914.3	517.6
10	3,369.6	573.4

SECTION V: QUALITATIVE INFORMATION

Here I report on the introduction of qualitative information into the demand model. Our intention was to develop variations in the demand model that would incorporate social, psychological, and economic indices about the student choosers. It appears, though, that the questions appearing in the SCOPE high school questionnaire had not been based on well defined indices. And, in order to incorporate qualitative information we had to construct our own indices. Rather than abandon the qualitative project, we proceeded by constructing a few indices of our own. We gingerly refer to this work as our exercise in amateur sociology.

Three models are compared. The first is the conditional logit model, the second is the conditional logit model with a correction to account for the possibility that all the probabilities for a particular choice may be off by a constant. The third model incorporates the qualitative information about the choosers into the second model. Statistical estimation procedures for the choice-type correction and the qualitative-information corrections are developed below. Then, the results are discussed and presented.

Models and Estimation Procedures

Consider three alternative models.

1. The first model is the conditional logit model. For each student i, $\vec{X}_i = (X_{i1}, \ldots, X_{iJ_i})$ has a multinomial distribution with

$$\text{Prob}\{X_{ij} = 1, X_{ik} = 0 \text{ for } k \neq j\} = \phi_{ij}$$

and $\sum_{j \in J_i} \phi_{ij} = 1$, and $\phi_{ij} \geq 0$ for all i.

TABLE 8 Elasticity of the Probability of Enrolling in Type _j_ with Respect to Family Income

Y_i	$6,000				$12,000				$18,000			
A_i	375	475	575	650	375	475	575	650	375	475	575	650
Estimate for β^1	−3.592	−2.407	−1.301	−1.031	−3.592	−2.407	−1.031	−1.301	−3.592	−2.407	−1.031	−1.301
Column	(1)	(2)	(3)	(4)	(5)	(6)	(7)	(8)	(9)	(10)	(11)	(12)
1	.160	−.360	−.226	−.313	−.123	−.233	−.120	−.167	−.094	−.167	−.082	−.114
2	−.013	−.245	−.176	−.263	−.036	−.173	−.096	−.142	−.036	−.129	−.066	−.097
3		−.200	−.157	−.244		−.151	−.086	−.133		−.114	−.060	−.091
4			−.133	−.220			−.074	−.121			−.051	−.083
5	−1.160	.522	.152	.065	.536	.210	.068	.022	.345	.127	.044	.012
6		.161	−.003	−.090		.029	−.009	−.056		.006	−.007	−.039
7			.021	−.066			.003	−.043			.000	−.031
8		.924	.324	.237		.410	.154	.108		.260	.101	.070
9		.924	.324	.237		.410	.154	.108		.260	.101	.070
10				.237				.108				.070

TABLE 9 Elasticity of the Probability of Enrolling in Type j with Respect to the Cost of Type j

	$6,000				$12,000				$18,000			
Y_i												
A_i	375	475	575	650	375	475	575	650	375	475	575	650
Estimate for β^1	−3.592	−2.407	−1.031	−1.031	−3.592	−2.407	−1.031	−1.031	−3.592	−2.407	−1.031	−1.031
Column	(1)	(2)	(3)	(4)	(5)	(6)	(7)	(8)	(9)	(10)	(11)	(12)
1	0	0	0	0	0	0	0	0	0	0	0	0
2	−.127	−.091	−.047	−.048	−.064	−.047	−.024	−.024	−.043	−.032	−.016	−.016
3		−.131	−.059	−.062		−.067	−.030	−.031		−.045	−.020	−.021
4			−.071	−.076			−.036	−.039			−.024	−.026
5	−1.204	−.794	−.365	−.370	−.559	−.386	−.182	−.185	−.360	−.254	−.121	−.123
6		−.455	−.196	−.204		−.226	−.098	−.103		−.150	−.065	−.068
7			−.197	−.208			−.098	−.105			−.065	−.070
8		−1.206	−.511	−.523		−.582	−.253	−.260		−.382	−.168	−.173
9		−1.211	−.487	−.504		−.585	−.239	−.249		−.384	−.158	−.166
10				−.402				−.192				−.126

2. The second model will be called the constant augmented demand model. Simply described, the augmented logit model has a constant for each choice type j, k_j, added to the conditional logit model: $\vec{X}_i$ has a multinomial distribution with

$$\text{Prob}\{X_{ij} = 1, X_{ik} = 0 \text{ for } k \neq j\} = \phi_{ij} + k_j$$

and $\sum_{j \in J_i} \phi_{ij} = 1$, and $\phi_{ij} \geq 0$ for all i, and $\sum_j k_j = 0$.

3. The third model is the qualitative information demand model. In the third model indices are considered one at a time. Each index is separated into a set of disjoint answer categories, $r = 1, \ldots, R$. Each individual has an index value that allocates him or her to answer category r. Associated with category r is a constant, a_j^r. This constant is added to the augmented conditional logit model. Thus, $\vec{X}_i$ has a multinomial distribution with

$$\text{Prob}\{X_{ij} = 1, X_{ik} = 0 \text{ for } k \neq j\} = \phi_{ij} + k_j + a_j^r$$

and $\sum_{j \in J_i} \phi_{ij} = 1$, and $\phi_{ij} \geq 0$ for all i, and $\sum_j k_j = 0$.

We assume the students make their decisions independently of one another, so $\{\vec{X}_i\}$ are distributed independently. We turn now to the estimation of these models.

Let p_j denote the observed relative frequency of choice j for a student population, and p_j^r denote the observed relative frequency of choice j for the students who have a category answer r. n^r denotes the number of students in category r.

The observed relative frequencies are determined from the multinomial distributions by the expressions

$$p_j^r = \frac{1}{n^r} \sum_{i \in r} X_{ij}$$

and

(1) $$p_j = \frac{1}{n} \sum_i X_{ij} = \sum_r \frac{n^r}{n} p_j^r$$

In the constant augmented model the relative frequency for each choice type-answer response category has an expected value given by

(2) $$E(p_j^r) = \frac{1}{n^r} \sum_{i \in r} (\phi_{ij} + k_j) = \phi_{\cdot j}^r + k_j$$

The observed relative frequency for each category response has an expected value given by

(3) $$E(p_j) = \frac{1}{n} \sum_i (\phi_{ij} + k_j) = \sum_r \left(\frac{n^r}{n}\right)(\phi_{\cdot j}^r + k_j) = \phi_{\cdot j} + k_j$$

333 | Leonard S. Miller

In the qualitative information demand model, the expected values of these two relative frequencies are

(2') $\quad E(p_j^r) = \dfrac{1}{n^r} \sum\limits_{i \in r}(\phi_{ij} + k_j + a_j^r) = \phi_{\cdot j}^r + k_j + a_j^r$

and

(3') $\quad E(p_j) = \dfrac{1}{n} \sum\limits_{i}(\phi_{ij} + k_j + a_j^r) = \phi_{\cdot j} + k_j + a_j^r$

The expected value of the difference between the observed relative frequency of the choice type-answer responses and the observed relative frequency of the choice type responses, in both the second and third model is given by

(4) $\quad E(p_j^r - p_j) = \phi_{\cdot j}^r - \phi_{\cdot j}$ (for all k_j)

The value of the variance of this difference

$$\mathrm{Var}(p_j^r - p_j) = \mathrm{Var}\!\left[p_j^r - \sum\limits_{s}\left(\dfrac{n^s}{n}\right)p_j^s\right]$$

$$= \mathrm{Var}\!\left[\left(1 - \dfrac{n^r}{n}\right)p_j^r - \sum\limits_{s \neq r}\left(\dfrac{n^s}{n}\right)p_j^s\right]$$

(5) $\qquad = \left(1 - \dfrac{n^r}{n}\right)^2 \mathrm{Var}(p_j^r) + \sum\limits_{s \neq r}\left(\dfrac{n^s}{n}\right)^2 \mathrm{Var}(p_j^s)$

This value can be estimated from the expression

(6) $\quad \mathrm{Var}(p_j^r) = \left(\dfrac{1}{n^r}\right)^2 \sum\limits_{i \in r}(\phi_{ij} + k_j)(1 - \phi_{ij} - k_j)$

To obtain estimates for k_j in the second model, and the a_j^r values of the third model, we shall substitute the observed relative frequencies for the expected value of choosing j.

Thus, k_j is estimated from equation 3 by

(7) $\quad k_j = p_j - \phi_{\cdot j}$

and a_j^r is estimated from equations 2 and 4 by

(8) $\quad a_j^r = 3p_j^r - \phi_{\cdot j}^r - {}_{Kj} = (p_j^r - p_j) - (\phi_{\cdot j}^r - \phi_{\cdot j})$

From equations 8 and 4

$\quad E(a_j^r) = 0$

and from equation 8

$\quad \mathrm{Var}(a_j^r) = \mathrm{Var}(p_j^r - p_j)$

which can be estimated with equations 5 and 6.

In the following list, the 21 indices, their associated response categories, and a meaningful title appears. The actual questions and score weights which constitute each index appear in the author's appendix. When an index has two response categories, the observations have been separated at the mean index value into low and high responses. For example, for index 1, category 1 is low conservative, category 2 is high conservative.

Index	Categories	Interpretation
1	1–2	Conservative
2	3–4	Subindex of conservatism
3	5–6	Fate control
4	7–8	Self-motivation for problem solving
5	9–10	Broad academic interests
6	11–12	Parents' concern with education
7	13–14	Student response to parents' concern
8	15–16	Student academic desires
9	17–18	Index 7 + Index 8
10	19–20	Peer group response at the cost of studying
11	21–23	Actual high school program
12	24–26	Will you ever go to college?
13	27–34	Most satisfaction in life
14	35–40	When was post-secondary-school choice made?
15	41–42	Educational implications of preferred jobs
16	43–44	Educational implications of jobs to which the student is uncertain or indifferent
17	45–46	Student attachment to parents
18	47–48	Desire to sacrifice for future payoffs
19	49–50	Parents' higher education desires for student
20	51–52	Index 6 + ½ (Index 19)
21	53–54	Sex of student

After the indices had been separated into response categories, a few of the choice types consistently had only a few observations. We aggregated two of the choice types with two other types. The following list will help the reader to understand the tables to follow:

Choice Type	Meaning
1	No school
2	Low cost–low achievement
3	Low cost–medium achievement
4	Low and medium cost–high achievement
5	Medium cost–low achievement
6	Medium cost–medium achievement
7	High cost–low and medium achievement
8	High cost–high achievement

The constants, k_j, appear in the various parts of Table 10 which present choice type frequency statistics for the following samples: Sample II with the reported income conditional logit estimates, Sample II with the predicted income conditional logit estimates, and Sample I with predicted income conditional logit estimates, respectively. The choice type

TABLE 10 Differences between Observed and Predicted Frequencies by Option Type and Model

Type (J)	Observed	Predicted	Observed Relative	Average Predicted Relative	Constant k_j
Sample II: Reported Income Model					
1	131	127.2003	0.3493	0.3392	0.0101
2	80	66.4680	0.2133	0.1772	0.0361
3	20	19.0140	0.0533	0.0507	0.0026
4	17	20.2639	0.0453	0.0540	−0.0087
5	48	51.7918	0.1280	0.1381	−0.0101
6	37	35.3294	0.0987	0.0942	0.0045
7	18	39.9006	0.0480	0.1064	−0.0584
8	24	15.0197	0.0640	0.0401	0.0239
	375	374.9871	1.0000	1.0000	0.0000
Sample II: Predicted Income Model					
1	131	125.1724	0.3493	0.3338	0.0155
2	80	67.9257	0.2133	0.1811	0.0322
3	20	25.8627	0.0533	0.0690	−0.0156
4	17	24.5696	0.0453	0.0655	−0.0202
5	48	52.3310	0.1280	0.1395	−0.0115
6	37	34.3342	0.0987	0.0916	0.0071
7	18	31.1366	0.0480	0.0830	−0.0350
8	24	12.9148	0.0640	0.0344	0.0296
	375	374.2463	1.0000	0.9980	0.0020
Sample I: Predicted Income Model					
1	208	176.4025	0.5637	0.4781	0.0856
2	53	65.1246	0.1436	0.1765	−0.0329
3	8	20.5756	0.0217	0.0558	−0.0341
4	21	22.3369	0.0569	0.0605	−0.0036
5	20	37.9099	0.0542	0.1027	−0.0485
6	28	23.0234	0.0759	0.0624	0.0135
7	13	16.9878	0.0352	0.0460	−0.0108
8	18	6.6308	0.0488	0.0188	0.0308
	369	368.9910	1.0000	1.0000	0.0000

constants are determined by equation 7 as the difference between the observed relative frequency and the average demand predicted relative frequency. They appear in the final column of Table 10. Due to space limitations only the choice type–category response estimates, $a\,'_j$, for the Sample IIR (reported income conditional logit estimates) are included here.

The most extensive change in the predicted probability distribution occurs when direct information about the higher-education choice decision is asked for: the present desires of the students (Index 8), their present high school curriculum (Index 11), or a direct statement of the possibility of going to college (Index 12). This is not surprising. It is probably best to view these indices as tests of whether the qualitative demand corrections work. Still, it is interesting to note that high school curriculum can readily be incorporated into higher-education demand projections.

Parents' objectives are important (Index 19). If the parent had low educational objectives, the students were allocated away from higher education. The conditional logit estimate for no higher education goes up and the estimates for the local junior college, the medium cost–medium achievement institutions, and high cost–high achievement schools go down. Parents with high educational objectives for their children produced exactly the opposite effect. Parents' concern about the student's education (Index 6) did not seem to alter the conditional logit model. Since Index 6 was not effective, the sum of Index 6 and one-half of Index 17 was also not effective (Index 20).

Economists tend to measure the response to education as a response to some future labor market. A few of the indices are related to this relationship. One factor in this education–labor market relationship is the educational implications of the jobs students prefer. For students preferring jobs with high educational requirements, significantly more of them went to higher quality–higher cost colleges, and significantly fewer of them did not go to college. Students preferring jobs with low educational requirements behave in exactly the opposite manner (Index 15).

If the student demonstrates high indifference and uncertainty toward jobs with high educational implications, he or she shows significantly greater nonattendance at any college, and significantly lower local junior college attendance. The allocation is reversed for students with high indifference and uncertainty toward jobs with low educational implications (Index 16).

Another aspect of the education–labor market relationship has to do with when the student makes a career choice. The earlier the choice is made, the more positively altered were the higher cost and higher quality alternatives. Students who decide (or accept a decision) on a career before the seventh grade, attend highest-quality–highest-cost institutions in significantly greater numbers, and significantly fewer of them choose not to achieve higher education. If the student has made a career decision by the tenth grade, he or she chooses the no higher education alternative significantly less, but is not allocated to any particular institutional type. Students who have not yet made a career choice decide not to go on to higher education with significantly greater frequency, and they attend medium cost–medium quality schools with significantly less frequency (Index 14).

What may be the most interesting result of this section is that indices which we thought would have been significant were not. Fate control (Index 3), self-motivation at problem solving (Index 4), broad academic interest (Index 5), and time preference or sacrificing ability (Index 18) were examples of indices which did not alter the conditional logit estimates. Are these measures so poor as to have no marginal effect on choice type, or does the achievement variable already incorporate the information contained in the indices?

The Massachusetts study found that disaggregating their total sample by students' sex altered their results. We did not find this result; only the medium cost–low quality institutions seemed to be affected. Males went less frequently and females more frequently. This result was of some surprise to us too.

These results appear in Table 11. Each choice-type–answer response category contains a column of three entries. The upper entry is the equation 8 estimated choice-type–consumer-answer category constant, a^r_j. The middle entry is the ratio of the estimated constant to its variance (as determined by equations 5 and 6). This number is a t-squared, or chi-squared statistic with one degree of freedom. Constants significantly different from zero at the .05 level are denoted by an asterisk; constants different from zero at the .01 level are denoted by two asterisks. The lower entry in the choice-type–answer category classification is the ratio of the estimated constant, a^r_j, to its observed relative frequency, p^r_j.

NOTES AND REFERENCES

1. This project was carried out by Roy Radner at the University of California, Berkeley, and by the author when he was at Berkeley, and then at SUNY, Stony Brook. The work presented here is the result of a joint effort. I accept responsibility for any errors or omissions. I should like to acknowledge that discussions with Daniel McFadden, in the early phase of this study, were extremely important.

   For our first report see R. Radner, and L. S. Miller, "Demand and Supply in U.S. *Proceedings* 60 (May 1970): 326–334. For further developments see Roy Radner and

TABLE 11 Response Residuals, Chi-Squared, and Percentage of Observed Relative Frequency

	1	2	3	4	5	6	7	8	9
1	0.0034	-0.0026	-0.0423*	0.0709*	0.0117	-0.0146	0.0509	-0.0222	0.0162
	0.0188	0.0188	5.8174	5.8170	0.3543	0.3544	2.1772	2.1774	0.7993
	0.0108	-0.0069	-0.1577	0.1461	0.0321	-0.0443	0.1095	-0.0744	0.0412
2	-0.0162	0.0122	0.0156	-0.0263	-0.0176	0.0220	-0.0265	0.0116	0.0168
	0.5454	0.5452	1.0785	1.0789	1.0642	1.0639	0.8073	0.8070	1.1318
	-0.0869	0.0522	0.0721	-0.1268	-0.0874	0.0966	-0.1312	0.0529	0.0703
3	0.0048	-0.0036	0.0018	-0.0030	0.0114	-0.0142	0.0154	-0.0067	-0.0118
	0.1459	0.1459	0.0543	0.0544	1.4058	1.4059	0.9801	0.9803	1.6672
	0.0705	-0.0861	0.0284	-0.0852	0.1827	-0.3394	0.2505	-0.1349	-0.3268
4	-0.0024	0.0018	0.0073	-0.0122	-0.0079	0.0099	0.0129	-0.0056	-0.0078
	0.0336	0.0335	0.9484	0.9487	0.6738	0.6735	0.9306	0.9308	0.7057
	-0.0383	0.0546	0.1068	-1.7086	-0.2061	0.1831	0.4909	-0.1052	-0.2898
5	-0.0418*	0.0314*	-0.0136	0.0228	-0.0026	0.0032	-0.0421	0.0184	-0.0008
	4.3039	4.3024	0.9229	0.9223	0.0265	0.0264	2.3402	2.3393	0.0034
	-0.6730	0.1771	-0.1332	0.1331	-0.0200	0.0257	-0.4359	0.1296	-0.0063
6	0.0160	-0.0120	0.0146	-0.0245	0.0066	-0.0083	-0.0242	0.0106	-0.0049
	0.8375	0.8383	1.7811	1.7818	0.2408	0.2412	1.2511	1.2505	0.1529
	0.1285	-0.1513	0.1142	-0.4897	0.0692	-0.0814	-0.3946	0.0920	-0.0578
7	0.0378	-0.0285*	0.0053	-0.0088	0.0074	-0.0093	0.0174	-0.0076	-0.0040
	4.1326	4.1349	0.1936	0.1940	0.2638	0.2644	0.5544	0.5550	0.0863
	0.4059	-2.0302	0.0825	-0.4127	0.1547	-0.1936	0.3310	-0.1656	-0.1102
8	-0.0017	0.0013	0.0113	-0.0189	-0.0091	0.0113	-0.0039	0.0017	-0.0036
	0.0222	0.0222	3.3781	3.3781	1.2723	1.2723	0.1233	0.1233	0.2006
	-0.0191	0.0268	0.1263	-0.8843	-0.1573	0.1573	-0.1110	0.0222	-0.0719

TABLE 11 (continued)

	10	11	12	13	14	15	16	17	18
1	-0.0234	0.0296	-0.0298	0.0331	-0.0386	0.1455**	-0.1095**	0.0972**	-0.0731**
	0.7994	1.8211	1.8213	2.6377	2.6380	31.4333	31.4341	14.3660	14.3665
	-0.0815	0.0705	-0.1071	0.0825	-0.1336	0.2415	-0.6889	0.1908	-0.3193
2	-0.0243	0.0067	-0.0068	-0.0273	0.0319	-0.0448*	0.0337*	-0.0253	0.0190
	1.1322	0.1234	0.1235	2.3848	2.3842	4.0143	4.0137	1.2861	1.2857
	-0.1379	0.0287	-0.0351	-0.1415	0.1345	-0.2329	0.1473	-0.1233	0.0866
3	0.0171	0.0018	-0.0018	0.0232*	-0.0271*	-0.0276*	0.0208*	0.0165	-0.0124
	1.6670	0.0281	0.0281	5.4442	5.4446	5.3445	5.3442	1.8667	1.8669
	0.2179	0.0374	-0.0306	0.3121	-0.9362	-2.2209	0.2468	0.2660	-0.2660
4	0.0114	-0.0009	0.0009	-0.0054	0.0064	-0.0049	0.0037	-0.0049	0.0037
	0.7055	0.0063	0.0063	0.2923	0.2922	0.1872	0.1871	0.1740	0.1739
	0.1580	-0.0230	0.0161	-0.1570	0.1099	0.0	0.0460	-0.2638	0.0565
5	0.0012	-0.0297	0.0299	-0.0160	0.0187	-0.0012	0.0009	-0.0419*	0.0315*
	0.0033	2.7848	2.7837	0.9331	0.9324	0.0033	0.0032	4.1839	4.1825
	0.0104	-0.3492	0.1746	-0.1543	0.1199	-0.0090	0.0070	-0.5184	0.1925
6	0.0072	0.0026	-0.0027	-0.0101	0.0118	-0.0669**	0.0503**	-0.0449**	0.0337**
	0.1526	0.0314	0.0316	0.5291	0.5285	15.8874	15.8847	7.0849	7.0829
	0.0610	0.0276	-0.0262	-0.1201	0.1020	-5.3876	0.3078	-1.2039	0.2330
7	0.0057	0.0047	-0.0047	0.0014	-0.0017	0.0117	-0.0088	0.0049	-0.0037
	0.0859	0.0861	0.0864	0.0091	0.0092	0.4268	0.4274	0.0737	0.0740
	0.0880	0.1102	0.0883	0.0319	-0.0320	0.3757	-0.1446	0.1321	-0.0662
8	0.0052	-0.0149	0.0150	0.0012	-0.0014	-0.0118	0.0089	-0.0017	0.0013
	0.2006	2.7215	2.7215	0.0211	0.0211	1.6045	1.6045	0.0289	0.0289
	0.0609	-0.4000	0.1647	0.0189	-0.0224	-0.6323	0.0903	-0.0342	0.0171

TABLE 11 (continued)

	19	20	21	22	23	24	25	26	27
1	-0.0070	0.0115	0.1419**	-0.1209**	0.1773**	-0.0554**	0.2156**	0.1947**	-0.0221
	0.1648	0.1647	10.1793	37.4128	14.3806	19.7618	7.8939	8.9772	0.0315
	-0.0212	0.0302	0.2249	-0.9197	0.2766	-0.2177	0.2875	0.2954	-0.0608
2	0.0001	-0.0002	-0.0545	0.0478**	-0.0717	0.0475**	-0.1874**	-0.1654**	0.0381
	0.0001	0.0001	2.0350	7.8659	3.4058	20.2618	9.1808	8.4261	0.1076
	0.0005	-0.0009	-0.2695	0.2035	-0.4302	0.1895	-3.3738	-1.8190	0.1396
3	-0.0089	0.0146	-0.0047	0.0068	-0.0135	-0.0052	0.0256	0.0142	0.0315
	1.1142	1.1140	0.0845	0.5812	0.5213	1.3046	1.0172	0.3749	0.2376
	-0.2078	0.2078	-0.1963	0.0902	-0.5253	-0.0967	0.4610	0.3129	0.3468
4	0.0014	-0.0023	0.0073	-0.0020	-0.0026	-0.0033	0.0346**	-0.0061	-0.0087
	0.0313	0.0314	0.2803	0.0528	0.0356	0.8703	7.6775	0.1138	0.0519
	0.0252	-0.0821	0.6153	-0.0260	0.0	-0.0610	1.2456	0.0	0.0
5	-0.0087	0.0142	-0.0501	0.0259	-0.0167	0.0132	-0.0674	-0.0333	-0.0254
	0.3750	0.3746	2.2290	2.7438	0.2269	2.2310	1.5756	0.5643	0.0663
	-0.0778	0.0918	-0.6010	0.1721	-0.1445	0.0905	-1.2133	-0.4891	-0.2797
6	0.0136	-0.0222	-0.0303	0.0316*	-0.0537*	0.0027	-0.0245	0.0020	0.0925
	1.3840	1.3849	1.7746	6.3972	3.9918	0.1483	0.4998	0.0027	1.2872
	0.1170	-0.3159	-1.2721	0.2040	-2.0937	0.0247	-0.8818	0.0224	0.5085
7	0.0023	-0.0038	0.0158	-0.0090	0.0075	-0.0078	0.0310	0.0271	-0.0509
	0.0355	0.0357	0.3777	0.4465	0.0716	1.1947	0.6859	0.4976	0.2978
	0.0416	-0.1084	0.6629	-0.1365	0.2920	-0.1540	1.1163	0.5969	0.0
8	0.0072	-0.0118	-0.0255**	0.0198**	-0.0268**	0.0083**	-0.0275*	-0.0333*	-0.0550
	1.0814	1.0814	7.0962	8.1452	7.0412	7.7016	4.7912	5.2247	1.4123
	0.0988	-0.2398	0.0	0.1761	0.0	0.1023	0.0	0.0	0.0

TABLE 11 (continued)

	28	29	30	31	32	33	34	35	36
1	0.0436	-0.0173	0.0283	-0.1254	-0.1219	0.0099	-0.1456	0.1779**	0.0666
	1.0592	0.0310	1.2905	3.5570	1.1286	0.0227	2.2551	8.8559	3.7256
	0.1034	-0.0494	0.0752	-0.7105	-0.5283	0.0306	-0.7278	0.3216	0.1492
2	-0.0511	0.0000	0.0091	0.1494*	-0.1120	-0.0216	-0.0373	-0.0068	-0.0191
	1.9653	0.0000	0.1769	5.5296	1.4242	0.1352	0.2017	0.0176	0.4065
	-0.3032	0.0001	0.0416	0.3908	-1.4558	-0.1227	-0.2798	-0.0320	-0.0928
3	0.0081	0.0465	-0.0192	-0.0003	0.0409	0.0215	-0.0023	0.0449	-0.0206
	0.1690	1.0457	2.5065	0.0002	0.7467	0.3403	0.0014	3.1880	1.5206
	0.1349	0.4650	-0.5284	-0.0111	0.5318	0.2440	-0.0339	0.5279	-0.5770
4	0.0024	-0.0168	-0.0036	-0.0325	0.0407	0.0225	0.0426	-0.0140	0.0219
	0.0163	0.2714	0.0894	0.7361	0.2343	0.3345	0.3555	0.2833	2.2883
	0.0661	0.0	-0.0991	-1.1049	0.2645	0.2551	0.3196	-0.6560	0.4895
5	-0.0067	0.0340	0.0076	-0.0588	-0.0204	0.0211	0.0298	-0.0859	-0.0104
	0.0375	0.2276	0.1409	0.9599	0.0594	0.1731	0.1400	3.3008	0.1311
	-0.0503	0.2265	0.0544	-0.6664	-0.2655	0.1795	0.2238	-2.0182	-0.0728
6	-0.0261	0.0081	-0.0097	0.0419	0.1497*	-0.0443	0.0479	-0.0931**	-0.0333
	0.9526	0.0175	0.3257	1.0257	4.2624	0.6605	0.4890	5.9325	2.2733
	-0.4328	-0.0806	-0.1002	0.3566	0.6487	-0.5015	0.3596	0.0	-0.6211
7	0.0347	-0.0472	-0.0067	0.0171	0.0208	-0.0200	-0.0291	-0.0355	0.0061
	1.4220	0.4957	0.1390	0.0971	0.0569	0.1534	0.1647	0.6596	0.0647
	0.4796	0.0	-0.1590	0.1939	0.2708	-0.6800	0.0	-1.6699	0.1364
8	-0.0049	-0.0073	-0.0057	0.0085	0.0022	0.0108	0.0938	0.0124	-0.0112
	0.1001	0.0502	0.3114	0.0789	0.0016	0.1015	2.3481	0.3832	1.0293
	-0.1022	-0.1460	-0.1036	0.0964	0.0285	0.1223	0.4692	0.1942	-0.4191

TABLE 11 (continued)

	37	38	39	40	41	42	43	44	45
1	-0.0767*	-0.0390	-0.1543*	-0.0589	0.0539*	-0.0461*	-0.0673*	0.0439*	-0.0137
	4.0463	0.6497	5.1214	0.7674	5.0180	5.0184	6.1921	6.1917	0.3939
	-0.2540	-0.1561	-2.0835	-0.2161	0.1123	-0.1941	-0.2553	0.1082	-0.0463
2	0.0336	-0.0023	-0.0295	0.0048	-0.0189	0.0161	0.0554*	-0.0361*	0.0109
	1.0524	0.0029	0.2239	0.0062	0.8186	0.8183	5.5131	5.5139	0.3309
	0.1345	-0.0115	-0.1989	0.0225	-0.0881	0.0758	0.2103	-0.2001	0.0531
3	0.0016	0.0037	-0.0235	0.0138	-0.0088	0.0076	-0.0116	0.0075	0.0079
	0.0083	0.0248	0.3558	0.1122	0.6007	0.6006	0.7330	0.7329	0.5629
	0.0312	0.0732	-0.6357	0.1520	-0.2549	0.1092	-0.2446	0.1317	0.1155
4	-0.0198	0.0050	-0.0237	0.0135	-0.0065	0.0056	0.0204	-0.0133	-0.0093
	1.2669	0.0272	0.1945	0.1427	0.3388	0.3386	2.1469	2.1473	0.7710
	-0.9490	0.0601	-0.3203	0.2229	-0.5658	0.0754	0.2522	-0.6053	-0.1769
5	0.0502	0.0277	-0.0132	-0.0280	0.0076	-0.0065	-0.0006	0.0004	-0.0083
	2.8685	0.4776	0.0573	0.2482	0.1550	0.1552	0.0007	0.0007	0.2239
	0.3010	0.1846	-0.1780	-0.3077	0.0548	-0.0548	-0.0053	0.0026	-0.0793
6	0.0364	0.0019	0.0937	0.0593	-0.0031	0.0026	0.0071	-0.0046	0.0138
	2.0378	0.0027	2.3612	1.6004	0.0373	0.0372	0.1432	0.1435	0.8747
	0.2691	0.0164	0.4218	0.3911	-0.0381	0.0232	0.0620	-0.0528	0.1090
7	-0.0143	0.0182	0.0375	0.0077	0.0056	-0.0048	0.0031	-0.0020	-0.0079
	0.2791	0.2451	0.3543	0.0214	0.1079	0.1082	0.0239	0.0241	0.2486
	-0.4583	0.2733	0.3376	0.1272	0.1619	-0.0811	0.0512	-0.0514	-0.1495
8	-0.0111	-0.0152	0.1130*	-0.0122	-0.0298**	0.0255**	-0.0067	0.0044	0.0066
	0.6233	0.3018	4.6417	0.1446	10.2959	10.2959	0.3445	0.3445	0.5554
	-0.2653	-0.1824	0.4358	-0.2015	-5.1510	0.2240	-0.1104	0.0662	0.0697

TABLE 11 (concluded)

	46	47	48	49	50	51	52	53	54
1	0.0140	-0.0270	0.0231	0.1462**	-0.0996**	0.1297**	-0.0855**	0.0157	-0.0145
	0.3939	1.2922	1.2920	28.7357	28.7364	21.7866	21.7873	0.4750	0.4751
	0.0346	-0.0915	0.0583	0.2497	-0.5291	0.2300	-0.4111	0.0457	-0.0411
2	-0.0112	0.0258	-0.0221	-0.0612*	0.0417*	-0.0429	0.0283	0.0371	-0.0342
	0.3311	1.5553	1.5558	6.8404	6.8395	3.1802	3.1796	3.4574	3.4581
	-0.0505	0.1114	-0.1114	-0.3722	0.1692	-0.2205	0.1254	0.1483	-0.1907
3	-0.0081	0.0045	-0.0039	-0.0045	0.0031	0.0024	-0.0016	0.0022	-0.0020
	0.5630	0.1503	0.1503	0.1281	0.1280	0.0366	0.0366	0.0374	0.0374
	-0.2146	0.0710	-0.0868	-0.1138	0.0487	0.0519	-0.0280	0.0387	-0.0387
4	0.0096	0.0171	-0.0147	-0.0016	0.0011	0.0027	-0.0018	-0.0102	0.0095
	0.7708	2.0887	2.0891	0.0191	0.0191	0.0519	0.0520	0.8283	0.8280
	0.2526	0.2279	-0.7406	-0.1243	0.0166	0.1362	-0.0292	-0.2633	0.1843
5	0.0086	-0.0288	0.0247	-0.0101	0.0069	-0.0295	0.0194	-0.0460*	0.0424*
	0.2236	2.2171	2.2161	0.2210	0.2207	1.8197	1.8188	5.9976	5.9962
	0.0566	-0.2769	0.1661	-0.0902	0.0494	-0.3136	0.1291	-0.3939	0.3063
6	-0.0141	0.0263	-0.0225	-0.0464*	0.0316*	-0.0423*	0.0279*	0.0174	-0.0160
	0.8755	2.6448	2.6462	6.6906	6.6887	5.5925	5.5909	1.2816	1.2823
	-0.2013	0.2070	-0.3036	-1.0066	0.2348	-1.0504	0.2033	0.2085	-0.1422
7	0.0081	-0.0103	0.0088	-0.0011	0.0007	0.0103	-0.0068	-0.0245	0.0226
	0.2480	0.3494	0.3488	0.0034	0.0034	0.2954	0.2959	2.1349	2.1333
	0.1867	-0.2225	0.1778	-0.0553	0.0110	0.3071	-0.1182	-0.6297	0.4006
8	-0.0068	-0.0077	0.0066	-0.0213*	0.0145*	-0.0305**	0.0201**	0.0083	-0.0077
	0.5554	0.6102	0.6102	4.5642	4.5642	9.5548	9.5548	0.7872	0.7872
	-0.2090	-0.1327	0.0948	-1.0806	0.1544	-4.5465	0.1977	0.1153	-0.1362

NOTE: Single asterisks indicate .05 level of significance. Double asterisks indicate .01 level of significance.

Leonard S. Miller, *Demand and Supply in U.S. Higher Education* (Berkeley, Calif.: Carnegie Commission on Higher Education, 1975) and Leonard S. Miller and Roy Radner, *Demand and Supply in U.S. Higher Education: A Technical Supplement* (Berkeley, Calif.: Carnegie Commission on Higher Education, 1975).
negie Commission on Higher Education, 1975).

2. Robert Campbell and B. W. Siegel, "The Demand for Higher Education in the United States 1919–1964," *American Economic Review* 57 (June 1967): 482–494.
3. Stephen A. Hoenack, *Private Demand for Higher Education in California*, Office of Analytical Studies, University of California. The document bears no date, but I believe the study was completed in 1967.
4. *Higher Education In the Boston Metropolitan Area*, Metropolitan Area Planning Council for the Commonwealth of Massachusetts Board of Higher Education, Volume VI of The Board of Higher Education Series, 1969.
5. Weights were set equal to the percentage of freshmen on each campus who lived with their parents and the percentage who did not live with their parents.
6. Hoenack, *Private Demand for Higher Education*, Appendix 4, pp. 3–4.
7. The wage rate effect was stronger in southern than in northern California. A 1 per cent increase in wages in the hometown area decreased the proportion of eligibles enrolling away from home by 3 to 5 per cent in the south, and decreased enrollment in the north by approximately 1.75 per cent.
8. *Higher Education in Boston*, pp. 38–39.
9. Harvey Galper and Robert M. Dunn, Jr. "A Short-Run Demand Function for Higher Education in the United States," *Journal of Political Economy* 77 (September/October 1969): 765–777.
10. For an excellent review of the topic see R. D. Luce, and P. Suppes, "Preference, Utility, and Subjective Probability," pp. 249–410 (see Sec. 5). Chapter 19 in R. Duncan Luce, Robert R. Bush, and Eugene Galanter, eds., *Handbook of Mathematical Psychology*, Vol. 3 (New York: John Wiley and Sons, 1965). In this paper we shall only be referring to models with constant utility functions. Random utility functions offer an alternative method of handling stochastic choice processes. For a discussion and comparison see Luce and Suppes cited above or H. D. Block and J. Marschak, "Random Orderings and Stochastic Theories of Responses," in Ingram Olkin et al., eds., *Contributions to Probability and Statistics, Essays in Honor of Harold Hotelling* (Stanford, Calif.: Stanford University Press, 1960). The development of this section follows Block and Marschak's presentation.
11. This choice model is weaker than the nonstochastic theory, for in nonstochastic theory j preferred to k implies j is chosen over k with probability 1. In the weak model, j is preferred to k with a probability only greater than one-half.
12. Block and Marschak, "Random Orderings." They credit R. D. Luce, *Individual Choice Behavior* (New York: John Wiley and Sons, 1959) with having most fully developed the strict constant utility model. Another property of the strict model shown by Block and Marschak is that the strict model implies that the probability of choosing j from a set K, where $K \subset J \subset A$ is the same as choosing j from the set J.
    This condition is referred to as the "independence of irrelevant choice" or the "irrelevance of added alternatives" condition.
13. Daniel McFadden, "On Measuring Design Criteria for Public Projects," Working Paper dated April 10, 1967 (processed), and "The Revealed Preferences of a Government Bureaucracy," Technical Report No. 17. Project for the Evaluation and Optimization of Economic Growth, Institute of International Studies, University of California, Berkeley (processed). The existence of McFadden's procedures for estimating the parameters was one of the key factors which made the demand estimates reported in this paper feasible. His work and his direct help on the project are

appreciated. McFadden calls his estimation procedure "conditional logit estimation." ϕ_{ij} is the conditional probability that student i chooses alternative j from the set J_i of alternatives open to him. R. D. Luce has shown (in *Individual Choice Behavior*) that the distribution function for the odds of the binary choice between j and k, in a strict model, can yield a "logistic curve."

14. *1962 SCAT-STEP Supplement*, Educational Testing Service, Princeton, N.J.; Berkeley, California, 1962. The specific linear predictors estimated were

$SAT_{Verbal} = -1,472.14 + 6.57 \, SCAT_{Verbal}$: 560 observations

$SAT_{Math} = -1,651.96 + 6.99 \, SCAT_{Quantitative}$: 513 observations

15. For a more complete statement of the predicted income models and results see Leonard S. Miller, "Predicting Family Income in the SCOPE Sample," Working Paper No. 7, Stony Brook Working Papers, April 1970 (Stony Brook, N.Y.: State University of New York, 1970) or Leonard S. Miller and Roy Radner, *Demand and Supply in U.S. Higher Education: A Technical Supplement* (Berkeley, Calif.: Carnegie Commission on Higher Education, 1975).

7 | COMMENTS

Stephen A. Hoenack

University of Minnesota

The private demand for higher education is an important topic which has received insufficient attention from economists. Public policy towards higher education could almost certainly be improved if the enrollment effects of a number of controllable variables were taken into account. For example, analysis of the effects of tuition charges on enrollments can form the basis of a policy of using flexibly administered higher-education prices. Such a policy could be used to allocate enrollments among educational programs in a manner which would ensure that student subsidies are no higher or lower than necessary to achieve desired enrollments.

Another example is in decision making regarding where to locate campuses. Estimates of the effects of travel costs on enrollments could be most helpful for this purpose.

Other policy-controllable variables which have enrollment effects include the nature of the high school curriculum and the timing and amount of career counseling provided.

In analyzing some of the complexities of student behavior, Miller's model of demand for higher education does a better job than previous models. The decision of whether to go to college is complicated because it involves a choice among the different types of schools for which the student is qualified as well as the choice of whether to go. The importance of this fact can be seen in the following question: Do students first choose to go to college and then decide which college to attend, or do the particular college options available to them affect their decision to go to college? In order to address such a question, econometric analysis of demand must direct itself to the determination of joint probabilities of various types of college attendance and to the hypothesis that college attendance involves sequential decision making. To my knowledge, Miller's model is the first one which explicitly takes into account the determination of joint probabilities of college attendance. This is an important advance over previous work.

Another important aspect of Miller's research is its incorporation of social and psychological determinants of the demand for college attendance, including factors related to the high school curriculum and environment. It is important to estimate the effects of these variables for two reasons. First, they more fully (and accurately) specify demand relationships and, thus, improve the estimates of the effects of costs on attendance. Second, variables such as high school curriculum and career counseling may, themselves, be desirable subjects of policy control.

In his research, Miller was confronted with some difficult problems with measures of students' families' incomes. Miller did what I suspect is the only existing empirical analysis of the differences between student- and parental-reported family incomes. He also developed an income predictor for students whose parents did not respond to a questionnaire requesting income data. Most important, Miller estimated his equations with different income data so that the reader can see the effect of alternative estimates on the results.

With regard to the specification of the effects of educational costs and family income on college attendance, Miller's estimating equations express the effects of these two variables through the ratio of educational costs to family income. This ratio is a special case of possible relationships between costs and income on college attendance choices. The most familiar way of envisioning the influences of costs and income on college attendance is in an equation in which each of these variables is entered individually and is not interacted with the other. Note that in this case the effect of either variable is independent of the level of the other variable. However, these are good a priori grounds for believing that the effects of costs and income are not independent of each other. While there are good a priori reasons for assuming an interactive relationship between the effects of costs and income on college attendance choices, there are not, to my knowledge, a priori grounds for specifying any particular form of this relationship. Miller's equations express a particular relationship in which one coefficient entirely determines the influences of both income and costs on the demand for college attendance. It would be worthwhile to test this hypothesis through the estimation of attendance equations in which educational costs and family income are entered separately, as well as interacted through the ratio variable. In addition, specifications of interaction terms alternative to the ratio form, such as multiplicative relationships, could be attempted. For such purposes it would be important to have wider ranges of sample cost data for each type of institution.

Much the same type of comment could apply to the student-institution achievement interaction variable. Incidentally, it would be interesting to test the hypothesis that the effect of the institutional component of this variable would differ according to the type of institution.

In summary, I believe that empirical analysis of the private demand for higher education is an important topic and that Miller's work is a valuable contribution.

8

JUNE O'NEILL
Council of
Economic Advisers

Productivity Trends in Higher Education

The relation between growth in output and growth in inputs in colleges and universities is of particular interest from the standpoint of public policy. The cost of higher education relative to the costs of other goods and services is in large part determined by relative rates of productivity change.[1] Since higher education has been heavily subsidized by public funds and private philanthropy, change in its price is of more than routine interest.

The traditional organization of the higher education establishment into public or private nonprofit institutions lends additional interest to the study along with additional difficulties. Economic research on productivity has generally dealt with private firms for whom pecuniary profit maximization is presumed to be a major goal. The goals of a subsidized, nonprofit firm may be more diffuse, and it is then a question whether such firms have the same incentives to minimize the costs of a given output or to pursue new and cheaper methods of production as energetically as those motivated by profit. Thus, a differential trend in productivity between higher education and other industries could be the result of differences in incentives as well as differences in the underlying technological production possibilities.

NOTE: This paper is based on research supported by the Carnegie Commission on the Future of Higher Education and was written while the author was at the Brookings Institution. Helpful suggestions were received from Dave M. O'Neill and Barry Chiswick. The views expressed, however, should not be interpreted as reflecting the views of the Carnegie Commission, the Brookings Institution, or of those who gave comments.

This paper presents estimates of the rate of growth of output and input in higher education over the period 1930–67. The results should be viewed as preliminary because the measures are far from perfect, particularly the measurement of output. Thus, the finding that output has grown at about the same rate as inputs suggests that productivity change may have proceeded at a lower rate in higher education than elsewhere, although a better measure of output might alter the finding.

I. DEFINING AND MEASURING OUTPUT

The definition and measurement of a unit of an industry's output is often a controversial issue. The proper unit is not always apparent (consider the medical care industry) nor is the extent or manner in which the qualitative aspects of the good should be measured.

In this paper, output is confined to the educational output of colleges and universities or what roughly corresponds to the instruction students buy with their time and tuition. Other outputs are produced by institutions of higher education and it is sometimes hard to draw a line between the purely instructional and other services. Whereas education may be viewed as the transmission of knowledge, and research as the production of knowledge, there can be considerable overlap between the two. Moreover, occupational guidance, future business contacts, and the atmosphere of a private club may be among the by-products of a college education. If the inputs that produce these other outputs cannot be separated from the purely educational inputs then, at least conceptually, these other outputs may be treated as qualitative aspects of the educational service. The problem is not unique to education—television may provide more than entertainment; a meal in a restaurant, more than nourishment.

Schools typically sell courses, so a simple quantitative measure of output would show the number of students times the number of courses per student per year. This is essentially the student load carried by schools and it may be conveniently expressed by standardized credit hours.[2] In any year, students in the United States are enrolled in disparate courses of study—resident or extension, degree-credit or non-degree-credit, part-time or full-time, summer and regular academic year. By assigning different numbers of credit hours to these different types of enrollments, I first derived a simple quantitative count (akin to full-time equivalents) reflecting the student course load carried each year, from 1929–30 to 1967–68.[3] In this initial form, the measure is equivalent to counting the number of aspirins as the output of the aspirin industry, or the number of automobiles as the output of the automobile industry. Obviously the measure will be deficient for measuring productivity change, and deficient to the extent that the "quality" of a standardized credit hour has changed over time.

Measuring the "Quality" of Output

By quality change economists mean a change in the ability of a given quantity of a good or service to satisfy some consumer want or "ultimate end". One approach to measurement of quality is to try to measure some aspects of the ultimate end or want more directly—as when student test scores are used as an indicator of the quality of a school's instruction. The other major approach, and one used more by economists and compilers of price indexes, is to specify various quality dimensions of the good or service (e.g. horsepower of the car, the "grade" of the meat, etc.) and then look to the market for information on how consumers value increments in these dimensions. Indeed relative prices of variants of a good, differing in particular specifications, are taken as indications of the relative quality of the variants. Adjustments can then be made for changes in price over time which are due to changes in the quality of a good, arising from changes in the mix of its specifications.

Of course, there are problems. The investigator must identify the relevant variants of commodities before they can be priced and it is possible that the more subtle specifications are missed in compiling existing price indexes. Another serious difficulty is that the relative prices consumers are willing to pay reflect relative utility only when the market is in equilibrium—a criterion seldom strictly met. The method fails particularly when new goods, or new substitutes for old goods, are introduced. While consumers are in the process of substituting the new for the old, prices will not be in equilibrium and price differentials will underestimate quality differentials. For this reason, quality change may be underestimated; and the greater the pace of new introductions, the greater the underestimate.[4]

The absence of a market price system in higher education adds an additional difficulty in estimating change in the quality of its output. Because of the variation in subsidies from school to school, differences in tuition charges need not bear any relation to quality differentials. Admissions are not rationed solely by price but also by various other devices.

Relative costs of different kinds of schooling may be substituted for relative prices in estimating "quality" differences, although this procedure raises problems. Without a market test, higher costs could possibly reflect inefficiencies in the use of resources rather than higher quality, since different kinds of schools may maximize different kinds of functions, and it is not clear what role the strictly objective factors play in the various functions. And, of course, relative cost data pose the same difficulties as relative price data do for constructing price indexes (e.g. relative costs change over time). However, cost differences are probably the most accessible route to measuring quality change in higher education arising from change in the mix of different kinds of schooling.

Pervasive cost differences have been found among different grade levels (upper- and lower-division undergraduate and graduate instruction) and among different types of schools (public and private universities, other four-year and two-year schools). Using available, but very limited cost studies, I have made a crude adjustment in the credit hours measure for change in the grade-level mix and change in the mix of schools.

More refined adjustments for change in the output mix can be made as the information becomes available. Thus, using data on the costs of different subjects, change in quality due to change in the subject mix can be added. Having adjusted credit hours for grade level, and subject, and possibly for type of school, one would have an output measure with a quality adjustment similar in spirit to that currently made for most goods. The question is then: What aspects of quality are omitted from the measure and how serious are the omissions in education versus other industries?

Unfortunately, I do not think the question is answerable, at least not with currently available information. Most price indexes, hence real output measures, are faulty for reasons given above, and we do not have any way of knowing the magnitude of the bias. By taking account of more subtle changes in specific aspects of automobiles (horsepower, weight, and length), Griliches adjusted the automobile Consumer Price Index and estimated lower rates of price increase for automobiles than the official indexes had indicated.[5] However, the technique leaves some questions unanswered and has not been widely duplicated for other goods. More elusive qualities of the "ultimate-end" variety (such as comfort and quiet for cars) are usually just not measurable at all.

Moreover, education is probably among the more complex goods and services with a larger component of elusive and unmeasurable quality characteristics. Narrowing down the education service to a specific subject, grade level, and type of school still leaves much room for quality variation.

Colleges and universities transmit knowledge. There are, however, alternative means of acquiring knowledge, such as books, television, family, and friends. Why, then, do people attend schools? Presumably, schools are more efficient through conserving the student's time and by allowing for the sharing of market inputs. Schools also provide evaluations—certifications to prospective employers and to other schools on the expertise of the pupil.

Qualitative change in school services should not be confused with change either in the quality of the knowledge itself or in the characteristics of the pupil, since these are not usually inputs controlled by the school. Thus, it would be incorrect to attribute the fruits of expenditures on research in science as a quality improvement in education, nor should quality change in students be counted as a change in output. An improvement in the writing style of authors or in the reading ability of book buyers would not be counted as a change in the output of the book-printing industry. However, knowledge has changed dramatically and students have changed too. Since different transmission processes may be required for the new knowledge or for the new types of student, evaluating quality is especially difficult. The speed and success with which schools adapt to these changes would actually be another, although difficult to measure, aspect of their quality.

Two measures—earnings and test scores—are often proposed for estimating the more elusive quality characteristics of school output. However, for the purpose of measuring quality change over time, both measures are at present inaccessible. Changes in the earnings differential between college graduates and high school graduates can hardly be attributed to changes in the quality of schools alone. Changes in the demand for different kinds of labor, changes in the physical supply of the two groups, and changes in the personal characteristics of the two groups are likely to dominate trends in earnings differentials over time, and since only physical supply changes can be readily measured, the separation of the unique effect of school quality on earnings differentials would appear to be a formidable task.

Tests of cognitive achievement could be administered to a cohort at high school graduation and then to the same cohort at different stages of college. Differential scores (college versus high school) could then be compared for different cohorts over time. The type of test would have to be such that it would be independent of changes in informational subject matter. It is well established that student characteristics dominate any explanation of differences in student achievement.[6] Therefore, for purposes of comparing results over time, it would be essential to know the relation between score improvement and starting level. Then, while a change in cohort score improvement may indicate the direction of quality change, the problem of measuring the exact value of the resulting change in output would remain. It would appear that these are difficult demands to meet.

II. DEFINING AND MEASURING INPUTS

For the purpose of estimating productive efficiency, it is necessary to identify and measure all the inputs which have been organized to produce the corresponding output. I have measured real inputs in higher education as total compensation to the factors (the sum of current operating expenditures and estimated capital costs), deflated by relevant factor price indexes.[7]

It should be noted that, due to data limitations, students' time is omitted from the measure. Since education is a highly time-intensive good, the omission would be serious if significant changes have occurred in the amount of student time spent in acquiring a credit relative to the growth of other inputs. However, no information could be obtained on this question.

With respect to the input measure actually used, two problem areas may be identified. First, the inputs used to produce instructional services may not have been properly separated from the inputs used to produce research and other jointly produced output. Second, the price deflators may be inadequate.

The decision about what portion of total expenditures to attribute to student instructional services involved some guesswork, since the financial statements of colleges (at least as reported by the Office of Education) do not provide very refined detail on the breakdown of expenditures by type of output. I have confined expenditures on student instruction to the following reported categories: instruction and departmental research, libraries, plant operation and maintenance, and general administration. The last three categories (sometimes referred to as overhead or indirect costs) include some expenses properly attributable to extension and public service and, also, to organized research. To adjust for this, I subtracted an amount equal to 5 per cent of extension expenditures and 15 per cent of organized research expenditures from the sum of the four categories.[8]

Since colleges and universities appear to have expanded their services over time, it is possible that some of the increase in the included inputs should not have been attributed to student instruction. This may be especially relevant for services such as job placement and the different types of counseling, which are not included in the measure of output. Working in the other direction is a possible downward bias in the measurement of input growth due to the possible transfer of some research activities, formerly classified as departmental research but reclassified into the organized research accounts as outside financing grew over time.

The capital input was measured as the deflated services of the capital stock and thus includes: (1) depreciation of the reproducible assets (buildings, improvements, and equipment), and (2) foregone interest on total capital assets (reproducible assets plus land), which would be equivalent to the return that the capital could earn if invested elsewhere in the economy.[9]

Depreciation was taken as 2 per cent of the gross value of buildings and 5 per cent of the gross value of equipment per year. Net replacement cost was used to approximate the market value of the capital assets and a conservative 5 per cent was used as the return to capital.

The selection of a measure of the capital input is a complex and controversial issue. However, in practice, the rate of growth in the net capital stock deflated, in the gross capital stock deflated, and in deflated capital costs, were all very close, about 4.2 per cent a year between 1930 and 1967.

Price indexes again present a problem. The deflator for physical capital is undoubtedly downward biased, due to the well-known bias in construction cost indexes. This results in a probable underestimate of the rate of growth of the real capital stock and, therefore, of deflated capital costs.

The deflator for educational operating expenditures is essentially a weighted average of separate indexes of faculty salaries, nonfaculty salaries, and supplies and services. The faculty salary index is itself a weighted average of separate salary indexes for full professors, associate professors, assistant professors, and instructors. Both the faculty and nonfaculty salary indexes have two known biases that work in opposite directions. The indexes were based on annual (or academic year) earnings, hence the well-known decline in hours worked over time suggests that hourly salaries actually increased faster than indicated. On the other hand, some of the observed increase in annual salaries is probably due to an increase in the educational level, and presumably the quality, of both faculty and nonfaculty workers. There is not enough information on the magnitudes of the two events to decide whether the opposite working biases were completely offsetting. However, whereas failure to account for hours worked biases change in the *quantity* of inputs upward, failure to adjust for educational level biases the *quality* dimension of inputs downward.

The overall input price index is necessarily crude, since there was not sufficient information to identify in detail all of the different inputs represented in operating expenditures.

III. SOME TENTATIVE ESTIMATES OF TRENDS IN PRODUCTIVITY

The quality of educational data along with the enormous conceptual problems makes measurement in this area hazardous. In reading this section, one should keep in mind all the qualifications previously mentioned.

Between 1930 and 1967, credit hours increased at an average annual rate of 4.8 per cent (Table 1, row 1). At the same time the average annual increase in total real inputs was 5.1 per cent. Therefore, taking the residual as a measure of productivity change leaves a seeming decline in productivity of −0.3 per cent a year. However, the choice of terminal years does influence the rate of change calculated this way.[10]

For some subperiods, small positive increases in the residual emerge (1954–67, 1954–60, 1960–67). An index of credit hours per unit of input recorded biennially over the same time period (annually from 1965–66 to 1966–67) suggests that there has probably been no trend, although there have been fluctuations (Table 2). These fluctuations correspond, as one would expect, to those unusual fluctuations in enrollment accompanying unusual events—depression, World War II, postwar GI boom. (See the index of credit hours, Table 2.)

Adjusting output for two kinds of quality change alters the results in the expected directions, but the magnitudes of these effects are very small. The two adjustments use cost differences by grade level as an indication of quality differences (as explained above). First an adjustment for changes in the graduate-undergraduate mix was made for the period 1930–67. Then, a further refinement was introduced by adding an adjustment for changes in the lower-division–upper-division mix of undergraduate credits (only for the period 1954–58).

The first adjustment necessarily assumes that costs, and therefore quality, are constant throughout the four years of undergraduate training, differing only between the graduate and undergraduate levels. Graduate costs were estimated to be three times as much as undergraduate costs.[11] Accordingly, the adjustment procedure gives graduate credit hours during the regular session a weight of three and undergraduate credits a weight of one. All summer credits were counted as undergraduate credits (weight of one).

The second adjustment allows for higher costs (and higher quality) in the upper division of undergraduate instruction. Upper-division costs were estimated to run 50 per cent higher than lower-division costs.[12] So the adjustment procedure gives a value of one to lower-division credits and a value of 1.5 to upper-division credits.[13] Graduate credits in four-year colleges and universities were given a value of 3.75, which retains the original 3 to 1 relationship between graduate and four-year

TABLE 1 Average Annual Percentage Rates of Change in Alternate Measures of Credit-Hour Output, Total Inputs, and of Residual, All Colleges and Universities, 1930–67 and Selected Subperiods (per cent)

	Period[a]					
	1930–67	1930–40	1940–54	1954–67	1954–60	1960–67
Total credit hours						
1. Unadjusted	4.8	3.1	3.2	8.0	6.6	9.1
2. Graduate adjusted	5.0	3.1	3.5	8.1	6.6	9.4
3. Standard lower-division units	–	–	–	8.0	6.7	9.2
Total inputs						
4.	5.1	3.1	4.2	7.7	6.3	8.9
Residual[b]						
Using as output:						
5. Unadjusted credit hours	–0.3	0.0	–1.0	0.3	0.3	0.2
6. Graduate adjusted credit hours	–0.1	0.0	–0.7	0.4	0.3	0.5
7. Standard lower-division units	–	–	–	0.3	0.4	0.3

SOURCE: O'Neill (1971).
    Row 1.   Based on Appendix A, Table A-10.
    Row 2.   Based on Appendix A, Table A-10. Undergraduate and summer credits given a weight of one, graduate credits given a weight of three.
    Row 3.   Based on Appendix A, Tables A-12, A-13, A-14. All credits in two-year schools are given a weight of one, all undergraduate and summer credits in four-year colleges and universities are given a weight of 1.25, and all graduate credits are given a weight of 3.75.
    Row 4.   Based on Appendix D, Table D-1.

[a] The dates refer to the academic year ending in the year indicated.
[b] Average annual percentage change in credit-hours output minus average annual percentage change in inputs.

TABLE 2   Indexes of Credit Hours per Unit of Input and of
          Credit Hours, All Colleges and Universities,
          1929–30 through 1966–67

Year	Index of Credit Hours per Unit of Input (1929–30 = 100)	Index of Credit Hours (unadjusted) (1929–30 = 100)
1929–30	100	100
1931–32	94	106
1933–34	88	96
1935–36	96	110
1937–38	101	124
1939–40	100	135
1941–42	93	127
1943–44	81	109
1945–46	104	153
1947–48	123	240
1949–50	110	241
1951–52	96	206
1953–54	87	211
1955–56	94	251
1957–58	90	282
1959–60	89	310
1961–62	90	353
1963–64	87	411
1965–66	93	519
1966–67	90	571

SOURCE: O'Neill (1971); Appendix Tables A-10 and D-1.

undergraduate costs. Thus, all credits are actually expressed as lower-division equivalents.

The two adjustments are extremely crude, based as they are on very limited data on differential costs. Apart from difficulties already noted, the cost studies used may not be sufficiently representative of all schools and cost differences may have changed considerably over time.

Although graduate credit hours grew at roughly twice the rate of total credit hours, they account for only a small portion of the total (7.1 per cent by 1966–67). Thus, the adjustment for the increase in graduate credits raises the measures of output growth and of productivity change, but only by a trifle. Since lower-division credits increased relatively rapidly, a consequence of the expansion of junior colleges, the adjustment for this factor almost cancels out the effect of the graduate-undergraduate adjustment, at least for the period 1954–67.

Further adjustments can also be made by disaggregating by type of school. Table 3 gives a summary of change in an index of output per unit of input, for both groups and for public and private institutions considered separately. The patterns of change have been different in public and private schools. In public schools, growth in output appears to have lagged behind growth in inputs from the 1930s to the 1950s, while inputs increased less rapidly than output from the 1950s to the 1960s. For private schools, the pattern is reversed although the changes are small. Within public institutions, there has been a large shift towards junior colleges, which are the lowest cost institutions even after adjusting for grade-level mix. Since this shift would largely cancel out the increase in graduate instruction, productivity in public institutions is biased upwards in Table 3 relative to private institutions.

Since enrollment has grown much more rapidly in public institutions (and especially public two-year colleges) which are lower-cost, and therefore likely to be lower-quality institutions, failure to adjust for the change in mix of schools would bias the aggregate measure of productivity change upward.[14] I have calculated a crude index of output per unit of input where output is adjusted for change in the mix of graduates

TABLE 3 Indexes of Output per Unit of Input Using Alternate Measures of Output, Public and Private Institutions, Averages of 1930–34, 1954–58, 1960–64, 1966–67 (1930–34 = 100)

Type of Output Adjustment and Period[a]	All Institutions	Public Institutions	Private Institutions
Unadjusted credit hours			
1930–34	100	100	100
1954–58	97	85	108
1960–64	94	86	98
1966–67	97	90	94
Graduate adjusted credit hours			
1930–34	100	100	100
1954–58	101	89	112
1960–64	100	92	104
1966–67	104	97	100

SOURCE: O'Neill (1971); Appendix Tables A-10, A-15, D-2, D-3.
[a] The data refer to the academic year ending in the year indicated.
   1930–34 = the average for 1930, 1932, 1934.
   1954–58 = the average for 1954, 1956, 1958.
   1960–64 = the average for 1960, 1962, 1964.
   1966–67 = the average for 1966, 1967.

and upper- and lower-division undergraduates, and, in addition, where output per unit of input is calculated as a weighted average for the following types of school: private university, private four-year college, private two-year college, public university, public four-year college and public two-year college.[15] With the average of the years 1954–58 as the base of 100, the index falls to 97 for the period 1960–64 and to 98 for the period 1966–67. Thus, for the period 1954–67, the effect of the added refinements of adjusting for mix of schools as well as change in the grade mix of students, is to lower the rate of productivity increase compared to that observed when no adjustment in credit hours is made at all (as in the upper part of Table 3).

As noted above, it should be possible to extend the cost-differences approach to make additional compositional adjustments for quality change in output due to change in the mix of subjects taught. However, available information does not indicate that such an adjustment would alter the results very much. Most cost studies show that courses in the physical and biological sciences and in health professions have the highest costs. The proportion of all bachelor's and first professional degrees granted in these areas seems to have declined somewhat over time (from about 17 per cent of all degrees in the 1930s to 13 per cent in the 1960s), with a resulting small shift towards degrees in lower-cost subjects— education, business and social sciences.[16] The same tendency is evident amongst Ph.D.'s. However, it is possible that the amount of science taken has increased for all students, regardless of field of degree, which might offset the shift towards lower-cost degree majors.

Further disaggregation than the broad adjustments given here would then be one approach to future research on productivity change in higher education. However, the potentially more serious sources of bias in the measures of output and productivity change probably lie in failure to account for quality change that is unrelated to grade level, type of school, or subject. And this brings us once more to the elusive areas of quality measurement. As discussed earlier, sophisticated studies of student achievement, holding precollege endowments constant, may in the future provide a way to estimate quality change in post-high-school education.

Although it is quite possible that quality has increased, there is still a question as to whether these quality changes would be sufficient to bring the estimate of growth in output per unit of total input up to the rate of the economy as a whole. To meet this mark, the rate of growth of the quality of output in higher education would have had to average between 1 and 1.5 per cent a year over the period 1930–67 (more, if quality of output is underestimated in other industries too, which is likely).[17]

IV. THE ORGANIZATION OF HIGHER EDUCATION AND INCENTIVES FOR CHANGE

The relation between the market structure of an industry and its rate of technological change has long interested economists. However, most discussion has been confined to the effect of differences in structure within the private profit-making sector of the economy and controversy has revolved around the question of whether technological advance is more compatible with bigness and monopoly or with competition (see, for example, Mansfield, ed. 1968).

Differences in the goals and structure of public and private nonprofit firms raise issues about which economists know very little. Within the private-for-profit sector there is the presumption that, although the degree of incentive may vary, the lure of profits and the rigors of competition provide powerful incentives for efficiency. According to this view, the constant search for lower cost (higher profit) methods of production promotes technological advance, whether it take the form of more subtle changes in business organization or of more dramatic changes in machinery and combinations of inputs.

Colleges and universities operate in a strikingly different atmosphere, where profits are not expected (indeed, they are frowned upon), and where public and private contributions are an important source of revenue. Of course, it is possible for state legislatures and private contributors to withhold funds when inefficiency is discovered. And this possibility probably does serve to restrain overt extravagance. However, outside funding depends largely on other considerations, and it is unlikely that the personal incomes of university administrators are as closely tied to the discovery of cost-saving innovations and factor substitutions as are those of entrepreneurs in private enterprise.

Numerous examples of what would appear to be inefficient practices have been cited by students of the higher education industry. Perhaps the most striking is the diffusion of the management role. Faculty are quasi-administration, quasi-employees and their self-interest may well conflict with optimum cost minimizing behavior. (For a more detailed critique of various practices, see Harris 1969; Schultz 1968.)

However, one can never be certain on the basis of a priori models of motivation or on the basis of ad hoc examples. Indeed, counter-examples are cited by those who stress that cost saving is primarily impeded by underlying technological restraints in higher education (Bowen 1968; Baumol 1967). Champions of this view point out that those forces influencing resource saving which are present in much of the economy simply do not apply to education. The "production process," as it were, is constrained by the basic requirement of one teacher to so many pupils and not much can be done to alter that basic fact without affecting the quality of the instruction. Consequently, substitution of physical capital for labor, or one type of capital or labor for another, are not as viable options as they are in the industrial world. Those who follow this line of reasoning conclude that as a result of this state of affairs, productivity change in education is doomed to be lower than that in the rest of the economy.

A number of questions may be raised. Colleges and universities use many resources other than teachers to supply the educational product; faculty salaries account for less than half of total educational costs. Without even changing pupil-teacher ratios, economies may be achieved in administration or in the use of libraries and physical capital. Furthermore, the relevant question with respect to quality change and pupil-teacher ratios is whether a given change in the ratio changes costs by more or less than it changes quality. Finally, I am not aware of any overwhelming amount of experimentation with nontraditional forms of instruction which would conserve teacher time. Nor are we, as part-time armchair entrepreneurs, likely to think of such things with the same urgency as would be the case if our incomes depended on it.

Since speculation cannot resolve the question, systematic and objective empirical studies that compare cost differences and productivity-change differences among edcational institutions producing similar outputs, but in which administrators operate under different personal-incentive environments, are needed. One of the few such studies compares costs in Navy training schools with costs of similar programs in private proprietary schools (D. O'Neill 1970). The results indicate substantially lower costs in the private schools although it could not be determined whether the quality of output was the same in both kinds of schools.

Very few colleges are private profit-making schools. Indeed the case of Marjorie Webster Junior College, a school excluded from even the chance of applying for accreditation solely on the grounds of its being a profit-making institution, suggests that the fewness of such schools may be in part the result of restrictive behavior by the college community (see Koerner 1970). However, many technical proprietary schools offer courses similar to those in the public junior colleges and these can be compared. Also, colleges and universities vary considerably in their reliance on student fees, endowment, gifts and state and local funds. Detailed study of schools classified by type of funding might provide insight into differential costs and rates of change in output per unit of input.

To sum up, there is a possibility that the rate of productivity change in higher education, even if positive, has not kept pace with the rate of productivity change elsewhere in the economy. Observers of the educational scene have offered various reasons why the productivity of resources in education might lag behind the rest of the economy.

The clarification of the issue has important implications for future decisions on methods of financing higher education. If present methods of financing (which give large sums directly to institutions) are found to affect incentives adversely and, in turn, to impede efficiency and productivity change over time, this could be counted as a cost of this kind of financing package, to be balanced against the advantages. Other financing schemes, such as giving aid directly to students, may have more beneficial effects on incentives and therefore lead to cost saving in the long run.

NOTES

1. The price of a product will obviously change depending upon change in the prices of inputs (including materials) used in its production and changes in the amount of output produced per unit of input. For a more elaborate discussion of the relationship, along with empirical results (see Kendrick 1961).
2. Woodhall and Blaug used a measure similar in spirit to measure the output of British universities: degrees awarded, weighted by length of course required for the degree, and including an allowance for "wastage"—those who did not complete the degree (Woodhall and Blaug 1965). One difficulty with the degree measure is that one may not be able to match the student load accurately with inputs for the appropriate year. Also, in the United States, where a very large percentage of students do not obtain degrees, and where the number of years taken to obtain a degree is extremely variable, the measure would be exceedingly cumbersome to put into standardized form.
3. The methods and data sources used to convert enrollment data into credit hours are described in detail in (O'Neill 1971). Note that the credit hour measure may be viewed as an alternate—and possibly more convenient—way of estimating comprehensive full-time equivalent enrollment.
4. For an interesting exchange on problems of measuring quality and constructing welfare-oriented price indexes see (Griliches 1964) and the comments following by (Jaszi 1964) and (Denison 1964). For some evidence showing that the Consumer Price Index may sometimes overstate quality improvements see (Triplett 1971).
5. The Griliches method is particularly useful for estimating quality changes that result in changes in the mix of characteristics which are so inherently a part of the basic commodity that they are not sold separately and therefore would not be counted as specifications in the making of official price indexes. Griliches uses multivariate techniques to impute shadow prices to these characteristics (Griliches 1964).
6. For a review of the literature referring specifically to higher education see (Berls 1969).
7. See (O'Neill 1971) for a detailed description of the construction of the index.
8. The data on expenditures are taken from publications of the Office of Education and have been adjusted and reported by O'Neill (1971). Note that current operating expenditures on student instruction accounted for only 50.7 per cent of total current expenditures in 1966–67.

9. The capital stock was estimated by cumulating increments of investment adjusted for price changes and depreciation (the perpetual inventory method). (See O'Neill, 1971 Chapter III for full details.)

10. Woodhall and Blaug concluded that there had been a *decline* in output per unit of input in British universities. However, their finding could be due to their choice of terminal years if British universities followed cyclical patterns similar to American colleges and universities. For the years that they selected (1938–52; 1952–62; 1938–62) output per unit of input declined in the United States too.

11. The adjustment factors used here are based on unit-cost differences found in a study of public institutions in Michigan. (See O'Neill 1971 for further details.)

12. Ibid.

13. All credits taken in two-year schools were counted as lower-division credits. Undergraduates and summer credits in four-year schools were assumed to be divided equally between upper and lower division.

14. The fact that private schools continue to attract even a shrinking portion of all students is a bit of circumstantial evidence of higher quality in private schools compared to public ones—especially when one considers that the ratio of tuition in the two sectors is much greater than the ratio of costs. Tuition and fees per credit hour in all private schools were 4.2 times as much as in public schools in 1966–67. Costs per lower-division credit were only 1.2 times greater in private than in public schools in the same year.

15. Index derived from Table 28 (O'Neill 1971). Fixed weight average is a weighted average across the six types of schools using the 1954 distribution of credit hours (adjusted for mix of credits by grade level).

16. From the beginning of the century to the 1930s the decline in health professions particularly (and also law) and the rise of education and business was still more dramatic. For the distribution by field of B.A.'s and first professionals (and also Ph.D.'s) by five-year periods from 1911 to 1953 see (Wolfle 1954, Appendix B). For more recent data see the Office of Education series on *Earned Degrees Conferred*.

17. Denison (1962, p. 224) gives estimates of growth in output per unit of input in the economy (for the period 1929–57) which range from .82 to 1.15 per cent a year depending upon the assumptions used to obtain measures of growth rates in output for those sectors of the economy where no direct output measures exist (e.g. government and nonprofit industries). While no comparable estimates exist for the whole period 1930–67, it seems likely that productivity growth during the sixties may have exceeded the trend for the 1929–57 period. It should be noted that Denison's estimates are based on a measure which relates changes in real output to changes in total factor input, and which counts changes in the quality of a factor as growth in the amount of that factor.

REFERENCES

Baumol, William J. "Microeconomics of Unbalanced Growth: The Anatomy of Urban Crisis," *American Economic Review* 57 (June 1967): 415–426.

Berls, Robert H. "An Exploration of the Determinants of Effectiveness in Higher Education." In *The Economics and Financing of Higher Education in the United States*. A compendium of papers submitted to the Joint Economic Committee, 91st Congress, 1st Session, Washington, D.C. 1969.

Bowen, William G. *The Economics of the Major Private Universities.* Berkeley, Calif.: Carnegie Commission on Higher Education, 1968.

Denison, Edward F. "Comment" to Griliches paper (Griliches 1964).

————. *The Sources of Economic Growth in the United States and the Alternatives Before Us.* Supplementary Paper No. 13. New York: Committee for Economic Development, 1962.

Griliches, Zvi. "Notes on the Measurement of Price and Quality Changes." In *Models of Income Determination.* Studies in Income and Wealth, Volume 28. New York: NBER, 1964.

Harris, Seymour E. "Financing Higher Education: An Overview." *The Economics and Financing of Higher Education in the United States.* A compendium of papers submitted to the Joint Economic Committee, 91st Congress, 1st Session, Washington, D.C. 1969.

Jaszi, George. "Comment" on Griliches paper (Griliches 1964).

Johnson, Harry G. "Correspondence on Productivity Trends in British University Education." *Minerva* 4 (Autumn 1965): 95–98.

Kendrick, John W. *Productivity Trends in the United States.* New York: NBER, 1961.

Koerner, James D. "The Case of Marjorie Webster." *Public Interest* 20 (Summer 1970): 40–64.

Mansfield, Edwin, ed. *Monopoly Power and Economic Performance.* New York: W.W. Norton and Co., 1965.

O'Neill, David M. *Meeting the Navy's Needs for Technically-Trained Personnel: Alternative Procurement Strategies.* CNA Research Contribution No. 151. Arlington, Va.: Institute of Naval Studies, Center for Naval Analyses, 1970.

O'Neill, June. *Resource Use in Higher Education: Trends in Output and Inputs 1930–1967.* Berkeley, Calif.: Carnegie Commission on Higher Education, 1971.

Schultz, Theodore W. "Resources for Higher Education: An Economist's View." *Journal of Political Economy* 76 (June 1968): 227–247.

Triplett, Jack E. "Determining the Effects of Quality Change on the CPI." *Monthly Labor Review.* Washington, D.C.: U.S. Bureau of Labor Statistics, May 1971.

U.S. Office of Education. *Enrollment for Advanced Degrees.* Washington, D.C. Published annually since 1959.

Wolfle, Dael. *America's Resources of Specialized Talent.* New York: Harper and Brothers, 1954.

Woodhall, Maureen, and Blaug, Mark. "Productivity Trends in British University Education, 1938–62" *Minerva* 3 (Summer 1965): 483–498.

8 | COMMENTS

George B. Weathersby
University of California

In general, this is a provocative and well-written report summarizing a massive study of educational costs and outputs over the past forty years. Essentially, the reported results of essentially no productivity gains (or even slight productivity losses) over this period seem to confirm Radner's observation that the relationship between educational inputs and outputs has changed very little from the days of Socrates to our own. While this paper is well girded with caveats, qualifications, and disclaimers, there remain several areas of potential difficulty which are discussed below. These are not criticisms of O'Neill's paper alone but are more generally applicable to basic definitions, data, and their interpretation. Finally, I conclude with some general comments on policy analysis and the educational industry.

COMMENTS SPECIFIC TO THIS PAPER

O'Neill begins by declaring a public policy focus for her paper and then concentrates almost exclusively on institutional efficiency. In other words, all of the costs and outputs are viewed from the institutional perspective. Therefore, only direct operating and capital costs were considered, with no adjustment for either direct social costs or social opportunity costs, and the only outputs considered were full-time equivalent student years, which were derived from full-time and part-time head count enrollments by an assumed credit-hour equivalency. Research, public service, extension, regional economic development, and all other noninstructional outputs were ignored. To the extent that these noninstructional outputs have constituted an increasing proportion of the total outputs of higher education over the past forty years—casual empiricism suggests that they have—then the results reported in this paper underestimate the actual productivity increases of higher education.

The use of student credit hours (SCH) through the full-time student year concept as an output measure is subject to challenge. The credit value of a course is often determined arbitrarily by faculty members, in a manner unlinked to its resource use or to the production process. Some schools have assigned the same unit value to all courses regardless of their frequency or duration of meeting. Independent study is a growing component of many schools' instructional program with some schools reporting over one-third of their total SCH's in independent study. Typically, the credit value of a student's independent efforts is personally negotiated between each student and faculty member and is again independent of the resource use or relative productivity.

Focusing on the SCH ignores attrition. While the SCH is a process measure of sorts, it contains little information about the progress of students through an institution or the number of students who successfully complete their degree program. Roughly one-half of the entering freshmen do not receive a bachelor's degree. This may be irrelevant to an institution because degrees are free, or nearly so. (The recent decision by many law schools to provide former LL.B. recipients with a J.D. for only twenty-five dollars established a market price for doctorates at major institutions for the first time.) However, many public agencies and private firms have been persuaded that certification is valuable. Occupational placement and mobility depend far more on degrees than on SCH's. Manpower planning depends far more on degrees than on SCH's. I believe that many aspects of public policy depend far more on degrees than on SCH. This is not to argue that SCH's are meaningless, but that their public policy significance beyond the institution is somewhat limited.

The joint input/joint output problems are either handled arbitrarily (libraries, administration, and extension) or are ignored completely. The efficacy of this is again a matter of perspective. Most institutions of higher education are small, with enrollments of less than two thousand students, with undergraduate instruction as the institutions' main mission. Many of these schools are private and church-related. On the other hand, most college students and most resources are found in large institutions offering a wide range of instructional, research, and public service activities, and which are predominately public. Joint output activities abound in such schools. Once again, ignoring these joint outputs would bias productivity estimates downward.

As pointed out in the paper, using cost as a proxy for quality is problematical at best because it obscures the very relationship one is seeking—the relationship between efficiency and quality. It is all too easy to label any relative increase in resource use as an increase in quality with no supporting evidence. Alternative measures of quality that one might use are the ratio of the number of applicants to the size of the entering class, the student admit/accept ratio, the number of faculty applications/vacancy, or the number of job offers/junior faculty members. An index of institutional quality constructed by David Brown some years ago may be somewhat anachronistic but may still be useful.

In another vein, the dollar value of the capital facilities recorded on institutional ledgers may seriously overestimate both their value and their cost to the institution. Since 1963, the federal government has supported the construction of new educational facilities under the auspices of the Higher Education Facilities Act. This act provided that the federal government would bear the bulk of the costs of approved facilities. Therefore, while the total cost reported on the books of the institution might accurately reflect the market value of the facility, they could also overstate the cost to the institution by a factor of four to ten times.

Another interesting problem associated with physical facilities is the extensive use of restricted funds for capital outlay. Often the marginal utility to the institution of restricted funds is much less than their face value. A tragicomic example of this is one public institution whose largest bequest was a $10 million gift to be used exclusively for a canon law library. Although medieval church law is neither a major nor a rapidly growing field in a modern, socially conscious law school, this institution did accept the gift. However, when questioned, some faculty and administrators would have eagerly preferred $1 million or even $200,000 in an unrestricted gift. Because there were no other alternative uses of the money available, $10 million for libraries was added to the books even though neither the direct cost to the institution nor the value to the institution even closely resembled $10 million.

These last two points are only two obvious examples of one of the major pitfalls in meaningfully comparing institutional cost data—the changing mix of institutional revenues. In many respects, an educational institution is a little like a hungry family; it essentially spends all that it makes. In this sense, unit costs are more accurately described as unit revenues. Meanwhile, the O'Neill study used institutionally reported expenditure levels without adjusting for the different and changing mix of the sources of funds; the inclusion or exclusion of self-supporting enterprises, such as dormitories, cafeterias, hotels, hospitals, and even airlines further bias the results. In some institutions, the ratio of total expenditures per student is as much as twice the ratio of instructionally related expenditures per student, whereas in other institutions the two measures are nearly identical. If the appropriate data were available, only the instructionally related expenditures should be compared with the instructional outputs (ignoring joint outputs again). Furthermore, if the proportion of non-instruction-related expenditures has increased in the last forty years, then the reported productivity figures would be biased downward once more.

Finally, as the paper points out, in the recent past the acquisition of resources for education has not depended upon demonstrated efficiency. Therefore, one should not be surprised when there is no consistent pattern of efficiency demonstrated.

BROADER COMMENTS ON EDUCATION AS AN INDUSTRY

One conclusion that seems apparent, particularly from the papers by Levin and O'Neill, is that the theory of the firm is an incomplete and possibly inappropriate paradigm for *policy* analysis in education—particularly higher education. It is unnecessary to repeat here the many ways in which education falls short of the competitive market assumptions, or to speculate on what minimum behavioral assumptions are necessary for a rational analysis of public sector resource allocation.

However, we are presented with no evidence that either the variables chosen or the educational processes modeled in these papers are appropriate in the judgment of those who must use the analysis or that decisions based on these analyses would be significantly different from those made without these results. We are caught in a strange paradox of demanding a fistful of computer-calculated test statistics to indicate the statistical significance of a variable in a relationship, without presenting a shred of empirical evidence that any of these variables are relevant for policy purposes.

The quantitative analysis of cause and effect relationships undoubtedly has an important role to play in policy analysis but it is not yet in the proper context. Basically, we have no reference for the relevance of any particular variable or relationship without specifying the set of decisions and the level of decision making one is trying to affect. This seems to be the essential first question for meaningful policy analysis.

9

ROBERT M. OLIVER
University of California, Berkeley

and

DAVID S. P. HOPKINS
Stanford University

Instructional Costs of University Outputs

I. INTRODUCTION

The purpose of this paper is to develop a simple model that evaluates the instructional costs of educating student cohorts enrolled in an institution of higher education. We have the additional objective of analyzing some of the cost implications of new operating policies and plans that modify the content, number, and type of degree programs available to these cohorts. Although the data we use is specifically adopted from sources at the University of Colorado, the University of California (Berkeley Campus), and Stanford University, the underlying model of the

NOTE: Part of this report was prepared while Robert M. Oliver was on sabbatical leave at the University of Colorado. The work was partially supported by the National Science Foundation under Grant GK-23153, and by the U.S. Army Research Office-Durham under Contract DA-31-124-ARO-D-331 with the University of California. Reproduction in whole or in part is permitted for any purpose of the United States Government. David S. P. Hopkins's research was partially supported by the IBM Corporation under a Postdoctoral Fellowship.

educational process and the mathematical methods that we use to evaluate these costs may be applicable to other private or public educational institutions. Since our emphasis is on finding a scheme for predicting budgets under specified policy constraints, no judgment is made or implied regarding the quality of educational programs. The assumption is that quality standards determine some of the constraints on feasible operating policies and that these may obviously differ from one institution to another.

Throughout this paper, student cohorts are identified by their status upon entering and by the sequence of educational programs which they undertake at the educational institution in question. For example, one cohort might consist of students who enter the lower division, continue into the upper division, and obtain a bachelor's degree. A second cohort might be students who enroll for the first time at the upper-division level and drop out prior to receiving a degree; still a third example is a junior transfer who receives his bachelor's degree and then continues for an additional period of time in order to receive his master's degree. Although we do not do so in this paper, it is possible to define a cohort by means of a finely divided classification which identifies such things as the student's major; his precise status, such as second quarter, third year; his educational background, two years of high school, three years of preparatory school; and even socioeconomic factors such as income and educational background of parents. We have chosen to restrict the problem and data requirements to a manageable level, but at the same time, to select aggregations that allow us to evaluate the costs of administrative and institutional policies, such as the implementation of year-round operations, the imposition of various enrollment ceilings, the adoption of new undergraduate and graduate programs or the alteration of dropout rates through selective admission policies.

As the reader will see, cohorts are defined in a way that makes it simple and straightforward to calculate the unit cost of educating a student member of that cohort. This accounting is straightforward when the life history and costs of each student cohort are independent of all others. Unfortunately, this is seldom the case, and possibly the most important feature of our model and its findings is the recognition that different degree programs have substantial interactions with one another. Changes in the unit costs of one program usually affect a large number of cohorts and hence the total costs of educating different student cohorts. This feature is particularly important when a fraction of the students being educated are themselves used as teachers.

It is common practice in many institutions to allocate a large amount of historical accounting data in such a way as to come up with a cost per student for every year that he attended the institution in question. The emphasis in this paper is quite the opposite: first of all, we are more interested in estimating and analyzing the unit costs of educating a particular student during his lifetime at the institution than we are in obtaining the unit cost of enrolling a student for a single time period. The connection between the two types of costs is not always obvious; while lifetimes of the student at the institution enter the former calculation, they are not involved in the latter. In our experience, calculations of the latter type always make it difficult to distinguish between the unit costs of those students who do, or do not, drop out, so that the effect of attendance patterns on unit costs is not explicitly made. Secondly, we are much less interested in manipulating large amounts of historical accounting data than we are in obtaining order-of-magnitude estimates which reveal the underlying structure of marginal and unit costs and the impact that new institutional policies have upon these costs. For example, if dropouts affect enrollment levels in a reasonably predictable way, we are interested in understanding how costs of educating different types of students are sensitive to policies which affect these dropouts.

In the remainder of this paper, we assume that "instructional cost" refers only to the direct salary cost of students and faculty who engage in the instruction of students at a given institution. While we do not become involved in such computations, standard accounting techniques for converting these direct labor costs into a total instructional budget that includes related items, such as expenditures for nonacademic staff and office space, do exist.

The organization of this paper is as follows: Section II discusses related work on university cost models. Notation and terminology are introduced in Section III, which we then use in Section IV to formulate a mathematical model of student flow patterns and costs on a network characterized by the degree programs available to student cohorts. The flows and costs have an apparent multi-commodity structure which can lead to interesting and nontrivial interpretations for shadow prices associated with final demands, admissions and enrollment ceilings. Section V gives source data for behavioral and institutional parameters and the unit cost data for campuses that we study in Section VI. The data and the model are used to analyze instructional costs at each institution if one were to adopt the policy recommendation made by the Carnegie Commission on Higher Education [1971] that lower-division programs be reduced from two years to one year. The paper concludes with a bibliography.

II. RELATED WORK

Some interesting papers on unit costs as they relate to productivity in education may be found in UNESCO [1967]. In this volume, the paper by de Escondrillas describes two types of aggregate unit costs that are commonly used for monitoring educational institutions: cost per student year and cost per graduate. These are computed by dividing the total annual operating cost by either the total enrollment or by the total number of students graduating per year. Observe that the latter computation has the effect of attributing the cost of all students who do not complete the curriculum (i.e. dropouts) to those who do. Moreover, de Escondrillas did not discuss specific uses for each type of unit cost. That it is important to decide a priori on the type of cost most pertinent to a given study was demonstrated in the paper by Chau who used real data to calculate both the cost per student year and the cost per departing student in the primary school systems of Cameroun and Senegal. The results showed Cameroun to be more "efficient" with respect to the first criterion, and Senegal with respect to the second. Finally, the paper by Gern analyzes various components of the cost per student year, such as the cost of teachers, capital equipment, and construction and mainte-nance of buildings, in order to isolate the factors that influence them. Gern also suggested a number of different unit cost comparisons which might be made for the purpose of identifying efficient alternatives, for example between similar institutions in a given country, between differ-ent countries, or between different teaching techniques.

Several cost simulation models have recently been developed for institutions of higher education to calculate costs in terms of levels of instructional activity. Although the details of these models are not gen-erally available in the open literature, mimeographed reports, such as Weathersby [1967] and Judy [1969], have been widely circulated. Tak-ing student enrollments to be the measure of instructional activity, these models determine instructional costs in the following manner: let $x(t) = [x_j(t)]$ be an n-dimensional column vector of student enrollments at time t (by grade level, major department, etc.) and let $y(t) = [y_i(t)]$ be an m-dimensional column vector of faculty staffing levels at time t (by rank, department, etc.). The assumption is made that $y(t)$ is linear in $x(t)$, i.e. given $x(t)$, one can compute $y(t)$ by the rule

$$y(t) = Mx(t)$$

where $M = [\mu_{ij}]$ is an $m \times n$ matrix of faculty-student ratios. Given an m-dimensional row vector of average faculty salaries, s, one obtains the total instructional cost for time period t, $C(t)$, by taking the vector product

$$C(t) = sy(t) = (sM)x(t)$$

In such a scheme, the unit (per period) cost of instruction for students in category i is expressed by the ith component of the vector (sM). We emphasize that the elements of sM are holding costs, not product costs.

This basic model was extended by Koenig et al. [1967] to include equations that describe the transitions of students as they flow through the system. These authors made the following assumptions regarding student attendance behavior: (1) each student's progress through his educational program does not depend on any other student's progress; and (2) a student's status at time $t + 1$ does not depend on his status *prior to* time t. Under these assumptions, it is reasonable to postulate the existence of a Markov-like transition matrix $P = [p_{ij}]$ whose (i,j)th element is the fraction of students in state i at the beginning of period t that will be in state j at the beginning of period $t + 1$. If $z(t) = [z_i(t)]$ is an n-dimensional column vector of new admissions during period t, student enrollments at $t + 1$ are related to the enrollments at t by the equations

$$x(t + 1) = P'x(t) + z(t)$$

where prime denotes matrix transposition. These authors were particularly interested in describing the cumulative instructional costs invested in students as they flow through the system. Thus, defining $\hat{c}_i(t)$ to be the average *cumulative* educational investment in students in state i at the end of period t and assuming that new students have accumulated the same average investment as those who entered previously, they described the conservation of money flows for each state j as follows:

$$\hat{c}_j(t + 1)x_j(t + 1) = \sum_i \hat{c}_i(t)[p_{ij}x_i(t)] + \hat{c}_j(t)z_j(t) + \left(\sum_k s_k \,\mu_{kj}\right)x_j(t + 1)$$

[total cumulative investment in students in state j in period $t + 1$]

= [total cumulative investment prior to $t + 1$ in continuing students who are in state j in period $t + 1$]

+ [total cumulative investment in new students entering at state j at the end of period t]

+ [value added during period $t + 1$]

While their purpose was to investigate cumulative educational investments regardless of where these investments were made, we are interested only in those investments made by the given institution. Therefore, it is appropriate to delete the second term in the above equation. If we then divide both sides by $x_j(t + 1)$, we obtain a set of linear equations that describe the propagation of the unit cumulative investment in students in the various states j:

$$\hat{c}_j(t + 1) = \sum_i \hat{c}_i(t)\left[\left[\frac{p_{ij}x_i(t)}{x_j(t + 1)}\right]\right] + \sum_k s_k \mu_{kj}$$

Observe that in order to calculate numerical values for the $\hat{c}_j(t)$ in this recursive relationship, it is necessary that we first be given values for investments in the initial period, $\hat{c}_i(0)$.

Models of this type are cross-sectional in the sense that the elements of M and P are estimates of ratios observed at a particular point in time or are, at best, the average of a small number of time periods. They tend to suffer from the real difficulty that cross-sectional data is sensitive to historical institutional policies, and it is often difficult to examine the cost implications of new operating policies. In the Koenig model, for instance, the meaning of the quantity $\hat{c}_i(t)$, computed for a group of students undifferentiated by where they entered the system, is not clear. Nor is it clear how the $\hat{c}_i(t)$ will be affected by changes in student admission and dropout rates.

Because these models are usually formulated to include a great deal of detail (i.e. numerous categories of students and faculty), they are costly to implement. An additional drawback is that, at such levels of disaggregation, the existence of widespread substitutability between members of a university instructional staff would seem to contradict the assumption of a single-efficient-point technology in which resource inputs are always used in fixed proportions; in addition, it may be unreasonable to assume that individual instructional programs exhibit constant returns to scale. These issues are discussed at greater length in Hopkins [1971].

Sengupta and Fox [1969] formulated a linear programming model to determine optimal policies for the recruitment of new faculty and the allocation of total faculty time to various instructional and research activities over a four-year planning period. Although they were not concerned directly with the costs of educating students, these were included as debit items in their maximand. The remaining coefficients in the objective function corresponded to the value added by "producing" a graduate from a bachelor's, master's, or doctoral program, this quantity being measured as the difference in expected discounted lifetime income due to the earning of the degree. The constraints specified demands for faculty time in teaching, research, and administration; available supplies of faculty time; undergraduate and graduate student admission quotas; and various technological restrictions. A major weakness of this model is its omission of the effects of dropouts and student lifetimes, for it assumes that admissions are equivalent to degree outputs and that all students are enrolled in a given degree program for the same period of time.

Our model in this paper differs in several ways from earlier ones and offers an alternative way to calculate the cost of educating a student at a given institution. First of all, the model is longitudinal rather than cross-sectional in nature. That is to say, student cohorts and the unit cost of educating a student cohort are defined over the lifetime of the cohort in question, not at a single point in time. Attrition rates and other factors related to student attendance patterns are defined for each student cohort; again the relevant time period is the lifetime of the cohort at the institution.

Secondly, we are concerned with the interactions that occur when an institution is in equilibrium with respect to student flows, enrollments, and various parameters of student behavior. We assume that input flows, output flows, enrollments, cohort lifetimes, and dropout rates are the same in each time period and make a concerted effort to attribute costs to the actual output flow rates of the instructional process, namely various types of degree recipients and dropouts per unit time.

Finally, our model is highly aggregated in the sense that individual departmental majors are not taken into account. Thus, we are interested in the implications of new policies at the campus-wide level, not at the departmental level. In this sense, it is similar to one developed earlier by Oliver, Hopkins, and Armacost [1970] expressing the enrollments of students, the number of teaching staff, and the flow rates of students who eventually drop out in terms of the final demand for degree recipients at various degree levels.

The size of our model is such that the number of policy variables that can be identified and studied is of the order of ten or twenty, not hundreds or thousands; the amount of data that must be collected and analyzed does not obscure one's understanding of the budgetary flow process; and it is possible, with a minimal amount of computation and analysis, to identify the effects of certain proposed policies.

III. NOTATION AND TERMINOLOGY

For our purposes it is convenient to represent the educational system by a directed flow network $[N, M]$, where N denotes an unordered set of nodes and M is an ordered set of chains. In this scheme, each node is equivalent to an educational program (e.g. the successful completion of upper division, or the termination of master's studies prior to completion of the degree requirements), while a chain corresponds to the sequence of programs pursued by a specific cohort of students (e.g. entrance at the upper-division level, successful completion of upper-division followed by admission to a master's program, with termination as a master's dropout).

We define a *chain* in M as a sequence of distinct ordered nodes in N, where the first node of the chain is the *origin* node and the last node of the chain is the *destination* node. All other nodes on a chain are intermediate nodes. To uniquely speci£ ↷ chain in our networks it is sufficient to list the sequence of nodes that comprise the chain.

Figure 1 illustrates the basic network used in analyses and calculations throughout this paper. Nodes $1'$, $2'$, $3'$, $4'$ are dummy nodes used to denote common origins for admissions to lower-division, upper-division, master's and doctoral degree programs, respectively. Nodes 1, 2, 3, 4 represent the programs associated with completion of the above while 5, 6, 7, 8 are the programs identified with dropouts at these same levels. Nodes 9 and 10 represent graduate students that are employed as teaching assistants during part of their career at the institution. Although the teaching assistantship is depicted in Fig. 1 as taking place at the end of a graduate student's career, we recognize that the sequence may differ in individual cases. It can be shown that the equations we obtain in the model of Section IV do not depend on the actual timing of the teaching assistantship.

There are 12 chains having origin node $1'$, 11 chains with origin node $2'$, 9 chains with origin node $3'$, and 3 chains with origin node $4'$. Three typical ones are

$\{1', 5\}$ with destination node 5,
$\{3', 3, 8\}$ with destination node 8,
$\{1', 1, 2, 3, 4, 9\}$ with destination node 9.

The first chain represents the student cohort that enters at the lower division and drops out before completing the lower division. The second chain represents a student who enters the institution, obtains a master's degree and drops out from the doctoral degree program. The third chain represents the student cohort that enters at the lower division, completes the lower division, upper division, master's degree, and Ph.D., and is employed as a teaching assistant before leaving the institution.

Associated with each node are the scalar quantities L_i: the *enrollment* in the program represented by the ith node; v_i: the *lifetime* required for completing the program at the ith node; g_i: the total *flow rate* entering the program at the ith node; and c_i: the *unit* (lifetime) *cost* of the program at the ith node. Finally, for certain nodes we specify *exogenous supplies* a^i or *exogenous demands* b^i. Lifetimes, costs and enrollments at dummy nodes are zero.

Associated with each chain are the scalar quantities: h_j^k—the flow on the jth chain in the set of chains M^k having origin node k; and C_j^k—the unit cost of the jth chain having origin node k.

Associated with the network is the vector $h = (h_1^1, h_2^1, \ldots, h_j^k, \ldots)$ which specifies the *flow pattern* at the educational institution, the

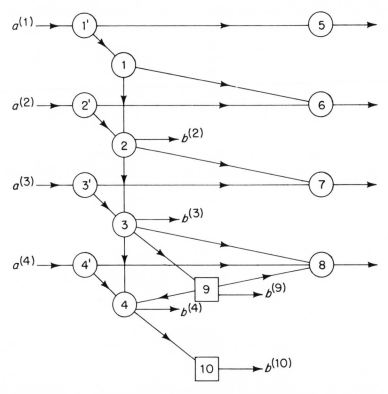

FIGURE 1   The Network of Student Cohorts and Programs

incidence matrix B that defines the network configuration of the institutional programs and flow patterns and finally the scalar C which represents the total instructional costs of educating all student cohorts. These variables are summarized in Table 1.

IV. A COHORT MODEL

The assumptions of the paper are:

A1: Flows and stock levels are sufficiently large so that a deterministic analysis is reasonable.

A2: An equilibrium exists with respect to flows, enrollments, lifetimes, costs, and student dropout rates over time.

A3: Student dropouts from a given program are specified as a fractional flow rate of all students enrolling in that program and having a common origin node.

TABLE 1 Summary of Notation

1.	N:	The set of nodes in the network $[N,M]$
2.	M:	The set of chains in the network $[N,M]$
3.	i,j,k:	Indices referring to nodes, chains, origins
4.	M^k:	The set of chains originating from node k
5.	N^k:	The set of chains ending in node k
6.	c_i:	The unit (lifetime) cost of the ith node
7.	L_i:	The enrollment at the ith node
8.	v_i:	The lifetime in the ith node
9.	g_i:	The total flow entering the ith node
10.	a^i:	The exogenous flow (admissions) into the ith node
11.	b^i:	The exogenous flow (final demands) from the ith node
12.	h_j^k:	The jth chain flow with origin k
13.	C_j^k:	The unit cost of the jth chain with origin k
14.	$h = \langle h_1^1, h_2^1, \ldots, h_j^k, \ldots \rangle$:	The vector of chain flows on the network, i.e. the flow pattern
15.	C:	The total network cost
16.	$B = [b_{ij}]$:	The node-chain incidence matrix

A4: Technological requirements are specified in terms of teacher-student ratios.

A5: The unit cost of a cohort equals the sum of unit costs of the sequence of programs that define the cohort.

In our model there are four types of equations and inequalities that must be satisfied by student flows. As the reader will see, all of these are linear in the chain flows h_j^k. The first two types of equations are inhomogeneous: admission equations require that chain flows with a common origin satisfy certain equalities or inequalities, whereas final demands imposed exogenously on the educational system constrain chain flows with a common destination node. The third type expresses a dropout cohort flow in terms of all other flows having the same origin node. Finally, we impose technological requirements on teaching assistants. In the last two cases, the equations in chain flows are homogeneous.

In order to conserve flows among student cohorts, it is useful to specify a node-chain incidence matrix B^k for the kth origin node of the network. The elements of each such incidence matrix are given by

(1) $\quad b^k_{ij} = 1$ if node i is in chain j with origin k
$\qquad\ = 0$ otherwise

To simplify notation for those cases where we include all origins we write

(2) $\quad B = [B^1; B^2; \ldots ; B^k; \ldots]$

Thus the augmented matrix B has columns identical with columns of B^k. Since a row corresponds to a node and a column corresponds to a chain, summing entries of B in a particular column gives the number of nodes in that chain, while summing a row of B gives the number of chains passing through a given node.

Using this notation one can write the supply and demand equations in terms of the chain flows and the flows entering or leaving each node of the network. If a^k is the total admission rate originating at the kth node, then a^k is simply the sum of all chain flows originating at k, i.e.

(3) $\quad a^k = \sum_{j \in M^k} h^k_j \qquad k \in N$

Similarly, when N^k denotes the set of all chains with destination node k, then

(4) $\quad b^k = \sum_{j \in N^k} h^l_j \qquad l \in N$

denotes the total final demand with destination k. In (4) we retain the convention that the index l refers to origin nodes on chains in N^k. Equations 3 and 4 represent the inhomogeneous conservation equations for admissions and final demands. In general there are as many constraints of type (3) or (4) as one chooses to impose. If no constraint is imposed, no equation is written. Furthermore, if a^k or b^k are lower or upper bounds, the appropriate inequalities are substituted for equalities.

We denote the average enrollment level at each node by the product of the lifetime at each node with the total flow into the node (Assumption A2). If we denote the total flow into node i by g_i and the expected lifetime by v_i, then

(5) $\quad L_i = g_i v_i \qquad i \in N$

where the total kth origin flow into i is

(6) $\quad g^k_i = \sum_{j \in M^k} b^k_{ij} h^k_j$

and the total flow into node i from all origins is

(7) $\qquad g_i = \sum_{k \in N} g_i^k = \left| \sum_k \sum_j b_{ij}^k h_j^k \right.$

Specification of dropouts is, by Assumption A3, simply a matter of expressing the flow rate of dropouts in terms of the total flow on chains having the same origin node and enrolling in the same program. For instance, the flow rate of students who enter as freshmen and drop out from upper division is proportional to the total freshmen admission rate. In general, if the jth chain with origin node k corresponds to a flow of dropouts we write

(8) $\qquad h_j^k = \alpha_j^k \left[\sum_l h_l^k \right]$

where α_j^k is the fractional dropout rate and the summation extends over chains $l \in M^k$ containing the program of interest. If, as is often the case, the term in brackets is given and fixed, as in equation 3, then the flow rate h_j^k of the dropout cohort is explicitly calculable. If, on the other hand, the chain flows within the brackets are a priori unknown, then equation 8 can be viewed as a single homogeneous equation restricting a subset of the chain flows with a common origin.

If technological requirements are specified (Assumption A4) as a ratio of teacher inventories required to instruct a given enrollment of students, say

(9) $\qquad L_m = \mu_{mn} L_n$

then (5) and (7) yield a homogeneous equation in chain flows as follows

(10) $\qquad \begin{aligned} L_m - \mu_{mn}L_n &= v_m g_m - v_n \mu_{mn} g_n \\ &= \sum_k \sum_j (v_m b_{mj}^k - v_n \mu_{mn} b_{nj}^k) h_j^k = 0 \end{aligned}$

or

(11) $\qquad \sum_k \sum_j (b_{mj}^k - v_m^{-1} v_n \mu_{mn} b_{nj}^k) h_j^k = 0$

Generalizations of (9) lead to essentially the same structure as that of (11). If, for example, teachers at node m instruct several student cohorts in programs at several nodes

(12) $\qquad L_m = \sum_n \mu_{mn} L_n$

and equation 11 becomes

(13) $\qquad \sum_k \sum_j (b_{mj}^k - v_m^{-1} \sum_n \mu_{mn} v_n b_{nj}^k) h_j^k = 0$

Just as a chain can be written as a sequence of distinct nodes, the *unit or average cost* of the jth chain with origin k can be written as the sum of the unit costs of the distinct nodes that comprise that chain, i.e.

(14) $C_j^k = \sum_i c_i b_{ij}^k \quad j \in M^k$

where c_i is the unit (lifetime) cost of the ith node. It is now possible to write total costs of the instructional program in two ways: the first is to multiply all chain flows having a common origin node by the unit cost of the appropriate chain and then sum over origin nodes to obtain the total cost

(15) $C = \sum_k \sum_{j \in M^k} C_j^k h_j^k$

To formulate (15) in terms of unit node costs one makes use of (14) and (6) to obtain

(16) $C = \sum_k \sum_{j \in M^k} \sum_i c_i b_{ij}^k h_j^k$

$\quad\quad = \sum_i \sum_k c_i g_i^k = \sum_{i \in N} c_i g_i$

Thus, an alternative expression for total network cost is to multiply the unit cost of each node by the total flow entering each node and sum over nodes.

In the remainder of this paper, we assume that node costs are proportional to teacher salaries, s_i, node lifetimes, v_j, and teacher-student ratios, μ_{ij}; i.e.

(17) $c_j = (\sum_i s_i \mu_{ij}) v_j$

in other words, the unit cost of a chain does not depend upon the chain flow. For this reason, policies which might affect enrollment levels, degree output rates, admission rates, staffing levels, and so on, *do not* affect the *unit* costs of a chain but *may* affect the total costs or budgets which have to be allocated to produce the chain flows.

The reader should note that a given node may be a member of many chains; thus, changing a node cost will, in general, affect the unit costs of many chains in the network. For example, node 4 in Figure 1 is the destination node for 7 chains and is an intermediate node for 7 additional chains, for a total of 14 chains. To put it another way, any change in the costs of educating doctoral graduates will affect the costs of 14 out of a total of 35 different student cohorts that are educated at the institution. On the other hand, node 5 is a member of only a single chain; altering the costs of lower-division dropouts will affect the costs of that particular student cohort and of no other.

Our formulation of the input-output model is expressed as a set of linear equations in unknown nonnegative chain flows h_j^k. For given right-hand sides of equations 3 and 4, i.e. given admissions and/or demands, the problem is one of finding flow patterns $h = (h_1^1, h_2^1, \ldots, h_j^k, \ldots)$ satisfying equations 3, 4, 8, and 13. Once a feasible flow pattern is found it is a simple matter to compute enrollments from equations 5 through 7. In our experience, it has always been the case that these inequalities contain a large set of feasible solutions, i.e. the number of degrees of freedom is large. Stated another way, we have not yet found an institution where administrative restrictions overconstrain the system of inequalities.

Administrative and institutional policies can affect the model structure in three ways: (1) by altering parameters such as lifetimes, v_j, dropout fractions, α_j, and teaching ratios, μ_{ij}; (2) by imposing constraints of various types, e.g., an enrollment ceiling,

$$\sum_{j \in N} L_j = \text{a constant}$$

or a budget restriction such as equation 16, or altering the types of teachers assigned to students such as equation 13; finally, (3) the cohort flows and programs in chains can be altered by choosing different network configurations which change the incidence matrix $[b_{ij}^k]$. Since the model is a multi-commodity network flow problem with each origin-destination pair serving as a single commodity, it will not, in general, be true that a feasible flow pattern is obtained by superposing cohort flows that are feasible with respect to each commodity. In general such flow patterns violate equations 3 or 4 or 13.

How are these models similar to or different from the cross-sectional models of Section II? (1) The model in this section is formulated in terms of chain *flows*, not *stock levels*. (2) Parameters such as α_j or v_j are based on *longitudinal*, not *cross-sectional* data. α_j is the fraction dropping out over the lifetime of a cohort, not the fraction of enrollments dropping out in one time period. (3) Our chain flow model is not generally linear in policy variables. By comparison, $x(t)$ in the first equation of Section II is often viewed as a policy variable, with $y(t)$ being calculated in terms of $x(t)$ and M being estimated from historical data. Once historical policies have been established, M is fixed and $y(t)$ is linear in $x(t)$. In our model, neither the enrollments nor the cohort flows are policy variables; rather, they are dependent variables which are functions of the policies discussed in the previous paragraph. Such policies not only determine some of the coefficients in the system of constraints but also possibly the set of constraints themselves. Finally, (4) adding or removing programs that constitute a chain, force particular elements of b_{ij}^k to be 0 or 1, and thus alter the coefficients and the number of cohorts in equations 3 through 16. In general, a feasible cohort flow is not a linear function of these *policy* variables.

V. SOURCES AND ANALYSIS OF INSTITUTIONAL DATA

The model described in Section IV was implemented using data for the 1969–70 academic year from Stanford University (SU) and the University of California, Berkeley campus (UCB). Several data sources at each institution were used to estimate parameters in the model for that institution. When good data were not available for estimating a parameter we relied on the judgment and intuition of persons familiar with campus operations and made no attempt to organize a large-scale data collection and analysis effort. We have used three additional assumptions. These are: (1) we allocate the entire salary cost of the faculty to instructional outputs; (2) the salary of a given faculty member is allocated to the various student levels in proportion to the formal courses that he teaches; and (3) the nontenure and tenure faculty inputs for teaching assistants are the same as those for other graduate students enrolled in the same degree program. Since none of these assumptions is crucial to the theoretical discussion of Section III, it is important that the reader bear in mind the distinction between formulation and implementation. Were it desirable to do so, one could modify or remove any of these three assumptions.

A. Stanford University

Our data for Stanford does not include students or faculty at the Stanford Medical School or at the various overseas campuses which have a total enrollment capacity of approximately 400 undergraduates.

1. Student Enrollments and Flow Rates

The enrollment, admissions, and graduation figures shown in Table 2 were obtained from sources in the Registrar's Office and the Graduate Study Office. Students classified as "Terminal Graduates" were included in graduate enrollments. Admission and degree flows during the year begin with the Summer Quarter of 1969 and end with the Spring Quarter of 1970. Separate figures for master's and doctoral admissions and enrollments were not available. Also, it should be mentioned that the total fall enrollment has been virtually constant during the past five years.

Observe that the Stanford enrollment is almost evenly divided between undergraduate and graduate programs and that most undergraduates are admitted as freshmen with only a small fraction entering as junior transfers. This contrasts with many state universities which are

TABLE 2 Stanford University 1969-70 Enrollments and Flow Rates

Student-Level	Fall 1969 Enrollment	1969–70 Admission Rate	1969–70 Degree Output Rate
Lower division	2,949	1,696	–
Upper division	2,782	167	1,515
Total undergraduate	5,731	1,863	1,515
Master's	} 5,163		1,555
Doctoral			441
Teaching assistants,	465		
Total graduate	5,628	2,227 [a]	1,996
Total students	11,359	4,090	3,511

[a] Of this total graduate admissions, approximately 260 students earned their bachelor's degree from Stanford.

required to draw a significant portion of their undergraduates from junior colleges within the state.

2. Student Dropout Fractions

For the dropout equations, we required estimates of thirteen distinct fractions, α_j^k. For each origin k, these correspond to dropouts that occur in each level at or above the level of admission. For example, there are four dropout cohorts and chains in Figure 1 for $k = 2'$, upper-division admissions. These correspond to dropouts at upper division, $\{2', 6\}$; master's, $\{2', 2, 7\}$; doctoral, $\{2', 2, 3, 8\}$; and doctoral following a master's teaching assistantship, $\{2', 2, 3, 9, 8\}$.

The dropout fractions estimated for Stanford appear in Table 3. The fractions α_1^1 and α_2^1 were obtained directly from a Registrar's study of successive freshman cohorts entitled "Survival of Freshmen Who Enter Autumn Quarter to Baccalaureate Degree Objective." Although the report did not state at what stage the dropouts occurred, there is much

TABLE 3 Stanford University Dropout Fractions

Origin k:	1	1	1	1	1	2	2	2	2	3	3	3	4
Chain i:	1	2	3	4	5	1	2	3	4	1	2	3	1
α_i^k:	.15	0	.05	.45	.45	.15	.05	.45	.45	.05	.45	.45	.45

evidence to indicate that almost all occur during the first two years following admission; therefore, the entire observed dropout fraction was allocated to the lower division, i.e. we set $\alpha_2^1 = 0$. The dropout fraction α_1^2 was taken directly from a Registrar's study of 1967–68 junior transfers.

Data on graduate dropouts was not differentiated according to the level at which students first entered the system. Therefore, it was assumed that the fraction who drop out at each graduate level is the same irrespective of the level at entrance. The master's dropout fraction represents an educated guess by the Head of the Graduate Study Office, while the doctoral dropout fraction was estimated from a study of doctoral students entering under the Ford Foundation Four-Year Guaranteed Assistance Program in the Humanities and Social Sciences. According to the Dean of the Graduate Division, this figure represents a low estimate of the overall fraction because it was derived with reference to a special cohort that was being provided with substantial financial aid as an incentive to complete the degree program.

Using the admissions rates from the second column of Table 2, the master's and doctoral graduation rates from the third column of Table 2, and the dropout fractions from Table 3, one can compute the steady-state output rate for bachelor's degrees. This computed value is 1,584, which seems reasonably close to the observed 1969–70 value of 1,515. In view of the many short-run fluctuations in flows and enrollments that occur even under a fixed enrollment ceiling, we judged this to be a good "fit" of model predictions and real data.

3. Student Lifetimes

The values for lifetimes in each program, v_j, were selected on the basis of discussions with persons familiar with Stanford operations. These are shown in the third column of Table 4. The only group of students for which lifetimes have actually been recorded are those receiving a Ph.D. According to a study by the Graduate Division entitled "Time Required for the Ph.D. at Stanford," the average length of attendance for all students receiving doctoral degrees in the 1967–68 academic year was 4.5 years. This figure was reduced to 4 years in our computations because, in many cases, a one-year half-time teaching assistantship (treated separately in our model) was included in the recorded data.

Observe that the estimated lifetime for lower division is actually less than the customary two years. This is primarily due to the fact that a substantial proportion of Stanford freshmen enter with advanced standing. There is a similar, yet less pronounced, effect from the group who spend their sophomore year at an overseas campus.

TABLE 4 Stanford University Student Lifetimes, Teacher-Student Ratios, and Unit Program Costs

Node j	Program	Lifetime (v_j)	Teacher-Student Ratios (Fall 1969)				Unit Node Costs (c_j)
			Teaching Assistants (μ_{1j})	Nontenure Faculty (μ_{2j})	Tenure Faculty (μ_{3j})		
1	L. D. Grad.	1.8	.137	.009	.017		\$1,279
2	U. D. Grad.	2.0	.013	.020	.037		1,909
3	Master's Grad.	1.7	.004	.016	.047		1,839
4	Doctoral Grad.	4.0	.004	.016	.047		4,328
5	L. D. D/O	1.2	.137	.009	.017		853
6	U. D. D/O	1.0	.013	.020	.037		954
7	Master's D/O	1.0	.004	.016	.047		1,082
8	Doctoral D/O	2.0	.004	.016	.047		2,164
9	T. A. (Master's)	1.0	—	.016	.047		1,073
10	T. A. (Doctoral)	1.0	—	.016	.047		1,073

If one computes steady-state flows consistent with the actual admissions rates and master's and doctoral graduation rates for 1969–70 and with the attrition rates in Table 3, and then converts these to enrollments using the lifetimes in Table 4, one obtains the figures 6,098 for undergraduate enrollment and 5,213 for graduate enrollment, exclusive of teaching assistants. The corresponding actual enrollments in the fall of 1969 were 5,731 undergraduates and 5,163 graduates. Again, the agreement between calculations and data is quite good.

4. Teacher-Student Ratios

The parameters μ_{ij} represent ratios of teacher inventories to student inventories. Instructional costs are computed in our model with reference to the following three categories of faculty: teaching assistants ($i = 1$), nontenure regular faculty ($i = 2$), and tenure regular faculty ($i = 3$); we did not include special temporary appointments such as lectureships and instructorships, because they are relatively small in number at the campuses we studied and policies regarding their use differ widely among institutions.

While separate data were available at each institution on the inventories of teachers by rank and students by level, it was necessary to devise a rule for allocating the total inventory of teachers of a given rank to students of each level. We chose to allocate each teacher on the basis of the classes he taught in the fall of 1969. That is, we first assigned each course taught by a given faculty member or teaching assistant to the student level represented by the majority of the students enrolled in that course (i.e., lower division, upper division, or graduate) and then allocated the individual to student levels in the same proportions as his courses. Summing up these allocations over all individuals of a given rank yielded the desired total allocations.

At Stanford, the source for our data was the Registrar's report on fall 1969 courses of instruction. These figures include persons with visiting and acting titles who were teaching at that time. We had to treat teaching assistants as a special case, because, out of a total of 465 teaching assistantships recorded in the Graduate Student Support Table for 1969–70 (Dean's Office, Graduate Division), only 99 appeared in the Registrar's report. Therefore, we allocated all 465 T. A.'s in the proportions established by the data on the smaller sample contained in the Registrar's report. Once allocated, these fall 1969 teacher inventories were divided by the appropriate fall 1969 enrollments from Table 2 to obtain the teacher-student ratios shown in Table 4.

Observe that our data did not permit us to compute separate ratios for different classes of graduate students. Thus, our figures assume that the same number of faculty of each rank are required for the instruction of a doctoral student as for a master's student. Also teaching assistants are assumed to have the same requirements for regular faculty as do other graduate students. In spite of these limitations, however, the trend in the computed ratios appears quite logical. That is, teaching assistants are used almost exclusively for instructing lower-division students, nontenure faculty are associated more with upper-division and graduate students, while tenure faculty are employed in increasing proportions as one proceeds from the lowest to the highest student level.

5. Unit Node Costs

Annual salaries of \$2,100 for teaching assistants, \$11,500 for nontenure faculty, and \$19,000 for tenure faculty were used together with the lifetimes and teacher-student ratios from Table 4 to compute the unit node costs of Equation 17. These are displayed in the last column of Table 4. These faculty salaries were obtained from two sources. For teaching assistants, we divided the total allocation for teaching assistant salaries in the 1969–70 Instructional Budget by the total number of teaching assistants shown in the 1969–70 Graduate Student Support Table. For regular faculty, we used the mean academic salaries reported for the year 1969–70 by the Controller's Office, rounded to the nearest \$500.

The results conform to a logical ordering of unit instructional costs. The unit costs of degree programs vary from \$1,839 for a master's degree to \$4,328 for a Ph.D., with the cost of a bachelor's degree appearing in between at \$3,188 (for those who enter as freshmen). Due to shorter lifetimes, the unit costs of dropouts are around one-half the unit costs of the corresponding degree programs.

B. The University of California, Berkeley Campus

1. Student Enrollments and Flow Rates

The quantities in Table 5 were obtained directly from 1969–70 *Campus Statistics* (Office of Institutional Research), except for the teaching assistant inventory which came from the November, 1969 Payroll Accounts. Flows correspond to the period: summer 1969 through spring 1970. Again, separate figures for master's and doctoral admissions and enrollments were not available. As was the case with Stanford, the total fall enrollment at UCB has changed only slightly from its 1965 level.

TABLE 5 University of California (Berkeley) 1969–70 Enrollments and Flow Rates

Student Level	Fall 1969 Enrollment	1969–70 Admission Rate	1969–70 Degree Output Rate
Lower division	7,198	4,250	–
Upper division	10,918	2,925	5,107
Total undergraduate	18,116	7,175	5,107
Master's ⎱			2,358
Doctoral ⎰ 8,940			859
Teaching assistants	1,032		
Total graduate	9,972	4,067 [a]	3,217
Total students	28,088	11,242	8,324

[a] Of this total graduate admissions, approximately 800 students earned their bachelor's degree from Berkeley.

In contrast to Stanford, Berkeley is predominantly an undergraduate institution; undergraduates outnumber graduates by a ratio of nearly two to one. In addition, Berkeley accepts a significant portion of its undergraduate admissions as junior transfers.

2. Student Dropout Fractions

All dropout fractions shown in Table 6 were estimated from cohort studies performed by the Office of Institutional Research on undergraduates admitted in 1965 and graduate students admitted in 1960. Since the graduate student cohort study did not provide enough information to yield unique fractions for all dropout cohorts, the values of α_3^1, α_2^2, α_1^3, and α_1^4 in Table 6 are based partly on experience and judgment. In comparing Table 6 with Table 3, we observe that the Berkeley dropout fractions are uniformly higher than their Stanford counterparts, as one might expect.

If one uses the 1969–70 Berkeley admission rates from Table 5, the dropout fractions in Table 6, and some additional information contained

TABLE 6 University of California (Berkeley) Dropout Fractions

Origin k:	1	1	1	1	1	2	2	2	2	3	3	3	4
Chain i:	1	2	3	4	5	1	2	3	4	1	2	3	1
α_i^k:	.30	.20	.30	.55	.55	.25	.30	.55	.55	.30	.55	.55	.45

in the graduate student cohort study, one obtains the following steady-state degree output rates: bachelor's, 4,574; master's, 2,122; and Ph.D., 772. Again, the discrepancy between these computed flow rates and their actual 1969–70 values shown in the third column of Table 5 is of the order of 10 per cent.

3. Student Lifetimes

With the exceptions of v_3, v_4, v_9, and v_{10}, which were obtained directly from the graduate student cohort study, lifetimes were estimated on the basis of discussions with persons familiar with Berkeley campus operations. These are displayed in the second column of Table 7. Using these lifetimes, one can convert the steady-state flows corresponding to 1969–70 admission rates to enrollments, obtaining values of 18,161 for undergraduates and 9,247 for graduates, excluding teaching assistants. The agreement between these computed values and the actual fall 1969 enrollments shown in Table 5 is excellent.

4. Teacher-Student Ratios

Due to data limitations, the Berkeley faculty was allocated to student levels in a slightly different manner from that used at Stanford. The essential difference is that, whereas at Stanford each faculty member was allocated according to the level of students enrolled in the courses he taught, at Berkeley the total inventory of faculty in each category was allocated to lower-division, upper-division, and graduate *students* in proportion to the total number of classroom contact hours spent by members of that category in lower-division, upper-division, and graduate division *courses*. Thus, we assumed a one-to-one correspondence between student level and course level and allocated the teaching assistants and regular faculty (including visiting and acting appointments) reported in the fall 1969 Schedule of Classes on the basis of the contact hours reported in the same document. These allocations were then divided by the fall 1969 enrollments from Table 5 to yield the teacher-student ratios shown in Table 7. Observe that these ratios exhibit exactly the same trends as did those computed for Stanford.

5. Unit Node Cost

The average salary for teaching assistants was obtained in the following way: the 1969–70 full-time equivalent (FTE) salary reported by the Chancellor's Office was multiplied by the ratio of FTE teaching assistants reported in the 1969–70 Instructional Budget to head-count teaching assistants reported in the fall 1969 Payroll Accounts. The average

TABLE 7 University of California (Berkeley) Student Lifetimes, Teacher-Student Ratios, and Unit Program Costs

Node j	Program	Lifetime (v_j)	Teacher-Student Ratios (Fall 1969)			Unit Node Costs (c_j)
			Teaching Assistants (μ_{1j})	Nontenure Faculty (μ_{2j})	Tenure Faculty (μ_{3j})	
1	L. D. Grad.	2.0	.098	.013	.018	$1,642
2	U. D. Grad	2.1	.024	.018	.031	1,861
3	Master's Grad.	1.8	.007	.014	.074	2,912
4	Doctoral Grad.	4.0	.007	.014	.074	6,472
5	L. D. D/O	1.0	.098	.013	.018	821
6	U. D. D/O	1.0	.024	.018	.031	886
7	Master's D/O	1.0	.007	.014	.074	1,618
8	Doctoral D/O	2.0	.007	.014	.074	3,236
9	T. A. (Master's)	1.0	—	.014	.074	1,595
10	T. A. (Doctoral)	1.0	—	.014	.074	1,595

regular faculty salaries were supplied by the Office of the Vice President for Academic Affairs and were based upon all faculty engaged in instruction during the 1969–70 regular academic year (i.e. excluding the summer quarter). The resulting figures were $3,300 for teaching assistants, $11,400 for nontenure regular faculty, and $19,400 for tenure faculty.

Using these salaries and the lifetimes and teacher-student ratios from Table 7, we computed the unit node costs displayed in the last column of that table. Observe that although they are ordered in the same way, the unit costs for degrees at Berkeley are significantly higher than at Stanford, except in the case of junior transfers earning a bachelor's degree. This finding is explained by the combination of two factors, for both the lifetimes and the tenure faculty-student ratios are generally greater at Berkeley than at Stanford. Thus, for example, a large discrepancy occurs at the doctoral level, where although the lifetimes are identical, one finds nearly 60 per cent more tenure faculty per student at Berkeley than at Stanford.

C. A Comparison of Unit Chain Costs

The unit chain costs for each institution are shown in Table 8 along with the chain descriptions. These figures were obtained by inserting the node costs from Tables 4 and 7 in equation 14 of Section IV. It is clear that they obey the following ordering scheme: each chain has a higher unit cost than all other chains made up of a subset of its nodes; moreover, the unit cost of any chain that ends in a dropout node is strictly less than the unit cost of the chain that has the same origin, passes through the sequence of nodes, and ends with the corresponding graduate node. Obviously, the least expensive way for an educational institution to meet final demands for degrees is to admit students at the highest level appropriate to the degree, and then to prohibit degree-winners from continuing further. However, several factors contribute to make this an unrealistic solution. (1) There are many reasons for preferring to admit freshmen instead of junior transfers to the undergraduate program. (2) Master's graduates are generally free to decide whether they wish to continue in the doctoral program. (3) There exist well-established teaching assistant ratios for different undergraduate cohorts. (4) Enrollment ceilings force certain cohorts to contribute to undergraduate as well as graduate enrollments. The reader may be troubled by the assumption that, for instance, the costs of a master's and doctoral program are strictly additive for those students who pursue both degrees. While this represents an abstraction from reality, we do not believe it influences our cost estimates in a significant way.

TABLE 8 Unit Chain Costs

Origin k	Chain j	Description of Cohort[a]					SU	UCB
							Unit Chain Costs(C_j^k)	
1	1	LD	UD				$3,188	$3,503
1	2	LD	UD	M			5,027	6,415
1	3	LD	UD	M	D		9,355	12,887
1	4	LD	UD	M	D	TA	10,428	14,482
1	5	LD	UD	M	D	D/O	7,191	9,651
1	6	LD	UD	M	TA		6,100	8,010
1	7	LD	UD	M	TA	D	10,428	14,482
1	8	LD	UD	M	TA	D TA	11,501	16,077
1	9	LD	UD	M	TA	D D/O	8,264	11,246
1	10	LD	UD	M	D/O		4,270	5,121
1	11	LD	UD	D/O			2,233	2,528
1	12	LD	D/O				853	821
2	1	UD					1,909	1,861
2	2	UD	M				3,748	4,773
2	3	UD	M	D			8,076	11,245
2	4	UD	M	D	TA		9,149	12,840
2	5	UD	M	D	D/O		5,912	8,009
2	6	UD	M	TA			4,821	6,368
2	7	UD	M	TA	D		9,149	12,840
2	8	UD	M	TA	D	TA	10,222	14,435
2	9	UD	M	TA	D	D/O	6,985	9,604
2	10	UD	M	D/O			2,991	3,479
2	11	UD	D/O				954	886
3	1	M					1,839	2,912
3	2	M	D				6,167	9,384
3	3	M	D	TA			7,240	10,979
3	4	M	D	D/O			4,003	6,148
3	5	M	TA				2,912	4,507
3	6	M	TA	D			7,240	10,979
3	7	M	TA	D	TA		8,313	12,574
3	8	M	TA	D	D/O		5,076	7,743
3	9	M	D/O				1,082	1,618
4	1	D					4,328	6,472
4	2	D	TA				5,401	8,067
4	3	D	D/O				2,164	3,236

[a] LD = Lower-division graduate   LD D/O = Lower-division dropout
UD = Upper-division graduate   UD D/O = Upper-division dropout
M = Master's graduate   M D/O = Master's dropout
D = Doctoral graduate   D D/O = Doctoral dropout
TA = Teaching assistant

Inter-institutional comparisons are also revealing. Chain costs at Stanford are in the range $853 to $11,501, while those at Berkeley range from $821 to $16,077. In nearly all cases, the unit chain costs are substantially higher at Berkeley than at Stanford, due to the higher program (node) costs, which we discussed earlier.

VI. AN ANALYSIS OF THE CARNEGIE UNDERGRADUATE PLAN

In this section, we use the numerical data of Section V and apply the model of Section IV to obtain some preliminary estimates of the unit and total instructional costs that would result from the adoption of the Carnegie Commission recommendation [1971] that the lower division be effectively reduced from a two- to a one-year program. In all cases that we discuss, we estimate lower bounds for the resulting instructional budget.

To understand how these recommended policies can be incorporated within the model of Section IV, it may be useful to characterize the structure of solutions of constraints that we have discussed in Section IV.

Table 9 lists the coefficients of 20 equations in 35 chain flows (cohorts). There are 5 dropout equations for the lower division, 4 dropout equations for the upper division, 3 dropout equations for master's degree candidates and 1 dropout equation for doctoral students. There is 1 technological constraint on teaching assistants, 1 enrollment ceiling constraint, 1 constraint on admissions to upper division, 2 constraints on admissions to graduate programs and 2 constraints on final demand for doctoral graduates. Flows are nonnegative, which is a simple way to require that students flow in the direction of the arrows of the network in Figure 1. While these constraints are obviously not representative of all educational institutions, they seem realistic for the three campuses which we studied.

In summary there are 20 linear constraints on 35 nonnegative chain flows to describe each institution. It is interesting to note that only the technological constraint (15), the enrollment ceiling (16) and the requirements on final demands (19 and 20) prevent the system of equations from being decomposed into four independent subproblems with solutions a function only of origin-dependent parameters. The reason that the system of equations cannot be decomposed is that (1) students in lower- and upper-division programs affect the number of teaching assistants in graduate cohorts, (2) an enrollment ceiling places a constraint on the total number of students, including teaching assistants, and (3) constraints on the output flows of a particular type of student, say

TABLE 9 Stanford University Constraints (BCC)

Chain Flow	Chain 1 h_1^1	2 h_2^1	3 h_3^1	4 h_4^1	5 h_5^1	6 h_6^1	7 h_7^1	8 h_8^1	9 h_9^1	10 h_{10}^1	11 h_{11}^1	12 h_{12}^1
LD D/O	-.177	-.177	-.177	-.177	-.177	-.177	-.177	-.177	-.177	-.177	-.177	
LD UD D/O		-.053	-.053	-.053	-.053	-.053	-.053	-.053	-.053			
LD UD M D/O			-.818									
LD UD M D D/O				-.818								
LD UD M TA D D/O					1							
UD D/O												
UD M D/O							-.818					
UD M D D/O								-.818				
UD M TA D D/O									1			
M D/O										1		
M D D/O											1	
M TA D D/O												1
D D/O												
Technological	-.274	-.281	-.299	.701	-.290	.719	.701	1.70	.710	-.278	-.260	-.165
Enroll. ceiling	3.8	5.5	9.5	10.5	7.5	6.5	10.5	11.5	8.5	4.8	2.8	1.2
Junior transfers	1	1	1	1	1							
Internal grad. adm.						1	1	1	1			
Ext. grad. adm.							1	1				
Fin Dem PHD			1	1								
Fin Dem PHD TA								1				

TABLE 9 (continued)

Chain / Chain Flow	13 h_1^2	14 h_2^2	15 h_3^2	16 h_4^2	17 h_5^2	18 h_6^2	19 h_7^2	20 h_8^2	21 h_9^2	22 h_{10}^2	23 h_{11}^2	24 h_1^3
LD D/O												
LD UD D/O												
LD UD M D/O												
LD UD M D D/O												
LD UD M TA D D/O												
UD D/O	-.177	-.177	-.177	-.177	-.177	-.177	-.177	-.177	-.177	-.177		
UD M D/O		-.053	-.053	-.053	-.053	-.053	-.053	-.053	-.053			
UD M D D/O			-.818	-.818						1		
UD M TA D D/O					1						1	
M D/O							-.818	-.818	1			
M D D/O												
M TA D D/O												-.053
D D/O												
Technological	-.026	-.034	-.051	.949	-.043	.966	.949	1.949	.957	-.031	-.013	-.007
Enroll. ceiling	2.0	3.7	7.7	8.7	5.7	4.7	8.7	9.7	6.7	3.0	1.0	1.7
Junior transfers	1	1	1	1	1	1	1	1	1	1	1	
Internal grad. adm.		1	1	1	1	1	1	1	1	1		
Ext. grad. adm.				1								1
Fin Dem PHD							1					
Fin Dem PHD TA								1				

TABLE 9 (concluded)

Chain Flow	25 h_2^3	26 h_3^3	27 h_4^3	28 h_5^3	29 h_6^3	30 h_7^3	31 h_8^3	32 h_9^3	33 h_1^4	34 h_2^4	35 h_3^4	rhs
LD D/O												0
LD UD D/O												0
LD UD M D/O												0
LD UD M D D/O												0
LD UD M TA D D/O												0
UD D/O												0
UD M D/O												0
UD M D D/O												0
UD M TA D D/O												0
M D/O	−.053	−.053	−.053	−.053	−.053	−.053	−.053	1				0
M D D/O	−.818	−.818	1									0
M TA D D/O					−.818	−.818	1					0
D D/O									−.818	−.818	1	0
Technological	−.025	.975	−.016	.993	.975	1.975	.984	−.004	−.018	.982	−.009	0
Enroll. ceiling	5.7	6.7	3.7	2.7	6.7	7.7	4.7	1	4	5	2	11,359
Junior transfers												167
Internal grad. adm.	1	1	1	1	1	1	1	1	1	1		260
Ext. grad. adm.	1	1	1	1	1	1	1	1	1	1	1	1,968
Fin Dem PHD	1											116
Fin Dem PHD TA		1								1		325

doctoral graduates, place restrictions on chain flows having a common destination rather than a common origin.

It is interesting to see how a lower bound for the instructional budget and a feasible solution of the system of equations in Table 8 can be generated. Consider, in the case of Stanford University, the chain costs in the first column of Table 8, and the 1969–70 graduation rates of Table 2. To estimate the cost of producing 1,515 bachelor's degrees, 1,555 master's degrees and 441 doctoral degrees, one could select the three cheapest chains ending in nodes 2, 3, 4 with costs

$$C_1^2 = 1,909, \ C_1^3 = 1,839, \ C_1^4 = 4,328$$

By forcing all students to use these three programs one obtains an unrealistically low instructional budget of

$$(1,515)(\$1,909) + (1,555)(\$1,839) + (441)(\$4,328) = \$7,660,428.$$

This estimate is approximately $3.2 million less than the actual 1969-70 budget of $10.9 million. What accounts for this large difference? With the unrealistic flow pattern we have just used, the university is divided into three independent components in which no students receiving one degree continue at the same institution to obtain a more advanced degree. There are no dropouts from any program and the total enrollment capacity of 11,359 is underutilized by approximately 4,300 students. Neither teaching assistants nor associates are involved in the instruction of undergraduate programs and no recognition is made of the value that teaching experience has upon the quality of education of a graduate student. We hasten to point out that each of these requirements costs money; the magnitude of the additional costs can also be estimated and we proceed to do so.

By requiring that no more than 167 junior transfers be admitted to Stanford, chain $(1',1,2)$ with a unit cost of $3,188 rather than $1,909 is introduced for the production of bachelor's degrees. By requiring that admissions to Stanford graduate schools must have a nominal flow of Stanford's undergraduates, we introduce a large number of chains with unit costs beginning at $3,748 and ending as high as $11,501.

The recognition of distinct final demands for doctoral students with or without teaching-assistant experience forces the use of chains such as $(4',4,10)$ with a unit cost of $5,401. Once the reader is convinced that such chain flows are desirable it is then a simple (but tedious) matter to consider all the associated dropout cohorts and their costs. Generally speaking, for every chain flow that results in some degree recipient there is a corresponding dropout flow.

By the time some minor readjustments in the flow patterns are made to meet the constraints of Table 9, one moves from the unrealistic budget estimate of $7.3 million to the more realistic estimate of $10.82 million.

A similar set of calculations for the Berkeley campus begins with a budget estimate of $21.93 million for positive flows on the three cheapest chains and increases to an estimate of $31.56 million when one includes the appropriate teacher-student ratios, enrollment ceilings, dropout flows and restrictions on junior transfers. In each case, the second estimate that we derive is still less than the instructional budget one obtains for actual 1969–70 fiscal operations. In the 1969–70 Stanford Budget, instructional salaries, excluding the Medical School, sabbatical leaves, and overseas campuses amount to $10,900,000; Payroll Accounts in November of 1969 give an instructional budget at Berkeley of $31,692,600. Both figures are in close agreement with estimates from the model.

Comparative solutions for enrollments, degrees, and cohort costs for Stanford University, the University of California at Berkeley, and the University of Colorado at Boulder are summarized in Table 10. Columns headed by BCC denote quantities predicted by our model before the Carnegie Commission recommendation is implemented while ACC denotes after Carnegie Commission. The fifth and sixth columns in the table refer to an unpublished study made by students in a graduate Operations Research course at the University of Colorado. It should be mentioned that the constraint set of the Colorado model differs from that used to analyze the Stanford and Berkeley campuses. In the first case, an enrollment ceiling is *not* imposed and the following are specified: total output rates for bachelor's, master's, and doctoral degrees, a ratio of entering junior transfers to entering freshmen and a ratio of external graduate admissions to internal graduate admissions.

Consider the following solution of the Stanford tableau in Table 9:

$$h_1^1 = 1,311, \ h_2^1 = 112, \ h_{10}^1 = 6, \ h_{12}^1 = 252, \ h_2^2 = 2$$
$$h_6^2 = 133, h_{10}^2 = 7, h_{11}^2 = 25, h_1^3 = 1,108, h_9^3 = 58$$
$$h_1^4 = 116, h_2^4 = 325, h_3^4 = 361, \text{ all other} \ h_j^k = 0$$

Elements in the first column of Table 10 are derived from these flows and the chains of Table 8 in the following way: Enrollments are obtained by substituting these chain flows in equations 5 and 6 with lifetimes from Table 4. Undergraduate degrees are obtained by summing h_1^1 through h_{10}^1 and h_1^2 through h_{10}^2. Master's degrees are obtained by summing h_1^1 through h_9^1, h_2^2 through h_9^2 and h_1^3 through h_9^3. Doctoral degrees sum the flows h_3^1, h_4^1, h_7^1, h_8^1, h_3^2, h_4^2, h_7^2, h_8^2, h_2^3, h_3^3, h_6^3, h_7^3, h_1^4 and h_2^4. Cohort costs are obtained by multiplying these chain flows by their unit costs in Table 8. In those cases where a cohort receives an undergraduate degree and then enrolls in graduate programs, we allocated the program cost to the appropriate category of degree-winner or dropout. For example, the cohort flow $h_{10}^1 = 6$

TABLE 10 Enrollments, Degree Rates, Costs of Degrees and Dropouts before (BCC) and after (ACC) Carnegie Commission Recommendation

	Stanford		University of California (Berkeley)		University of Colorado (Boulder)	
	BCC	ACC	BCC	ACC	BCC	ACC
Enrollments						
Lower division	2,874	2,194	7,302	5,647	8,906	5,379
Upper division	3,166	3,930	10,994	12,771	6,574	6,574
Graduate	5,317	5,233	9,792	9,670	2,447	2,384
Total	11,357	11,357	28,088	28,088	17,927	14,338
Degrees/Year						
B.S., B.A.	1,571	1,953	4,603	5,359	2,640	2,640
M.S., M.A.	1,355	1,354	1,751	1,751	814	814
Doctoral	441	441	859	859	302	302
Total	3,367	3,748	7,213	7,969	3,756	3,756
Cohort costs (in millions of dollars)						
Undergraduate degrees	4.83	5.01	12.52	12.57	—	—
Undergraduate dropouts	.24	.30	3.22	3.38	—	—
	5.07	5.31	15.74	15.95	—	—
Graduate degrees	4.89	4.80	12.32	12.12	—	—
Graduate dropouts	.86	.86	3.50	3.50	—	—
	5.75	5.66	15.82	15.62	—	—
Total	10.82	10.97	31.56	31.57	16.78	14.33
Instructional Cost/Degree (in dollars)						
Undergraduate	3,225	2,720	3,419	2,977	—	—
Graduate	3,201	3,151	6,061	5,987	—	—
Combined	3,211	2,927	4,374	3,962	4,469	3,815

results in $6 \times \$3,188 = \$19,128$ for undergraduate degree costs and $6 \times \$1,082 = \$6,492$ for graduate dropout costs.

To see how one calculates parameters relevant to the Carnegie Commission plan, consider the lifetime of node 1, the lifetime for the lower division program. This lifetime affects (1) the technological constraint associated with teaching assistants that are required to instruct lower-division students (see equation 11 or 13 of Section IV) and (2) the total lifetimes of all chains which contain node 1; thus, the coefficients of the first eleven chain flows passing through node 1 are reduced in the enrollment ceiling constraint which is obtained by substituting chain lifetimes rather than unit costs in equation 15. Finally, (3) the unit costs, as defined by equation 14 in that section, are also modified. In summary, the reduction in lower-division lifetimes affects the total lifetimes and unit costs of 11 out of 35 possible chains, and affects a single technological constraint for teaching assistants. We display the least-cost budgets, enrollment levels, graduation rates, and costs of educating the dropout and degree-winning cohorts in the ACC columns of Table 10.

The lower-bound estimates that we have just described can be routinely calculated by using a linear programming algorithm to minimize the sum of costs of all chain flows, i.e. the total instructional cost of equation 15 in Section IV, subject to the constraints of equations 3, 4, 8, and 13 in the same section. Chain costs used are those of Table 8, with the modifications described above for calculations based on the Carnegie plan; all parameters used in the constraints are derived from the appropriate terms in Tables 2 through 7 of Section V. For example, the magnitude of the coefficient of the first chain flow in the first restriction of Table 9 is $\alpha_1^1 (1 - \alpha_1^1)^{-1} = .1765$.

It appears that the major impacts the Carnegie Commission recommendation would have if adopted in the long run are the following: (a) At both Stanford and Berkeley the flow rate for graduating B.S. degrees would increase substantially, from approximately 1,571 per year to 1,943 per year at Stanford, from approximately 4,603 to 5,359 per year at Berkeley. (b) There would be an increased flow rate of the number of students that drop out each year at each institution. At Stanford, the lower-division dropout flows would increase from 252 to 320 per year; at Berkeley, from 1,292 to 1,698 per year. (c) Lower-division enrollments would decrease and admissions would increase because of the reduction in lifetime to complete the lower-division programs. At Stanford, lower-division enrollments would decrease from 2,874 to 2,194; at Berkeley, from 7,302 to 5,647. (d) If enrollment ceilings were maintained at their current levels, as well as current restrictions on junior transfers, upper-division enrollments would increase from 3,166 to 3,930 at Stanford, from 10,994 to 12,771 at Berkeley. This increase is due, of course, to the increased admission rate into the lower-division program. (e) Unless different admission policies were adopted, the graduate components at both institutions would remain roughly the same, with one important exception—(f) the enrollments of teaching assistants would decrease at Berkeley from 1,042 to 921 and at Stanford from 458 to 374. In both cases, the decrease is due to the fact that there is a substitution of small teacher-student ratios at the upper division for large teacher-student ratios at the lower division which more than offsets the increased upper-division enrollments discussed in (d). (g) The total instructional costs increase slightly at both institutions—by approximately $150,000 per year at Stanford and by $25,000 per year at Berkeley; this small increase in total instructional budget is offset by (h) the very large increases in total degree rates at both institutions; from 3,367 to 3,748 at Stanford, and from 7,213 to 7,969 at Berkeley. The net result which should be of primary interest to educational administrators is (i)—unit costs of all degree recipients decreases from $3,211 to $2,927 at Stanford and from $4,374 to $3,962 at Berkeley. To state it in another way, it appears that if the total degree output rates were held constant at their current values, the total instructional budget could decrease substantially at both institutions.

REFERENCES

Carnegie Commission on the Future of Higher Education [1970]. "A Chance to Learn: An Action Agenda for Equal Opportunity in Higher Education." Special Report. New York: McGraw-Hill.

———. [1971]. "Less Time More Options: Education Beyond the High School." Special Report. New York: McGraw-Hill.

Sengupta, J. K., and Fox, K. A. [1969]. *Economic Analysis and Operations Research: Optimization Techniques in Quantitative Economic Models.* Amsterdam: North-Holland.

Hopkins, D. S. P. [1971]. "On the Use of Large-Scale Simulation Models in University Planning." *Review of Educational Research* 41 (Dec. 1971): 467–478.

Judy, R. [1969]. "Systems Analysis for Efficient Resource Allocation in Higher Education: A Report on the Development and Implementation of CAMPUS Techniques." Paper presented to the Conference on Management Information Systems: Their Development and Application to the Administration of Higher Education. Washington, D.C.

Koenig, H.; Keeney, M.; and Zemach, R. [1968]. "A Systems Model for Management, Planning, and Resource Allocation in Institutions of Higher Education." Final Report, National Science Foundation Project C-518. Michigan State University: East Lansing.

Oliver, R. M.; Hopkins, D. S. P.; and Armacost, R. L. [1970]. "An Equilibrium Flow Model of a University Campus." *Operations Research* 20 (Mar.-Apr. 1972): 249–264.

UNESCO [1967]. *Educational Costs and Productivity.* Paris: International Institute for Educational Planning.

Weathersby, G. [1967]. "The Development and Applications of a University Cost Simulation Model." Office of Analytical Studies. University of California, Berkeley.

9 | COMMENTS

Colin E. Bell

University of Tennessee, Knoxville

There is little controversy inherent in the description of the Oliver-Hopkins model. Given their assumptions, their equations appear to be correct. However, considerable controversy arises when it comes time to apply a model such as this one or any of a myriad of other mathematical models which simulate the operation of a university system. In this note, then, I wish to comment on the applicability of the Oliver-Hopkins model. Later I shall discuss the workings of the model and some of the inevitable shortcomings of a model of this size.

The Oliver-Hopkins model provides a contrast to many large-scale simulations which cost hundreds of thousands of dollars to build and require thousands of data inputs. Such simulations have been built by Weathersby [3], Koenig et al. [2], Judy [1], and others. They rely on a sequence of linear transformations and thus require that several large input-output matrices be specified. The volume of computer output can be overwhelming, although to a certain extent there can be an advantage in having information more disaggregated than in the Oliver-Hopkins model.

Input-output matrices in the large simulations are filled with data based on historical policy trends. Without guessing coefficients out of the blue, it is difficult to eliminate the effect of presently irrelevant past policies in the simulated future. This shortcoming which Oliver and Hopkins point out in the other models is also present in theirs, where presumably cost and dropout rate estimates have their basis partly in historical trends. However, the size of this model allows for much more experimentation with different assumptions.

Constant returns to scale are assumed both in this model and in the large-scale simulations. It would add unreasonable computational complications if this assumption were changed. A decision maker should be sobered by this and by many other restrictive assumptions.

All of these models are designed to assist university administrators in their decision making. To this end, they should provide outputs which are neither misleading as regards accuracy nor too voluminous. The decision maker must interpret output of these models in light of possible future trends, which cannot possibly be incorporated directly into the model.

For a moment, let us consider applying these models at a point in time ten years ago in an attempt to predict future student enrollments and various costs. We could use input data based on past enrollments, student-faculty ratios, faculty salaries, building costs, and so on, and could project certain changes in these input measures over past trends. However, could we have reliably quantified the effects of such external environmental changes as the abolition of student draft deferments, the changing public attitudes toward education and resulting budget cuts, greatly decreased demand for Ph.D.'s, mass unemployment in the aerospace field, and increased concern with various forms of environmental pollution? My impression is that there are many future influences external to the university that cannot be adequately incorporated in any present model. Such influences introduce a great deal of uncertainty into any future cost or enrollment estimates and add futility to the process of calculating volumes of "precise" estimates based on past trends and detailed disaggregated present figures. The calculations of a large-scale simulation are analogous to an engineer's painstaking calculation of one figure to seven significant digits when it must then be added to another figure with only three-digit accuracy. The size of the Oliver-Hopkins model represents a better match between input precision and detail and the predictive power of the output.

To further simplify computations, there are no time dependencies included in Oliver and Hopkins's inputs. The assumption that flows are stable from year to year allows for computing characteristics of the resulting equilibrium. Thus, rather than answering specific questions about enrollment patterns and costs in 1972, 1973, 1974, et cetera, this model examines the equilibrium which would result from continued use of a given policy and thus gives a picture of the direction in which such a policy is leading.

The most impressive features of this model then are its size and its computational simplicity. The idea of computing steady-state characteristics associated with the system, although not at all new to operations researchers, has appeal in reducing the computational burden. However, there are disadvantages arising from the fact that these computations do not comment on the feasibility of immediately implementing the policy which looks good at equilibrium. Perhaps the current state of the system prohibits the use of a policy which would eventually meet all of the constraints if allowed to run long enough.

There are a couple of puzzling features as regards the cost arguments in this paper. The authors give a lower bound on the Stanford instructional budget and then show how constraints cause more expensive chains to enter the picture. It is clear that an upper limit on junior-college transfers forces the school to give expensive four-year B.A.'s. However, the requirement of admitting some Stanford undergrads to graduate school does not increase the budget in this model. The cost of educating one student from freshman to Ph.D. does not differ from the cost of educating one student through a B.A. and another from a B.A. to a Ph.D. The costs of these alternative means of producing one B.A. and one Ph.D. could be made to differ by assuming different dropout rates in graduate school for Stanford graduates and others. Depending on these specific rates, a least-cost production policy might call for admitting either as many Stanford graduates into graduate school as possible *or* as few as possible. Thus a wide policy swing depends on whether Stanford graduates are more or less likely than others to drop out of graduate school.

This model allows dropout rates from a given program to depend on a student's status when he first enters the institution as well as on the program he is currently enrolled in. It is only when this former type of dependence is very real that the model is sensitive to the past history of any given student. Then the optimal policy (although not necessarily the budget figure) is very sensitive to different dropout-rate values. If, on the other hand, the dropout probability depends only on the current program of a student, the cost of any policy with the same enrollment levels in each program is the same regardless of the past history of students.

The problem of assigning instructional costs to students in various programs is a somewhat sensitive one but not nearly as difficult as the problem of measuring the value of a student's experience as a function of contact hours with faculty and faculty salaries. I was pleased to see Oliver and Hopkins stay away from that issue; my experience with UCLA data showed that educational values could be assigned to students in different ways to reach whatever pet conclusion one had in mind.

In focusing on one institution, the authors naturally find that that institution can attain a desired degree output at minimum cost by admitting as many undergrads at the junior level as possible and avoiding the costs of educating lower-division students—many of whom drop out and none of whom earn a degree while in lower division. In judging, for example, whether this is a wise policy for a public university, one must really compare the savings to costs of providing lower division schooling in other public institutions such as community colleges. It is natural also that an institution can save money by abbreviating the lower division to one year. Again, to really judge the advantages of this policy one should compare the budget savings to the value of the "year of education lost" to the student.

The constraint for junior-college transfers is expressed as an equality constraint (i.e. exactly 167 should be admitted). It might be that with different cost assumptions, the shadow price of changing that requirement to 168 would be negative. The argument that it is unlikely that the real shadow price will be more than 2 or 3 times the estimate computed by the model seems to need more justification (Stanford's shadow price is more than ten times Berkeley's).

Many different constraints could be placed on the output of an institution through this model. It appears most natural from the network diagram (Figure 1) to place lower bounds on $b^{(2)}$, $b^{(3)}$, $b^{(4)}$, $b^{(9)}$, and $b^{(10)}$ (or perhaps equality constraints). Yet it seems hardly more reasonable to constrain $b^{(2)}$ than to constrain the total flow out of node 2. In the first case, the university has a responsibility to send a minimum number of B.A. graduates from the graduation ceremony immediately into the real world; in the second, there is a responsibility to send a minimum number to the graduation ceremony. As the authors point out, the location of those constraints influences shadow prices.

As I have mentioned, the form of an optimal operating policy is very sensitive to the various dropout-rate values. It would be valuable to find out whether shadow prices are equally sensitive.

In conclusion, I am pleased with the size of this model. It lends itself very well to all sorts of sensitivity testing. Thus an administrator making use of it is in a good position to evaluate how big a grain of salt must be swallowed with the output. It is important that no operations research model be accepted by practitioners on blind faith; this model's simplicity and sensitivity-testing features guard against that possibility in an admirable manner. However, lacking personal computational experience, I still have some questions as to the outcome of many sensitivity tests.

REFERENCES

1. Judy, R. (1969). "Systems Analysis for Efficient Resource Allocation in Higher Education: A Report on the Development and Implementation of CAMPUS Techniques." Paper presented to the Conference on Management Information Systems: Their Development and Application to the Administration of Higher Education, Washington, D.C.
2. Koenig, H.; Keeney, M.; and Zemach, R. (1968). "A Systems Model for Management, Planning, and Resource Allocation in Institutions of Higher Education." Final Report, National Science Foundation Project C-518. East Lansing, Mich.: Michigan State University.
3. Weathersby, G. (1967). "The Development and Applications of a University Cost Simulation Model." Berkeley, Calif.: Office of Analytical Studies, University of California.

Estelle James

State University of New York
at Stony Brook

My comments on the interesting paper by Oliver and Hopkins fall into two categories. First, I shall give some general critical reactions, as an economist, to the operations research models which are much in vogue these days for experimental planning and budgeting in higher education. These reactions, which focus on some conceptual ambiguities in the definition and measurement of costs, apply to a broad class of models, including the one developed by Oliver and Hopkins. Secondly, I will make a few brief points specific to the paper under discussion.

The university is a multi-product institution and any attempt to measure unit costs must take cognizance of all the major outputs to which resources are allocated or else the resulting cost figures will be grossly distorted. Oliver and Hopkins have decided to aggregate over all departments—which produce different outputs using vastly different inputs—in order to make their problem more manageable. Changes in university costs and resource requirements generated by a varying departmental mix are therefore exogenous to, and unpredicted by, their model.

I am more concerned, however, about the ease with which they (and many others) have overlooked the fact that considerable university resources are spent on nonteaching activities such as research and administration. According to data which I have collected at Stony Brook, the faculty—the resource with which Oliver and Hopkins are primarily concerned—spends barely 50 per cent of its time on classroom instruction, and even less if one takes account of holidays, summers, and sabbaticals.[1] Thus, allocating the full faculty cost to teaching seems unwarranted.

Research and teaching activities of the faculty are not inherently tied together in fixed proportions; indeed, we find liberal arts colleges which produce undergraduate education exclusively and institutes which specialize in research. Graduate schools usually produce some research— presumably, the faculty cannot teach graduate students how to do research without doing some themselves—but the exact mix varies among institutions. Thus, research may be viewed as an output, albeit difficult to measure, or, alternatively, as an input into the graduate program. Its input into undergraduate teaching, particularly at lower-division levels, is probably much less. (I say "probably" because this is basically an empirical question about which one can only make assumptions until an operationally sound means of testing the hypothesis is devised.)

Whether this explicit treatment of research makes any difference depends, of course, on the question being asked. When estimating unit costs, ignoring research overstates the *absolute* cost of teaching in general and teaching undergraduates in particular. It does not, however, significantly alter the *relative* instructional costs of two schools with a similar teaching-research mix and a similar undergraduate-graduate mix. Stanford and Berkeley have similar mixes, so the specific comparison that Oliver and Hopkins make is probably unbiased. If, on the other hand, they had chosen to look at two institutions with different product mixes, their approach *would* have distorted these relative costs. For example, when comparing lower-division teaching costs at a university and a community college, Oliver and Hopkins would probably predict much higher figures for the former than the latter, whereas in studies that I have made, program costs were often the same or higher at the community college. I would thus view the choice between these school types by a legislature as a decision about the optimal product mix for the institution and the state, rather than a response to differential costs of undergraduate education.

Similarly, an increase in teaching loads at a given institution would reduce faculty costs for each student or degree in the Oliver-Hopkins model, whereas I would view this primarily as a shift in product mix, to a higher teaching/research ratio. Any cost-saving for a given enrollment would be attributed to a lower quantity of research and to a lower quality of graduate education—a more accurate and useful way of looking at the matter, in my opinion.[2]

Faculty spend their time, too, on administrative activities—curriculum planning, recruitment, and so forth. Oliver and Hopkins simply ignore this, implying that such activities are current costs which should be allocated among various student cohorts in the same proportion as teaching time. I suggest that much of this administrative activity may more properly be regarded as an investment in the future research and teaching functions of the university than regarded as an input into its present instructional functions. If the university were to close down next year there would be no need to introduce new courses, revise requirements, hire additional faculty, and so on. Such costs are thus relevant only when considering whether to extend the life of the institution into the future, and not when discussing its current operations. This year's research and teaching depends, of course, on past administrative inputs, but by now these are sunk costs. Furthermore, there is no reason to believe that the "depreciation" of these past administrative activities is exactly equal to, and therefore measurable by, the current activities. The distortion is particularly significant in an old, declining institution or in a young, growing university, of which we have many today.

The multi-product nature of a university comes to the fore again when dealing with the cost of teaching assistants. Teaching assistants have been variously interpreted as a "slave labor" input into the undergraduate program or as "parasites" who are paid in excess of their true marginal product. Oliver and Hopkins adopt a variant of the former, considering teaching assistants a cost of undergraduate education, without even mentioning other definitions. I prefer to value the input of teaching assistants into the undergraduate program according to the market price of equivalent resources. The difference (if any) between this figure and the total payment to teaching assistants represents a subsidy to graduates, a portion of forgone earnings which is borne by the university rather than the student, or, alternatively, a purchase by the university of the student input into its graduate program. Using the wage for moonlighters at a nearby community college and for high school teachers in the area as a proxy for market value, I found that, in general, only half of the cost of teaching assistants at Stony Brook should be allocated to the undergraduate program. The remainder should be considered a cost of, or transfer payment to, the graduate students.

I have, in effect, been arguing that the operations research models in general, and Oliver-Hopkins in particular, overstate the real undergraduate instructional costs at a university by ignoring its joint supply of multiple products.[3] The key distinction between money and real (opportunity) costs is overlooked in other ways as well. I would question, for example, whether we are justified in using annual salaries as an index of faculty services, and wage differentials as an index of real cost differences. Since faculty tends to be hired on a long-term contractual or tenured basis, the university reaches its hiring decision on the basis of lifetime wages and expected performance, and current wages are not necessarily tied to current performance. Although the university will not become a "net lender" to the professor, who is free to leave, the professor may become a "net lender" to the university, knowing that he will afterwards be compensated. Thus, wages of young people may be less, and of older people more, than their current productivity. On the other hand, tenured professors are buying insurance as well as wages with their lifetime services, so the latter is understated by looking at the wage payment alone. Similar comments regarding the complex measurement problem might be made about other university resources which are not included in the Oliver-Hopkins model and which, therefore, will not be discussed here.

It is true, of course, that the university administration may be more interested in money than in social costs. More generally, there are many levels of decision makers at a university, and costs relevant at one level may not be relevant at another. Consequently, we must distinguish not simply between social and private costs but also among private costs perceived by varying decision makers. For example, the secretarial staff may be considered a variable cost to the central campus administration, a constraint to the department chairman who is not permitted to hire additional people, and a free good to the professor as he ponders whether to have a manuscript typed. Benefits of different activities also vary among decision makers, depending on the precise consequences and objective functions involved. Therefore, in building a useful operations research model one must clearly and consistently specify the decision maker for whom it is intended, in order to ascertain the appropriate set of costs, constraints, and goals. Oliver and Hopkins score well on this point, with one exception noted below.

Returning to the paper directly at hand, I have only a few specific criticisms. These could be handled easily in theory, but sometimes at the cost of a rather more complicated model.

1. No note is taken of faculty inputs into the graduate program other than regular course work; e.g. time spent advising students and supervising theses without corresponding credit hours appears to be omitted. This may help explain why the Oliver-Hopkins differences between undergraduate and graduate costs are not as great as other sources claim.

2. Although graduate students who serve as teaching assistants are recognized to spend a longer lifetime at the institution, it is also assumed that their annual course load and faculty input are the same as for non-teaching-assistants. Thus, the cost to the institution of educating a Ph.D. who has served as a teaching assistant is considerably greater than educating one who hasn't. Empirically, I wonder whether teaching assistants tend to take fewer courses and use less faculty time per year, which would reduce somewhat the unit cost for that cohort.

3. I am troubled by the possible emphasis on destination modes, particularly for the lengthy chains which include one or more intermediate degrees. If one is interested in finding the least-cost method of obtaining a fixed number of degrees, I presume that such intermediate degrees would also count. I see no reason, for example, why Berkeley should prefer taking a

Stanford B.S. into its Ph.D. program, rather than its own (as the discussion on page 396 seems to imply), in order to meet specific degree constraints.

For the educational system as a whole, such emphasis on final rather than intermediate destinations might be useful (stemming from national manpower needs) but for a single institution it is difficult to justify. Conversely, a single institution may, following Oliver and Hopkins, focus on different entry points and ignore the previous investment in human capital embodied in their students, but for the system as a whole such previous investment is fully relevant. As discussed above, a model builder should determine whose viewpoint he is adopting and consistently use that same viewpoint, while contrasting it, if he desires, with the viewpoint which would be appropriate to a different decision maker.

4. In the Oliver-Hopkins model, costs of all degrees are additive and independent of where the student's earlier work was done. This strikes me as a somewhat questionable assumption, especially when dealing with M.A.'s and Ph.D.'s. In many fields, one goes directly from a B.S. to a Ph.D., sometimes picking up a master's en route at virtually no extra cost. The lifetimes associated with these two programs are then not sequential but simultaneous, and the corresponding costs should not be added together. Furthermore, students switching institutions after the master's may require greater time toward completion of the Ph.D. than those continuing on at the same school. Such interaction between program costs and points of entry or destination may be important for certain policy questions but is not explored by the Oliver-Hopkins formulation.

5. I should like to underscore the word of caution Oliver and Hopkins rightly extend about interpreting their shadow prices and other results, which depend so critically upon the particular constraints assumed. For example, their very low shadow price for a junior transfer is based on a constant enrollment figure, thereby implying fewer freshmen. If we held the number of freshmen constant and broke the enrollment ceiling instead, the shadow price on junior transfers would be much higher. Conversely, if we held degrees constant instead of enrollment, increasing junior transfers would actually have a negative shadow price, since this is the cheapest way of granting a given number of bachelor's degrees. Similarly, if one examines the effects on total instructional costs of the Carnegie Commission recommendation to compress lower-division work to one year (Table 10), one gets completely divergent results depending on whether an enrollment constraint or degree constraint is assumed. Thus, this analysis can certainly be useful, but the structure of the model and changes resulting therefrom must be clearly specified and understood.

Finally, I should emphasize that many of the above observations belong more to the domain of economists than operations research specialists, so it is hardly a surprise that they have not been dealt with in the operations research literature on education. Oliver and Hopkins have developed a promising way of applying network theory to educational planning. Every attempt should be made by economists to provide conceptually meaningful inputs for their model.

NOTES

1. I am referring here to the faculty budgeted under "departmental instruction" not "organized research." While some research is funded separately, much of it is financed out of the regular departmental budgets at most universities. My particular results for Stony Brook, as well as the broader conceptual and measurement problems outlined in this comment, are discussed by me in the following Stony Brook working papers: "Resource Allocation and Costs in Higher Education"; "Some Notes on the Faculty as a University Resource"; and "Methods of Resource Measurement and Allocation."

2. Parenthetically, I am worried when an adjustment for research is not made in other contexts as well. For example, subsidies to undergraduates at state universities are frequently overstated for this reason; community college students are subsidized at least as much, contrary to the usual impression. The social rate of return to college teaching is understated if it is based on an unadjusted calculation. Changes through time in faculty-student ratios and teaching productivity, two topics discussed at this conference, might well have looked different if an explicit correction for research costs had been attempted. I also wonder whether this measurement problem might help to account for the apparent lack of connection between level of college expenditures and quality of educational output in cross-sectional studies. The "high-spending" universities may be the research-oriented institutions, whose true teaching costs are relatively overstated, and we may be observing, in part, that research is not an important input into undergraduate education.

3. To indicate the rough order of magnitude of this effect, my own figures for undergraduates are approximately 60 per cent of those of Oliver and Hopkins. My graduate costs are also somewhat less, unless research is counted as an input into graduate study, in which case, costs of a master's or Ph.D. skyrocket by a multiple of six.

10

ROY RADNER
University of California,
Berkeley

Faculty-Student Ratios in U.S. Higher Education

1. INTRODUCTION

It usually requires no special effort to interest academics in the subject of faculty-student ratios, at least at the level of faculty club or cocktail party conversation. We feel threatened by any decrease in the faculty-student ratio, and we consider any increase to be a sign of increasing quality. On the other hand, if the ratio is low, we can boast to the legislature of our "efficiency."

An interest in forecasting the demand for teachers leads naturally to an interest in the patterns of variation of student-teacher ratios among institutions and through time. More generally, it leads to an interest in the relations among inputs and outputs in higher education, or, as the production economist might put it, in the "technological possibilities" that have been observed within the education sector. Of course, there are many nonhuman inputs into the educational process, but the human ones are probably still the most important. In any case, the everyday

NOTE: This paper is based on research supported by the Carnegie Commission on the Future of Higher Education and also by the National Science Foundation. The material presented here forms part of a more extensive report that Leonard S. Miller and I have prepared for the Carnegie Commission: *Demand and Supply in U.S. Higher Education* (New York: McGraw-Hill, 1975). The data processing and regression analyses for Section 4 were done by Sunny Yoder, whose contribution to this research has been considerable.

415

mythology of education suggests that the relations among the human inputs and outputs have remained at the heart of the educational process since at least the time of Socrates and may even have changed very little from his day to ours!

On the other hand, the measurement of "quality" of inputs and outputs may not have advanced much either during the past twenty-five hundred years, nor shall we in this paper contribute to the solution of this important problem. I, like most other educators, cling to the hypothesis that an educational institution *can* do more to increase the quality of its output than merely select students with higher initial "ability." But quantitative confirmation of this hypothesis still seems to elude those who have studied the question carefully.[1]

Relative to the magnitude of the various problems to which I have referred, the goal of the present study is quite modest. We shall try to "explain" the variation in numbers of faculty, both among institutions of higher education and through time, as a function of numbers of students enrolled, and in terms of several other institutional variables, such as ratings of graduate schools, faculty salaries, size, type of control, and so forth.

Although our data are crude and subject to considerable error, some conclusions may be ventured. First, during the period 1950–67, there seems to have been a downward trend in faculty-student ratios, except in private universities. This trend appears both in aggregate data and in individual data for a sample of institutions (Section 2).

However, the variation in faculty-student ratios among institutions, even within standard categories (classified by control and level), is striking. A major part of this report (Sections 3 and 4) is devoted to trying to relate this variation to variation in other institutional variables by a cross-section analysis of a 1966 sample of institutions. This cross-section analysis reveals the presence of "increasing returns to scale" in the relation between faculty "inputs" and student enrollment, except in the universities and in public master's-degree-level institutions, and (curiously enough) the public four-year institutions. The other groups all show some evidence of fitting the "economizing model," in which institutions substitute higher salaries, or a greater percentage of Ph.D.'s on the faculty, for higher faculty-student ratios.

Finally, we have had some success, in the case of the universities, in estimating separate "faculty input coefficients" for undergraduate and graduate education and in showing how these coefficients depend on other institutional variables. If our estimates are not unduly inaccurate, the university faculty input coefficients for undergraduate education are somewhat lower than those for private master's degree level institutions and private four-year institutions with high faculty salaries, but are above those for other types of institutions. Furthermore, the university faculty input coefficients for graduate education appear to be from two to four times as large as those for undergraduate education (in the universities).

2. RECENT HISTORICAL TRENDS IN FACULTY-STUDENT RATIOS

2.1. Summary

We present here evidence from two sources on trends in faculty-student ratios during the period 1950–67. Roughly speaking, during this period, faculty-student ratios declined in public universities and in institutions other than universities, and increased somewhat in private universities. However, there was considerable variation within each major category of institution. This variability declined somewhat in the undergraduate categories but remained relatively stable in the universities. In Sections 3 and 4, we try to relate this variation among institutions to variations in institutional variables.

2.2. Evidence from the Office of Education Statistics

We first consider estimates of faculty-student ratios calculated from statistics on numbers of faculty and students published by the Office of Education. For these estimates, institutions have been grouped in six categories, based on a two-way classification: (a) public, private; and (b) universities, "other four-year colleges," two-year colleges. For each of the years 1957, 1963, and 1967, and for each of the six categories, we have estimated the ratio of total full-time-equivalent faculty to total full-time-equivalent students. The results are presented in Table 2.1. It should be emphasized that these estimates may be subject to considerable error because of the noncomparability of statistics in different years and the difficulties of estimating full-time equivalents.

Table 2.1 indicates that faculty-student ratios fell in all categories except that of private universities. In this last category, the ratio increased from 1957 to 1963 and then fell between 1963 and 1967.

In interpreting Table 2.1 and subsequent tables, it may be useful to have in mind some sample numbers relating faculty-student ratios to student-faculty ratios:

Faculty-student ratio	.04	.05	.06	.07	.08	.09
Student-faculty ratio	25.0	20.0	16.7	14.3	12.5	11.1

TABLE 2.1   Total Faculty-Student Ratios

	—Universities—		Other Four-Year ——Colleges——		Two-Year ——Colleges——	
	Public	Private	Public	Private	Public	Private
1957	.078	.085	.065	.078	.053	.080
1963	.066	.099	.058	.074	.051	.067
1967	.060	.089	.056	.069	.046	.056
Per cent change 1957–67	−23	+5	−14	−12	−13	−30

SOURCE: Estimated from Office of Education Statistics. See the appendixes to Chapter 6 of Roy Radner and Leonard S. Miller, *Demand and Supply in U.S. Higher Education* (New York: McGraw-Hill, 1975).

2.3. Evidence from the "ACE Sample"

We consider next a sample of 372 colleges and universities taken from a larger set of more than 900 institutions for which data were available[2] on numbers of faculty and students for the years 1950, 1954, 1958, and 1962. These 372 institutions included all those in the larger set that either (a) were purely undergraduate institutions or (b) had substantial graduate enrollment in each of the four years mentioned above but were neither purely graduate schools nor primarily religious or professional schools. In this paper, these two groups will be called "undergraduate schools" and "universities," respectively; there are 259 "undergraduate schools" and 113 "universities." With a few exceptions, we had data on numbers of faculty and students for each of the 372 schools for each of the four years. Thus, we were able to avoid the problems of possible changes in numbers and classification of institutions. On the other hand, our sample is not random, and it may well not be "representative."

After further subdividing the undergraduate schools and universities into public, private nonsectarian (hereafter called "private"), and private sectarian (hereafter called "sectarian"), we calculated the average and the standard deviation of each of the faculty-student ratios for the resulting six groups for each of the four years in our observation period (1950–62). The results are presented in Table 2.2.

The mean faculty-student ratio clearly fell in each of the under-graduate groups, with the greatest decline (28 per cent) in the public schools and the smallest decline (14 per cent) in the private schools. The

TABLE 2.2 Averages and Standard Deviations of Faculty-Student Ratios

| | Undergraduate | | | Universities | | |
	Public	Private Nonsectarian	Private Sectarian	Public	Private Nonsectarian	Private Sectarian
Mean of faculty-student ratio						
1950	.0939	.1016	.1031	.0833	.1111	.0782
1954	.0859	.0963	.0973	.0785	.1244	.0868
1958	.0742	.0934	.0859	.0777	.1263	.0845
1962	.0674	.0875	.0809	.0766	.1266	.0956
Standard deviation of faculty-student ratio						
1950	.036	.031	.033	.030	.062	.039
1954	.039	.028	.030	.029	.072	.037
1958	.028	.031	.023	.029	.074	.037
1962	.027	.022	.018	.030	.066	.041
Number of institutions in group						
1950	45	51	162	51	46	13
1954	45	51	162	54	46	14
1958	44	51	162	54	46	14
1962	45	51	162	55	45	14

mean faculty-student ratio also fell slightly in the public universities, but rose in the other universities. In both undergraduate schools and universities the private schools ended the period with the highest ratios; and the public schools, with the lowest. Of course, one suspects that the increases in the universities are due to the increased fraction of the total enrollment represented by graduate students.

The variability of the faculty-student ratios, as well as their means, declined in the undergraduate-school groups, but remained relatively stable in the university groups. On the whole, there was considerable variation in the ratios, with the means roughly only two to four times the standard deviations. In 1962, the private universities had the lowest ratio of mean to standard deviation (1.9), whereas the sectarian undergraduate schools had the highest (4.5).

All in all, we have a picture of declining faculty-student ratios in undergraduate schools and in public universities, and of increasing ratios in private sectarian and nonsectarian universities. The downward pressure on the faculty-student ratios seems most pronounced in the case of the public schools, both undergraduate and universities. Within each of the groups there is considerable variation in the faculty-student ratio. Our task in the subsequent sections will be to try to relate this variation—over time and within groups—to variation in institutional variables, and in the case of the universities, to changes in the undergraduate-graduate student mix.

3. UNDERGRADUATES AND GRADUATES: THE FIXED-COEFFICIENT MODEL AND ITS DIFFICULTIES

3.1. A Simple Fixed-Coefficient Model

It is generally believed that graduate students take up more faculty time, per student enrolled, than do undergraduates. In the language of activity analysis, we might say that the training of undergraduates and graduate students are two different "activities," with different (faculty) input coefficients. This suggests the simple linear relationship

(3.1) $\quad F = a_u U + a_g G$

where, for a given institution, at a given date

F is the number of (full-time equivalent) faculty;

U, G are the numbers of enrolled (full-time equivalent) undergraduate and graduate students, respectively; and

a_u, a_g are the faculty input coefficients for undergraduate and graduate teaching, respectively.

If observations were available on a given school for several points of time, during a period in which the input coefficients remained constant but the ratio of undergraduate to graduate students was changing, then the input coefficients could be estimated from, say, a regression of F on U and G. Which particular regression would be appropriate would depend on the particular stochastic specification of the relationship (3.1). Alternatively, if observations were available at a given point of time on each of a set of schools believed to have common input coefficients, then the coefficients could be estimated from a "cross-section" regression.

The situation we are considering is illustrated in Figure 3.1, which is based on a simple transformation of equation 3.1 into a relationship involving student-faculty ratios. Define

$$U^* = \frac{U}{F} \qquad G^* = \frac{G}{F}$$

Then, dividing both sides of equation 3.1 by F gives

(3.2) $1 = a_u U^* + a_g G^*$

All (nonnegative) pairs (U^*, G^*) satisfying (3.2) would lie on a single line, as in Figure 3.1. The line might be thought of as the "output transformation locus" per unit of teacher input. The slope of that line would equal the negative of the ratio (a_u/a_g), and the intercepts on the U^* and G^* axes would be $1/a_u$ and $1/a_g$, respectively. The figure represents a situation in which a_g is greater than a_u.

3.2. Problems in the Use of Time Series Data

Observations on a single school at different points of time would yield (U^*, G^*) pairs all lying on the same line, if the input coefficients remained constant during the period, and if there were neither "disturbances" in the input-output relationship nor errors in the measurement of the variables. However, suppose there were a time trend in the input coefficients. A smooth trend would produce a situation such as that illustrated in Figure 3.2. Successive solid lines in the figure represent different transformation loci, and correspond to successive pairs (a_u, a_g), but we have only one observation on each line (one observation for each point of time). In the situation depicted by the figure, the ratio of graduates to undergraduates (equal to G^*/U^*) is also increasing smoothly. The result is that observed (U^*, G^*) pairs appear to fall on a single (dotted) line, which corresponds to a (a_u, a_g) pair that is a very

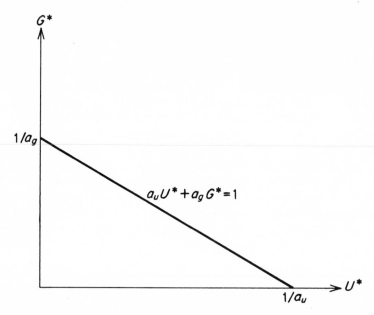

FIGURE 3.1 Locus of (U^*, G^*) Pairs for Constant Input
Coefficients

poor (indeed biased) estimate of the true average (a_u, a_g) pair over the period of the observation.

Even if the input coefficients remain constant during the observation period, random disturbances (or errors of measurement) may obscure the underlying relationship. It is clear that for a given variability of the disturbances, the greater the variation in the undergraduate/graduate ratio, the easier it will be to estimate the input coefficients. This is illustrated in Figures 3.3a and 3.3b. In Figure 3.3a, the undergraduate/graduate ratio is practically constant over the observation period, and it is impossible to get a good estimate of the input coefficients (i.e. it is impossible to estimate the relationship 3.2). In Figure 3.3b, there is a great variation in the undergraduate/graduate ratio, so that the relationship can be reliably estimated in spite of the random disturbances.

Unfortunately, a school that is experiencing large changes in its undergraduate/graduate ratio is also likely to be experiencing "structural" or quality changes that will affect its input coefficients. Therefore, in the presence of random disturbances, we are likely to face a dilemma in which either the input coefficients are stable but we cannot estimate them, or they are not stable but we cannot identify the pattern of change.

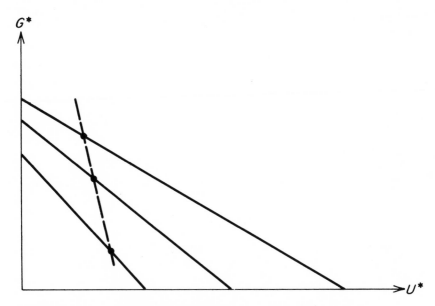

FIGURE 3.2 The Case of a Smooth Trend in the Input Coefficients

Examination of the data reveals that we are indeed faced with this dilemma, as I shall now show. First, note that for a least-squares fit of relation 3.2, the appropriate measure of stability (i.e. lack of variation) of the undergraduate/graduate ratio in a set of observations $[U^*(t), G^*(t)]$ is the coefficient

$$r = \frac{\Sigma U^*(t)G^*(t)}{[\Sigma U^*(t)^2 \Sigma G^*(t)^2]^{1/2}}$$

Note that r has the form of a correlation coefficient, except that the moments are around zero instead of around the means of the variables. if $r = 1$, then all of the pairs $[U^*(t), G^*(t)]$ lie on a common ray through the origin; the greater the variation of the undergraduate/graduate ratio in the sample, the closer will r be to zero.

In our sample of 113 universities, r ranged from 1.0 to .80, and was at least .88 in all but five cases. Figure 3.4 shows the scatter diagram of (U^*, G^*) observations for five selected universities, with r ranging from .88 to .999. In all but one of these cases (South Carolina State College), there is clearly no possibility of estimating the individual input coefficients from the observations. Even in the case of South Carolina State College, a line fitted to the four points would imply that the undergraduate faculty input coefficient is larger than the graduate

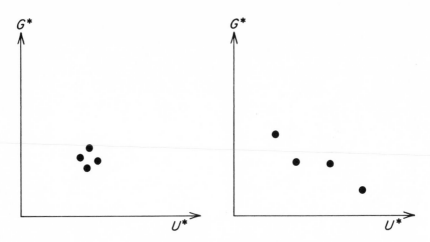

FIGURE 3.3a Small Variation in *U*/*G* **FIGURE 3.3b** Large Variation in *U*/*G*

coefficient. These selected schools are typical, and an examination of the observations for the entire set of schools shows that in most of the cases there is no clear basis for estimating the input coefficients, either because the variation of the random disturbances is too large, or because there have been changes in the coefficients, or both. We are, of course, handicapped by the smallness of the sample, but even with more observations during this twelve-year period, it seems unlikely that reliable estimation would be feasible.

3.3. Problems with the Use of Cross-Section Data

As already noted in Section 3.1, one could estimate equation 3.1 or 3.2 from a cross section of universities at a given point of time, provided one had a set of institutions that were approximately homogeneous with respect to input coefficients.

For this purpose, we looked at the Higher Education General Information Survey (HEGIS) data for the year 1966. Our sample included 55 public universities and 38 private universities. (A number of universities covered by HEGIS were eliminated from our sample because they did not have substantial "standard" graduate programs or because data on other variables, used in the analysis discussed in Section 4, were not available. For definitions of the data and sources, see Chapter 7, *Demand and Supply in U.S. Higher Education*.)

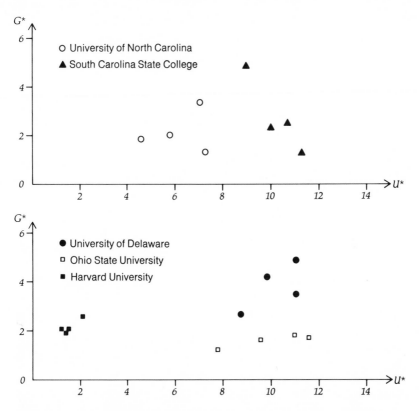

FIGURE 3.4 Scatter Diagrams of $(U^*(t), G^*(t))$ Pairs for Five Selected Universities, for $t = 1950, 1954, 1958, 1962$

To see how well the data might fit equation 3.2, we plotted a scatter diagram of (U^*, G^*) pairs for each of the two groups of universities, public and private. (Recall that $U^* = U/F$ and $G^* = G/F$.) The two scatter diagrams are shown in Figures 3.5a and 3.5b, respectively. Figure 3.4 reveals tremendous variation in the pairs (U^*, G^*), even among institutions with the same undergraduate/graduate student ratio. (Recall that institutions with the same U/G ratio will lie on the same ray through the origin.) It is clear that equation 3.2 does not fit either of the scatter diagrams (with a line like that of Figure 3.1).

Of course, one expects the input coefficients to vary among institutions and to be related more or less to various institutional characteristics. This is confirmed in a rough and informal way by an examination of Figure 3.4. In each half of the figure, if we compare those institutions at

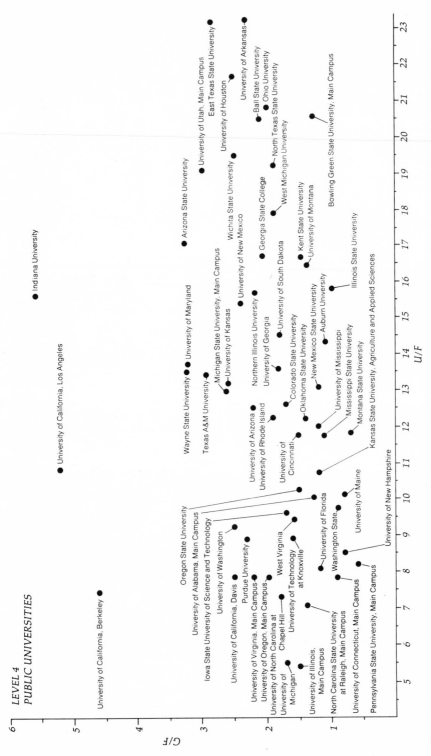

FIGURE 3.5a Scatter Diagram of (U/F, G/F) for Public Universities

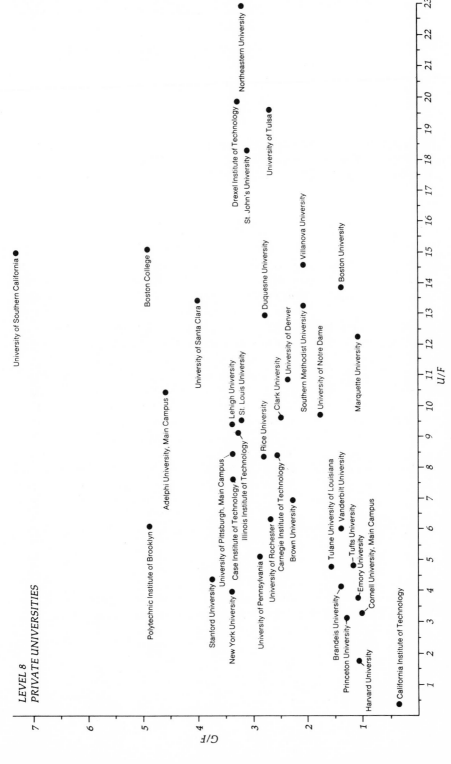

LEVEL 8
PRIVATE UNIVERSITIES

FIGURE 3.5b Scatter Diagram of (*U/F*, *G/F*) for Private Universities

or near the "southwest" boundary of the scatter diagram with those near the "northeast" boundary, we find that the first set has a higher concentration of "prestige" institutions than the second. An attempt to relate the input coefficients to other institutional variables will be described in the next section.

4. THE RELATIONSHIP BETWEEN INPUT COEFFICIENTS AND OTHER VARIABLES: A CROSS-SECTION ANALYSIS

4.1. A Variable Input Coefficient Model

In the previous section, we saw that variations in student-faculty ratios were far from explained by variations in the undergraduate–graduate-student mix, but that for schools with the same mix the ratios appeared to be related to other school characteristics. In the context of the activity analysis model, this could be expressed by saying that the "crude" numerical input-output coefficients, in terms of numbers of faculty, undergraduates, and graduates, depend on the "quality" of the inputs and outputs, and possibly on other school characteristics as well. Why not try to relate these input-output coefficients directly to these other variables?

Unfortunately, there are few, if any, accepted measures of the quality of inputs and outputs, nor do we have available data on many of the more promising measures. However, many people have found it reasonable to suppose that institutions with the same average faculty salaries, the same per cent of faculty with the Ph.D. degree, and so on, tend to have the same quality of inputs and outputs, or at least that the variation in quality among institutions that are similar in these characteristics is less than among the set of all institutions.

Consider again the linear relationship 3.1,

$$F = a_u U + a_g G$$

where F, U, and G represent the full-time-equivalent numbers of faculty, undergraduate students, and graduate students, respectively. For each institution, let W and Z be two vectors of measurements of institutional characteristics (there may be some characteristics common to both vectors), and assume that the input coefficients are related to these characteristics, as follows:

$$(4.1) \quad a_u = h_0 + h \cdot W, \qquad a_g = k_0 + k \cdot Z$$

where h_0 and k_0 are parameters, h and k are vectors of parameters, and

(4.2) $h \cdot W = \sum_j h_j W_j,$

(4.3) $k \cdot Z = \sum_j k_j Z_j$

Combining equations 4.1 and 4.2, and adding a constant term c, yields the equation:

(4.4) $F = c + (h_0 + h \cdot W)U + (k_0 + k \cdot Z)G$

The constant term, c, if different from zero, could reflect the presence of increasing or decreasing returns to scale (if c is positive or negative, respectively). An alternative measure of returns to scale could be obtained by setting $c = 0$ but including a measure of "size" in the vectors W and Z.

Finally, it should be noted that equation 4.4 could be applied to purely undergraduate institutions to examine how variation in faculty student ratio (a_u) is related to institutional characteristics.

Equation 4.4 can easily be fitted by least squares, since the equation is linear in the parameters to be estimated. However, if the vectors W and Z contain measurements in common, problems of multicollinearity may arise (they may, and do, arise in any case, for other reasons!).

For the components of the vector W we have taken the variables

PHD = fraction of the faculty holding a Ph.D. degree
SAL = average faculty salary
U = undergraduate

For the components of the vector Z we have taken

$QUAL$ = measure of the quality of the graduate program (see below)
SAL = average faculty salary
G = graduate

The variable $QUAL$ is an index derived from two measures: (1) an overall index derived from the departmental ratings in the 1966 American Council on Education report on quality of graduate education in the United States, the so-called Cartter Report,[3] and (2) the numbers of Woodrow Wilson and National Science Foundation Fellows electing to go to a given institution. Unfortunately, we were not able to obtain a comparable measure of quality of undergraduate programs.

With these "explanatory variables," equation 4.4 takes the form

(4.5) $F = c + h_0 U + h_1 (SAL)(U) + h_2 (PHD)(U) + h_3 U^2$
          $+ k_0 G + k_1 (SAL)(G) + k_2 (QUAL)(G) + k_3 G^2$

In the regressions that we shall report, two restrictions were imposed. First, we did not include both the constant term, c, and the size variables, U^2 and G^2, in the same regression. Second, we found that the two variables $(SAL)(U)$ and $(SAL)(G)$ were too highly correlated to permit reliable estimation of their coefficients separately; therefore, we imposed the restriction that $h_1 = k_1$, which is equivalent to replacing the two above variables by the single variable $(SAL)(STUD)$, where $STUD = U + G$.

4.2. The Sample

For our cross-section analysis, we used a sample of institutions for which HEGIS data were available for the year 1966. These institutions were grouped in a two-way classification, by "control" (public or private) and by "highest degree granted" (two year, bachelor's, master's, Ph.D.). Actually, for the second classification we use the following corresponding terms: two year, four year, M.A., Ph.D. (or university). For all institutions except the universities, "private" means "private nonsectarian." The "private universities" include both nonsectarian universities and those sectarian universities that did not have primarily religious programs of education. We did not include all institutions of higher education covered by the HEGIS data. In particular, we did not include: (1) institutions with less than 300 undergraduates, (2) institutions beyond the two-year level that were very specialized or were primarily vocational, (3) institutions for which the data on some of our variables were missing or were obviously in error. In some cases we supplemented our main body of data with material from other sources. Finally, the category "private four year" was divided into two groups, according to whether the average faculty salary was above or below $8,000 per year.

Table 4.1 shows the classification of institutions and the number of institutions in each category.

The variables used were those described in Section 4.1. They are listed here again, together with the corresponding scaling factors, where applicable. (See Chapter 7, *Demand and Supply in U.S. Higher Education*.)

TABLE 4.1 Classification and Numbers of Institutions

	Two Year	Four Year		M.A.	Ph.D.
Public	185	51		134	55
Private	34	44[a]	47[b]	62	38

[a] Average salary less than $8,000.
[b] Average salary greater than or equal to $8,000.

F	Full-time-equivalent number of faculty, $\times\ 10^{-2}$
U	Full-time-equivalent number of undergraduates, $\times\ 10^{-3}$
G	Full-time-equivalent number of graduate students, $\times\ 10^{-3}$
$STUD$	$U + G$ ($STUD = U$ for levels 1, 5, 2, and 6)
PHD	Fraction of the faculty who hold Ph.D. degrees
$QUAL$	An index of quality of the graduate program (see Section 4.1)
SAL	Average nine-month (or nine-month equivalent) faculty salary, $\times\ 10^{-4}$

Tables 4.2 and 4.3 show the means and standard deviations, respectively, of the variables for each level. The statistics for the mean faculty-student ratios are also shown. In interpreting these statistics, the reader must keep in mind the scaling factors. In addition, in comparing the mean faculty-student ratios with those reported in Table 2.1, one must keep in mind that Table 4.2 gives the means of faculty-student ratios for individual institutions, whereas the ratios reported in Table 2.1 are ratios of total faculty to total students in a given category of institution. We see that the mean faculty-student ratios for 1966 in Table 4.2 are generally lower than the *corresponding* ratios for 1962 reported in Table 2.2, thus suggesting an extension of the downward trend. On the other hand, the fact that the mean ratios for 1966 are generally higher than the (total) ratios for 1967 reported in Table 2.1 is probably more a reflection of the difference in the method of averaging than a reflection of any trend (although other information suggests that the downward trend has indeed continued beyond 1966).

4.3. Results of the Regression Analyses for the Undergraduate and Master's Level Institutions

For each of the categories other than the two Ph.D. levels (public and private universities), we fitted by least squares the following two regression equations:

(4.6) $\quad F = h_0 STUD + h_1(SAL)(STUD) + h_2(PHD)(STUD) + h_3(STUD)^2$

(4.7) $\quad F = c + h_0 STUD + h_1(SAL)(STUD) + h_2(PHD)(STUD)$

Generally, we found that the specification without the constant term (4.6) gave a slightly better fit, although the differences in fit were not very great. In each category, the fit was quite good; in the set of seven categories the multiple correlation (R^2) ranged between .904 and .986.

In Table 4.4 the estimates of the regression coefficients are given for specification 4.6. In order to conserve space, we have reported only one set of estimates for each category of institution. In selecting the set of estimates to present for each particular category, we restricted ourselves to specifications that included only "explanatory" variables yielding

TABLE 4.2 Sample Means

Level	F (×10⁻²)	U (×10⁻³)	G (×10⁻³)	STUD (×10⁻³)	F/STUD (×10)	PHD	QUAL	SAL (×10⁻⁴)
1. Public two year	0.935	2.213	0.	2.213	0.489	.041	–	0.835
5. Private two year	0.464	0.842	0.	0.842	0.661	.039	–	0.715
2. Public four year	0.963	1.849	0.	1.849	0.556	.243	–	0.815
6L. Private four year	0.566	0.972	0.	0.972	0.634	.263	–	0.705
6H. Private four year	0.747	1.091	0.	1.091	0.783	.447	–	0.951
3. Public M.A.	2.382	3.891	0.359	4.249	0.588	.356	–	0.924
7. Private M.A.	1.379	1.872	0.166	2.038	0.753	.457	–	0.937
4. Public Ph.D.	10.085	11.290	1.909	13.200	0.742	.513	.581	1.048
8. Private Ph.D.	9.027	5.869	1.998	7.869	1.492	.589	.896	1.121

NOTE: Figures in parentheses under variable names indicate the scaling factors.
SOURCE: Higher Education General Information Survey, 1966.

TABLE 4.3 Sample Standard Deviations

Level	F $(\times 10^{-2})$	U $(\times 10^{-3})$	G $(\times 10^{-3})$	$STUD$ $(\times 10^{-3})$	$F/STUD$ $(\times 10)$	PHD	$QUAL$	SAL $(\times 10^{-4})$
1. Public two year	0.864	2.549	0.000	2.549	0.131	0.055	—	.154
5. Private two year	0.265	0.601	0.000	0.601	0.294	0.063	—	.096
2. Public four year	0.591	1.355	0.000	1.355	0.115	0.102	—	.134
6L. Private four year	0.264	0.578	0.000	0.578	0.146	0.106	—	.086
6H. Private four year	0.336	0.883	0.000	0.883	0.192	0.182	—	.170
3. Public M.A.	1.752	2.548	0.607	2.989	0.193	0.126	—	.128
7. Private M.A.	0.842	1.286	0.281	1.455	0.287	0.173	—	.138
4. Public Ph.D.	7.370	5.161	1.610	6.583	0.253	0.079	.602	.075
8. Private Ph.D.	9.340	3.965	1.974	5.334	2.669	0.146	.662	.175

NOTE: Figures in parentheses under variable names indicate the scaling factors.
SOURCE: Higher Education General Information Survey, 1966.

TABLE 4.4 Regressions for Nonuniversity Groups

Level	STUD times[a]				n	R^2	a^*_{STUD}[b]
	1	SAL	PHD	STUD			
1. Public two year	.667 (.00)	−.197 (.00)		−.013 (.00)	185	.956	.446
5. Private two year		1.062 (.00)	−1.443 (.04)	−0.126 (.00)	34	.904	.491
2. Public four year	.291 (.00)	.279 (.05)	.336 (.02)	−0.028 (.00)	51	.986	.496
6L. Private four year, SAL < $8,000	.760 (.00)			−0.137 (.00)	44	.967	.496
6H. Private four year, SAL > $8,000	1.075 (.00)	−.495 (.00)	.657 (.00)	−.101 (.00)	47	.979	.677
3. Public M.A.	.174 (.03)	.435 (.00)		−.006 (.04)	134	.969	.525
7. Private M.A.		.394 (.00)	.852 (.00)	−.022 (.03)	62	.947	.668

[a] For items where two numbers appear, the upper number is the regression coefficient for the corresponding variable in the regression equation

$$F = h_0 STUD + h_1(SAL)(STUD) + h_2(PHD)(STUD) + h_3(STUD^2)$$

The number in parentheses is the significance level of the coefficient. For two-year and four-year colleges, "STUD" means undergraduates only. For M.A.-granting colleges, STUD = U + G. All variables are scaled as in Table 4.2.

[b] a^*_{STUD} is the derivative of the regression equation with respect to STUD, evaluated at the sample means of the explanatory variables.

statistically significant coefficients, and among such specifications we chose the one that gave the best fit. Since the correlations between some of the explanatory variables were rather high, we had in some instances problems of multicollinearity; these problems are discussed in Section 4.5, where we also present some examples of regressions with coefficients that are statistically not significant. In any case, in none of the specifications reported in Table 4.4 could the fit be significantly improved by adding more variables.

Table 4.4 also shows the corresponding estimates a^*_{STUD} of the derivative of the regression equations with respect to the variable $STUD$, i.e. $a^*_{STUD} = dF/dSTUD$; this derivative has been evaluated at the sample means of the explanatory variables. Thus a^*_{STUD} is the "marginal input coefficient." Notice that a^*_{STUD} is not in general equal to the input coefficient, a_{STUD}, since the input coefficient itself depends on the variable $STUD$. Indeed, since (by Section 4.1)

$$a_{STUD} = h_0 + h_1 SAL + h_2 PHD + h_3 STUD$$

(4.8)

$$a^*_{STUD} = h_0 + h_1 SAL + h_2 PHD + 2h_3 STUD$$

the two coefficients are related by

$$a^*_{STUD} = a_{STUD} + h_3 STUD$$

We see from Table 4.4 that h_3, the coefficient of $STUD^2$, is significant in every case, and negative. This indicates that in each of the nonuniversity categories there was a measurable effect of *increasing returns to scale* to the faculty input. We see, too, that this effect was more pronounced in the case of the private institutions than in the case of the public ones. This is no doubt related to the fact that the average enrollments in the public groups were consistently higher than those in the corresponding private groups (see Table 4.2).

If we compare the marginal input coefficients of Table 4.4 with the mean faculty-student ratios of Table 4.2, we see that the marginal coefficients are consistently lower than the average coefficients. This is, of course, consistent with the effect of increasing returns to scale. The ranking of the 7 nonuniversity groups is roughly the same by the marginal as by the average coefficients, but the exceptions to this are revealing. Table 4.5 gives the two rankings, with the number "1" corresponding to the largest coefficient. The most obvious discrepancies in the two rankings occur in the case of the private two-year and the public M.A. groups. Table 4.2 shows, however, that these two groups have the lowest and highest mean enrollments, respectively, of the seven groups. Thus it would appear that, although the private two-year institutions have relatively low marginal input coefficients, their average coefficient is high because of their small average size. An analogous, but reverse, argument would seem to apply to the public M.A. group.

435 | Roy Radner

TABLE 4.5 Rankings of Nonuniversity Groups by Marginal and Average Input Coefficients

Level	Ranking by Marginal Input Coefficient	Ranking by Average Input Coefficient
Public two year	7	7
Private two year	6	3
Public four year	4–5	6
Private four year: low salary	4–5	4
Private four year: high salary	1	1
Public M.A.	3	5
Private M.A.	2	2

Before studying the "effects" of salary and per cent of faculty with the Ph.D., it might be useful to speculate on some a priori models. The first, which might be called the "prestige model," postulates that high faculty-student ratios, high salaries, and high percentage of faculty with the Ph.D. are all trappings of a high-prestige institution, so that one would expect the coefficients h_1 and h_2 to be positive. The second model, which might be called the "substitution model," postulates that salary and per cent Ph.D. are measures of "quality," and that quality of faculty inputs can be substituted for quantity, so that one would expect h_1 and h_2 to be negative. Of course, in the "substitution model" one would want to control for the quality of output, which we have not been able to do here.

Table 4.4 does not show any consistency among the groups in the signs of h_1 and h_2. Public four-year, private M.A., and (in part) public M.A. institutions seem to follow the "prestige model," whereas the two-year and the high-salary private four-year institutions show evidence of "substitution," with respect to one of the variables. It should be pointed out that most of the so-called high-prestige liberal arts colleges fall into the private M.A. group, since they typically give some beginning graduate work. The low-salary private four-year institutions do not show a significant effect of either salary or per cent Ph.D. on the input coefficient.

4.4. Results of the Regression Analyses for the Universities

For each of the two university categories we fitted by least squares the following two regression equations:

$$(4.9) \quad F = h_1(SAL)(U + G) + h_0U + h_2(PHD)(U) + h_3U^2 + k_0G$$
$$+ k_2(QUAL)(G) + k_3G^2$$

$$(4.10) \quad F = c + h_1(SAL)(U + G) + h_0U + (PHD)(U) + k_0G + k_2(QUAL)(G)$$

Again, we found in general that the specification without the constant term (4.9) gave a slightly better fit. The fits for the universities were not quite as good as those for the other groups, but were still quite good.

In Table 4.6 the estimates of the regression coefficients are given for specification 4.9. For each group, we have given more than one set of estimates in order to illustrate some of the problems that we face.

Recall that for the case of the universities, one of the tasks we set ourselves was to estimate the separate effects of U and G on the numbers of faculty. Thus we aim not only to get a good "fit," but also to get reasonable estimates of the marginal input coefficients a^*_u and a^*_g. (See Sections 3 and 4.1. The marginal input coefficients are defined just as in equation 4.8.)

Examination of Table 4.6 shows that, although each regression equation shown gives a reasonably good fit, not all the specifications lead to sensible values for the marginal input coefficients. For example, the second specification for each of the two groups is the same as equation 3.1, i.e.

$$(4.11) \quad F = a_uU + a_gG$$

The resulting estimates of a_u and a_g are reasonable for the public universities, but not for the private universities. The first specification for each of the two groups does lead to reasonable estimates of the marginal input coefficients:

	a^*_u	a^*_g
Public universities	.596	1.166
Private universities	.575	1.983

However, one would have expected a^*_u to be larger for the private than for the public universities; it is generally believed that classes are smaller and teaching loads are lighter in private universities than in public universities. These faculty input coefficients for undergraduate education are somewhat smaller than the coefficients for the private M.A. and high-salary private four-year groups, but larger than those for the other groups. It should be emphasized that the data on "faculty" did not include teaching assistants, teaching associates, or teaching fellows; to that extent the input coefficients underestimate the instructional inputs. On the other hand, the data for "faculty" include faculty in organized research units.[4]

We do not find evidence of significantly increasing returns to scale in either undergraduate or graduate education at the mean values of the

TABLE 4.6 Regressions for the Universities

Level	U times:				G times:				n	R^2	a^*_u	a^*_g
	1	SAL	PHD	U	1	SAL	QUAL	G				
4. Public Ph.D.		.569 (.00)				.569 (.00)	.982 (.00)		55	.907	.596	1.166
	.497 (.00)				2.330 (.00)				55	.887	.497	2.330
8. Private Ph.D.		.513 (.00)				.513 (.00)	1.572 (.00)		38	.782	.575	1.983
	.217 (.45)				3.416 (.00)				38	.702	.217	3.416
		2.395 (.00)	-3.358 (.01)	-0.039 (.09)		2.395 (.00)			38	.808	.249	2.685

NOTE: The regression equation is given by 4.9. Numbers in parentheses are significance levels. See Table 4.4 for other explanatory notes.

explanatory variables (except in the case of the third regression for the private universities, which does not in any case yield sensible values of the input coefficients). The universities, of course, have much larger enrollments, on the average, than do the other groups (see Table 4.2).

If we accept the first regression in each of the two university groups as valid, then the universities appear to fit the "prestige model" quite well. The variable $QUAL$ represents the combined judgments of faculty peers and prospective graduate students concerning the "quality of the faculty in graduate programs," and therefore would seem to be a measure of the quality of faculty input. (It should not be necessary to insist here on the uncertainties surrounding the meaning of this measure!)

4.5. An Analysis of Elasticities

Although the regression coefficients discussed in Sections 4.3 and 4.4 give a fairly good qualitative idea of the relationships between the input coefficients and the "explanatory" variables, it is difficult to interpret their numerical magnitudes. For this reason we calculated the *elasticities* of the input coefficients with respect to each explanatory variable in the appropriate regression equation. Recall that the elasticity of an input coefficient, say a, with respect to a variable, say X, is defined by:

$$(4.12) \quad \text{elasticity} = \frac{d\log a}{d\log X} = \frac{X}{a} \cdot \frac{da}{dX}$$

Thus, for small changes, the elasticity equals the percentage change in the input coefficient associated with a 1 per cent change in the explanatory variable.

Table 4.7 shows the elasticities of a^*_{STUD} with respect to the explanatory variables SAL, PHD, and $STUD$ in the regression equations determined by the coefficients in Table 4.4, taking the estimates of a^*_{STUD} from the same table, and taking the variables at their sample means. Table 4.8 shows the corresponding elasticities for the two university groups, using the first regression for each group in Table 4.6.

In the nonuniversity groups, the elasticities of the input coefficients with respect to $STUD$ are largest (in magnitude) for the private two- and four-year institutions, and lowest for the public M.A. and two-year institutions. Indeed, although the regression coefficient for $STUD$ is statistically significant in the case of the public M.A. group, the corresponding elasticity is rather small in magnitude. It is interesting that with regard to the variable PHD, the private two-year group has the largest regression coefficient but the smallest elasticity (in magnitude). Generally, the elasticities with respect to SAL are larger in magnitude than those with respect to PHD.

TABLE 4.7 Elasticity, Coefficient of Variation, and Probable Per Cent Variation: Nonuniversity Groups

Level	Elasticity of a^*_{STUD} with Respect to:			Coefficient of Variation			Probable Per Cent Variation of a^*_{STUD} with Respect to:		
	SAL	PHD	STUD	SAL	PHD	STUD	SAL	PHD	STUD
1. Public two year	−0.368		−.129	.184		1.152	−.068		−.149
5. Private two year	1.546	−.114	−.432	.134	1.598	0.715	.207	−.182	−.309
2. Public four year	0.458	.165	−.209	.164	0.419	0.733	.075	.069	−.153
6L. Private four year			−.537			0.594			−.319
6H. Private four year	−0.695	.434	−.325	.178	0.408	0.809	−.124	.177	−.263
3. Public M.A.	0.766		−.097	.138		0.703	.106		−.068
7. Private M.A.	0.553	.583	−.134	.147	0.379	0.714	.081	.221	−.096

TABLE 4.8 Elasticity, Coefficient of Variation, and Probable Per Cent Variation: Universities

| | Elasticity of: | | | Coefficient of Variation | | Probable Per Cent Variation | | |
| | a^*_u with Respect to | a^*_g with Respect to | | | | a_u | a_g | |
Level	SAL	SAL	QUAL	SAL	QUAL	SAL	SAL	QUAL
4. Public Ph.D.	1.000	.511	.489	.072	1.036	.072	.037	.507
8. Private Ph.D.	1.000	.290	.710	.156	0.739	.156	.045	.525

In the two university groups, the graduate input coefficient is about equally elastic with respect to *SAL* and *QUAL* in the public universities, but almost two and one-half times as elastic with respect to *QUAL* than *SAL* in the private universities.

Further insight into the relative importance of the explanatory variables can be obtained by taking account of the dispersion of the explanatory variables in the sample. To measure the relative dispersion of a variable we used the *coefficient of variation*, equal to the ratio of the standard deviation to the mean. For the nonuniversity groups (see Table 4.7), the overall picture is that *STUD* has the largest coefficients of variation, and *SAL* the smallest. In the universities, the coefficient of variation was considerably larger for *QUAL* than for *SAL*.

To "correct" the elasticities for differences in relative dispersion, we measure the "probable per cent variation," defined by

(4.13)   probable per cent variation = (elasticity) × (coefficient of variation)

This last measure can be interpreted as an approximation to the per cent change in the input coefficient associated with a change in the explanatory variable equal to 1 per cent of its standard deviation. The figures for probable per cent variation are also given in Tables 4.7 and 4.8. It is interesting to note in Table 4.8 that, when measured by the probable per cent variation, the association of *QUAL* with the graduate input coefficient is considerably more "important" than that of *SAL*. Also, the probable per cent variation of the undergraduate input coefficient with respect to *SAL* is larger than that of the graduate input coefficient.

4.6. Multicollinearity and Other Specification Problems

The pattern of correlations among the variables is such that in many instances it is not evident which selection of explanatory variables is "best." Examples of this are shown in Table 4.9.

In the first example (private Ph.D.), the coefficient of (*STUD*)(*SAL*) is not very significant (statistically) when introduced in addition to (*G*)(*QUAL*); but if the variable (*U*)(*PHD*) is then introduced, the coefficient of (*STUD*)(*SAL*) becomes more significant, and the coefficient of (*G*)(*QUAL*) loses its significance. Similar problems arise in the other examples.

For each group of institutions, quite a few different regression specifications were tried. In choosing the ones we have presented here, we considered not only the criterion of goodness of fit, but also the plausi-

TABLE 4.9 Examples of the Effects of Multicollinearity

Level	U times:				G times:				Constant Term	R^2
	1	SAL	PHD	U	1	SAL	QUAL	G		
8. Private Ph.D. [a] (with constant term)							2.574 (.00)		3.898 (.00)	
		.372 (.07)				.372 (.07)	1.989 (.00)		1.770 (.29)	
		1.623 (.02)	−3.199 (.06)			1.623 (.02)	.978 (.17)		2.893 (.10)	.819
8. Private Ph.D. [b] (without constant term)		.529 (.00)				.529 (.00)	1.891 (.00)			
		1.459 (.04)	−2.206 (.17)			1.459 (.04)	1.151 (.11)			
		1.790 (.02)	−2.319 (.16)	−.028 (.26)		1.790 (.02)	.727 (.36)			.811
6L. Private B.A. [c]	.406 (.00)								.171 (.00)	
	.189 (.32)	.283 (.25)							.183 (.00)	
	.203 (.44)	.241 (.34)	.107 (.49)						.173 (.00)	.965
4. Public Ph.D. [d]		1.004 (.00)			−4.432 (.00)	1.004 (.00)	2.375 (.00)			
	1.149 (.06)	−.094 (.87)			−3.441 (.02)	−.094 (.87)	2.809 (.00)			.928

NOTE: See Table 4.4 for other explanatory notes.
[a] Correlation between (G)(QUAL) and (U)(PHD) is .398.
[b] Correlation between (STUD)(SAL) and (U)(PHD) is .913, and between U^2 and (G)(QUAL) is .202.
[c] Correlation between U and (U)(SAL) is .986.
[d] Correlation between U and (STUD)(SAL) is .976.

bility of the resulting estimates of the input coefficients. We have already alluded to this in the discussion of the regression estimate of equation 4.11.

One may wonder how it is that the regression estimate of 4.11 for the public universities could give plausible results, whereas the scatter diagram in Fig. 3.5a is so diffuse. Related to this is the fact that regressions of $F/STUD$ on the other variables invariably gave poor fits (for all groups of institutions). This suggests that, in the regressions in which F is the independent variable, those institutions in each group that have relatively large numbers of faculty and students may have a "disproportionate" influence on the results. However, we have not yet sufficiently explored this problem to come to a conclusion.

Finally, we should mention that treating undergraduate and graduate students separately in the M.A.-level institutions did not give good results. It would appear that in this group of institutions, it is not possible, with these data, to obtain reliable estimates of a_u and a_g separately.

NOTES

1. Alexander W. Astin, "Undergraduate Achievement and Institutional 'Excellence,'" *Science* 161 (Aug. 16, 1968): 661–667.
2. *American Universities and Colleges* (Washington, D.C.: American Council on Education, 1952, 1956, 1960, 1964). Numbers for faculty and students are "head counts," and not full-time equivalents.
3. Allan M. Cartter, *An Assessment of Quality in Graduate Education* (Washington, D.C.: American Council on Education, 1966).
4. Variations in reporting practice prevented us from excluding research faculty in any consistent manner. Thus our faculty figures reflect the "research style" of each institution.

10 ‖ COMMENTS

Gus Haggstrom
The Rand Corporation

Roy Radner's paper provides an admirable study of faculty-student ratios over the period 1950–67, together with an enlightening cross-sectional analysis of the 1966 institutional data in which he attempts to explain the variation in these ratios among institutions in terms of other variables.

In reporting the behavior of faculty-student ratios over time, Radner begins by presenting Table 2.1, which contains his estimates of faculty-student ratios by institutional category for the years 1957, 1963, and 1967. The table suggests that faculty-student ratios have been dropping rather consistently between 1957 and 1967 in all categories except the private universities.

This table is of particular interest to me because of its relevance to projecting the future demand for college teachers and because of the uncertainties involved in estimating the ratios from the available data. As Radner points out, the data published by the Office of Education both on enrollments and on numbers of faculty lack year-to-year comparability, so that his estimates may be subject to considerable error. Having recently attempted to construct a similar table from the same sources, I understand his misgivings about the reliability of the estimates. The 1966 and 1967 Office of Education surveys on numbers of faculty seem almost to have been designed to frustrate attempts to compare them with the notably consistent biennial surveys up to 1963. My estimates of faculty-student ratios for the period 1957–67 are given in Table 1. The estimates in parentheses in Table 1 were derived independently by June O'Neill and were published in her book *Resource Use in Higher Education* (Berkeley, Calif.: Carnegie Commission on Higher Education, 1971).

Although the sets of estimates are not strictly comparable because of differences in our definitions (in particular, June O'Neill's estimates of FTE faculty include junior faculty), the time trends for my estimates tend to confirm Radner's calculations for the four-year colleges. On the other hand, whereas Radner's estimates show a steep decline in the faculty-student ratios for the two-year colleges between 1963 and 1967, my estimates show a slight increase, and June O'Neill's estimates show a substantial increase in faculty-student ratios for the public two-year institutions between 1963 and 1966.

Tables 2 through 4 provide some background information for analyzing the behavior of the faculty-student ratios over time. From Table 2, which shows the number of institutions within each category, we note that the number of public two-year institutions increased by 73 per cent between 1957 and 1967, despite the fact that many two-year colleges became four-year institutions during this period. Thus, the category of public two-year institutions

TABLE 1 Faculty-Student Ratios by Institutional Category, Aggregate U.S., 1957–67

	Universities		Other Four-year Colleges		Two-Year Colleges	
	Public	Private	Public	Private	Public	Private
1957	.083 (.086)	.095 (.101)	.067 (.067)	.079 (.081)	.049 (.048)	.066 (.075)
1959	.078	.096	.063	.078	.049	.058
1961	.074 (.083)	.100 (.111)	.059 (.061)	.074 (.077)	.049 (.045)	.053 (.059)
1963	.070 (.080)	.105 (.114)	.058 (.060)	.074 (.078)	.048 (.045)	.054 (.060)
1966	.063 (.079)	.091 (.118)	.057 (.060)	.070 (.076)	.048 (.050)	.058 (.058)
1967	.064	.089	.056	.069	.049	.058
Per cent change 1957–67	−23	−6	−16	−13	0	−12

included a high proportion of new campuses which had not yet had an opportunity to achieve a degree of efficiency through experience in faculty utilization and economies of scale. Incidentally, the counts of the two-year colleges do not include the many two-year branch campuses of universities. The faculty and students in the two-year branches are included in the calculation of the faculty-student ratios for the universities.

Table 3 suggests one reason why the faculty-student ratios for the private universities have behaved differently from those of the other categories. The private institutions had a much higher proportion of graduate students in 1957, and in absolute terms they have shown the largest increase in the proportion of graduate students between 1957 and 1967.

On the other hand, Table 4 shows that the private universities have shown

TABLE 2 Number of Institutions within Each Institutional Category, Aggregate U.S., 1957–67

	Universities		Other Four-Year Colleges		Two-Year Colleges	
	Public	Private	Public	Private	Public	Private
1957	82	59	286	969	302	241
1959	82	59	290	1,009	332	243
1961	83	60	293	1,022	348	238
1963	88	58	299	1,058	377	260
1966	92	65	313	1,112	479	276
1967	93	64	323	1,113	522	267
Per cent change 1957–67	13	8	13	15	73	11

TABLE 3 Ratio of Full-Time Equivalent Graduate Resident Enrollment to Total Opening Fall Full-Time Equivalent Enrollment by Institutional Category, Aggregate U.S., 1957–67

	Universities		Other Four-Year Colleges		Two-Year Colleges	
	Public	Private	Public	Private	Public	Private
1957	.099	.152	.038	.029	–	–
1959	.114	.170	.042	.033	–	–
1961	.120	.175	.047	.034	–	–
1963	.118	.194	.052	.036	–	–
1966	.140	.222	.052	.042	–	–
1967	.148	.221	.057	.044	–	–
Per cent change 1957–67	49	45	50	52	–	–

the smallest rate of increase in average total enrollment per institution between 1957 and 1967. According to my estimates, among the private universities almost 40 per cent of the increase in full-time equivalent enrollment per institution was at the graduate level.

Since the behavior of faculty-student ratios derived from aggregate totals for institutional categories may be distorted by the inclusion of new institutions and changes in institutional classification (say, from two-year to four-

TABLE 4 Average Full-Time Equivalent Enrollment per Institution (Ratio of Aggregate Full-Time Equivalent Enrollment to Number of Institutions in the Category), Aggregate U.S., 1957–67

	Universities		Other Four-Year Colleges		Two-Year Colleges	
	Public	Private	Public	Private	Public	Private
1957	8,600	6,330	1,720	620	930	270
1959	9,310	6,600	2,020	660	950	300
1961	10,570	7,000	2,310	740	1,080	350
1963	12,400	7,500	2,710	790	1,260	360
1966	16,020	8,300	3,660	920	1,680	440
1967	17,050	8,690	3,950	950	1,770	470
Per cent change 1957–67	98	37	130	53	90	74

year or from private to public control), it is important to supplement them by longitudinal studies of individual institutions. Radner has done this for 372 institutions for which he has relatively complete data for the years 1950 to 1962. (See Table 2.2.) The institutions in his sample constituted only about one-sixth of all institutions listed in the *Higher Education Directory* of the Office of Education in 1962 and, as Radner points out, they surely do not constitute a representative sample. Nevertheless, the conclusions seem clear. There was a sharp reduction in the aggregate faculty-student ratios at the primarily undergraduate institutions throughout the period. There was a smaller but consistent drop in these ratios for the public universities, and there was a relatively consistent increase in the ratios for the private universities.

It is regrettable that the time period covered by Table 2.2 ends in 1962, and I hope that Radner will attempt to update his study soon to include data for the late 1960s. A comparison of this table with my Table 4 on the average FTE enrollment per institution suggests that the decreases in the faculty-student ratios between 1950 and 1962 are approximately proportional to the increases in average enrollment per institution. Thus, Table 2.2 seemingly presents very strong evidence of sizable returns to scale, but Radner is apparently unwilling to draw this conclusion from his study. For reasons to be discussed below, I share Radner's caution in ascribing the drops in faculty-student ratios to economies of scale.

As an indication of more recent trends in faculty-student ratios, Hans Jenny and Richard Wynn in a new book *The Golden Years* report the results of a longitudinal study of 48 small private four-year liberal arts colleges over the period 1960–68, during which time the aggregate enrollment for this group of colleges increased 29 per cent. The aggregate faculty-student ratios for the group barely changed at all during the eight-year period. On the other hand, the faculty-student ratios for the individual institutions fluctuated widely over time with some showing large increases between 1960 and 1968 and others showing large decreases. Jenny and Wynn provide a plot of percentage growth in FTE faculty between 1960 and 1968 versus percentage growth in FTE enrollment for the 48 colleges which shows almost no relationship between these two variables. This study suggests that the reduction of faculty-student ratios may be unrelated to economies of scale.

How then can one explain the behavior of the faculty-student ratios by institutional category over the period 1957–67? One approach is suggested by the following identity:

$$C/S = (C/C_F)(C_F/F)(F/S)$$

Here

C = instructional costs;
S = number of students;
C_F = total cost for faculty salaries; and
F = number of faculty.

I contend that the individual institutions operate under certain constraints that limit increases in instructional costs per student over time. Indeed, some governors and boards of trustees are not above fixing (or at least assessing) next year's budget for instructional costs by combining an enrollment projection with a modest increase in the present instructional cost per student. I believe that, in general, the budgetary constraints upon the public institutions were much more restrictive than those for the private institutions during the period 1957–67. For one thing, the public institutions had to accommodate much larger increases in enrollment during this period. (See Table 4.) Between 1957 and 1966, according to estimates by June O'Neill, instructional costs per credit hour rose by 34 per cent in the public institutions and by 57 per cent in the private institutions.

On the right-hand side of the identity are three factors: (1) the ratio of instructional costs to the expenditure for faculty salaries (this ratio should be relatively constant over time); (2) the average faculty salary; and (3) the faculty-student ratio. Since faculty salaries are not as directly subject to the same budgetary constraints that affect instructional costs per student, they are more susceptible to external factors such as the state of the labor market for highly trained manpower. In fact, faculty salaries did rise very rapidly between 1957 and 1967 (at an annual rate of close of 6 per cent per year), partly as a result of the extreme shortage of college teachers during a period of rapid enrollment growth. It follows from the above identity that faculty-student ratios had to decrease in those institutions where the increases in faculty salaries were far in excess of increases in instructional costs per student. Given the recent change in the job market for college teachers, we may very well see a change in the behavior of faculty-student ratios over time.

The last part of Radner's paper deals with the cross-sectional analysis of the institutional data for 1966. He provides an insightful discussion leading up to the linear model specified by equations 4.1–4.4. First, I have some reservations about his basic equation

$$F = a_u U + a_g G$$

since this relationship attributes increases in faculty entirely to enrollment increases, ignoring the role of research activity in creating new faculty positions. I should have preferred to see either a third term on the right side of the equation measuring the institution's research activity or a reduction in the number of faculty on the left side of the equation to account for differences in average teaching load among the institutions. However, perhaps neither of these preferences are realizable due to the unavailability of suitable data.

The results of his regressions as summarized in Tables 4.4 and 4.6 lack a consistency across categories that suggests a lack of fit (despite the high values of R^2) perhaps due to the inappropriateness of the model. In Table 4.4 there seems to be a general consistency among the nonuniversity groups in the regression coefficients that indicates increasing returns to scale for faculty inputs. However, the strength of the relationship may be exaggerated by the omission of a key variable (e.g. the age of the institution or a measure of the degree of budgetary constraint that has affected the institution in the past).

It is interesting that the corresponding regressions for the universities summarized in Table 4.6 do not provide evidence of returns to scale. However, here the multicollinearity among the independent variables may be preventing a cogent analysis. To skirt this difficulty, Radner might have based his analysis on an equation of a slightly modified form:

$$F = a_s(STUD) + a_g[G - c(STUD)]$$

with c equal to the overall proportion of graduate students for institutions of the same type.

In summary, I think the paper sheds a lot of light on the subject of faculty-student ratios, but I am hopeful that Radner will attempt to update his work with more recent data and provide more insight into some of the many questions that remain unanswered in this area.

Kenneth D. Roose

Economic and Educational Consultant

Student-faculty ratios in higher education are worthy of study and analysis. For one thing, the data, although subject to considerable measurement and definitional error are generally available across the levels and variety of higher education. For another, the ratios, themselves, can be interpreted as proxy measures of such factors as efficiency, financial insufficiency, and prestige. For still another, they supply evidence of the wide diversity in the circumstances under which higher education is carried out.

What additional light, then, does Radner throw upon the input-output relationships of students and faculty in higher education? In general I think he would agree that his study tends to confirm what has already been thought to be true: faculty-student ratios declined during the period, 1950–67, with contrary trends for private universities during part of the period;[1] ratios vary considerably even within an institutional category; faculty input coefficients and consequently costs for graduate education appear to be from two to four times as large as those for undergraduate education in the universities. Undergraduate-graduate student ratios are poor predictors of faculty input coefficients; and prestige institutions have lower student-faculty ratios both at undergraduate and graduate levels than do other types of institutions.

Where Radner tests relatively unexplored relationships such as increasing returns to scale through tradeoffs of rising salaries and growing numbers of Ph.D's for larger faculties, the numerical results, although often statistically significant, still tend to be suggestive only of possible relationships rather than conclusive or definitive. In a comparison of faculty input coefficients in public and private universities, however, he arrives at results that are inconsistent with what we already believe to be obvious relationships. Therefore he rejects his finding that the marginal input coefficient of faculty to undergraduate students in private universities is smaller than in public universities. Incidentally, as Radner points out, because of the ambiguities involved in the definition and measurement of student enrollments and faculty size, his data may be subject to considerable error. For this reason alone interpretation of the data must be qualified.

Beyond these observations about his specific findings, I consider the most interesting parts of the paper those that lead to further speculation about possible root causes of the present financial crisis in higher education. Surely the declining productivity in private higher education as well as the modestly rising productivity in public higher education, as revealed in these faculty-student ratios, must be instrumental in the growing financial bind. Moreover, the evidence on increasing returns to scale, particularly in the case of private institutions, clearly would appear to reflect underutilization of faculty. Since the student-faculty ratio is an obvious and reasonably objective measure of productivity trends, it is not surprising that public and private institutions as well are being forced to take a hard look at teaching loads, faculty size, courses offered, and so on.

Another point of considerable interest in this paper is Radner's evidence that quality or prestige considerations have such a positive impact on faculty costs. In the university syndrome, drives for salary and prestige, particularly prestige in the private universities, contribute markedly to growing costs and declining physical productivity.

This leads me to some final observations about quality of output and the influence of environment, especially the faculty, upon the quality of the output. As Radner rightly points out, the studies of undergraduate students by Alexander Astin and others have shown little relationship between institutional excellence and undergraduate achievement. If allowances are made for the ability of the student upon entering, then his performance upon graduation appears to be unrelated to the alleged quality or prestige of his institution. Since this thesis has not been seriously contradicted, then the moves to rationalize the use of educational resources by raising student-faculty ratios may not have deleterious or even perceptible effects on the quality of the output. Moreover, studies of class size have not demonstrated the superiority of the small class for the learning process. If, in addition to these considerations, more than lip service is paid to the desirability of building student independence and self-reliance, then serious questions must be raised about the dramatically higher costs associated with graduate education. If student ability is a powerful determinant of the educational outcome, if the student demand increasingly is for relatively more independent study, and if there are strong philosophical and educational arguments supporting this trend, then why must we have such high faculty-student ratios at the undergraduate level and accept ever-rising ratios at the graduate level?

NOTES

1. See William Baumol, *AAUP Bulletin* (American Association of University Professors), Spring 1968.

PART
FOUR | Policy Issues

11

JOSEPH N. FROOMKIN
Joseph Froomkin, Inc.

Policy Issues in the Education Industry

Economists have a great deal to contribute to the formulation of policy issues when they look at education through the prism of industrial analysis. Besides analyzing the demand and supply of factors used by, or produced by, education, they can throw some light on the effect of educational inputs on achievement, especially that of slow learners. Economists are brave enough to ask what is optimized. They have already contributed much to the "gutsy" issues in education, namely, whether the level of quality of resources makes a difference in terms of educational outcomes. They may further contribute to answering the bothersome question of what would be produced by allocating a richer or better mix of resources to slow learners, as contrasted to investing the same resources to benefit the gifted.

Currently, we are just scratching the surface in the analysis of education as an industry. In order to sharpen the issues which are high on society's agenda, it may be well to describe the present pressures on the educational establishment and point out how they are affecting the problems which economists are expected to tackle. In the past twenty years, education in the United States has been geared to do the things which it knows best how to do, namely streaming large numbers of students through educational institutions. The coverage of American education has become well-nigh universal between the ages of six and sixteen, and an increasing proportion of children below that age, as well as those above it, are now participating in the educational experience.

455

The present dissatisfaction with the state of events can be traced to the criticism that education still acts as a sorting device, benefiting the gifted more than the slow learners, and the children of the rich more than the children of the poor. It has been argued that this is an important failing of the educational system.

At the same time, as attendance rates have swelled, and costs per student have continued going up, the resources assigned to education have increased substantially. Especially in the postsecondary area, there is increasing difficulty in providing the funds for rising enrollments.

In a nutshell, education is being asked to equalize opportunity and control costs at the same time. Can economists contribute to the achievement of these goals?

The first step in this direction is to build models which describe what is happening in the educational process. The value of modeling the system is twofold. In the first place a model can handle various pieces of the system and, if broad enough, quantify the consequences of different combinations of resources. Second, a broad-based model may help bring together disparate pieces of information and test whether they are consistent with each other.

CLARIFICATION OF THE CONCEPT OF EQUALITY OF EDUCATIONAL OPPORTUNITY

Before discussing which models have to be built and which issues they ought to address, a clarification of the concept of equality of educational opportunity is essential. It lies at the very heart of defining what outputs of education economists ought to be measuring.

Most discussions concerning the improvement of the educational process are conducted in the context of equalizing educational opportunity for children of various social classes. Even this objective is often stated imprecisely. In some instances, it implies that children from various socioeconomic groups ought to benefit from the same number of years of education. In other instances, the objective is translated to mean that children of the poor and children of the rich should attain the same level of schooling, say twelve grades of education. In yet other cases, equality of educational opportunity is taken to mean a state of affairs where, irrespective of social background, children who have equal achievement, or equal intelligence, benefit from the same number of years of education, or reach the same level of schooling. Depending upon the definition which is adopted, the implications for the goals of education reform are substantially different.

The different implications of these standards for policy are best illustrated with actual examples. According to the U.S. Census of 1960, for instance, the attainment of the children of the poor was well below that of the children of the rich. While only 4 per cent of the children of rich parents, those with incomes of $10,000 or more, were in grades below the mode for their age, 37 per cent of the children of the poor were in grades lower than the mode for their age. The children of parents with incomes of less than $3,000 a year were likely to be one grade behind the average of the population. The children of the poor generally start school later than the children of the rich, according to the information of the U.S. Census, and they are more likely to repeat grades.[1]

The children of the poor are also more likely to discontinue their education at an earlier stage. Among young adults aged twenty to twenty-four who were high school dropouts in the United States in 1962, nearly eight out of ten were the children of high school dropouts.[2] Two factors conspired to limit their educational attainment. In the first place, the atmosphere of the home and the aspirations of the parents were not conducive to the continuation of the education of such young people. Parents with less education generally aspire to lower levels of attainment for their children, and the aspirations of the parents are generally shared by their offspring. This state of affairs is illustrated by Table 1, which gives the latest available data about the plans of twelfth-grade students

TABLE 1 College Aspirations for High School Seniors by Mothers' Educational Attainment and College-Going Plans of Seniors, 1966

A. Per Cent of Mothers Wanting Seniors to Attend College

| | Education Attainment of Mothers | | | |
	0–8 Years	9–11 Years	12 Years	1 or More Years of College
Male	73	84	91	98
Female	60	72	87	97

B. Per Cent of Seniors Planning to Attend by Mothers' Aspirations

| | High-School Seniors' Plans | |
Mothers' Wishes for Seniors	College	No College
College	82	16
No College	18	84

SOURCE: Unpublished tabulations from Special U.S. Census Bureau Survey.

in 1966. The lower the educational attainment of the mother, the lower the expectation for postsecondary education of both the parent and the child.

The second cause for the weaker persistence of children of the poor in the educational process is their generally lower achievement in school. This lag has been documented convincingly by a number of studies, and is illustrated below by data collected by the American Institute of Research in a large-scale study conducted in the early 1960s. Table 2 presents a matrix showing the dropout rate between the tenth and twelfth grades by socioeconomic status and by achievement on a nationally standardized test. The sixteen cells of the table divide the population into four socioeconomic groups and four roughly equal achievement groups.

The data in the table show that in 1960 the dropout rate between grades ten and twelve was six times as high in the lowest socioeconomic group as in the highest socioeconomic group. If the comparison between socioeconomic status (SES) groups is made while taking achievement into account, a different picture emerges. The dropout rate in the low socioeconomic group compared to the high SES group was double in the bottom half of the ability distribution, and roughly five times higher in the top half. Thus, about half the difference in the dropout rate between the upper and lower socioeconomic groups is explained by differences in achievement and the rest by differences in socioeconomic status.

There is some evidence that since the 1960s the dropout rate of higher-ability students has declined considerably, especially in the third quartile of the population. In 1967, by contrast with 1960, the number of students who failed to complete twelfth grade after starting this level declined drastically in the third quartile. There are considerable grounds for hypothesizing that the possibility of enrollment in postsecondary institutions favorably affects the retention rate. While this development

TABLE 2 Dropout Rates Between Tenth and Twelfth Grade by Ability and Socioeconomic Status (Per Cent)

Socioeconomic Status Quartiles	Ability Quartiles				
	Low	2	3	High	Total
Low	28.8	15.2	10.8	5.6	19.0
2	21.6	11.9	5.7	3.2	10.4
3	17.4	8.6	4.4	2.0	8.1
High	13.5	6.5	2.0	1.4	3.2

SOURCE: Project Talent, 1965.

may be a harbinger of what social programs can achieve in equalizing the number of years attained, we still have very little indication of the usefulness of additional years of education for persons with different levels of achievement or intelligence.

Some preliminary data on the earnings of males in the late 1950s and early 1960s is highly disquieting, and tends to indicate that additional years of schooling are not likely to contribute to earnings for persons whose general level of ability is low. Data from the U.S. Social Security System analyzed by Cutright indicates that the marginal contribution of additional schooling over and above primary education is much higher for males in the high-ability ranges than for those whose ability is mediocre or low[3] (see Table 3). Thus, it is not at all clear to what extent equalizing the number of years of school attended can serve to equalize incomes. Probably, to reach that goal, the equalization of achievement must be increasingly emphasized.

In theory, it is possible to equalize achievement by (1) introducing remedial measures which will equalize the learning rates of different groups of the population, or (2) applying a higher level of resources to those groups where there is a greater incidence of slow learners. These policies can be oriented to raising the average of a group, but it is unlikely that they will eliminate the variability within groups unless very precise, individualized prescriptions are worked out for each member.

EQUALIZING LEARNING RATES

There is now some evidence that human learning characteristics are shaped by the environment, and may be affected by efforts expended in

TABLE 3 Illustrative Contributions of Education to Income by Ability Quartile (Dollars)

| | Ability Quartiles | | | |
	Low	2	3	High
Primary School	1,238	539	215	191
Some High School	6,113	738	947	1,213
High School	2,081	1,860	1,308	na
College	–	–	2,848	3,456

na = not available.

SOURCE: Adapted from Phillip Cutright, *Achievement, Mobility, and the Draft, Their Impact on the Earnings of Men* (Washington, D.C.: Department of Health, Education and Welfare, Social Security Administration, O.R.S., Staff Paper 14, 1972).

the early life of a child. Benjamin Bloom of the University of Chicago has provided some evidence that one-half of the human traits of intelligence are formed by the age of four.[4] It is precisely in these critical years that environmental factors may determine future learning characteristics.

Bloom's hypothesis of the development of human characteristics can, with some license, be represented by the equation $h = a^{\alpha}$, where h is the learning rate, a is age, and α is an exponent equal to ½. The resulting formula shows that human characteristics related to learning are accumulated extremely rapidly during the first few years of life and more slowly later. Table 4 shows the rate at which these characteristics are accumulated.

If it is assumed that efforts or expenditures are more likely to affect the learning rate of a child during the period when these characteristics develop fastest, expenditures at a later age are less likely to affect human characteristics of learning than outlays earlier in life. If the effects on characteristics are proportional to the effort expended, i.e. a multiplicative model where the exponent of the resource function is one, the formula can be rewritten as $h = Ea^{1/2}$, when E is the unit of effort expended. We shall refer to E, for convenience, as a year of effort. Some arithmetic examples may illustrate the implications of this "learning curve" for educational policy.

Assume that in some social classes the effect of the environment is such that it produces a learning rate only seven-tenths that of the learning rate for other social classes. (This estimate is roughly in line with the Coleman Report's findings for the relative learning rate of children of poor parents. We shall not consider in this paper the effect of different genetic endowment or biological factors.) How much effort is required to bring h from .7 to 1.0? It can be estimated that in order to

TABLE 4   Rate of Accumulation of Human Characteristics Related to Learning (Increments of ½ for Ages One to Eighteen)

Age	Increment	Age	Increment	Age	Increment
1	1.000	7	.196	13	.141
2	.414	8	.183	14	.136
3	.318	9	.172	15	.131
4	.268	10	.162	16	.128
5	.236	11	.154	17	.123
6	.216	12	.148	18	.119

reach the desired level, the effort must be increased 43 per cent. ($E_1 a^{1/2}$; .7 $E_2 a^{1/2}$, $E_1/E_2 = 1.0/.7 = 1.43$, i.e. $1.43 E_2 a^{1/2} = E_1 a^{1/2}$)

Pushing this analysis further, we can also calculate the amount of effort needed to have the average development of the slower group catch up. If more effort is expended during the first year, the answer is 43 E_1, as was shown earlier. If one neglects to take remedial action during the first year, the area under the growth curve at the end of year two of life is .7 × 1.414 or .9898, i.e. .4242 units behind. The learning development rate in the second year is again 70 per cent of .414, equal to .2970. In order to catch up during this year, an additional 1.429 years of effort is required. Instead of adding .43 units of effort two years in a row, an additional effort of .57 units is now required. If the remedial effort is postponed to the third year, the child is likely to be .520 units behind, and with a learning rate of .2236, require 2.34 years of additional effort. In other words, by accepting this model, one perceives that in this case postponement has doubled the required effort.

At a later age, say nine, the needed effort is of gargantuan proportions. If the children's average learning rate was .7 during nine years, this segment of the population is now 2.7 years behind, and the equivalent of 23.2 units of effort is required to close the gap. This is a formidable, if not impossible, challenge.

The challenge becomes even more awesome when one assumes that the outcome of additional efforts is not simply multiplicative, but that incremental efforts have a smaller effect on the development of learning characteristics. For instance, if an exponent of .5 is attached to the effort function, and the expression is rewritten as $L = E^{1/2} a^{1/2}$, more than double the effort (1/.72) is required to achieve the required results. The effect of postponement would then be even more dramatic. We would require roughly six units of effort to make up the differences in the second year, and the cost of doing nothing during the first year would be equivalent to the cost of four years of effort. The crucial unresolved issue in the whole matter of affecting human characteristics is whether a group can be brought to a higher learning rate permanently, or whether the effect is a temporary one, with additional infusion of resources needed to keep the learning rate up.

Because of the somewhat primitive analysis to date, however, we can only make wild guesses about what is likely to happen to experiments that try to affect the learning rate. On the other hand, the impact of changing learning rates on the level of required additional effort is not to be underestimated. If the difference in learning rates between social groups can be reduced by one-half through enrichment by age six, it can be hypothesized that the learning rate of deprived populations, now approximated by the coefficient of .7, could be increased to .85. This increase could dramatically reduce the outlays needed for remediation.

In all probability, the learning process does not depend merely upon the student's ability or speed of learning. To some extent, it also depends upon the stock of knowledge which has been accumulated up to a given time. Perhaps it can be represented as a function of both the learning rate and the previous stock of knowledge S.

$$\Delta S_j = S_{jt} - S_{jt-1} = (\alpha E_{tj} a^{1/2} + \beta S_{jt-1}) E_j$$

A given unit of learning ΔS_j will require an amount of effort proportionate to the sum of $(\alpha E_{tj} a^{1/2} + \beta S_{jt-1})$. If this formulation is accepted, the postponement of offering a given unit 1 till βS_{jt-1} reaches a certain level will allow a smaller expenditure of effort to be expended to master it than if it is presented to the student earlier.

The considerations above are put forward to make a simple point: it is quite likely that production functions in education are not uniform for children of different ages or of different abilities.

TOWARDS AN ECONOMIC ANALYSIS OF THE EDUCATIONAL PRODUCTION FUNCTION

The role of education (measured by scholastic achievement tests) as a neutral filter has been demonstrated by Case in an imaginative analysis of the Equal Opportunity Report. Case found that the children of parents with a low educational attainment stayed the same number of standard deviations behind the children of rich parents from grades one through nine. Only in grade twelve, after the worst students had dropped out, was the difference between children of parents with a grade-school education and those with a college education somewhat narrower than at grade one.[5]

Among educators, this gap has been ascribed to the failure of the school and the family, but it remains for an economist to try to quantify the interaction between family and school and to attempt to assign some numerical values to the influence of these two important factors in determining achievement.

Denis Dugan, while a Brookings fellow, spent a year at the Office of Program Planning in the U.S. Office of Education trying to estimate production functions which would take into account the contribution of both the home and the school. In a nutshell, Dugan's models try to estimate the contribution to children's attainment made by parents as well as by schools.[6] This is a much more realistic description of the situation than one which assumes that all learning originates in the school. Using information from the Equal Opportunity Survey, Dugan attempted to explain inequalities in educational outcomes as a function of both parental investment, during preschool and school years, and school investment.

The value of parental investment was measured by a proxy of average earnings of persons with different levels of education. School investments were considered to be equal for children in all social classes. As with many pioneering efforts, many factual and methodological questions can be raised about the precision or even reasonableness of the estimates, but the present writer, who helped develop the Dugan model, believes this approach throws more light than confusion on the dynamics of learning.

Fundamental to the whole model is the estimate of parental contribution to children's learning. The model assumes that parental contribution or investments could be measured by, or at least scaled in proportion to, the opportunity cost, i.e. the market price of the time which the parents devote to the cognitive activities of their children during the years from birth to age eighteen. These expenditures are then lumped with the costs of formal education to arrive at a total cost.

In this expanded view of the educational process, total educational investment is substantially greater than formal school expenditures. For instance, at grade nine, the cumulative value of parental investment is roughly $19,800, or 81 per cent of the total educational investment—totaling $24,500—for a child whose parents are college graduates, as contrasted to 53 per cent—i.e. $5,500 of a total of $10,500—for a child whose parents had less than an eighth-grade education. These startlingly high estimates of parental contribution to education were derived on the basis of fairly conservative assumptions. Thus, it was assumed that a mother spent 43 per cent of her time in the preschool period with her child or children. In cases where several preschool children were in the house simultaneously, the mother's time was allocated partially to each child. During the period of formal schooling, 5 per cent of the mother's time was allocated to educational activities of children and 5 per cent of the father's time was allocated to the educational activities of children. The parental services were divided up among the children in the family.

In the calculations which related the stock of services to the attainment of the child, the contributed services of both parents and of the school were compounded at a rate of interest of 5 per cent to differentiate services provided in different time periods. In effect, the method of accumulating these services took into account the alternative investment opportunities available to both parents and society.

These estimates were used to derive a set of production functions which explained the achievement of students as a function of the capital embodied in their education. Suffice it to say here that one model which attempted to explain the difference in resources was in a linear multiplicative form, and the other was of a nonlinear character. This later model was transformed into the linear-in-the-logarithms function, which can be estimated by regression analysis.

While the linear model assumes equal returns in all ranges of the "production function," the nonlinear model implies decreasing returns to scale. Intuitively and empirically the nonlinear model seems to describe the learning process somewhat more realistically and accurately, since the regression coefficients for this model are somewhat higher than those for the linear model.

Using the empirical results of this model, it is possible to calculate the amount of expenditures which may be required to close the gap between a disadvantaged group and one which is relatively more advantaged. Below we cite some examples, taken from the United States experience, of expenditures which would be required to equalize the achievement of black children—whose parents on the average have less education—and that of white children.

The cumulative investment which would be required to equalize achievement between these two groups by grade nine (age fifteen) is $6,999 according to the linear model, and $18,177 according to the nonlinear model. There are two reasons why the required expenditures are higher with the nonlinear model. In the first place, the marginal rate of substitution is less favorable, i.e. lower, for school expenditures, as compared to parental outlays, in the nonlinear model. Second, the effectiveness of resources applied in the school increases less than proportionately when incremental expenditures are added to school resources.

There are several ways of looking at the results of the model. If the resources of the white home environment were made available to blacks, it would appear that 90 per cent of the difference could be made up by the infusion of parental resources. In other words, even then, something extra is needed to have black students come up to the white average.

Another way of looking at the results of such an analysis is to examine how much of the achievement gap could be closed by increasing school resources. Again, the empirical results, for whatever they may be worth, indicate that most of the gap between whites and blacks in the United States can be closed if resources are increased by 75 per cent with the linear model, and that even an increase in resources of 150 per cent would not quite close the gap with the nonlinear model.

An interesting implication of the model is that cultural differences play a role in the effectiveness of parental investments. To what extent those differences are due to differences between black and white cultures and to what extent they are a reflection of the rural origins of many blacks deserves further investigation. The higher than expected educational attainment of Jewish and Oriental children has often been cited as an exogenous cultural factor. Yet, we have very little information on the power of this factor in producing learning.

The analysis above is only a step in the right direction in analyzing learning in a realistic context. It would be well if the model were broadened to take into account the contribution of children's school peers to their attainment. An analysis of the Equal Opportunity Report indicates that the influence of the school cannot be separated from the social background of the student. As Alexander Mood has pointed out: "Speaking very roughly, when one looks at variations in achievement scores between pupils, about 65 per cent of it occurs between pupils in the same schools and about 30 per cent of it occurs between schools."[7]

Such a study of tradeoffs should be very high on the agenda of the economics profession because economists handle problems sequentially, having been trained to accept the ceteris paribus assumptions. Their conclusions, right or wrong, are easier to understand and are more likely to have an impact than those of other social scientists.

MORE ON PRODUCTION FUNCTIONS

It may appear paradoxical that a concluding paper of a conference dealing with education as an industry should raise more problems than it can answer. Yet it should be realized that economists have only begun to analyze the problems of education as an industry. Up to now, most of the economic analyses of education discussed cost/benefit problems where the assumption was that the output of education and costs are uniform for the purposes at hand. The opening up of the topic of education as an industry makes it imperative to look at a new set of problems.

Once one starts looking at differences in costs caused either by variations in the number of factors applied or in their quality, the definition of production functions becomes even more difficult. We are currently not too sure about how the factors should be combined or what attributes of production factors should be measured. Henry Levin has pointed out that teacher quality plays an important part in determining the student outcomes.[8] A similar finding was documented by Piccariello in a study of deviant schools, where the achievement of children was one standard deviation above or below the one expected, given the school's socioeconomic composition.[9]

Those economists who have worked with educational production functions have often suspected that some factors which are currently being used to improve performance are probably redundant and contribute little or nothing to the learning process. By contrast, other factors which are not measured play an important part in determining achievement.

Attempts to determine tradeoffs between capital and labor have been especially frustrating. There are some indications that the value of school plant plays no role in influencing achievement.[10] There is little or no information about the effect of adding educational hardware in the school setting, or its role in affecting learning. Anyone who has ever ventured into the schools to observe what happens must conclude that variations between schools may be caused more by variations in the way personnel or equipment is used than by variations in the level of resources devoted to teaching. The presence or absence of a language lab, for instance, does not foretell the possible achievement of students in foreign-language studies. In many schools, the labs exist but are not used. These variations in practice have discouraged investigations of capital/labor tradeoffs in schools.[11] Only if we moved to teacher-proof systems of instruction might such analysis become easier.

Perhaps while we think of new methods of tackling this difficult problem, we may wish to analyze variations between schools at a lower level of generality. Economists have been known to make contributions in understanding the effect of organization upon output. Investigation of the organization of the American school may not be out of place. For instance, analyzing the findings of the international study of mathematical achievement may yield some interesting insights.[12] If this study is to be trusted, our educational system is not producing achievement which is anywhere near the acceptable level. Thirteen-year-olds in the United States perform well below Japanese students of the same age. The lower achievements were especially surprising since our standard of living is higher, our teachers are trained longer, and the resources we spend on education are higher.

The chairman of the International Project for the Evaluation of Educational Achievement (International Education Association), Benjamin Bloom, has hypothesized that the organization of the classroom had a great deal to do with the gap in achievement. Based on some educational theories of John B. Carroll,[13] he and his students have been running experiments to change the competitive atmosphere of the classroom to a cooperative one. They have also organized a hierarchy of remedial services to insure that students understand basic concepts before moving on to more complex applications. I understand that the results so far have been encouraging.

Perhaps if labor economists become interested in this problem, they may contribute to improving the effectiveness of schools. They may also contribute to a reorganization of curriculum choices. A cafeteria approach to curriculum may be hampering teaching and learning. The effects of multiple-course objectives upon motivation must be traded off against the difficulty of teaching under circumstances where multiple roll calls, administrative announcements, and cumbersome traffic regulations dominate the management concerns of the school.

The popular notion that a principal can make or break a school may also require examination by economists. Are there optimum ratios of supervisor to teacher? To what extent is it possible to trade off supervisory personnel at a lower pay for supervisory personnel who are paid relatively more?

While an analysis of education as an industry has been started for elementary and secondary education, little effort to link inputs with outputs has been evidenced in postsecondary sectors. The studies of Astin and his associates appear to indicate that there is a very high correlation between entering freshmen's Scholastic Aptitude Test scores and Graduate Record Examination scores.[14] This stability seems to hold for a large number of schools, irrespective of the level of resources expended.

These results are equivocal because the majority of postsecondary institutions cater to relatively homogeneous student bodies in terms of ability. We also know that the resources expended on education are roughly proportional to the ability of entering freshmen. Able students enjoy more resources expended than those who test less well.

An interesting hypothesis has been advanced by Lloyd Humphreys in an unpublished paper on the nature of intelligence. Humphreys claims that the effect of good schools should not be considered neutral and that the expenditure of resources has prevented the student body from regressing toward the mean. Humphreys' hypothesis certainly deserves testing. It would be interesting to rescale our expenditures with this hypothesis in mind and come up with a price for excellence, or at least above-average achievement. In order to perform this analysis, we would have to disaggregate the data from the less prestigious colleges and try to isolate the outcomes of students of above-average abilities in settings where expenditures are below average.

The whole matter of outcomes in higher education is extremely vexing. Postsecondary education has been justified on a variety of grounds, many of which appear to be intuitively reasonable. Some of these have since proved wrong, while others cannot be readily quantified. The most attractive argument for justifying further schooling is the demand for skilled manpower in a highly technological society. This argument is heard less and less these days as the output of postsecondary education is meeting, if not exceeding, the demand for professional, technical, and managerial workers. Forecasts of these developments were heard, but not heeded, some seven to ten years ago.[15]

Another argument used to justify postsecondary education is increased social awareness, translated into more frequent or more enlightened voting. Schultz has pointed out, in that connection, that this is one of the more expensive ways of getting high voter participation.[16]

Another argument, and this does seem to hold water, is that higher educational attainment results in longer participation in the labor force for men, i.e. greater flexibility and adaptability to change. For women, the results are even less equivocal. Labor participation for women of all ages substantially increases as their educational attainment rises.[17]

It may be reasonably argued that it is too early to ask the question: "What are we buying?" before homework has been completed on the costs of various levels and kinds of education. Although we do know that instructional costs vary both by level of instruction—lower-level undergraduate, upper-level undergraduate, and graduate students—and by type of curriculum—humanities, social sciences and physical sciences—the variations between individual institutions may dwarf the variations between levels and disciplines. A study at the U.S. Office of Education, which attempted to classify institutions along conventional lines—universities, four-year liberal arts colleges, teachers' colleges and junior colleges—threw very little light on why costs varied. It did raise some questions. Thus, private institutions spent somewhat more on undergraduates than state institutions; on the average, the cost of instruction of lower-level undergraduates is no less in junior colleges than in state institutions; and so on.[18]

Perhaps the data were equivocal and inconclusive because rough measures were used to allocate costs between graduate and undergraduate students. It may not be sufficient to divide salaries of senior faculty by the number of credit hours paid for by graduate students to derive a credit-hour cost. The status of the graduate student in a university is more complex. If my impression is correct, the presence of graduate students may reduce the cost of teaching undergraduates. Also, much of the funded research of senior faculty would probably be priced out of the market if they did not have access to cheap graduate-student labor. This question is raised despite the fact that I have little hope that it will be researched.

Without good cost information, we are left with the impression that bachelor's, master's, and doctorates cost vastly different amounts to produce. The variation is present within the same school and is probably even wider between schools. The costs to students also vary widely. The amount of the subsidy, i.e. costs less tuition, seems to favor able students. Able students get more resources expended on them. Generally, they do not pay the full excess cost of these resources. We are thus left with the unresolved question of whether the traditional pattern of rich schools attracting gifted students is justifiable, or whether we are pandering to an intellectual elite, largely the children of the well-to-do.

AN UNCONVENTIONAL VIEW OF EXTERNALITIES

It is now fashionable to look at the spillover effects of industry. We are just as worried about automobile exhaust fumes as about the car's cost in getting us to and from work. In the case of education, one of the externalities, the effect of education on income distribution, has not received the attention that it deserves.

In the elementary- and secondary-school sectors, additional attention should be paid to achievement levels. Currently, most of the analysis of returns to education has assumed that the number of years of schooling is what matters. In the postsecondary sector, where some part of the education is subsidized, though only a fraction of the population participates in the postsecondary experience, an even closer analytic look at what is produced is advisable.

Conventional cost/benefit analysis in which additional income was ascribed to a college education was based on the experience of a period during which (a) college places were rationed, and (b) subsidies, though substantial, did not provide subsistence allowances to the majority of needy students. Under those circumstances, it was quite likely that returns to postsecondary education would be high. In the first place, only the most able students with low-income parents gained access to postsecondary education; second, fewer college-educated persons were produced than were demanded by a society in which technology was advancing rapidly.

It would be interesting to describe a system where the differentials in incomes are kept to a minimum and the required number of college students are educated. In order to achieve this goal, every subsequent level of attainment should either cost less than the previous one, or have a lower internal rate of return. Subsidies are an obvious way to achieve this goal. It was argued elsewhere that subsidies to college students will reduce income differentials because the amount invested will be reduced, even if the expected rate of return does not change. It is also quite likely that the existence of subsidies will tend to depress the expected internal rates of return. The internal rate of return may very well depend upon the amount of the investment and the risk of not completing college for financial reasons. Thus, subsidies may have secondary income-leveling effects.[19]

From a policy point of view, it is imperative to estimate which proportion of the eligible population would be attracted to college, given different levels of subsidies, and what their subsequent earnings would be. It is quite likely that subsidies to students are going to claim large sums of public budgets because the student's investment, i.e., the cost of tuition and living expenses, is probably going to be an increasing burden to a larger number of American families. It has been creeping up as college costs escalate more rapidly than they were projected to in 1969, and an increasingly large proportion of personal income may be consumed by college expenses.

It may be necessary to estimate the burden of college expenses in relation to discretionary purchasing power—a concept developed by the National Industrial Conference Board—to quantify the amount remaining in the hands of consumers after net contractual savings and outlays for essential goods and services have been made.

In 1965–66, full-time undergraduate student costs were estimated at $4.9 billion, or 1.8 per cent of discretionary purchasing power. In 1968–69, they rose to $6.6 billion and amounted to 2 per cent of discretionary purchasing power. By 1975–76, it is quite possible that undergraduate costs will amount to $11.8 billion and may claim as much as 3.4 per cent of discretionary purchasing power. Even when grants and loan funds are subtracted from undergraduate outlays, the discretionary purchasing power devoted to paying for student undergraduate instruction is found to have risen 1.4 per cent to 1.7 per cent in 1969.[20]

Although these percentages seem small in relation to total discretionary purchasing power, it should be remembered that only one family in ten has children in college at any one time. Hence, possibly as much as one-third of the discretionary income of a typical family with children in college may be consumed by undergraduate outlays in 1975–76.

The increasing burden of college expenses, even in the upper-income groups, is no longer a trivial issue. An examination of costs is especially timely because of the new trend toward substituting loan funds for grants to the majority of the students. The current administration's proposals also place fairly low ceilings on the total amount of grants and loans available to all students, thus forcing a large number of children to attend low-cost community-type institutions.

The reasonableness of this policy, in the light of probable declines in the relative benefits of a college education, calls for some careful examination. The whole matter of available spaces, available subsidies, and the future supply of college-educated personnel should be viewed in the context of (a) meeting the social aspirations of Americans for a college degree, and (b) what they will actually receive if they get one, both in monetary and psychological terms.

CONCLUSIONS

Economists have tended to be very pleased when they could fit functions to the behavior of students or institutions so as to show that these groups' activities could be explained in rational terms. Beyond that, only a small number of economists have tried to crack the difficult problem of the educational production function.[21] Others have tried to measure the effects of changing the resource mix, or the levels of resources expended upon the education of slow learners, euphemistically called the disadvantaged.[22]

All of these efforts are to be welcomed, and they do contribute toward a better understanding of education as an industry. Yet they fall short of the goal of providing policy prescriptions, which may result from broader and more ambitious modeling of the process of learning and its consequences.

This paper has argued that a better understanding of learning theory may contribute to the building of more realistic educational production functions. It has implied that simple models of learning would prompt investment early in life, rather than later on. Also, it has indicated that the curriculum for slow learners must be special, not only in content, but also that its "power" should be several times higher than that of conventional curricula.

The implication of models of learning which broaden the relevant inputs to both family and school make this last argument even more compelling. For instance, in the Dugan model, in order to close the gap between blacks and whites and keep remedial expenditures at a reasonable 25 per cent of regular outlays, a technology 1.5 to 2.0 times as effective as the one used today must be devised.[23]

Since economists are generally concerned with tradeoffs, it would be well to look at tradeoffs in curriculum structure, organization of the classroom, school socioeconomic composition, and the relevant variables in the educational production function to devise an effective educational system. Only very modest beginnings have been made in this direction.

In the elementary and secondary educational sector, arguments about quantifying the outputs of the educational system beyond reading, writing, and arithmetic, to encompass other outputs such as citizenship, career orientation, and life adjustment, have been so free-form as to discourage economic analysis. While economists have been rightly discouraged by the vagueness of the debate on outputs, they should join it if for no other reason than to introduce educators to the concept of joint products. If educators were made to realize that a semiliterate person is less likely to make a satisfactory adjustment to the twentieth century world, this would dampen the ardor of those who argue that adjustment should be emphasized at the expense of reading.

The financial crisis in postsecondary education, which is already upon us, will certainly require even more attention to the outputs and purposes of colleges and universities. Issues such as the equalization of income will probably be mentioned more often in the face of a more generous supply of college graduates relative to demand.

Some recent projections for 1980, prepared by my staff and myself, place the supply of persons with bachelor's degrees at roughly 7 per cent over the demand for persons with this educational attainment. Thus, it is quite likely that the opportunities for college graduates to find employment in professional, technical, and managerial occupations will decrease considerably. The unemployment rate, which was practically nonexistent among these categories in the 1960s, may then go up drastically in the 1970s. (In the first year of this decade, unemployment among professional, technical, and kindred workers increased from 1.0 to 2.5 per cent.) These projections are based on naive extrapolations of past trends. It is quite possible that the lower B.A. recipients may fill less-skilled jobs. It is also possible that the more generous supply of college graduates in relation to demand may retard earnings growth for this type of labor.

Looking at education as an industry, it would be interesting to study how individual colleges and universities will be able to differentiate their product from that of others. Pressure to differentiate products is much more likely to be present in a buyer's market. It will also be interesting to see to what extent the customers of the institutions will be able to gauge the advantages to be gained from attending expensive versus cheap schools. The behavior of consumers of various types of postsecondary education is hence likely to become more important to institutions.

The reluctance of state legislatures and private donors to escalate their support to this sector will either: (1) force students and their families to shoulder a larger share of postsecondary costs, or (2) have the federal government carry an increasing burden in financing students. Unless there are drastic changes in the attitudes of the federal government, the level of support per student which it is willing to shoulder is not likely to meet the institutions' rising deficits per student. Could it be possible that expensive institutions will have unfilled places? No one is ready to make this forecast yet. But such an eventuality is not ruled out.

The problems of education in the next decade will be serious. Now is the time to build a macromodel, based on the scattered findings of micromodels such as the ones presented at this conference.

NOTES AND REFERENCES

1. U.S. Bureau of the Census, *1960 Census of Population*, PC(2)5a, Table 5.
2. U.S. Bureau of the Census, "Education of Fathers and Sons," Series P–20, No. 132.
3. Present writer's estimates of differentials from Social Security records, adapted from Phillip Cutright, *Achievement, Mobility and the Draft, Their Impart on the Earnings of Men* (Washington, D.C.: Department of Health, Education, and Welfare, Social Security Administration, O. R. S. Staff Paper 14, 1972).
4. Benjamin S. Bloom, *Stability and Change in Human Characteristics* (New York: John Wiley and Sons, 1964). See also J. McV. Hunt, *Intelligence and Experience* (New York: Ronald Press, 1961).
5. C. Marston Case, "A Revision of the Equal Opportunities Survey Estimates of the Relationship Between Child's Achievement and Father's Education," J. Froomkin and D. J. Dugan, editors, "Inequality: Studies in Elementary and Secondary Education" (U.S. Department of Health, Education, and Welfare, U.S. Office of Education, June 1969, processed).
6. Denis J. Dugan, "The Impact of Parental and Educational Investments Upon Student Achievement," ibid.
7. Alexander Mood, "Introduction," in George W. Mayeske et al., *A Study of Our Nation's Schools* (Washington, D.C.: Department of Health, Education, and Welfare, Office of Education, 1971), p. iii.
8. Henry Levin, "Recruiting Teachers for Large City Schools" (Washington, D.C.: Brookings Institution, 1968, processed).
9. Harry Piccariello, "Productivity of Schools," in "Inequality: Studies in Elementary and Secondary Education" (see note 5).
10. James S. Coleman et al., *Equality of Educational Opportunity* (Washington, D.C.: U.S. Department of Health, Education, and Welfare, U.S. Office of Education, 1966), p. 22.
11. Anthony Ottinger and Selma Marks, "Educational Technology, New Myths and Old Realities," *Harvard Educational Review* 38 (Fall 1968): 697 ff.
12. Torsten Husén, editor, *International Study in Mathematics* (New York: John Wiley, 1967), vol. II, esp. 31 ff.
13. John B. Carroll, "A Model of School Learning," *Teachers College Record* 64 (May 1963): 723 ff.
14. Alexander W. Astin, "Undergraduate Achievement and Institutional 'Excellence'," *Science* (August 16, 1968).
15. A. J. Jaffe and Joseph Froomkin, *Technology and Jobs* (New York: Praeger, 1968, chapter 14); also Neil H. Rosenthal and Janice H. Niepert, "Matching Sheepskins and Jobs," *Monthly Labor Review*, 91 (November 1968), p. 10.
16. Theodore W. Schultz, "Resources for Higher Education—An Economist's View," in *Financing Higher Education* (Princeton, N.J.: Educational Testing Service, 1971).
17. Malcolm S. Cohen, Samuel A. Rea, Jr., and Robert I. Lerman, *A Micro Model of Labor Supply*, BLS Staff Paper 4 (Washington, D.C.: U.S. Department of Labor, Bureau of Labor Statistics, 1970).
18. Joseph Froomkin, *Aspirations, Enrollments and Resources* (Washington, D.C.: U.S. Department of Health, Education, and Welfare, U.S. Office of Education, 1970, chapter 4).
19. ———, "Allocation of Resources to Education—Towards a Theory of Subsidy," *Budgeting, Programme Analysis and Cost Effectiveness in Educational Planning* (Paris: Organisation for Economic Cooperation and Development, 1968).
20. ———, *Aspirations, Enrollments and Resources*, p. 100 (see note 18).

21. Jesse Burkhead, Thomas G. Fox, and John W. Holland, *Input and Output in Large-City High Schools* (Syracuse: Syracuse University Press, 1967). Samuel Bowles, "Towards an Educational Production Function," in W. Lee Hansen, ed., *Education and Human Capital* (New York: NBER, 1970), pp. 11–61. Elchanan Cohn, "Economics of Scale in Iowa High School Operations," *Journal of Human Resources* 3 (1968): 422–34. Herbert J. Kiesling, "Measuring a Local Government Service: A Study of School Districts in New York State," *Review of Economics and Statistics* 49 (1967): 356–67.

22. Kiesling's paper for this conference is in this tradition.

23. Dugan, "Impact of Parental and Educational Investments" (see notes 5 and 6).

11 ‖ COMMENTS

Jerry Miner
The Maxwell School of
Citizenship and Public Affairs,
Syracuse University

Froomkin points out that his paper raises more problems than it can answer. In a discussion of policy toward the education industry, such a conclusion should be neither surprising nor disturbing. The important issue is whether the problems raised and the ways in which they are presented contribute to possible solutions. In the following remarks, I first discuss Froomkin's paper in terms of its contribution to better understanding and resolution of policy issues in the education industry, and then indicate some of my own views as regards a useful framework for these purposes.

This paper, as most of those presented at the conference, views the study of education as an industry primarily from the standpoint of the educational production function. Also, as in the other papers, education is virtually identified with formal schooling. As a result, the discussion of policy issues in education becomes almost inseparable from the problem of the proper specification of the production and cost functions of schools. Froomkin appears to share the general presumption that, difficult as the task may be, once these functions are specified, educational policy can proceed in accordance with the well-known principles of economic maximization. Henry Levin's contribution to the conference provides a thorough exposition of the application of these principles to education.

The propriety of concern for educational production functions can scarcely be questioned. Warnings about pitfalls in both the estimation and use of empirical studies of such functions may serve to improve the techniques employed and the sophistication with which results are related to policy. When, however, the subject is "policy issues" one hopes for more than another interpretation of the implications of input-output relations for re-source allocation decisions in schools.

Froomkin does provide, early in the paper, an indication of his conception of the essential policy problem in the education industry: "Education is being asked to equalize opportunity and control costs at the same time." He suggests that the first step that economists can take to solving this problem is, "to build models which describe what is happening in the educational process." If I interpret Froomkin correctly, the economists' models should treat equality of educational opportunity as the objective function. But, as Froomkin shows by reference to a variety of data and analysis, years of schooling received, performances on test scores, dropouts, earnings for those with equivalent years of schooling but differential test scores, and virtually all other operational measures of educational opportunity, reveal it to be concentrated among those already privileged and powerful.

What is to be done? Froomkin, if I read him rightly, suggests compensa-tory remedial and enrichment programs. However, he finds no basis in the empirical studies of school production functions for decisions about the character, intensity, and timing of such programs. Under these circum-stances, he turns to learning theory to provide estimates of the nature of the required enrichment or remedial training.

This is rather like using engineering specifications to estimate production functions in manufacturing, and its results are at least as arbitrary. This is not to say that learning theory is irrelevant to the matters at hand. But, because Froomkin chooses so general a learning hypothesis (learning rate $= \sqrt{age} \times$ educational effort) his conclusion is trivial and without sig-nificant policy implications: "it is quite likely that production functions in education are not uniform for children of different ages or of different abilities." We do not need learning theory to draw such conclusions. Instead of substituting the most general of hypotheses about learning for empirical analysis of the schooling process, what is needed are attempts to substan-tiate detailed hypotheses which relate specific learning situations to particu-lar consequences or outcomes.

Froomkin next takes up the problem of the interaction of the school, the pupil, and society in the determination of scholastic achievement. Scholastic achievement, a proxy for educational opportunity, should be equalized. If the school is to accomplish this, it is necessary to distinguish in-school from out-of-school influences. Here, however, Froomkin prefers parameters de-rived empirically rather than from learning theory. In this context, Froomkin reports on an approach he and others have developed for summarizing family influences on pupil achievements in a single continuous variable representing the amount of parental investment in their childrens' education. For the first time in the paper, the idea that education can be other than schooling arises, but only to avoid biasing estimates of the effects of in-school factors. My objection to the concept of parents' investment in chil-drens' education is that it, too, is so general that it ignores important underlying details. Of course, the variable, as measured, works in regression analysis of pupil achievements; it essentially substitutes for conventional socioeconomic (SES) status variables. To achieve the full potential of this sort of approach in the explanation of scholastic achievement requires rather detailed specifications of the amount and type of interaction among family members and the prevalence of such interactions across families.

The method reported on by Froomkin, however, incorporates none of this. A measure of educational investment derived by assuming that all parents spend equivalent time in educational activities with their children, and then weighting this equal time by the differential potential earning power of the parents, can reveal nothing about the different achievements accomplished through various types of parent-child interactions nor about the prevalence of such productive practices among various groups in society.

A better specified measure of parental investment would permit, among other things, a test of the significance of the association of pupil performance and parental attitudes toward school as found in the Plowden Report on *Children and Their Primary Schools* in England. The strongly positive association of students' performance and favorable attitudes of their parents toward schools may be a reflection of the time spent by such parents in educational activities with their children. If so, it would cast doubt on the policy of attempting to change the attitudes of parents of low SES and suggest instead the need for changes in their behavior.

Froomkin concludes by pointing to some of the problems which remain unresolved due to lack of knowledge of the educational production function. These include the inability to specify tradeoffs among school inputs, especially between labor and capital and among types of labor, the ignorance of the effects of alternative organizational structures, the failure to establish a hierarchy of goals, and even the mundane matter of the costs of existing school programs.

Policy conclusions deal primarily with suggestions for further study. Thus, Froomkin worries about the projected surplus of secondary school graduates in relation to the rising costs of college education. This leads him to wonder how colleges will vary their products to avoid unfilled places or how future earnings of college students may be affected. He regards the application of learning theory to education as potentially highly fruitful. Finally, he avers, "Now is the time to build a macromodel based on the scattered findings of micromodels. . . ." But, this conclusion hardly seems warranted by what has gone before. We have little firm knowledge of production relations in schools, no model of the interaction of schools and other sources of education, and, most important, no substantive treatment in Froomkin's paper of the interrelation of educational outputs and the economy or society. Without specification of the structural relations between education and manpower, output, and economic growth, it is difficult to conceive what a macroeconomic model of education might be like. Surely, such macromodels cannot be built solely out of the findings of micro cost or production models. One component of a macro educational model would, of course, encompass production of education, but this part would have to be structurally integrated within a wider system whose elements are not mentioned.

It is probably evident by now that my major reservations about the present paper concern the omission of what appear, to me, to be the truly important issues of policy for the education industry. To treat schooling as the totality of the education industry diverts attention from perhaps the most basic policy question. What are the consequences of alternative mixes of educational modes? These include formal schooling for the young; informal education in homes, churches, and community organization, and through personal interactions; books, television, and other media; job-related education; and organized adult education—in specialized schools or through other institutions, including labor organizations and the military. Possibilities here encompass both combinations of modes and the timing of exposure to various modes over the lifetime of the individual. A recent study of the Educational Policy Research Center of Syracuse University has shown more people involved in the educational periphery than in the formal educational core. The identification of education with schooling so narrows the alternatives that the analysis of policy choices in the education industry tends to degenerate into studies of school production functions and their inevitably ambiguous implications for policy.

Even taken on its own terms, Froomkin's perspective does not at all recognize contemporary criticism of the school as an organization which promotes conformity and individual repression. Policy toward education as an industry cannot ignore the role of schools in fostering racism and stultifying intellectual and emotional growth. Without accepting in full the views of Kozol, Silberman, Kohl, Illich, and others, economists concerned with policy must look beyond the resources needed to attain minimum standards, or to achieve equality in the performance of schools or of pupils, to the question of whether any of these performances are personally or socially destructive. Clearly, this point is related to the previous one. If the production function in schools cannot be altered to reduce their destructive effects to tolerable limits, greater emphasis on alternative educational instruments is called for. Limitations of measures of output to pupil performance provides no information on these vital matters.

A most useful area of policy-oriented research would be to examine the organizational, staffing, and other implications of some of the more radical proposals for school reform. So far, little is known about differences in the administrative and personnel requirements of various proposals for extensive modification of the conventional classroom situation. No amount of empirical analysis of existing schools will provide cost and output information about as yet untried models. Ultimately, pilot studies may yield some of this information, but preliminary analysis can suggest what one or another of these alternatives would look like in operation, and what might be its input requirements and organizational character.

If the school is to change—not simply to provide all with equal opportunity but to enhance human potential—new forms of control, governance, and finance are necessary. Here is a vital area for policy, and although Froomkin makes mention of school organization as a factor influencing productivity, he does not discuss alternatives and their possible significance. In addition to the conventional concerns of public versus private operation and finance of schools (i.e. the problem of pricing) we need to turn our attention to how such arrangements as a school inspectorate, central influence over curriculum and location of school buildings, and nationwide collective bargaining for teachers might influence what happens in classrooms. Evidence of many of these matters is available from comparative analysis of education, especially in Western Europe. For example, the studies of comparative pupil achievement by the International Association for the Evaluation of Educational Achievement hold promise of exposing relations between achievement and types of school organization and control with which we in the United States have had little or no experience.

Finally, in addition to looking at the school within the context of the entire educational system and at its social, cultural, and political effects, policy requires attention to linking skills learned in school with future demands for them. Policies toward schools must be concerned with curriculum, with the mix of special and general training and the timing of specialization, with the availability of places in various fields in higher education, and with incentives for students. All these, in turn, must be rationalized with sources of training other than schools. Froomkin touches on some of these points, but his overriding concern for internal production relations leads him to gloss over them.

Equality of schooling is an important concern. We must know something of the consequences of inputs on outputs in schools. The education industry, however, extends far beyond the formal school. Proper concern for the inputs provided and the outputs produced by schools greatly transcends the question of whether all pupils enjoy equal amounts of either. If the future of our society is dependent upon education to a substantial degree, discussions of it, especially by economists, must concern the relations of the school and other educational institutions to the economic and social order and to the determination of man's place in it.

J. Alan Thomas

University of Chicago

Economists have already made important contributions to the study of policy issues in education. Most of their theroretical and empirical contributions to the examination of such issues have been at the macro level, utilizing rate-of-return techniques to assess the effect of investments in education. As a result of the work of Becker, Dennison, Hansen, and others, we are now able to address ourselves, although crudely, to such important policy questions as: How much should society invest in education as opposed to other public and private undertakings? How should resources be allocated among the various levels of education? What is the cost/benefit relationship associated with major technological alternatives, such as the increased use of educational television? Is the productivity of educational systems increasing or decreasing over time?

Since this conference has been devoted to the analysis of education as an industry, Froomkin's paper is properly concerned with micro- rather than macroanalysis. He discusses economic production functions, which provide a means to deal with problems of resource allocation within educational systems. While these studies are still at an early stage, the work of Kiesling, Levin, and others may well lead to better resource allocation within schools and school districts.

As a person whose prime interest is in the improvement of education, I welcome the contribution which Froomkin describes. In my opinion, economists are uniquely able to deal with the kinds of issues that govern the development and operation of educational systems. In particular, they can attempt to deal with the recalcitrance of systems that appear to be committed to practices leading to constant or even decreasing productivity.

The difficulties facing economists as they approach these problems are immense. In particular, they must recognize that the main dependent variables at their disposal (in particular, student achievement) are psychological and not economic. Furthermore, the independent variables also tend to be based on psychology and sociology rather than economics. The tools of microeconomics can therefore be applied to education, but a great deal of patience and a willingness to work with scholars from other disciplines are required. In other words, production-function studies can be most meaningful when approached from an interdisciplinary framework.

A prerequisite for success is an understanding that important and sophisticated work has already been conducted by scholars in other fields. The literature in child development is extensive.[1] There are numerous empirical studies dealing with the education of the disadvantaged. Research into the relationship between learning patterns and students' backgrounds is well advanced.[2]

However, these psychological studies usually ignore such basic economic concepts as cost, and hence the feasibility of proposed treatments is often doubtful. Economists with their tools of marginal analysis can provide an input which is indispensable if psychological studies of learning are to be put into practice. Since most empirical work in education has lacked an economic dimension, new experiments which identify the parameters of production functions, and which can determine the degree to which one set of inputs can be substituted for another are required.[3] This approach appears much more promising than the continued mining of questionable cross-sectional data.

NOTES AND REFERENCES

1. For example, see R. Hess and V. Shipman, "Early Experience and the Socialization of Cognitive Modes in Children," *Child Development* 36 (1965): 869.

2. For example, see Kenneth Eelles, Allison Davis, Robert J. Havighurst, Virgil E. Herrick, and Ralph T. Tyler, *Intelligence and Cultural Differences* (Chicago: University of Chicago Press, 1950); Susan S. Stodolsky and G. S. Lesser, "Learning Patterns in the Disadvantaged," *Harvard Educational Review* 37 (1967): 546–93.

3. William Garner has begun such a study, "Identification of an Educational Production Function by Experimental Means," Ph.D. dissertation in progress, Department of Education, University of Chicago.

Index

Ability, dropout rates by, 458

Absolute inequality aversion-constant, 230

"ACE sample," 420–22

Achievement, 53–93; computer-assisted instruction and, 209–18; decisions governing enrollment in higher education and, 55–66; determinants of, 72–77; higher education demand and, 318–25; implications of analysis of, 77–78; IQ and, 202; output of, 161, 193, 195; standardized, 161–63; teacher experience and, 86–87

Admissions standards, graduate school, 15

Aggregation results on higher education demand: achievement, 318–25; detailed state, 310–18

Aid to Families with Dependent Children (AFDC), 259, 261, 266, 272

Aigner, D. J., 157, 176, 185n

Alcaly, Roger, 272

Allocative efficiency, 153–54, 168, 169, 191–92, 195; maximization of, 171

American Council on Education, 429

American Institute for Research, 133n, 253, 458

Anderson, Kent, 249n

Aptitude influences: on higher education decisions, 65; on higher education rationing, 71

Arithmetic, computer-assisted instruction in, 204–205; differential performance in, 245–46; gains in, 209–13

Armacost, R. L., 377

Army Research Office, U.S., 371n

Arrow, Kenneth, 155

Astin, Alexander W., 98, 136–38

Atkinson, A. B., 218, 222–24

Atkinson, Richard C., 201–47

Attrition from Ph.D. programs, 19–27

Average input coefficients, ranking of nonuniversity groups by, 436

Average production isoquants, 165

Averch, Harvey, 249n, 251

Baird, Leonard, 136–41

Ball, J., 233, 238n

Barro, Stephen, 249n

Bartell, Ernest, 53n

BASIC, 207–208, 216

Baumol, William J., 150, 197, 361

Bayer, A. E., 137

Becker, Gary, 82n

Becker, Howard S., 172, 478

Behavioral assumptions on efficiency, 156–61; incentives and reward structures in, 160; knowledge of production set and, 157; little or no competition and, 158–59; prices of inputs and outputs and, 159–60; signals of success or failure in, 160–61; standardized achievement and, 161–63; substantial management discretion and, 158

Bell, Colin E., 405–408

Bell, Terrel, 149

Berkeley, University of California at, 3–51, 338; Carnegie undergraduate plan and, 401–404; Center for Research and Development in Higher Education of, 307; departmental behavior at, 6–27; differences in departmental performance at, 3–6; instructional costs at, 371, 406–407, 411–12; student dropout fractions for, 391–92; student enrollment and flow rates for, 390–91; student lifetimes at, 392; teacher-student ratios at, 392; unit chain costs at, 394–96; unit node costs at, 392–94

Berls, Robert H., 363n

Binary numbers, 207

Black students, home environment of, 464

Blalock, H. M., Jr., 139

Blaug, Mark, 363n, 364n

Block, H. D., 304, 345n

Bloom, Benjamin S., 184n, 460, 466

Boardman, Anthony E., 185n

Boneau, C. A., 214n, 215n

Boston Metropolitan Area, 54, 57, 78–79, 85; statistical characteristics of data on, 79–82

Boston Standard Metropolitan Statistical Area (SMSA), 55, 57, 60, 77, 80

Bouton, Jim, 284

Bowen, William G., 361

Bowles, Samuel S., 92, 150–52, 162, 163, 166, 174, 175, 185n, 198, 203, 271

Brandle, John, 282

Brewster-Zacharias Plan, 90

Brian, D., 205

British universities, 364n

Brookings Institution, 349n, 462

Brown, Byron, 150

Brown, David, 28–29, 39, 40, 367

Brown, Murray D., 137, 185n

Burkhead, Jesse, 150

Butler, C., 231

Cain, Glen G., 151, 175, 185n

California: computer-assisted instruction in, 209, 210, 220–21, 245–46; compensatory education in, 249–90; Department of Education of, 184; Department of Finance of, 17; Division of Compensatory Education of, 249n; higher education demand in, 307, 310–13, 317; University of, 296–97, 306, 371n. See also Berkeley, University of California at

Callahan, Raymond, 88, 89

Cameroun, primary schools in, 374

Campbell, E. Q., 203

Campbell, Robert, 295–96, 301, 302

Campus Statistics (Office of Institutional Research), 390

Caplow, T., 11, 13

Carlson, Richard C., 186n

Carlson, Sune, 184n

Carnegie Commission on Future of Higher Education, 293, 373, 349n, 415n; undergraduate plan of, 396–404, 412

Carnegie Corporation of New York, 249n

Carnoy, Martin, 149, 174

Carpenter, Margaret (Polly), 249n

Carroll, John B., 466

Carroll, Stephen, 249n

Cartter, Allan, 28

Cartter Report, 13, 39, 40, 48, 431

Case, C. Marston, 462

Categories, comprehension, 206

Census, U.S., 457

Chain, definition of, 377

Chain flows, 384

Chalupsky, Albert B., 162

Change, incentives for, 361–63

Chemistry faculty and students, interviews with, 44–46

Chemistry Ph.D. candidates, 4–5, 21–22, 24, 26–27

Chicago, University of, 460

Chickering, A. W., 137

Children and Their Primary Schools (Plowden Report), 476

Chiswick, Barry, 349n

Chu, S. F., 157, 176, 185n

Classroom instruction, compensatory, 262–63

Cohn, Elchanan, 155

Cohort model, 379–84

Coleman, James S., 93n, 152, 159, 185n, 203, 209

Coleman Report, 237, 278n, 280n, 283, 460

Colorado, University of, 371, 401

College aspirations of high school seniors, 457

Colleges, 48, 116–18, 231, 401, 409–10, 413n, 460. See also Berkeley, University of California at; Higher education (various entries); Stanford University

Comanor, W., 157

Compensatory education, 249–90; coordination and leadership variables in, 263–64; data collection on, 258–60; description of process for, 252–53; description of six best projects for, 268–69; diagnosis by psychologists of need for, 264; equipment for, 263; factors associated with successful, 254; gain scores and, 273–74; individual instruction in, 254–56; instructional intensity by type of instructor for, 262; means, standard deviations, and description of variables for, 265–66; methodological considerations for research on, 251–52; model for, 252–54; organization of report on, 250; percentage of instruction in regular classroom for, 262–63; performance measure for, 260–61, 275–76; pooling of grade data on, 274–75; prior findings on, 253–54; program management and coordination for, 256–58; purpose of study of, 250; socioeconomic variables and, 261–62; use of educational materials and equipment in, 263; weighting and, 276–77. *See also* Computer-assisted instruction

Competition among schools, 158–59

Comprehension categories, 206

Comprehension sentences, 206

Computer-assisted instruction (CAI), 194, 201–47; achievement gains from, 209–18; in arithmetic, 204–205, 209–13, 245–46; assessment of differential performance in, 209–26, 245–47; in computer programming, 207–209, 216–18, 246–47; costs of, 227–40; per student cost, 234–36; in reading, 205–207, 213–16, 246; reduction in inequality through, 218–26, 229; in rural areas, 231–36

Computer programming. *See under* Computer-assisted instruction

Constant absolute inequality aversion, 230

Constant relative inequality aversion, 229

Consumer Price Index, 352, 363n

COOP (California Cooperative Primary Reading Test), 214–15

Corazzini, Arthur, 53n

Cronbach, Lee J., 273

Cross-sectional data, uses of, 384, 426–30

Curriculum: for computer-assisted instruction, 228, 231; graduate school, 16

Cutright, Phillip, 459

Cyert, Richard M., 184n, 186n

Dahl, R. A., 155

Daniere, Andre, 97

Data collection on compensatory education, 258–60

Demand: exogenous, 378; for higher education, 293–348; for Ph.D.'s, 28–29

Denison, Edward F., 363n, 364n

Department of Labor, U.S., 28

Departments, graduate school: admissions standards of, 15; curriculum of, 16; differences in attrition patterns of, 23–27; individual faculty members in, 12–15; information available to students from, 16; invest-

ment model of graduate student behavior in, 9–12; performance of, 3–6; resources of, 17; success rates of, 19–23

Design, instructional, 255–56

Destination node, definition of, 378

Dispersion of variables, 80

Donaldson, Ted, 249n

Downs, Anthony, 184n

Dreeben, Robert, 162

Dropout fractions, 458; at Berkeley, 391–92; at Stanford, 386–87

Dugan, Dennis J., 59–93, 183n, 462, 471

Duncan, O. D., 139

Dunn, Robert M., Jr., 302

Efficiency in education, 149–90; allocative, 153–54; behavioral assumptions and, 156–61; data availability, 159–60; educational production functions and, 151–53; empirical application of, 175–83; frontier estimates for, 176–83; incentive and reward structures for, 160; lack of knowledge of production set and, 157; lack of substantial management discretion and, 158; little or no competition and, 158–59; sample for, 175–76; scale and, 155; signals of success or failure and, 160–61; social welfare, 154–55; standardized achievement as educational output and, 161–63; technical, 153–54; technical inefficiency in producing achievement and, 163–70

Elashoff, R. M., 214n, 215n

Elasticities: in cross-sectional analysis of faculty-student ratios, 439–42; of higher education demand, 325–30

Electrical engineering faculty and students, interviews with, 49–50

Elementary and Secondary Education Act (ESEA) (1965), Title I of, 92, 202, 250, 252, 276, 283

England, primary schools in, 476

English department faculty and students, interviews with, 46–49

English Ph.D.'s, 4–5, 32, 41; placement of, 42–43

Enrolled student time per degree, 5

Enrollment: decisions governing, *See* Higher education enrollment decisions; flow rates and, 390–91; representation of, 378

Equal Opportunity Report, 462, 465

Excess demand, ranking of disciplines by, 29

Exogenous demands, 378

Exogenous supplies, 378
Expenditures per pupil, 76
Experience of teachers, 86–87; relative prices and marginal products for, 183

Faculty, graduate school: interviews with, 41; prestige maximization by, 12–15
Faculty-student ratios, 415–50; ACE sample on, 418–20; cross-sectional analysis, 428–44; elasticities of, 439–42; fixed coefficient model for, 420–28; instructional costs and, 389–90, 392; multicollinearity and other specific problems of, 442–43; Office of Education statistics on, 417–18; problems in use of cross-sectional data on, 424–28; problems in use of time series data on, 421–24; recent historical trends in, 417–20; regression analysis for undergraduate and master's level institutions, 431–36; regression analysis for universities, 436–39; sample for, 430–31; variable input coefficient model for, 429–30
Failure, signals of, 160–61
Family: higher education decisions and, 61, 64, 65; income of, 57–58, 77; rationing and, 71; scholastic achievement and, 76–77; size of, 58, 76–77
Farrell, Michael, 153, 157, 185n
Far Western Regional Laboratory, 278n
Feldman, K. A., 136–38
Fixed-coefficient model: problems in use of cross-sectional data in, 424–28; problems in use of time-series data in, 421–24; simple, 420–21
Flow rate, students', 378; enrollment and, 390–91
Ford Foundation Four-Year Guaranteed Assistance Program in the Humanities and Social Sciences, 387
Fox, K. A., 376
French Ph.D. candidates: annual production of, 33–34; attrition pattern of, 25, 27, 32; success rate of, 21–23
Friedman, Milton, 150, 182n
Frontier and average production isoquants, 165
Frontier and average production relations, 179–80
Froomkin, Joseph N., 455–80
Full time equivalent (FTE) faculty, 14; funding for, 17
Furby, Lita, 273

Gain scores, 273–74
Gallup, George, 149, 150, 159
Galper, Harvey, 302
Garner, William, 480n
German Ph.D.'s, 32; annual production of, 35–36
GIGO (Garbage In Garbage Out) production function, 198
Gini coefficients, 204, 218–22, 243
Gintis, Herbert, 162, 174, 184n, 198
Gittell, Marilyn, 159, 160
Goodrich, H. B., 97
Grabowski, Henry, 53n
Grade data, pooling of, 274–75
Graduate Record Examination, 98, 467
Graduate school attendance, investment in college training and, 95–147; data sources on, 99; determinants of, 142–45; empirical results of, 108–24; estimation technique for, 145–46; functional form and estimation procedure for, 101–102; linear model of, 108–16; logit analysis of, 127–33; measures of input for, 102–108; measures of output for, 99–101, 141–42; multicollinearity and the interpretation of empirical results in, 146–47; nonlinearities of, 118–24; other studies of, 96–99; principal component analysis of, 127; production function and, 145; public and private colleges compared, 116–18
Graduate school departments. See Departments, graduate school
Graduate students: interviews with, 41–50; investment model of behavior of, 9–12
Greer, Colin, 149
Griliches, Zvi, 153, 162, 172, 352, 363n
Guszak, Frank J., 256, 269
Guthrie, James W., 151

Haggstrom, Gus, 447–52
Hall, Lady, 185n
Hansen, W. Lee, 53, 289, 478
Hanushek, Eric Alan, 92, 150–52, 159, 161, 183n, 191–96, 271, 278n
Harris, Seymour E., 361
Hartley, Harry J., 160
Harvard University, 48
Hawkridge, David G., 162, 253–54, 258
Hawthorne effects, 245
Head Start Programs, 290
Health, Education and Welfare Department, U.S., 149, 160

Hedrick, Charles L., 184n, 186n
Herriott, Robert E., 172
Heyns, Barbara L., 84–89
Higher education, estimation of demand for, 330–38; organization of, 361–363
Higher education demand, 293–348; achievement aggregation results for, 318–25; alternative specifications for, 309–10; data and sampling on, 307–308; detailed state aggregation results on, 310–18; elasticities of, 325–30; models and estimation procedures for, 302–307, 330–38; qualitative information on, 330; review and critique of literature on, 295–302
Higher Education Directory (Office of Economic Opportunity), 450
Higher education enrollment decisions, 55–72; environmental influences, 61, 64, 65; family income and, 57–58; family size and, 58; market and nonmarket rationing in, 66–72; per cent nonwhite in community and, 58; regression analysis of, 59–62; Scholastic Aptitude Test scores and, 58, 63; school environment and, 62–63
Higher Education Facilities Act, 367
Higher Education General Information Survey (HEGIS), 133n, 141, 426, 432
Higher education investments, 95–147; determinants of graduation and graduate school attendance and, 142–45; empirical results on, 108–24; estimation technique for, 145–46; logit analysis of, 127–33; measures of educational output, 141–42; model of, 99–108; multicollinearity and, 146–47; other studies of, 96–99; principal component analysis of, 127; production function and, 145
Higher education output: analysis of unit chain costs in, 394–96; Carnegie undergraduate plan and, 396–404; cohort model of, 379–84; notation and terminology for, 377–79; quality of, 351–53; related work on, 374–77; sources and analysis of institutional data on, 385–96
Higher education output trends, 349–69; defining and measuring inputs for, 354–55; defining and measuring output for, 350–53; organization and incentives for change in, 361–63; tentative estimates of, 356–60
Higher Horizons project, 284
History Ph.D. candidates, 4–5
Hobson, C. J., 203

Hoenack, Stephen A., 296–302, 306–307, 346–48
Holland, J. L., 98
Hollander, T. Edward, 159
Hopkins, David S. P., 371–413
Humphreys, Lloyd, 467
Hunt, Shane, 96–97

Iannacone, Laurence, 159
IBM Corporation, 371n
Identification of letters, 206
Illinois: higher education demand in, 307, 310–12, 314, 317; University of, 231
Incentives in education, 160, 361–63
Income: higher education decisions and, 57–58; illustrative contributions of education to, 459; scholastic achievement and, 77
Individualized instruction, 254–56
Industry production surface, approximation of, 170
Inequality: computer-assisted instruction in reduction of, 218–26; Gini coefficient of, 219–22; value explicit measures of, 222–26
Information available to graduate students, 16
Inputs in education production: in higher education, defining and measuring, 102–108, 254–55; management discretion over obtaining, 158; means of, and standard deviations, 103, 104; prices of, 159–60; teacher, 193–94; technical inefficiency and, 167, 168
In-service training, 258
Instructional costs of university outputs, 371–413; Carnegie undergraduate plan and, 396–404; cohort model for, 379–384; notation and terminology for, 377–79; related work on, 374–77; student dropout fractions and, 386–87, 391–92; student enrollment and flow rates and, 385–86, 390–91; student lifetimes and, 387–89, 392; teacher-student ratios and, 389–90, 392; unit chain costs in, 394–96; unit node costs in, 390, 392–94
Intensity, instructional, 255, 262
International Project for the Evaluation of Educational Achievement (International Education Association), 466, 478
Investment model of graduate student behavior, 9–12
Investments in higher education, 95–147; data sources on, 99; determinants of graduation and graduate school attendance and, 142–45; empirical results on, 108–24; estimation

technique for, 145–46; functional form and estimation procedure for, 101–102; linear model of, 108–16; measures of input for, 102–108; measures of output for, 99–101, 141–42; multicollinearity and, 146–47; non-linearities in, 118–24; other studies of, 96–99; principal component analysis of, 127; production function and, 145; public and private colleges compared, 116–18

IQ, 202

Isoquants, 165

Jackson, Philip W., 162
James, Estelle, 408–13
Jamison, Dean T., 201–47
Jaszi, George, 363n
Jencks, Christopher, 151, 159, 160
Jenny, Hans, 450
Jensen, Arthur R., 202, 203, 280n
Jerman, M., 205
Jewish children, educational attainment of, 464
Judy, R., 374, 405

Kain, John F., 151
Karpoff, Peter, 97
Karweit, Nancy, 159
Katzman, Martin, 150
Keith, John, 53n
Kelley, Allen C., 201n, 240–45, 289
Kendrick, John W., 363n
Kentucky, computer-assisted instruction in, 209
Kershaw, J. A., 160
Kiesling, Herbert J., 150, 151, 155, 202–203, 236, 244, 249–90
Kleindorfer, George B., 151
Klevorick, Alvin K., 53n, 141–47
Knapp, R. H., 97
Knight, Frank, 185n
Koenig, H., 375, 376, 405
Koerner, James D., 362
Krathwohl, D. R., 184n

Lau, Lawrence, J., 157
Law, Alex, 249n
Leadership variables in compensatory education, 263–64
Learning-related characteristics, rate of accumulation of, 460
Leibenstein, Harvey, 153, 157, 185n, 192
Lekan, H. A., 202
Letter identification, 206

Levin, Henry M., 149–98, 203, 282, 368, 465
Levine, D. B., 219
Levy, Frank, 90–93
Lifetimes, student, 378; at Berkeley, 392; at Stanford, 387–89
Lindblom, C. E., 155
Linear model of investments in higher education, 108–16
Linn, R. L., 137, 139
Little, I. M. D., 155
Logit analysis, 127–33
Longitudinal data, 384
Lorenz curve, 204, 218–20, 243
Lorton, P., 208
Los Angeles County Department of Compensatory Education, 249n
Luce, R. D., 345n, 346n
Lyke, Robert F., 159, 160

McCormack, William, 249n
McFadden, Daniel, 304, 338n, 345n
McGee, R., 13
Machine readiness in computer-assisted instruction, 206
McKean, R. N., 160
McPartland, J., 203
Management discretion, 158
Mansfield, Edwin, 361
March, J. G. A., 186n
Marginal input coefficients, ranking nonuniversity groups by, 438
Marginal products, 182; relative prices and, 183
Marjorie Webster Junior College, 362
Market higher education rationing, 66–72
Marschak, J., 304, 345n
Masia, B. B., 184n
Mason, W., 162
Massachusetts: Board of Higher Education of, 53n, 297–301; higher education demand in, 307, 310–12, 315, 317–18
Maximization: of allocative efficiency, 171; of prestige, 12–15
Mechling, Jerry, 97
Merton, R. K., 12
Metropolitan Area Planning Council, 297, 298
Metropolitan Readiness Test (MET), 213
Michelson, Stephan, 150–52, 175, 185n, 201n, 209, 251
Michigan, public institutions in, 364n
Miller, Leonard S., 293–348, 417n, 426, 432
Miner, Jerry, 474–78

Mississippi, computer-assisted instruction in, 209–11, 213, 220–21, 245–46
Mobility, 261–62
Model-33 teletypewriter, 232
Mongello, Beatrice O., 184n
Mood, Alexander M., 203, 465
Mooney, Joseph, 6
Morningstar, M., 205
Morrison, Donald F., 134n
Muller, Jurgen, 185n
Multicollinearity, 444–45; investments in higher education and, 146–47
Multiplexing and communication system for computer-assisted instruction, 228, 233, 234, 235
Murnane, Richard, 150
Mushkin, Selma, 160

National Academy of Sciences, 40
National Industrial Conference Board, 470
National Research Council, 32
National Science Foundation, 201n, 371n, 417n, 431
Navy training schools, 362
Nelson, Valerie, 162
Nerlove, Marc, 157
Newberry, D., 218
Newcomb, T. M., 136, 137
Newhouse, Joseph, 280n
New York City school system, 184n
New York Higher Horizons project, 285
Nonmarket higher education rationing, 66–72
North Carolina, higher education demand in, 307, 310–11, 316–18

Office of Analytical Studies, 296
Office of Economic Opportunity, 288, 290
Office of Education, 133n, 162, 173, 363n, 364n; faculty-student ratio, statistics of, 419–20, 447, 450; National Center for Educational Statistics of, 133n; Office of Program Planning of, 462; Survey on Equal Educational Opportunity of, 175
O'Neill, June, 349–69, 447, 451
O'Neill, Dave M., 349n, 362
Opportunity costs of computer-assisted instruction, 236–38
Oriental children, educational attainment of, 464
Origin node, definition of, 377
Output, educational, 151–53; choice of combinations of, 156; instructional costs of, 371–

415; means of, 103, 104; measures of, 99–101, 141–42; prices of, 159–60; "quality" of, 351–53; standardized achievement as, 161–63

Pace, C. R., 137, 138
Panos, R. J., 137
Peck, Kim, 141n
Perl, Lewis J., 95–147, 150
Peterson, R. E., 136
Pfanzagl, J., 224
Pfouts, Ralph W., 184n
Ph.D. production process, 3–52; admissions standards and, 15; analysis of objective function of departments in, 17–19; curriculum and, 16; demand for Ph.D.'s and, 28–29; differences in attrition patterns in, 23–27; differences in departmental performance in, 3–6; individual faculty members and, 12–15; information available to students in, 16; interviews with faculty and students on, 41–50; investment model of graduate student behavior and, 9–12; placement of Ph.D.'s and, 32–41; resources and, 17; success rates in, 19–23; supply of Ph.D.'s and, 29–32; theory of departmental behavior in, 9–18
Phonics, 206
Piccariello, Harry, 202, 465
Pincus, John, 184n
Pittsburgh, University of, 133n
Placement of Ph.D.'s, 32–41
PLATO IV, 231
Plowden Report, 476
Policy analysis, 368–69
Policy issues in education, 77–78, 455–80; concept of equality of educational opportunity in, 456–59; cost-benefit problems of, 465–66; curriculum and, 466–67; economic analysis of, 462–65; effect of organization and, 466; equalizing learning rates as, 459–62; higher education outcomes and, 467–68; production functions and, 462–69; unconventional view of externalities and, 469–70
Policy variables, 384
Political science Ph.D.'s, 4–5, 32, 37–38
Pollak, William, 160
Potter, J., 233
Prestige, departmental, 12–15
Prestige groupings: academic placements in, 41; definition of, 40
Prestige Index of colleges and universities, 39

Prices: input and output, 159–60; relative, 183

Principal component analysis, 127

Private colleges. *See* Colleges

Production functions, educational, 145, 151–53

Production set, lack of management knowledge of, 157

Program management for compensatory education, 256–58

Project on Econometric Models of Higher Education, 293

Project Talent, 133*n*, 137, 141, 147, 307

Psychologists, diagnosis of need for compensatory education by, 264

Public colleges. *See* Colleges

Radner, Roy, 308, 338*n*, 415–50, 426, 432

Rand Corporation, 249*n*, 278*n*, 279*n*

Rapp, Marjorie, 249*n*

Rationing of higher education, 66–72

Reading, computer-assisted instruction in, 205–207, 213–16, 246

Regression analysis: of faculty-student ratios, 431–39; of higher education decisions, 59–62

Relative inequality aversion, constant, 229

Relative prices, 183

Report on Doctoral Programs (National Research Council), 32

Research assistanceship (RA) positions, 14

Resources, departmental, 17

Reward structures, 160

Ribich, Thomas, 249*n*, 272, 282–86

Richards, J. M., Jr., 138

Riew, John, 155

Rivlin, Alice M., 184*n*

Roberts, A. Oscar H., 162

Rock, D. A., 137, 139

Rogers, David, 160

Roose, Kenneth D., 450–52

Rural areas, costs of computer-assisted instruction in, 231–36

Ryder, Gerald, 249*n*

St. John, Nancy H., 172

Saks, Daniel, 150

Salter, W. E. G., 157, 185*n*

Satellite system for computer-assisted instruction, costs of, 234

Scale, efficiency and, 155

Scanlon, William J., 53

Schoenfeldt, L. F., 137

Scholastic achievement, 53–93; computer-assisted instruction and, 209–18; expenditures per pupil and, 76; family income and, 57–58, 77; family size and, 58, 76–77; higher education demand and, 318–25; implications of analysis of, for policy considerations, 77–78; IQ and, 202; market and nonmarket rationing and, 66–72; methodology for study of, 73–74; per cent nonwhite in community and, 58, 76; regression analysis of, 59–62; Scholastic Aptitude Test scores and, 58, 63; school environment and, 62–63

Scholastic Aptitude Test (SAT), 72–78, 80–82, 84, 90, 92, 94, 294, 309, 310, 318, 320, 467; means of, 75

School environment, influences of, 61–64, 71

School to College: Opportunities for Post Secondary Education (SCOPE), 294, 307, 330

Schrag, Peter, 159

Schultz, Theodore W., 361

Schultze, Charles L., 184*n*

Science (magazine), 98

Sen, A., 238*n*

Senegal, primary schools in, 374

Sengupta, J. K., 376

Sentences, comprehension, 206

"Sesame Street" (television show), 209*n*

Sex factors in higher education demand, 299, 301

Shellhammer, Tom, 249*n*

Siegel, B. W., 295–96, 301, 302

Sietsema, John P., 184*n*

Sight-word vocabulary, 206

Silberman, Charles, 149

SIMPER (Simple Instruction Machine for the Purpose of Educational Research), 207–208

Singer, N. M., 219

Size of family: higher education decisions and, 58; scholastic achievement and, 76–77

Slimick, J., 208

SLOGO (Stanford LOGO), 207–208

Smith, Adam, 150, 182*n*

Social mobility, 87

Social Security System, U.S., 459

Social welfare efficiency, 154–55, 156, 191–92

Socioeconomic status: compensatory education and, 261–62; dropout rates by, 458; higher education demand and, 301

South Carolina State College, 425

Snyder, E. E., 137

Spanish Ph.D.'s, 29

Spelling patterns, 206

Standardized achievement, 161–63

Stanford Achievement Test, 210–15; average grade placement scores on, 211, 213
Stanford Reading Test, 259, 260, 274–75, 287
Stanford University, 240; Carnegie undergraduate plan and, 400–404; Institute for Mathematical Studies in the Social Sciences of (IMSSS), 201n, 202, 204, 205, 207, 208, 232, 238n; instructional costs at, 371, 406–407, 412; student dropout fractions for, 386–87; student enrollment and flow rates for, 385–86; student lifetimes at, 387–89; teacher-student ratios at, 389–90; unit chain costs at, 394–96; unit node costs at, 390
Stark, Rodney, 3, 23, 48
State University of New York (SUNY), at Stony Brook, 409–10, 413n
Stifle, J., 231
Stochastic choice theory, 303–307
Stock levels, 384
Stout, Robert T., 151
Strict utility model, 303–304
Student dropout fractions, 458; at Berkeley, 391–92; at Stanford, 386–87
Student enrollment and flow rates: at Berkeley, 390–91; at Stanford, 385–86
Student lifetimes, 378; at Berkeley, 392; at Stanford, 387–89
Success: Ph.D. program rates of, 19–23; signals of, 160–61
Suppes, Patrick, 201–47, 345n
Supplies: exogenous, 378; of Ph.D.'s, 29–32
Syracuse University, Educational Policy Research Center of, 477

Taubman, Paul J., 162
Teachers: experience of, 86–87, 183; verbal score of, 183
Teacher-student ratios. See Faculty-student ratios
Teaching assistantship (TA) positions, 14
"Teamwork," 256–58
Technical efficiency, 153–54, 191–96
Terminal equipment for computer-assisted instruction, cost of, 227, 232
Thomas, J. Alan, 150, 478, 480
Tiebout, Charles M., 184n
Timmer, C. P., 157, 185n
Title I. See Elementary and Secondary Education Act
Toder, Eric, 185n

Triplett, Jack E., 363n
Turner, William, 249n, 270

UNESCO, 374
Unit chain costs, 394–96
Unit cost, representation of, 379
Unit node costs, 390, 392–94
Universities. See Colleges
Utility maximization theory, 12

Value explicit measures of inequality, 222–26
Variable input coefficient model, 431–32
Variation, coefficient of, 444
Verbal score of teachers, 183
Vocabulary, sight-word, 206

Wales, Terence J., 162
Wargo, Michael J., 162
Watley, D. J., 138
Watts, Harold W., 151, 175, 185n, 197–98
Weathersby, George B., 366–69, 374, 405
Weighting, 276–77
Weiler, Daniel, 184n
Weinfeld, F. D., 203
Weisbrod, Burton A., 53, 249n, 272, 286–90
Wells, S., 203, 218, 238n
Werts, C. E., 138
Whelchel, B., 218
Wilbur, Norma, 249n
Wiley, David E., 201n, 245–47
Williams, Andrew T., 155
Winkler, Donald R., 150
Winsten, C. B., 185n
Wolfle, Dale, 364n
Woodhall, Maureen, 363n, 364n
Woodrow Wilson Fellows, 6, 431
World War II, 356
Wynn, Richard, 450
Wynne, Edward, 159

X-efficiency, 192

Yale University, 48
Year of admission, outcome of doctoral studies by, 4
Yoder, Sunny, 415n
York, R. L., 203
Yotopoulas, Pan A., 157

Zinn, K. L., 202